The
Writs of
Assistance
Case

The Writs of Assistance Case

M.H. SMITH

University of
California Press
Berkeley
Los Angeles
London

University of California Press
Berkeley and Los Angeles, California

University of California Press, Ltd.
London, England

Copyright © 1978 by
The Regents of the University of California

ISBN 0-520-03349-3
Library of Congress Catalog Card Number: 76-48365
Printed in the United States of America

1 2 3 4 5 6 7 8 9

To MARY CAROLINE SMITH

Contents

Acknowledgments

This book owes much to the generosity of those who own or control materials it deploys. Accordingly, my grateful thanks are due, in the United States, to Columbia University, the Butler Library; Harvard University, the Houghton Library; the Huntington Library; the Massachusetts Historical Society; the Historical Society of Pennsylvania; Princeton University; and, in this country, to His Grace the Duke of Buccleuch and Queensberry; the Earl Fitzwilliam and his Trustees, and the Director of the Sheffield City Libraries; the Trustees of the National Library of Scotland; Oxford University, the Bodleian Library; the British Library Board; the House of Lords Record Office; the Public Record Office and the Controller of H.M. Stationery Office.

In addition, facilities have been allowed me, invariably with the utmost helpfulness, by the American Antiquarian Society; the Boston Public Library; the Harvard University Archives; the Grand Lodge of Massachusetts, A.F. and A.M.; the New York Public Library; the Library Company of Philadelphia; Yale University; Cambridge University, the Squire Library; the Honourable Societies of the Inner Temple and of the Middle Temple; London University, the Institute of Advanced Legal Studies and the Institute of United States Studies; Manchester College Library, Oxford; Rhodes House Library, Oxford; the Scottish Record Office. Again, my warmest thanks. In H.M. Customs and Excise they go especially to the library and archives staffs, and to Mr. G. F. Gloak, of the Solicitor's Office. (Of course, no responsibility for what is said in this book rubs off on to anyone in the department.)

My American research activity was mostly in Boston. Officers of the Commonwealth of Massachusetts to whom I am under considerable obligation include the Clerk of the Supreme Judicial Court for Suffolk County, Mr. John E. Powers, and, in the Massachusetts State Archives, Mr. Leo C. Flaherty. The then editor-in-chief of the Adams Papers, Mr. Lyman H. Butterfield, very kindly enabled me to examine the original of John Adams's notes of the writs of assistance hearing. In the Massachusetts Historical Society I have had the benefit and pleasure of conversations with Mr. Butterfield and with his immediate colleague, Mr. Marc Friedlaender; Mr. John D. Cushing and Mr. Malcolm Freiberg have been unstintingly liberal with their great learning on the judicial system of provincial Massachusetts and on the fated career of Thomas Hutchinson; and I hesitate to think how much else would have escaped me but for the advice and help of Miss Winifred Collins. During the years of my shuttling back and forth across the Atlantic the Society was in the stewardship of Mr. Stephen T. Riley. To him, and to Mrs. Riley, I am very beholden indeed; most of all, for a valued friendship.

It has been my good fortune to meet many professional scholars at various points along the line. I warmly appreciate their courtesy and helpfulness. And I ought not to omit specific acknowledgment of a number of improvements kindly suggested by Professor Thomas G. Barnes, of the University of California at Berkeley, as the book neared completion. Certainly I must also record my thanks to my old friend, Professor Alfred M. Gollin, of the University of California at Santa Barbara, whose zestful interest was a stimulus and a tonic throughout.

Mrs. Anne Brookfield did most of the typing; and I am grateful for all the skill and care that went into it.

Broxbourne, Hertfordshire   M.H.S.

Abbreviations

Add. MSS	Additional manuscripts, British Library
BEP	*Boston Evening-Post*
BG	*Boston Gazette*
BNL	*Boston News-Letter*
BPBA	*Boston Post-Boy and Boston Advertiser*
BWNL	*Boston Weekly News-Letter*
DAJA	*Diary and Autobiography of John Adams*, L.H. Butterfield, ed., L. C. Faber and W. D. Garrett, assistant eds., 4 vols. (Cambridge, Mass., 1961)
Holdsworth, HEL	*History of English Law*, by W. S. Holdsworth, 17 vols. (London, 1903-72)
JHR	Journal of the House of Representatives (the Massachusetts Historical Society reproductions cited were edited by Mr. Malcolm Freiberg)
LPJA	*Legal Papers of John Adams*, L. K. Wroth and H. B. Zobel, eds., 3 vols. (Cambridge, Mass., 1965)
LWJA	*Life and Works of John Adams*, C. F. Adams, ed., 10 vols. (Boston, 1850-56)
MA	Massachusetts Archives
MHS	Massachusetts Historical Society
MHSC	*Massachusetts Historical Society Collections*
MHSP	*Massachusetts Historical Society Proceedings*
SCM	Superior Court Minutes
SCR	Superior Court Records See pages 231-32
SF	Suffolk Files

1

〜〜〜〜〜
〜〜〜〜〜

Bearings

〜〜〜〜〜
〜〜〜〜〜

I N 1767, on the initiative of Charles Townshend, gadfly chancellor of the exchequer, Westminster enacted a package of legislation new-modeling the customs regime in the American colonies. A group of import duties was introduced, and, with it, large organizational change. Till now, enforcement of the imperial system of shipping, trade, and revenue regulation had been a responsibility of the English board of customs commissioners in London; henceforth it would be for a separate American board, located at Boston. Also in the package was this:

> Writs of Assistants, to authorize and impower the Officers of his Majesty's Customs to enter and go into any House, Warehouse, Shop, Cellar, or other Place, in the British Colonies or Plantations in America, to search for and seize prohibited or uncustomed Goods . . . shall and may be granted by the Superior, or Supreme Court of Justice having Jurisdiction within such Colony or Plantation. . . .

Customs law enforcement had long been a fertile region of colonial unruliness. If the new taxes did not promise trouble enough, this power to search for smuggled goods, offensive both to local interests and to the sanctity of hearth and home, could not fail to open up yet another dimension of colonial indignation and contentiousness. Nor did it: controversies aroused by the Townshend customs search legislation form part of a tradition of United States origins regularly commemorated in histories of the revolutionary period.

Tar and feathers had their place in the tensions between American colonists and custom house agents of British authority in the years approaching the Revolution. Opposition to search, however, belonged more to the war of words. It was not so much physical resistance to break-ins on the spot as argumentation against the piece of paper that made them legally possible, the writ of assistance (a more usual spelling than the 1767 act's "Assistants"). The scene of contest was not the street, but the courtroom.

The crux of the numerous forensic debates over the Townshend writ of assistance was the American customs commissioners' insistence that the writ should be general and open-ended, so as to be available whenever and wherever the customs officers believed smuggled goods to lie hidden away. American judges, whom the Townshend legislation had made responsible for issuance of the writ of assistance, and who may not have been best pleased by this mandated participation in an unpopular cause, professed much embarrassment and perplexity about an instrument that smacked so strongly of a general search warrant. Many were as good as their hesitations. Reports of judicial unwillingness to issue writs of assistance other than for a single sworn occasion were already reaching the commissioners in Boston in the spring of 1768.[1] Rhode Island, Connecticut, Maryland, and South Carolina prevaricated, temporized, or somehow else omitted to play along. The Supreme Court of Pennsylvania was explicit: "I have laid the matter before our attorney general and another eminent Lawyer," wrote Chief Justice William Allen to the Philadelphia custom house, "who both concur with me in Opinion that such a general Writ as you have demanded is not agreable to Law." Contributing to the customs commissioners' difficulties was the fact that neither the 1767 legislation nor any comparable enactment in England said exactly what the writ of assistance was. Materials on the subject were not totally lacking in Boston, but how much they might weigh against all those powerful misgivings to the south was uncertain. So the commissioners referred the problem to their superiors, the Treasury at Westminster.

In due time it was laid before the principal law officer of the crown, the attorney general of England, William De Grey. The Treasury put it to De Grey that

> if such a General Writ of Assistants is not granted to the Officer, the true Intent of the Act may in almost every Case be evaded, for if he is obliged,

1. These and subsequent reports to the commissioners are copied, excerpted, or otherwise set forth in the commissioners' own reports to Westminster, which survive in various bundles in the Public Record Office's T1 series: in particular, T1/465, 471, 491, 492, 493, and 501. In the present chapter additional notation on the American resistance to the Townshend scheme for customs search will be made only as it may seem useful.

For the American resistance see "Writs of Assistance as a Cause of the Revolution," contributed by O. M. Dickerson to R. B. Morris, ed., *The Era of the American Revolution* (New York, 1939). Also, pp. 500-511 in the appendix, "Writs of Assistance," by Horace Gray in Samuel M. Quincy, ed., *Reports of Cases argued and adjudged in the Superior Court of the Province of Massachusetts Bay, between 1761 and 1772 by Josiah Quincy, Junior* (Boston, 1865). (The Gray treatise in *Quincy's Reports* will often be cited in the course of this book.)

every time he knows, or has received Information, of Prohibited or
unaccustomed Goods being concealed, to apply to the supreme Court of
Judicature for a Writ of Assistants, such Concealed Goods may be conveyed away before the Writ can be obtained.

The attorney general was reminded that issuance of writs of assistance in England was a simple once-for-all routine, with no question
of a separate application, still less a full-scale judicial hearing, whenever a customs officer had reason to go out on search. Surely,
suggested the Treasury, it should be the same in America? In an
Opinion dated 20 August 1768 De Grey agreed. The American
judges, to many of whom the writ of assistance was new, evidently
had misunderstood it; let them be shown a copy of the English writ
and its mode of issuance explained to them.[2]

But the Americans still would not fall into line. The only success
was South Carolina, which did at length give in. But there was a
minus even for this solitary plus. The New York judges, who first
time round had agreed to a general writ, on learning that it was too
unlike the English prototype changed their minds and dropped the
thing altogether. Rhode Island kept a posture of equivocal inaction.
Connecticut likewise wore the customs men down (meanwhile consulting its agent in London and campaigning among other colonies
for solidarity).[3] Maryland and Pennsylvania remained unmoved.[4] In
New Jersey, North Carolina, and Delaware the local customs officers
seem not to have had optimism enough even to apply for the writ. [5]
Reaction in the distant south was more explicitly negative. Georgia's
court had a majority unshakeably against the general writ. East
Florida's chief justice wrote that he did not consider himself "justified by Law to issue General Writs . . . to be lodged in the Hands, &

2. See Appendix A, and *Quincy's Reports*, 452-54. On 1 September 1768 the Treasury
sent a copy of the De Grey materials "and also a Copy of the form of the Writt of
Assistance as it issues out of the Court of Exchequer here" to the American customs
commissioners, directing them "to send Copies of the same to your principal Officers in
each colony": T28/1.

3. See also O. Zeichner, *Connecticut's Years of Controversy 1750-1776* (Chapel Hill,
1949), 82-83, 132-34; the Pitkin papers in Connecticut Historical Society, *Collections* XIX
(Hartford, 1921), 118-19, 142, 151, and *passim*; the Trumbull Papers, *MHSC* fifth series
(1885), IX; and *Quincy's Reports*, 501-7.

4. The Supreme Court of Pennsylvania was, however, willing to issue writs good for the
one time only. A specimen, dated 2 June 1769, is in the Historical Society of Pennsylvania,
Custom House Papers X, 1174; and is reproduced in MHS, British-American Customs
Records 1765-1773.

5. A report by the American customs commissioners 20 October 1772 states that no
applications for writs of assistance appeared to have been made in these three colonies:
T1/492.

to be executed discretionaly, (perhaps without proper Foundation) at the Will of subordinate Officers, to the Injury of the Rights of His Majesty's other loyal Subjects." Specially worrisome to the customs commissioners was judicial intransigence in Virginia, which had more custom houses than any other colony. In fact, it was on Virginia's account that they bleated to Westminster a second time.

In July 1769 the commissioners complained to the Treasury that the one-time-only writ, which was all that the Supreme Court of Virginia had been willing to countenance, was "calculated to impede and obstruct the execution of the Revenue Laws." Perhaps reluctant to affront Attorney General De Grey with so stark a demonstration of his policy's failure, the Treasury did not move at once. Almost two years were allowed to pass, by which time there was a new attorney general. They bade he be asked; "which measures it may be proper to take to oblige such of the Supreme Courts of Justice as have refused to do so, to grant Writs of Assistance according to the directions of the Act of Parliament, & the Opinion of the late Attorney General. . . ." But Edward Thurlow in 1771 was as circumspect as William De Grey in 1768. The Treasury might grate and growl, but what came forth from the attorney general was a bland resolve to see, hear, and speak no evil. It seemed "strange indeed," Thurlow wrote, "that any Judge in the Colonies should think the Laws of the Mother Country too harsh for the temper of American Liberty. I am therefore inclined to suppose that they proceed upon a meer mistake of the Law."[6] All that could follow from this limp response was yet another round of futile endeavor in the courts. The hapless American customs commissioners were told in April 1773 of attitudes in Virginia as hard as ever, the bench "inflexibly adhereing to their former Opinion" and expressing the desire that the local customs staff "wou'd not again trouble them on the Subject."[7]

So much for Westminster's supposition that judicial hostility in America to general customs search with writ of assistance was innocent error. Not that Attorney General Thurlow can have been too convinced of it himself. Included in his Opinion was a glimpse of the bleak reality:

6. T27/30. See Appendix B; and Dickerson, *op.cit.* (n. 1 above), 69-71.

7. Extract of letter 24 April 1773 from Cary Michell and Samuel Allyne, respectively collector and comptroller, Lower James River, to the American customs commissioners, enclosed with the commissioners' letter to the Treasury, 14 June 1773: T1/501. See also Dickerson, *op. cit.,* 71-72.

I know of no direct, and effectual means, in the ordinary course of Law, to compel the Judges of the chief courts in the Colonies. . . . Upon a case of obstinate and contumacious refusal to execute an English act of Parliament, I apprehend the Judges might be impeached, But this is a measure of punishment, not of controul.

Short of shipping the recalcitrant judges to England for impeachment trial by the House of Lords, which improbable maneuver would need the collaboration of the House of Commons besides, there was really nothing open to Thurlow but anodyne make-believe. Behind the face-saving pretense that American antagonism toward the general writ of assistance signified nothing worse than persistence in simple mistake lay the uncomfortable awareness that on this troublesome subject the legal system had toppled over the edge.

In some cases openly, in others by dragging of feet, judges in colonial America thus were defying and defeating British overlord-ship years before a single soldier took to the field; and with legal process so highly thought of in the nation ahead it seems apt that the definitive break of 1776 should have been actively anticipated, in however small a way, in courts of law. But not many of the judges would have seen themselves as pioneers of revolutionary schism. Chief Justice Allen of Pennsylvania became a loyalist. Among the occupants of the Virginia bench was none other than the governor, Lord Botetourt. And it is instructive to see something that Botetourt wrote about his judicial colleagues' cast of mind on the writ of assistance: "the Bench . . . are always of opinion to make the Law the rule of their conduct. . . ."[8] What motivated the American judges' opposition was not spearhead radicalism, but a genuine belief that the general writ did not accord with true legal principle.

Only a few years were to pass when proscription of all manner of promiscuous searches and seizures became a more or less standard item in constitutions of the now independent states; and not many more when the Fourth Amendment to the Constitution of the United States was to enshrine it nationally:

The right of the people to be secure in their persons, houses, papers, and effects, against unreasonable searches and seizures, shall not be violated, and no Warrants shall issue, but upon probable cause, supported by Oath or affirmation, and particularly describing the place to be searched, and the persons or things to be seized.

8. *Quincy's Reports*, 510.

However, while Fourth Amendment constitutionalism (so to call it) doubtless owed something to recollections of the intercolonial stand against the Townshend writ of assistance, that inspirational obduracy was not wholly homegrown. In the middle 1760s general powers of search and seizure had been a heady subject in England. Intrusions on to private premises by the agents of a government bent on scourging the journalistic excesses of John Wilkes had led to robust judicial and parliamentary denunciations of general warrants as contrary to law. Whiffs of those excitements got over to America good and strong, and in time to energize opposition to the Town-shend search power of 1767 and its concomitant writ of assistance.

Still, there was another experience behind Fourth Amendment constitutionalism; this one exclusively American, and remembered for other matters of consequence as well. It too had centered upon customs search and the writ of assistance under courtroom debate.

Conspicuously missing from the roll of colonies that held out against the Townshend general writ of assistance was Massachusetts Bay. Not normally backward in pre-revolutionary activism, in this one respect Massachusetts gave the frustrated American customs commis-sioners no trouble at all. Massachusetts already had the writ of assistance, and the general writ at that; so in the Bay province — and in New Hampshire, which had followed its more populous neigh-bor — there was not so much occasion for courtroom agitations such as those in colonies where the Townshend scheme for customs search had come as something entirely new. But the Massachusetts writ had a story of its own; and it is this that the present book is about.

In 1761 writ of assistance search was the subject of courtroom debate every bit as intense as any that took place in colonies to the south seven to a dozen years later. Moreover, the writs of assistance case in Boston in 1761 far outclasses the post-Townshend inter-colonial stand in emphasis accorded to it by history; and this not-withstanding the paradox that opposition to the Townshend design succeeded where the Boston protest had not. The intercolonial bag of victories over the Townshend writ is material mostly for the specialist historian. The blast against the Massachusetts general writ of assistance in 1761, for all its failure in terms of immediate practical purpose, hit the historical jackpot. It is in all the books. Much of its fame is the doing of one witness. Among those present in the courtroom was John Adams, then a fledgling lawyer of twenty-five. Adams was not the flashiest of the founders of the Republic, but he knew how to turn a phrase. "Then and there was the first scene of the first Act of Opposition to the arbitrary Claims of Great Britain," he recalled fifty-odd years after, "Then and there the child Independence was born."[9]

Another and less exuberant assessment might be ventured. It was in the writs of assistance case in Boston in 1761 that the American tradition of constitutional hostility to general powers of search first found articulate expression. The intercolonial rejection of the Townshend writ of 1767 had the recent Wilkesite general warrant cases in England to draw upon, but in 1761 those great landmarks of the common law were still in the future. The Massachusetts protest anticipated them. It was an American original.

Either way, and however else its significance might be interpreted, the writs of assistance case is tackled in this book mostly as a historical phenomenon in its own right. It presents a fairly knotty exercise in factual and legal discovery. Aside from the courtroom argument and its inevitable sophistications, the case was in various ways the product of a remarkably sulfurous politico-economic mix, spiked with circumstantial accident and human idiosyncrasy, that happened to be brewing in Boston around 1760. And this melee of a setting is in turn incapable of being understood save by reference to events years before. On the legal side there has to be archaeology, even; with excavatory work in England for the writ of assistance itself.

Faring forward to the Massachusetts scene in 1761 means starting from several places, some of them a long way back. However, if there was a single matrix for the whole miscellany of elements and factors making toward the writs of assistance case, it was the imperial system of trade regulation.

9. John Adams to William Tudor, 29 March 1817: *LWJA* X, 248. Adams's words have been quoted and endorsed in the United States Supreme Court: see the judgment of Bradley J. in *Boyd v. U.S.* (1886) 116 US 616 ("the famous debate . . . was perhaps the most prominent event which inaugurated the resistance of the colonies to the oppressions of the mother country").

2

Groundworks of Empire

I N AN AGE when liberty was the boast of Britishers on both sides of the Atlantic, business activity among them nevertheless endured a massive apparatus of regulatory laws. What dictated this paradox was a national ambition that Great Britain — England, until the union with Scotland in 1707 — and its overseas dependencies should constitute an economic whole, a kind of pan-Atlantic stockade self-sufficient against the foreigner and capable of beating him off, with such territorial and other increments of victory as might be, by naval and military power.

Emphatically, the mode and style of eighteenth-century empire were not freedom of trade. Interventionist autarky was visited even upon inland industry. American iron manufacture, for example, was curtailed in the larger interest. In Great Britain itself the cultivation of tobacco was forbidden. However, internal restrictions were not numerous. The real weight of the imperial system was at the ports, where the procedural mechanisms of the customs organization, designed primarily for purposes of revenue but readily adaptable to controls of a nonfiscal sort, were practically part of the natural order.

In terms of the basic governing legislation the imperial economic system originated in the Restoration period. Endeavors to promote English shipping and overseas trade to the special advantage of Englishmen went back to the middle ages; and a disposition toward national monopoly in colonial commerce had exhibited itself in the earlier years of the seventeenth century. An act of 1651 gave effect to the principle of favoring English ships in the carrying trade, and had it not been that legislation of the Interregnum no longer counted as law this could be taken as the foundation of the imperial system. [1]

---

1. *Acts and Ordinances of the Interregnum 1642-1660* II (London, 1911), 559.

As things happened the job had to be done again, with improvements as the opportunity offered, on the king's return in 1660. Henceforth and for many years — long after the American breakaway — trade with British territories overseas was almost entirely for British-built ships that were also owned, skippered, and for the most part manned by British nationals.

More distinctively economic — the shipping monopoly had a strong defense pigmentation — were two other components of the imperial system: enumeration and the staple. Enumeration was the word associated with the principle, also embodied in the Navigation Act of 1660, that certain colonial products, tobacco for one, should be exported to British destinations only;[2] and in 1673 enumeration was supplemented by a regime under which the products then listed bore an export duty, known as a "plantation duty," on such of them as were shipped to another colony rather than bound for the metropolitan country itself. The enumerated list (though not the plantation duties correspondingly) was added to from time to time in the passage of years. The staple originated in an act of 1663. Here the principle was that England should be the source of most of what the colonies needed to import from across the Atlantic, or if not the source the entrepôt. Virtually everything destined for a British colony from continental Europe had to go first to a port in Great Britain and be reshipped from there. As with enumeration so with the staple; time brought changes of scope (in 1721 goods from east of the Cape of Good Hope were included), but these served to underline the principle, not to modify it.

Of course, it was not by coercive regulation alone that Britain came to be the market or the clearinghouse for so much of the colonies' overseas trade. Trade between the metropolitan country and the colonies was also stimulated by a structure of fiscal devices — bounties and preferential duty rates, for example — the effect of which was to make it especially profitable to abide by the system. And much of it would have taken place anyway, regardless of the constraints or inducements of the system, just because it was good business.

Enforcement in the colonies of the acts of navigation and trade was originally the responsibility of the governor. Vestiges of this old

---

2. Some exports were prohibited absolutely: colonial woolens, for example. The present point, however, has to do with the steering of trade rather than with stamping bits of it out.

regime continued throughout, together with the functionary, known as the naval officer, who did the actual work. Well before the end of the seventeenth century, however, the men in charge were the board of customs commissioners in England, who had their own staff of surveyors-general, collectors, and so on down the line, located at colonial ports.

Those outposted customs officials did not have much revenue to collect, however. There were the plantation duties on certain products exported elsewhere than to Great Britain, but there was little enough in these, especially in colonies to which such products were not indigenous. The only other regular duties in mainland America — before the 1760s, that is, and not including imposts levied by colonial legislatures for their own local purposes — were from the Molasses Act of 1733. The Molasses Act duties were import duties at prohibitively heavy rates on molasses, sugar, and spirits produced in foreign territories close by; their object (how far it succeeded is another matter) was to force New England distillers of rum, for which molasses was the base material, into using molasses from the British West Indies. Small yield from the plantation duties and the Molasses Act duties was, in a sense, according to the book. The duties had not been conceived as revenue raisers. Rather the opposite, in fact. They existed not to exploit the traffic at which they were directed but to discourage it. They are best thought of as mechanisms of trade regulation operating by fiscal means.[3]

The customs officer in America looked still less like a tax gatherer in relation to importations from across the Atlantic, when all he did was stand guard on the staple and check that the incoming goods had been shipped from or via Great Britain. However, first appearances were not all. That there was no money to collect (which largely remained true even after a few import duties were introduced in the 1760s) did not mean that the customs process in America had no revenue function. There was more to the staple than furtherance of British trade, shipping, and port interests. Commercial policy had considerable influence on the elaborate network of import duties, export duties, and drawbacks (repayments of duty wholly or in part, notably import duty on goods re-exported) that, together with

3. As time passed and fiscal pressures intensified, original objectives became overlaid, or were lost sight of. In the early 1760s the Treasury was expressing serious concern that "the revenue arising . . . in America & the West Indies amounts in no degree to the sum wch. might be expected from them": C. Jenkinson to customs commissioners, 21 May 1763, in T11/27. The Sugar Act of 1764 was a consequence.

peripheral fiscal devices such as bounties and the plantation duties, constituted another component of the imperial system; but it was not the be-all and end-all. The fact that practically every item of merchandise entering or leaving Great Britain attracted some kind of revenue incident had a rationale of its own as well. This could not have been simpler: the government needed the money. So, when a cargo from Great Britain to America bore an export duty, or, if it were a re-export on part-drawback, what remained of an import duty, there was something in it for the exchequer. Alternatively, a cargo that arrived in America direct from continental Europe would have bypassed the mechanism set up in Britain for taxing it, leaving the imperial finances that much the poorer. The importance of the staple's fiscal side shows forth from mid-eighteenth-century British government records, in worried references to money lost through low enforcement performance in the colonies.[4] Clearly, to whatever extent the customs officer in America might succeed in intercepting a cargo that transgressed the staple he did a job for the revenue, three thousand miles though he was from Great Britain, the fiscal as well as the political and economic center of the imperial system.

The standard and principal sanction against violations of the acts of navigation and trade, in England and the colonies alike, was a form of penalty that had been a feature of customs law since the thirteenth century. Actually, it rather neatly fitted the offense. Things that had no right to be where they were, having been wrongfully imported or brought forward for exportation, were seized and forfeited.

However, denoting as it did loss of ownership, customs forfeiture signified something much more positive than logical nicety. The Anglo-American tradition has always made disturbance of property rights a matter for considerable puffing and blowing. On customs forfeiture no less an authority than Magna Carta is in point. The charter as adopted by Edward I in the Statute of Westminster of 1275 included these words: "And no . . . Man be amerced, without reasonable Cause and according to the Quantity of his Trespass; that is to say, every free Man saving his Freehold, a Merchant saving his

---

4. For example: customs commissioners to Treasury, 16 September 1763, in T1/426; and Sir Charles Hardy, governor of New York, to Board of Trade, 15 July 1757, extracted at folios 507-510 in Add. MSS 32890. See also T. C. Barrow, *Trade and Empire: The British Customs Service in Colonial America 1660-1775* (Cambridge, Mass., 1967), 151.

Merchandise . . . ." Peremptory confiscation of something that had been smuggled was all too likely to breach the principle thus enunciated, since the offending article probably would be some merchant's merchandise. It is noticeable that when, a little later in 1275, provision was made for certain customs duties (the *antiqua custuma*), the forfeiture penalty attaching to them was given color of parliamentary approval. From that time on, customs forfeiture was invariably a matter of specific statutory enactment.[5]

Nor, even with forfeiture authorized by act of Parliament, was it enough for the customs officer simply to seize the offending thing. Seizure was a mere taking of possession; it did not constitute transfer of ownership.[6] In order that property should pass there had to be a court process. This process of "condemnation" (as it was called) was pronounced upon by one of the judges in the famous ship money case, *R. v. Hampden*:

> The King's majesty . . . can neither take any lands or goods from any of his subjects, but by and upon a judgment on record, (according to our daily experience in the exchequer), there must precede some judgment in that or some other court of record, whereby his majesty may be intitled either to the lands or goods of a subject, as namely where seizure of goods is made for his majesty either upon outlawries, attainders, or matters of like nature; as in cases of seizures in the court of Exchequer, where seizures are given by statutes; yet without a judgment in that court upon a trial for the king the goods are not to be recovered for the use of the king as forfeited.[7]

As this statement indicates, condemnation proceedings for customs seizures were taken in the Court of Exchequer rather than in the Court of King's Bench or the Court of Common Pleas, the other two courts administering the common law (the centralized body of judge-made law that had overshadowed local or feudal jurisdictions to

---

5. Sir Matthew Hale, "Concerning the Custom of Goods Imported and Exported," in F. Hargrave, ed., *Law Tracts* (Dublin, 1757), 144, 170. Volume 64 of the Selden Society's *Select Cases in the Exchequer Chamber (II)* (London, 1945), 35, notes a judgment in 1475 indicating a common law forfeiture of uncustomed imported merchandise; but the correct reference almost certainly was the act 12 Edw. 4, c. 3, which introduced forfeiture in relation to a wide range of uncustomed goods. The Hale view, that customs forfeiture is always statutory, is the true one. See also *A-G v. Lade* (1745) Park. 57. For the parliamentary status of the 1275 customs grant, see Hale, *op. cit.*, 146; D. E. C. Yale, ed., *Hale's Prerogatives of the King* (Selden Society vol. 92, London, 1976), 287 and n. 3; W. Stubbs, *Constitutional History of England* II (Oxford, 1880), 118.

6. See n. 7.

7. (1637) 3 St. Tr. 1201-1202, *per* Denham B., *diss.* And Hale, *op. cit.*, 226: "the king's title is not compleat, till he hath a judgment of record to ascertain his title . . . ."

become the law common to the whole of the country and to all men). For one thing, the Court of Exchequer specialized in cases touching revenue and other duties belonging to the king. For another, it had a ready-made procedure, the information *in rem*, which was easily adaptable to customs forfeitures.[8]

It was usual for condemnation proceedings for the forfeiture of a customs seizure to be initiated by the man who did the seizing. The proceedings being by way of information (a way of getting a matter to trial without a grand jury process), he was known as the informer. The situation was not without hazards. If the case were defended and went against the informer he would have a bill of legal costs to meet; and his position in common law was also that the seizure he had failed to justify constituted a trespass, for which he was liable in damages.[9] On the other hand, the game could be well worth the candle. For the successful informer (and many condemnations went undefended, because of the smuggler's unwillingness to reveal himself) there were rich pickings. He was beneficiary of a mode of law enforcement that was commonly resorted to in times when nothing in the nature of a regular police organization existed. In essence it was law enforcement by private enterprise. The law would create an offense, make it punishable by a monetary exaction, and apportion a share of the money to any individual who troubled to seek out the offense and prosecute it. This so-called "popular" or *qui tam* process was adapted for use in customs law enforcement. In England most customs seizures condemned as forfeited were divided equally between the crown and the private pocket of the customs man who brought the proceedings. In the colonies it was generally a three-way split; the acts of navigation and trade gave one-third each to the king, the governor of the particular colony, and the customs man.

In the early decades of the imperial system condemnation proceedings in the colonies tended to be stultified by the unwillingness of juries, perhaps inspired by fellow-feeling, to return a verdict

8. For the application of the information *in rem* to revenue forfeitures see chapter 13 of *Treatise on the Exchequer* by Sir Jeffrey Gilbert (London, 1758). In *Scott v. Shearman* (1775) 2 W. Bl. 977, Blackstone J. judicially affirmed his *Commentaries'* approval of the Gilbert account.

9. *Leglise v. Champante* (1728) 2 Str. 820. The act 19 Geo. 2 c. 35 (1746) modified the common law position in England, to the extent that if the court certified probable cause for the seizure an action for damages was in effect barred. Like provision was introduced into the colonies in 1764, and contributed to American grievances: *cf. LPJA* II, 125, 224; and chapter 14 n. 32 below.

against the putative smuggler. The year 1696 saw the enactment of a comprehensive body of customs enforcement law for America which aimed to equip the customs organization there with broadly the same enforcement powers as in England. This policy was subject to an important exception however. In England, as hitherto in America, condemnation proceedings took place according to common law process, which implied a jury trial (in contested cases). The act of 1696 envisioned customs officers in America bringing condemnation proceedings in courts where that discommodious institution had no place. These courts would exercise admiralty jurisdiction, outside the common law tradition.

Admiralty jurisdiction had to do with seafarers and ships and maritime casualties in general (including, for example, prize in time of war). The ways of admiralty courts had a cosmopolitan quality, and affinity with the so-called civil law derived from the legal thinking of ancient Rome. Though English common law has proved capable of transplantation and is today the basic legal mode in many parts of the world, it must yield pride of place in this respect to the jurisprudential framework which continental scholars have been adducing from Roman law since the early middle ages. The civil law thus reconstructed is the foundation of many a modern legal system: it made convenient borrowing for countries in need of a more or less ready-made package of developed law. More particularly, it has always been a matrix for admiralty practice everywhere. Even in England, whose own common law was indigenous and not greatly affected by the Roman influence,[10] it made sense that the law that often bore upon seagoing foreigners from continental Europe should partake of the civil law style that such persons were accustomed to. Besides, courts of admiralty afforded a number of practical advantages. For example, a crew in dispute about wages with the master of a ship could sue him jointly in the admiralty court; in a common law court each man would have to bring his own separate action. Again, in a milieu where men were always on the come and go across the sea it was a convenient principle of the admiralty process that the ship herself could be immediately fixed upon as a kind of surrogate defendant; the common law operated for the most part *in personam*, going for the man and his pocket rather than directly for his physical property (the Court of Exchequer's procedure *in rem* was of very

10. The Court of Exchequer presumably borrowed "condemnation" from admiralty practice somewhere back along the line, for the term belongs more to the civil law than to the common law. Paradoxically however the old-time Roman *condemnatio* was pecuniary and not *in rem*: Gaius, *Institutes*, 4.48.

limited and specialized application). To the policymakers of 1696, however, the advantage offered by admiralty jurisdiction over customs forfeiture in the colonies was more earthy: the civil law tradition of admiralty courts did not know the jury. The judge decided everything.

Two essentials followed from the policy of 1696. One was that courts of the orthodox admiralty type had to be established in America. Ordinary cases of an admiralty provenance — disputes over seamen's wages, collisions at sea, and so forth — were of course nothing new there, but generally they had been adjudicated in common law fashion, with a jury; what Westminster was now purposing necessitated a chain of true admiralty courts — actually, vice-admiralty courts, since the colonial governors to whom they nominally belonged were commissioned vice-admirals, not admirals — conducted on civil law lines. (And the courts thus constituted would be free of local influence not only through having no jury, but for the additional reason that the judge himself was beholden to no one in the colony; he would owe his appointment to London, and get his income not by vote of a colonial assembly but from fees in his court.) The other essential was that the new vice-admiralty courts should have the necessary customs jurisdiction. This did not belong to them naturally, of course; it had to be legislated for. Accordingly, provision for it was included in the 1696 legislation.

Insofar as customs forfeiture could be made a go of by an efficacious condemnation jurisdiction it posed a further problem. The seizure of offending goods was not always a simple matter of intercepting them at ship's side. Often they would be stored away ashore. It was one thing for a customs officer to know or suspect where smuggled goods lay concealed, but quite another for him to go in and seize them.

This is as good a point as any at which to quote the well-known declamation of the elder Pitt:

> The poorest man may in his cottage bid defiance to all the forces of the Crown. It may be frail — its roof may shake — the wind may blow through it — the storms may enter — the rain may enter — but the King of England cannot enter — all his force dares not cross the threshold of the ruined tenement.[11]

11. It was cited judicially from Brougham's *Statesmen in the Times of George III* by Lord Denning M. R. in *Chic Fashions (West Wales) Ltd. v. Jones* [1968] 2 Q.B. 299, 308. The basics of the matter were stated more prosaically by Lord Camden C. J. in *Entick v. Carrington* (1765) 19 St. Tr. 1066: "By the laws of England, every invasion of private

Pitt's manner may have been slightly overblown, but what he said was true enough. The occasions when the common law sanctioned a power of entry and search on a man's property were few. Certainly search for smuggled goods was not one of them. The only instance in any degree comparable occurred with stolen goods. For these the common law did allow the issuance of a search warrant (possibly on the principle that respect for one form of property ought not to thwart protection of another), but that was as far as it went. If there was to be a power of entry and search for smuggled goods that the common law courts would recognize it must be given by statute.

Such was the common law position on customs search in England and the colonies alike. An act for customs search warrants was passed in 1660;[12] and when in 1662 a comprehensive corpus of customs enforcement law was enacted it included the power of entry with which the writ of assistance was associated.[13] But the acts of 1660 and 1662 were for England only. Provision for the colonies was more than thirty years distant. The *Act for preventing Frauds, and regulating Abuses in the Plantation Trade* of 1696 [14] − its title significantly resembling that of the English act of 1662, *An Act for preventing Frauds, and regulating Abuses in his Majesty's Customs,* and similarly shortened in common parlance to the Act of Frauds − included power of entry and search in its general objective of creating in the colonies a compendium of customs enforcement law comparable to that in England.

More of how the imperial system and the grand designs of 1696 actually worked appears in later chapters, but first it is desirable to get into focus the writ of assistance itself. This will be the endeavor of chapter 3. Part and parcel of the originating history of the writ is the anatomy of the two enactments for customs entry and search in England, in 1660 and 1662; that will take a further chapter. These historico-legal exertions will help clear the way for what lies farther ahead, the writ of assistance in pre-revolutionary Massachusetts.

---

property, be it ever so minute, is a trespass. No man can set his foot upon my ground without my licence, but he is liable to an action, though the damage be nothing."

    12. 12 Car. 2, c. 19. In *Acts and Ordinances of the Interregnum 1642-1660,* I (London, 1911), at 163-65, there is an ordinance of the Long Parliament appointing "commissioners" to prevent smuggling. It gave a power of search "in the day time, to, goe and enter into all, or any Cellars, Vaults, Ships, Warehouses, or other places . . . to see, Surveigh, and make search for any . . . prohibited Goods . . . ." This, though passed by the lords and commons, did not have the royal assent; and, naturally, it lost all force of law at the Restoration.

    13. 13 & 14 Car. 2, c. 11.

    14. 7 & 8 Gul. 3, c. 22.

3

The Customs Writ of Assistance

Under the common law, the judge-made jurisprudence that characterized the English legal system, the only things for which a power of search was available were things that had been stolen. If a power of search for anything else were to be recognized in the common law courts, it had to be legislated for in Parliament. Legislation for search for smuggled goods in England was on the statute book when Parliament sought to duplicate the English customs regime in the colonies, in 1696. Particularly in point were the two enactments of 1660 and 1662. The interrelation between these was to have some bearing on the American controversies around a hundred years later; it will be described in chapter 4. Resultant problems for the draftsman of the Act of Frauds of 1696 when he endeavored to export English-style customs search to the colonies will become apparent in chapter 6, where the advent of the Massachusetts writ of assistance is considered.

First, however, it is necessary to establish the legal credentials of the customs writ of assistance. These, and the origins and juridical nature of the writ, are the concern of the present chapter.

The 1660s brought forth a good many statutory enactments on powers of entry on to private property. There was much besides the customs legislation of 1660 and 1662. The regulation of a certain trade might be facilitated by its authorities being given statutory power to enter premises in order to inspect specimens of the product.[1] Statutory protection of timber for shipbuilding extended to search by warrant of particular places where unlawfully cut wood was suspected to be.[2] The notorious Licensing Act of 1662 provided for access to places thought to harbor uncensored press material. [3]

---

1. For example, baize-making (12 Car. 2, c. 22, s. 5); 13 & 14 Car. 2, c. 7 permitted wardens of the curriers' company to search for illicit export consignments of leather.

2. 15 Car. 2, c. 2, s. 3.

3. 13 & 14 Car. 2, c. 33.

Another act of 1662 enabled the dwellings of persons considered "dangerous to the Peace of the Kingdom" to be searched for arms.[4]

The significance of all this legislation is that there had been very little like it before. Hitherto the English statute book had hardly anything on powers of entry and search. The year 1660 appears to have been the first time that legislation for power of customs search was found necessary. Even the weighty customs enforcement statute of 1558[5] was silent on this aspect of its subject. Yet a power to move in and seize the offending goods was essential if forfeiture, long a fundamental institution of customs enforcement law, was to bite to full effect.

It would have been incongruous that Tudor government, not generally lacking in muscle, were worse off in customs enforcement powers than the comparatively constrained regimes of the later Stuarts. And of course it was not so. Powers of entry and search in the service of executive government were not an invention of the 1660s. They had existed long before that. What was new was that they had to be legislated for.

An instructive illustration of search in former times centers on a figure of unique eminence in the common law. He was the judge and jurist Sir Edward Coke. The uniqueness of Coke is that his writings rank practically as law. Unlike legal systems of Roman derivation, traditionally more open to the influence of academic commentary, English common law is resistant to learned disquisitions from outside the courtroom. The material of the common law is the actual decision in a concrete case in court, and the reasoning then and there expounded by the judge (and published in a recognized series of law reports). If there is an exception to this principle it is Coke's *Institutes of the Laws of England.* Indeed, as will be seen later in this chapter, Coke's extrajudicial *Institutes* enshrine the doctrinal source of the customs writ of assistance. However, present interest is not with Coke the master common lawyer but with Coke the archantagonist of the prerogative claims of the earlier Stuart kings.

Coke lived from 1552 to 1634. After a highly successful career at the bar and in government, during which periods he was as fervent a

---

4. 13 & 14 Car. 2, c. 3.

5. 1 Eliz. 1, c. 11. There appears to have been a brief spasm of legislative activity on powers of search in 1604, early in the reign of Elizabeth's successor: 2 Jac. 1 c. 20 (regulation of the "Art or Mystery of Painting"), and 2 Jac. 1, c. 22 (leather cutting). And another in 1622: 21 Jac. 1, c. 18 and c. 19 (respectively, woolen cloths and commissioners in bankruptcy). Such specimens are not numerous, however, or related to smuggling.

supporter of kingly rule as the next man with a way to make, he went on to the judicial bench. His period as chief justice, first of the Common Pleas and then of the King's Bench, was marked however by an enthusiasm for his specialty, the common law, even at the expense of the royal interest; and in 1616 James I dismissed him. The rest of his active life was spent in legal writing and in leadership of parliamentary opposition.

Though Coke's last few years were passed in retirement the royal finger remained on him. His immense learning made him an object of more than ordinary apprehension: "he is held too great an oracle amongst the people," said Charles I in 1631.[6] The king was at this time directing that watch be kept on Coke's state of health, so that when the old man's time at last came suitable action might be set on foot. And, accordingly, three years later:

> Upon his death-bed Sir F. Windebank . . . by an order of the Council came to search for seditious and dangerous papers. By virtue whereof he took Sir Edward Coke's comment upon Littleton . . . his comment upon Magna Charta, etc. . . .[7]

In this disagreeable little episode may be seen how such matters as entry and search were managed in those days. For, aside from the irony that the great opponent of regal power should suffer from that same power even in death, there was nothing widely out of the ordinary about the search for Coke's papers. Other instances of this mode of action are to be found in plenty in the *Acts of the Privy Council* for the period. A businessman in trouble with the authorities might have his premises ransacked for account books.[8] Secretly imported bibles were another subject of search.[9] And it is unnecessary to look further than these *Acts of the Privy Council* for witness to the fact that search for uncustomed goods, notwithstanding the absence of authority for it in statute, was anything but unknown in those times.[10]

The driving principle behind all such violations of domestic privacy is made plain in a particularly striking example. In 1637 the Privy Council directed their clerks "to make your immediate repayre to the dwelling house of Doctor Everite at Fulham or els where, and

6. Holdsworth, *HEL* V, 454.

7. *Ibid.*, 455 n. 1. See also *Calendar of State Papers, Domestic Series 1629-31* (London, 1860), xxvi, xxvii, 490; and the 1634-35 volume (London, 1864), 165.

8. *Acts of the Privy Council, June 1630 - June 1631* (London, 1964), 10-11.

9. *Ibid.*, 189-190.

10. *Cf.* p. 30.

to sease into your Custodie all his papers and writings, and to bring away wth you such of them, as may concerne the State . . . ."[11] Nor was it the council alone that sponsored invasions of private dwellings in the interests of "the State." In 1636 Sir Francis Windebank, off his own bat as secretary of state, ordered that an approach be made to one Leonard Wolley of St. Martin's Lane in London for the surrender of "the Lieger book of Alvingham Priory in the County of Lincolne wch being a record of great consequence is not fitt to remaine in the hands of a private man"; if Wolley refused to give up the book "then you are to search for the same and having found it to seize and take itt into yor Custody and bring it to mee to be ordered as his Maj^tie shall please to appoint."[12] Authority for people's houses to be searched *pro bono publico,* exercised by the king's council, the secretary of state, or anyone else, was not to be found in the common law. Nor had statute given it. It was a matter of the crown, through its agents, asserting an undefined power to safeguard good public order when the ordinary law seemed not to measure up.

With such residual power available to day-to-day executive government, insufficiency of common law and statute was of no great consequence. What explains the profusion of search legislation in the Restoration period is the fact that this standby power could no longer be relied upon. There had been an important change.

Any law-making or regulatory regime depends upon a court being willing to authorize penal sanctions against persons who violate or impede it. This is what was lacking in prerogative directives — orders in council, royal proclamations, and so forth — in Charles II's time. The only courts with relevant jurisdiction were the courts of common law, where the royal say-so alone did not count for much. The common law attitude was reflected in the statement of Coke C.J. in *The Case of Proclamations,* in 1611:

> The King by his proclamation or other ways cannot change any part of the common law, or statute law, or the custom of the realm . . . also the King cannot create any offence by his prohibition or proclamation, which was not an offence before . . . that which cannot be punished without proclamation cannot be punished with it . . . .[13]

11. British Library, Stowe MSS, 576.
12. *Ibid.*
13. 12 Co. Rep. 74.

Royal proclamations and the rest could underline what was already authentic law, and by doing so make a violation the more serious; but that was all. To a common law court the only true lawmaker was Parliament. A common law court would not regard it as wrong for a householder to bar the way of someone whose only claim to be allowed to come in and search was a piece of paper issued on the bare executive fiat of the crown.

Under Charles II's predecessors it had been different. In those days the doctrinal inhibitions of the common law courts did not have this limiting effect on governmental action. Prerogative authority had enforcement agencies to match. The Court of Star Chamber, whatever its general value and contemporary esteem as a tribunal for tackling wrongs that might otherwise pass unremedied or unpunished, owes its traditional reputation to its amenability to the requirements of executive government. Proceeding without a jury, and on occasion pretty peremptorily, the Star Chamber came to be much looked to for the upholding of royal or conciliar policy. In modern terms this collateral system of law might be thought of as a kind of criminal *droit administratif.* Historically however it perhaps is better seen in terms of the medieval dichotomy of *jurisdictio* and *gubernaculum,* which the late Professor C. H. McIlwain highlighted from the writings of the thirteenth-century English jurist Henry de Bracton: *jurisdictio,* the exercise of public power according to strict rule and form; *gubernaculum,* a residual police power untrammeled by doctrine or methodology and exercised at the royal discretion in the interest of good public order.[14] Star Chamber (and various other tribunals of more or less similar orientation) was a manifestation of this indeterminate power of *gubernaculum.* Fostered by the Tudors after the country had been almost torn apart by internal strife, its processes long served to offset the constricting formalism of the common law courts' *jurisdictio.* But the time arrived when this medieval pair, *jurisdictio* and *gubernaculum,* could no longer jog along in tolerable double-harness. The break came in 1641. More and more the king had relied upon extraparliamentary lawmaking for the routine government of the country, and hence upon the Court of Star Chamber for the concomitant judicial processes. In 1641 Parliament forced the king's assent to an act that abolished the Star

14. *Constitutionalism: Ancient and Modern* (Ithaca, 1947), chapters IV and V.

Chamber and other tribunals identified with the years of prerogative oppression. The common law courts' insistence upon statute as the one and only external source of law had brought them a powerful ally. From now on they and they alone would be the forum in which executive government must make good its claims to power.[15]

The importance of the act of 1641 to constitutionalism in the Anglo-American tradition could scarcely be overstated. For ever afterward, the crown had only such power as the common law acknowledged and gave effect to. With common law *jurisdictio* the permanent and sole mode of public law enforcement, and with statute as the only means of enabling it to do new things, executive government in England came to rely as never before upon the exclusive legislative power of Parliament. Nor was there any going back on this at the Restoration. Lack of a system of prerogative courts was part of Charles II's inheritance. The act abolishing the Star Chamber may have been forced upon his father, but it had been lawfully passed; there was no repudiating it as a product of a revolutionary and illegal regime. In any case there was little serious attempt to repeal it and bring back the courts in which the word of the king or his executive agents might pass for law. The politicians in Parliament now had a monopoly of law-making power, and they were not anxious to give it up.

---

15. Thus the beginning of the "rule of law" as expounded in A. V. Dicey, *Law of the Constitution* (8th ed., London, 1915).

It is interesting to see this foggy expression applied differently in a prerogativist counterpart to the common law *Case of Proclamations* (see p. 20). *Acts of the Privy Council 1613-14*(London, 1921), 211-19, show James Whitlocke before the council for having written critically of a royal commission into corruption in affairs of the Navy. The attorney general's allegations and argument (which the council appear to have accepted) included this:

"[Whitlocke] had affirmed and maintayned by the said writing that the Kinge cannot ... meddle with the bodies goodes or landes of his subjects but only by indictment, arraignement and tryall, or by legall proceedinge, in his ordinary Courtes of Justice, laying for his ground the Statute of Magna Charta: *Nullus liber homo capiatur,* etc., which posicion, in that generall and indeffinite manner, was ... not only grossely erroneous, and contrary to the rules of Lawe, but daingerous, and tendinge to the dissolvinge of government.

First, for that *lex terrae,* mencioned in the said statute, is not to bee understoode only of the proceedinges in the ordinary Courtes of Justice, but that his Majestie's prerogative and his absolute power incident to his Soveraignty is alsoe *lex terrae,* and is invested and excercised by the lawe of the land, and is parte thereof. And ... the opinion broached by ... Whitlocke did manifestly (by consequence) overthrowe the Kinge's martiall [naturall?] power, and the authoritie of the Councell Table, and the force of his Majestie's proclamacions and other accions and direccions of State and policie, applied to the necessitie of tymes and occasions, which fall not many tymes within the remedies or [sic] ordinary justice, nor cannot be tyed to the formalities of a legal proceedinge. ..."

Of course, real life does not always go according to the book. That the judicial limb of the king in council was not stitched back on after the Restoration did not mean that government under Charles II faithfully abstained from practices not sanctioned by common law or parliamentary enactment. Loss of its judicial power-base notwithstanding, the king's lawful and effective prerogative was still considerable; besides, the newly magnified citadels of power, Parliament and the courts of common law, were by no means immune from royal influence offstage. And adjustment to an untried and unfamiliar style of government was not achieved overnight. In the constitutional half-light of Restoration England the prime maxim of executive government seems to have been that, provided it could be gotten away with, anything went. Still, about entry and search of houses there was a certain *rigor juris* almost from the start.

An interesting insight into the climate around entry and search may be gained from, curiously enough, a royal proclamation. Royal proclamations were no less abundant under Charles II than in earlier reigns, and perhaps not all of them were strictly in line with the common law rule that while proclamations might underline the law they could not change it. But this particular proclamation was deeply impregnated with the Cokeian principle. Shortly after the king's return to the throne certain unregenerate elements in London had been gathering arms in preparation for an insurrection. The proclamation, issued some months afterward on 17 January 1661, takes up the story:

> We have been necessitated to cause diligent search to be made for such arms, and to secure several persons, whom We had good cause to suspect to be engaged in the said wicked and traitorous designs: Which nevertheless We desired might be done in so orderly a manner as such an exigence would bear, and not to the terrifying, disturbance, or injury of any of Our good subjects . . . .

Unfortunately, the purity of the king's intentions had not been paralleled in the consequent action:

> And we being given to understand, that during those late Commotions, several Persons have been imprisoned by Souldiers and others, their Houses searched, and their Goods taken away without lawful Authority . . . . These are strictly to charge and Command all Officers and Souldiers, and all other Persons whatsoever . . . to forbear to molest or trouble any of Our good Subjects, either in their Persons or Estates, and not to presume to apprehend any Armes whatsoever, or to search any Houses, without a lawful Warrant . . . .

(The "lawful Warrant" thus contemplated for the future presumably would be the warrant that the common law authorized for the taking of a criminal, which an insurrectionist doubtless would be.) Further admonitions followed:

> And We will that the said Warrants be always directed to some Constable, or other known Legal Officer: and that no Souldiers do otherwise interpose or meddle with the execution of any of the said Warrants, than by aiding and assisting of the said Constable, or other such known Legal Officer or Officers, as aforesaid: And all Military Officers and Souldiers are hereby commanded to be aiding and assisting to such Constables, or other Legal Officers, being by them thereunto required: And We do hereby declare, that as well as all who shall hereafter be so hardy as to offend against this Our Proclamation, shall not onely not receive countenance from Us therein, but shall be left to be proceeded against according to Our Laws, and incur Our high displeasure, as persons doing their utmost to bring scandal and contempt upon our Government.

It is not to be supposed that this proclamation was inspired solely by royal outrage at the excesses that had taken place. The insistence upon due legal form even when the "exigence" had been nothing less than the prevention of an armed uprising is better ascribed to the strength of contemporary sentiment on entry and search and removal of property (especially by soldiers, perhaps: the ruderies of Cromwell's major-generals were still a recent memory).[16]

What most signifies is the sequel. A few months after this proclamation Parliament was prevailed upon to enact that those responsible for the disorders condemned in it should be "saved harmless and indemnified in that behalf."[17] One catches the whiff of a deal behind the scenes: the king's men would be rescued just this once, but the king had to make it plain beyond all possibility of retraction that such gross violations of hearth, home, and property should never happen again. The thing to notice however is that without the interposition of Parliament the intrusions upon the disaffected Londoners threatened to be the subject of actions for damages at common law. Had the courts of common law been disposed to acknowledge new categories of peremptory entry and search the indemnifying legislation would have been unnecessary. After all,

16. This text was taken from an original print of the proclamation in the British Library. The climate of the times is evidenced by the king's speech as reported in *Commons Journals* 3 March 1662: "I need not tell you, that there is a Republican Party still in the Kingdom which have the Courage to promise themselves another Revolution. . . ." And for contemporary sensitivity on search powers see various cases in Kelynge's Reports: *e.g., Gardiner's Case* at 46-47.

17. 12 Car. 2, c. 6.

what more deserving a cause than suppression of a violent insurrection? But there it was. However amenable to crown pressure judges may have been in some respects, and even though common law doctrine was by no means incapable of absorbing useful inventions of the Court of Star Chamber, the contemporary mood did not encourage expectations of judge-made extensions to the law of entry and search.

Unaccommodating attitudes toward powers of entry and search were all one with the common law's ancient preoccupation with maintenance of the peace: few things were more likely to cause violent disturbance than intrusion upon a man's home and family. In the 1660s the common law attitude not only made it the more necessary that any new power of entry and search should be legislated for properly and in due statutory form, it also tended to influence the terms of the legislation itself. This was very evidently the case with the legislation for customs search.

It is worthwhile to observe in some detail how common law sentiment affected the shaping of the legislative provision that first made mention of a customs writ of assistance. This was section 5(2) of the Act of Frauds of 1662, which read as follows:

> And it shall be lawful to or for any Person or Persons, authorized by Writ of Assistance under the Seal of his Majesty's Court of Exchequer, to take a Constable, Headborough or other Publick Officer inhabiting near unto the Place, and in the Day-time to enter, and go into any House, Shop, Cellar, Warehouse or Room, or other Place, and in Case of Resistance, to break open Doors, Chests, Trunks and other Package, there to seize, and from thence to bring, any Kind of Goods or Merchandize whatsoever, prohibited and uncustomed, and to put and secure the same in his Majesty's Store-house, in the Port next to the Place where such Seizure shall be made.

The four passages underlined will suffice to indicate how the drafting was influenced by current common law thinking.

To take the last of them first. Since far back in the middle ages, when strong-arm techniques of dispossession were often resorted to among the landed classes, the courts of common law, whether in obedience to statute or from natural inclination, had strongly discountenanced forcible entries on to land;[18] and although occasions did exist when the common law sanctioned force in the pursuance of

18. See Holdsworth, *HEL* II, 452-53.

a power of entry, they were not numerous and were vouchsafed only under stringent conditions. The draftsman of 1662 could not have assumed that the courts would show greater liberality (if that is the word) toward a statutory power that spoke merely of entry. If anything, it was more likely that a bald reference to a power of entry would be construed as intending peaceable entry only. But a right to use force was essential if a power of entry to search for smuggled goods were to serve its purpose effectively: to await a freely opened door would often be self-defeat. Section 5(2) had therefore to neutralize the prospect of judicial disallowance of force by specifically providing for force. Even so, however, "to break open Doors . . ." was authorized only "in Case of Resistance."

In the limitation of section 5(2) power of entry to daylight hours the influence of common law thinking is reflected differently. Here it was not so much common law doctrine as the more or less personal predilection of a contemporary judge and jurist almost as exalted in the annals of the common law as the institutional Sir Edward Coke himself. Holdsworth, indeed, rated him, "as a lawyer, Coke's superior . . . the first of our great modern common lawyers." [19] This considerable figure was Sir Matthew Hale. In his *History of the Pleas of the Crown* Hale discoursed in some detail upon the common law provisions for power of entry on to private premises, in particular upon the common law search warrant for stolen goods. One of his comments was this:

> It is fit that such warrants to search do express, that search be made in the day-time, and tho I will not say they are unlawful without such restriction, yet they are very inconvenient without it, for many times under pretense of searches made in the night robberies and burglaries have been committed, and at best it causes great disturbance. [20]

It is unlikely to have been accidental that a principle which the most highly regarded lawyer of the time believed should govern search for stolen goods was given expression as unquestionable law in the drafting of legislation on search for smuggled goods.

In providing for the use of force, section 5(2) as it were overbore the common law position. In stipulating that its power of entry held good only in the daytime it accorded with the common law, or, at any rate, with the opinion of the greatest exponent of the common law then living. The two other section 5(2) passages underlined for

19. *Ibid.* VII, 594-95.
20. Hale, Vol. II (London, 1736), 150.

special attention, that "any Person or Persons" might be qualified to use the power of entry given by the section, and that he must have with him a "Constable . . . or other publick Officer inhabiting near unto the Place," combine to show further how the draftsman came to terms both with the practical necessities of customs search and with the cross-current of common law thought.

In the royal proclamation quoted on pages 23 and 24 the king repudiated the rough behavior of soldiers and others employed in seeking out arms in the houses of suspected subversives. The proclamation went on to indicate that in future there would be no searches of houses save by lawful warrant, such warrant being "always directed to some Constable, or other known Legal Officer." Much the same sentiment was reflected in one of Sir Matthew Hale's prescriptions for common law search warrants:

> They ought to be directed to constables and other public officers, whereof the law takes notice, and not to private persons . . . .[21]

With views such as these prevalent in the highest counsels of the kingdom, a statute that provided for powers of entry and search without stating by whom they might be exercised would run the same sort of risk as if it remained silent on the use of force: the risk of the courts construing it more narrowly than its begetters intended and confining its powers of entry and search to persons who could be regarded in law as "public officers." The point is, the men who obviously ought to be authorized to conduct searches for smuggled goods — the ordinary custom house staff — might well not answer to the designation "public officer." It sharpened the problem that in 1661 the customs had been put into farm, an arrangement whereby the king made over future duty receipts to private contractors in return for advances of ready cash; as agents of the farmers customs men could be only private persons themselves. A way of ensuring that customs searchers were not faulted for want of status as public officers was to have section 5(2) say explicitly that they could be "any Person or Persons."

This neutralization of common law predisposition was not, however, as total as at first appears. For one thing, a later section of the act restricted the right to seize — at common law this right was open to anyone willing to undertake the responsibility of getting the seizure condemned in court — to customs men proper, which in turn

21. *Ibid.*

meant that the section 5(2) power of entry, the purpose of which was to enable a seizure to be made, was likewise limited in practice to persons with a special occupational interest in customs law enforcement. The common law was also accommodated in the fact that the person exercising the power of entry must be accompanied by a "Constable . . . or other publick Officer." If the customs man could not himself rank as a public officer the next best· thing was that he should have with him someone who undoubtedly did.

Also, the accompanying public officer had to be "inhabiting near unto the Place." With this the completing segment of the picture falls into position. It is again relevant to recall the royal proclamation of January 1661 saying that the search warrants it contemplated should be "directed to some Constable, or other known Legal Officer." Here the thing to notice is the word "known." So far as the law could ensure it, the householder should be able to identify as someone respectable the man who came to the door and asked to be let in. As Hale hinted when recommending that search be restricted to the daytime, there was a risk that an ostensibly lawful entry might in fact be a ruse for a burglary. Reviewing, long afterward, enactments such as section 5(2) of the Act of Frauds of 1662, Mr. Justice Blackstone (Sir William Blackstone, of *Commentaries* fame) remarked: "The spirit of all the revenue laws is, that the accompanying officer must be an officer of the place, that the subject may not be unreasonably terrified at his house being entered . . . by mere strangers." [22] The stipulation in statutory provisions for entry and search that there must be "assistance" (as the function of just being present was sometimes called) by a local public officer can be seen as a sensible and practical device for minimizing the alarm and disturbance that violation of a man's home might so easily cause.

It was one thing for section 5(2) to make its power of entry conditional upon a constable or other local public officer being in attendance, but another to see that he actually came. It was not to be expected that he would drop everything and step along merely at the bidding of a man who claimed to be a customs officer. After all, there was nothing in it for him; the actual seizure would be made by the customs man and the customs man would get the proceeds. What was needed was something that the customs man could produce to

22. *Hill v. Barnes* (1777) 2 W. Bl. 1135, 1137.

satisfy the constable that his duty was indeed to do as the man said. Such as, for instance, an obviously authoritative document. Here was where section 5(2)'s stipulation for a writ of assistance came in.

The customs writ of assistance was a document that in the name of the king ordered a wide variety of persons to help the customs man make his search. Stripped of its prolix recital about the appointment, responsibilities, and powers of the customs commissioners and their understrappers, the specimen writ reproduced in Appendix C amounts to no more than this simple directive. That it was addressed not only to the indispensable local public officer but to all manner of functionaries and private folk besides probably owed something to the suggestions of history.

It was not new in England that a generality of persons, public and private alike, should be obligated to assist in the enforcement of law and the promotion of good order. Communal responsibility for maintenance of the public peace went back long before the Norman Conquest (a notable manifestation of it, the grand jury's presentment of suspects for trial, survives in many common law jurisdictions — though not, as it happens, the English — to this day). There were circumstances, having to do with a breach of the peace or the arrest of a felon, in which the common law entitled a constable to call upon bystanders for a helping hand. For centuries the duties of a sheriff had been the subject of a "patent of assistance," by which all manner of men were enjoined to aid and assist that rather lone public man-of-all-work. Nor were these piecemeal examples all.

Requisitioned assistance, for whatever objective pursued, was a fairly common feature in the modes of executive rule that came to grief in 1641. When the king's government still had a judiciary in partnership it would issue directives on widely various public subjects and bring to account anyone who did not obey; not infrequently those directives included a "clause of assistance," the purport of which was to enjoin all and sundry to aid and assist the bearer in the business stated. A clause of assistance was tacked on to the Privy Council's order in 1637 for the search of Doctor Everite's house, quoted on page 19: "And these are further to will and require all Maiors, Sheriffs, Justices of Peace, Bayliffs, Constables &c and all other his Maties Officers and loving subjects whome it may concerne, to bee ayding and asisting unto you, in the exeqution of this warrant." There were similar conciliar injunctions to give assistance in relation to the impressment of seamen, the seduction of ordinance workmen, and search for an illicit "Engine for the making of Needles." [23]

Especially relevant to the present purpose is an "open warrant" issued in 1629 (about the time when Charles I's irregular collection of tunnage and poundage was arousing strong indignation). [24] It began with a grumble about merchants in London landing imported goods at unauthorized places at night so as to evade customs duty, and also about "many disorderly people frequenting the waterside" in order to mock and harass the customs officers. Henceforth the king's messengers would act as auxiliaries to the customs officers "for the taking and keeping possession of all such goodes as have not payd all the duties payable for the same." They might search for "such goodes" too. Thus:

> it is further ordered that the Messingers upon notice given of any such goodes which have beene . . . landed or howsed without payment of all the duties aforesaid shall enter into any Shippe, hoye, barque, boate or any other Vessell, as also into any Shopp, howse, warehouse, seller, soller, or any other place to try and make diligent search in any trunke, cheste, press or any bulke whatsoever, for any goodes as well going out of this Kingdome as coming into the same which hath not paid all the duties aforesaid, and any such goodes so found, to seaze, attach and carry away to his Majesties Storehouse there to be kept . . . .

A further responsibility of the messengers was to arrest anyone who resisted or who abused and disturbed the customs officers. Lastly, the warrant widened its coverage with a clause of assistance:

> the Sherriffes of London and all other His Majesties Officers and loveing Subjects being required there unto shall be aydeing and assisting unto the Officers and messingers aforesaid wheresoever there shall be occasion in any part of his Majesties Dominions in this behalfe, as they will answer to the contrary in their perills.

One wonders whether this conciliar instrument of 1629, which conferred an almost open-ended power of entry and search for smuggled goods, backing it up with an admonition to everyone to be aiding and assisting, may not have been in the mind of the authorities when, some thirty years later, endeavors were again being made to improve the effectiveness of the customs enforcement regime. Of course, the resemblance between the "open warrant" of 1629 and

23. *Acts of the Privy Council May 1629-May 1630* (London, 1960), 4 (seamen), 5 (workmen), 126 (needle engine).
24. *Ibid.,* 1135.

the writ of assistance mentioned in the act of 1662 was not one hundred per cent. The warrant constituted in itself the definitive conferment of a power of entry and search by the king's prerogative, whereas the writ merely referred to a power given elsewhere, namely, in section 5(2) of the 1662 act. To this extent, indeed, it might have been section 5(2) rather than the writ of assistance that mirrored the 1629 warrant. But in that each pronounced a generalized command to assist, the warrant and the writ were practically identical; and the possibility seems fairly strong that recollections of the 1629 council warrant inspired the distinctive technique of customs search adopted in 1662.

An important question remains, however. The writ of assistance envisioned in the act of 1662 was not found ready and waiting in the old books of the law. Since the abolition of the prerogative-oriented courts in 1641 the only law in point was the common law. At no time had the common law provided a power of its own for customs entry and search, and it is not to be supposed that its antiquities would somehow have included an instrument associated with a power that in common law had never existed. How then did this new-fangled writ of assistance come into being?

In common with the generality of royal writs, the customs writ of assistance was in essence a communication in the name of the king. A royal writ might be to any of a multitude of purposes, its legal significance depending on the case. Though a letter to a foreign prince gained little by being called a writ, other documents answering to this designation were the bedrock of the country's judicial system. In the final analysis the legal weight of a royal writ was no more and no less than what a court of law acknowledged it to be. The courts would not necessarily take a writ at its own valuation. It did not at all follow that a writ that ostensibly altered a person's legal position — for example, a writ originating an action for damages against him on certain facts being established — would actually do so. In the words of Maitland, "the fact that a writ was penned, and that it passed the seal, was not a fact that altered rights . . . it had still to run the gauntlet in court, and might ultimately be quashed as unprecedented and unlawful." [25] It was only common sense, after all. Without this judicial veto, administrative authorities who made

25. F. W. Maitland, "The History of the Register of Original Writs," in *Select Essays in Anglo-American Legal History* II (Boston, 1908), 558; also 559-60.

out and issued writs — the clerks of chancery, as it might be — would have had what amounted to a law-making power of their own. [26]

So too the customs writ of assistance needed more behind it than the mere fact of its issuance. That it was the work not of the clerks in the chancery but of an official of the Court of Exchequer, the king's remembrancer, did not affect the circumstance that, if challenged, its substantive legality would have to be demonstrated in judicial process. Ordinarily, of course, the authenticity of a writ bearing upon a man's legal position could be established by that kind of writ having been included in the registers of writs published for practitioners; that a writ appeared in these compilations meant that the courts had accepted it as legally satisfactory. But there was no possibility of the customs writ of assistance being found in any of the old books, since the statutory power of entry and search to which it related did not exist until 1662. For its acceptability as an instrument having legal force one has to look elsewhere.

A lead is given in the English attorney general's Opinion, referred to in chapter 1 and reproduced in full in Appendix A. In 1768, it will be recalled, Attorney General William De Grey was consulted about the recalcitrance of judges in the American colonies toward the writs of assistance wished upon them by the Townshend legislation of the previous year. De Grey's Opinion is as informative a statement of the juridical provenance of the customs writ of assistance as has ever been committed to paper. (Not that it tells a great deal, even at that.) According to De Grey, the customs writ of assistance "was founded upon the Common Law." That is to say, the writ was not so much acknowledged as actually created by the common law.

In the brief sketch of Sir Edward Coke earlier in the chapter it was remarked that his extrajudicial *Institutes* were generally accepted as tantamount to authoritative common law, and that it was in them that the doctrinal source of the customs writ of assistance was to be found. A passage in the Third Institute reads:

> And here is a secret in law, that upon any statute made for the common peace, or good of the realm, a writ may be devised for the better execution of the same, according to the force and effect of the act.[27]

Here was common law doctrine from which the customs writ of assistance could take its rise. The writ clearly satisfied the first of the

26. By the end of the thirteenth century formulation of writs had also become a subject of parliamentary regulation (as in Statute of Westminster II, 1285, c. 24).

27. At 162.

three requirements set forth in Coke: it would be difficult to deny that the Act of Frauds of 1662 was "for the good of the realm." The second requirement, that the writ be "for the better execution" of the act, could have been satisfied by the simple fact that the power of entry and search that the act provided had expressly been made dependent on a writ of assistance. On the third requirement some elaboration is necessary.

The writ needed to be "according to the force and effect of the Act," but nothing in the 1662 act that has been seen thus far warrants its actual purport: a directive to all manner of persons to give assistance. And there is something else. In his 1768 Opinion Attorney General De Grey went on to say that disobedience of the writ was "a Contempt of the Court"; [28] if each and every person in the almost infinite multitude to whom the writ of assistance was addressed were liable to imprisonment in the event of refusal to do its bidding, clearly there must be more to the wording of the writ than the invention of the official who penned it, or what of the common law doctrine in the *Case of Proclamations* outlawing the creation of punishable offenses by executive or administrative fiat? The "force and effect" of the 1662 act that constituted the third requisite to the legal validity of the writ of assistance were a long way down from section 5(2) and its power of entry and search. They were near the end of the act, in section 32:

> And be it further enacted and ordained, That all Officers belonging to the Admiralty, Captains and Commanders of Ships, Forts, Castles and Block-houses, as also all Justices of the Peace, Mayors, Sheriffs, Bailiffs, Constables and Headboroughs, and all the King's Majesty's Officers, Ministers and Subjects whatsoever whom it may concern, shall be aiding and assisting to all and every Person and Persons which are or shall be appointed by his Majesty to manage his Customs, and the Officers of his Majesty's Customs, and their respective Deputies, in the due Execution of all and every Act and Thing in and by this present Act required and enjoined . . . .

This statutory obligation to give assistance probably could have warranted writs of assistance related to anything and everything the

---

28. De Grey may have been well up on the law of contempt, through participation in a potentially leading case on the subject, the abortive *R. v. Almon* (1765); for which see Holdsworth, *HEL* III, 391-94, and the works there cited; also J. C. Fox, *History of Contempt of Court* (Oxford, 1927), 109-110. And in another of the cases arising from John Wilkes's tussles with the government, *Leach v. Money* (1765) 19 St. Tr. 1002, the question of general warrants was "very strenuously argued" by De Grey A. G.: Lord Campbell, *Lives of the Chief Justices of England* II (London, 1849), 461.

customs authorities did under the 1662 act. And though in practice there were no other writs of assistance than the ones issued by the Court of Exchequer for use in section 5(2) entry and search of premises, those writs were drafted in terms that associated them with search of ships also (for which the act made separate provision — without, however, actually stipulating for a writ of assistance — in section 4). But that is by the way.

The originating logic of the writ of assistance was that the customs officer might summon assistance the more effectively. By being shown the writ, public officers and others would be put on notice of an obligation to go along with the customs officer or otherwise facilitate his task. However, there was another logic too; in the opposite direction. As a common law instrument, the writ of assistance was not in the English language. It was in Latin, or, to be accurate, a weird approximation to Latin in which apostrophes were substituted for case-endings and which had recourse to English whenever the draftsman was not sure of the right Latin word. Unintelligibility was further advanced by the calligraphy in which this strange argot was set forth. It was another part of the medieval hangover or throwback characterizing so many English institutions that different agencies of the crown — including the courts — might have their own distinctive kind of handwriting, so stylized as to be practically indecipherable to persons unfamiliar with it. The office of the king's remembrancer in the Court of Exchequer, where the customs writ of assistance was prepared, affected a kind of "chancery hand," an elegant but almost unreadable script used by the clerks in the office of the lord chancellor. What with the barbarous near-Latin and the difficult writing, the text of the writ of assistance can have conveyed very little to most of the people whom the customs officer presented it to. A justice of the peace of some education, or a sheriff whose duties often brought him into contact with the ways of government, might be able to make out what the writ was saying; but to the lowly constable, and the even lowlier headborough ("a petty constable," the *Oxford English Dictionary* calls him), the whole thing would be a mystery.

The truth is, a good many of these functionaries would be illiterate even in English; and the significance of their being unable to comprehend the language and script of the writ of assistance was therefore not great. One suspects that what the writ actually said was less important in practice than the sheer visual impact of the thing, and here the king's remembrancer did a really magnificent job. The writ was a large sheet of vellum, some two-and-a-half feet wide by two feet deep, bearing an ornate portrait of the monarch and, suspended from a stout plaited cord, a massive waxen seal. With this daunting paraphernalia thrust under his nose, he would be a bold constable who refused to take the customs officer's word for what it was all about.

Nor when Parliament at last decided upon reform and enacted that from the beginning of 1733 the language of the common law should be English, and chancery script no more, would even a literate person have found it easy to tell exactly what the writ of assistance said. One has only to attempt to read through the English writ of George III, reproduced in Appendix C. The writ's prolix recital of attendant but superfluous detail — for example, the particulars of the customs commissioners' patent of appointment — rendered its unpunctuated text practically as unreadable as ever. If some resolute spirit did manage to persevere right through, he would probably finish in such a state of mental fatigue as to be very little wiser than when he started. Even in English, the writ of assistance was a document more impressive than understandable.

Not that it mattered much. As in the old Latin style so in the new English, if by the mere charisma of its appearance the writ enabled the customs officer to get the necessary assistance and set to work in peace it served its turn.

If its impact upon the humble laity was little other than totemistic, the customs writ of assistance has never been too luminous among the learned either. Updated versions or variants of it are still used for search purposes in the United Kingdom and elsewhere, yet legal commentary on it is exceedingly sparse. The most extensive treatment of it — and this strongly angled to events in pre-revolutionary America — has been that given by Horace Gray (later chief justice of Massachusetts and an associate justice of the United States Supreme Court), which appeared in 1865.[29] In England there is scarcely a legal treatise that gives the writ of assistance as much as a passing mention.

The customs writ of assistance, it must be emphasized. As if to

29. As an appendix to *Quincy's Reports* (*cf.* chapter 1, n. 1), 395-540.

thrust this writ of assistance into deeper obscurity, for centuries there have existed miscellaneous other instruments of the same name. For example, the writ by which judges and law officers of the crown are bidden attend as "assistants" to the House of Lords at the opening of a Parliament is sometimes called a writ of assistance. Some writs of assistance have had to do with sheriffs. One of them ordered the sheriff to assist a debtor to the king in recovering money that the debtor himself was owed, so that he in turn might settle with the king. Another directed the sheriff to help a man into possession of property adjudged to him by a court of chancery. Yet another was to the purpose that the sheriff should assist in levying exactions for which his predecessor was accountable.[30]

The only English book to set forth a specimen customs writ of assistance last came from the presses in 1725. This was a book on exchequer practice by one William Brown, and, as there will be cause to note later on, Brown's specimen was not a very satisfactory one. The almost total disregard of the customs writ of assistance in recognized books of legal forms and precedents can perhaps be rationalized on the lines that these books were not so much academic treatises as practitioners' manuals, and since the content of the writ was of practical interest only to the solicitor to the customs commissioners there would have been little point in including it in a work of general use. At bottom, however, the reason for the dearth of information and commentary on the customs writ of assistance may be that, aside from a smallish number of more or less incidental references, mostly in the later years of the eighteenth century, there has been almost nothing in the English law reports to nourish learning on this unfamiliar instrument. The power associated with the writ was mentioned when the Commons were debating Walpole's abortive excise scheme in 1733 (search of premises was one of the points of opposition).[31] And, as will be recounted in chapter 8, the writ attracted notice in a London periodical some years later. But how little there was on it may be judged from the fact that as late as 1785 Lord Mansfield, chief justice of the King's Bench and a very considerable common lawyer, was in such doubt as to the historical provenance of the writ that he postponed judgment until counsel had

30. 1 Ann. stat. 1, c. 8 (continuation of legal processes, etc., after demise of the crown; see p. 273 below) seems to have differentiated kinds of writs of assistance. *Cf.* E. R. Adair and F. M. G. Evans, "Writs of Assistance, 1558-1700," in *English Historical Review* (1921), 356.

31. *Parliamentary History* VIII (London, 1811), 1268-1320; and *cf.* p. 111 below.

researched into it (to no great profit, as it turned out). [32] And some forty-five years later, in 1830, the writ was still a subject of puzzlement and doubt on the bench. Thus Lord Tenterden C. J. in *R. v. Watts and Watts:*

> A writ of assistance is certainly an ancient writ. It is mentioned in the statute 13 & 14 Car. 2 c. 11 s. 5. It was probably in the same form at that time as at the present, and it seems to be mentioned in that statute as a matter then known and in use, but whether precisely in the same form as at present, has not been ascertained. [33]

As has been seen, the writ of assistance of the kind Lord Tenterden was talking about, the customs writ of assistance, was not really as ancient as all that (though some of the other documents which also and confusingly answered to the name of writ of assistance did indeed date back into the middle ages). His lordship would have done better to adopt a suggestion that Lord Mansfield had let fall in the earlier case, namely, whether the customs writ of assistance "was not founded entirely on the Statute of Charles II, and framed from the general directions of that Act."

The two cases just cited, *Cooper v. Boot* in 1785 and *R. v. Watts and Watts* in 1830, are virtually the only cases in the English law reports in which the customs writ of assistance has come under discussion. Though rather short on illumination in some respects both of them afford useful signposts away from a fallacy which has sometimes darkened thinking, that the writ was a species of search warrant.

The comments of Lord Tenterden C. J. in the *Watts* case go on: "The writ . . . does not give nor profess to give any power to search or seize . . . ." What signifies in these words is the denial, the refutation of any notion that the writ in itself constituted the customs officer's authority to enter and search. A search warrant, on the other hand, did exactly that. Upon being challenged to show by what right he intruded the holder of a search warrant would produce his warrant, whereas the customs officer with a writ of assistance would point to section 5(2) of the Act of Frauds of 1662. In the earlier case, *Cooper v. Boot,* Lord Mansfield C. J. was quite explicit. The case had to do with liability in trespass of excise officers who had executed a search warrant without finding anything. A similar question having

---

32. *Cooper v. Boot,* 4 Dougl. 339, 346-47; also, as *Cooper v. Booth,* 3 Esp. 135.
33. 1 B. & Ad. 166, 175.

been put (for the sake of argument) in relation to a customs writ of assistance, Mansfield finally dismissed it as irrelevant. "The writ of assistance . . . is no warrant," he said, "it is general, and leaves all to the discretion of the custom-house officers." [34] Here was another difference between a warrant and the writ of assistance. A warrant left little to discretion. It was a firm directive that a search be made, obligating the holder specifically.

So resilient is the fallacy that regards the power of entry and search associated with the writ of assistance as given by the writ itself, emphasis seems admissible. "The Power of the Custom House Officer," said Attorney General De Grey in his 1768 Opinion,

> is given by Act of Parliament, not by This Writ, wch. does nothing more than facilitate the Execution of the Power by making the disobedience of the Writ a Contempt of the Court; the Writ only requiring all Subjects to permit the Exercise of it to aid it. The Writ is a Notification of the Character of the Bearer to the Constable & others to Whom He applies & a Security to the Subject agst. others Who might pretend to such authority.

The act referred to was of course the Act of Frauds of 1662, section 5(2): "it shall be lawful to or for any Person or Persons authorized by Writ of Assistance under the Seal of his Majesty's Court of Exchequer, to take a Constable, Headborough or other Publick Officer inhabiting near unto the Place, and in the Day-time to enter, and go into any House . . . ." If it were necessary to demonstrate De Grey's statement that "the Power of the Custom House Officer is given by Act of Parliament, and not by this Writ," the task would not be difficult. The effect of section 5(2) was that action on the face of it trespassorial should nevertheless be lawful, if the person engaging in it had a writ of assistance and a local public officer were in attendance. That the power of entry thus legalized depended upon these preconditions does not mean that it was created by them. Still less by only one of them. In the case of the local public officer this is perfectly plain: nobody would suppose that he was the source of the customs officer's power. But it is equally true of the writ of assistance.

The error that the writ of assistance constituted the customs officer's power of entry and search probably owes something to a

---

34. Twenty years earlier Mansfield's thinking apparently had not advanced thus far. In *Leach v. Money* (n. 28 above, c. 1026): "there are many cases where particular acts of parliament have given authority to apprehend, under general warrants; as in the case of writs of assistance . . . ."

semantic accident. Section 5(2) of the 1662 act spoke of persons "authorized by Writ of Assistance." Modern usage might well take this as meaning that his authority came from the writ. However, the writ of assistance "authorized" its bearer only in the sense, long obsolete today but still current in the seventeenth century, of vouching for him. Hence De Grey's comment: "The Writ is a Notification of the Character of the Bearer . . . ." The writ was a sort of identity card by which the customs officer could establish himself as a man to be heeded.

There was perhaps one way in which the writ of assistance had the quality of a search warrant: the man whose premises were to be entered was presented with a document that assured him that the entry was not trespassorial or in breach of the peace, and in effect warned him to let the bearer of the document in. But that was as far as similarity went. Juridically, the search warrant and the writ of assistance were poles apart. In a sense that had no application to the writ of assistance, issuance of a warrant was generally exercise of a jurisdiction. This was certainly so in the case of the search warrant for stolen goods issued by justices of the peace under the common law; and it was so, too, in the cases where statute had drawn upon the common law model to bestow authority to issue search warrants for other things. The justice had to be shown cause — a statement on oath was the common law norm — before he issued the warrant. His issuance of a warrant was not a merely mechanical function. There was an element of consideration and decision in it. "A search warrant is partly a ministerial and partly a judicial act," [35] as it has been said in the English courts.

By contrast, issuance of the writ of assistance was exclusively "ministerial" (or, in more modern terminology, executive or administrative). There was nothing judicial about what took place in the king's remembrancer's office. It was just a matter of penning the writ and affixing the Court of Exchequer seal to it. Even if it had been the practice to issue a writ of assistance related to one particular occasion only, the king's remembrancer had no jurisdiction to say whether the occasion were appropriate or not. Any question as to the legal validity of the writ would be for determination by judicial process afterward. It was the same principle noticed earlier in relation to writs purporting to affect legal rights as between private persons: clerks might frame a writ, but it was for the courts to say if

---

35. *Webb v. Ross* (1859) 4 H. & N. 115, *per* Martin B.

it was valid. The writ of assistance was in no danger of successful attack, of course. It was backed foursquare by the "secret in law" enunciated in Coke's Third Institute.

It may be that much of the silence and misunderstanding enveloping the customs writ of assistance is that the "secret in law" has been too well kept. Some might hesitate to take the "secret" at face value anyway, for Coke was not always above resorting to originality.

But the "secret" looks authentic enough. In Fitzherbert's *La Novel Natura Brevium,* published in 1609, there was a precedent of a writ framed on the Statute of Northampton II, 1328. A copy of Fitzherbert in the British Library has pages interleaved with folios of manuscript commentary. Opposite the Statute of Northampton writ there is a manuscript citation of Coke's "secret in law," and the remark "ceo brev. ft. frame gr . . . selong le effect d'Act." (Norman French, as well as Latin, was an affectation favored by the common law.) The handwriting is that of Sir Matthew Hale, who was not a man to follow even the mighty Coke against his own judgment.[36]

There is another thing. Section 5 of the Act of Frauds of 1662 prescribed that the writ of assistance it spoke of should be under the seal of the Court of Exchequer. Assuredly such a novelty would not have been introduced without the knowledge and approval of the chief baron of the court (chief judge, that is to say: judges in the Court of Exchequer were called barons). In 1662 the chief baron was Sir Matthew Hale.

36. In *History of the Pleas of the Crown* II, 113, Hale, affirming that common law search warrants for stolen goods existed, made no bones about contradicting a statement by Coke that no search warrants at all were available at common law.

Eighteenth-century editions of Fitzherbert took to incorporating notation said to be Hale's; but not the references to Coke's "secret."

4

The Originating Legislation

VERY RELEVANT to how customs search turned out in the American colonies in the eighteenth century was how it had started in England in the 1660s.

Though the question centers upon the Act of Frauds of 1662 and the politico-administrative conditions of the period, it is best approached in the light of a slightly earlier statute, the *Act to prevent Frauds and Concealments of his Majesty's Customs* of 1660. This act, mentioned in chapters 2 and 3, merits inspection in some detail.

Although the journals of the respective houses of Parliament were usually little more than a bare-boned record of business done, the legislative history of the 1660 act is fairly full. Immediately upon the restoration of the monarchy in the spring of 1660 the commons granted the king a range of customs duties on practically everything entering or leaving the country. The following September they were affronted to learn of a quantity of foreign tobacco having been "landed, and secretly carried away . . . without due Entry, or paying of Customs or Excise . . . ." The house ordered it to be seized, but was told that it could not be gotten at: the culprit merchant, James Haberthwaite, it was reported, "keeps his Doors against the Officers." Haberthwaite was within his rights; the act imposing the duty provided for forfeiture of offending goods, but it said nothing about invading private property in pursuit of them, and if "the Officers" had nevertheless made their way in they would have had no defense to an action for trespass. Immediate action was taken to remedy the deficiency. Within barely a week, the House of Lords having sat specially, the 1660 act for customs search was in the statute book.[1]

Henceforth it would be legally possible to track down "any Goods

---

1. Acknowledgments to: J. R. Frese, "Early Parliamentary Legislation on Writs of Assistance," *Colonial Society of Massachusetts Publications* 38 (1959), 317-59.

for which Custom, Subsidy or other Duties" were "due or payable by Virtue of the Act passed this Parliament," such goods having been "landed or conveyed away without due Entry thereof first made, and the Customer or Collector, or his Deputy agreed with." "Oath thereof" had to be made before the Lord Treasurer, a baron of the Exchequer, or the "Chief Magistrate of the . . . Place where the Offence shall be committed, or the Place next adjoining thereunto," who would

> issue out a Warrant to any Person or Persons, thereby enabling him or them with the Assistance of a Sheriff, Justice of Peace or Constable, to enter into any House in the Day-time where such Goods are suspected to be concealed, and in case of Resistance to break open such Houses, and to seize and secure the same Goods so concealed; and all Officers and Ministers of Justice are hereby required to be aiding and assisting thereunto.

A curious feature of this legislative *tour de force,* propelled through Parliament with such imperative urgency, was that it was scheduled to last only a year or so at most. In section 3 the act set a term on its own life: "this Act," it said, "shall continue in Force unto the End of the first Session of the next Parliament, and no longer." Why there should have been such a limitation is not clear. It would hardly have been that this particular parliament, being unsure of its own legal status (having been convened when the king was still in exile), was unwilling to venture a permanent provision: other acts it passed had no automatic expiry written into them. Nor can it be supposed that the confirmatory act passed by a normally convened Parliament the following year would have the effect of making the 1660 provision for customs search warrants perpetual; the time limit was confirmed along with everything else. Two possible explanations suggest themselves. Men in the know may have been aware of plans, which materialized in the Act of Frauds of 1662, for comprehensive legislation to strengthen customs enforcement in all its aspects; so the small 1660 act and its search warrant perhaps were conceived as a mere stopgap. Alternatively, the word might have gotten around that the customs were shortly to be put into farm, which transference to private management meant that the distinctively public interest in maximizing revenue yield by enhanced enforcement procedures would be lessened. A mode of enforcement that trenched upon the rights of hearth and home was one thing when directly and exclusively for the public benefit; it was quite another when the principal interest served was substantially a private one.

Whatever the reason for the 1660 act being only temporary, the fact is that in 1662 fresh provision for customs entry and search of premises was made. The terms of section 5(2) of the Act of Frauds of 1662 bear repeating:

> And it shall be lawful to or for any Person or Persons, authorized by Writ of Assistance under the Seal of his Majesty's Court of Exchequer, to take a Constable . . . or other publick Officer inhabiting near unto the Place, and in the Day-time to enter . . . any House . . . or other Place, and in Case of Resistance to break open Doors, Chests, Trunks and other Package, there to seize, and from thence to bring, any Kind of Goods or Merchandize whatsoever, prohibited and uncustomed, and to put and secure the same in his Majesty's Store-house . . .

There is an obvious question. Why had the 1660 precedent been succeeded by something so different?

Some enlightenment is to be found in Attorney General William De Grey's 1768 Opinion on American uncooperativeness over the Townshend writ of assistance:[2] "The Writ is not granted upon a Previous Information, nor to any Particular Person, nor on a special occasion. The inconvenience of that was experienced upon the Act of 12 C.2. C.19, the present Method of Proceeding adopted in Lieu of what That Statute had prescribed." In 1771 judges in America were still holding out against general writs of assistance, and it fell to De Grey's successor, Edward Thurlow, to elaborate further upon the relation between the writ of assistance enactment of 1662 and the search warrant act of 1660. Thurlow thought the Americans had made the mistake of looking to the 1660 act for the provenance of the writ instead of to the act of 1662,

> not observing, as it should seem, that the first act has a different object, and proceeds by different means. These were found useless, and inconvenient; and, to remedy the mischief, the second act was made, on which the present writ of assistance in England is founded.[3]

As the crown's principal advisers on legal matters, De Grey and Thurlow would have had access to whatever records remained of the origins of the acts of 1660 and 1662. The view each of them expressed, that the operation of the 1660 act had proved unsatisfactory, therefore seems reliable enough. Unfortunately however neither explained exactly what was wrong.

2. Appendix A; and see pp. 2-3 and 38.
3. Appendix B; and see pp. 4-5.

Conjecture draws first upon the unfavorable common law attitudes to intrusion on to private property that in chapter 3 were seen
to have done much to shape writ of assistance entry and search in
section 5(2) of the Act of Frauds of 1662. It is not surprising to find
signs of the same influence in the 1660 act for customs search
warrants. For example, as it was in 1662 so it had been in 1660,
entry must be in the daytime, and force was permissible only "in
Case of Resistance": one recalls Sir Matthew Hale's concern about
householders being startled into nocturnal disturbance of the peace,
and the courts' ancient dislike of the use of force. Included in the
common law predisposition was the view that a man's house should
not be invaded by strangers whose authority and identity as public
officers were not apparent; and the policy of the 1660 act was, as
that of the 1662 act would be, to stipulate that the intruder from the
custom house must be accompanied by an officer of the peace,
whom the householder would be more likely to recognize. Both acts
imposed a corresponding obligation upon constables and so forth to
"assist" accordingly. Here, however, a significant difference is to be
noticed. The 1660 act did not anticipate the problem that the 1662
act actually provided against: the constable's unwillingness to do as
the customs man said. Unlike the 1662 act the 1660 act said nothing
about the customs man having a writ of assistance, with which he
could put the reluctant constable on specific and immediate notice
of an obligation to step along. The document contemplated by the
1660 act was a warrant authorizing the customs man to enter "with
the Assistance of a Sheriff, Justice of Peace, or Constable," and that
was all.[4] That 1660-style customs search really did pose this sort of
problem is indicated by the curious document reproduced in Appendix D, which appears to have been a hybrid variant of a 1660
warrant, directed not to a customs officer but to the constables of a
certain parish, ordering them to assist him (and if it came to using
force, to do the actual seizing). As a quasi-administrative instruction
to subordinate officers of the peace this may have been valid enough,
but its legality as a 1660-type search warrant is very questionable.
Resort to so dubious an instrument seems inexplicable save on the
hypothesis of uncooperativeness among constables in the operation
of the 1660 act.

4. Such a writ was theoretically possible, nevertheless: by reference to the requirement
included in the 1660 act that "all Officers and Ministers of Justice . . . be aiding and
assisting . . . ."

So much for one of the bugs in the 1660 act. Another had to do with the actual issuance of the warrant. Promptness of action was essential to successful customs search. Unless the offending goods were found and seized quickly they would be gone, either in the normal course (they had been smuggled to be sold, not stored up) or because word had gotten round that the customs were on the trail. Under the 1660 act, the difficulty of procuring a warrant might often cause a search to fail for being too late. The authorities whom the act empowered to issue warrants were few and in most places far between. Jurisdiction was limited to "the Lord Treasurer, or any of the Barons of the Exchequer, or Chief Magistrate of the Port or Place where the Offence shall be committed, or the Place next adjoining thereunto." In London, the largest port in the country and the area where the need was the greatest, this restriction would not have mattered much; the Lord Treasurer and the barons of the Exchequer were only a mile or so upriver, at Westminster. But elsewhere in the country there was no one to apply to other than an appropriate "Chief Magistrate." Aside from possible difficulty in identifying this personage (arguably, for example, he could only be the lord lieutenant), the number one on a county bench might live a day's ride away.

Practical clumsiness probably weighed most against the act of 1660 as a model for 1662. But, in the words used by Attorney General Thurlow, the two enactments were different not only in "means" but in "object."

The range of goods for which search warrants might be issued under the 1660 act was defined thus: "any Goods for which Custom, Subsidy or other Duties are due or payable . . .," having been "landed or conveyed away without due Entry thereof first made . . . ." Power of search under the 1660 act was available only in relation to goods involved in an offense against the revenue. Nothing was said of a further category of goods susceptible of customs enforcement action, prohibited goods. Prohibited goods were goods imported or brought forward for exportation in violation of a law by which such movements were forbidden or restricted. Some prohibitions were imposed as it were for their own sake, because national policy held it undesirable that the particular categories of goods to which they applied should be allowed into the country — or, as the case might be, out of it. (There was a statutory prohibition on the exportation of gunpowder, for instance.) Other prohibitions, however, depended not upon what the article was but upon facts or circumstances attending it: its place of origin or destination, for example, or its mode of transportation. Prohibitions of this kind were an important feature of the regulatory regime of navigation and trade: goods transported in violation of, say, the national shipping monopoly in the colonial trade, or the transatlantic staple, were deemed prohibited. To goods thus offending the respective statute commonly attached the sanction of forfeiture. This meant of course that the customs authorities would purpose to seize them. But since the 1660 act spoke only of goods in breach of the revenue law, its search provision apparently did not apply to goods seizable as prohibited. Possibly the act had been rushed through Parliament too fast.

However it may have been with the 1660 act, the new provision for customs entry and search, in section 5(2) of the Act of Frauds of 1662, did not omit reference to prohibited goods.

Indeed not. True, the power of entry and search introduced in 1662 was free from the practical cumbrousness of the act of 1660; all that difficulty, for instance, of having to get specific warrants from inaccessible magistrates was discarded in favor of a once-for-all writ of assistance. But the subject of the new power,

> any Kind of Goods or Merchandize whatsoever, prohibited and un-customed

was so worded that whereas the 1660 act had not provided for prohibited goods, the 1662 act provided for nothing else.

Even on first impression the 1662 form of words has something curious about it. It reads as though the draftsman had belatedly tumbled to the obvious fact that the power of entry could not be good for literally *any* "Kind of Goods or Merchandize whatsoever" and had added the qualification "prohibited and uncustomed" as a hasty afterthought. That, however, was at most a small inelegance. What matters is the wording of the qualifying phrase itself. There was an inescapable double-barreledness about "prohibited and un-customed." On a strict interpretation — indeed, on the plain meaning of the phrase — the only things that could be legitimate quarry under the section 5(2) power of entry were things that were *both* prohibited *and* uncustomed. From this it follows that the power could properly be invoked for undutied goods only if they happened to be prohibited as well.

While prohibited goods might be uncustomed, if only in the sense that they had not gone through the appropriate customs control procedure, it was by no means the case that everything that unlawfully escaped duty ranked as prohibited. Indeed, in England it was not so much as probable. In 1661 a number of ancient statutory prohibitions on various specified manufactures were reactivated. These were backed by forfeiture, and may therefore have been a factor in the prominence given to prohibited goods in the 1662 provision for customs search; even so, the great majority of products remained unaffected by them. The burgeoning legislation on navigation and trade was a fertile source of prohibitions of the *sub modo* sort; but comparatively few can have materialized in England, where, in contrast to the colonies, the emphasis of the imperial system was revenue rather than regulation. Overall, then, most of the things smuggled into or out of England were "uncustomed" only, and the "prohibited and uncustomed" formula was too narrow for them.

That the power of entry and search in section 5(2) of the Act of Frauds of 1662 was drafted so as to have no application to straight revenue smuggling was not necessarily, or even probably, inadvertent. It was after all a fairly sophisticated piece of work, involving resourceful exploitation of Coke's "secret in law" for the writ of assistance, and almost certainly the scrutiny of no less a luminary than Sir Matthew Hale, as chief baron of the Court of Exchequer. So crass an error as "prohibited and uncustomed" when "prohibited or uncustomed" was meant would not have been likely at that level of legal skill; still less since elsewhere in the act (in relation to search on board ship, for example) "prohibited or uncustomed" was the phrase chosen. The chances are that the draftsman knew well what he was doing. Earlier in the chapter it was suggested as a possible reason for the brief life written into the 1660 act on search for undutied goods that Parliament, apprehending that the customs duties were shortly to be put in farm, preferred not to sanction violation of hearth and home for the sake of private investment. If there was anything in this it would also have applied to the search legislation of 1662, for by then the farm was in operation. A power of customs entry for search for prohibited goods was unobjectionable, if not positively desirable, since prohibition was a matter of public interest exclusively. But goods that were undutied represented a mere private loss, in regard to which so serious an encroachment upon another man's private rights was less acceptable. Such ratiocination is not fanciful. As was seen in the last chapter, entry and search of people's houses was a sensitive subject in this period.

Legally speaking, the position of customs search in the years after 1662 cannot have been robust. The original act of 1660 under which search warrants might be issued for undutied goods had lapsed, and the writ of assistance mode of search under the Act of Frauds of 1662 appeared to apply only to the comparatively small number of smuggled items that could be deemed "prohibited." In strictness, things that had become liable to forfeiture for having dodged customs duty — which was the case with most smuggled items in England at that time — lay beyond the range of seizures that could properly be the subject of customs entry and search.

It is in point to notice something that happened in 1685, on the accession of James II. The first act of James's first Parliament was to endow him with a revenue; and he was given duties of tunnage and poundage similar to those given to his brother in 1660. The interesting thing is that this act went on to revive the search warrant act of 1660, saying that it would "be of full force and effect during His Majesties Life . . . ." It would now be legally possible for a customs officer to obtain a search warrant for undutied goods.

Besides underlining the position that since the expiry of the 1660 act in 1662 there had been no legal foundation for customs search for goods that were simply undutied (and not prohibited as well), the 1685 legislation fits in with a change that had taken place in the crown's relation to undutied goods. At the time of the 1662 act it might not have greatly mattered to the government that the new writ of assistance mode of entry and search was not angled to revenue law: customs revenues were in farm and refinements of enforcement practice were more for the private farmers to bother about. But in 1685 this was no longer the situation. In 1671, the customs had been taken out of farm, and restored to crown management under a board of customs commissioners. It then ceased to be a matter of letting someone else do most of the worrying about revenue smuggling. The problem was squarely and exclusively the government's.

Yet when the opportunity came in 1685 for legislation to widen the scope of customs search, why should action have been limited to reviving (of all things) the clumsy and discredited search warrant act of 1660? Why was a decent job not made of it? Such as, for instance, amending section 5(2) of the Act of Frauds of 1662 so that the constrictive "prohibited *and* uncustomed" formula were replaced by "prohibited *or* uncustomed"? The explanation perhaps lay in a sagacious awareness of actuality. Whatever the limitations upon customs search in strict law, it is not necessarily to be supposed that practice at the ports was overmuch inhibited by observance of them. Evidence exists that even the topmost levels of government were not quick to apprehend that the 1660 act had set a short term upon itself;[5] and it seems reasonable to surmise that not all customs officers and local magistrates, having gotten used to 1660-style search warrants, realized that such things ought to have stopped as long ago as 1662. Similarly with the 1662 writ of assistance mode of customs search. A hard-nosed appraisal of the "prohibited and uncustomed" formula might cause uneasiness in a lawyer's chambers or in the higher echelons of the customs administration; but rarified statutory interpretation was not the forte of the workaday customs officer in the outfield, who probably was content to assume that entry and search with his impressive writ of assistance was good for seizures of all sorts. A background of widespread customs search actually and notoriously going on, but with nonexistent or highly dubious legal justification, makes sense of the 1685 decision. The authorities would have been conscious that explicitly and manifestly new legislation on customs search might provoke embarrassing questions — and perhaps litigation — on the lawfulness of all the searches with warrants and many of the searches with writ of assistance that customs officers had been engaging in for years. Better, then, a quiet regularization of 1660-type warrants; and a blind eye toward the strict rights and wrongs of writ of assistance activity.

The position created in 1685 remained substantially unchanged for many years. The provisions in the customs search warrant act of 1660 were reenacted again and again, and it was not until the time of George I that a suitable opportunity for transmuting the inconvenient "prohibited and uncustomed" in the act of 1662 into a more accommodating "prohibited or uncustomed" became available.[6] In

5. Lord Treasurer Southampton was issuing warrants, presumably in the belief that the 1660 act was still operative, many months after its expiry. See a specimen dated 14 October 1663 in *Calendar of Treasury Books* I, 352 (and others in the same volume).

6. See p. 513 and chapter 21, n. 3; *cf* also chapter 18, n. 20.

the meantime the deeply unsatisfactory state of the law had be-
deviled the Act of Frauds of 1696, the broad aim of which was to set
up in America a customs enforcement regime as like as possible the
English original of 1662. It would be extravagant to claim that the
troubles over customs search in eighteenth-century America — in
particular, the writs of assistance case in Boston in 1761 — would
not have happened but for the "and" in "prohibited and uncustomed" not being an "or"; all the same, as will be suggested in
chapter 7, this unhappily worded formula in the Act of Frauds of
1662 underlay an even worse text on customs search in the act of
1696, to which not a little of the difficulty in America can be traced.

Imperial Mechanisms

It is a notorious fact of American colonial history that the imperial system of trade regulation, in terms of coercive enforcement (voluntary observance induced by commercial considerations and the system's positive benefits presented a healthier aspect), was badly deficient. The object of the present chapter is to suggest some reasons for this state of affairs, with special attention to those most relevant to conditions in New England in the middle decades of the eighteenth century.

Responsibility for enforcement of the acts of navigation and trade in the colonies still lay to some degree upon governors, specifically in the functions, deriving from the very early years of the system, that the so-called naval officer carried out on the governor's behalf. For the most part however powers and duties of enforcement were vested in the customs organization, presided over by the customs commissioners in England (until November 1767, when an American board of commissioners started up). The English commissioners were instituted in 1671, when the customs duties ceased to be in farm; and soon after, by the act of 1673 whose "plantation duties" naturally implied agencies of collection, officers of the commissioners were given their first formal foothold in the colonies. The Act of Frauds of 1696 equipped the customs organization in the colonies with an armory of enforcement procedures and powers broadly comparable to that which existed in England under a similarly named act of 1662.

The English board of customs commissioners was located in London. No sign exists that any of the commissioners journeyed to inspect their establishments in America. For the practicalities of what was doing or needed doing they relied on resident surveyors general. Dispersed under one or other of the surveyors general — and

it illustrates how far-flung the dispersion tended to be that till well
into the 1760s the Boston-based man's territory stretched from the
remote Canadian north down through New Jersey — were some
thirty-odd custom houses on mainland America. At these operational
points the staff commonly included a collector, a comptroller (who
jointly with the collector headed the custom house, and saw to its
accounts), a surveyor and searcher (the latter office having long
ceased to signify the rummaging of ships and now denoting simply
documentary check of export cargoes), and miscellaneous understrappers.

Whatever salaries might go with their jobs, custom house operational staff depended greatly on fees: that is, fees pertaining to
necessary procedures in the process of clearing a ship and her cargo
into or out of the port. It was in the nature of this situation that
custom houses were geared more to the handling of legitimate traffic
than to the detection and suppression of smuggling. Of course,
profitable smuggling predicated reasonably convenient lines of access
to commercial centers, and the impossibility of patrolling the entire
American littoral and its vast wildernesses must not be seen out of
proportion. All the same, at many ports there were too many creeks,
protuberances, and islets in the neighborhood for adequate watch to
be kept; and the generality of custom houses in America seem to
have had no one whose paid job consisted wholly in invigilating
nearby coasts and waters for clandestine comings and goings. The law
of averages doubtless saw to it that the smuggler ran into the customs
now and then, but mostly, one imagines, it worked in his favor; the
more so because it was not by speculative prowling but by attending
to ships and cargoes properly clearing in the port that customs
officers got their livelihood.

What however of personal profit sharpening the edge of antismuggling enterprise? From the earliest days of the system, a customs officer who seized something and could get it condemned as
forfeited would gain one third of the proceeds for his own pocket.
True, before the reforms initiated for America in 1696 condemnation had always depended upon the verdict of a jury and was
therefore all but unattainable; but did not the reforms include
provision for condemnation proceedings to be brought in vice-admiralty courts, sitting without a jury and under the presidency of a

judge hand-picked in England? Such indeed had been the intention; but how it turned out in practice was quite another thing.

Much responsibility rests with a man of some fame in early American history, Edward Randolph. Ill-fame would be nearer the mark, perhaps: "a *Blasted Wretch*, followed with a sensible Curse of GOD wherever he came; Despised, Abhored, Unprosperous," was Cotton Mather's assessment of him.[1] Randolph was an Englishman who in 1696 could draw upon twenty years' experience of America, Massachusetts in particular. His opinion of the bay colonists was reciprocally low. It went back to 1676, when he undertook some sort of government mission to visit New England and report on matters there. Possibly it was his obvious lack of sympathy with local interests that earned him the appointment soon afterward of collector of customs for that region. Located at Boston, he discharged his duty with uncompromising zealotry for some eleven years; however, on the collapse of the Dominion of New England (which luckless experiment he had done much to facilitate) he was thrown into jail by the triumphant Bostonians and sent home. In 1692 he was back in America, promoted surveyor general of customs. Both as collector and as surveyor general he ceaselessly bombarded the authorities in England with accounts of the endeavors and difficulties of a conscientious revenue man. Such was his reputation as an expert that, visiting England in 1695, he was called in to help prepare the new colonial code of customs enforcement law.

No one knew better than Randolph the frustrations of a customs officer seeking condemnation of a seizure before an American jury, and he it was to whom this part of the work was given. It seems that his idea was not for vice-admiralty jurisdiction but for colonial courts of exchequer, the creation of which he had for some time been urging from across the water.[2] However, this did not get past the

---

1. *Parentator* (1727), quoted in R. N. Toppan, ed., *Edward Randolph; Including His Letters and Papers from . . . America . . .* I (Boston, 1898), 207n. Randolph was disfavored elsewhere too, apparently. The governor of Bermuda called him to his face: "old Dogg, old Rogue, Villain, Rascall &c threatening to pull off his Nose": *ibid.*, 165. For Randolph at large see M. G. Hall, *Edward Randolph and the American Colonies 1676-1703* (Chapel Hill, 1960).

2. The idea was not wholly his own, though. Hall (*Edward Randolph and the American Colonies*, 163-64) indicates that Randolph had formerly favored vice-admiralty courts, but came to share the preference for exchequer courts felt by his friend Governor Francis Nicholson of Maryland. The exchequer courts idea caught on with the customs commissioners too (*ibid.*).

crown's legal advisers, and on 27 March 1696, when the bill was already well on its way through Parliament,

> Mr. Randolph was called in [and] asked if he had prepared a Clause for a Court of Admiralty it is he says provided in the Act of K. Ch. 2d — he proposes words to be inserted in the Bill. [3]

One senses a certain foot-dragging. Disputatiousness, even. The act of Charles II under which, according to Randolph, vice-admiralty jurisdiction was already possible was presumably the 1663 Staple Act — of all the acts of navigation and trade perhaps the most at risk of violation — whose condemnation formula for forfeitures spoke of "any of his Majesty's Courts" in the colonies: words which Randolph may have thought sufficiently wide to include any and all colonial vice-admiralty courts that might be set up in the king's name. Nevertheless, and work of supererogation though Randolph apparently believed it to be, provision was duly made in section 7 of the Acts of Frauds of 1696 for ". . . all the Penalties and Forfeitures before mentioned . . . to be recovered in the Court of Admiralty held in his Majesty's Plantations . . . ." Ironically, this formula was also to prove wanting. As will emerge from the chequered story of Staple Act enforcement in eighteenth-century Massachusetts told in the next chapter, section 7's package of "Penalties and Forfeitures before mentioned" arguably did not include enough. [4]

It could be a question, perhaps, whether Randolph did not draft with forked pen. He was a strong character, not given to giving up. Conceivably, he purposely narrowed the scope of American admiral-

---

3. MS journal of the House of Lords, 22 November 1695 to 1 September 1696, f. 522: House of Lords Record Office.

4. See p. 83 for how Staple Act forfeitures were in doubt. Enumeration forfeitures were in like case.

In 1702 the English attorney general, Edward Northey, advised that section 7 gave American vice-admiralty courts "jurisdiction of all penalties and forfeitures for unlawful trading": G. Chalmers, *Opinions of Eminent Lawyers* II (London, 1814), 190. But this was not the definitive view: contrast the advice of Richard West, counsel to the Board of Trade, in 1720 (*ibid.*, 200-215), which construed the various enactments on condemnation jurisdiction in the colonies heavily against the vice-admiralty courts.

Northey may have thought to counter the effect of his also having advised that colonial vice-admiralty courts were outside the Staple Act's provision for its forfeitures to be triable "in any of his Majesty's Courts in such of the . . . Lands, Islands, Colonies, Plantations, Territories or Places where the Offence was committed, or in any Court of Record in England, by Bill, Information, Plaint or other Action, wherein no Essoign, Protection or Wager of Law shall be allowed." Vice-admiralty courts were out on the reasoning that since essoigns and the other repudiated archaisms pertained to the common law, "any of his Majesty's Courts" must be understood as contemplating common law courts only. Probably enough, this was also the reasoning behind the brush-off to Randolph in 1696.

ty jurisdiction in artful anticipation of practical circumstances forcing Westminster back to his own previous preference for colonial
exchequer courts. There would have been a double edge to the 1696
act spelling out, plainly and incontrovertibly, an exclusive and universal admiralty jurisdiction in customs matters. Randolph would
have known that admiralty courts of a kind already existed in
America: disputes of the ordinary admiralty type — over seamen's
wages, for instance — were inevitable in a maritime milieu, and there
had to be some court ready to adjudicate them. He would have
known, too, that colonial judicatures handling admiralty cases sometimes did so in a common law way, with a jury.[5] The setting-up of
new vice-admiralty courts on the authentic civil law pattern was
bound to take a year or so; if in the meantime those pre-existing
jury-ridden courts of admiralty successfully appropriated the freshly
enacted customs jurisdiction to themselves, condemnation of forfeitures would be as infrequent as before. Hence the attractiveness of a
jurisdiction formula that left room for exchequer courts to be moved
in alongside, where the customs interest would be served properly.
Admittedly, such courts would have juries (for although the Court of
Exchequer in England sometimes sat without a jury, a jury verdict in
a contested customs condemnation case was indispensable); nevertheless, if, as Randolph envisioned, these colonial exchequer courts were
presided over by strong judges sent from England and subjected to
"certain Rules & Methods to direct the Judg & Jury from wch they
are not to deviat,"[6] all would be well.

This conjectured explanation of Randolph's unsatisfactory draftsmanship does not really run, however. Whatever problems and hazards the establishment of American vice-admiralty courts might present were as nothing to the fearsome unpracticality of instituting in
the colonies replicas of the uniquely arcane processes of the Court of
Exchequer. Into which, moreover, would need to be woven some
sort of regime for curbing wrongheadedness in juries — and this at a
time when the classic vindication of a juror's independence, *Bushell's
Case* in 1670,[7] was still within living memory. Imagining how thoroughly the law officers of the crown drubbed Randolph's vision of

5. C. M. Andrews, *The Colonial Period of American History, IV, England's Commercial
and Colonial Policy* (New Haven, 1938), 224-25. For a somewhat different view as respects
Massachusetts, see L. K. Wroth, "The Massachusetts Vice-Admiralty Court," in G. A. Billias,
ed., *Law and Authority in Colonial America* (Barre, Mass., 1965), 35.

6. Randolph to customs commissioners, 27 June 1692: A. T. S. Goodrick, ed., *Edward
Randolph . . .* VII (Boston, 1909) (the same series as in n. 1 above), 356.

7. Vaugh. 135.

colonial exchequer courts, one can be pretty confident that not even
that resilient operator could any longer hold to it seriously. There is
no sign of it featuring in discussion when he produced his "Clause for
a Court of Admiralty"; at that point he probably had no hope of it
at all. In short, what did for section 7 of the Act of Frauds of 1696
was ham-fistedness rather than guile.

Not that the blame was Randolph's alone. To draft legislation is
not to pass it. Those parliamentary interlocutors who overbore
Randolph's protest that the Staple Act already provided for vice-
admiralty jurisdiction were soundly advised, as time was to confirm;[8]
which makes it the more puzzling that the draft clause they required
of him should not have been just as thoughtfully scrutinized and its
defectiveness put right. (After all, Randolph was not professionally
equipped as a legislative draftsman, whereas among the legislators
themselves was one of the foremost lawyers of the period, Sir John
Holt.) Nor was the subject of the clause a recondite technicality that
a bored or impatient house might understandably let through on the
nod. It purposed to deprive people of their property without a jury
verdict, and in a court of admiralty at that. Either count was a
sufficient alert, one would have supposed, for lawyer-parliamen-
tarians at least. The very necessity for a judicial process of condemnation was a matter of common law;[9] it was contrary to logic, a
perversion even, that the process should be in other than common
law form. Furthermore, it was an offense against history as well as
against logic and doctrine. The victory was secure and far in the past,
but there had been no competitor the practitioners of the common
law had fought so long and strenuously as courts of admiralty. All
this is not just to marvel that the legislators of 1696 acquiesced in so
conspicuous an affront to the English legal-political inheritance as
admiralty jurisdiction over property rights ordinarily pertaining to
the common law (in a small way it had been countenanced in England itself).[10] A greater wonder is that, the decision for an admiralty
customs jurisdiction in America having been made, care was not
taken to make the statutory text for effecting it beyond all possibility of doubt or challenge. A particle of common sense reflection
surely would have warned the 1696 legislators to get section 7 ab-

8. See n. 4 above.
9. See p. 12 above
10. 22 and 23 Car. 2, c. 26 (1670).

solutely watertight. Otherwise their countrymen across the water, resenting both deprivation of property without jury trial and that the alien process took place in courts historically obnoxious to the common law, could be expected to move in on the section with every stultifying trick in the book (and the common law in America had all the weaponry with which it had battled successfully against admiralty encroachments in England a hundred years and more ago). That the architects of section 7 of the Act of Frauds of 1696 passed into law this spatchcock tissue of imprecision and error was a major cause of their intentions for customs condemnation to bypass the fatal colonial juryman coming to so little.

There was another inbuilt weakness as well. It related to the central figure upon whom the whole system was planned to pivot, the vice-admiralty judge. The idea was that this presiding functionary, patented by the High Court of Admiralty in England, could be relied upon — independent as his process would be of the jinxing proclivities of a jury — to do the right thing by the crown and its customs officers. But it did not always work out like that. Cases were different with different men, naturally. It is not possible to generalize from, for example, Roger Mompesson, an early appointee from England, who is on record as an upholder of jury trial in customs condemnation cases.[11] A less idiosyncratic phenomenon, however, especially when local men came to be appointed, was for a vice-admiralty judge to bend with political or mercantile sentiment in his neighborhood.[12] To begin with, the post carried no regular salary and the fees attaching to it were no higher than colonial legislatures chose to permit. Then again, where the judge was a lawyer whose livelihood depended mainly on private practice he was not likely to be too assertive in an unpopular cause. It was said of one: "this Gentlemen is a constant practising Attorney, in all the King's Courts here, so that when anything comes before him in the Court of Vice-Admiralty, where his Clients are concerned, he is under a strong temptation, to be in their Favour, to His Majesty's Dishonour, & to the great Discouragement of His Majesty's Officers of the Customs, & should he not so act he must lose a great number of Fat Clients, who are of much more value to him than his post of Judge of the

---

11. Andrews, *op. cit.* (n. 5 above), 259-60.

12. See A. M. Schlesinger, *The Colonial Merchants and the American Revolution* (New York, 1918), 46; and, rather differently, C. Ubbelohde, *The Vice-Admiralty Courts and the American Revolution* (Chapel Hill, 1960), 205-206.

Vice-Admiralty."[13]   One can only assume that the policymakers of 1696 saw such situations as a calculated hazard; in one manifestation or another they were quite predictable.

Of course, though no doubt responsible for the originating idea, customs condemnations were not the entirety of jurisdiction in the post-1696 colonial vice-admiralty courts. Entrenched common law interests notwithstanding, the vice-admiralty courts succeeded in fair measure to the kinds of cases that fell naturally within their scope: disputes over seamen's wages, salvage, prize (in wartime), and so forth. The late Professor C. M. Andrews's researches into colonial vice-admiralty court records persuaded him that in these matters of ordinary admiralty jurisdiction the courts did pretty well.[14]

Customs cases were comparatively few. "Even in Massachusetts, probably the chief offender among the colonies, the great majority of cases concerns wages, desertions, assault upon the high seas, the other matters that fall within the class of strictly marine causes. The number of trials for illegal trading, recorded in the proceedings of the vice-admiralty courts (as far as we have them) of Rhode Island, Pennsylvania, Maryland, South Carolina and Antigua, is very small, amounting to less than five per cent of the whole." In New York the percentage was negligible (though this was "probably due, in part at least, to the fact that many trials for evasion of the acts of trade at the port of New York came before the mayor's court there"). This evidence afforded no certain test of the situation — indeed, "evasion was often possible with the connivance of officers and many a ship escaped detection altogether" — but, Professor Andrews was inclined to think, it did perhaps suggest that the colonists' reputation for smuggling was overdone. An alternative interpretation seems possible however. The smallness of the proportion of customs cases in the vice-admiralty court records could be an indication not so much of the volume of unlawful trading carried on as of customs officers' unwillingness to invoke so vulnerable and uncertain a jurisdiction.

In course of time acts of Parliament were passed to widen the scope of the staple and to lengthen the list of enumerated products, but in none of them was the opportunity taken to repair the deficiencies of the past and provide properly for vice-admiralty

13. Governor Jonathan Belcher (Mass. and N.H.) to Admiralty, 31 January 1742: Adm. 1/3817.

14. *Op. cit.* (n. 5 above), 240-41.

jurisdiction. And, as if by some malignant magic, the result of the one important addition to the acts of trade that did give colonial vice-admiralty courts firm jurisdiction over its forfeitures was the introduction of a new element — almost a new dimension — of toxic depression into custom house morale.

The Molasses Act of 1733 imposed customs duties on importations into the American colonies of molasses, spirits, sugar, and certain sugar products, originating in neighboring foreign colonies. It had been passed largely for the benefit of the British West Indian sugar-planting interests, and its chief design was that rum distillers in the northern colonies should in future use British West Indian molasses, which remained free of import duty, in preference to foreign, which was to bear a very heavy duty indeed. Importations in violation of the act were subject to forfeiture in any colonial court of record or "in the Court of Admiralty in his Majesty's Colonies or Plantations in America (which Court of Admiralty is hereby authorized, impowered and required to hear and finally determine the same). . . ." No foothold here for attack on vice-admiralty jurisdiction.

On paper, the operation of the Molasses Act was as satisfactory as its draftsmanship was tight. From the very beginning the duty collected under it was negligible: £2.5s. in 1735, for example, and absolutely nothing in 1739. To eyes that looked no further this was perfectly splendid: such infinitesimal duty receipts meant that hardly any foreign molasses was being imported, so the New England distillers must have switched to British. The truth was quite the opposite, of course. The act was not working at all. The northerners had long been accustomed to the cheaper foreign product, and they were using immense quantities of it still. What the derisorily small duty receipts really signified was a massive unlawful trade.

A deepening rot in custom house morale began to set in. Not all or even most of these illicit importations were clandestine, and simply unknown to the custom house. Foreign molasses continued to come into American ports almost as openly and freely as ever. An illustration of how it was done and gotten away with has been given in a noted history of the West Indies:

> Jamaica was a center for much clandestine trade with the foreign sugar islands. Masters of vessels from the Northern Colonies were often indulged to enter and clear these vessels at one and the same time, and they frequently cleared out their ships as having on board the commodities of

Jamaica when in fact they had no such produce aboard or even design to take any but, indeed, carried empty casks for holding and money for purchasing molasses, sugar, and other products of the French islands. But by means of their cockets [export documents] obtained in Jamaica they easily entered the Northern colonies with such sugar etc., as the produce of Jamaica.[15]

The customs officer at the northern port might feel sure that the cargo was foreign and the British West Indian export document a fabrication, but what could he do? He could seize the cargo and go to the vice-admiralty court without fear of the jurisdiction being faulted; the judge might be one of the more benign, and, besides, the Molasses Act had placed the burden of proof upon his opponent. But that spurious certificate of British West Indian origin would put the ball right back into his court. And fatally, before even the most well-disposed judge. To assert the document's falsity was to be expected to prove it. It needs little effort to imagine the formidable difficulties confronting a customs officer in the northern colonies who sought to prove that a man who signed a document somewhere down in the Caribbean had not told the truth. The cost alone of such an exercise might be prohibitive. Faced with this sort of situation the customs officer seeking a condemnation under the Molasses Act was no better off than under the older acts of trade.

Practical difficulties over condemnation were only part of the trouble. An equally damaging consequence of the Molasses Act was corruption. Whether because false clearance documents were not always available, or from some other originating cause, a kind of unofficial customs tariff developed at ports where molasses came in. Foreign molasses was admitted on payment of a sum far less than the proper duty, which went more into the private pocket of the customs officer than into the official coffers of the custom house. In slight extenuation it should be said that the customs officer did not always appropriate these payments in full. So at any rate it would appear from a letter from the newly appointed surveyor general for the northern district, John Temple, written early in 1762 to the customs commissioners:

15. F. W. Pitman, *The Development of the British West Indies 1700-1763* (New Haven, 1917), 278.

Governor Francis Bernard of Massachusetts, 3 November 1764, Bernard Papers IV: "These Clearances are found in all the ports in North America. It seems they have been purchased at Eustatia at about 20 portugal pieces of 3/6 each."

The Bernard Papers are among the Sparks manuscripts of Harvard University; and the extensive use of them in this book has the kind permission of the Houghton Library.

Very soon after my arrival I discover'd that it was the practice, in several Custom Houses to admit foreign Rum, Sugar and Molasses, on a partial Duty, instead of Receiving the Six pence p gall for molasses, nine pence p gallon for Rum, & 5/- per hund. for Sugar Their method was to receive only about a 5th or 6th part of the Duty and by that practice they have collected some little money for the Crown and remitted it home, and have taken some merritt for themselves for Collecting it without Acquainting you the practice by wch it was collected . . . .[16]

But it would be innocent to suppose that these fragmentary contributions to the Molasses Act receipts represented the whole of the amount actually collected.

The customs commissioners themselves were under no illusion as to the true state of affairs. Commenting in 1763 on the operation of the Molasses Act they were candid about "The Collusive Practices of the Officers of the Customs . . . who, at this Distance from Inspection, are too easily led off from their Duty, to their Interest, in a Country where the strict Observance of the Former, is rendered highly difficult and obnoxious."[17] With this from the top echelon of the customs service there is no need of further testimony to the fact — historically notorious, in any case — that the Molasses Act of 1733 represented in practice little other than a custom house racket.

But the act could never have worked anyway. The aim was to break and recast a firmly established pattern of commerce in a region with not much diversification of economy — far more than the modest custom house staffs, even though expanded a little for the purpose, could possibly have accomplished. And again in fairness to those remote agents of empire the truth has to be told that until the 1750s, when in desperation for revenue London began thinking hard, the men at the top gave not two straws about the Molasses Act and how it was working. It has been noticed that to those who preferred to turn a blind eye the minuscule receipts could be a cause of comfort rather than of concern. On the witness of an insider, the executive authorities in England had been indifferent to the act from its inception. This man was Henry Hulton, one of the ill-fated American customs commissioners. Before going to America in 1767 Hulton had served several years as "plantation clerk" to the English commissioners in London. It was the responsibility of the plantation clerk to look after the commissioners' overseas business. Having had

16. 1 January 1762: letter-book of John Temple in MHS. See also T. C. Barrow, *Trade and Empire* . . . (Cambridge, Mass., 1967), 142 *et seq.*

17. To Treasury, 21 July 1763: T1/426.

access if not to contemporary papers then at least to the folk-memory of the office, Hulton was well placed to know what he was talking about. He said of the origins and early days of the Molasses Act:

> The Ministry having granted the Planters their desires took no measures to inforce the Act, but winked at the prostitution of the National authority, at the connivance of the Officers of the Customs, and the illicit Commerce of the People; which introduced a depravity of Morals, and alienated the Subjects from their duty to Government.[18]

Some additional officers were appointed, to be paid out of the revenue, "but many of these soon gave up their Offices on their being no prospect of their receiving any Salary on those terms." Remembering what Edward Randolph had had to contend against one need not take too literally Hulton's judgment that in the Molasses Act lay "the Source of Smuggling and corruption." But there is a ring of truth in this brief factual commentary on the attitude of an administration which in 1733 had had the West Indian planters on its back for several years and wanted nothing so much as to get them off. "John Marshall has made his decision," President Andrew Jackson is supposed to have said of a Supreme Court decision he did not care for, "Now let him enforce it." Such was the spirit, by the look of things, of the British government in relation to the Molasses Act.

The Molasses Act was not of indefinite duration, and it came up periodically for renewal. The West Indian planters strove for something stronger, but in vain. When the time came, as it did in the 1760s, for legislation to raise a revenue on all colonial importations of molasses, British as well as foreign, the administration moved energetically enough. But there was no tangible advantage to the British government in fostering the philosophy of 1733. The Molasses Act served a purely private interest for the most part, and there had never been much in it for the crown. To discourage importations of foreign molasses was fine for producers in the British sugar territories, but all it could mean to the government was an enlarged colonial customs establishment that had somehow to be paid. And since the more effective the act the less money it brought in, from the Treasury point of view the case for strengthening it was not compelling.

18. "Some Account of the Proceedings of the People of New England from the Establishment of a Board of Customs in America to the breaking out of the Rebellion in 1775," from the André Coppet Collection of American Historical Manuscripts in Princeton University Library (microfilm in MHS).

Everything considered, it is small wonder that in practice the Molasses Act was left to sink to its own level, and that the level was pretty low. The colonial custom houses had been saddled with an unworkable folly, of which little else could be made than a private dollar or two on the side.

Other examples of weakness or vulnerability in the enforcement of the imperial system are not far to seek.

The system's heavy dependence on documentation was prolific of hazard. False documentation occurred not only in the Molasses Act connection; it could be encountered in practically any part of the system where origin or destination was in point, and where — as was inevitably the case — customs checks and controls looked mostly to certificates of one sort or another from across the sea. And then there was the special problem of the bond, a customs control document very widely used. A bond was an undertaking under seal, perhaps backed by a surety, to pay the crown a certain sum of money in a stated eventuality — as it might be, that a certificate of landing of enumerated goods in Britain was not produced to the customs at the outward colonial port within a given period. The difficulty here was not so much falsification as the custom house's inveterate bugbear, attitudes in the ordinary American court. Action for the bond penalty was intrinsically a common law matter, and a vice-admiralty court had poor claim to jurisdiction. Accordingly, the customs had little choice but to bring it in one of the ordinary courts of the colony. With what slender hope appears in a report by the customs commissioners in 1759, on a question of putting enumeration bonds in suit: "these prosecutions must be carried on in the ordinary course of proceedings in the colonies, where, it is apprehended, that Verdicts, upon points of this Nature, are not so impartial, as in England."[19]

Also there were internal or organizational weaknesses in the customs service. Loose-jointed structuring made for lack of drive, and modern-style bureaucratic hierarchy was not much in evidence in eighteenth-century custom houses. Of course, directives were received from the commissioners in London, and a colonial custom house located in the port where a surveyor general had his headquarters might experience special pressures. But the custom houses seem to have not been so much organic units as congeries of more or less independent functionaries, with or without subordinate staff, each

19. To Treasury, 10 May 1759: T1/392.

having his own part of the work and his own fees. In fact, the mode and outlook of the times did not greatly conduce to strong control from above. It could be very difficult to dismiss a man, for one thing. If he had been appointed by London the Treasury would have to be persuaded, and perhaps a political patron placated. Another inhibition all of a piece with eighteenth-century attitudes is illustrated by an episode in England. A quantity of iron had been seized by an officer of the customs at Liverpool; the commissioners wished it to be restored, but "as the law gives the Officers a property in all Goods seized by them, we did not think it expedient to order Mr Rogers to deliver the Iron against his Consent."[20] Departmental policy even at the topmost level had to yield to the lowly officer's rights of property.

Then there was the practice, equally characteristic of the period, whereby the principal posts in the customs diaspora, notably collectorships and comptrollerships, were executed by deputy, the absentee holder of the office doing no more than milk the emoluments. A list of colonial absentee incumbents drawn up in 1763 showed that Thomas Clift, collector for Rhode Island, had not been near the place in more than twenty years.[21] Nathaniel Ware, comptroller for Boston, had been away seven or eight.[22] Too much must not be made of the evils of deputyism (though in time the British government clamped down upon it); there is no reason to suppose that the principal would have done better than the stand-in at the actual work. But on the whole it cannot have been good for efficient and steady direction of custom house endeavor to have the men in charge mere surrogates at will.

Outside the custom house the scene might be one of debilitating harassment, present or potential. Colonial legislatures were sometimes disagreeably assertive in the regulation of custom house fees. It was not unknown, either, for a governor to allow his own responsibility for the acts of navigation and trade (or the perquisites attached to it) to bring him into collision with the custom house.[23] And quite aside from extraneous vexations such as these, there was the human fact that members of the custom house, like everyone else, had to come to terms with life around them and somehow shake down with the people next door. "We are here removed at a great distance from

20. T1/485 (1771). Cf. 6 Geo. 1, c. 21, s. 43.

21. List of officers absent from the colonies, 8 March 1763: Add. MSS 38335.

22. Ibid.

23. Barrow, op. cit. (n. 12 above), 92-94.

our superiors," wrote one customs officer from New England, "and continuing long in the same Place degenerate into Creols, and at length forget Mother Country and her Interests."[24]

The frequency of war, practically a constituent of the imperial system, added to the strain. In the Hobbesian melee that characterized relations among rivals for empire the price of sovereignty was eternal belligerence. Most of the time, of course, war was not so much formally declared as being prepared for. In these periods of nominal peace there was normally no proscription on export trade in nonenumerated commodities from the mainland British colonies to incipiently enemy colonies, notably of France. It was by this means that much of the immense import of molasses into New England was paid for. The formal outbreak of war rendered such commerce illegal, but, as when the Molasses Act duties came in, an established pattern of trade was not readily broken. It was particularly unfortunate that agricultural produce exported from British America was used for the sustenance of the enemy's troops; but it was also the case that another component of the system, restrictions upon imports into Great Britian, blocked recourse to the best alternative market.[25] In those relatively undiversified colonial economies people still had to make a living, war or no war, in the only way they had. A certain degree of fig-leaf cover was afforded by flags of truce, and — for a time — by contriving shipments via a neutral territory. But it remained the case that wartime conditions automatically created a large additional category of unlawful trading, if not as one of the contradictions of the imperial system then certainly as a result of the inability of that complex artefact of principles and concepts to keep in gear with life.

The fact that the imperial economic system worked at all in the American colonies owed much less to coercive sanction applied by the customs enforcement regime than to the enjoyment of commercial advantage (fortified here and there by such contrivances as bounties and preferential duty rates) and, in some areas, to the financial hold of the metropolitan country. When, in the 1760s, attempts were made to strengthen the fiscal component of the system by means of improved enforcement measures, the response

24. Undated (but possibly 1755), "Extract of a letter from New England" in Add. MSS 33029.

25. Not that surplus for export was always available: see R. Hofstadter, *America at 1750* (New York, 1973), 145,

was unsatisfactory; but that is another matter. Until that time the system ticked over largely on its own economic momentum.

Largely, but not entirely. If the enforcement regime was ineffective all the time and everywhere there could hardly have been occasion for the great eruption against it in Boston in 1761. Indeed, the fact that a prominent feature of the 1761 set-to was the writ of assistance, a fairly sophisticated piece of customs weaponry, is a sign that in Boston at least the enforcement regime was alive and kicking. Seizure in particular, the distinctive sanction of customs law, was very much a reality in the Bay province; were it otherwise the searches for which the writ of assistance was required would have been pointless.

The origins of this Boston phenomenon will now be considered in some detail.

6

The Boston
Vice-Admiralty Court

THE WRIT of assistance in pre-revolutionary Massachusetts signified seizure that stuck. It would have been useless to search out
things for seizure if there had not existed the means of getting them
condemned as forfeited.

Needless to say, it was not in the provincial courts of common law
that condemnation could be obtained; the juryman was as unhelpful
as ever. The condemnation jurisdiction that sustained the regime of
seizure was in the Boston court of vice-admiralty.

The vice-admiralty jurisdiction had not always been so effective.
The transformation, historically important as a wellspring of the Bay
province's distinctive discontents, evolved from a tangle of laws
unsatisfactorily drafted and imperfectly understood, and from the
personal dispositions of particular men.

The Boston vice-admiralty court had its origin in the system of
colonial vice-admiralty courts inaugurated soon after the Act of
Frauds of 1696, and was in trouble practically from the start. It
quickly found an enemy in the courts of common law. With the
establishment of a proper admiralty jurisdiction the provincial common law courts stood to lose much of the ordinary marine business
that had hitherto gone to them, and they did not delay in making
their displeasure felt. "The conflict began as early as 1705-1706,"
said the late Professor C. M. Andrews, "with a sharp difference of
opinion regarding the right of the vice-admiralty to entertain trials
between whale fishermen . . . ."[1] In the 1720s the vice-admiralty
court got into another thicket of controversy, about its part in the
enforcement of the crown interest in the woods and timber of New

1. *The Colonial Period of American History* IV, 263.

England. A further source of travail was legislation enacted by the province for the regulation of court fees.

But most of the obloquy and assault was against the court's jurisdiction over violations of the acts of trade. This too seems to have started quite early. Customs law enforcement was the context of a Board of Trade record recalling that "in the year 1720 a Memorial was presented to the Lords of the Admiralty by the Judge and the Advocate of the Province [*sic*] Court at Boston complaining against the frequent Encroachments which they affirmed the Judges of the Provincial Courts made upon *His Majesty's Authority and the Admiralty Jurisdiction* discharging persons imprisoned by the Admiralty for Debts and Penalties due to His Majesty and by granting Prohibitions to the Proceedings of their Court." In 1726 Vice-Admiralty Judge John Menzies was again protesting to Westminster, though with the only practical consequence that the Massachusetts House of Representatives expelled him from membership.[2] Too many of his fellow-members were content that the customs jurisdiction of his court remain as weak as possible. That way their illicit cargoes would be safe.

The provincial judges released persons imprisoned by the court of vice-admiralty under the time-honored process of *habeas corpus.*[3] But it was "Prohibitions" that bulked largest in the common law attacks on the court. The writ of prohibition was the principal instrument with which the common law courts in England had asserted their ascendancy over the admiralty courts and done battle against other courts besides, back in the time of the Tudors and early Stuarts. In essence it was a directive by a senior court of common law that a tribunal of inferior standing desist from adjudicating a cause which in the judgment of the common law court did not lawfully pertain to it. Though the writ of prohibition in Massachusetts might on occasion be directed to, say, a court of probate,[4] its

2. C05/216 for the 1720 reference, and Andrews, *op. cit,* 264-65 for the 1726. See also J. H. Smith, *Appeals to the Privy Council from the American Plantations* (New York, 1950), 515.

Menzies was a member of the Faculty of Advocates in his native Scotland: E. Washburn, *Sketches of the Judicial History of Massachusetts* (Boston, 1840), 176. This civil law background was of course just the thing for an admiralty judge.

3. Refractory witnesses imprisoned by the vice-admiralty court for contempt were thus released because the vice-admiralty marshal, into whose charge they were committed, lacked authority to keep them in the ordinary jail and did not have one of his own: Shirley to Admiralty 3 October 1743, in Adm. 1/3817; and see undated memorial of William Bollan in C05/894.

4. SCM VII *Johonnott et al. v. Stride* (1741) seems to be a case in point.

most frequent target was the court of vice-admiralty. At the behest of an unwilling defendant in a vice-admiralty process the Superior Court of the province, "wishing to maintain the Laws and Rights of . . . . Courts of Record," would order the vice-admiralty court to "meddle not further" pending determination of its right to jurisdiction, and invite the judge and other officers of the vice-admiralty court to attend and show, if they could, that the case was indeed cognizable there.[5] An adverse determination meant that this "temporary" writ of prohibition would be declared final. Oftener however persons to whom the temporary writ was addressed simply obeyed the order to "meddle not further" and let it go at that.

Just as the Superior Court's writ of prohibition might be used against other courts than the court of vice-admiralty, so it was not always customs cases that attracted the writ to the vice-admiralty court; an early case was about a drift whale.[6] But undoubtedly it was the vice-admiralty court's customs jurisdiction where the common law was at its most stultifying. Common law laced with provincial politics, it should be understood. Violators of the acts of trade included men of considerable standing in the province; it was their influence that got Vice-Admiralty Judge Menzies expelled from the House of Representatives. They could also make themselves felt when the salaries of the Superior Court judges came up for annual vote in the Assembly. Thus, it was said of the court of vice-admiralty in 1733, "The Jurisdiction is at present entirely unsettled by the Constant prohibitions of the provincial Judges in all Cases concerning Breaches of Trade, tho' never so plainly giv'n by Act of Parliament to be try'd by the Court of Admiralty, such prohibitions being popular things, and all Officers here being Creatures of the House of Representatives."[7]

These words were by William Shirley, then advocate general. The advocate general, or king's advocate,[8] was the lawyer who handled cases in the vice-admiralty court on behalf of the crown. (Shirley had

---

5. A footnote to *Scollay v. Dunn* (1763) in *Quincy's Reports*, 74-83, gives the text of a typical writ of prohibition to the Boston vice-admiralty court.

6. Andrews, *op. cit.* (n. 1 above), 261.

7. William Shirley to Duke of Newcastle, 1 July 1733, in C. H. Lincoln, ed., *Correspondence of William Shirley* I (New York, 1912), 2-4. And see n. 38 below.

8. The alternative usages presumably were suggested by the designation of the corresponding figure in England, the king's advocate general (until 1872, when the office was abolished, a law officer of the crown, together with the attorney general and the solicitor general). See J. Ll. J. Edwards, *The Law Officers of the Crown* (London, 1964), 2, 131-33.

·

in fact stepped down to the position, having for a brief period been vice-admiralty judge.) The political heat on the Boston vice-admiralty court seems to have lessened during the 1730s, and it may be a token of this that considerable local approval supported the elevation in 1741 of a man conspicuously associated with the vice-admiralty court, Advocate General Shirley, to the governorship of the province. Nevertheless the court's customs jurisdiction was still far short of satisfactory when, ten years after his 1733 lamentation, he had occasion to write again.

Governor Shirley had been asked by the Board of Trade, "What Methods are used in the Province under your Government, to prevent Illegal Trade, and are the same Effectual." He weighed in with a will. His reply, dated 26 February 1743, consisted of a letter of his own and a long and closely argued letter on the state of the vice-admiralty court's customs jurisdiction by his successor as advocate general (and future son-in-law), William Bollan.[9] The message that Shirley and Bollan strove to get across was that unless Parliament were prevailed upon to legislate for colonial vice-admiralty courts to have overall and unassailable jurisdiction over violations of the acts of trade, the imperial system would soon cease to mean much. (Violations, that is to say, which gave rise to the seizure and forfeiture of things involved in them.) A class of violations upon which Governor Shirley and Advocate General Bollan placed special emphasis related to the staple, the constituent of the imperial system that required practically all transatlantic importations into the American colonies to have been shipped from Great Britain. To Shirley these violations of the staple threatened Britain's own market in America, her entrepôt profits from re-exports, and finally her very dominion. Bollan saw the Staple Act of 1663 (still the basic and governing enactment, even though the scope of the staple had since been widened to include goods of Indian and eastern origin as well as European) as "the main Ligament whereby the Plantation Trade is fastened and secured to Great Britain."[10] Yet it was being evaded with impunity. Ships had

---

9. CO5/883 (Shirley); CO5/753 (Bollan; date likewise 26 February 1743): both reproduced in M. Jensen, ed., *English Historical Documents* IX (London, 1955), 370-76.

10. People were getting dangerous thoughts, according to Bollan:

the Persons concerned in this Trade are many, some of them Men of the greatest Fortunes in this Country, & who have made great Gains by it, & having all felt the Sweets of it, they begin to espouse & justify it, some openly some covertly & having persuaded themselves that their Trade ought not to be bound by the Laws of Great Britain, they labour & not without Success, to poison the Minds of all the Inhabitants . . . . And as Examples of this Kind soon spread their Influence on the other

been arriving direct from Holland and other foreign countries in Europe "with Reels of Yarn or Spun Hemp, Paper, Gunpowder, Iron & Goods of various Sorts used for Men & Women's Cloathing"; some of these illegal importations came even from Spain, with which country Great Britain was at war. Bollan did not rest his case on the existing legislation being unclearly worded and vulnerable to perverse interpretation. The difficulty with these highly injurious violations was, flatly, that they were "not cognizable in the Court of Admiralty." And Governor Shirley, whatever he may have thought ten years previously, likewise appeared to accept that in law the vice-admiralty court was deficient in jurisdiction over violations of the staple. The vice-admiralty judge himself, Robert Auchmuty, gave the same impression when on a visit to England in 1743. Having been in touch with the Board of Trade Auchmuty sent them an account of various weaknesses in the customs enforcement regime in America, to which he appended a statement purporting to set forth which of the acts of navigation and trade made forfeitures recoverable in common law courts exclusively and which allowed jurisdiction to vice-admiralty courts; included in the former category was the Staple Act.[11]

On the united testimony of the governor of the province, the judge of vice-admiralty, and the advocate general, the Boston vice-admiralty court in the earlier 1740s was in poor shape as an agency for enforcing the staple.

Did they but know it, Governor Shirley and his companion partisans of stronger vice-admiralty jurisdiction had already missed out.

On 8 May 1742 Sir Dudley Ryder, the attorney general of England, wrote to the lords of the Admiralty enclosing the draft of a bill — not his original handiwork but heavily recast by him — which spoke of "Doubts and Disputes" over the construction of the acts of trade and "the Power, Authority, and Jurisdiction of the . . . Admiralty Courts in America." The purpose of the bill was to "obviate such Doubts and Disputes for the future, and to ascertain, establish and enlarge the Power, Authority and Jurisdiction of the said Courts." After the amending pen of Ryder himself had been applied, this went even to the extent of denying a concurrent jurisdiction to

---

Plantations around, 'tis too plain almost to need mentioning that if care be not soon taken to cure this growing Mischief the British Trade to these Plantations & their proper Dependance on their Mother Country will in a great Measure ere long be lost . . . .

11. CO5/883: letter dated 31 May 1743.

the colonial common law courts. Allow a concurrent common law jurisdiction, said Ryder, and "the Provincial Courts will claim all the Jurisdiction they have hitherto insisted on . . . I take the view of the Bill to be to give the cognizance of all matters of trade to the Admiralty Courts exclusive of other Courts in the Plantations."[12]

What gave rise to this radical proposal does not appear. Conceivably it was connected with a law case recently received by the Privy Council, as the ultimate judicial tribunal for the overseas empire, on appeal from New York. This case concerned a writ of prohibition issued and confirmed in New York against vice-admiralty jurisdiction over the *Mary and Margaret,* a sloop seized by the customs for smuggling foreign goods in violation of the staple. The collector of customs at New York, Archibald Kennedy, was appealing to have the vice-admiralty jurisdiction upheld. As the leading counsel for Kennedy before the Privy Council, Attorney General Ryder would have had good reason to acquaint himself with the shaky and uncertain position of the customs jurisdiction of the colonial vice-admiralty courts. (And, as the case turned out, good reason to deplore it: Kennedy lost.)[13]

Nothing came of Ryder's draft bill. Legislation was indeed passed in the summer of 1742 "further regulating the Plantation Trade,"[14] but it was very meager by comparison. Additional procedures and precautions against foreign-owned ships were set forth, and provision made for the dutiability of goods taken as prize; but not a sign of measures to strengthen the colonial vice-admiralty courts.

As with its origins, one can only speculate why the draft bill met this fate. Atavistic revulsion elsewhere in the ministry, perhaps, against so cavalier an ouster of the venerated common law by the old alien rival. A more down-to-earth explanation, however, is that there was a war going on and the colonists' active good will was too valuable to be put at hazard by legislation certain to be vehemently disliked. Sir Robert Walpole might have passed from the political scene but his maxim lived on: *quieta non movere.*

If the attorney general of England, located at the center of power, could not get action, a colonial governor and a pair of his understrappers were unlikely to do any better. Some five years later Governor Shirley tried again. In 1748 he wrote the Board of Trade calling

12. Adm. 7/298.
13. For the *Mary and Margaret* case see J. H. Smith, *op. cit.* (n. 2 above), 515-17. William Bollan's 1743 letter to the Board of Trade (n. 9 above and text) touched upon the New York proceedings.
14. 15 Geo. 2, c. 31.

attention to the "casual Omissions & ambiguous Expressions, which the Judges of the Provincial Courts here take advantage of, to break in upon the Jurisdiction of the Court of Admiralty by their Prohibitions." Recalling the evasions described in William Bollan's letter of 26 February 1743, Shirley went on: "I would now observe that this Evil is daily increasing, of wch I have frequent Complaints from the Officers of His Majesty's Customs; and if the Growth of it is not soon stopp'^d by some proper Act . . . for giving the Courts of Admiralty in the Colonies a general Jurisdiction (in express Terms) of all Branches of the Several Acts for the Preservation of the Plantation Trade, the Execution of 'em here will soon become impracticable, as it is indeed already in many principal Points . . . ." He rounded off by suggesting that further details be obtained from Bollan, still nominally advocate general but now resident in London as agent for Massachusetts.[15]

Shirley was no more successful than in 1743. The time when Parliament at last legislated for a stepped-up customs jurisdiction in colonial vice-admiralty courts was still fifteen years in the future.

Yet, long before the 1764 reforms the Boston vice-admiralty court was condemning Staple Act forfeitures, the centerpiece of Governor Shirley's worries in the 1740s, as a matter of routine.

Positive evidence of this may be seen in the contemporary press (the court's records for this particular period did not survive the Stamp Act disturbances of 1765).[16] By the end of the 1750s it was commonplace for Boston newspapers to carry advertisements by the

---

15. C05/886. Letter dated 6 February 1748. It appears from this that Bollan's 1743 representations (n. 9 and n. 10 above) would be shown to the Duke of Newcastle; hence, presumably, their inclusion in the Newcastle papers (Add. MSS 32890). Replying 18 June 1748 (C05/918) the Board of Trade said that they would "take into . . . consideration Mr. Bollan's Observations." Upward of ten years later — sixteen after Bollan actually wrote — Westminster was still mulling: T1/392. See also Andrews, op. cit. (n. 1 above), 267-68.

Abolition of the tea drawback by 18 Geo. 2, c. 26 (1744) doubtless had intensified smuggling in America; and it is problematical whether an alleviating measure in 21 Geo. 2, c. 14 (1747) made much difference. See Hoh-cheung and L. H. Mui, "Smuggling and the British Tea Trade," *American Historical Review* LXXIV (1968).

16. According to Governor Francis Bernard (to Gen. Gage, 27 August 1765: Bernard Papers V), writing of the sufferings of William Story, deputy register of the vice-admiralty court, in the Stamp Act disturbances, "all the records . . . of the Admiralty, were burnt before his door." John Adams (*LWJA* X, 354) believed all the court records to have been "hurried away to England . . . never to be seen again in America." The loss was exaggerated by both Bernard and Adams. Useful remnants of the records remain in the Office of the Clerk of the Supreme Judicial Court for Suffolk County, in Boston: see L. K. Wroth, "The Massachusetts Vice-Admiralty Court," in G. A. Billias, ed., *Law and Authority in Colonial America* (Barre, Mass., 1965).

register of the vice-admiralty court about custom house seizures, either calling upon an unknown owner to put in a defense against condemnation proceedings or telling of the condemnation of a seizure and offering the goods for sale.[17] These advertisements usually gave "for unlawful importation" as the ground of seizure. Sometimes it was clear that the unlawfulness of the importation consisted in a violation of the Molasses Act, but many of the seizures advertised were of commodities that could not possibly have arrived in America other than by crossing the Atlantic. Some of these seizures could have been because the ship that brought them did not comply with the nationality laws, but it is a safe assumption that most were for violation of the staple.

Occasionally another type of official advertisement appeared. The custom house itself might insert a notice inviting information that might lead to a seizure. A telling example occurred early in 1753. The collector of customs for Boston, Sir Henry Frankland, baronet, announced as follows:

> Whereas, I am informed there still continues to be carried on an illicit trade between *Holland* and other parts of Europe, and the Neighbouring Colonies; and that great quantities of *European* and *Asiatick* Commodities are clandestinely brought from thence into this port by land as well as by sea . . . I . . . give this publick Notice That, if any Person or Persons will give me Information where such Goods are concealed, that they may be proceeded against according to law, they, upon Condemnation, shall be very handsomely rewarded, and their Names concealed; And I hereby direct all the Officers of the Customs within my District to be very vigilant in discovering and seizing all such Contraband Goods.[18]

The "Contraband Goods" in question obviously were goods that had violated the staple. And given the unchanging attitudes of the colonial juryman, it scarcely needs saying that the condemnation of which the collector spoke was condemnation by the court of vice-admiralty.

17. The court's record of a condemnation in default of a claimant commonly included a reference to the impending proceedings having been advertised in the press: see, *e.g.,* *Frankland v. a Sloop,* 22 October 1743, in Court of Admiralty Records V (on which see n. 20 below). Research through the advertisements is the more laborious because there is no depending upon the one newspaper always carrying them. Whether a particular paper was or was not given the business could be a matter of judicial patronage or, possibly, political influence: *cf. Lambert v. Sloop Conclusion,* 23 July 1744, *ibid.;* and the "Journal of the Times" 14 April 1769 (see p. 470) in *BEP* 12 June 1769.

18. The advertisement may be seen in *BG* 20 February 1753; but it was run several weeks, and not only in the one newspaper.

Although the fact of the Boston vice-admiralty court's effective jurisdiction over violations of the staple in the 1750s seems well enough established by newspaper evidence, evidence from a different source is worth noticing. It is in a letter written in April 1756 by a Boston merchant, Henry Lloyd, to a Rhode Island merchant, Aaron Lopez, through whom he had been obtaining supplies of Bohea tea. Lloyd had run into problems. He told Lopez: "the difficulty of Importation is very great, the Officers on an Information having been this day in pursuit of some I have by me, but having a Cockett [in essence a certificate of shipment from a British or British colonial port] for it I sav'd it, notwithstanding if you are determined to send any must caution against venturing too much in one bottom, as it is an unsettled point here whether in a Court of Admiralty, a Cockett will screen it, if can't be proved to be Legally Imported from Great Britain . . . ."[19]

Lloyd's letter is of interest not only for its clear indication that the Boston vice-admiralty court was handling violations of the staple (for tea was certainly subject to that regime). There is the toughness of the court's attitude for one thing: even though the defendant produced documentary proof of a lawful route, he might be required to back it up with more. Also, Lloyd's reference to it being "an unsettled point" whether a cocket would suffice to signify compliance with the staple suggests that proceedings for condemnation of goods in violation of the staple were still something of an innovation.

An important question comes squarely into view. In fact it suggested itself two paragraphs back, with the Frankland newspaper advertisement in 1752. What had happened since 1748, when Governor Shirley was still lamenting the inadequacy of the vice-admiralty court's customs jurisdiction, that the court was now able to take even Staple Act violations, the principal subject of Shirley's concern, more or less in stride?

It should be stressed that the jeremiads despatched to the British government in the 1740s were substantially truthful. Some supporting evidence, of a negative kind, lies in the fact that in this period newspaper advertisements about Staple Act condemnation cases in the Boston vice-admiralty court were few and far between. Other and

19. "Commerce of Rhode Island," *MHSC* seventh series IX, 65-66. See also B. M. Bigelow, "Aaron Lopez: Colonial Merchant of Newport," *New England Quarterly* IV (1931).

better evidence is in one of the few vice-admiralty records to have escaped destruction, a book that shows business transacted in the court over 1740-47. The detail varies, and coverage in the last two years is scanty and obviously incomplete;[20] but for the most part the material looks full enough. It confirms that at least where Staple Act forfeitures were concerned the jurisdiction of the court was not doing as well as it might.

In some ways the court appears to have been prospering. There were plenty of straight admiralty cases, about seamen's wages and so forth. There are also signs of a fairly lively customs jurisdiction. Within limits, this is not surprising. The Molasses Act of 1733 was explicit that colonial vice-admiralty courts should have jurisdiction over its forfeitures; and while evasion of the act was as rife in Massachusetts as anywhere there was always the odd importer who, preferring not to bother with false documentation or to tip the customs officer, took his chance on smuggling his molasses secretly and now and then had a cache seized. Again, vice-admiralty jurisdiction over violation of the requirements as to British construction, ownership, and manning of the carrying ship was reasonably clear, even in the opaque Act of Frauds of 1696.[21] Less expectedly, the court record occasionally tells of almost piratical venturesomeness into matters where vice-admiralty jurisdiction had really no right at all. In 1743 the court condemned a quantity of coffee "for unlawfull importation." This, it would seem, was under an act of 1732 which prohibited coffee to be imported unless shipped from Great Britain, the forfeiture penalty "to be sued for, recovered and adjudged, in any Court of Record in any of his Majesty's Dominions in Europe, or in any of his Majesty's Plantations . . . ."[22] Not on any reckoning did courts of vice-admiralty rank as courts of record.

And less expectedly still — having regard to the tale of woe

20. In fact, the volume is entitled "Court of Admiralty Records 1740 to 1745 vol. V." Other volumes (cf. n. 16 above) include vol. II (1718-26), vol. III (1726-33), "Admiralty Book of Accts. of Sales," and a few miscellaneous records surviving or postdating the Stamp Act disturbances.

21. See, e.g., Frankland v. Sloop Dover, 2 September 1746. Cf. Wroth, op. cit (n. 16 above), 34.

22. Frankland v. Coffee, May 1743. The act was 5 Geo. 2, c. 24 (extended in point of time by 11 Geo. 2, c. 18, 19 Geo. 2, c. 23, etc.). What distinguishes this case from a Staple Act one is that the vice-admiralty record does not use its customary Staple Act formula. which invoked an unloading before report as ground for forfeiture (see pp. 78-82 below).

On courts of record see Holdsworth, HEL V, 157 et seq. Authoritative exposition of the common law might be a characteristic that is relevant here.

recounted by Governor Shirley, Judge Auchmuty, and Advocate General Bollan — the 1740-47 record includes a dozen Staple Act cases. However, the proposition still holds that what Shirley and his men said about the court's Staple Act jurisdiction was substantially true; these dozen cases notwithstanding, the jurisdiction was far from healthy. All save one of the Staple Act cases were either undefended or compounded. (Composition was a familiar customs practice: instead of taking a seizure to formal condemnation the customs officer and the owner made a deal for the restoration of the seizure on payment; in order that the king — and in the colonies the governor — should not be defrauded of his share in the proceeds the bargain had to be given judicial sanction.)[23] In other words, only where they would not be called upon to fight the case through to a judicially considered decision did customs officers venture upon Staple Act enforcement. Or, to put it yet another way, the Boston vice-admiralty court was not averse to asserting a Staple Act jurisdiction in cases where no one was going to contest it, or challenge it by a writ of prohibition in the Superior Court. Seen in this light, the undefended and compounded cases in the 1740-47 record do not falsify the Shirleian lamentations. On the contrary, they tend to confirm that whenever the owner of a potential seizure looked like putting up a fight the custom house backed away. If the vice-admiralty jurisdiction were tried and formally found wanting they could hardly invoke it even for their undefended cases and compositions. Better these occasional profits than none at all, even though it meant letting flagrant violations of the staple go unpunished.

The question remains, though: what happened that violations of the staple, barely touched in the 1740s, featured regularly in vice-admiralty condemnations in the 1750s? A start toward the answer may be discerned in the one Staple Act seizure in the 1740-47 record that actually went the length of a full trial.

This was the seizure of the brigantine *Hannah* by Peter Brasier, tide surveyor at the Boston custom house, in December 1741. Brasier sought vice-admiralty condemnation of the *Hannah*, together with her tackle and certain "junk" that she had on board,

23. An undefended case: *Frankland v. Lighter, Raisins & Yarn*, 20 May 1746. A compounded case: *Paxton v. Ship Sophia*, involving a miscellaneous cargo — which included salt, one of the few products excepted from the staple (Charles Paxton, more of whom in the course of the book, was at this time surveyor and searcher of customs at Salem).

ffor that the said Junk & sundry other Commodities all of the Growth
production & manufacture of Europe ... were Imported in the said
Vessell into this Province from Rotterdam ... wch Junk & other Commodities were not Laden & Shipped on Board the said Vessell in Great
Britain Wales or the Town of Berwick upon Tweed and also ffor that ...
the said Vessell came into this Province & there divers Goods & Commoditys were taken out of & unladen from the said Vessell ... wch Goods &
Commoditys were unladen from the said Vessell before the Master or
Commander thereof had made known to the Governor of the said Province
or to the person or officer by him thereunto authorized & appointed the
aforesaid arrival of the said Vessell contrary to the form of the Stat in that
Case made and provided . . . .

Thus the court record for 22 January 1742.

A point to notice is that two grounds of forfeiture were asserted:
first, goods of European origin imported without having been on-
shipped from Great Britain; second, the *Hannah* had unloaded some
of her cargo before reporting her arrival. Both relate back to the
Staple Act of 1663. In section 6 the act prescribed forfeiture of ship
and goods for the offense of actual importation from continental
Europe otherwise than via Great Britain and in compliance with the
requirements as to British nationality laid upon the ship. Section 8
prescribed forfeiture of ship and staple goods for nonobservance of a
regulatory procedure under which no ship or vessel coming into a
colony might "lade or unlade any Goods or Commodities whatsoever, until the Master ... first have made known to the Governor ...
or such Person or Officer as shall be by him thereunto authorized
and appointed, the Arrival of the said Ship or Vessel [giving certain
other particulars besides] ."

The owners of the *Hannah* having decided to contest the condemnation suit, Brasier — through his counsel, Advocate General William
Bollan — proceeded to establish his case. The going was heavy. Bollan
himself alluded to this in 1743 when he urged the Board of Trade to
promote legislation for stronger vice-admiralty jurisdiction; the
Hannah, he said, was "the only Vessel, which has been condemned
for being employed in this illicit Trade" (that is, trade in violation of
the staple), and "the only thing, which worked her Condemnation,
was our catching some of the Crew flying & holding them by such
compulsory Process as we could not have had any where but in the
Admiralty Court"; "by their Oaths [we] proved such Facts against
her that she was condemned." Other evidence of how Brasier and
Bollan had to sweat for victory is in the vice-admiralty court record.

If, as Bollan said, some members of the crew of the *Hannah* were taken into custody they were none too ready to talk. The condemnation proceedings began on 12 January, but it was not until 6 March, after repeated adjournments "by reason that Witnesses could not be found," that one Richard Barry was prevailed upon to supply the required testimony. He had boarded the *Hannah* at Rotterdam, whence she sailed with a cargo of paper, sponges, and other products. Though she had touched at Deal on the south coast of England it was only because of contrary winds, and no customs officers had come aboard. Across the Atlantic she stopped at Cape Cod, but without unloading anything, and after a few days proceeded to Nantasket, south of Boston, and there remained at anchor four or five weeks. In that period her hold was opened several times, and paper and other cargo taken out. Although he had sailed as a passenger, Barry helped in the unloading into boats for Boston and on to a neighboring island. Four days after Barry's testimony (which was given in the vice-admiralty register's office, not in open court), Judge Robert Auchmuty issued a decree of condemnation of the *Hannah* and the "junk" still on board her.

Condemnation in the *Hannah* case had been a laborious and close-run thing, with so much having to be proved and with such difficulty. It is small wonder that the custom house afterward shied away from contested Staple Act cases: they were too problematical. A few moments' reflection is in point, however. The trudge retracing every stage in the *Hannah*'s voyage, from the departure from Rotterdam through the failure to clear in Great Britain and at last to the discharge of cargo off Nantasket, had reference to only one of the two Staple Act grounds of forfeiture which Brasier had set forth in his information, the section 8 unloading before report. Little or none of this was necessary to the other ground of forfeiture, the section 6 forfeiture of ship and goods for importation in violation of the staple. Section 6 forfeiture was within the benefit of a provision in the Act of Frauds of 1696, the statute governing customs enforcement generally: "where any Question shall arise concerning the Importation or Exportation of any Goods into or out of the ... Plantations, in such Case the Proof shall lie upon the Owner or Claimer . . . ." Why, one cannot but ask, was this advantage not exploited in the *Hannah* case? Why, with section 6 forfeiture so comparatively easy in terms of proof, should Brasier and Bollan have gone through all that bothersome business to establish a section 8

forfeiture (for, of course, the statutory shift of proof had no application where the operative occurrence was not an importation but an
unloading)? And thereafter, why should the customs authorities,
whom the *Hannah* experience understandably had made wary of
contested section 8 condemnation suits, have been at least equally
reluctant to seek condemnation under section 6, where proof was so
much less a problem?[24]

The strangely atrophied condition of section 6 forfeiture in the
1740s puts the vigorous and effective Staple Act enforcement of the
1750s into even sharper contrast. There can be little doubt that
insofar as they related to the Staple Act the vice-admiralty advertisements about the condemnation or sale of things "for unlawful
importation" were accurately worded, and that the offense was
indeed importation contrary to section 6 (and not unloading contrary to section 8, with all the concomitant problems of proof).
Collector Frankland's notice in the newspapers in 1753 is a useful
illustration of the move to section 6. He offered rewards for information leading to the condemnation — no doubt in the vice-
admiralty court — of European and Asiatic goods clandestinely
brought in "by land as well as by sea." In the case of landward
smuggling section 8 proof, which turned on the unlawful unloading
of a ship, would take on yet another dimension of impossibility;
obviously it can only have been straight importation contrary to
section 6 that Frankland had in mind. Then there was the letter by
Henry Lloyd in 1756, also quoted earlier. Lloyd spoke of seized
goods having to be "proved to be Legally Imported from Great
Britain." A dual confirmation, this, of a section 6 orientation: actual
importation as the operative factor, and the burden of proof in court
shifted from the customs officer to his opponent.

It seems necessary, then, if the transformation of the Staple Act
enforcement around the turn of the 1750s is to be understood, not
so much to observe section 8 forfeiture up against intolerable diffi-

24. The proof problem would have been less difficult if Brasier had limited the seizure
to the *Hannah* herself, releasing her residual "junk" cargo. While section 8 forfeiture of the
carrying ship arose merely from an unlawful loading or unloading, its application to goods
depended upon their having violated the staple (proof of which meant tracing back through
the successive stages of their voyage).

That a ship could be forfeited under section 8 regardless of the wrongfulness or
innocence of her cargo seems to have been exploited in Boston for the seizure of vessels
used for smuggling in violation of the Molasses Act 1733, which had no provision of its own
for forfeiture of vessels: see, *e.g., Frankland v. Sloop Speedwell and Molasses*, 13 August
1742 (undefended).

culties of proof as to account for the custom authorities' unwillingness in the 1740s to invoke the less burdensome section 6.

When in the late middle ages and after the common law courts in
England were elbowing the courts of admiralty into permanent
subordination, they did not rely wholly on doctrine of their own
invention. They made much of two statutes of Richard II, enacted in
1389 and 1391, the effect of which was that admiralty courts should
confine themselves to things "done upon the sea" and should have
no jurisdiction, save in a narrow criminal range, over "things arising
within the bodies of the counties," including creeks and the mouths
of rivers. These medieval enactments were considered law in colonial
America; and the records of provincial Massachusetts show them
featuring frequently in writs of prohibition against the vice-admiralty
court.[25]

To invoke the acts of Richard II was to protest that because the
matter at issue had not arisen out to sea a court of admiralty had no
business with it; and this seems to be the light in which to see why
the 1740-47 record of the Boston vice-admiralty court is so empty of
forfeitures imposed by section 6 of the Staple Act of 1663. The
operative element in a section 6 forfeiture was an importation.
Understood as an actual landing of goods, an importation had necessarily to be "within the bodies of the counties" since every point on
the coast was in one county or another. And from this it presumably
appeared to follow that a section 6 importation forfeiture was barred
to the vice-admiralty court by the acts of Richard II.[26]

25. The acts were 13 Ric. 2 c. 5 and 15 Ric. 2 c. 3. In 1536 statute subjected admiralty
criminal process to jury trial. In England, that is: for the colonial position see *LPJA* III,
277-78.

According to Richard West, counsel to the Board of Trade, 20 June 1720, the acts of
Richard II were "not introductive of new laws, but only declaratory of what the common
law was before," and "they are of force even in the plantations ...": G. Chalmers, ed.,
Opinions of Eminent Lawyers II (London, 1814), 200-215. For the acts in Massachusetts
see, *e.g.*, *Norton v. Jekyll* (1728) SCR 1743-47, 294-95; *Stephen's Case* (1756) SF 76066.
However, "Justice Story urged that the limiting acts of Richard II were not in force in the
colonies": Wroth, *op. cit.* (n. 16 above), referring to *DeLovio v. Boit*, 7 Fed. Cas. 418.

26. In 1726, the English attorney general (Philip Yorke, later Lord Hardwicke L. C.)
advised that "importation" was "always accounted from the time of the ship's coming
within the limits of the port, with intent to lay the goods on land": Chalmers, *op. cit.* (n. 25
above), 280. This doctrine did not become known in Massachusetts apparently. In *The
Freemason*, 1763, the Boston vice-admiralty court held that there could be a Staple Act
importation without a landing; Governor Francis Bernard (*Quincy's Reports*, 393) told of
counsel having argued about this "for two whole days"; which indicates that the idea was
new in Massachusetts. *Cf.* chapter 9, n. 71 and text.

The logic also holds for forfeitures under section 8 of the Staple Act, where the operative element centered upon a loading or unloading of the carrying vessel. It was a common smuggling technique (the *Hannah* case was an instance) for the incoming ship to anchor some distance from land and discharge her cargo into small boats clandestinely sent out to meet her. Practically all the Staple Act cases in the 1740-47 record that speak of foreign goods from Europe do so in terms of a wrongful unloading. Why else than that section 8 was in mind as the forfeiture provision? Furthermore, because forfeiture occasioned in this manner was something that had arisen out to sea the acts of Richard II did not apply; and, accordingly, the vice-admiralty court felt free to officiate.[27]

So, as a framework for the Boston vice-admiralty court's abstention from section 6 forfeitures in the 1740s the acts of Richard II check and double-check.

The framework was out of true, however.

Here the focus shifts from the section 6 forfeitures the vice-admiralty court stayed clear of and toward the section 8 forfeitures it ventured into. It is immaterial that the venturesomeness was not all that thrustful (virtually all cases were either undefended or compounded). What signifies is that jurisdiction was exercised at all.

The source of the jurisdiction needs to be identified. On this the 1740-47 record is not too explicit, and leaves digging to be done. But this is no great problem. Only two candidate possibilities present themselves: the Staple Act's own jurisdictional formula, and the provision for vice-admiralty jurisdiction over a broader generality of customs forfeitures in section 7 of the Act of Frauds of 1696. Both of these may be remembered from the account in chapter 5 of how Edward Randolph, when assisting in the preparation of the 1696 legislation, was disabused of the idea that the Staple Act formula would cover the new American vice-admiralty courts, and how he thereupon produced the draft of a supposed catchall customs jurisdiction for them.[28] It will also be recalled, from earlier in this present chapter, that in 1743 the Boston vice-admiralty judge himself

27. That seizures of goods under section 8 were nevertheless infrequent is a sign not so much of uncertainty about the vice-admiralty court's jurisdiction as of the custom house's inability to gather proof of the origin of the goods and their movements on the other side of the Atlantic: *cf.* n. 24 above and text.

28. See pp. 53-54 above.

indicated that the Staple Act envisioned its forfeitures as triable in common law courts exclusively. The Staple Act's formula eliminated, it can only have been the 1696 catchall that the vice-admiralty jurisdiction over Staple Act forfeitures — such as it was in the 1740s — drew upon.

Much to the point are the terms of section 7 of the Act of Frauds of 1696, which provided for "all the Penalties and Forfeitures before mentioned . . . to be recovered . . . in the Court of Admiralty held in his Majesty's Plantations . . . ." Inasmuch as this formula might have been stretched to include Staple Act forfeitures — for in fact it was just the act itself, without anything about its forfeitures, that had been "before mentioned" — it surely included them all. On this showing, the Massachusetts differentiation between Staple Act forfeitures as they belonged to section 6 or section 8 meant construing the one statutory text in two opposite ways. The contradiction was not warranted anywhere in the 1696 act itself; the only discernible rationale was in the importation/unloading dichotomy reflecting the influence of the acts of Richard II.

First reaction might be to puzzle what gave those oldsters from the middle ages the strength to bite a piece out of more up-to-date legislation. But the objection goes deeper than that. The essential concern of the acts of Richard II was with jurisdiction that might colorably have been claimed by admiralty courts as pertaining to their natural and proper business; it was to be reserved to courts of common law, save only where the matter in dispute had arisen out to sea. Condemnation of customs forfeitures was not part of an admiralty court's natural inheritance on any argument. A requirement of the common law, it belonged squarely in a common law court;[29] the common law's claim to it needed no vindication by the acts of Richard II. And one can get to the same point from another direction. An admiralty court could assert a customs condemnation jurisdiction only in the event that statute had displaced the common law's presumptive monopoly (whether totally, or sufficiently to permit admiralty jurisdiction as an alternative). In instances where statute had thus provided, with the common law ousted or bidden move over and make room, the acts of Richard II had no application: there was nothing for them to champion.

The split vision which by dint of the acts of Richard II read the

29. *Cf.* pp. 12-13 above.

jurisdictional formula in section 7 of the Act of Frauds of 1696 as enabling the Boston vice-admiralty court to deal with some Staple Act forfeitures but not others, made no sort of sense.

The foregoing analysis, which interpreted Staple Act forfeitures into the vice-admiralty jurisdiction authorized by the 1696 act, and which denied the acts of Richard II power to pull any of them out again, would not have been likely to commend itself to Boston lawyers allied to the merchant interest. Nor would the more obvious objection that in confrontation with a later statute it should have been the acts of Richard II that yielded, not the other way about. Be pure doctrine what it might, a vice-admiralty court at liberty to handle all Staple Act forfeitures, instead of just the occasional undefended or compounded case, would have been bad for business.

Remaining for consideration is why the Boston vice-admiralty court's handling of Staple Act cases should have been tolerated — acquiesced in, indeed: witness the compositions — at all. The wobbliness of the position was not wholly, or even mainly, a matter of misconceived notions about the acts of Richard II. A more fundamental instability went to the question whether the jurisdiction the court was invoking — section 7 of the Act of Frauds of 1696 — really did cover Staple Act forfeitures, that is, to the highly dubious extension of section 7's "all the Penalties and Forfeitures before mentioned" to Staple Act forfeitures when what actually had been "before mentioned" was not the forfeitures but the act itself. However, the adversaries of customs enforcement seem not to have followed through.

The account of the *Hannah* case in Advocate General Bollan's 1743 representations for legislation to improve customs jurisdiction in colonial vice-admiralty courts included a curious comment: "The Condemnation of this Vessel was owing in a great Measure to Accident; the Advocate employed by the Claimers not knowing that upon Application to the Superior Court here, he might have had a Prohibition to the Court of Admiralty." The *Hannah* case was about violation of the staple, of course; and Bollan, who in another passage complained of the 1696 act being "obscurely penn'd in the Point of the Admiralty's Jurisdiction," presumably saw danger to a Staple Act forfeiture of the *Hannah* in the textual insufficiency of section 7. As well he might, for it was only on a very loose construction of the

1696 act's words that the vice-admiralty jurisdiction could stretch so far. By much the same token however — that the vulnerability of the jurisdiction would have been equally evident to any competent lawyer — one wonders whether it might not have been Bollan himself who failed to size up the situation. Temptation may have been resisted rather than opportunity lost. Again it is useful to picture the situation from the viewpoint of a Boston lawyer mindful of his merchant clientele at large. The "Advocate employed by the Claimers," while fully aware of the prohibition possibility, might just as consciously have opted against it (adopting instead the tactic — which, as Advocate General Bollan acknowledged, nearly succeeded — of confounding the custom house on problems of evidence and proof). Release of the *Hannah* might be a cast-iron certainty if he asked the Superior Court to denounce the vice-admiralty jurisdiction; but a disquieting corollary was possible too. A prohibition granted on the ground that the jurisdictional formula in section 7 of the Act of Frauds of 1696 did not empower American vice-admiralty courts to adjudicate Staple Act forfeitures would amount to formal and explicit avowal that the staple, perhaps the most important constituent of the imperial system, was incapable of effective enforcement. The least to be expected was a considerable strengthening of the case for legislative reform on customs condemnations, shortly to be urged on the British government by Governor Shirley and the vice-admiralty establishment. And should there result a newly enacted and prohibition-proof vice-admiralty jurisdiction for customs cases across the board, damage to the Boston commercial interest in general surely would far outweigh the immediate one-off benefit enjoyed by the owners of the *Hannah*. Calculation of net advantage along some such lines as these may explain how, more generally and throughout the 1740s, the Boston vice-admiralty court was suffered to handle the occasional compounded Staple Act case.

Assuming that the vice-admiralty court's self-contradictory and doctrinally unsound position on Staple Act forfeitures could not continue undisturbed forever, one would logically suppose the resolution, when it came, to be downward and out. Yet that was not the way it happened. In the event, the beggarly condition of the vice-admiralty court on Staple Act enforcement did not collapse into nothingness. On the contrary, the 1750s saw the court adjudicating Staple Act forfeitures of all sorts and in full measure. That the transformation cannot be accounted for by logic or objective legal probability is a reminder that life sometimes cuts across both. Human agency was what turned the trick in the end.

According to Advocate General Bollan in 1743, if a prohibition against the vice-admiralty court had been applied for in the *Hannah* case the Superior Court of Massachusetts would have complied. Custom house timorousness over Staple Act forfeitures right through the 1740s doubtless was conditioned by the same downbeat frame of thinking. Conversely, that in the 1750s Staple Act forfeitures became more or less routine business in the vice-admiralty court is a sign that fear of Superior Court disapproval was no longer being felt. Hereabouts lies an important key.

In his diary for 1752, one of the judges of the Superior Court, Benjamin Lynde junior, included the following entry:

> In May Chambers Russell Esq Appointed Judge of our Supr Court where had been a vacancy from Judge Dudley's Death & Judge Sewall made Ch. Justice tho Coll Saltonstall his Senr Judge.[30]

This reconstitution of the Superior Court could scarcely fail to have a bearing on the court's attitude to the court of vice-admiralty. The newcomer to the bench, Chambers Russell, was the judge of vice-admiralty himself. And Russell (who had succeeded Robert Auchmuty in 1747) would continue to be judge of vice-admiralty, his Superior Court judgeship notwithstanding. The tonic to custom house nerve and initiative is obvious. Fear of the Superior Court's writs of prohibition need reign no longer. In a challenge to the vice-admiralty court on Staple Act jurisdiction Judge Russell's colleagues on the Superior Court surely would not deny him the benefit of the doubt.

The other appointment, of Judge Stephen Sewall as chief justice, also is to the point. With Russell one of their number it would have been awkward for the Superior Court judges to be other than reasonably accommodating toward the vice-admiralty court. With Sewall presiding it was unthinkable. Sewall was by nature the last person to court unpleasantness: he was too nice a man. Besides, there could well have been a special amity between Sewall and Russell: some little time after Russell went on the Superior Court he befriended young Jonathan Sewall, a promising nephew of the chief justice, "received him into his family, instructed him in law, fur-

---

30. In MHS. The new appointments were taken up at Ipswich 2 June 1752: SCM X, 1748-56.

nished him with books, and introduced him to practice at the bar."[31] By reason not only of Chambers Russell's appointment to the Superior Court but also of Stephen Sewall's promotion as chief justice, the Boston vice-admiralty court had become safer from common law spoliation than ever before.

Russell's membership on the Superior Court did not mean that writs of prohibition to the vice-admiralty court ceased altogether; issuances occurred from time to time on a variety of subjects (though it is interesting that an attempt in 1755 to secure prohibition of two forfeitures arising from section 6 of the Staple Act came to nothing).[32] As for Russell personally, he seems to have been a decent enough man in private life, and it is only fair to mention that he showed scruple about absenting himself from the Superior Court when a matter in which he had an interest was to be dealt with.[33]

Yet, as will be seen later in the book, some of his notions of judicial propriety were pretty odd.[34] And apparently they did not always measure up even to the standards of his own day. Thus the *Boston Gazette* for 20 September 1756 commented on his tandem judgeships of vice-admiralty and the Superior Court:

> We cannot as yet acquaint the World that the Hon. J-e R-s-l has resign'd either the Post of J-e of the A-y, or J-e of the S-r C-t — as it has long been expected he would; If these two Places should at last appear to him INCOMPATIBLE (especially in a Time of War) it is hoped his Honour will not fail very soon to exhibit such a noble Example of Disinterestedness and Self-Denial.

One suspects that the writer was not motivated by principle alone, and that apprehension or experience of a revivified vice-admiralty jurisdiction came into it too. In any case Russell did not take the

---

31. *LWJA* IV, 5 (John Adams's preface to the 1819 edition of his "Novanglus" papers).

32. *Scollay v. Dunn* (1763), *Quincy's Reports,* 74-83, affords an illustration. Also *Stephen's Case,* n. 26 above. For the unsuccessful section 6 cases (by John Wheatley and Thomas Mitchel), see SF 74984; SCR 1757-59, 155; SCM XII, 8-9.

33. So it would appear from a petition that a substitute for Russell be appointed in a Superior Court case involving the vice-admiralty court: 44 MA 454, reproduced in *Quincy's Reports,* 550. See also C05/823, Minutes of Council (Massachusetts) 16 August 1762: Samuel Danforth "to be a special Justice . . . in the room of Chambers Russell Esqr . . . who declines sitting . . . ." On the other hand, there is nothing in the court record to show that Russell absented himself when the Superior Court, at Charlestown 30 January 1759, upheld inferior court judgments he had obtained (as a private litigant) against Zachariah Shed and Benjamin Shattuck: SCR 1757-59, 511.

34. Pages 168-69 below. In *BG* 11 April 1763 James Otis junior asserted that the two judgeships were so far incompatible that the vice-admiralty one was vulnerable to a *supersedeas,* eliminating it. This writ had been used in the common law attacks on admiralty in England, until prohibition proved more reliable: Holdsworth, *HEL* I, 553.

hint; far from resigning one of his judgeships he held on to both of them to the end of his life.

Rebuke followed Russell even into the grave. When he died on a visit to England in November 1766 the Boston press was not totally wanting in the customary civilities (an "upright and truly amiable Character, in public and private Life": *Boston Evening-Post*), but that unequivocal organ of whiggism, the *Boston Gazette*, gave no more than the bare facts, and a week later came out in full flood against "a new kind of star chamber which had been erected without law, and held in conjunction with the late surveyor-general and the late judge of admiralty" (which reference plainly was to events of the 1750s, for "the late surveyor-general" could only have been Thomas Lechmere, who retired in 1761 after many years of service and whose successor was still in office). James Otis senior remarked in a letter to James Otis junior: "I am sorry for poor Judge Russells Death so far as relates personally to him and his Relations: but whether the Country will have Reason to mourn him is to me uncertain all things Considered . . . ."[35]

By the time Russell died the unpopularity of vice-admiralty courts in the colonies was greater than ever: Parliament had at long last gotten round to strengthening and widening vice-admiralty jurisdiction over violations of the acts of trade, and vice-admiralty courts were to have been the forum for enforcement of the Stamp Act. No doubt all this deepened the disfavor in which Judge Russell was held. But it may not have been these latter-day developments alone that John Adams had in mind when, musing in his diary some years later, he named Chambers Russell as one of "the original Conspirators against the Public Liberty."[36]

If the regeneration of the Boston vice-admiralty court in the 1750s can be traced to Vice-Admiralty Judge Chambers Russell's appointment to the Superior Court, and in a lesser degree to the out-of-turn promotion of Judge Stephen Sewall as chief justice, its true begetter was the man in whose gift these appointments lay, Governor William Shirley.

35. *BEP* 19 January 1767. *BG* 19 and 26 January 1767. Otis: 24 January 1767, MHS Otis Papers II, 137. An annotation by Harbottle Dorr (see p. 499 below) to *BG* 19 January 1767 was more ungenerous: "Judge Russell's Death could not be much lamented, as it was supposed that He with Charles Paxton went home to get an establishment made to pay Judges &c. &c. &c." See also *BG* 9 November 1767. (Paxton's 1766-67 visit to England features in chapter 18.)

36. *DAJA* II, 90.

Born in 1694, Shirley was an English barrister who emigrated to Boston in 1731 with the good will of the Duke of Newcastle but little else. By any standard, he was a man of parts. Sheer ability and a desire for work that stretched him no doubt accounted for much of the drive that, in ten years, propelled him upward (though not without disappointments on the way) to the governorship of Massachusetts. There may have been something slightly abnormal in his appetite for advancement that caused him to dispatch his wife to England in the cause; and the accent on money in that lady's assiduous endeavors suggests what that something was.[37] But Shirley's governorship, when he actually got to it, was not marked by especially conspicuous obsession with personal gain; and his earlier concern to better his finances may not have been all that far out of proportion to his domestic responsibilities. Still, his salary as governor — £1,000 sterling, assuming the province assembly agreed to vote it — was not so princely that he could afford to neglect the extra emoluments of the office. Chief among these was the one-third share in custom house forfeitures that the various acts of navigation and trade appropriated to the governor's private purse. Custom house forfeitures depended upon the condemnation jurisdiction of the court of vice-admiralty: Governor Shirley had good reason of his own for wishing to make the jurisdiction as effective as possible.

Though on the Staple Act the vice-admiralty court was still pretty ineffective when Shirley became governor in 1741, the overall condition of the court seems to have improved since the times of Judge Menzies and his immediate successor Nathaniel Byfield[38] in the

37. Among Shirley's disappointments were: customs jobs at Boston (C05/899; Belcher to Newcastle 30 June 1733); the naval officership (*ibid.*, Shirley to Newcastle, 2 January 1738); royal woods and lands appointments (G. A. Wood, *William Shirley, Governor of Massachusetts 1741-56* (New York, 1920), 65; and Add. MSS 32688, Shirley to Newcastle 4 August 1733); chief justiceship, New York (Add. MSS 32691; Newcastle to Mrs. Shirley, 23 July 1738). Perhaps his strongest aspirations were toward customs collectorships, notably at Boston (see C05/753: petition of Shirley 6 May 1737).

Frances Shirley's redoubtable efforts on her husband's behalf were part of a larger scene of complex pan-Atlantic intrigue for the removal of Governor Belcher, variously from his two governments of Massachusetts and New Hampshire. (This duality did not survive Belcher: Shirley got Massachusetts only; New Hampshire went to Benning Wentworth.)

38. Byfield was Menzies's predecessor as well as his successor. Originally commissioned as vice-admiralty judge in 1702 after three years as deputy (apparently he was the choice of Edward Randolph: Toppan, *Randolph* V, 137), he had resigned in 1714 because he could not get a salary (so he himself said, in the letter about to be quoted; but Washburn, *Judicial History of Massachusetts*, 179, has him superseded for his "political opinions"). In 1728, on Menzies's death, he came back; as he put it in a letter to the Admiralty on 21 February 1732, "being disengaged from other Business, & in easy Circumstances, and having a sincere Desire to Serve the King and his People": Adm. 1/3878. Byfield soon had cause to repent his

1720s and early '30s, and when Shirley, as advocate general, was writing so bitterly of the crippling of the court by politically motivated common law harassments. The middle and later 1730s had been a period of much flux in the public life of the province, and the comparative calm in which the vice-admiralty court now worked perhaps owed something to the complex chemistry of events a remove or two away.[39] But a more proximate cause was to be found in the court itself, in the amenable disposition of Judge Robert Auchmuty. Like Shirley and Bollan, Auchmuty was an emigré barrister from England. His association with the vice-admiralty court went back to the 1720s, first as advocate general and, from 1733, on changing places with Shirley, as judge. Auchmuty it was who attracted the comment from former Governor Jonathan Belcher in 1742: "this Gentleman is a constant practising Attorney, in all the King's Courts here, so that when anything comes before him in the Court of Vice-Admiralty, where his Clients are concerned, he is under a strong temptation, to be in their Favour, to his Majesty's Dishonour, & to the great Discouragement of his Majesty's Officers of the Customs, & should he not so act he must lose a great number of Fat Clients."[40] In the same letter to the Admiralty Belcher wrote of the vice-admiralty judge's "unfaithfulness in not discharging his

---

public spirit. On 8 October 1730 he and various officers of the vice-admiralty court were complaining to Governor Belcher of "the Treatment your Memorialists for these few years past have met with from the Honourable the Provincial Judges" and threatening to protest to the Privy Council against the Superior Court's prohibitions: SF 30398. And, as the 1732 letter went on to say, Byfield and his officers were indicted for taking allegedly illegal fees. (See also SCM III, 1729-30; SF 33289; and William Shirley, in the letter in the text to n. 7 above, telling in 1733 how Byfield, now dead, had had "prosecutions Civil and Criminal" commenced against him, and had "before his Death . . . spent two hundred pounds New England Currency in the Defence of himself and his Officers . . . .")

39. An account of Massachusetts and Boston politics in the 1730s is in chapter 6 of G. B. Warden, *Boston 1689-1776* (Boston, 1970). One factor in the vice-admiralty court's changed fortunes may have been the death, in 1737, of Elisha Cooke, an early Boston political boss and an old enemy of the court (over its White Pine Acts jurisdiction). Another foe who may have been quietened was Nathaniel Cunningham, a Boston merchant. Cunningham, an associate of Cooke, had been a leader in the attacks on Judge Byfield at the beginning of the decade (see n. 38 above) — Byfield and the vice-admiralty staff, that is. A key figure among the latter was the court's executive officer, the marshal, Charles Paxton (see in particular SF 33289). In 1738 Cunningham married Paxton's widowed sister, Susan Gerrish. It would have made a strange start to married life for him to be still hounding his bride's brother with writs. *Cf.* chapter 11, n. 26.

40. *Cf.* chapter 5, n. 13. Belcher's animus may have been sharpened by a suspicion that the campaigners who succeeded in dislodging him as governor in 1741 had included Auchmuty; but the animus was not new. In 1739 he had written of Auchmuty as "the unjust Judge": "The Belcher Papers," *MHSC* sixth series VII (1894), 239. In the late 1730s

trust upon the Seizure of a Ship." The Admiralty itself reprimanded Auchmuty in 1738 for his handling of condemnation cases under the White Pine Acts: he had given conflicting decisions on the same evidence.[41] The spirit of accommodation in which Auchmuty approached his responsibilities may have earned him the displeasure of Governor Belcher and the Admiralty, but it could well have lessened the political fire against his court. Local political interests had had to be rough with Menzies and his equally stiff-necked successor Nathaniel Byfield. With Robert Auchmuty, however, the merchant-politicians could do business.[42]

The worst days of political hatchet-work on the vice-admiralty court now past, the newly appointed Governor Shirley may have entertained some hope of serving both the imperial cause and his own pocket by revitalizing the court's jurisdiction over Staple Act forfeitures. The amenability of Judge Auchmuty may have come into it too. If he could be bent perhaps he could be straightened, or even bent the other way. Certainly Auchmuty was not well positioned to withstand pressure from Shirley. For one thing, he was anxious that the son of the displaced Governor Belcher, Andrew Belcher, incumbent register of the vice-admiralty court, should be ousted too, to make room for one of his own sons, Samuel Auchmuty; an ambition that stood no chance without the new governor's blessing. Yet the judge was now more vulnerable than ever to the displeasure of his superiors. As if his standing had not been weakened enough already, notably by dubious conduct in office, he had recently been involved in a promotion, known as the Land Bank, for issuing paper money on the security of little more than hopes of good times ahead; and this venture had been heavily frowned upon — indeed, sat upon — by

---

Auchmuty verged on dismissal through disarray in his private affairs: indebtedness, and involvement in unseemly litigation. "The King, Belcher wrote the Admiralty, should not be served by insolvents": J. A. Schutz, *William Shirley, King's Governor of Massachusetts* (Chapel Hill, 1961), 30-31.

41. Wood, *op. cit.* (n. 37 above), 78.

42. They could also expect some sympathy from his deputy judge, George Cradock. Though the Molasses Act 1733, unlike the more basic acts of navigation and trade, was incontrovertibly clear that its forfeitures were subject to vice-admiralty jurisdiction, judicial zeal in the Boston vice-admiralty court may have been tempered by the circumstance that Cradock himself set up as a distiller in 1739: *A Report of the Record Commissioners of the City of Boston*, covering 1736-42 (Boston, 1886), 202. Cradock's daughter Deborah married Auchmuty's son Robert (himself a future vice-admiralty judge) in 1751, whereupon the distilling business seems to have become a joint Cradock-Auchmuty venture (at any rate till 1753, when Cradock possibly dropped out): biographical card in MHS, citing Suffolk deeds 80.73 and 87.256. Robert Auchmuty senior had died in 1750.

all manner of right thinkers in high places; and former Governor Belcher's ongoing denunciations of Judge Auchmuty to Westminster naturally did not fail to brand him as "one of the principal Actors in that vile, fraudulent Affair."[43] Auchmuty probably needed Governor Shirley's protective good will over the Land Bank as much as his active patronage in the registership matter. And such perhaps was the backdrop to the apparently unprecedented seizure and vice-admiralty condemnation in the *Hannah* case in the winter of 1741-42. The new governor had come to office in the summer of 1741 anxious to stop and cash in on Staple Act violations. The custom house bestirred itself accordingly with the brigantine *Hannah*; and it would be unrealistic to assume that the governor's interest was wholly absent from the mind of Judge Auchmuty when at length he allowed himself to be prevailed upon to give a decree of condemnation.

The first phase of Governor Shirley's campaign for effective vice-admiralty jurisdiction against violations of the British staple was a failure. As it panned out, the forfeiture of the *Hannah* did not herald anything remotely resembling a general clampdown on Staple Act violations. Shirley's 1743 effort, in which Judge Auchmuty again collaborated, for legislative strengthening of vice-admiralty jurisdiction, was even more abortive. His renewed attempt in 1748 did no better. But by now his ultimate strategy may have begun to form. Here Auchmuty's contribution was more negative; in 1747 he lost the vice-admiralty judgeship, leaving the way clear for Governor Shirley to introduce the fateful figure of Chambers Russell.[44]

Chambers Russell attributed his appointment as vice-admiralty judge to the recommendation of William Bollan.[45] It is not hard to understand why Governor Shirley listened. Russell would not be

---

43. Note 40 above. And on 27 January 1742 Belcher explicitly recommended Auchmuty's dismissal as judge for being "one of the Principal Actors and Promoters, of this wicked Projection": Adm. 1/3817.

44. In theory, a plan to double up the vice-admiralty judgeship with a seat on the Superior Court could have been envisioned with Auchmuty as the incumbent. And Shirley was ready enough to make use of him in some ways: Auchmuty's presence in England in 1743 (p. 71) was occasioned by the governor having sent him as joint province agent to argue for the province in a boundary dispute with Rhode Island; and he also took soundings at Westminster for the Louisbourg expedition of 1745. However, his unsatisfactory general reputation (n. 40 above) would have told against him for the Superior Court. As it was, in 1747 he lost even the vice-admiralty judgeship (in circumstances unknown to the present writer).

45. CO5/755, fols. 825-29; and see chapter 9, n. 52.

another practicing lawyer, whose eye in customs cases might squint too much in the direction of private clients. In fact he was not a lawyer at all. It was nothing uncommon in colonial America for laymen to be appointed to judicial office, and presumably a layman could pick up a sufficiency of the Romanish admiralty jurisprudence no less than of English common law. As a man of inherited substance Russell would be independent of sectional interests anyway. His money originated from the West Indies trade, and no doubt he understood the ways of that particular world; but he had no special affinity with merchants. Though not unconcerned with politics (he had sat in the House of Representatives), his natural orientation seems to have been more rural than urban.[46]

At about the same time he went to the vice-admiralty court Russell was made a judge of the Middlesex Inferior Court. It seems possible that Governor Shirley's idea was to groom his man in the common law, with a view to higher things in the future. Russell was not appointed to the very next Superior Court vacancy, however. This in fact arose quite soon — too soon, perhaps, for the novice lay judge to show how he was making out with his double assignment of admiralty and common law; anyway, the post went to another man, John Cushing, and Russell's elevation had to wait until 1752.[47]

There was that other Superior Court appointment, too: Judge Stephen Sewall to be chief justice. The gentleness of Sewall's character as a factor in the court's new benignity toward the vice-admiralty court was commented upon earlier. His considerable reputation as a scholar could be seen as justifying his preferment, but perhaps another element came into Governor Shirley's decision to uplift him out of turn. "If there was anything habitual to him, which could be called a fault," said Sewall's obituaries in 1760, "it seems to have been an excessive self-diffidence. Had he this quality in a less degree, he might, probably, have engaged deeper, and more vigorously than he did, in the police, and public affairs of the government . . . ." Perhaps a certain innocent amenability would have been in character, too. To a governor packing a court Sewall may have seemed useful material.

46. For Russell generally see C. K. Shipton, *Sibley's Harvard Graduates* IX (Boston, 1956), 81 *et seq.*

47. *BEP* 31 August 1747 for Russell's Middlesex appointment. In 1749 and 1750 he gained experience by doing turns as "special" — *i.e.*, stand-in — judge on the Superior Court: W. H. Whitmore, *The Massachusetts Civil List 1630-1774* (Albany, 1870), 73.

In form, the appointment of Russell to the Superior Court and the promotion of Judge Stephen Sewall to be chief justice, were made not by Governor Shirley but by Lieutenant Governor Spencer Phips. Shirley had been in Europe since 1749, for work on a boundary question with the French. But there can be no doubt that in substance the choice was Shirley's. Before leaving America Shirley was careful to instruct Phips that judicial vacancies that occurred in his absence should be filled only if it were absolutely necessary, and even then only "during your Honor's Continuance in the Administration."[48] Even if the Sewall and Russell appointments had not been sufficiently important to warrant consultation with the governor anyway, the fact that they were not limited to the lieutenant governor's period in the chair would be enough to signify that in making them Phips was merely the instrument of Shirley. There is further circumstantial evidence in the long period of time that elapsed between the occasion for the appointments — the death of Chief Justice Paul Dudley in January 1751 — and when they actually took place in May 1752. Plainly, much of this time was taken up by letters passing back and forth across the Atlantic.

The appointment in 1752 of Vice-Admiralty Judge Chambers Russell to the Superior Court, backed up by the promotion of Judge Stephen Sewall as chief justice, was deeply significant for the court's orientation. The days of responsiveness to elected politicians in the legislature were past. Henceforth the leaning would be toward the executive government. Peter Oliver, the next appointee, was a government-minded man, and Thomas Hutchinson, the next after that, more government minded still. But the immediate effect was the stimulus to custom house enforcement activity, against the vexations of which the Bostonians were at length to rise up in wrath. The hard things said of Judge Russell by John Adams not only ranked this catalytic figure in the 1752 transformation among "the original Conspirators against the Public Liberty"; Russell was merely one of the "subordinate instruments" manipulated by that "crafty, busy, ambitious, intriguing, enterprising, man"; Governor William Shirley.[49]

The next chapter will show further evidence of Governor Shirley's enterprise in matters of customs law enforcement.

48. 11 September 1749: *Shirley Correspondence* (n. 7 above) I, 490.

49. *LWJA* IV, 18-19. At *DAJA* I, 109, John Adams quotes Oxenbridge Thacher (for whom see chapter 14 below): "Shirley never promoted any Man for Merit alone."

7

Beginnings of the Massachusetts Writ of Assistance

Dᴏᴄᴜᴍᴇɴᴛꜱ variously called writs or warrants of assistance were known in colonial America long before the controversies, first in Massachusetts and later almost everywhere else, in the middle eighteenth century.[1] As in the maturity of the imperial system, in its infancy also, searching places where smuggled goods might lay stored could be a sore problem for the customs authorities.[2] However, while the statutory provision for entry and search with writ of assistance in England — section 5(2) of the Act of Frauds of 1662 — may have fretted customs officers in America into trying to mock up something similar, the 1662 act did not apply in America in those early years and until the passage of the Act of Frauds of 1696 it could not even be said to.[3] Details need not be gone into; the

1. The most abundant source of information is probably the unpublished dissertation by the Reverend Dr. J. R. Frese, S.J., in the Harvard University archives: "Writs of Assistance in the American Colonies 1660-1776." Also of interest is the "writ of assistance" common in colonial Pennsylvania, addressed to "all Judges, Justices, Magistrates . . . and all other persons whatsoever . . . ," bidding them "be aiding and assisting" the sheriff "in all things that to the office of sheriff . . . do . . . belong lawfully." See W. H. Egle, ed., *Commissions issued by the Province of Pennsylvania* . . . (State Prints of Pennsylvania, 1896). Like comparable writs of assistance in England (see p. 36), these writs of assistance were not related to customs law enforcement.

2. Edward Randolph, for one. The seven volumes of R. N. Toppan and latterly A. T. S. Goodrick, eds., *Edward Randolph . . . His Letters and Official Papers* . . . , (Boston, 1898-1909) include much on Randolph's search problems. See also B. Bailyn, *The New England Merchants in the Seventeenth Century* (Cambridge, Mass., 1955), 165, 178.

3. In 1682 the Massachusetts governor was explicit that the 1662 act did not apply there (Toppan, *Randolph* III, 165); and a writ of assistance granted by the Council of Maryland to Surveyor General Patrick Mein in 1686 (*Maryland Archives* V 523-24) stopped well short of implying that Mein had a lawful power of search; the most it enjoined assistance for was "the detecting and seizing of any prohibited and uncustomed goods." Randolph in Boston also could get "warrants of assistance," at any rate for search of ships. The governor had queried the law on "assistance . . . to seizures in Cellars": Toppan,

pre-1696 tantalizations of the customs organization bore little relation to the eighteenth-century events more central to the subject of
this book.

To recapitulate the essentials. The characteristic institution of
customs law enforcement, seizure of offending ships and cargoes, was
viable only if the customs officer could be confident of following it
up with the necessary court process of condemnation; unless the
spoils of a seizure were condemned as forfeited he not only forwent
his one-third share (in the profits that did not materialize), but also
stood vulnerable to an action for damages. Condemnation by a
common law court was usually out of the question (at any rate in a
contested case), because it depended upon the verdict of jurors who
were likely to favor the custom house's adversary. In a vice-admiralty
court, on the other hand, condemnation was decided by the judge
alone. The early 1750s brought a boost to the position of the
vice-admiralty court at Boston. Condemnation of seizures, notably
Staple Act seizures, became a regular thing; and customs enforcement activity increased accordingly.

It was natural that this newly profitable endeavor was not directed
exclusively at red-handed capture of seizable goods at ship's side. An
illicit cargo remained just as liable to forfeiture if it had been taken
ashore unnoticed and now lay stored in some merchant's warehouse
or wherever. But in order to make seizure of offending goods the
customs officer first needed to have access to them; and legal
mechanism for him to go in and search gained in importance. Thus it
came to pass that, at length and after one or two false starts, the writ
of assistance arrived on the Massachusetts scene.

The customs writ of assistance that was to prove so troublesome in
Massachusetts resulted from an encounter between two men outside
a merchant's warehouse in Boston in the middle 1750s. The incident,
prefaced with a background sketch, is described in Hutchinson's
History of Massachusets-Bay:

Randolph II, 168. A warrant of assistance by a Massachusetts magistrate was addressed only
to officers of the peace — subordinates whom he could obligate by directive. The Maryland
Council's writ extended "to all other persons . . . whom it may concern." That this —
somewhat guardedly worded — command had no backing in statute (see pp. 33-34 above)
perhaps signifies that conciliar authority in the colonies, having been left untouched by the
abolition of the English conciliar jurisdictions in 1641, retained a clout that it had lost in
England.

The collectors and inferior officers of the customs, merely by the authority derived from their commissions, had forcibly entered warehouses, and even dwelling houses, upon information that contraband goods were concealed in them.

The people grew uneasy under the exercise of this assumed authority, and some stood upon their defence against such entries, whilst others were bringing their actions in the law against the officers, for past illegal entries, or attempts to enter.

When Mr. Shirley was in administration, he, as the civil magistrate, gave out his warrants to the officers of the customs to enter.

This appears more extraordinary, as Mr. Shirley was a lawyer by education, and was allowed to be a man of good sense. These warrants, however, were in use some years. At length, the surveyor and searcher being one day about to break open a warehouse, upon an information of iron imported from Spain being concealed there, a gentleman, who was brother to the owner of the warehouse, and also a friend to the surveyor and searcher, enquired what authority he had to enter, and, thereupon, he shewed the governor's warrant. The gentleman, who knew the information to be ill-founded, sent for the keys, and caused the warehouse to be opened; and, at the same time, assured the surveyor, that, if he had forced an entry, an action would have been brought against him, his warrant being of no value.

This put the governor upon examining the legality of his warrants, and caused him to direct the officers to apply for warrants from the superior court; and, from that time, writs issued, not exactly in the form, but of the nature, of writs of assistance issued from the court of exchequer in England.[4]

This account has unique authenticity. The "gentleman" who intercepted the break-in of the warehouse and who questioned the legality of the governor's warrant was Thomas Hutchinson, the writer himself. Both Hutchinson and the "surveyor and searcher" whom he came upon at the warehouse merit attention.

Thomas Hutchinson, destined to be the last civilian governor of the province of Massachusetts, was a person of consequence when barely out of his twenties. Born in 1711 a descendant of antinomian Anne Hutchinson, noted hell-raiser in the religious life of early New England, he himself was as conformist as they came. Graduating from Harvard College in 1727 he spent several years exclusively in the family merchant business. His career as a public man appears to

4. *The History of the Colony and Province of Massachusets-Bay.* The edition cited in this present book is by L. S. Mayo (Cambridge, Mass., 1936), the third volume. The three volumes were originally published in 1764, 1767, and 1828, respectively. The Proceedings of the American Antiquarian Society for April 1969 include "Additions to Thomas Hutchinson's 'History of Massachusetts Bay,'" edited by Catherine Barton Mayo.

have begun in 1737, when he became a selectman of the town of
Boston. Soon afterward he was elected to the province House of
Representatives. On the death of his father in 1739 he became
reasonably well-heeled in his own right; and thereafter more and
more of his time was spent on public affairs. In 1740 Hutchinson
went to England to argue the cause of Massachusetts in a boundary
squabble with New Hampshire. In 1742 he was back in America and
again in the House of Representatives, of which he was soon to be
speaker. His role as high-level man-of-all-work continued: he was on a
commission to treat with the eastern Indians, for example; and in
1745 he managed the province lottery. By the end of the decade,
however, his popularity had taken its first serious tumble. Currency
reform, of which he was the province's leading exponent, bore hard
upon the populous debtor class, and in the 1749 election his seat in
the House was whipped from under him. But there was no keeping a
useful man down, and in the same year he was elected (by the House
itself) to the other branch of the General Court, the Council. This
probably suited Hutchinson's inclinations well enough. Like the
House of Representatives, the Council was a legislative branch of the
General Court, the overall organ of government under the Massachusetts province charter; but it also did duty as the consultative body
to whom the governor, a royal appointee, looked for advice and
consent in matters of executive action. Three years later, in 1752,
Hutchinson boxed the governmental compass by becoming a judge.
Two judges, in fact. His uncle having died, he succeeded him in the
not inconsiderable offices of justice of common pleas (a court of
civil jurisdiction) and judge of probate, both for the county of
Suffolk, the principal county in the province. That Hutchinson was
not a lawyer by education was no problem: lack of legal training was
not a bar to colonial judicatures. Nor did his judicial offices disqual-
ify Hutchinson from membership of the Council. Another important
assignment was as one of the Massachusetts representatives at the
Albany conference in 1754: the plan for a colonial union produced
at that abortive gathering owed much to the work of Hutchinson. A
still greater intensification in his public work from about that time
forward may have resulted from the death of his wife, to whom he
was deeply attached, in 1753. Unlike most widowers of the time
Hutchinson did not remarry, but seemingly found sufficient domestic felicity in the companionship of his children, and other compensation in public work and private historical scholarship. Voracious-
ness for office was a charge most often levied against him in years to

come; but against the motives usually imputed to him — love of power, jobbery for the benefit of his relatives, and so forth — ought to be set the possibility that, at bottom, Hutchinson's undoing lay in nothing much worse than an innocent gluttony for work he believed himself good at. However, in the 1750s the tragic dénouement was many years off:[5] he was still very much the up-and-coming man.

The customs officer whom Thomas Hutchinson came upon at the warehouse was Charles Paxton. Paxton too was to have a considerable future in the events leading to the American Revolution, if only for his part in the appointment and the affairs of the ill-starred American board of customs commissioners under the Townshend legislation of 1767. (According to a historian of the American loyalists, "As far as individual men are concerned . . . Charles Townshend, in England, and Charles Paxton, in America, were among the most efficient in producing the Revolution.")[6] Paxton was born in New England in 1708. In his early twenties he was appointed marshal of the vice-admiralty court at Boston. The responsibilities of the post — broadly, the execution of the court's decrees — naturally involved Paxton in the common law imbroglios that broke out between the court and the Boston merchants around this time. The job was worth (in commissions and so forth: there was no salary) some £40 sterling a year. As vendue master in charge of sales decreed by the court — of customs forfeitures, for example — he earned a little more. Later he picked up a pair of court jobs on the common law side: cryer of the Superior Court and of the Court of General Session, respectively. Presumably these paid him a little too. At one point he appears to have ventured into commerce.[7]

5. The most recent major study of Hutchinson's later career is B. Bailyn, *The Ordeal of Thomas Hutchinson* (Cambridge, Mass., 1974). Malcolm Freiberg's dissertation (Brown University, Providence, R.I.), "Prelude to Purgatory: Thomas Hutchinson in Provincial Massachusetts Politics 1760-1770," was in 1950. Articles by Mr. Freiberg include "Thomas Hutchinson: The First Fifty Years (1711-1761)": *William and Mary Quarterly* XV third series (1958), and "How to become a Colonial Governor: Thomas Hutchinson of Massachusetts": *The Review of Politics* XXI (Notre Dame, Indiana, 1959).

6. L. Sabine, *Biographical Sketches of Loyalists of the American Revolution* II (Boston, 1864), 154. Townshend and Paxton are well bracketed here. There was a long-standing personal connection between the two men, which culminated, under Townshend's chancellorship of the exchequer in 1766-67, in Paxton exercising the influence referred to in and in his becoming one of the American customs commissioners. See n. 8 below; also p. 458 and chapter 18, n. 26.

7. Paxton was among the signers of a "Letter from several Merchants at Boston . . . to the Merchants in London," dated 19 August 1741, seeking help in suppressing debased Connecticut and Rhode Island paper money that circulated in Massachusetts. Other signers included John Erving (of whom more later, particularly in chapter 9) and James Bowdoin: C05/883.

But what Paxton had really set his heart upon was a place in the customs. Despite dogged sponsorship by Governor Jonathan Belcher in the 1730s,[8] the favorable regard of Governor William Shirley in the 1740s,[9] and trips to England on his own account,[10] it proved a long haul. Not until 1752 — though he had held the like post at Salem and Marblehead, the port next up the coast from Boston about twenty miles away, a year or two — did he become surveyor and searcher at the province's principal shipping center. However, the timing was lucky for him. It was about now that the dispositions that strengthened the Boston vice-admiralty court's customs jurisdiction were taking place. The recent appointment of Vice-Admiralty Judge Chambers Russell to double up as a judge of the Superior Court meant that vice-admiralty condemnation of customs seizures was less liable to harassment by common law prohibitions. Of course, it was not only the contriver of this new order, Governor Shirley, who stood to profit by it; another one-third share of the condemned seizure went to the customs officer whose enterprise had brought the whole thing about. His seizures reasonably sure of condemnation in the vice-admiralty court, Charles Paxton was well set for a remunerative career.

Paxton went about his rewarding duties with such energy and resource that for an instant one might wonder whether Boston was not under visitation by the reincarnate spirit of Edward Randolph, its custom house tormentor of seventy years before. But Paxton was no Randolph. The architect of the customs regime in the colonies had been a man of considerable force of character. Paxton was above all a pussyfooter. "Shew me the man in this province, or on this continent who knows him," said Sam Adams of him, "that will not allow, he is the most *insincere* plausible, and insinuating of mankind, and yet such is the art of the man, that let any person thus well acquainted with him, give him but a few moments of his company [Paxton] is sure to catch him — the poor Gentleman comes away deluded (in spight of his senses) nay absolutely satisfied that not

8. "The Belcher Papers," *MHSC* sixth series VII (Boston, 1894), 33, 401-403, 514, 517. Probably it was through Belcher, of whom the then Viscount Townshend was patron, that Paxton first formed his own connection with the Townshends (*cf.* n. 6 above).

9. Shirley to Admiralty, 14 November 1743: "Diligence, Fidelity and good conduct"; courage too: Adm. 1/3817. See J. A. Schutz, *William Shirley, King's Governor of Massachusetts* (Chapel Hill, 1961), 68.

10. Belcher Papers, n. 8 above. And in Josiah Willard to Thomas Hill, 23 June 1750: "By Charles Paxton Esqr a Passenger in the Ship Britannia . . .": C05/886.

only he, but all the world have abused the poor innocent . . . ." [11]
Not at all the Randolph style. Nor, in fact, did Paxton and his
unctuousness get away with it every time. There is an anecdote of
how he

> one day, having fleeced a very wealthy gentleman, met him, and with the
> impudence of *Beau Nash and Tobit's Dog* but in the antique aukward air
> of the last century, accosted him with 'Mr —, your most obedient humble
> servant, Sir' — Yes, yes, answered the other, 'every man's humble servant,
> but no man's friend' . . . ." [12]

Most of Charles Paxton's bad press — and few figures in the revolutionary period can have had worse — was in the years following
1767, when he was promoted to be one of the new American
commissioners of customs. But it started long before that. In 1756,
quite early in his unpopular career, the *Boston Gazette* was taking
him to task for concentrating his seizure efforts on some merchants
and improperly exercising "a *dispensing* Power" on others. [13]

It could be, perhaps, that Paxton had not yet perfected any such
discretionary mode of operation at the time of the incident at the
Hutchinson warehouse. Or perhaps that attempt was some sort of
mistake or aberration. To the world at large Paxton may have been
"no man's friend"; but his relations with Thomas Hutchinson seem
always to have been cordial. Indeed, in his account of the warehouse
incident, Hutchinson referred to himself as a friend of Paxton, and in
private correspondence he wrote of "My good friend Mr Paxton with
whom I have been intimate ever since we were boys and to whom I

---

11. *BEP* 12 December 1768, article signed "Candidus" reproduced in H. A. Cushing,
ed., *The Writings of Samuel Adams* (New York, 1904), 259-64. In the article Paxton is
"Squire Froth," a sobriquet that went back to a lampoon of Paxton (unsigned, but
conceivably by Adams himself) in *BG* 2 March 1761. *Cf.* p. 172 below. "Froth" often did
duty for Paxton in the antiestablishment Boston press: see, *e.g.*, p. 503 below. It may have
caught on even in custom house circles: witness a reference to "the example of Charles
Froth . . . under the circumstances of Candidus" in a letter from Inspector-General Thomas
Irving to Charles Steuart, 4 September 1769: National Library of Scotland, Steuart Papers
5025.

12. *BG* 6 November 1769, "Anecdotes of the Cabal." This particular anecdote was still
kicking forty years on: "When I was a boy there lived at Boston a certain person called
Charles Paxton . . . known . . . by everyone as everybodys humble Servant but nobodys
Friend" (Thomas Aston Coffin to "Margaret," 2 October 1809; Coffin Papers, MHS).

13. 6 December. Paxton had advertised a reward in *BEP* 29 November 1756 for
information about illegal importations of tea, yarn, and other goods from Holland. The
Gazette's open letter "To Mr P-X-N" speculatively inferred "secret agreements" to wink at
"the *Hambourgh, French, Spanish, Portuguese,* and *Danish* branches of illicit Trade."

It will be noticed that the unlawfulness of all this import traffic consisted in violation of
the British staple.

can deny nothing."[14] The good terms between Hutchinson and Paxton would hardly have lasted as they did — right through to the end, when the former governor and the former customs official were disconsolate loyalist refugees in England — if Paxton had kept up a bothersome interest in the trading practices of the Hutchinson family business. If there was truth in the *Gazette*'s allegation of more or less corrupt partiality in Paxton's law enforcement activities, what likelier beneficiary than Hutchinson?[15]

Another rumination suggests itself. The birth of "the child Independence" has been identified with the hearing on writs of assistance in Boston in February 1761. Presiding over that hearing was Thomas Hutchinson, now chief justice of Massachusetts; and the case is often known as "Paxton's Case." It is curious that an encounter between these same two men, Hutchinson and Paxton, should have been the occasion for the writ in the first place.

Uniquely valuable though it is, Thomas Hutchinson's account of the advent of the writ of assistance is pretty skeletal; and much of what follows in this chapter will be by way of amplifying comment on it, drawn from other fragments of evidence. Perhaps the first point for clarification is timing, in particular that of the crucial warehouse incident between Hutchinson and Charles Paxton which signaled the beginning of writs of assistance issued by the Superior Court of Massachusetts.

Not that the clarification can be one hundred per cent. On 23 November 1761 the *Boston Gazette* reported the final outcome of the writs of assistance case, and in a series of disgruntled observations recalled that the "Power now granted, was never asked for, or if asked, was constantly deny'd for this long Course of Years, until *Charles Paxton,* Esq; whose Regard for the Liberty and *Property* of the Subject, as well as the *Revenue of the King,* is well Known, apply'd for it in 1754 — it was granted by the Court in 1756, *sub silentio* . . . ." Against this statement that Paxton applied for the writ in the year 1754 there is the fact, witnessed by the surviving document itself,[16] that the petition upon which the writ was actually granted to him was addressed to the Superior Court on circuit "at York in and for the County of York on the third Tuesday of June

14. To William Wood, December 1764: MA 26, 123-24.
15. See n. 37 below, and text.
16. In Misc. MSS., MHS. Reproduced in *Quincy's Reports,* 402.

1755." Nothing to corroborate the story of a 1754 application has been discovered, and it is probable that the *Gazette* made a mistake. If, as the account in Hutchinson's *History* indicates, Paxton had been able to get a gubernatorial search warrant it would have been an uncharacteristically impertinent initiative for him to have gone to the Superior Court, without special reason, asking to be given something better.

It is unlikely too that the warehouse incident that gave rise to his petition in June 1755 was other than very recent. The petition was made to the Superior Court sitting at York. York is in Maine, and quite a journey from Boston even by today's standards; that Paxton could not wait the few weeks when the court would be back in Boston suggests an immediacy of purpose inconsistent with a matter that had been hanging fire many months. Conceivably he was in York already, in his capacity as cryer of the Superior Court, but it does not seem probable that the requirements of that minor office would normally keep him away from his substantive custom house and vice-admiralty work in Boston when the court was out on circuit. A far stronger probability is that the York application involved a special errand, hotfoot at that.

Also relevant is the position of Governor Shirley. The challenge at the warehouse, says Hutchinson, "put the governor upon examining the legality of his warrants, and caused him to direct the officers to apply for warrants from the superior court; and, from that time, writs issued, not exactly in the form, but of the nature, of writs of assistance issued from the court of exchequer in England." In June 1755 Shirley was making ready to absent himself from the province again, this time on military duty (as it turned out, as major general in command of the whole British army in America). That he attached serious importance to customs powers of search is evidenced by the warrants he had gone out on a limb to issue. It would have accorded with this purposeful interest that, his warrants no longer passing unchallenged, he wished the application to the Superior Court for the writ of assistance to be put in hand at once, so that everything might be settled before he went away. He would be leaving on Saturday 28 June.[17] If the court dealt with the application at York on the Tuesday of the preceding week there should be ample time for word to get back to him. Seen against this background Paxton's approach to the court at so remote a venue makes sense. And by the

17. *BEP* 30 June 1755.

same token — the haste of it all — it seems safe to conclude that the Hutchinson-Paxton encounter at the warehouse dates from almost immediately before. To put it at the beginning of June 1755 would not be far wrong.

However, the Superior Court did not rise to the occasion at their York sitting. Perhaps because something so novel as a petition for a writ of assistance required the kind of learning and books that were available only at the province capital, the judges took no action till they returned to Boston.[18] To borrow from Horace Gray:

> this case first appears on the records of the Court at the ensuing August term in Suffolk, (which the docket shows to have been held by *Sewall* C. J., *Lynde, Cushing & Russell*, J. J., and which was finally adjourned on the 30th of August,) in this form:
>
>> "UPON READING the petition of Charles Paxton Esquire wherein he shewed that he is lawfully authorized to execute the office of Surveyor of all Rates Duties and Impositions arising & growing due to his Majesty at Boston in this Province, and could not fully exercise said office in such manner as his Majestys Service and the Laws in such cases require, unless said Court who are vested with the power of a Court of Exchequer for this province would grant him a writ of Assistants, he therefore prayed that he and his Deputies might be aided in the Execution of said office with his District by a writ of Assistants under the Seal of said Court in Legal form and according to Usage in his Majestys Court of Exchequer & in Great Britain. ALLOWED, AND 'TIS ORDERED BY SAID COURT that a writ be issued as prayed for."[19]

What discussion may have taken place in Boston is unrecorded.

Uncertainty as to precisely when the warehouse encounter took place extends to the actual issuance of the writ. The original draft of the writ (to be considered in detail shortly) is undated, and it affords no indication of when the writ proper was delivered to Paxton. It seems probable, however, that Paxton had to wait several months before the writ, ordered by the Superior Court in August 1755, was actually in his hands. That the *Boston Gazette* was wrong in giving the year of Paxton's application as 1754 does not mean that it was wrong about the year of issuance being 1756. At the resumed hearing of the writs of assistance case in November 1761 one of the counsel, Oxenbridge Thacher, asserted that the writ of assistance "was never

---

18. Also the court may have been rather busy at York, with several lawsuits in progress between respective proprietors of the Kennebec Purchase and of land on the Kennebec and Sagahadoc rivers: *BEP* 15 September 1755. (*Cf.* chapter 17, n. 74.) The SCM indicate that the sitting lasted into four days; they say nothing of Paxton or the writ of assistance.

19. *Quincy's Reports*, 403.

applied for, nor ever granted, till 1756."[20] Thacher's misstatement that the year of application was 1756 is as irrelevant to the present question as the *Gazette*'s error in making it 1754: the question being not when the writ was applied for but when it was issued. What does signify is the fact that both Thacher and the *Gazette,* one supposes independently of each other, show the answer to be 1756.

In view of Governor Shirley's personal involvement, in particular that it was on his direction that the application for the writ had been made, subordinate figures may have decided it only proper that the actual issuance of the writ should await his return from military duties. Shirley arrived back in Boston from his ill-fated expedition early in 1756. Issuance of the writ shortly thereafter would fit in with the statements of Oxenbridge Thacher and the *Boston Gazette* that 1756 was the year it happened.

The original draft of the writ of assistance ordered by the Superior Court of Massachusetts in August 1755 is among the records preserved in the court archives of Suffolk County in Boston. It is in the handwriting of the attorney general of the province, Edmund Trowbridge.

Appointed attorney general in 1749, Trowbridge had the reputation of a considerable lawyer, much given to out-of-the-way learning.[21] Something so obscure and unfamiliar as the customs writ of assistance was right up his street, it might be supposed. But in fact he did not do too well with it. The comments in chapter 3 on how scarce information on the customs writ of assistance had always been included a reference to a specimen reproduced in a book by William Brown, first published in 1688 under the title *Compendium of the Several Branches of Practice in the Court of Exchequer at Westminster.* Until the publication in Horace Gray's treatise, in which a writ of assistance in the name of Queen Victoria was set forth, the Brown specimen was the only one ever to have reached the printed page. Trowbridge's draft for the Massachusetts writ of assistance was taken, in translation, from the weird, truncated, partly anglicized

20. *Ibid.,* 51-52.

21. According to Chief Justice Parker of Massachusetts in 1813, Trowbridge was "perhaps the most profound lawyer of New England before the Revolution"; F. W. Gwinnell, "The Bench and Bar in Colony and Province (1630-1776)," in A. B. Hart, ed., *Commonwealth History of Massachusetts* II (New York, 1928), 176. Contemporaries sometimes knew Trowbridge as Edmund Goffe; he had formerly called himself Goffe, after his great uncle and guardian. He was at the Superior Court at York in June 1755: SCM.

Latin of the *Breve Assisten' pro Officiar' Custum'* in Brown's little book. The texts are in Appendix E, and it straightway appears that this *breve assisten'* was not a satisfactory model.

The flaw lies in the things which the Trowbridge/Brown writ commanded assistance in the search for: "any Goods, Wares or Merchandizes . . . hid or concealed, having been imported, Ship't or laden in order to be exported from or out of the said Port . . .": things, that is to say, awaiting exportation or re-exportation. But it was not this sort of cargo that Charles Paxton went after at Boston; the problem there was with simple inward smuggling. Trowbridge's fidelity to the Brown *breve* betrayed him into error. What Brown had managed to find as a specimen writ of assistance to put in his book was a very peculiar specimen indeed. A point to notice in its mass of near-Latin is that this writ related specifically to the port of Dover. Dover was the nearest port in England to mainland Europe, and considerable entrepôt trade went on there. For a few years in the Restoration period it had been able to offer free port facilities for this. The particular form of writ of assistance that Brown got hold of could well have been invented for the situation that resulted when those facilities ceased. Entrepôt goods that previously touched in at Dover without involvement in the revenue mechanism now had import duty charged upon them, to be recovered as drawback when they were shipped out again. Drawback was notoriously vulnerable to abuse,[22] through fraudulent manipulation of goods when they were in the trader's custody awaiting re-exportation. The customs had a responsibility to see, as far as they could, that drawback was not paid on — for example — a hundred casks of French wine when ten of the casks were now filled with water. Obviously there were severe practical limitations upon what was possible by way of physical examination at the outgoing ship's side. It was useful, then, for the customs to be able to make their way into places where export or re-export goods were stored, to check that all was as it should be and that no fraudulent substitution had been going on. And it was particularly useful in the special circumstances of Dover where, one would suppose, a large increase in drawback traffic had occurred practically overnight. This was probably the true orientation of the writ of assistance in William Brown's book.

Nor did this old and peculiar writ of assistance specify anything about the holder actually seizing the goods he went in to inspect — in

---

22. This was a factor in Walpole's excise scheme in 1733. See n. 26 below and text.

Massachusetts the only possible object of an entry and search. Indeed, one might question the legal force of such a writ even in England. No doubt the substantive statutory obligation to aid and assist the customs in all things, imposed upon "all the King's . . . Subjects whatsoever whom it may concern" by the Act of Frauds of 1662, was sufficient warrant for a writ of assistance angled to the prevention of drawback fraud. But an obligation upon the public to give assistance was one thing, and a power in customs officers to enter upon private property quite another; how far customs officers might enter premises merely for checking up on drawback goods is very questionable. Brown's *Breve Assisten' pro Officiar' Custum'* was an oddity from the beginning; and by the middle of the eighteenth century it was at best an historical curio even in England. In Massachusetts it made no sense whatever.

It is curious that Attorney General Trowbridge should have allowed himself to be led so badly astray by the Brown *breve*. His Massachusetts writ of assistance was by no means wholly a blinkered translation.[23] Manifestly appropriate adaptations were attended to. A reference to Charles Paxton as surveyor of customs for the port of Boston was substituted for the reference to the Dover customs men. Trowbridge originally mentioned "Officers of Vice-Admiralty within said Province" among the miscellaneous addressees of the writ, but struck this out (possibly because the only officer of vice-admiralty to whom these words could meaningfully relate was Paxton himself, as marshal of the vice-admiralty court). He again departed from Brown in the recitation of the public officers qualified to accompany Paxton in the search of premises: Brown, following the substantive statutory power in section 5(2) of the Act of Frauds of 1662, naturally had included headboroughs; Trowbridge began by writing them into the Paxton writ too, but crossed them out: this particular grade of constable was nonexistent in Massachusetts. But when he came to the real substance of the writ, the operation the writ was designed to facilitate, he closed his mind and stuck to the *breve*. Of course, it was no part of Trowbridge's responsibility to know all the finer requirements of customs enforcement practice, but so much accent on exportation and re-exportation surely should have struck him as somewhat off-key for Massachusetts. It is difficult to believe that if Trowbridge had realized that the writ of assistance was a comparatively modern instrument, related to and no older than the

23. See also Appendix E(i) notes.

Act of Frauds of 1662, he would not have drafted the Paxton writ in closer conformity both with the terms of the act and with what customs search in Boston was actually for, namely, the seizure of illicit incoming traffic. The truth seems to be that Trowbridge did not understand the true juridical nature of the writ but regarded the Brown *breve* as an authentic precedent, however fossilized and inaptly worded.

The writ of assistance thus made an inauspicious start in Massachusetts. But at least it introduced a semblance of stability into what had been an awkwardly volatile situation. It displaced the vulnerable gubernatorial warrants, themselves introduced, according to Thomas Hutchinson, to supersede a practice under which customs officers assumed a power of forcible entry *ex officio* and which had been resisted physically or contested at law. So much shifting of position suggests one thing very clearly: uncertainty as to what the law on customs entry and search of premises, especially where force might be involved, really was.

Unsatisfactory draftsmanship in the Act of Frauds of 1696 bedevilled enforcement of the acts of trade, apropos the customs jurisdiction of colonial vice-admiralty courts. It was the culprit here too. Power of entry and search was one of the subjects of section 6. Earlier sections of the act having mentioned the various acts under which goods might be prohibited or dutiable, section 6 set forth that ships lading or unlading in a colonial port, and their masters, should be liable to "the same Rules, Visitations, Searches, Penalties and Forfeitures" as applied in England under the Act of Frauds of 1662; and it went on to provide that customs officers in the colonies

> shall have the same Powers and Authorities, for visiting and searching of Ships, and taking their Entries, and for seizing and securing or bringing on Shore any of the Goods prohibited to be imported or exported into or out of any of the said Plantations, or for which any Duties are payable, or ought to have been paid, by any of the before mentioned Acts, as are provided for Officers of the Customs in England by the said . . . Act made in the fourteenth Year of the Reign of King Charles the Second, and also to enter Houses or Warehouses, to search for and seize any such Goods.

The words underlined clearly denoted an intention that customs officers in the colonies should have some power of search on land. And that was as far as clarity went. The impression conveyed is that search on land as well as on board ship should be the same in the colonies as in England under the act of 1662, but it is an impression that quickly gives way to doubt. This syntax is not right, for one thing. It is in fact impossible to tell for certain exactly how the words "and also to enter Houses or Warehouses, to search for and seize any such Goods" should be read in relation to the rest of the text. If a replica of the 1662 power of entry was intended, why the limited reference to "Houses or Warehouses" when the 1662 power applied to "any House, Shop, Cellar, Warehouse or Room, or other Place"? Above all, why was the intention not spelt out plainly and unequivocally?

The point was taken in chapter 5 that the 1696 act's faulty provision for vice-admiralty jurisdiction could have been a matter of calculated ulterior design (on the part of Edward Randolph, who preferred a different kind of jurisdiction). Similarly one now hesitates to attribute the delphic perplexities of the provision for entry and search to mere carelessness, and suspects that a straight extension to the colonies of the 1662 provision was deliberately fudged. The draftsman of 1696 was faced with a real problem in this area. Peripheral difficulties that could have been gotten over by small adjustments in the 1696 drafting can be discounted, of course: for example, the 1662 act's stipulation that the writ of assistance should be under the seal of the Court of Exchequer, an institution whose processes did not run in the colonies, was a detail easily capable of being written out of the 1696 legislation. The problem was much more serious and intractable than this. It can conveniently be seen in terms of contrast. Search of ships presented no difficulty. The 1662 act, in section 4, had provided a power of shipboard search for goods "prohibited *or* uncustomed"; and it was therefore simple for the 1696 act to give "the same Powers and Authorities, for visiting and searching of Ships" in relation to "any of the goods prohibited to be imported or exported into or out of any of the said Plantations, or for which any Duties are payable, or ought to have been paid . . . as are provided for the Officers of the Customs in England [by the act of 1662]." But a similarly simple extension of the 1662 formula for entry on land was impossible. Here it was not goods "prohibited *or* uncustomed" but goods "prohibited *and* uncustomed." Chapter 4 showed that although this double-barreled requirement might have suited the conditions prevailing in England in 1662, times soon changed and it became embarrassingly insufficient: so much so that the intrinsically unsatisfactory customs search warrant act of 1660

had to be resurrected to supplement it. Obviously, if the 1696 act
had extended section 5(2) of the 1662 act to the colonies, "prohib-
a like (if lesser)[24] problem there. Yet it would not have been practical politics, either, to have made the 1696 legislation say that the
power of search now to be introduced into the colonies should be
the same as that of 1662, but with "prohibited or uncustomed"
instead of "prohibited and uncustomed." The position in England
had to be borne in mind. There the law of 1662, "prohibited and
uncustomed" and all, would remain as before. Even with the revived
act of 1660 — indeed, all the more because of it — the law on
customs search on land in the metropolitan country was in a condition where the less said and seen of it the better. It would not have
been prudent for the 1696 provision to spotlight the deficiencies of
its 1662 stablemate.

There is further reason to believe that the 1696 act's baffling
draftsmanship was no accident. The words from section 6 quoted
two paragraphs ago were only a fragment of the whole. In its entirety
section 6 was a series of regulatory and other provisions, all strung
together in a single sentence of more than five hundred words. The
piece about search occurred about one-third of the way through this
teeming verbiage, where its impossible construction was much less
apparent than when extracted and examined in isolation. The section
is reproduced in full in Appendix F, and the reader may judge for
himself; but well might the calculation have been that of the few
whom that daunting density of letterpress did not deter on sight
fewer still would persevere to the end and remain in fit mental
condition to cavil at a point of syntax two-thirds of the way back.
Not least would this go for the members of Parliament by whom
clause 6 had to be passed, and whose scrutiny the draftsman might
hope were not at its sharpest: for if the fudge on search powers did
not get through on the nod it might not get through at all. Technique
was the word, perhaps.

Eventually it came about that in Massachusetts section 6 of the
Act of Frauds of 1696 was interpreted and applied as if it plainly did
extend the English search provision of 1662: writ of assistance and

---

24. Lesser, because much of the smuggling into America was to be of goods both
prohibited (by reason of direct shipment from continental Europe) and uncustomed (if only
for having bypassed the customs process in Great Britain). Not so for Molasses Act
smuggling, though; Molasses Act goods were dutiable at prohibitively heavy rates, but they
were not in themselves prohibited to be imported.

everything else (including the use of force). Until that time, however, customs search in the province could be said to have been in a jurisprudential no-man's-land. Indeed, that the statute most directly pertinent presented so forbidding a puzzle may be a root cause of the instability of practice before the authorities at last plumped for the writ of assistance.

The life put into the Boston vice-admiralty court's customs jurisdiction in 1752 was an important element in the developments on customs search in the early and middle 1750s, but it was not everything. Revenue search was the subject of considerable public atmospherics at this time, and not only because of rows and litigation over customs officers' forcible search as it were *ex officio*. An important contributory factor was a noisy controversy that arose from the province's own taxation system.

In the year 1754 war against the French plainly was not far off, and defense expenditure necessitated reform in the province's defective excise revenue. Included in the new scheme was a move to close a loophole through which significant quantities of wine and spirits had hitherto passed into consumption untaxed. The excise on wines and spirits had been charged only on supplies sold through licensed outlets in domestic quantities (less than thirty gallons); the reformed scheme would charge domestic supplies obtained by other means. Small-time interests enthusiastically supported the scheme, as consumers who had no choice but to buy their liquor at duty-paid rates from retailers. Merchant interests opposed it, as consumers who had been able to tap their domestic supplies duty-free from commercial stocks. Governor Shirley sensed big political trouble over a control mechanism under which the householder would submit to the excise collector an annual return of his ménage's consumption of wines and spirits ("inconsistent with the *natural Rights* of every private Family,"[25] and so forth). Accordingly, he put a temporary stop on the bill, and canvassed public opinion in the towns.

The resulting furor was reminiscent of the tremendous excitements that attended Sir Robert Walpole's attempt to reform the excise in Great Britain just over twenty years earlier; and in a

25. Shirley's speech "to both Houses of Assembly" on 17 June 1754, in *BEP* 24 June. For the story in general see P. S. Boyer, "Borrowed Rhetoric: The Massachusetts Excise Controversy of 1754," *William and Mary Quarterly* XV third series (1964). *Cf.* chapter 16, n. 43 below.

specially curious way. Though neither Walpole's nor the Massachu-setts excise scheme in fact provided for promiscuous search of private dwellings, people insisted on believing otherwise.[26] The clamor against the Walpole scheme was strident enough to be heard in New England. In June 1734 the *Boston Gazette* had this:

A RECEIPT TO BE HAPPY

How pleasant is it, to behold on shore
The diving Bark, and hear the Billows roar!
Not that I'm pleased with other mens distress,
But glad to find the load I bear is less.
While all the fools, and more than half the wise,
Are puzzled at the bugbare word EXCISE;
Serene, I live a private country mouse,
Nor officers, nor coxcombs haunt my house . . . .

Massachusetts' own scheme for excise reform brought less compla-cent pieces from the printing presses.

Governor Shirley's moratorium, from June to December 1754, was a period of vigorous pamphleteering. The evils of excise search were a recurrent theme, though with even less justification than in Britain. In the Walpole scheme there had been at least some provision for search (of places set aside for the handling or storage of excisable products). In the Massachusetts reform of 1754 there was none. Nevertheless, in Massachusetts as in Britain, the opposition was not to be done out of a telling point by considerations of mere fact. Thus "A Letter from a Gentleman to his Friend, Upon the Excise-Bill now under Consideration," published in Boston as a broadsheet on 7 June 1754: "But besides the Excise itself, the propos'd Manner of exact-ing it, is what cannot but give very great Disgust, that it should be in the Power of a petty Officer to come into a Gentleman's House, and with an Air of Authority, demand an Account upon Oath of the Liquor he has drank in his Family for the year past . . . ." Another anonymous broadsheet, "The Relapse," spoke of the bill violating the "interior transactions" of the family. Of course, opponents of the bill were not always so crass as to claim that it provided powers of search when a plain reading showed that it did nothing of the kind. They saw powers of search rather as something which the

---

26. The essence of Walpole's scheme was that tobacco and wine should be subject not to a customs duty on importation but to an excise duty when afterward removed from bonded warehouse. (Elimination of drawback fraud was part of the purpose: see n. 22 above.) For obdurate incomprehension of what was proposed, see Sir John Barnard M.P. at c. 1317, *Parliamentary History VIII* (London, 1811), 12 March 1733.

new-style excise would inevitably move toward: For example, in "Some Observations on the Bill" published in Boston: "such a Law, when once passed, would lay a sure Foundation for destroying every other natural Right . . . ." And then words which almost could have come from the writs of assistance debate seven years later: "Such a Law is entirely unconstitutional, and therefore unknown, and never so much as once attempted in the *English Constitution*. It is *essential* to the English Constitution, that a Man should be safe in his own House: his House is commonly called his Castle which the Law will not permit even a Sheriff to enter into, but by his own Consent, unless in criminal Cases." The thin end of the wedge again: "But what avails it him, that he is safe within those Walls from an Attack upon his Person and Property, if at the same Time he must be oblig'd to give an account of his innocent Transactions there — of his *private Oeconomy* in his Family, and that upon Oath too, or else be obliged to pay a heavy Fine? If an account of one thing in the house, why not of all? . . . It is an old Maxim with regard to things in their own Nature bad, and apt to increase in their pernicious Effects, *Obsta principiis,* which may be expressed in a homely English Proverb, *Nip them in the Bud.*" Threatened invasion of hearth and home also featured in the pamphlet war's noisiest fusillade: "The Monster of Monsters: A true and faithful NARRATIVE of a most remarkable Phaenomenon lately seen in this METROPOLIS, to the great Surprize and Terror of HIS MAJESTY'S good Subjects: Humbly DEDICATED to all the Virtuosi of New-England, by Thomas Thumb, Esq." This lampoon on the excise bill dissensions so incensed the House of Representatives that two men suspected of responsibility for it were put in jail. It told of two groups of women, spoof-named members of which were easily identifiable as leading participants in the excise bill controversy, at odds over "a MONSTER of the most hideous Form, and terrible Aspect." This monster — a figure for the excise bill perhaps inspired by a like reference to Walpole's excise scheme in the English press twelve years before[27] — had been acclaimed "in a large Assembly of Matrons." However, "a middle-aged Gentlewoman of a more refined Taste" spoke up in opposition. "What would become of us all," asked Mrs. Gracca, "if he should break his Chain, get out of his Cage, and range about at large, seeking whom to devour! Doors and locks, and Bolts, and Bars, would be no Security against him. He (having a Faculty of contracting and enlarg-

27. See R. Turner, "The Excise Scheme of 1733," 42 *English Historical Review* (1927).

ing himself at Pleasure) would easily climb into our Bed Chambers;
and tho' we should hide ourselves down in our *Wine Cellars* among
the *Casks;* he would find us out even there . . . ."

The campaign against the excise bill failed and the bill was signed
by Governor Shirley in December 1754, but it showed how acutely
sensitive people in Massachusetts could be to anything that seemed
to threaten the sanctity of their dwellings. A practical illustration is
on record, too. Though also in a setting of province revenue enforcement, this episode, which dates around December 1755, has affinity
with the mention in Thomas Hutchinson's *History* of how customs
officers, seeking to make forcible entries "merely by the authority
derived from their commissions," had encountered resistance and
litigation and had thereafter obtained warrants from Governor Shirley, "as the civil magistrate." It arose from the province's tax on
imports. For some years past the Impost and Tunnage Act passed
annually by the province legislature had provided that the enforcement officers should be "impowered to search in all suspected
places" for goods that had improperly escaped the province import
tax. The *Journal of the House of Representatives* tells of a petition
by one Hayward Smith, deputy impost officer, to the effect that in
December 1755 he had led a party to Taunton and other places in
pursuit of undutied importations of rum and wine, when he and his
men were "plainly told by several Persons that they had large
Quantities of Rum in their Cellars which had paid no Duties, and had
threatened to shoot them if they should pretend to break open their
Doors." The House appointed a committee to consider Smith's
petition; what the committee reported seems nowhere recorded, but
the next Impost and Tunnage Act supplemented province revenue
officers' powers of search by explicit sanction of force. Something
essentially similar in a new excise enforcement mechanism, also
legislated for in 1756, perhaps was a measure of vindication for those
who had predicted that the excise reform of 1754 would soon be
followed by added powers of search.[28]

It seems reasonable to conjecture — firm evidence has not been

28. *Cf.* an historical curio in the old Massachusetts colony's enforcement regime for its
impost on wine. Enacted law gave a revenue officer the power and duty "to goe into all
Houses or Cellars where he knoweth or suspecteth any wine to be, and . . . seize upon such
wines as are not entred . . . And all Constables and other Officers are heerby required to
assist and ayd the Officer . . . helping to break open such Houses or Cellars, if the Owners of
such wines shall refuse to open their doors or deliver their keys in a peacable way . . .": *The
Book of the General Lawes and Libertys . . . of the Massachusets* as published in 1648 and
in facsimile by the Huntington Library (T. G. Barnes, ed., San Marino, 1975), p. 27.

found — that it was roughly in the same period as these agitations over province revenue search that the two preliminary modes of forcible search recounted by Hutchinson came and went: customs officer's commission and governor's warrant.

One can work backward from a proposition established earlier: that the writ of assistance superseded the gubernatorial warrant early in 1756. Thomas Hutchinson in his *History* said the warrants "were in use some years." Governor Shirley was absent in Europe four years up to August 1753. On the basis that Hutchinson's "some years" could have been as few as two and a bit, it could be that Shirley began issuing his warrants in the late summer of 1753, soon after his return. In 1752 the appointment of Vice-Admiralty Judge Chambers Russell to serve also on the Superior Court had made vice-admiralty condemnation of customs seizures safe from common law prohibitions; seizure now being worthwhile, search for seizable things also would be stimulated. One remembers from chapter 6 the newspaper advertisement by Collector Frankland in February 1753 ordering "all the officers in my district to be very vigilant in discovering and seizing all . . . contraband goods": this could easily have been interpreted as a directive for stepped-up search activity. Opposition would not have been long in showing itself, so that when Governor Shirley returned in the summer of 1753 forcible search on an *ex officio* footing was pretty well played out. If forcible search was to continue as a means of maximizing the new profitability of seizure there needed to be more impressive authority than a mere customs officer's commission; and the governor's warrants were brought in as the answer (until scotched by the challenge at the Hutchinson warehouse in mid-1755).

Interaction between the excise bill controversy and the various developments in the law and practice of revenue search, provincial and custom house, also is hard to gauge precisely. The Hayward Smith incident at Taunton at the end of 1755 and the consequent legislation on province revenue search in 1756 may have been the last repercussions from the scares of 1754. At the beginning, however, it could have been somewhat the other way round. Some day an exhaustive scrutiny of the coastal counties' inferior court records [29] may reveal details of those lawsuits which Hutchinson in his *History* says were brought against customs officers who had ventured on *ex officio* forcible entry; but, on the strength of Hutchinson's bare-boned account, it is at least an open possibility that this litigation

29. *Cf. LPJA* I, xxxiv.

took place before the excise bill and helped feed nervousness about powers of search into the agitations that burst forth when the bill appeared.

In relation to the challenge at the Hutchinson warehouse, which put an end to the gubernatorial warrant phase of customs search, the influence of the excise bill controversy was not a matter of ambient atmosphere. The afterglow may have been still warm enough at the end of 1755 to arouse the indignation of the chawbacon assailants of Hayward Smith out in the sticks; but the Boston sophisticate who boldly and effectively declared Governor Shirley's warrants to be "of no value" drew on more than stale populist rhetoric. The assurance with which Thomas Hutchinson felt able to speak can have come only from special knowledge of the law on revenue search. That "middle-aged Gentlewoman of . . . refined Taste" who had declaimed against the Monster of Monsters rooting around ladies' bedchambers and household wine cellars had taken trouble to bone up on the underlying legalities; what "Mrs Gracca" had found out about revenue search law at the time of the excise bill controversy was available to Thomas Hutchinson at his brother's warehouse a few months later — for she was he.

It remains to speculate what colorable legal justification might have been conjured forth for these two try-ons to get off the ground at all.

That Thomas Hutchinson is a reliable if a not very communicative witness to customs officers having "forcibly entered warehouses, and even dwelling houses" on nothing more than "the authority derived from their commissions" can be assumed from his direct personal knowledge of the lawsuits he said had resulted: from 1752 he had been a judge in one of the (so-named) inferior courts likeliest to have tried them.

It is a verifiable fact, too, that customs officers' commissions in mid-eighteenth-century America did recite that the holder had

> power to enter . . . into any House Shop Warehouse Hostery or other place whatsoever . . . to make diligent search into any Trunk Chest Pack Case Truss or any other parcel or package whatsoever for any Goods Wares or Merchandize prohibited to be imported or exported or whereof the Customes or other Duties have not been paid, and the same to Seize . . . ."[30]

30. This particular excerpt is from Surveyor General Thomas Lechmere's commission to George Cradock, as deputy collector at Boston in December 1759: SF 172363; closely resembling it is Surveyor General John Temple's commission to Timothy Folger (Nan-

However, it is another fact that a power of search was not something a customs officer's commission could snatch out of the air: there had to be statutory foundation for it. Here was a curious thing. Some commissions cited no statute at all for the power of search they asserted; and where that was not the case and the commission did identify the statute it drew upon, that particular statute in fact said nothing whatever about a power of search. The commission issued to Benjamin Hallowell junior as comptroller, Boston, in 1764[31] included the more or less standard formula for search of "any Shop, House, Warehouse, Hostery or other place . . . ," invoking the old act of 1673, *for the Encouragement of the Eastland and Greenland Trades and for better securing the Plantation Trade.* This was the act under which the customs service in America had first been set up (on the introduction of the plantation duties), by virtue, however, of no more than the laconic formula: "this whole Business shall be ordered and managed . . . by the Commissioners of the Customs in England." Presumably the view was that if the 1673 text was elastic enough to cover the establishment of an entire regime of customs enforcement in the colonies, it could stretch to powers of search.

The situation just described can be traced back to the early years of the imperial system, when the 1673 act was literally all the legislation that was available to the customs commissioners for their responsibilities in America.[32] Yet in the meantime the Act of Frauds of 1696 had been passed, ideally to give customs officers in America an explicitly legislated apparatus of control and enforcement mechanisms comparable to those in England. The defectiveness of the 1696 provision for power of search has been one of the themes of

tucket) in 1764: *LPJA* II, 160-61, n. 45. Both these commissions went beyond a surveyor general's authority (*ibid.,* 147-73: *Folger v. Sloop Cornelia;* and Treasury ratification of former surveyor generals' appointees, by letter to the American customs board 20 January 1769: T28/1); though of course that is not to the present point.

31. See *Quincy's Reports,* 433. This was an unquestionably authentic commission by the customs commissioners in London. The surveyor generals' commissions in n. 30 above were of the sort that mentioned no statute.

32. Surveyor General Mein's commission in 1685 (*Maryland Archives* V, 521; and n. 3 above) asserts a power of search deriving from the 1773 act. But that of his predecessor, William Dyer, in 1683 seems not to have done: Andrews, *Colonial Period of American History* IV, 164. And Edward Randolph's commission as collector in 1678 certainly had not: MHS Misc. III. The innovation may have been prompted by Randolph's inability, deepened perhaps by obstructionist moves in the Massachusetts legislature, to persuade the governor to give him search warrants (Toppan, *Randolph* III, 165; Goodrick, *Randolph* VI, 100), and by the Treasury's unresponsiveness to the situation evidenced by inapplicability of the 1662 Act of Frauds to America (Goodrick, *ibid.,* 106).

this chapter. Contemporary unease with it may be why the provision got not so much as a mention in customs officers' commissions, the commissioners preferring to continue to cite the act of 1673 (itself far from ideal).

And it seems that, with moderation, this purported power of search *ex officio* might have been gotten away with. This is suggested by something from Connecticut. In March 1769, Duncan Stewart, the collector of customs at New London, was conferring with the judges of the Superior Court of Connecticut on their reluctance to issue writs of assistance under the Townshend legislation of 1767. "I do not see why the Collector needs be uneasy," came the comment from Judge Robert Walker, "as he has still the same powers as Officers of the Customs formerly had, that is, to enter into houses & by their own Authority."[33]   What went wrong in Massachusetts perhaps was that moderation ceased to be observed. According to the account in Hutchinson's *History,* the "assumed authority" that people bridled at was customs officers having "forcibly entered warehouses, and even dwelling houses . . . ." The operative word, one suspects, is "forcibly." Whatever argument there might have been for extrapolating a power of search out of the sprawling generality of the 1673 act, sufficient perhaps to ward off challenge, it most certainly did not extend to vindicating the use of force. Again calling to mind Collector Frankland's advertisement in February 1753, which urged all customs officers "to be very vigilant in discovering . . . contraband goods," one can imagine some of them so fired with enthusiasm as to read this not merely as an order to make searches but as implying that what their commissions said about a power of search meant a power to break in. To such "assumed authority" local reaction would have been emphatic. It needed little more than a riffle through familiar lawbooks — Hale's *History of the Pleas of the Crown,* for instance — for any lawyer worth his fee to see that a power of forcible entry was by no means to be inferred from a power of entry, and that without clear statutory authority it could not lawfully exist.

To pass to the second of the false starts: "When Mr. Shirley was in administration, he as the civil magistrate, gave out his warrants to the officers of the customs to enter." It is hard to better Hutchinson's

33. Stewart denied that this authority existed. Technically he was right; but Judge Walker may have been well enough informed on actual practice. By a colleague on the judicial bench, that is to say: Judge Eliphalet Dyer was a former customs comptroller at New London. T1/471.

own comment: "This appears more extraordinary, as Mr. Shirley was a lawyer by education, and was allowed to be a man of good sense."

The text of Governor Shirley's warrant has not survived and no direct means exists of telling what legal framework he considered himself to be working in. There may be an indication of it, nevertheless, in something else from Thomas Hutchinson. Not Hutchinson as historian, but Hutchinson as recently appointed chief justice of the Superior Court. In a verbatim report of the resumed hearing of the writs of assistance case in November 1761, Chief Justice Hutchinson answers a point that the writ of assistance had been unknown in Massachusetts before 1756 and that its validity was the more questionable because of nonuser. "The Custom House Officers have frequently applied to the Govenour for this Writ," states Hutchinson C. J., "and have had it granted them by him, and therefore, though he had no Power to grant it, yet that removes the Argument of Non-user." And the answer given on behalf of the crown also is relevant: "As for the Argument of Non-user, that ends whenever the Law is once executed; and this Law has been executed in this Country, and this Writ granted, not only by the Governor, but also from this Court in Ch. Justice Sewall's Time."[34] These statements about the writ of assistance having been granted by the governor obviously had reference to the practice adopted by Governor Shirley when forcible search *ex officio* ran into trouble. And it is equally plain that Hutchinson was identifying the writ of assistance under consideration by the Superior Court with the "warrant" that he himself had seen and challenged in the warehouse encounter with Charles Paxton upward of six years before.

At the warehouse Hutchinson would hardly have been in a position to challenge the legality of Governor Shirley's warrant without first informing himself of its contents. Before denouncing it as "of no value" he needed to have read what it said. The later fact that he was able to think of it as the same kind of thing as the Superior Court's writ of assistance suggests that its text was to the same general purport as that of the writ. The essential feature of a writ of assistance was a directive to assist a customs officer. Chapter 4, it may be recalled, spoke of a magistrate's warrant that also had this feature. The specimen of this warrant reproduced in Appendix D is addressed to the constables of Stepney, in the English county of Middlesex; it recites that Andrew Bull, a customs officer, had sworn

34. *Quincy's Reports,* 52

to the likelihood of undutied imported liquor being in a certain house, and orders the constables "in his Majesty's Name . . . to assist the said Andrew Bull in the entering of the said House, and . . . search for the said Barrels of Liquor . . ." To this extent, at any rate, the Stepney warrant was of the nature of a warrant of assistance. And it happens to have been readily available for Shirley to meditate upon; notwithstanding its distinctively English provenance it was set forth in a book published in America and much in use there as a kind of magistrate's manual. This book was *Conductor Generalis: or the Office, Duty and Authority of Justices of the Peace, etc.* A lawyer of Shirley's practical experience would certainly have known of *Conductor Generalis;* and since no lawyer would invent the text of a legal instrument if he could find a suitable model to borrow from or adapt it seems likely enough that the warrants issued by Governor Shirley for the search of buildings for contraband owed something to the Stepney warrant of assistance (so to call it) in *Conductor Generalis.* The more so by reason of the words in the Stepney warrant: "and in Case you meet with any Resistance . . . you do enter the said House by Force": very probably it was because customs officers ran into trouble over using force in *ex officio* search that gubernatorial warrants had been resorted to.

In chapter 4 the Stepney warrant was associated with the act of 1660 (set out on page 42), under which certain personages in England had jurisdiction to issue search warrants for undutied goods. It was not entirely clear that the Stepney warrant was legally valid even in England. The validity of a comparable warrant in America, where the 1660 provisions did not apply, must be more uncertain still. However, Shirley's warrant would have been less a straight adaptation of the *Conductor Generalis* specimen than a fairly wide variant. Plainly, the statutory foundation for this warrant to the constables of Stepney went back to the act passed specially for customs search warrants in 1660. Shirley would have apprehended that the 1660 act (and *a fortiori* acts to similar purport that succeeded it), which appeared to have reference only to England, probably did not apply in Massachusetts, on the common law principle that legislation enacted after the settlement of a colony applied there only in the event of specific provision to that effect. Therefore he must turn to the power of entry and search in the Act of Frauds of 1662, which could be said to have application in the colonies by virtue of what the Act of Frauds of 1696, obscurely worded though it was, seemed to intend in this respect. The document predicated by the 1662 act was a writ of assistance, directed to (among others) constables; and to that extent the *Conductor Generalis* specimen might answer. But unlike its 1660 forerunner the 1662 act said nothing about oaths and appeared to leave its power of entry and search unrestricted in this way. Accordingly, while a warrant founded on the 1660 act had necessarily to be circumscribed by reference to the particular occasion for it, and such was the case with the *Conductor Generalis* specimen, such a restriction was not appropriate to the document contemplated by the 1662 act. Thus it may have come about that Governor Shirley left his warrants general in form and effect.

How might they have been illegal? Chief Justice Hutchinson gives a clue: Shirley "had no Power to grant it." The 1662 act expressly laid down that the writ of assistance should be from the Court of Exchequer, which identity no governor of provincial Massachusetts conceivably could pretend to.

However the gubernatorial warrants might be viewed, one has to agree with Thomas Hutchinson that they came strangely from a lawyer of Shirley's standing: for a man who had been a practicing barrister such liberties with the law were truly surprising. Nor was Governor Shirley always heedless of rights of security against intrusion. The aftermath of an abortive Land Bank scheme in the 1740s had included a bill passed by the Assembly for tidying up loose ends. Shirley rejected the bill because of, as he put it, "the extraordinary powers . . . for carrying it into Execution." The first of these powers, as set forth by Shirley in a report to the Board of Trade, was a power "to break open Doors, Chests, &c in order to seize the Effects, Books and Papers of the late Directors" of the Land Bank.[35]

If, as is possible, Shirley's disapproval of "extraordinary power" of search in the Land Bank affair was a politic gesture to populist elements disappointed by the destruction of the Land Bank, why should he have risked flouting public opinion in the matter of search by customs officers? The explanation perhaps is of a piece with his anxiety to get the customs jurisdiction of the Boston vice-admiralty court on to an effective footing: the one-third share of customs forfeitures that went into the governor's pocket. It was entirely

---

35. Letter dated 7 November 1743, C05/884. Reproduced in C. H. Lincoln, ed., *Correspondence of William Shirley* I (New York, 1912), 108.

consistent with the maneuverings of this "crafty, busy, ambitious, intriguing, enterprising, man"[36] that, having at last succeeded in fortifying the court process upon which his one-third perquisite depended, he followed through with whatever were necessary to maximize its yield. The more contraband customs officers sought out and seized, the greater the profit to Governor Shirley. It was natural that when their search activities ran into difficulty he did what he could to help, even though it was more than he ought.

That fateful encounter between Thomas Hutchinson and Charles Paxton at the warehouse in the summer of 1755, which marked the end of the gubernatorial warrant and the beginning of the Superior Court's writ of assistance, also is worth pondering a little. As will become apparent, the part played by sheer chance in the writs of assistance controversy was almost uncannily large. It could be that Hutchinson simply happened to be passing his brother's warehouse at the moment Paxton was about to break in. Yet there was something suspiciously pat about it. Paxton, says Hutchinson, was acting "upon an information of iron imported from Spain" being concealed in the warehouse. Hutchinson "knew the information to be ill-founded, sent for the keys, and caused the warehouse to be opened" (and presumably demonstrated to Paxton that it contained no illicitly imported iron). One cannot help wondering how Hutchinson could have been so certain that his brother's warehouse was not harboring contraband, or, as he put it, that Paxton's information was "ill-founded."

In all likelihood the house of Hutchinson was no more free from the taint of illicit trade than the next merchanting concern. Smuggling begets smuggling: if through smuggling a trader can supply goods at a lower price than his competitor the competitor must follow suit or lose business. As for Thomas Hutchinson himself, a modern commentator has observed that when historians "remark that he was esteemed for his probity and at the same time was as deep in the Holland smuggling as the rest of the merchants, they are probably correct." In 1745 he sailed pretty near the wind in the matter of exporting axes under a flag of truce. In 1749 Sir Henry Frankland, collector of customs at Boston, wrote of an endeavor some years before to force a change in registership of the vice-admiralty court as having been defeated "by a petition of a Few Merchants here": such petitions, said Frankland, "are very easy to be

36. John Adams, *LWJA* IV, 18-19.

obtained as the Merchants here are generally Smugglers." The petitioning merchants had included Thomas Hutchinson.[37]

The possibility cannot be ruled out that the Hutchinsons had had forewarning, and got the offending iron out of the warehouse before Paxton arrived. On this hypothesis, Thomas Hutchinson could have stayed around to prevent Paxton breaking into the now innocent warehouse — indeed, to scold him with talk of legal action. Why should Hutchinson have put himself to this trouble? Two answers suggest themselves. He was friendly with Paxton, as he makes a point of saying. And it would not have looked well to have it bruited about in open court that the Hutchinson family were thought by the custom house to have engaged in illicit trade — least of all in the Suffolk court of common pleas where Thomas Hutchinson himself had sat as a judge since 1752.

And there was a fair chance that sooner or later someone would challenge the governor's warrant in Hutchinson's court, which would be something of an embarrassment to a judge with political affiliation toward the government. A discreet reference back to Shirley, through Paxton, was much to be preferred to a noisy courtroom debate which — given that Hutchinson was right in believing the warrant bad in law — could end only in mortification for the governor.

Though Hutchinson is clear that his admonition to Paxton at the warehouse resulted in the introduction of the writ of assistance, he does not say that when denouncing the governor's warrant as illegal he advised adoption of the writ of assistance instead. Having warned Paxton off the warrant, he may well have left it to the authorities to find their own alternative. After all, it was bold enough in a layman to question the handiwork of the lawyer-governor without presuming to venture into something so novel and so recondite as the writ of assistance. Besides, if Hutchinson was still involved in illicit trade, it was hardly to his interest to promote a more effective counter-smuggling device.

Yet perhaps there was more than met the eye in the part he

37. Holland smuggling: C. K. Shipton, *Sibley's Harvard Graduates* VIII (Boston, 1951), 151. An admittedly unfriendly contemporary, William Palfrey, was explicit that Hutchinson "constantly practis'd all the various methods of Smuggling:" G. M. Elsey, "John Wilkes and William Palfrey," *CSM Publications* 34 (1943), Palfrey to Wilkes, 23-30 October 1770. But see also M. Freiberg, "Thomas Hutchinson: The First Fifty Years . . ." (n. 5 above). Flag of truce: P. O. Hutchinson, ed., *The Diary and Letters of Thomas Hutchinson* I (London, 1883), 52-53. Frankland: letter to Admiralty, 5 February 1750, Adm. 1/3882; petition, Adm. 1/3817.

played. In this period he was very close to Edmund Trowbridge, the attorney general, the man who actually prepared the writ of assistance. Trowbridge had the reputation of a lawyer of considerable and unusual learning. Possibly it was under the tutelage of Trowbridge that Hutchinson — who was not given to intellectual arrogance — could feel so confident that the governor's search warrant was legally unsound. One wonders whether Trowbridge may not have actually engineered a challenge to the warrant as an opportunity to show his own virtuosity in matters of unfamiliar legal technicality.[38] If so he overreached himself; for, as has been seen, the writ of assistance he produced was badly wide of the mark.

38. See p. 226 below.

8

The Onset of the Case

SEVEN WRITS of assistance were issued by the Superior Court of Massachusetts in the period between the Paxton original in 1755 or early 1756 and the public hearing on the writ in February 1761: in January 1758 to Richard Lechmere at Salem; in February 1758 to Francis Waldo, who had recently persuaded the Treasury to give Falmouth a custom house and appoint him collector; in January 1759 to James Nevin at Newbury; in February 1759 to Thomas Lechmere, surveyor general, and William Sheaffe, acting collector at Boston; and in March 1760 to George Cradock, taking a turn as acting collector at Boston, and William Walter at Salem.[1]

This modest profusion of writs of assistance is of a piece with the resurgence of the Boston vice-admiralty court's jurisdiction over Staple Act seizures. Confident that the vice-admiralty court would award them a decree of forfeiture, customs officers throughout the province naturally turned to the writ of assistance as a means of maximizing this source of personal profit — their one-third share — and the effectiveness of the imperial system.

However, for about three years after the advent of the writ of assistance the busiest of the Massachusetts custom houses had only

1. *Quincy's Reports,* 405-406. Waldo's representations, which the Treasury approved on 21 October 1757, are in T11/25. They described the mischief to be combated: "it is become a common practice for Ships in the Clandestine trade, belonging to Boston, New York, and other Southern ports in their return from Holland etc to put into these Eastern harbours, and employ coasters to distribute along the continent their contraband merchandise, in great Security, under cover of Deals or other Woods, whilst these foreign Traders proceed to the Ports, they respectively belong to or are bound to and enter themselves in Ballast. Besides these Vessels belonging to Subjects of his Majy foreign Bottoms have discharged Cargoes of Rum Sugar and Molasses in some of the harbours aforesd and then released for Louisbourg etc." Also, "a very pernicious [trade] has of late much prevailed from . . . New England to Louisbourg, giving them Supplies of the best provisions of cash in Exchange for french Rum, Sugar and Molasses, the produce of their Islands in the West Indies."

For comment on William Walter, see n. 23 below.

one of these valuable instruments, Charles Paxton's. From the issuance of the first writ in 1755 and up to early 1759, when Surveyor General Lechmere and Acting Collector Sheaffe obtained writs, customs search in the port of Boston was the prerogative of Paxton alone. This unique advantage helped consolidate Paxton's near-monopoly of the profits of seizure, including receipts from compromise settlements agreed out of court, and to account for the greater prosperity he was now enjoying.

Paxton had been fortunate. That he could practically corner the profits of seizure owed not a little to the distractions and protracted absence of the head of the customs establishment for the port of Boston, the collector, Sir Charles Henry Frankland, baronet. Frankland had been oddly placed domestically. Residing with him was a child named Henry Cromwell, of uncertain relationship to him, but whose adoptive surname betokened their common blood descent from Oliver Cromwell. Whatever good will this ancestry might have brought Frankland, for in Boston the memory of the lord protector was warmly cherished, soon suffered a reverse by more determinate evidence of the sort of individual he was. Frankland entered into a liaison with a young girl, Agnes Surriage, whom, so the story goes, he had encountered when she was scrubbing the floor of a tavern in Marblehead, and who before long was living under his roof; disparity of rank inhibited the baronet from actually marrying her. Opinion in the puritan capital was affronted, and in 1752 the incontinent collector removed his unseemly household from Boston out to Hopkinton. Two years later the ménage removed to England, apparently in connection with a lawsuit there; and after that Frankland and Agnes did the grand tour. Boston did not see him again until August 1756, and even then it was not for long. Within eighteen months he quit the collectorship and went to Europe for good.[2] A new collector did not arrive until September 1759.

2. See E. Nason, *Sir Charles Henry Frankland Baronet or Boston in Colonial Times* (Albany, 1865). Nason ascribes the paternity of Henry Cromwell (whose mother was not Agnes Surriage, of course) to Collector Frankland. But E. L. Pierce, *The Diary of John Rowe* (Cambridge, Mass., 1895) suggests Sir Thomas Frankland, an uncle whose baronetcy the collector succeeded to in 1747. Uncle Frankland, a commissioner of customs, presumably helped Charles Henry into the collectorship too (on condition, one is prompted to speculate, that he took the child with him to Boston, three thousand miles out of embarrassment's way). The Cromwell line was through Oliver's daughter Frances.

Nason's book was a source for a salty-saccharine ballad by Oliver Wendell Holmes, "Agnes." Here is a sample of "This old New England-born romance of Agnes and the

Frankland had not been wholly indifferent to making seizures on his own account,[3] and had he been on hand more he might have queered Paxton's pitch. William Sheaffe, who was commonly Frankland's stand-in, was perhaps too meek a character to try to assert himself as if he were a real collector;[4] and Paxton was left with most of the spoils. (It was when Frankland was absent in Europe, in the summer of 1755, that Paxton made his bid for the original writ of assistance.) In course of time, around 1760, other custom house functionaries took a hand in seizures, but even then the enterprise often was a joint one with Paxton participating.

Paxton went about his business with a certain professionalism. His association with newfangled instruments of customs search — first governor's warrants, and then the writ of assistance — is in itself a sign of this. But he did not stop there.

Seizure, the main sanction of customs law, depended upon the thing being physically accessible: hence the need for powers of entry and search. But even so, it was one thing to have a legal power of entry and another to know when and where to make use of it. Random searches on the off-chance might often be so much wasted effort, and no amount of legislation could lead a customs officer to

---

Knight" (the shining armor image required Frankland's demotion from baronet, presumably):

> The old, old story — fair and young
> And fond, — and not too wise, —
> That matrons tell, with sharpened tongue
> To maids with downcast eyes.

A still more sentimentalized account of the affair is in the novel *Agnes Surriage*, by E. L. Bynner (London, 1886).

3. Several are shown in the extant fifth volume of the vice-admiralty court records: cf. chapter 6, n. 20. For a later example see *BWNL* 18 April 1754.

4. "The baronet had no idea of spending his time in an office, so he drew the salary and left the work to Sheaffe:" C. K. Shipton, *Sibley's Harvard Graduates* VII (Boston, 1945), 254. Sheaffe's diffidence was remarked by his wife, apropos of paying court to the American customs commissioners: "There is nothing like being acquainted . . . Mr. Sheaffe is of so backward a disposition, I am bound to exert myself . . .:" L. Sabine, *Loyalists of the American Revolution* II (Boston, 1864), 820. Sheaffe's all-round character seems to have been a cut above average in the Boston custom house, neither venal nor high-handed. Thus *BG* 19 October 1772, soon after his death: "justly esteemed for his obliging Behaviour to the People; and Readiness to promote and serve the Trade and Commerce of the Province. He never appeared at the Sales of forfeited Goods, to interfere and prevent an unfortunate Man the chance of purchasing his own Goods; — He valued the Esteem of the People more, than to insult the distressed and unfortunate . . . ." He died a poor man. Cf. chapter 18, n. 8.

where a particular lot of smuggled merchandise lay hidden. What was needed was a reliable tip-off. Hence the type of custom house advertisement that was discussed, in another context, in chapter 6: the advertisement in 1753 in which Collector Frankland gave "pubick Notice that, if any Person or Persons will give . . . Information where such [unlawfully imported] goods are concealed . . . they . . . shall be very handsomely rewarded, and their Names concealed . . . ." The informer was essential to the swinging enforcement regime of the Boston custom house in the 1750s.[5]

Charles Paxton became an arch-practitioner of search and seizure on information received. He went one better than Frankland. While not scorning the generalized advertisement for persons with information to contact him, he cultivated a specialist in the business. This was Ebenezer Richardson, a man more ill-famed in the lore of pre-revolutionary Boston than even Paxton himself. The blackest point in Richardson's dark career was conviction in 1770 for shooting and killing a young boy: mitigating circumstances saved him from the rope, however. An early instance of his attracting unfavorable notice occurred in 1751, when be broke out of Boston jail. Two years later he was rapped for a slight case of incest (the other delinquent was a kinswoman only by marriage). It could have been through this affair that the authorities began to regard Richardson as a useful sort of man. Edmund Trowbridge, attorney general of the province, wrote of him in 1761 as "having about Seven Years Agoe been very serviceable to me in detecting a Conspiracy to Father a bastard Child on the Parson of a parish wherein he himself had been and other persons in higher Stations were engaged." And, Trowbridge went on, "perceiving he was well apprised of the manner in

5. English authority was to establish that a fruitless entry and search grounded an action for damages (much as did a seizure that failed of condemnation). "There was a case of *Shipley v. Redmain* in the Common Pleas, T. 5 Geo. 3 before Lord Camden, on a writ of assistance, when it was considered to be settled law that a person acting under the writ, and finding nothing, was not justified:" Plumer, *arguendo*, in *Cooper v. Boot* (1745) 4 Dougl. 339; see also his argument in 3 Esp. 135. "And any person so authorized by writ of assistance may search in the day-time, and accompanied by a peace-officer. But he is still only justifiable in an action of trespass by the event:" De Grey C.J. (who, as attorney general, had advised on writs of assistance in America: *cf.* chapters 1, 3, and 18) in *Bostock v. Saunders* (1773) 2 W. Black, 912 and 3 Wils. 434. *Cf.* also *R. v. Akers* (1790) 6 Esp. 125n. And see p. 424 below.

Section 32 of the Act of Frauds of 1662, the statutory foundation for the customs writ of assistance (see pp. 33-34 above), went on to provide that all who duly assisted the customs officer" shall be defended and saved harmless by Virtue of this Act." This protection did not extend to the officer himself.

which goods and merchandizes were illegally imported in the province I thought he might also be serviceable to the officers of the Customs and recommended him accordingly and promised to give him Advice and Assistance so long as he behaved well . . . ." That it was Charles Paxton to whom Trowbridge recommended him is on record from Richardson himself. The recruitment of Richardson was a kind of consummation. Trowbridge had drafted Paxton's writ of assistance, and now he was following through with help for Paxton to put the writ to best use.[6]

How informers such as Richardson were remunerated was shown in the Frankland advertisement. When the goods they had informed about were actually seized and condemned they would get a reward from the proceeds. Here, as will be seen in more detail later in the book, Paxton had gotten his system buttoned up rather too well. He was not content to pay for information out of his own one-third share, but often contrived to swing it on to the king's share. This practice was to be attacked in a lawsuit against him in 1761, adding to the unpopularity he had already earned by employing so notorious a reprobate as Ebenezer Richardson.

No direct evidence has been found of how Paxton's and the other pre-1761 writs of assistance were used in actual practice, but one guess may be ventured. The purport of a writ of assistance was that the customs officer wishing to exercise his statutory power of entry should be given all necessary assistance: in particular, by a local peace officer. Signs of Charles Paxton having used his writ of assistance in this way (rather than simply as a kind of *laissez-passer*) are suggested by documentation connected with the 1761 lawsuit. Set forth were several vice-admiralty condemnation cases over the years 1753-60 in which excessive costs allegedly had been allowed. The bill of costs in each case was broken down into considerable detail.

6. The homicide is treated in *LPJA* II 396-430 (which quoted John Adams on Richardson: "His life would exhibit an atrocious volume"); for the technical incest see *ibid*, p. 397, n. 4. Richardson's 1751 jail escape is reported in *BG* 10 December 1751. *BEP* 5 February 1753 implies that he had since escaped from Cambridge jail too, the report being of the conviction of his brother Timothy for "conveying Tools" to him. Trowbridge's testimony on Richardson, dated 18 March 1761, is in T1/408. Richardson's statement is in a petition, dated 19 January 1775, which besought Lord Dartmouth for British government aid ("your Petitioner gave Information of siverl breches of the Acts of Trade — and . . . was thereupon cried out against as an Informer and frequently abused by the people"); he got £10: T1/517. His services were not to the custom house exclusively. The Massachusetts Accounts for 1757-58 (C05/853) include the entry: "Paid Ebenr. Richardson for informing against & convicting Simon Davis & Son of counterfeiting . . . £25."

Three of them, in the years 1757-60, told of a fee for the sheriff or deputy sheriff's "assistance." It seems possible that the assistance thus paid for was assistance enjoined by the writ of assistance.[7]

Based as it was upon an old and idiosyncratic model, the writ of assistance devised for Massachusetts in 1755 cannot be supposed to have been wholly in line with contemporary practice in England.[8] How close or remote it was would be a principal question in the great debate of 1761; but there was one respect in which the Massachusetts writ and the English were identical. Both belonged to a class of legal instruments which at common law ceased to have effect when the monarch in whose name they had been issued died. However, logic had long since given way to practical convenience; an act of 1702,[9] which was expressed to apply in America as well as in England, included writs of assistance in a catalogue of instruments and processes that henceforth were to remain valid for six months after the current reign ended. George II, in whose name Paxton's and the other writs of assistance had been issued, died on 25 October 1760, and the news of his death reached Boston on 27 December. Accordingly, it was only a matter of time before new writs, in the name of George III, had to be applied for.

The Superior Court's records of the writs of assistance case are sparse. But some exist, and among them is an undated "memorial" which the surveyor general of customs addressed to the court at its sitting "at Boston . . . on the third Tuesday of February, 1761":[10]

> THE MEMORIAL of Thomas Lechmere Surveyor General of His Majesty's Customs for the Northern District of America. WHEREAS a petition is enter'd in this Honble Court sign'd by a great number of Merchants and Traders belonging to the Town of Boston praying to be heard upon the Subject of Writs of Assistance Your Memorialist therefore prays that Council may be heard on his Majesty's behalf upon the same Subject: And that Writs of Assistance may be granted to him and his Officers, as usual.
> THOs LECHMERE.

7. The lawsuit features in chapter 9 (mostly).

8. For one thing, the writ in England was not made out to one named individual specifically: any person legally competent to make a customs seizure could use it.

9. 1 Ann., stat. 1, c. 8. The two houses of the Massachusetts legislature put much thought into a bill "for preventing and removing all Doubts and Disputes" about writs and the like issued in the name of George II when in fact he was dead; eventually however the Council negatived it (20 January 1761: C05/822). There was another act, 6 Ann. c. 7, under which Parliament, the Privy Council, and crown offices survived the demise of the crown. For corresponding measures in Massachusetts see proclamations by Governor Francis Bernard: BPBA 19 October 1761.

10. SF 100515.

This memorial of Surveyor General Lechmere is the only official record of the customs authorities having asked for writs of assistance following the news of the death of George II. Not that the king's death was explicitly mentioned, even then: that it came into the matter at all has to be inferred from the fact that if nothing had happened to invalidate the existing writs there would have been no point in Lechmere requesting another supply.

Indeed, Lechmere's request "that Writs of Assistance may be granted to him and his Officers, as usual," seems almost to have been added by way of afterthought. First in line was another request, "that Council may be heard on his Majesty's behalf" on the subject of writs of assistance. The stimulus for this was stated to be that "a great number of Merchants and Traders belonging to the Town of Boston" had already petitioned to be heard.

This petition also survived.[11] Undated, like Lechmere's memorial, it was signed by sixty-three persons, headed by one Thomas Greene. Although Lechmere described them as Boston merchants and traders they described themselves as "Inhabitants of the Province of the Massachusett's Bay." Endorsed "Greene & al petition ab[t] Writ of Assist[s]" the petition read as follows:

> To the Honb[le] the Justices of the Superior Court of Judicature, Court of Assise & General Goal Delivery to be holden at Boston within & for the County of Suffolk on the third Tuesday of February ADom. 1761
>
> THE PETITIONERS Inhabitants of the Province of the Massachusett's Bay Humbly Pray that they may be heard by themselves and Council upon the subject of Writs of Assistance & your Petitioners shall (as is Duty bound) ever pray;

and then followed Greene's and the other signatures.

A further source of evidence is the *History of Massachusets-Bay* by Thomas Hutchinson, who, as chief justice of the province, had been the man actually presiding over the writs of assistance case. According to Hutchinson, "Upon application made to the court by one of the custom-house officers, an exception was taken to the application; and Mr. Otis desired a time might be assigned for an argument upon it . . . ."[12] It is not obviously remarkable that Hutchinson puts the "application by one of the custom-house officers" prior in time to the "exception" that was taken to it. One does notice however that with the memorial in which Surveyor General Lechmere asked for

---

11. Long enough, anyway, for Horace Gray to reproduce it on pages 412-13 of *Quincy's Reports*.

12. Page 68.

writs of assistance and the Greene petition for a hearing the sequence was the other way.

The suspicion thus raised that there was more to the onset of the writs of assistance case than the Greene petition and the Lechmere memorial is fed by other considerations. For some five years the Superior Court had been issuing writs of assistance for the asking. Only as recently as March 1760 writs of assistance had been issued, to George Cradock at Boston and William Walter at Salem, apparently without incident or protest of any kind. Yet, within no more than ten months, there was this clamor for a courtroom debate. Writ of assistance search cannot but have been unpopular at any time. If grounds for challenging the writ existed, why were they not tried out until the beginning of 1761? Turning again to Surveyor General Lechmere's request for writs of assistance one now wonders whether there may not be more significance than meets the eye in the way he put it: that writs might be granted "as usual." What might have happened that Lechmere apprehended departure from the norm?

Evidently, a new factor had come into play.

A key to what this was is in Thomas Hutchinson's *History of Massachusets-Bay*.

Describing the progress of the hearing before himself and his brother judges in February 1761 Hutchinson tells of an objection to writs of assistance that were "of the nature of general warrants." The existence of precedents for writs of this kind was conceded, "but it was affirmed, without proof, that the late practice in England was otherwise, and that such writs issued upon special information only." To this there was appended a footnote: "The authority was a London magazine." If Hutchinson had made this footnote a little more communicative the illumination it affords to the origins of the writs of assistance case would have shone forth long ago. The reference was not to some unidentified periodical from London but to a quarterly publication, carrying miscellaneous articles of topical and general interest, which bore the actual name *The London Magazine*. Particularly in point was an article in the issue for March 1760.

This article — it is reproduced in full in Appendix G — was concerned with an act that had recently been passed at Westminster "for the more effectual preventing the fraudulent importation of cambrics and French lawns."[13] In the words of the act, cambrics and

13. 32 Geo. 2, c. 32.

French lawns which had been improperly brought into Great Britain "shall be forfeited, and shall be liable to be searched for and seized in like manner as other prohibited and uncustomed goods are . . . ." When this legislation was still going through Parliament, the article related, merchants trading in draperies petitioned the House of Commons that "they might have leave to be heard by their counsel" in protest against the measures envisioned in the bill, notably with regard to search of premises. The merchants got their hearings, but the bill went through, search provisions and all. Consisting as they did simply of a blanket adoption of pre-existing provisions for search and seizure of "prohibited and uncustomed goods," they struck the *London Magazine* writer as a subject for explanatory comment, including a brief disquisition upon the writ of assistance: "As to a writ of assistance from the Exchequer, in pursuance of the act of the 13th and 14th of Charles II. cap. 11., I believe, it was never granted without an information upon oath, that the person applying for it has reason to suspect that prohibited or uncustomed goods are concealed in the house or place which he desired a power to search . . . ."

The *London Magazine* article was copied in full in the *Boston Evening-Post* for 19 January 1761 – in nice time for the public hearing on writs of assistance only four or five weeks ahead. But it would have been circulating privately long before that. Excerpts from the *London Magazine* often appeared in the Boston press, normally around three months after the month of publication in England.[14] Why the March 1760 article took so much longer is a matter for speculation, and the fact of its having done so may or may not be significant. But that the March issue of the *London Magazine* actually arrived at Boston at the normal time, and was available for private reading there from around the end of June, there can be no reasonable doubt.

So, in the middle of 1760, Bostonians were reading a respected journal from England in which it was stated as the belief of a writer who seemed to know his stuff that the writ of assistance in its home territory was never issued without sworn information as to the specific occasion for it. On this showing the "general" writ of assistance that the Superior Court of Massachusetts had been issuing

14. By way of example: the *London Magazine* for March 1758 was referred to in *BEP* 15 June; for September 1760 in *BEP* 28 November; for May 1761 in *BEP* 27 August; for August 1761 in *BEP* 31 December.

these past four years was at variance with the authentic English prototype. It now needs no effort of the imagination to understand why a writ issued routinely in March 1760 should have been so vigorously disputed only a few months later. Or, in the shadow thus cast on the future of the conveniently open-ended Massachusetts writ of assistance, why Surveyor General Lechmere made a point of asking that the new George III writs be "as usual."

After the *London Magazine* for March 1760 reached Boston the next writ of assistance application was bound to get a less easy reception. But this is not to say that this next application was one that followed upon the news of the death of George II. The unprecedented argumentation over writs of assistance early in 1761 related back to an application the previous fall.

The Superior Court records do not tell of this application. The prime source of evidence is John Adams. Aside from Thomas Hutchinson (who had presided as chief justice), Adams was the only person present at the hearing in February 1761 to put anything in writing about it. Indeed, it is to Adams's accounts and recollections of what was said in court that the writs of assistance case owes its fame. From time to time in the course of his long life he harked back to the case as a starting-point of the movement toward American independence. Adams's memory sometimes played him tricks, and his knowledge of the events that had impressed him so deeply was surprisingly incomplete. But on the point that the writs of assistance case originated not with the news of the death of George II late in December 1760 but some time before, John Adams's testimony is in essentials consistent and convincing. Here is one version of it, from his autobiography in 1802:

> The King sent Instructions to his Custom house officers to carry the Acts of Trade and Navigation into strict Execution. An inferiour Officer of the Customs in Salem whose Name was Cockle petitioned the Justices of the Superior Court, at their Session in November for the County of Essex, to grant him Writs of Assistants . . . . Some Objection was made to this Motion, and Mr. Stephen Sewall, who was then Chief Justice of that Court, and a zealous Friend of Liberty, expressed some doubts of the Legality and Constitutionality of the Writ, and of the Power of the Court to grant it. The Court ordered the question to be argued at Boston, in February term 1761. In the mean time Mr. Sewall died . . . .[15]

And in a letter from Adams to Dr. Jedidiah Morse in 1815:

15. *DAJA* III, 275.

In the month of February, 1761, the great cause of writs of assistance was argued before the supreme judicature of the province, in the council chamber in Boston; and this important question was tainted from the beginning with an odious and corrupt intrigue. Chief Justice Stephen Sewall, who was an enlightened friend of liberty, having great doubts of the legality and constitutionality of this projected writ of assistance, at November term, 1760, at Salem, where it was solicited by Cockle, a Custom-house officer, had ordered the question to be argued before the court at the next February term in Boston; but Sewall in the mean time died, and [Governor] Bernard . . . appointed Hutchinson, for the very purpose of deciding the fate of the writs of assistance, and all other causes in which the claims of Great Britain might be directly or indirectly implicated . . . .[16]

Adams returned to the subject of the writs of assistance case more than once in still later years, notably in letters to William Tudor (for a biography of James Otis junior). In March 1817 he told Tudor of the British government having ordered "the collector of the customs in Boston, Mr. Charles Paxton, to apply to the civil authority for writs of assistance . . . ." According to this version, Paxton "thought it not prudent to commence his operations in Boston." Instead,

he instructed his deputy collector in Salem, Mr. Cockle, to apply by petition to the Superior Court, then sitting in that town, for writs of assistance. Stephen Sewall was then Chief Justice of that Court, an able man, an uncorrupted American, and a sincere friend of liberty, civil and religious. He expressed great doubts of the legality of such a writ, and of the authority of the Court to grant it. Not one of his brother judges uttered a word in favor of it; but as it was an application on the part of the crown, it must be heard and determined. After consultation, the Court ordered the question to be argued at the next February term in Boston, namely in 1761.

In the mean time Chief Justice Sewall died, and Lieutenant-Governor Hutchinson was appointed Chief Justice of that Court in his stead. Every observing and thinking man knew that this appointment was made for the direct purpose of deciding this question in favor of the crown, and all others in which it should be interested . . . .[17]

16. *LWJA* X, 182-83. Morse had sought Adams's help in writing a history. For Adams's responsiveness to such requests, see L. H. Butterfield, "John Adams: What Do We Mean by the American Revolution?" in D. J. Boorstin, ed., *An American Primer* (New York, 1968), 246-48.

17. *LWJA* X, 246-47. Likewise in *ibid.*, 274-75, to Hezekiah Niles, of Baltimore, Md., publisher of the *Weekly Register*, 14 January 1818: "Mr. Cockle, a deputy under Mr. Paxton, of Boston, the collector of the customs, petitioned the Superior Court in Salem, in November, 1760, for such a writ." Also in W. C. Ford, ed., *Statesman and Friend —
Correspondence of John Adams with Benjamin Waterhouse 1784-1822* (Boston, 1927), 121 (Adams to Waterhouse, 25 June 1816). Somewhat earlier still: "the British cabinet ordered

These fairly extensive descriptions of the onset of the writs of assistance case are not free from error, but this need not be gone into now. More to the point is the central element common to all of them, namely, that the hearing in Boston in February 1761 related back to an application for a writ made by a customs man at Salem, Cockle by name, when the Superior Court was on circuit there the previous fall.

Something else has to be said. In the second and third of the quoted pieces John Adams stated flatly that it was for the sake of a decision favorable to the writ of assistance that Thomas Hutchinson was appointed chief justice in place of the deceased Stephen Sewall. The appointment was made in November 1760. Obviously, if Adams's allegation was to hold water a challenge to the writ of assistance must already have been in prospect. Perceiving this, mindful of Adams's tendency to factual mistake and aware that no application by Cockle at Salem is in the remaining records of the Superior Court, the skeptic might wonder whether the story of the Cockle application was not a little too pat. But the Adams evidence also includes material which dates not from his old age[18] but from the actual time of the writs of assistance case, before Hutchinson's orientation toward the British connection had become anything out of the ordinary or Adams's disapproval of him colored by events of the revolutionary years. Adams in fact first put pen to paper on the writs of assistance case as he sat in court listening to it going on. His sketchy contemporaneous notes were shortly afterward written up in what he called an "Abstract,"[19] the opening words of which were these: "On the second Tuesday of the Court's sitting, appointed by the rule of the Court for argument of special matters, came on the dispute on the petition of Mr. Cockle & others on the one side, and the Inhabitants of Boston on the other concerning Writs of Assistance." And here is how the Abstract had counsel for the crown

---

Charles Paxton and his Subordinate Cockle, to apply for Writs of Assistance . . .:" Adams to Benjamin Rush, 29 November 1812, in J. A. Schutz and Douglass Adair, eds., *The Spur of Fame. Dialogues of John Adams and Benjamin Rush, 1805-1813* (San Marino, 1966). And see n. 18 below.

18. Also there was this, to Mercy Otis Warren, 20 July 1807: "As early as 1760, orders came to Paxton and Cockle to demand Writs of Assistance . . . Judge Sewall died: Hutchinson was appointed Chief Justice on purpose, as I believed, to give judgment in favor of these writs:" *MHSC* fifth series IV (Boston, 1878), "Correspondence between John Adams and Mercy Warren," 339-40. And see Adams's letter of 4 October 1780 to the Dutch jurist Hendrik Calkoen, in *LWJA* VII, 226 (*cf. DAJA* II, 447, n. 5).

19. See Appendix I for the notes and Appendix J for the Abstract.

beginning his argument: "I appear on the behalf of Mr. Cockle & others . . . ."

The Superior Court's records — such as they are — of the Boston writ of assistance proceedings in 1761 are as silent on Cockle as were those of the sittings at Salem in October 1760. But what of that alternative first-hand source, the Hutchinson *History*? In this too there is no mention of Cockle by name. Hutchinson's lapidary account of the launching of the writs of assistance case may be recalled, however: "Upon application made to the court by one of the custom-house officers, an exception was taken . . . ."[20] First impression that the applicant custom house officer was Surveyor General Thomas Lechmere has already been discounted. (In any case, the hierarchically minded Hutchinson would scarcely have designated the head of the entire customs establishment from Newfoundland through New Jersey as "one of the custom-house officers.") That it was the man Cockle whom Hutchinson meant is a wholly reasonable supposition.

It remains to establish the identity of Cockle, and to weigh up various other elements in John Adams's testimony that indicate that the writs of assistance case took its rise not so much from the need for replacement writs for the new reign as from a single application when — as far as anyone in America knew — the old king was still alive.

James Cockle was hardly the "inferiour Officer of the Customs in Salem" that Adams dubbed him, and certainly he was not the deputy or subordinate of Charles Paxton at Boston. He was in his own right collector of customs at Salem and Marblehead, a port smaller than Boston but quite independent of it. As collector he was, if anything, a cut above Paxton, who had only the middling rank of surveyor and searcher.

Cockle also has some claim to recognition as one of the minor agents of irritation in the darkening days of provincial Massachusetts. Had he lasted longer he might have been almost the equal in public disesteem of Paxton himself. As it was he had only from 1760 to 1764 in which to earn his reputation. But even at that he did pretty well: "Mr. Cockle suspended from his Office yesterday at Salem," records the diary of the Boston merchant John Rowe for 29 September 1764, "which the people at that place Rejoyc'd at, by Firing

20. Page 68.

Guns — making Bonfires, Entertainments etc. . . . ."[21] Cockle's arrival in America from England in 1760 had been a little out of the ordinary too.

As a collector of customs Cockle was the appointee of the Treasury, which meant the Duke of Newcastle. He had been nominated by Lord Monson, whom Newcastle presumably wished to oblige or reward.[22] That there was an opening for Cockle at Salem resulted from an odd mistake. The mistake was that the previous collector of customs at Salem had died. This was William Bollan, the man who, under the governorship of his father-in-law, William Shirley, had so earnestly tried to get legislation to strengthen the customs jurisdiction of colonial vice-admiralty courts. Bollan, though still titular advocate general, had for years been living in London as the Massachusetts agent. On arrival there in 1745 he was given the Salem collectorship, the emoluments of this additional absentee appointment perhaps being in satisfaction of the understanding on which he had accepted the (unsalaried) advocate generalship back in 1742: "a yearly Salary of £300 or some valuable office in the Customs in America."[23] However, more to the point is Bollan's loss of the Salem job. The circumstances could date from 1755, when he told the Board of Trade of infirmity obliging him to retire "as soon as

21. Manuscript diary in MHS. Cockle's dismissal (for corruption) is described in J. D. Fiore, "The Temple-Bernard Affair," *Essex Institute Historical Collections* 90 (Salem, 1954), and H. B. Zobel, *The Boston Massacre* (New York, 1970), 20-21. *Cf.* chapter 18, n. 16.

Horace Gray, *Quincy's Reports*, 422, reproduces this spoof advertisement in *BG* 10 May 1762:

Port of C-k-le Borough

Now riding at Anchor and ready for Sailing, the Idiot of full Freight, with Ignorance, no Commission, few Guns; any necessitous Person that wants daily Sustenance may meet with suitable Encouragement by applying to J-s C-k-le the Commander, at the King's Arms in S-.

22. Governor Bernard to Richard Jackson, 30 November 1764: Bernard Papers III.

23. C05/894: Memorial by Bollan to the king in council (undated, but probably the latter half of 1767). Bollan had previously written to the Duke of Newcastle about, *inter alia*, his supersession as collector: Add. MSS 32974, 12 April 1766. *Cf.* chapter 17, n. 25.

Although Bollan visited America (in 1749, the memorial says; and for his reappointment as agent see *BG* 23 January 1750) it does not seem likely that he ever actually functioned as collector at Salem. One of his deputies was Richard Lechmere; latterly it was William Walter. In 1764 Walter gave up the customs service altogether, became an episcopalian parson, and took an appointment at Trinity Church, Boston: H. S. Tapley, "St. Peter's Church in Salem before the Revolution," *Essex Institute Historical Collections* 80 (Salem, 1944). *Cf.* C. W. Akers, *Called unto Liberty: A Life of Jonathan Mayhew 1720-1766* (Cambridge, Mass., 1964), 186.

properly, & justly may be." Seventeen fifty-seven saw him still in harness, but excusing himself from an engagement because of sickness. In 1761 young John Hancock was to write from London: "I frequently see Mr. Bollan . . . and he looks half Dead, and is kept alive merely by Mechanism." Reports on Bollan's condition reaching the Treasury had gone further. Thus, on 23 April 1760: "James Cockle appointed collector at Salem and Marblehead, . . . Wm. Bollan decd." Demonstrably, exaggeration had gotten badly out of hand. (Hancock himself probably overdid it in 1761, for in that same year Bollan was to prove sufficiently active to play a key role in the writs of assistance case.) But, although Bollan certainly was not deceased in 1760, for all the difference it made to the Treasury dispensation he just as well might have been. The mistake went unremedied. His Salem job was not restored to him. The new man Cockle — no absentee — moved quickly; appointed in April 1760, he was across to America and in post before the summer was out.[24]

Clearly, then, the customs officer at Salem whom John Adams repeatedly identified with the origin of the writs of assistance case was indeed around at the time. On why Cockle should have applied for a writ, however, the Adams testimony is less reliable. Adams saw Cockle as acting on some kind of special directive from the British government. If there was anything at all in this it was that William Pitt, secretary of state, had written to colonial governors in America on 23 August 1760, urging them to root out a persistent unlawful trade with the French. Great Britain and France were still at war, the British conquest of Canada notwithstanding, and more than anything else it was the "Provisions, and other Necessaries" obtained through this trade with the British colonies that kept the French war effort going in the American theater. Accordingly, said Pitt, governors were "to put the most speedy and effectual Stop to such flagitious Practices." As will appear in chapter 9, Pitt's letter elicited a mere bromide response from the governor of Massachusetts. But it could

---

24. Letter dated 21 March 1755: C05/887. Bollan to Board of Trade, 22 February 1757: C0391/64. "Letters of John Hancock," *MHSF* XLIII (1910), 193-200: John Hancock to Thomas Hancock, 14 January 1761. T11/26 (out-letters, customs).

In the memorial (n. 23 above) Bollan complained not only of the loss of the Salem collectorship in 1760 but also of his supersession as advocate general in 1767 (by Jonathan Sewall). What redress, if any, was given does not appear. Bollan's experience indicates that jobs such as his were not copper-bottomed properties. Or perhaps times were changing. In 1742, Thomas Leehmere was restored as surveyor general of the northern customs district of America after displacement "upon a false representation that he was dead:" *Calendar of Treasury Books . . . 1742-1745* (London, 1908) 34, 500.

not in any case have played a part in Cockle's applying for a writ of assistance. An application to the Superior Court on circuit at Salem could not have been later than 23 October, for that was the date of the court's last business there. At this time Pitt's letter had not yet arrived from England.[25]

Yet it is likely that Adams was right when he told of James Cockle having applied for a writ of assistance at Salem in the fall of 1760. Cockle had reason enough of his own to try to get a writ of assistance as soon as possible. He came to America badly in need of money. A friendly comment put it thus: Cockle "had the misfortune, before leaving England, to be involved in a Bankruptcy of his Brother, who under pretence of admitting him into partnership, made him subject to all his debts . . . ."[26] (When, four years later, he was dismissed for corruption, his fear of creditors was still so strong that he made for France or Holland rather than return to England.)[27] A man in Cockle's straitened circumstances would not have neglected any means of boosting the profits of his office. Prominent among these was the customs man's one-third share in condemned seizures (or whatever he could get by composition in lieu of condemnation process). A valuable tool in seeking out seizures was the writ of assistance. An early opportunity for Cockle to apply for a writ occurred on 21 October 1760, when the Superior Court visited Salem on circuit for two days. What more natural than that he should have taken it?

Another fairly constant element in John Adams's accounts of how the writs of assistance case originated was the doubts of Chief Justice Stephen Sewall. In one respect here, Adams was quite wrong; Sewall could not have had any say in the handling of Cockle's application for a writ at Salem in the fall of 1760, because he was dead. Not, however, that this discredits Adams's testimony one hundred percent. Sewall died on 10 September 1760 after an illness of only a week or so.[28] He had had plenty of time in which to read what the *London*

25. Pitt's letter is reproduced in *Quincy's Reports,* 407-8. Its arrival was notified by Governor Bernard to the Council on 31 October: C05/823. *Cf.* pp. 161-163 below.

26. Governor Bernard to Richard Jackson, 30 November 1764: Bernard Papers III. See also Tapley, *op. cit.* (n. 23 above), 354.

27. Bernard to Jackson, n. 26 above.

28. C. K. Shipton, *Sibley's Harvard Graduates* VI (Boston, 1942), 565. A significant slip of chronology occurs where, in another context, Adams refers to Sewall's death: "In December, 1760, or January, 1761, Stephen Sewall, chief justice, died, deeply lamented, though insolvent" (*LWJA* IV, 7).

Magazine for March 1760 said about the writ of assistance in England being special rather than general. The *London Magazine*'s implications for the writ of assistance his court had been issuing since 1755 would not have been lost on a person of his sensitivity and conscientiousness. That it caused him doubt goes without saying. (The Massachusetts writ, modeled as it was upon the curio *Breve Assisten' pro Officiar' Custum'* an old book on English exchequer practice, had never read quite right anyway.) And that Sewall ventilated his doubt in course of conversation in the summer of 1760 is credible enough too.

Furthermore John Adams seems to have been justified, up to a point and in an out-of-focus sort of way, in including the doubt felt by Chief Justice Sewall as a factor in the events that foreshadowed the writs of assistance case. Thomas Hutchinson's *History of Massachusets-Bay*, having told how a hearing on writs of assistance was asked for and arranged, adds this: "The motion was the more readily complied with, because it was suggested, that the late chief justice, who was in high esteem, had doubts of the legality of such writs." On the word of his successor, though Sewall was dead by when Collector Cockle put in his fateful application at Salem in October 1760 his doubt lived on, and to some effect.

But Hutchinson too leaves something more to be said. If Chief Justice Sewall knew of that disturbing *London Magazine* piece, his brother judges on the Superior Court also knew of it. With talk going round that the general writ of assistance might very well be unlawful, James Cockle's application for just such a writ could not have come at a worse time for the surviving four. Not one of them — Benjamin Lynde junior, John Cushing, Chambers Russell, or Peter Oliver — was a fully trained lawyer. It could be that they had Attorney General Trowbridge with them at Salem in October;[29] he had learning in plenty to draw upon in the ordinary way, but as the draftsman and probable instigator of the document now so deep in doubt he was not the best and most objective of advisers. The likelihood arises that the puzzled and uneasy four, preferring not to commit themselves on the inopportune problem posed by the Salem collector, laid it aside

---

29. The Superior Court record for Barnstable in May 1760 says, "The Attorney General being absent, the Court appoint James Otis Esq to Act as Attorney for the King this term." A like entry is in the record for Springfield in September, with Robert Auchmuty nominated. At Bristol on 15 October it was Samuel White. But at Salem the following week (as at Worcester in September) there was no stand-in attorney general, which could mean that Attorney General Trowbridge was there in person.

for consideration in Boston, the center of legal knowledge in the province. (In the meantime, moreover, they could hope to be given a new chief justice with whom to share, generously, this unwelcome responsibility.) Certainly there are indications, which will be discussed in later chapters, of the bench extending feelers for learned help soon after the circuit tour ended.

Mum was the word, naturally. It would not look well, in the court record or wherever, for the topmost judges in the province to admit to being jolted off course by a lay article in the public prints. And, insofar as their shilly-shallying did need accounting for, let the doubt about the writ of assistance be attributed to Stephen Sewall exclusively and the hesitation of his surviving colleagues to decorous respect for their departed chief.[30]

It is not to be supposed that challenge in the Superior Court was set on foot immediately word of Cockle's application got round.

Of course, the *London Magazine* for March 1760 had other readers in Boston besides the judicial establishment. All manner of persons, including such as had cause to disfavor effective customs search, doubtless could see in it the makings of an attack on the general writ of assistance. No more than the makings, though. The baldly expressed belief of an anonymous journalist that the writ of assistance in England was granted only ad hoc and on sworn suspicion was not much to go on. Even if among the custom house's numerous ill-wishers there were some who might have been willing to hire and actually pay for an attempt to mount a contest in court, any professional lawyer they engaged would see formidable difficulties: not least, a reluctance in the Superior Court to face the corollary of a definitive decision against Cockle, namely, the awkwardness and embarrassment of somehow revoking writs of assistance already in the possession of customs officers; a plate of crow altogether too heaped and indigestible. Opposition to the writ of assistance in the fall of 1760 probably amounted to no more than a diffuse and inchoate grumble.

Come the end of the year, however, the situation was different. The news late in December of the death of George II meant that all writs of assistance issued in his name expired; to the extent that the

---

30. *Cf.* the memorandum by William Bollan reproduced in Appendix H, which tells of "the court doubting suspended their determination til next term." The context, however, suggests that this was a reference not to the Cockle application at Salem but to the full-dress writs of assistance hearing at Boston in February 1761.

status quo was that much less inhibiting hopes for some sort of effective counteraction could have risen. For another thing, the new king was a very young man: if the Superior Court were not dissuaded from replacing the George II writs with George III writs exactly like them — good for the whole reign, plus six months — most Bostonians could reckon on being saddled with general customs search for the rest of their lives. But the most important transforming factor was the emergence of an experienced and considerable lawyer to articulate a researched case against the general writ of assistance (as he was to claim, without fee). Other events, which will be described in later chapters, had delivered James Otis junior into the service of the custom house's merchant adversaries.

Not that it was a matter of Otis and the merchants slotting into a public courtroom hearing that was already scheduled. Almost certainly, when the puisne judges of the Superior Court postponed the Cockle application from Salem to Boston they had no thought of a debate in open court. Consult with the bar they might, and perhaps invite the customs authorities to sustain the general writ of assistance in a formal legal presentation confuting what the *London Magazine* had said; but a public confrontation — James Cockle versus whatever objector — is most unlikely to have been envisioned. This need not have had anything to do with the want of an objector actually coming forward, or even with precedent (the very first application for a writ of assistance, by Charles Paxton in 1755, was also postponed from up country to the province capital; and there is no sign that the Boston deliberations on Paxton's application had been other than behind closed doors). A courtroom bout of the ordinary sort, with Cockle as one party and an objector the other, was up against an adventitious difficulty. Under a province enactment dating from 1701, the noncriminal jurisdiction of the Superior Court was almost wholly appellate; in general, the court could adjudicate at first instance only in cases that involved the crown.[31]

That a jurisdictional problem did exist, and how the writs of

31. *Cf. LPJA* I, xl, xli. Prohibitions perhaps were an exception of sorts (*cf.* p. 84 above); but there could be no place other than the Superior Court for them anyway, since a lower court could not claim the jurisdiction to which they naturally pertained (*i.e.,* jurisdiction at the King's Bench level).

The Superior Court's first-instance writs of assistance hearing cannot be rationalized in any such way, even though the writ was conceived as pertaining to that court exclusively: English process afforded no model. (This is not necessarily to stigmatize the hearing as heterodox; arguably it was an example of the common law shaking down to a different life in America.)

assistance case took place in spite of it, can be seen from Surveyor General Lechmere's "memorial." In this memorial, the supremo of the customs organization asked the Superior Court for a batch of new writs of assistance (in replacement, mostly, of those lapsing after the death of the king), and by reference to the petition already made to the court by Thomas Greene and others "praying to be heard upon the Subject of Writs of Assistance" himself requested the court "that Council may be heard on his Majesty's behalf upon the same Subject." What the surveyor general's intervention signified is plain. As now projected, the hearing had the crown as a party. The king's hat having been thrown into the ring, so to speak, the writs of assistance question answered to the one category of issues determinable by the Superior Court at first instance. The way had been cleared for an open-court debate.[32]

The Greene petition and the Lechmere memorial were earlier discussed in conjunction with the account of the onset of the writs of assistance case given in Thomas Hutchinson's *History of Massachusets-Bay*:

> Upon application made to the court by one of the custom-house officers, an exception was taken to the application; and Mr. Otis desired a time might be assigned for an argument upon it. The motion was the more readily complied with, because it was suggested, that the late chief justice . . . had doubts of the legality of such writs.

It was apparent that the "application" and the "exception" spoken of in that sequence were not identifiable as the Lechmere memorial and the Greene petition, which chronologically were the other way about. The relationship among these four can now be looked at again, through the refracting proposition that the whole thing was stage-managed.

Given that a lawyer of James Otis's standing would have been aware of the jurisdictional problem, he surely did not trouble himself and his merchant clients to the point of putting in a petition to the Superior Court — one has only to think of the labor of gathering some sixty-odd signatures — without having first gotten the problem out of the way. In other words, before Otis lodged the merchants'

---

32. That Cockle was in the crown service does not imply that his application was identifiable as the crown's. It is improbable, on precedent alone (see the previous "petitions" set forth in *Quincy's Reports*, 402-6), that his application was even expressed to be on behalf of the crown.

petition an understanding had been arrived at that Surveyor General Lechmere would respond in the name of the king so that the issue thus joined were indisputably susceptible of trial by the Superior Court.

Staff work behind the scenes is indicated by something else. The Greene petition and the Lechmere memorial each were addressed to the Superior Court at its sitting "on the third Tuesday of February . . . 1761." There was more to this particular day than is immediately apparent. What it was shows forth in the opening words of John Adams's abstract of the February proceedings: "On the second Tuesday of the Court's sitting, appointed by the rule of the Court for argument of special matters, came on the dispute . . . concerning Writs of Assistance." In 1759 the Superior Court had "determin'd that for the future the special pleadings shall come on the second Tuesday in each Term & continue from day to day till finish'd; & to allow the Bar the preceding Monday to prepare therefor."[33] The "third Tuesday of February . . . 1761" — 24 February — specified in the Greene petition and the Lechmere memorial was such a "special pleadings" day, as John Adams stated (the term having begun the Tuesday before). It looks as if prearrangement rubbed off on to the Superior Court, too. The day reserved for "special pleadings" could not have been bespoken without the court's prior approval. Furthermore, the court would hardly have given its approval — in Hutchinson's phraseology, complied with Otis's motion that "a time might be assigned for an argument" — while the jurisdictional problem was still unresolved.

One wonders, in passing, whether Hutchinson's reference to a "motion" by Otis may not signify some kind of preliminary or interlocutory proceeding in the Superior Court at which Otis presented and spoke to his clients' petition for a hearing. (There is no evidence one way or the other.) But in whatever circumstances the court's cooperativeness manifested itself it need not have been notably eager, even allowing that some of the judges had puzzlements they genuinely wanted removed. What Hutchinson says of the Otis motion being "the more readily complied with" because of the esteemed late chief justice's doubts may be fig-leaf cover for a grudging acquiescence. An acquiescence, that is to say, the true rationale of which the judges would have preferred not to be confronted with: the surveyor general's willingness to play along had not

33. See *Quincy's Reports*, 479.

so much enabled them to hold a public debate on the "exception . . .
to the application" of James Cockle as embarrassed them out of all
possibility of ducking it.

That, however, is as may be. What comes through incontrovertibly
is that by the time the Greene petition and the Lechmere memorial
were delivered to the Superior Court, probably in late January or
early February, a public hearing was already on the tapis. The
petition and the memorial served no other purpose than formal
documentation for the court's files. (Except that in the outcome the
court kept scarcely any other record of the writs of assistance case,[34]
and for the specially good turn they have therefore done history.)

Two postscripts.

The first has to do with Thomas Hutchinson's muttering manner
of telling the tale in his *History of Massachusets-Bay*. That his
footnote reference to "a London magazine" instead of the *London
Magazine* clouded rather than clarified can be shrugged off as a
mistake or a lapse of memory on a detail. However, indulgence is
more difficult toward obscurity in his substantive text. To quote yet
again:

> Upon application made to the court by one of the custom-house officers,
> an exception was taken to the application; and Mr. Otis desired a time . . .
> for an argument upon it. The motion was the more readily complied
> with . . . .

The criticism need not be labored that Hutchinson's silence on the
Greene petition and the Lechmere memorial leaves the reader to
discover them for himself and to see as best he may how the
"exception" and the Otis "motion" stand in relation to them. There
is another insufficiency of statement deserving attention. It lies in
Hutchinson's failure, if that is quite the word, to reveal that the
"application made to the court by one of the custom-house officers"
was the application that Collector James Cockle had made back in
October when the Superior Court was at Salem on circuit. Unless the

---

34. *Cf.* chapter 12.

The court's endorsement on the surveyor general's document (n. 10 above) is "Lechmere's petn.," which conflicts with his own word for it, "memorial." *Cf.* also a SCR index
reference to the November writs of assistance hearing, "Lechmere Surv. Genl. his petition . . ." (along with "Greene et al. Petn. . . ."): *Quincy's Reports*, 418.

That Lechmere used another word than "petition" underlines that his invocation of the
crown was no mere form, but was considered and significant: the king could not be thought
to petition in his own court.

Hutchinson reader happens to know — thanks to the invaluable Adams materials — that the application had been made some four months previous to the hearing the *History* was proceeding to describe, and in a different town, he might easily suppose that the events recounted (application, exception, motion, and so forth) all took place in rapid immediate sequence, and all at Boston. This misleading impression is unlikely to have been left through innocent error. Much more probably, calculation and purpose were at work in Hutchinson's constricted narrative. Illumination is from John Adams again, in the link he believed had existed between the writs of assistance case and Hutchinson being appointed chief justice. According to Adams, "Every observing and thinking man knew that this appointment was· made for the direct purpose of deciding this question in favor of the crown . . . ." This sort of talk going the rounds would not have missed the ear of Hutchinson himself. Nor were his many enemies and traducers men to let it be forgotten. Indeed, as the Adams testimony shows, it was still blackening his reputation fifty years and more after. The story that he was made chief justice in order to fix the writs of assistance question clearly was not something he would wish his *History* to add credence to. Yet this might well have followed if the book had been more expansive. It was public knowledge that he was given the chief justiceship in November 1760. For the *History* to have written of Cockle by name, with an indication that the application that originated the writs of assistance case had been lodged in October (and therefore was already pending in the Superior Court when the chief justiceship appointment occurred), would have been a foolish benefaction to the dirty-minded.[35]

The second postscript is on the puzzling helpfulness of Surveyor General Lechmere. Of course, it could be that Lechmere intervened out of dutiful concern for the future of customs law enforcement:

35. Hutchinson's uninformativeness on the Cockle application may have encouraged the erroneous tradition that the writs of assistance case originated with an application by Charles Paxton. In *Quincy's Reports,* at p. 51, "Paxton's Case of the Writ of Assistance" is the heading used for the account of the resumed hearing of the case in November 1761; and Josiah Quincy Junior's actual report begins: "CHARLES PAXTON, Esq., applied to the Superior Court for the Writ of Assistants, as by Act of Parliament to be granted to him." Quincy may have been misled by the fact that, after the case, it was Paxton to whom the first (George III) writ was issued — on the application, however, not of Paxton himself but of John Temple, who by now had succeeded the retired Lechmere as surveyor general: *Quincy's Reports,* 416.

replacement writs of assistance in the name of George III were needed for the proper functioning of the customs service, and they could hardly be obtained in circumstances of jurisdictional impasse (which quiet-lifers on the Superior Court bench might have been content to see continue indefinitely). But there is a different possibility. Lechmere was an elderly man, coming up to retirement. Many years had passed since he arrived from England; Massachusetts was now his home, and he planned to end his days there. The people he would be living among were hoping to rid themselves of general customs search once and for all, if they could get a hearing in the Superior Court. Lechmere's memorializing the court on behalf of the crown was what made the hearing possible. A timely gesture of friendliness and reconciliation?

To this second postscript, a tailpiece. Whatever the reason for the surveyor general's cooperativeness, it is droll to reflect that the historic writs of assistance case might never have happened but for good will on the wrong side.

9

Collateral Commotions

THE END of 1760 and the beginning of 1761 witnessed the onset of other forensic contests involving the Boston custom enforcement regime. Although these other lawsuits were in strictness independent both of each other and of the writs of assistance case there were elements of connection among all three, and it would be unreal to ignore them or to treat the writs of assistance case as isolated from them. To the governor of the province all were manisfestations of a larger "confederacy" directed against the custom house and its judicial arm, the vice-admiralty court. Whatever the justification for the epithet, if the writs of assistance case is to be understood in the round its companion controversies must be examined as well.

Human fortune and behavior added an important dimension. The complex was not made up of events alone.

It is convenient to view the scene through the experiences of a man who had the ill luck to be right in the middle of it.

Governor Francis Bernard was still a newcomer to Massachusetts when the "confederacy" against the custom house and the vice-admiralty court started up. Born in 1712 the son of an English country clergyman, he was educated at Westminster and at Christ Church, Oxford. He became a barrister in 1737, and practiced law in and around the cathedral city of Lincoln. Part of his work was with ecclesiastical affairs, and presumably it was this — for the canon law of the Church of England had affinities with the Roman legal tradition — that warranted the comment that Bernard "was bred a Civilian."[1] His marriage in 1741 to a kinswoman of Viscount Barrington, that most durable of politicians in the British ministry,

---

1. Henry Hulton's "Account:" see pp. 61-62 above and chapter 5, n. 18. For instances of Bernard deploying his civil law learning, see *LPJA* II, 333, and a letter to the Board of Trade, 2 July 1764, in Bernard Papers II.

engendered both a large family and employment in the government service for its maintenance. Through Barrington's good offices Bernard arrived in America in June 1758 as governor of New Jersey, in place of Jonathan Belcher, former governor of Massachusetts and New Hampshire, who had died the previous August. The fall of 1759 brought a minor general post among colonial governors, following the death of the governor of Jamaica. Thomas Pownall, who had succeeded — not to say ousted[2] — William Shirley as governor of Massachusetts in 1756, went to England in expectation of becoming governor of South Carolina. Francis Bernard got Lord Barrington to pull strings again, and on 13 November 1759 Lord Halifax, president of the Board of Trade, wrote to him to say that the Massachusetts post was his.[3] Pownall quit Boston early in June 1760 and Bernard moved in on 2 August.

A character sketch of Governor Bernard has been left to history by Henry Hulton, one of the American board of customs commissioners set up in 1767. Bernard, said Hulton,

> was an exceeding good Classic Scholar, and had a fine taste in Musick, and Architecture. As a friend, a Neighbour, and companion, no one was more easy and agreeable, without ostentation and ceremony, he lived with ease with his friends, told a thousand good Stories, and every body was pleased and happy in his Society. He was perhaps too open and communicative, a person of less abilities and merit than himself, with more address, art, and intrigue, might have succeeded better. He perhaps was not sufficiently disguised, and did not practise enough the courtly manner and courtly arts, for one in his Station.[4]

Thomas Hutchinson wrote to a friend a few months before Bernard's arrival, "People that know Mr Bernard say he is not a Man of Intrigue, that he loves to be quiet himself & is willing that other People should be so too."[5] The *Boston Gazette,* whose columns were

2. Shirley's undoing was primarily as commander-in-chief (pp. 103 and 188), but removal from America meant loss of his governorship as well. He clearly saw Pownall, then lieutenant governor of New Jersey, among the intriguers against him; by, *e.g.,* pamphleteering, and inducing in the New Jersey assembly "a diffidence in my conduct" (addressee unknown, 2 April 1756: SRO GD224/Box 8/24A). That his brother John was secretary to the Board of Trade (*cf.* n. 31 below) perhaps did something for Pownall's Massachusetts candidacy: on the other hand, when it came to South Carolina in 1760, see p. 160 and n. 33 below.

3. Bernard Papers IX.

4. "Account." n. 1 above. In Harvard College, the present Harvard Hall (reconstructed after a fire) was to Bernard's design. He also designed new wings for Thomas Hutchinson's house at Milton: Esther Forbes, *Paul Revere and the world he lived in* (Boston, 1942), 73.

5. To Israel Williams, 4 March 1760: MHS Williams Papers II.

later to revile Bernard with the utmost ferocity, by no means disfavored him at the beginning. On 2 March 1761 it carried an allusion to him as "facetious merry man, of an easy temper, and naturally well dispos'd . . . ." And for what physical appearances are worth, the portrait of Bernard in Christ Church, Oxford, has a reasonably friendly look about it.

The Hulton assessment suggested that Bernard's virtues were to some extent his undoing. Certainly there are signs of an excessively sanguine temperament betraying him into serious misjudgment of the task that faced him in Massachusetts. "I am very unacquainted with the Circumstances of that Government," he wrote to Lord Barrington in February 1760, "but have the pleasure of being assured that the Government is put into very good order by Mr Pownall, & that I shall have nothing to do but keep it so."[6] And in April, "As for the people I am assured that I may expect a quiet and easy administration."[7] A few days after arrival in Boston: "there are no disputable points of government remaining unsettled; & this people are better disposed to observe their compact with the Crown, than any other on the Continent that I know. I may add, that I enter upon the government, without any party being formed against me."[8]

Within six months of this high-riding optimism Bernard was writing of the fury of party having been turned against him, and of "a contention between the King's Authority and Law and the Subjects & Objects of them."[9] Bernard's shortsightedness and failure to size up a situation must not be overstated; much of what was to activate the "confederacy" at the end of the year could not possibly have been predicted in August by Bernard or anyone else. All the same, he really ought to have known better than to confide to his official superiors in England a belief — if considered belief it was, and not just exuberance over the new job — that the government of Massachusetts would be plain sailing, with no more than an occasional touch on the tiller. A letter from Lord Barrington on 22 February 1760 had a warning undertone that should have put him on his guard against facile first impression: "the most sanguine wish of your

6. 16 February 1760: Bernard Papers I. Halifax, when giving Bernard the Massachusetts governorship, had strongly recommended him to confer with Pownall before the latter's departure: "It is impossible to pursue a better Plan of Government than what he directed himself by" (letter at text to n. 3 above).

7. Bernard to Barrington, 19 April 1760: Bernard Papers I.

8. To Board of Trade, 18 August 1760: C05/891.

9. To ? 19 February 1761: Bernard Papers I.

friends cannot go farther than that the People over whom you are going to preside may think of you, & act towards you as you deserve."[10] Welbore Ellis, writing from England in July, was more direct: "I am sensible that you are now at the Head of a people very difficult to manage . . . ."[11] Above all, Bernard was related by marriage to Samuel Shute, a former governor of Massachusetts whose time in the province, some forty years before, had been marked by some very rough tussles with the local politicians. Altogether, Bernard's extravagantly up-beat expectations of "a quiet & easy administration" must have caused eyebrows to rise in England.

For generations past a "perpetual discordance," as John Adams called it,[12] had characterized relations between Massachusetts and Westminster, with scarcely a time when a dispute of some kind was not going on. If there was one root cause of this it may have been that New England had never fitted too well into the imperial economic system. Said an anonymous contributor to the Board of Trade archives in 1729,

> The more powerful our Plantations grow, the more it behoves us to have a watchfull Eye upon their Conduct, more especially such of them, as have few or no Staple Commodities of their own to Exchange with us, and whose product is generally the same with that of Great Britain, which lays them under strong temptations of interfering with us in our Manufactures, Commerce, Shipping and Navigation, as is very much the case of all the Colonys to the Northward of Virginia, but more particularly of the Massachusetts Bay.[13]

Another deep cause of trouble had been the trauma of 1684 in which Massachusetts lost its original colony charter. Its neighbors to the south, Rhode Island and Connecticut, had not been affected in this way, and in all but form were more or less independent republics; but the replacement charter by which in 1692 Massachusetts had become a province (somewhat on the Roman model, with its governor appointed by Westminster) was not quite so free and easy. For decades afterward encroachments upon powers intended for reservation to the crown, and resourceful exploitation of such local autonomies as the province charter did allow, were as if to recapture the colonial liberties of time long past.[14]

10. Bernard Papers IX.
11. 24 July 1760, *ibid.*
12. In a letter to Hezekiah Niles, 13 February 1818: *LWJA* X, 284.
13. C05/752 pt. 2, "Some Considerations upon the Present State of the Massachusetts Bay 1729."
14. The political state of things in Massachusetts was reported on by the Board of Trade to the king on 8 September 1721 (British Library, King's MSS 205): "altho' the Govern-

War conditions had been a fertile source of colonial discontent. In King George's war, rioting broke out in Boston over the activities of shore patrols of the Royal Navy in the taking of deserters and the impressment of colonial seamen;[15] and the victory of American arms at Louisbourg in 1745 quickened the colonists' resentments of the uppity British officer caste. (It did not help that Britain afterward handed Louisbourg back to the French.) The none too glorious defeat of Major General Braddock and the British in the 1755 run-up to the French and Indian war had added further spice to colonial umbrage. "I heard such relations from our provincial officers of the treatment they received from the regulars as made my blood boil in my veins," John Adams recalled, "Brigadier Ruggles with his whole brigade . . . was put under the direction of a British ensign, and employed to cut roads, when they were much more willing, and I believe much more able, to fight the French, than the British officers and soldiers who treated them so cavalierly."[16] Such slights may have rubbed off on to relations between Massachusetts and the British military at the political level, for the province's own top officers naturally gravitated to membership of the General Court

---

ment of this province be nominally in the Crown, and the Governor appointed by Your Majesty, yet the unequal balance of their constitution having lodged too great a power in the Assembly, this province is, and is always likely to continue in great disorder. They do not pay a due regard to Your Majesty's Instructions, they do not make a suitable provision for the maintenance of their Governor, and on all occasions they affect too great an independence on their mother Kingdom."

15. Adm. 1/388 has a letter, indistinctly dated but probably November 1747, in which Vice-Admiralty Judge Robert Auchmuty told the Admiralty how the trade of Boston was suffering for want of mariners: "The happy Expedition against Cape Britton greatly Exhausted this Government of their Men;" and "the repeated Demands lately made by his Majestys Capts for Manning his Majestys Ships" had resulted in opposition founded on an act of 1707 (6 Ann., c. 37), which had made impressment in America illegal and arguably did so still. *Cf.* the argument of John Adams and editorial comment in *R. v. Corbet* (1769) *LPJA* II, 276-335.

Massachusetts objection to impressment does not seem to have been deeply rooted in principle. On 23 March 1759, Captain Benjamin Hallowell, commander of the province ship *King George*, obtained the Assembly's agreement to his being empowered to impress men from incoming vessels: CO/821.

16. Adams to Mercy Otis Warren, 20 July 1807: "Correspondence between John Adams and Mercy Warren," in *MHSC* fifth series, IV (Boston, 1878), 339-40. Ruggles himself may not have minded much. In civil life a legal practitioner (attaining to a common pleas chief justiceship, indeed), he also opened an inn "and was remarkable for his personal discharge of the various duties of ostler, bar-keeping &c declaring, that he would not shew himself to be above his business": W. Tudor, *The Life of James Otis of Massachusetts* (Boston, 1823), 232. C. K. Shipton, *Sibley's Harvard Graduates* IX (Boston, 1956), 204-5, questions the authenticity of Adams's story about Ruggles.

For British military attitudes to Americans, see J. Shy, *Toward Lexington* (Princeton, 1965), 100.

(there being no professional province army, and in view of the General Court's close control of military expenditure).[17]

But another side may explain and to some extent excuse Bernard's unthinking hopes of amenability among his new charges. As against all the grievances that the war had bred and added to, a victorious end was now clearly in sight. Quebec had fallen to the forces led by Wolfe, and the French menace from Canada was at last over. A euphoria seems to have descended, masking the memory of old quarrels. The "perpetual discordance" gave way to general satisfaction in the triumph of arms. It was now a pretty good feeling to belong to the British Empire. Here is how John Adams felt at the end of the war. The earlier of the British commanders, he said, "Abercrombie, Webb, and above all Lord Loudon . . . gave me such an opinion and disgust of the British government, that I heartily wished the two countries were separate for ever. I was convinced we could defend ourselves against the French, and manage our affairs better without, than with, the English. In 1758 or 1759, Mr Pitt coming into power, sent Wolfe, and Amherst, and then conquered Cape Breton and Quebec. I then rejoiced that I was an Englishman, and gloried in the name of Briton."[18]   The great events in Canada were only recently past when Francis Bernard took up his governorship in Boston; and the scene overall perhaps was still rosy in the afterglow.

Shadows persisted, even so. The events in Canada did not alter the fact that Massachusetts, and in particular Boston, had for some time been touched by economic malaise. Herein lay the seedbed of the "confederacy" that the new governor was so soon to be railing against.

It would be too much to say that Boston was in a state of pronounced decline.[19]   The town was a very considerable center of commercial activity: distillation of rum; manufactures of various kinds (including furniture and footwear for other colonies); "next to Salem, the New World's chief continental fresh and cured fish emporium";[20]   shipbuilding; and an important depot for distribution of

17. See C. K. Shipton, *Sibley's Harvard Graduates* VII (Boston, 1945), 15.

18. Letter to H. Calkoen, 4 October 1780: *LWJA* VII, 266-67.

19. *Pace* a dolorous piece in *BEP* 21 May 1750: "The declining State of the Province, and the near Approach to *utter Ruin* to this (once flourishing) Town of Boston, are matters to obvious to be any longer conceal'd . . . ."

20. L. H. Gipson, *The Triumphant Empire: Thunder-Clouds Gather in the West, 1763-1766* (vol. X in fifteen-volume series, *The British Empire before the American Revolution*) (New York, 1961), 14.

merchandise from abroad. Yet in the ten years from 1750 Boston's population had fallen from 16,000 to 15,000. Its shipbuilding had diminished. Taxation was heavy, on account of the war (a measure of recoupment from Britain was to be expected, but the money had had to be paid out in the first place). And Boston was falling behind as a port. "After 1750, the economic health of the Massachusetts seaport was jeopardized as New York and Philadelphia merchants, exploiting the rich productive lands at their backs and capitalizing upon their prime position in the West Indian and southern coasting trade, diverted a significant portion of European trade from the New England traders"[21] (which in turn had significant effect upon the fortunes and attitudes of the dependent urban working population). Evidence of recent hard times in Boston is not far to seek: a glance down the advertisements columns of the Boston press in the earlier months of 1758 shows a chilling multiplicity of bankruptcy notices. In 1760 the worst of the depression may have been over (even allowing for a disastrous fire that swept the town in March of that year);[22] but it was still true that Boston had seen better days. And there were many people around to whom erosions of Boston's prosperity were causes of deepening discontent.

Already in existence when Governor Bernard took up his appointment was a body of merchants styling themselves "The Society for Encouraging Trade and Commerce." Indeed, on the very day the *Boston News-Letter* announced his arrival, 7 August 1760, the society was advertising a meeting of members "and all Gentlemen, Merchants, and others, who are disposed to join them." Precisely when this society of merchants was founded is not clear, but it could have had some lineal affinity with a group mentioned in a newspaper report from New York in 1756: "It is to be hoped that the most

21. J. A. Henretta, "Economic Development and Social Structure in Colonial Boston" *William and Mary Quarterly* XXII (1965), 79; and Gipson, *op. cit.*

In the war, additional demand on account of the troops pushed up the price of food; a situation made worse in 1759-60 by a bad corn harvest in Connecticut: extracts from letters, 24 August and 20 September 1759, from Francis Bolland of Boston, in Add. MSS 32901.

22. "In the minds of the Bostonians, the disaster reached epic dimensions and was compared to the burning of Rome under Nero, the London Fire of 1666 and the destruction of Lisbon by earthquake in 1755:" G. B. Warden, *Boston 1689-1776* (Boston, 1970), 150. The same work gives details of a widespread appeal that went out. Colonies which contributed did not include New Jersey, apparently. Governor Bernard's tardy and temporizing response to an approach from Governor Pownall (Bernard Papers I, Bernard to Andrew Oliver, 2 June 1760) cannot have told in his favor among the people he was about to join.

reputable Merchants in New York will follow the good Example given by those in Boston, by associating in order to put an end to a clandestine Trade, chiefly injurious to the Interest of Great Britain, and the fair Trader.''[23] The ''fair trader,'' protesting his innocence and abhorrence of smuggling, was to become a familiar figure in the Boston agitations of the later 1750s and early '60s.

The year 1756, which saw that newspaper reference to ''the most reputable Merchants'' in Boston having joined in opposition to smuggling, was a point in time when, because of the new reliability of the vice-admiralty court's forfeiture jurisdiction, customs enforcement had gotten into gear and was beginning to present a serious threat to the open disregard of the British staple, which only a few years previously had been widespread if not standard practice. Among the merchants were no doubt brave spirits who persisted, though more covertly than hitherto, in direct import trade from continental Europe. To others, however, forfeiture of a complete ship and cargo would represent too great a loss and too fearsome a risk. These latter were at an obvious disadvantage against their less timorous competitors, whose transatlantic merchandise had not borne the extra expense — including, probably, a net revenue charge — of detour to Great Britain and reshipment there. The anathemas of the ''fair Trader'' and ''the most reputable Merchants'' against ''clandestine Trade, chiefly injurious to the Interest of Great Britain'' (but also to their own) were only to be expected.

But it was not the local smuggler that vexed the Boston fair trader most. A greater menace lay outside Massachusetts.

In keeping with Rhode Island's chartered semi-independence, the custom house at Newport, though under the same London-based direction as its counterparts in Massachusetts, must have been as ineffective as any in America. John Temple, who took over as surveyor general of the northern customs district toward the end of 1761, found ''Scarce the appearance of a Custom House, not so much through the fault of the two Officers there, as to the Uncontrolled Licenciousness of the People, having no Constitution, or Laws that they value of a Civil Government, tis hardly to be expected they will pay a due Regard to the Acts of Trade, Enforcd by none but the two Custom house Officers Unsupported by the Power of the Colony, to a Man Interested directly or Indirectly in a Clandestine

---

23. *BEP* 21 December 1756.

Trade . . . ." Temple animadverted upon Rhode Island in another
letter: "the Custom house officers there can do nothing to any
purpose, an abandon'd little Collony with no Constitution as a Civil
Government & to a man determined to disregard the Kings Authority
in Every Respect, and to all intents and purposes they have been a
free port the last half century."[24]

The hard lot of Boston in comparison with the unofficial free port
status of Rhode Island was the burden of a long complaint by "A
FAIR TRADER" in the *Boston Gazette* for 7 December 1761:

> Is it not notorious that the Acts of Trade are no where executed, *with
> Rigor* but in this Province? . . .
>
> WE are watched with the utmost Severity — Private Informers, the
> Disgrace of Civil Society, are multiplied and well paid at *our own Cost* —
> Uncustomed Goods, when found, are seized to the utmost Farthing — if
> not found, the person suspected to have imported them is served with a
> Writ, as having sold them and the Money is attached in his Hands . . . .
> WRITS OF ASSISTANCE are now established and granted to the Officers
> of the Customs, who were tho't by many Persons, to have had full Power
> over us before — If it be said that all this is no more than the Law
> prescribes, I again ask, *Whether the Law is carried to these Extremities in
> any Province?* . . . Let us be on an equal footing with our Neighbours —
> Let no Indulgencies be given any where, and we are content without
> them — We want nothing but to be as free as others are, or that others
> should be restrained as we — This is reasonable WE HAVE A RIGHT TO
> CLAIM IT.

The contrast between the tough enforcement practices of the Boston
custom house and the complaisance at Rhode Island could well rank

---

24. To customs commissioners, 1 January 1762 and 25 November 1763, in "A Letter-book of Sir John Temple 1762-69 . . ." in MHS, Winthrop MSS XXVI.

See Dorothy S. Towle, ed., *Records of the Vice-Admiralty Court of Rhode Island 1716-1752* (Washington, D.C., 1936), 89, from which it appears that the records show only one illicit trade case, and that a matter for astonished comment by the victim: "few men in the Government has carried on a Greater Illicit Trade than the Deputy Collector." However, the Newport custom house seems to have been ready enough to seize cargoes intercepted from non-Rhode Island traffic: *BEP* 9 June 1755.

A general view of the situation in Rhode Island and Connecticut was sketched to the Treasury in 1756 by William Sholbrook, who, having recently come from those parts, hoped to be given a custom house job there. He had "seen many Clandestine practices to the prejudice of the Revenue of Customs," and reported "That the Inhabitants there are supplied chiefly with Linnen Teas & other Merchandize directly shipped from Holland . . . That they constantly supply the French islands with all sorts of provisions, and take their produce in Return vizt. Sugar Rum Coffee etc without interruption of the Customs Officers . . . :" T11/25. According to information collected by Charles Townshend's political factotum, John Bindley, Newport customs officers "compound for so much a year, and allow the People . . . an open Trade in all contraband and other Goods" (n.d.): SRO GD224/Box 8/34.

as a classic example of what a customs system should always be at pains to prevent. It is a commonplace of customs administration that nothing is more likely to cause trouble than differences of customs treatment as between neighboring ports serving more or less the same inland region. Importers will put up with all manner of impositions if they are sure that their competitors are no better off. But if some of those competitors are able to get their goods in more freely — whether in terms of duty payment or of convenience and speed — at the next port along the coast, the market becomes distorted. ("Vigour in one Part," said the anonymous New England customs officer quoted in chapter 5, "could only serve to banish Trade from that place without answering a common Good . . . .")[25] In these conditions it is only a matter of time before the customs organization gets into trouble.

The Boston merchants, whether as the "Society for Encouraging Trade and Commerce" or in less formalized groupings, were already a political force to be reckoned with when the Bernard administration began.

They had in fact brought their influence to bear very recently. In March 1760 the Assembly decided the province ship *King George* should sail to England and pick up the money that Parliament had voted to Massachusetts as compensation for war expenditure; it was also arranged that the departing Governor Thomas Pownall should be given a passage on board her. The day before the House of Representatives passed this measure, Thomas Hutchinson wrote in a letter, "The Change was in a flame & this Afternoon a Petition signed by 150 Merchants was offered to the Council desiring to be heard and tomorrow at 11 o Clock is assigned. I believe the Petition will have some influence but I have very little expectation of the Votes being stopped."[26] The merchants' stated objections[27] were that the ab-

25. Note 24. The point is brought out, too, in a bitterly sarcastic article in *BG* 21 December 1761: "And with regard to what is called the fair trade . . . that must fall of course very soon — for the *illicit goods* of all sorts which are imported in the other governments, will be afforded so cheap there, that no merchant here will think of sending for them, for they won't be able to sell them, to any profit — All purchases then, must go *out of the province* for whatever kind of goods they want . . . ."
Cf. a letter, 14 December 1764, in which Governor Bernard told Lord Hillsborough of foreign goods getting into Boston *via* Connecticut: C05/755.
26. To Israel Williams, 25 March 1760: MHS Williams Papers II.
27. *BEP* 14 April 1760.

sence of the *King George* from province waters would expose commercial shipping to greater risk from French privateers and cause underwriters to double their rates for insurance; when she arrived in England her crew might be impressed into the Royal Navy; the project was too expensive and not justified by the amount of the war compensation money to be collected. Hutchinson was right about the fate of the merchants' petition, for the Council came down in favor of sending the *King George* as the House had proposed.[28] But the final victory went to the merchants. On 7 April Pownall wrote to Andrew Oliver, secretary of the province, backing out of the arrangement. He esteemed the offer of the ship as an honor, "But as I am conscious that I have never yet once, since I have been in the Chair, sought or even mentioned in any Instance, my own Interest; I should be sorry, just at my going away, that any Thing meant to accommodate me, should interfere with the Interest of the Province, or even be represented by any to do so." To the Board of Trade he attributed his refusal to "so much animosity between some of the Merchants and the Court."[29] And as if to cap the merchants' triumph the two Pownallites who had sponsored the aborted trip, Benjamin Prat and John Tyng, were voted out of the House of Representatives in the May election.[30]

28. C05/821, Minutes of Assembly 25 and 26 March 1760. The Council were willing to hear up to ten of the petitioners ("Thomas Greene, Esq. & others:" though the first signer — see *BEP* 7 April 1760 — in fact was Thomas Lechmere, the surveyor general of customs who presumably had reasons of his own for preferring that the *King George* stay and protect the coast).

29. Pownall's letter to Oliver is in *BG* 21 April 1760; and that to the Board of Trade (20 May 1760) in C05/890. In *BEP* 12 May 1760 an unsigned article rejoiced that the "extraordinary proceeding . . . had been seasonably prevented, by the intervention of the merchants . . . ." And in the MHS edition (Boston, 1965) of *JHR* Mr. Malcolm Freiberg quotes a letter from Samuel Mather to Samuel Mather junior dated 7 June 1760, which touched upon Governor Pownall's departure: "It was observed, that but few of the Merchants attended him down the long Wharf; and that no one cried at his going aboard the Boat." (Pownall left in the *Benjamin and Samuel*, after a ceremonial dinner on board the *King George*: *BNL* 5 June 1760.)

In a letter to the Admiralty, 30 March 1760 (Adm. 1/3819), Pownall had sought protection against impressment of the *King George* crew in England; but he denied that she was the province's — rather than the king's — property.

30. Not that the electoral defeat of Prat and Tyng was all the merchants' doing. "The Tories cried out against their extravagance in supporting the appropriation for a statue of Lord Howe . . ." (in Westminster Abbey): C. K. Shipton, *Sibley's Harvard Graduates* VII (Boston, 1945), 598. See also *LWJA* X, 242-43. One of the contemporary lampoons on Pownall's administration, by Samuel Waterhouse, *Proposals for . . . the History . . . of Vice Admiral Sir Thomas Brazen . . .*, told how "Jack Swing" and "Bob Sprat" had supported the plan for shipping Pownall home in the *King George*. Prat had been one of

Francis Bernard was not ignorant of the *King George* affair when he arrived in August. He may well have had word of it from Pownall himself. When notifying Bernard of his promotion to Massachusetts from New Jersey Lord Halifax strongly recommended him to confer with Pownall; and the two governors did in fact meet on 10 April, in New London, Connecticut.[31] Thomas Pownall had urged a meeting in Boston, but Bernard saw objections to this. As he stated them they had to do with the undesirability of a governor-designate coming into the province in advance of being formally commissioned; but one wonders whether Bernard was not also concerned to stay clear of Pownall's particular spot of bother. Writing to Andrew Oliver on 15 June 1760, he reported receiving a letter from Lieutenant Governor — for such he now was — Thomas Hutchinson, apparently offering to send "the province sloop" to New Jersey to collect him: "All my concern has been, that I mayn't appear to have been a mover in this business, which, in my present situation, it is improper that I should be."[32] And, although the sloop was sent for him he did not risk embarrassment from arriving at Boston in her but disembarked en route and crossed into the province by land. A hardening of attitudes against Pownall at Westminster (he did not get the South Carolina governorship)[33] may have contributed to a continuing

Boston's leading attorneys: "*Sprat* . . . a clever fellow when he sail'd only in a merchant man . . . , but after he enter'd on board a man of war, he contemptibly enough affected to despise his former merchant-employers . . . ."

The lampoon was, however, not written from the merchants' standpoint. Waterhouse was of the tory — Hutchinsonian — faction whom also Pownall had offended. More of this in chapter 11.

And *cf.* n. 35 below.

31. Halifax to Bernard, n. 6 above. Meeting with Pownall: Bernard to Halifax, 31 March and to Barrington, 19 April 1760: Bernard Papers I. The two governors perhaps knew each other already. Pownall was from Lincolnshire, England, where Bernard had been in law practice. Certainly Bernard was friendly with Pownall's brother John, secretary to the Board of Trade.

32. Reasons for not going to Boston: Bernard to Halifax, n. 31 above. Letter to Oliver: Bernard Papers I.

33. P. O. Hutchinson, ed., *Diary and Letters of Thomas Hutchinson* I (London, 1885), 61, speaks of Pownall intriguing to cause trouble with the military, but there seems to have been a rebound: "To let him down lightly, he was nominated Governor of S. Carolina; but upon Gen. Amherst hearing of this nomination he said to Brigr. Ruggles, . . . 'Depend upon it, Mr Pownall will not go out a governor again to any of the American colonies.' " Nor did he (but see too Hutchinson to Israel Williams, 4 March 1760, in MHS, Williams Papers II, indicating that Pownall's own intention was to remain in England if he could). For Amherst's, and the military's, poor view of Pownall (having to do with Pownall's opening and destroying letters entrusted to him), see B. Bailyn, *The Ordeal of Thomas Hutchinson* (Cambridge, Mass., 1974), 369.

circumspection on the part of his successor. It helped, too, that the former governor's principal political henchman no longer had a base in the House of Representatives. "If he has shown any greater regard to T-g & his adherents than to other persons," a watchful Thomas Hutchinson reported of Governor Bernard on 25 August 1760, "it is not generally known. It is no small disadvantage to them that the Speaker & so many of the principal Members of the House dislike them, and he will be convinced that at least for this year he will not want them."[34]   In the Council (the upper house of the province assembly) a leading Pownallite had survived, in the person of Brigadier William Brattle, adjutant general, medico, and lawyer. "I find him mentioning many Facts . . . which he received from Mr Pownall among others the great usefulness of Br-le . . . ," Hutchinson went on to say. What success Bernard may have had in these soundings of opinion on Brattle is not recorded; but he did decide to do without Brattle and to cut right away from Thomas Pownall's men.[35]   It was a reasonable decision. Even at full political strength they had shown themselves unequal to the power of the merchants.

Writing to the Board of Trade on 18 August 1760, Governor Bernard felt able to say, "I enter upon this government without any party being formed against me . . . ."[36]   So far as it went this may have been true enough. The former governor's supporters were in eclipse, and it clearly was too early in the Bernard administration for new political alignments to have formed. But the merchant bloc that had lately flexed its muscles against the Pownallites was still there.

In keeping with his affability of temperament Governor Bernard hoped to found his administration on, as he put it, "the broad bottom of a Coalition."[37]   It would have been no more than prudent, in any case, to strive for some sort of accommodation with the merchant interest.

This perhaps is the light in which to view Bernard's handling of the letter from William Pitt, secretary of state, mentioned in chapter 8.

---

34. MHS, Williams Papers II.

35. Another Waterhouse lampoon (cf. n. 30 above), *Proposals for . . .* the *History of Adjutant Trowel and Bluster* (i.e., Brattle and James Otis junior) told how Governor Bernard "from the principles of *virtue, honour,* and *humanity,* inherent in him, despises the Adjutant and his adherents, for their mean, abject, base and servile disposition . . . ." More on Brattle later, particularly in chapter 11.

36. C05/891.

37. To A. Colden, New York, 11 May 1761: Bernard Papers I.

On 23 August 1760 Pitt had written to colonial governors on the subject of trading with the enemy. The minutes of the province Council for 31 October recorded that Pitt directed governors "to make inquiry into the State of the dangerous and Ignominious Trade carried on to the French Settlements particularly to the Rivers Mobile and Missisipi, and to take effectual Measures to discover the Persons concerned in such Trade, and to bring them to exemplary and condign Punishment, and further to investigate the various Artifices and Evasions, whereby they find means to cover their criminal Proceeding . . . ."[38] The Council thereupon appointed a committee "for the Purpose aforesaid." The committee reported on 7 November. They could not find, they said, "that there has been any illegal Trade, or any Trade at all, carried on by His Majesty's Subjects of this Province, either to the French Islands, or to the Rivers Mobille & Missisipi, or to any of the French Settlements on the Continent of America since the Commencement of the present War." Governor Pownall had allowed two flag-of-truce voyages, but that was all.[39]

When examining documentation of this period it is advisable to remember that favorite ploy of the colonists, legalistic economy of truth. Although the remit from Pitt plainly intended a comprehensive inquiry into trading with the enemy in all its forms, the committee chose to limit their report to the French islands and mainland settlements and the Mobile and Mississippi rivers. Their verdict that Massachusetts traders had no truck with these enemy areas cannot be flatly contradicted; but neither is it necessary to give more credit than is claimed. The report said nothing about trade with the French through neutral colonies. Monte Cristi on the island of Hispaniola, where neutral Spanish territory adjoined enemy French, comes particularly to mind. Monte Cristi was a notorious clearinghouse for illicit trade with the French. "This trade at Monte Cristi," said G. L. Beer, "was carried on mainly by New England and Middle colonies"; and he cited accounts of Massachusetts ships actually having been seen there.[40] The committee's report was not the blanket absolution it seemed.

---

38. C05/823.

39. *Ibid.* Pitt's letter is reproduced in full in *Quincy's Reports,* 407-8.

40. *British Colonial Policy, 1754-1765* (New York, 1907), 98. In Rhode Island the situation was so far out of hand that "rates of insurance on trips to the enemy islands were being openly quoted:" F. B. Wiener, "The Rhode Island Merchants and the Sugar Act": *New England Quarterly* III (1930), 466.

The significance of its silence on traffic with neutral colonies cannot have been lost on Governor Bernard. He had after all spent most of his working life as a practicing lawyer, and though a newcomer to Massachusetts he had served in America long enough to be well aware of what went on in the business world. Nor would it have been unknown to him that one of the members of the committee, John Erving, was a merchant who had lost a ship for illegal trading only a few months past.[41] Yet without batting an eyelid Bernard wrote back to Pitt that Massachusetts was wholly guiltless: "If I apprehended that there was the least danger that this trade would be carried on from this Province, I would, immediately communicate your orders by circular letters to the several officers of the ports within my government. But I apprehend that, as things are, such public notifications would answer no other purpose than to imply a charge against the Province of what I believe it is quite free from." The more so since he endorsed a copy of the committee's report,[42] it could be that in doing the merchants thus proud Bernard did himself harm. If, upward of two hundred years later, his reply to Pitt can be seen as the disingenuous whitewash that it was, assuredly his superiors at contemporary Westminster would not have been deceived by it.

For all his conciliatory endeavor Governor Bernard had little real hope of harmony with the merchants anyway. The cards were too heavily stacked against this. Even if accidents of fate had not brought forth activating factors of extraordinary turbulence (these to be described in due time), the simmering resentments of the merchants over their disadvantageous trading position were a clear portent of trouble. To be fair to him, Bernard was not slow to identify the central mischief of the situation and in urging Westminster toward remedial action. There would be no end to the problem, he wrote in May 1761, "till Rhode Island is reduced to the subjection of the British Empire; of which at present it is no more a part, than the Bahama Islands were, when they were inhabited by the Buccaneers."[43] Bernard was not without ideas of his own for reform;

41. Other members were Samuel Danforth, Ezekiel Cheever, James Bowdoin, and Thomas Hancock. The merchant community's interest indeed was not likely to be overlooked.

42. These Bernard materials are from *Quincy's Reports*, 408.

43. To John Pownall, 9 May 1761: Bernard Papers I.

"The Shipping of Boston has decreased of late, this is partly owing to the increase of the trade of other Towns in the Province, and partly to the illicit trade which is carried on in Rhode Island with greater security than it can be here .... The greatest difficulty which

but the foreseeable future boded continuing difficulty with the merchants of his own province. Those with nerve enough would maintain their competitive edge against Rhode Island by smuggling. And to all of them, smuggler and "fair trader" alike, the enforcement activity of the custom house and the vice-admiralty jurisdiction upon which it depended would fall into worse and worse odor. When it came to a showdown with those institutions of crown authority there was only one side the man who personified crown authority could be on.

Directly in the merchants' line of fire was the Boston vice-admiralty court. Had it not been for the regeneration of the court's customs jurisdiction in the early 1750s transatlantic importations might have remained practically unaffected by the requirements of the British staple; trade would have continued in its old unhindered way, and the de facto free port status of Newport, Rhode Island, would not have mattered. As things were, the Boston merchants could identify the vice-admiralty court as the fount and origin of their inequitable trading position and a prime cause of the town's downward economic drift.

As if to add to the gall of the Bostonians their neighbors and rivals to the south had recently broken loose from the one tenuous link which, if only symbolically, had signified that Massachusetts and Rhode Island were subject to the same regime of trade regulation. From the early years of the colonial vice-admiralty court system Rhode Island had been within the territory of the vice-admiralty judge at Boston. There might at times be a vice-admiralty court at Rhode Island, with its own judge, but both it and he were surrogates of Boston. As the notorious ineffectiveness of the Newport custom house bears witness, the customs jurisdiction of the vice-admiralty court at Rhode Island cannot have amounted to much. (Though a branch of the main vice-admiralty emporium at Boston, the court was of course subject to the Rhode Island common law courts, which would have had little hesitation in slapping prohibitions on a jurisdiction inimical to the colony's commercial interests.) Nevertheless, and

---

attends the execution of the Laws of trade here, arises from the great Liberty which is allowed in some other Colonies. The Merchants here complain, with great show of reason, of the hardship they suffer by being subject to restraints, which their Neighbours in ports almost under their Eye are quite strangers to . . .:" Bernard to Board of Trade, 5 March 1763, in BL King's MSS 205 and C05/891.

especially in time of war, an efficiently run vice-admiralty court could be very useful. Rhode Islanders made quite a profitable business of privateering; they would obtain letters of marque from the colonial government commissioning their ships to go out and seize enemy vessels, and the prize jurisdiction under which they secured the profits of their enterprise was proper to a court of vice-admiralty. The exigencies of this Rhode Island privateering were the cause of the development now being referred to. On 12 May 1758 the Lords Commissioners of the Admiralty recorded having received "Application . . . from the General Assembly, of the Governor and Company of the Colony of Rhode Island, and Providence Plantations in New England, setting forth that there no [*sic*] Judge of the Court of Vice-Admiralty in that Colony, but a Deputy, and he is much limitted, and controuled by his Superior, who lives out of the Government, that very great Damages, Delays, and Inconveniencies, as well as extravagant Expences have occurred to the Persons concerned in privateering, and therefore desiring that some suitable Person be appoin^{td} Judge within, and for that Colony . . . ." The application seemed "reasonable," and "John Andrews Esqr of the said Colony, a Gentleman of the Law, and of a fair Character" having been recommended, the lords commissioners ordered the judge of the High Court of Admiralty, Sir Thomas Salusbury, to issue letters patent to Andrews as "Judge of the Admiralty Court of the Colony of Rhode Island and Providence Plantations in the room of Chambers Russell Esqr . . . ." Salusbury was also "to insert a Clause in the said Patent revoking so much of the Patent to Chambers Russell Esq as appoints him Judge of the Vice Admiralty Court of the Colony of Rhode Island and Providence Plantations."[44] There is no sign of the Admiralty having consulted other departments — the Customs, the Board of Trade, and the Treasury — with an interest in the colonial vice-admiralty court system. Natural preoccupation with combating

44. Adm. 2/1056. Though Governor Hopkins of Rhode Island wrote to the Admiralty on 15 January 1759 (Adm. 1/3819) recommending a new register and a new marshal for the new court, it seems that these posts were left in Boston hands: C. Ubbelohde, *The Vice-Admiralty Courts and the American Revolution* (Chapel Hill, 1960), 30. And *cf.* p. 171.

Curiously, around this time the Admiralty took it into their heads to displace Charles Paxton as marshal of the Boston vice-admiralty court by "Mr. Steven Dollars": Adm. 2/1056, to Sir T. Salusbury, 6 August 1759. The present writer has discovered nothing about Dollars, and nothing to indicate that the Paxton removal ever took effect. (In fact, a George III patent "for Mr. Charles Paxton to be Marshall" at Boston was ordered on 15 July 1761: *ibid.*).

the enemy crowded out other considerations, possibly. (Privateers were of course a useful auxiliary arm.) There was not even any consultation with Vice-Admiralty Judge Chambers Russell; he knew nothing of the curtailment of his responsibilities until after it had been done. Commenting on the episode some years later he said that the hiving-off of Rhode Island had been no loss for him, for the fees it brought him were swallowed up by traveling expenses. "He did not think himself at liberty to remonstrate against it, after it had past. If he had had an opportunity, he should have shown that such an alteration would be much to the disservice of the King; as it would render that Court which was weak enough before much weaker." And, he added, "the Event has answered accordingly; for by this Alteration the Judge of that Court is so totally in the Power of that community that . . . no suit in the Admiralty Court is suffered to proceed which is not agreeable to the governing Powers of the People."[45]   In fact John Andrews did not prove as totally amenable to the Rhode Island merchants' wishes as might be supposed.[46]   And enough evidence has been seen of the chronically derelict condition of the acts of trade in Rhode Island to suggest that the 1758 change would not have made the vice-admiralty court significantly "much weaker" in this department.

Still, however little practical difference it made in terms of effectiveness of the acts of trade, the further license vouchsafed to Rhode Island by the establishment of a separate vice-admiralty court could only have thrown the plight of the Boston merchants into even sharper contrast. Nothing could have more cruelly underlined the prime reason for the vexations they labored under, the potency of the customs jurisdiction in their own vice-admiralty court. But for this their trade would have remained as free as it had been in the 1740s and perhaps as free as Rhode Island trade was now.

Discontents with the Boston vice-admiralty court were fed by how it actually worked.

It is only fair to keep in mind the fact that the court had to be self-supporting. Neither its judge nor any of his subordinates re-

45. Petition (1766) in C05/755. *Cf.* n. 52 below.
46. Ubbelohde, *op. cit.,* 30-32. Even so, there is the testimony in 1765 from the now somewhat regenerate Newport custom house that Judge Andrews and the advocate general "are natives of this place, and their Connections with the people are such that it influences them to a Disregard of the King's Service which they have upon different Occasions shown by favouring the Merchants to the prejudice of the Crown": T1/446.

ceived an official salary: what money they got came from a variety of charges exacted in a variety of circumstances. "Each step in the course of a trial carried a fee," says a modern commentator, "and although the aggregate of these fees might total only a small percentage of the profits of a large prize ship with a valuable cargo, in minor litigation they were proportionately higher."[47] The court not unnaturally took as much business as it could, even reaching out to bits of jurisdiction it had little or no title to. Thus, an act of 1742[48] "for further regulating the Plantation Trade" had provided a stand-by procedure for when proof of a ship's British nationality was not to hand, which involved the services of a customs collector: in Boston a move had been made to divert this work to the vice-admiralty court, where the charges were nearly four pounds sterling against the custom house's five shillings. An "address" sent by the Society for Encouraging Trade and Commerce to the Treasury in February 1762 (the origins of this useful compendium of contemporary dissatisfactions will appear in the next chapter) was explicit: "This being an Innovation which greatly affected the Property of the Merchants occasion'd a considerable Stir among them" (and they had in fact prevailed upon Governor Bernard to get this "great Grievance" stopped).[49] But even where its right to jurisdiction was indisputable the vice-admiralty court encountered resentment over the costliness of its processes. So much so, that exorbitance reached self-defeat. The court priced itself out of its own market. The Society for Encouraging Trade and Commerce's address told how the Boston merchants had for some years taken to "adjusting many of their Affairs in a private Way, which formerly were settled in that Court": "In Cases of Vessels or Goods sustaining Damage at Sea . . . they have found the Charges insupportable, inasmuch as after Deductions for Surveys, Apprizements, Storage and Custody of Goods, Commis-

47. Ubbelohde, op. cit., 20.
48. 15 Geo. 2, c. 31.
49. T1/415.
As with the petition for a hearing on writs of assistance (pp. 131-132 above) the leading signature was that of Thomas Greene. Governor Bernard gave an account of the ship's register affair in a statement dated 16 March 1761: T1/408.
Another of the society's complaints was of rapacious fees exacted by the vice-admiralty court for canceling ships' bonds (e.g., for the due arrival of an enumerated cargo) out of time. Here again jurisdiction seems dubious: bonds sounded in common law and equity rather than in the civil law.
The court's tendency to filch business was not new: an instance of it in the 1740s was seen in chapter 6 (p. 76).

sions and many other Charges which are always brought in and allowed there is generally but a small Proportion to be received." The merchants had resorted to outside arbitration, "from a proper Attention to their own Interest and to that of the Merchants and Underwriters in England, some of them having for the same Reasons forbid any of their Affairs being adjusted in the Court of Admiralty, if it could possibly be avoided, choosing rather to confide in the Honor and Judgment of private Men." Westminster probably was not surprised by this. Only a few months previously, in response to reports from Governor Bernard on the storms that were already assailing the Boston vice-admiralty court, John Pownall, secretary to the Board of Trade, commented: "the Fees & charges of proceeding in Admiralty Courts in the Plants in Genl are become so shamefully exorbitant, as to be matters of notice of Govt. & have been in one or two cases, pretty severely censured by the Council." [50]

But in Massachusetts there was also that special root cause of hostility toward the vice-admiralty court, the fearsomely effective customs forfeiture jurisdiction that rendered the Boston trader permanently one down to his rivals in Rhode Island. And the Bostonians had to suffer not only the commercial effects of this disadvantageous jurisdiction but also the way it worked. To a twentieth-century eye it looks little short of grotesque that the deputy judge of vice-admiralty should have been as closely associated with the custom house establishment as George Cradock. Though not a full-time regular member of the custom house staff, Cradock seems to have held himself on call for stand-in jobs: for example, for some nine months up to August 1760 he had acted as collector of customs at Boston. And the vice-admiralty judge proper, Chambers Russell, doubled up as a judge of the Superior Court (a circumstance that had done as much as anything, probably, to enable the vice-admiralty court to function effectively — that is, without fear of common law prohibition — on Staple Act forfeitures). In both men, incompatibility in the posts they held went with attitudes to the judicial office just as strange by modern standards. Deputy Judge Cradock told, without any discernible hesitation or embarrassment, how he met a custom house colleague on the steps of the vice-admiralty court one day and said to him: "I hope it will not be long before I shall have the pleasure of Condemning a large Seizure of yours." [51]   Judge Russell actually

50. 22 July 1761: Bernard Papers IX.
51. T1/408, deposition dated 24 February 1761.

made bias a matter of self-commendation. Petitioning Westminster in 1766 for a salary, he declared he "hath never, that he knows of, acquitted any goods in direct contradiction to. the Opinion of the Kings Advocate" (apparently on the principle — not that it explains much — that the judge thus "moderated between the King & the People").[52] Toward the end of 1761 a new surveyor general of customs relieved Deputy Judge Cradock from his acting collector-ship, it "being something improper, and likely to create a Riotous Disposition in the People, when he should act as Judge in Condemn-ing the Seizure that himself should make."[53] It has to be said, however, that contemporary supporting evidence of Cradock's incon-gruous pluralities as a subject of grievance is hard to find.[54] And if people tumbled to Judge Russell's squint-eyed stance between par-tiality on the one hand and impartiality on the other, there is no sign of its ever having been included in their protests against vice-admiralty excesses.[55] The fact is, hostility toward the Boston vice-admiralty court in the early 1760s was directed not so much at the quality of the judicial process as at things that happened down the line. And personalized not in the judge and deputy judge but in the court's multiple executive functionary — "Marshall . . . , Surveyor, Storekeeper and Vendue Master," as the Society for Trade's address to the Treasury catalogued him — Charles Paxton.

Paxton had been doing pretty well in recent years. Not so much from his vice-admiralty jobs, of course, as from his substantive

52. C05/755, fols. 825-29 (also referred to in n. 45 above). Cf., in the same bundle, a contemporaneous petition from Robert Auchmuty junior for a salary as advocate general; Auchmuty claimed he had "never yet proved unsuccessful in any attempt made in the Court of Admiralty in favor of his Majesty, though at Times opposed by the principal Gentlemen of the Bar."

A copy of Russell's petition, in the handwriting of William Bollan's amanuensis, is among the Townshend papers in the Scottish Record Office: GD224/Box 8/41. From this it appears that Russell petitioned both the Admiralty and, *mutatis mutandis,* the Treasury. He may have intended to back up his petitions with personal calls. He journeyed to England in the fall of 1766; however, shortly after arrival and before reaching London he died.

53. John Temple to customs commissioners, 1 January 1762, in "A Letter-book of Sir John Temple 1762-68:" MHS.

54. It may have moderated merchant sentiment against Cradock that he himself was in the distilling business: *cf.* chapter 6, n. 42.

55. In particular: that future scourge of the establishment, James Otis junior, himself a former acting advocate general (see chapter 15), presumably had reservations about pub-licizing a practice by which the advocate general was automatically deferred to: *cf.* p. 326.

Justifiably or not, Vice-Admiralty Judge Russell seems to have maintained a reputation for probity. In his 1766 petition for a salary he indicated discomfiture at the manner of his remuneration in customs condemnation cases: a percentage of the proceeds of forfeiture.

employment as surveyor and searcher of customs;[56] all the same, just as his custom house seizures mounted in number so did his fees for handling them in the vice-admiralty court. The address to the Treasury, which made no bones about identifying Paxton with practically everything wrong with the court, spoke sourly of his "ample Charges" in all his various executive capacities there, and his disposition toward "preying upon the Trade, and thereby adding to a large Fortune, which he is said already to have acquired." Improper favor in his custom house law-enforcement responsibilities had been charged against him several years back, and this point of grievance had not abated.[57]   A sober-toned piece in the *Boston Gazette* for 16 February 1761 implied corruption in Paxton's vice-admiralty work also ("seiz'd goods have been inventoried by false names in order that another disposition of them might be made . . .").

Nor do all the signs of venality come from Paxton's avowed enemies and a hostile press. Among the Dana manuscripts in the Massachusetts Historical Society is a letter written by William Fletcher, an expatriate New Englander merchant at St. Eustatius in the foreign Caribbean, on 20 January 1759, soon after Rhode Island got its own vice-admiralty court. Fletcher evidently feared disadvantage from the change. To a friend in Massachusetts he wrote: "I am sorry to find the Alteration made in the Court of Admiralty at Rhode Island — I flattering myself notwithstanding, shd any of my Interest

---

Inevitably this in-built temptation to him to condemn (for his fees on an acquittal stood to yield him much less) became another subject for popular dissatisfaction. But when, on 3 November 1764, the houses of assembly formulated a complaint against the "manifest tendency . . . to procure decrees of condemnation where there is no just cause," they were explicit that "with respect to the present Judge . . . , we apprehend he is not to be biassed by such a motive"; C05/892.

56. In T1/408 is a deposition sworn on 18 February 1761 in which Paxton says that since 1752 (when his Boston appointment began) he had "Seized prohibited Goods that have been Condemned in the Court of Admiralty to the Amount of Six thousand one hundred & twenty Six pounds 14/ lawfull money . . . ." His netted one-third share of this may have been modest enough; but one notices that Paxton's figure apparently did not include his takings from compositions, or his share in ship seizures and Molasses Act seizures (which were of uncustomed goods, not prohibited ones).

A further sign of Paxton's growing prosperity is his relinquishment of two of his pluralities: the cryership of the general sessions of the peace in 1753 (Suffolk minute book 1754-58) and the similar Superior Court post in 1755 (SCR 1755-56).

57. See chapter 7, n. 13; also n. 11 with reference to an attack on Paxton by Sam Adams in *BEP* 12 December 1768, which also declared Paxton to have been "as great a smuggler as any . . . (if knowing such acts to be done, and taking hush money makes an officer an accessory)." *BG* 21 December 1761 spoke of a "*little body* . . . suppos'd to have wisdom enough to determine what part of the contraband trade shall be indulg'd or eas'd . . . ."

be brought that way, the good influence of you & my other Friends will prevent my suffring." It says little for standards in public life that the addressee of this letter almost certainly was Edmund Trowbridge, the attorney general of Massachusetts. Also that, inasmuch as the innovation at Rhode Island was oriented to prize jurisdiction (the de facto free port status of the colony in relation to the acts of trade would of course remain as it was), the cooperation that Fletcher was soliciting from the topmost law officer of his native province was suggestive of trading with the enemy. Some of the grime perhaps rubs off on to Vice-Admiralty Judge Russell — another of Trowbridge's pals — who, when the vice-admiralty court at Rhode Island was still under his control, presumably could protect a favored "Interest" that had fallen to the prize jurisdiction there: indeed, the severance of Russell from the Rhode Island court may have been the originating cause of Fletcher's worry. More to the point, however, Fletcher probably knew that Attorney General Trowbridge had some pull with Charles Paxton (it was Trowbridge who introduced to Paxton the informer Ebenezer Richardson), and that although the Rhode Island vice-admiralty court was no longer under Judge Russell, Paxton continued as marshal there. In his capacity as executive factotum with responsibility for whatever prize goods were for disposal by the court Paxton would be well placed to rig bogus sales and prevent Fletcher "suffring." That Paxton was capable of whatever malpractice ensured him the approval of men of influential connection is all too easy to believe.

Altogether it was a sleazy business that Paxton was in, even disregarding what he may have gotten up to at Rhode Island. But come 1760-61 both he and the vice-admiralty regime at Boston were to experience the townsmen's resentments in action.

The Boston press still had not attained the strident outspokenness on public men and affairs that was so soon to characterize it. Indeed, it would be impossible to chart the electrifying controversies in the winter of 1760-61 from contemporary reportage in the newspapers. Of the writs of assistance hearing in February that occupied the Superior Court several days solid, and which afterwards became so famous, there is not a word. And the developing turmoil over Charles Paxton in the vice-admiralty court did not shout from the headlines either. How the newspapers tried to do justice to it is worth seeking out, nevertheless.

Some years later, when Paxton was even lower in popular disesteem, the townsfolk hanged him in effigy. It was a bit like that with
the Boston press's treatment of him now. The *Gazette* for 15
December 1760 came out with "a *Chinese* Allegory," the subject of
which was the destructiveness of a gnawing rat that had somehow
gotten inside a wooden statute; it was impossible to smoke or drown
him out without damaging the statue. The piece went on to speak of
"a kind of Rat here, as mischievous as perhaps in any Part of the
World . . . . This Rat is observ'd to infest our Ships, Wharves and
Warehouses . . . an amazing Devourer of almost every Kind of Merchandise . . . Brandy and other *distill'd Spirits,* he is particularly fond
of . . . Tea is another Article with which he is never satisfy'd . . . ."
Hitherto this Boston rat had been too much for "our *ordinary* Cats."
Lately, however, some people had "*smelt a Rat*" and had "procured . . . two or three Cats of a very *staunch Breed,* so that there is
Reason to hope, that the Rat will very soon fall a Victim; especially
as we know of no *Wooden Statue* in which he can take Refuge."
Extirpation of the Boston rat as a species of "*dangerous reptiles*" was
encouraged in a responding piece in the *Gazette* for 26 January. On 9
February the *Boston Evening-Post* joined in, with a verse about "the
pesky RATT, by *Edes* and *Gill* inserted," removing what little doubt
might have remained that the rat was Paxton.[58]   It ended:

> Plunder away ye *Ratts* of pray,
> Your Day *may* be but short
> For all do cry, drive, drive away,
> This RATT from ev'ry Port

The newspaper satirist having gotten away with it thus far, on 2
March the *Boston Gazette* devoted its entire front page, plus a little
of the back, to a scorching lampoon "Sketch of the History of
CHARLES FROTH, Esq;", wherein Paxton was no longer a mere rat
but "a man of abandon'd principles, and flagitiously wicked"; "his
character . . . remarkable for insincerity, pride, haughtiness and deceit"; "in wickedness and iniquity, neither Cataline, Jejanus or Judas
could exceed him, being perfidious and treacherous to the last

58. The piece began: "Ah THEA BOHEA: *Quid placet insigni ut decem Codices* PACI-
TONO?" Bohea tea featured regularly in the illicit trade from continental Europe; but what
may have been the ten codes so pleasing to Paxton is a puzzle. Also for speculation is
whether the writer of the original 15 December piece about the rat in the statue may not
have owed some of his inspiration to the recent fuss about the statue of Lord Howe in
Westminster Abbey (n. 30 above). Benjamin Edes and John Gill were the publishers of *BG.*

degree, as oppressive as a tyrant, and an intire stranger to truth . . . that none that ever knew him, would believe one single word of what he said."

It is a commentary on the climate in which the Boston press worked at this time that personalized or otherwise robust commentary on men of government should resort to spoof zoology and make-believe history. And, more particularly, that in the week following the "Froth" piece both the *Gazette* and the *Evening-Post* carried a sworn disclaimer of authorship by the prime suspect, James Otis. The 2 March lampoon had Charles Paxton in the lead role, of course; but also featured were Governor Bernard, as "Sir Wm. Slygripe" — the "facetious merry man . . ." noted on page 151 — and Lieutenant Governor and Chief Justice Thomas Hutchinson as "Sir Thomas Graspall, who was dictator general." But it may have been with "Mr. Justice Gnaw-Post, who was an admirable judge in casuistical cases" and of service to "Froth" in a variety of insalubrious enterprises, that the joke went dangerously too far. The likely identity of this unpleasing figure, his name evocative of the 15 December rat in the statue, would not have escaped the penetrating notice of that long-time helpmeet of Charles Paxton, Edmund Trowbridge; and Attorney General Trowbridge, a specialist in legal craft, certainly was not the man to be unaware that a law officer could sidestep the ordinary process of grand jury indictment and prosecute a criminal libel, and that the criminal quality of utterances against government and its men was for the bench — not a jury — to determine.

John Adams was to recall something of Trowbridge — "as ardent as any of Hutchinson's disciples" — around this period. After the surrender of Montreal in 1759 a youthful lawyer friend of Adams, Jonathan Sewall (later a loyalist, but "then a patriot"), expressed fears of what British intentions might be and urged Adams to write a newspaper piece. Adams suggested that Sewall do it himself. " 'Why', said Mr Sewall, 'I would write; but Goffe [Trowbridge] would find me out, and I shall grieve his righteous soul, and you know what influence he has . . .' "[59] Oxenbridge Thacher wrote to Benjamin Prat (the former Pownallite, now chief justice of New York) in 1762:

> I . . . hear that the press now is under the dominion of our great men, and that those printers who owe their first subsistence & present greatness to the freedom of their press refuse to admit any thing they suspect is not

59. *LWJA* IV, 6.

pleasing to our sovereign lords. I will lay a guinea that they are bound to that in good behaviour, and that our sovereign lord the kings attorney hath threatened them with a prosecution for past freedoms. So that future silence is the price of pardon. You remember he loves . . . to have his rod over a man.[60]

So it is not hard to understand the newspapers' reticence over the exploding turbulences in the winter of 1760-61, and their resort to obliquity and satiric parable. Rather the wonder might be that under the baleful gaze of Attorney General Trowbridge anything but the most subdued treatment was ventured at all.

As the Otis disclaimer signaled, commentary indicative of current political gunnery for Charles Paxton stopped with the "Froth" lampoon on 2 March. The fact remains, nevertheless, that readers between the lines were alerted as early as 15 December that the ineffable custom house freebooter and vice-admiralty racketeer might at last be coming up for his comeuppance.

What he experienced was not wholly new to Paxton. Long before he became — according to John Adams — "the essence of customs, taxation, and revenue" and was still just the vice-admiralty factotum, he had been under common law fire from a hostile merchant interest.[61] And somewhat as the merchants' campaign against the vice-admiralty men in the early 1730s had targeted on allegedly unlawful fees, so the 1760-61 onslaught had as its subject money that the vice-admiralty court was allowing Paxton to siphon off to his own use or purposes.

The present attack of the merchants centered upon two peculiarities of the Molasses Act of 1733 in the apportionment of the profits of forfeiture. Molasses Act forfeitures were subject to the usual three-way split — one-third each to the king, the governor, and the customs officer obtaining the condemnation — but whereas under other acts of trade the king's share went to the British exchequer, the Molasses Act made it over "for the Support of the Government of the Colony or Plantation where the same shall be recovered." The second peculiarity went in the opposite direction, so to speak. Ordinarily the costs of bringing a seizure to condemnation were deducted before there was any share-out, so that in effect they were charged equally upon all three shares. The Molasses Act, however,

60. *MHSP* first series 20 (1884), 46-47.
61. *LWJA* X, 298. *Cf.* chapter 6, nn. 38, 39.

specifically charged them upon the king's share alone (they bit into the other shares only if the king's share had been wholly consumed). So the greater the charges on a Molasses Act forfeiture the smaller the share to the province treasury.

This was the framework in which the Boston merchants built their case against Charles Paxton and the vice-admiralty court. The form their initiative took was a petition addressed to the General Court on 17 December 1760.[62] Appended to the petition were "Extracts from the records of the Court of Vice Admiralty," namely, detailed accounts of sales and charges that had arisen from six Molasses Act condemnations over the period August 1753 to May 1760, plus the account of the sale of a Molasses Act forfeiture in November 1760 for which the charges had not yet been settled. The complaint of the petitioners — "sundry Inhabitants of the Province," as they styled themselves — was that the six completed accounts showed excessive charges deducted against the king's share. The province treasury thus appeared to have received less than its lawful due. With a view to "a strict Enquiry" being made and the province recompensed the petitioners asked to be given a hearing. Their request was granted, and the Council and House of Representatives appointed a committee to go into the matter.

In its report the committee found "Wrong done to the Province . . . by Large and exorbitant Sums of Money said to be given to private Informers; for Condemnation Dues &c . . . and . . . by excessive Sums said to be paid to Attorneys, and for other Uses contrary to the Law of this Province made in the second Year of *George* the first, for settling and starting Fees in the Court of Admiralty." The province treasurer should be told to seek this money of "those Persons from whom it shall appear to be due," failing which "he should bring an Action or Actions at Common Law against such Persons, for recovering said Sum for the Use of the Province." A total of £475 9s. 11d. was said to be owed to the province. Of this a few pounds were put down to Sir Henry Frankland, the former collector of customs, now British consul general at Lisbon and far out of reach. About £127 was laid to the register of vice-admiralty and "the Court of Admiralty": insignificant and awkward targets,

---

62. The petition and what followed in the General Court are in JHR 1760-61 (Pt. 2 MHS print, Boston, 1966), 231-47. The contemporary print was sent to England, and is in T1/408. See also the brief account by William Bollan, presumably on what he had been told by Thomas Hutchinson, in Appendix H.

one would suppose. By far the greatest amount — £375 3s. 8d. — was laid at the door of Charles Paxton; and it was against only this prime bugbear of the Boston merchants that action was taken.

The "illegal Charges to be refunded by *Charles Paxton,* Esq." related in part to his fees as an officer of the vice-admiralty court for storage of the seized goods (it was civil law doctrine and admiralty practice that the court had custody of any article it was adjudicating upon).[63] Others related to what he had paid to his lawyers, allegedly in excess of what the legislation of the province allowed.[64] But for the most part they were recoupments of money paid for information as to where the offending goods could be found. It was not only because of their size that these payments for information bulked largest. That money otherwise due to the province should go into the pockets of informers such as the disreputable Ebenezer Richardson was a point of special vexation to the Boston public. To recall the newspaper piece by "Fair Trader," quoted on page 157: "Private Informers, the Disgrace of Civil Society, are multiplied and well paid at *our own Cost* . . . ." There was also a suspicion that Paxton's claims for information money, which the vice-admiralty court allowed on his sworn statement and without investigation, might have been fraudulently inflated if not totally bogus; it was even suggested that he split the spoils with the judge and the governor.[65]

63. A piece in *BG* 7 September 1761 complained of the vice-admiralty court (though without naming it), "where no distinctions are made between right and wrong, but every thing yields to the grand object in view, *private gain* — where the subject is grievously burdened with expences in getting his cause tryed, and generally suffers a decree against him without law or justice, and perhaps for no other reason than because his property is already in the hands of the court's officers . . . ."

64. The legislation was 1716-17, c. 7, apparently. Section 1 said that the various fees specified in the act were permissible "and none other." The act's regulation of fees was strongly oriented to the vice-admiralty court's condemnation of prize. Ten shillings was all it sanctioned to advocates otherwise, and what the judge might be paid was likewise pretty niggardly.

It is hard to be sure what the act intended (and the basic province act regulating court fees generally, c. 37 of 1692-93, naturally said nothing about the vice-admiralty court, which did not then exist). That the court did not interpret the act narrowly is understandable. The opposite attitude of the merchant-politicians in 1760-61, technical and perverse as perhaps it was, is understandable too.

65. Statement of Governor Bernard, 16 March 1761; and deposition of Ebenezer Richardson, 27 February 1761: both in T1/408. The Society for Trade's address to the Treasury, 18 February 1762, mentioned "a notable Instance of Mr. Paxton's particular Regard to himself . . . , by his libelling two Parcels of seized Brandy as distilled Spirits, alledging as a Reason therefor (in a large Company, the late Surveyor General [Lechmere] being present) that he got more Money by it for himself . . ." (the essential point in the province's litigation against Paxton).

In the end — February 1762, on appeal to the Superior Court — Paxton definitively defeated the province's claim against him. It all had been an acute embarrassment to Governor Bernard. This is not to echo the canard that the governor had shared in Paxton's ill-gotten profits: the seizures involved in the action had happened before Bernard's time, but it was no doubt part of his discomfiture that Paxton was the man in whose continuing enterprise lay the best hope for future income from the gubernatorial one-third share. And it is possible to suppose, too, a genuinely responsible concern in Governor Bernard lest a common law judgment that Paxton disgorge money awarded him by decree of the vice-admiralty court should diminish the court's viability, and serve to encourage further common law attacks on a jurisdiction uniquely identified with the imperial government at Westminster, to whom Bernard had a clear and direct duty. But Bernard was not a mere passive hand-wringing observer of these distressing events. He himself was a constituent element of the General Court to which the petition that began them had been addressed; and by a like token there could be no possibility of the province initiating a lawsuit without his positive assent.

"I thought it a cruel thing to force the Governor into this measure," wrote Thomas Hutchinson;[66] and assuredly it was an uncomfortable dilemma for Bernard to be instrumental in the chastisement of his valued coadjutor in the crown's service and — all the more ironically since he himself was the vice-admiral — proportionately to blame for whatever harm might result to the vice-admiralty court. Helpful opposition by Hutchinson in the Council notwithstanding, the merchant-politicians' move to get Paxton had too much steam behind it to be stopped. Resistance carried to the point of veto would have been altogether too damaging to the governor's hopes of

---

66. To Israel Williams, 21 January 1761: MHS, Williams Papers II.

On page 65 of his *History of Massachusets-Bay,* Hutchinson plays down the originating complaint. The Molasses Act "was always deemed a grievance"; but "The assembly had suffered the share given to the province to lie in the court." This is not borne out by the vice-admiralty accounts reproduced by the committee (in the materials cited in n. 62 above), which show the court ordering the register to pay the province treasurer whatever residue of the king's share there might be. The surviving "Admiralty Book of Accounts of Sales" (covering 1760-65) in the Suffolk County Court Records is inconclusive. But in *Frankland v. 16 h/h Molasses,* Judge Auchmuty decreed, 1 May 1747, the remainder of the king's share "into my own hands to be by Me applyed for the Government of this Province."

Neither the law nor the vice-admiralty accounts bear out Hutchinson's further statement (*ibid.*) to the effect that rewards to informers were charged exclusively to the king's share in non-Molasses Act cases. It could be however that the king's share was not milked until the three-way division had been entered and finalized in the accounts. See n. 75 below.

a harmonious administration. It would be inaccurate to say that Bernard wholly mishandled his part in the affair, but he cannot have earned himself much credit for purity of intention. The committee of the two houses of legislature had recommended that the action against Paxton should be brought by the province treasurer, Harrison Gray. Bernard argued that since the money to be sued for was technically the king's revenue the action was proper to the attorney general, Edmund Trowbridge. In the end Bernard gave way; but not before, one guesses, it had occurred to some people that there was more to his pernicketiness than a fine regard for constitutional logic. For example, that if he had succeeded in getting the suit into the management of Trowbridge, the punches against Paxton would have been pulled somewhat; the attorney general was not a salaried appointee of the houses of legislature, and at this time Trowbridge was very clearly identified with the establishment and custom house interest. Governor Bernard undoubtedly was in a quandary, but his approach to *Gray v. Paxton* — or *Province v. Paxton* as it afterward and more properly became — is not to be seen as just so much dither reflecting it.[67]

If the province's action against Charles Paxton disconcerted the governor for the repercussions it might have on the vice-admiralty court, another lawsuit almost simultaneously commenced rattled him still more. Anxious that the local result of this other case be appealed to the Privy Council at crown expense, Bernard declared: "If this Verdict can be maintained It is plain that there is an End of the Custom house & the Court of Admiralty here."[68] This menacing companion to *Province v. Paxton* was the case of *Erving v. Cradock,* a sequel to the events now to be related.

In April 1760 the brigantine *Sarah* arrived at Boston from Amsterdam, having called at Kirkwall, a remote port to the northward of Scotland.[69] Although in Great Britain and thus a port of onshipment for purposes of the Staple Act, Kirkwall was not overexacting in its standards of customs control. William Sheaffe, of the Boston custom house, found that not all of the cargo of the *Sarah* had been properly cleared for Boston, and afterward deposed as to what then passed between him and her owner, John Erving (the same John Erving, a

67. See p. 324, and chapter 17, n. 70.
68. Letter to T. Pownall, 28 August 1761: Bernard Papers II.
69. This paragraph draws upon depositions in SF 82173.

member of the Council, who some months later was to join in pronouncing Massachusetts guiltless of the forms of illegal trading remonstrated against by William Pitt). Erving inquired of Sheaffe whether the matter could not be put right by payment of duty or by the *Sarah* being permitted to take the offending cargo to St. John's in the West Indies, for which it was ostensibly intended. "I was of opinion it could not be done," said Sheaffe, "but I told him, I would Ask the advice of Mr Pratt the Advocate Genl . . . ." Prat — thus is the name usually spelt — "was of opinion that the Vessell should be seized." Sheaffe "accordingly went on board said Vessell & Seized her, in behalf of George Cradock Esqr Collector of the Customs at this port, who ordered an Officer to be put on board." Cradock, the deputy judge of vice-admiralty who sometimes helped out at the custom house, was at this time standing in as collector while the substantive holder of the office was on a visit to England. Erving went with the master of the *Sarah* to see Cradock at the custom house; Sheaffe said that Cradock was at first inclined to grant permission for the *Sarah* to proceed to St. John's with the cargo documented for that destination, "but finally refused, confirmed the Seizure, & seemed to entertain some Suspicion that there were other goods on board . . . & acquainted said Erving that he should order the Vessell to be unloaded, & searched." Erving, Sheaffe continued, "told him to do it at his peril, or words to that Effect. Whether any Violence was used by the Collector or his Officer I can't say, but the Vessell was unloaded, & the goods that were cleared for Boston were delivered to the Owners, others that were entered for St. Johns were taken into Custody, together with sundry packages that were found on board, for which there was no Cocket [export clearance document] . . . ." A deposition by the master, Alexander Smith, indicates that the seizure of the *Sarah* herself went smoothly enough (Sheaffe "made the mark of the broad arrow, with a piece of Chalk on the Mainmast"); but when, two days later on 26 April, two men from the custom house came to search her the atmosphere heated up a little, much as it had done when Cradock spoke of search to Erving. They told the mate to open the hatches, saying that if he would not "they would force them open themselves, and unload the Vessell, for they had orders to do so from the Collector . . . ." Neither side was willing to move, however. After a half hour or so Cradock arrived with Surveyor General Thomas Lechmere, and asked why unloading had not begun. It seems that "the Mate answered him and said that . . . he might do it himself, and stand all Damages that might happen." Lechmere now stepped in "and gave orders likewise that they should unload the Vessell, and seemed to be angry that they had not before." The customs men thereupon set to work, unloaded the *Sarah,* and removed her farther up the Long Wharf.

Benjamin Prat as advocate general filed an information against the *Sarah* and her seized cargo in the vice-admiralty court on 3 May 1760.[70] Possibly Prat took over because of the embarrassing unseemliness of Cradock appearing as prosecutor in the court where he so often presided as deputy judge. Or perhaps the case for condemnation was not all that cut-and-dried. According to Alexander Smith, at the interview with Cradock Erving had objected to the *Sarah* being unloaded "for that she had not broke bulk or committed any breach of trade." The argument of this objection no doubt was that without bulk having been broken (or an actual landing having taken place), goods were not "imported" into the province in violation of section 6 of the Staple Act of 1663, and that ground for forfeiture of the *Sarah* and cargo had therefore not materialized. The analysis in chapter 6 of the rebirth of the Boston vice-admiralty court's Staple Act jurisdiction indicated that section 6 forfeiture did not become firmly established till the early 1750s; in 1760 it was therefore still rather early for the custom house to have willingly ventured into counterargument on refinements about bulk not having been broken.

A glimpse of the situation is given in a letter written by Governor Bernard in 1763, about the recent seizure of the brigantine *Freemason* for violation of the staple. In the *Freemason* condemnation proceedings before Vice Admiralty Judge Russell it had been contended that ships direct from continental Europe "had a Right to come into this Port so long as they reported & did not break bulk." Bernard went on: "This produced a Question very interesting to the Crown, that is, whether a Vessell laden with prohibited goods and pretended to be found from a foreign European port to a foreign American port, might come, ever so much out of their way, into a British American port & there lie at anchor upon the credit of reporting her Cargo & pretended destination. The affirmative of this Question had been pronounced to be law in some popular declama-

---

70. *Quincy's Reports,* 554. On pages 541-72, immediately following Horace Gray's Appendix on writs of assistance, which is numbered I, is a further appendix, numbered II, relating to, *seriatim, Gray v. Paxton, Province v. Paxton, Erving v. Cradock,* and "Powers and Rights of Juries." Presumably this was the work of the editor, S. M. Quincy.

tions in the causes which were carried on here against the Custom house officers about 3 years ago: but there never was a cause, that I know, in which this point was adjudged."[71] Clearly Bernard had in mind the case of the *Sarah,* if only because that was the only one of its kind to feature in the controversies of 1760-61.

Bernard was right in implying that the point of breaking of bulk was not adjudicated upon in the *Sarah* case. There was in fact no judicial determination at all. Although, according to Alexander Smith, Cradock expected to get £2,000 sterling as his share from the condemnation proceedings, the proceedings never got to condemnation. The parties entered into a composition deal. "Mr *Erving* appeared personally in Court & prayed leave to compound, which being agreed to by the Governor & Collector as well as the King's Advocate, was allowed by the Court at one half of the value, which upon appraisement was ascertained at above £500 sterling. This sum Mr *Erving* paid into Court, & it was equally divided between the King, the Governor & the Collector." From the vice-admiralty court's book of accounts it would appear that Erving paid a total of £505 16s. 3d.; and that Cradock picked up no more than £160 3s. 6d. (Charles Paxton got £10 2s. 3¾d. "for his Extra Trouble & agreement," as marshal of the court.)

The essence of *Erving v. Cradock,* which came on ten months later, in March 1761, was an attempt by John Erving to renege on his composition agreement with George Cradock and get his money back. Erving's action in the Suffolk court of common pleas was for damages in trespass, the trespass consisting in Cradock having taken the *Sarah* and the other seized property and detained them "untill the said John made a fine by five hundred and fifty five pounds, four shillings, and four pence Sterling, with the said George for having the delivery of the said Brigantine . . . ."[72] The writ put Erving's damages at £1,000. The grounds upon which Erving asked for relief seem to have been the uncertain justifiability of the seizure under section 6 of the Staple Act, and "duress." Anyway, he won, and went on to sustain his victory when it was appealed in the Superior Court.

71. Bernard to Lord Halifax, 24 December 1763: C05/755; *Quincy's Reports,* 392-94. *The Freemason* is reported by Quincy at 387-94. Judge Russell's finding, that an actual landing was not necessary to an importation in violation of section 6 of the Staple Act of 1663, was upheld by the High Court of Admiralty in England: *LPJA* II, 238. (*Cf.* chapter 6, n. 26, and text.)

72. That the sum here cited was some £50 greater than the composition is explained, probably, by Erving's liability for costs: *Quincy's Reports,* 554.

Governor Bernard's move to have the case reviewed by the Privy Council — the overseas empire's final court of appeal — does not need much explanation. It had nothing to do with the personal position of Cradock. To Governor Bernard the gravity of *Erving v. Cradock* result lay in the damage it did to the court of vice-admiralty. If a composition agreement that had been sanctioned by the vice-admiralty court could be attacked and vitiated in the courts of common law, what binding finality could any decree of the vice-admiralty court be said to have? What customs officer dare invoke the court's jurisdiction for the condemnations of seizures if some kind of trespassorial action for damages might successfully follow against him? "They now begin to talk of bringing more actions against Custom house officers who have made seizures and have had them condemned or compounded in Court for them," Bernard wrote to the Board of Trade after the Superior Court jury had found against Cradock, "A Custom house officer has no chance with a jury, let his cause be what it will."[73] His Privy Council gambit succeeded, however. Faced with the uncertainty and the enormous cost of this process Erving threw in his hand; and in the words of a modern British writer, "the monstrous effort to destroy the [vice-admiralty] jurisdiction failed."[74]

Nor was the effort repeated. The crown's long pocket no doubt discouraged those other persons who talked of "more actions" subversive of the finality of vice-admiralty jurisdiction, even as it had daunted John Erving. And *Province v. Paxton* was by nature a one-off operation, dependent upon peculiarities of fact and of the Molasses Act; even if Paxton had not finally won out, the embarrassment to the vice-admiralty court would have been well short of fatal. But the outcome of *Erving v. Cradock* and *Province v. Paxton* was more relief than triumph for Governor Bernard. The equivocation of his performance in the launching of the province's litigation against Charles Paxton may have left him some claim to the benefit of the doubt. The move that checkmated Erving, however, would have been impossible without Bernard's active intervention: it had always been inevitable that the governor — any governor — would line up alongside an institution of British authority under attack; and here the gubernatorial hand was manifest beyond question.[75] Whatever hopes

---

73. 2 August 1761: Bernard Papers II.

74. A. B. Keith, *Constitutional History of the First British Empire* (Oxford, 1930), 333.

75. *BEP* 3 September 1770 carried a documented piece by "DETECTOR," animadverting upon how Governor Bernard, jointly with Surveyor General Lechmere, had caused Cradock's legal expenses (both in the province courts and for the projected appeal to the

Governor Bernard cherished toward amity with the merchant interest stood little chance after that.

By the spring of 1761 Governor Bernard was having a far more worrying time than could possibly have been foreseen on his arrival in August 1760. The rather fatuous optimism with which he came to his new appointment was bound to suffer deflation before long, but it would be unfair to fault him for failing to anticipate all the misfortunes that befell. The writs of assistance case was something of an exception, perhaps: the unsettling effect of the March 1760 *London Magazine* article was already being felt, and it was fairly certain that the next application for a writ of assistance would encounter difficulty. Merchant discontent was evident enough, too, but there was as yet no sign of its unmanageable eruptions in the form of common law litigation directed against the vice-admiralty court.

At the time and afterward Bernard wrote of the events of 1760-61 in terms of a "confederacy."[76] Indeed, as a modern commentator has said, "Bernard's fear of a conspiratorial faction is the main theme that runs through his extensive correspondence of the 1760s."[77] This kind of thinking toward disfavored political activity was common on all sides in the eighteenth century:[78] a disposition to see connection and pattern in events of like tendency was much of a piece with the contemporary Newtonian accent on cosmic synthesis. And if Governor Bernard saw the writs of assistance case, *Province v. Paxton,* and *Erving v. Cradock* as components of the Boston political orrery of 1760-61 he had some justification. Undeniably there were interactions and relationships amongst the various forensic assaults on the custom house and the vice-admiralty court.

Even so, as the next two chapters will demonstrate, a great deal turned upon accidents of human personality.

Privy Council) to be paid out of the king's share of the *Sarah* composition "or some other forfeiture." Whether this was generally known at the time does not appear. According to the 1770 piece, however, it was known to Lechmere's successor, John Temple, in the spring of 1762. (Temple disapproved and stepped in: perhaps this helped start the hostility that was to develop between him and Bernard; for another such possibility see chapter 18, n. 16, and text.)

76. See, *e.g.,* Bernard to ? 21 February 1761; Bernard Papers I; and to Board of Trade, 17 May 1765: C05/891.

77. B. Bailyn, *The Ideological Origins of the American Revolution* (Cambridge, Mass., 1967), 151n.

78. *Ibid.,* 144-59 and *passim. Cf.* G. S. Wood, *The Creation of the American Republic* (Chapel Hill, 1964), 40-41, 487-88; also Pauline Maier, *From Resistance to Revolution* (New York, 1972), 183-91 and *passim.* The theme occurs again in chapter 19 below.

10

~~~~~~~~~~~~~~~~~~~~~~~~~~
~~~~~~~~~~~~~~~~~~~~~~~~~

The Demon Collector

~~~~~~~~~~~~~~~~~~~~~~~~~~
~~~~~~~~~~~~~~~~~~~~~~~~~

Much of the turbulence that shook the Massachusetts governor and his establishment in the fall and winter of 1760-61 can be traced to a truly remarkable state of affairs in, of all places, the Boston custom house. The trouble centered upon the collector, under the surveyor general the topmost official there. His name was Benjamin Barons.

"Mr Barons has plaid the Devil in this Town," wrote Governor Francis Bernard on 19 January 1761. "He has put himself at the head of a combination of Merchants all raised by him with the Assistance of two or three others to demolish the Court of Admiralty & the other Custom House officers, especially one who has been active in making seizures."[1] To the governor Barons was the originating agent of practically all that went so calamitously wrong in those early months of his administration. Writing to his predecessor, Thomas Pownall, on 12 July 1761: "My acquaintance with Mankind has not been very extensive or very confined, but I can say that in all my knowledge of Men I never met with one like that Gentleman, so wonderfully wrong-headed & so wantonly mischevous. In direct Opposition to Common sense & reason, to his Obligations his Duty & his interest, did he make a formal attack upon the Government . . . . I can truly say that all the trouble I have had in this Government is owing to him & his Confederacy."[2]

Vividly though contemporary records describe episodes in Benjamin Barons's bizarre career as collector of customs at Boston from 1759 to 1761, not a great deal is known of his antecedents. His first appearance in the records did not augur well for his Boston job. Treasury papers for 1750 tell of a ship of his, the *George*, having been condemned in Boston — no doubt by the vice-admiralty

---

1. To John Pownall: Bernard Papers I.
2. Bernard Papers II.

court — for arriving without the requisite documentation attesting British ownership.[3] The fact that the Treasury remitted the king's share in the forfeiture indicates that the offense was only technical (in other words, the vessel in fact proved to be British); but the loss of two-thirds of the value of an ocean-going ship and her cargo was not something easily laughed off.

Barons next shows up as secretary to Rear Admiral Sir Charles Hardy, governor of New York 1755-57. The *Boston Gazette* referred to him as Sir Charles's brother-in-law.[4] Upon the governor's return to naval service in 1757 Barons presumably was out of work, but he seems to have stayed around New York a while. A letter from Thomas Hutchinson on 17 July 1758 spoke of an impending move to fire William Bollan from the Massachusetts agency in London (Bollan was seldom free from the threat of dismissal after his father-in-law William Shirley left the governorship in 1756); as to Bollan's successor, Hutchinson went on, "one Mr Barons now at New York has been mentioned to divers Gentlemen."[5]

At roughly the same time as Barons's secretaryship to Sir Charles Hardy ended, the collectorship of customs at Boston fell vacant. Sir Henry Frankland, the incumbent since 1741, had departed to become British consul general at Lisbon. Frankland in fact had been in Lisbon not long before, and had narrowly escaped death in the famous earthquake there. Agnes Surriage was with him, and it was to her he owed his survival. The entire experience so far disordered the baronet's sense of social propriety that he at last married his lowly born Marblehead protegée. The marriage perhaps explains Frankland's vacating his lucrative collectorship. Life in small-town society would be difficult for the new Lady Frankland. The gentlewomen of Boston might not be too gracious in yielding precedence to a person whose former status had not entitled her to so much as polite notice.

On the other hand, there may be truth in the statement of one commentator, that Frankland was "removed from office for inattention to his duties."[6] Traditionally no one had minded much if a custom house higher-up chose to absent himself and put in a deputy to do the work. In fact, around the time Frankland returned to

3. T11/23. See T. C. Barrow, *Trade and Empire* (Cambridge, Mass., 1967), 123; and C. M. Andrews, *The Colonial Period of American History*, IV, 172, n. 3.

4. 4 August 1760.

5. MHS, Williams Papers, II.

6. W. Warren, "The Colonial Customs Service in Massachusetts in its Relation to the American Revolution," *MHSP* XXXVI (Boston, 1913).

Boston from Europe his colleague Nathaniel Ware, comptroller of customs, left for an indefinite stay in England. Times were changing, though. However lackadaisical the attitude to such matters in the past, a more purposeful concern over customs law enforcement in the colonies was now in the air. "The war effort was beginning to take its toll, and the Treasury Lords were uneasy about their ability to meet the financial requirements imposed upon them," a modern commentator says; "Consequently a general tightening of the system was begun."[7] When the Treasury spoke other departments paid heed: not least the customs department, which was a kind of specialized branch of the Treasury. It is perhaps possible to discern a sharper professional outlook in some of the business of appointing a successor to Frankland. In 1758 and 1759 the Duke of Newcastle, who as first lord of the Treasury had the gift of customs appointments, received letters from a former collector of customs at Antigua, George Munro, alleging a promise to make him collector of Boston "if my Character answered."[8] That Munro's expectations were disappointed may be an indication that the needs of the work at Boston were being taken seriously. Another hopeful for the Boston collectorship was a man named Cary, reportedly a native of the town. Cary's sponsor, a Mr. Charles Spooner, wrote to Newcastle saying that "the Commissioners of the Customs had objected to him [Cary] on account of his commercial connexions." Spooner went on, "But the more material objection against him . . . is, that having been concerned in Trade to the Sugar Islands he may be tempted to encourage the illicit Trade carried on there between those Islands and the Continent of America."[9] It looks as if the customs commissioners were hoping for someone they could trust to do the Boston job properly.

However, the old ways of the world were dying hard. Whatever judicious weighing of candidates according to merit might have been going on, the actual disposal of this plum appointment proceeded on more traditional lines. Hopes and cerebrations among lesser persons were of little account when the Marquis of Rockingham put in a bid. Rockingham was out to do something for a certain George Quarme, an old tutor of his. Insofar as Quarme wanted a real job, a job involving work, it was in one of the revenue offices in England; his

7. Barrow, *op. cit.*, 165.
8. 1 March 1758, Add. MSS 32878; 16 March and 23 April 1759, Add. MSS 32889.
9. 11 March 1758, Add. MSS 32878.

interest in a customs post in the colonies arose only because there was no other foreseeable vacancy. And the Boston collectorship itself does not appear to have been his first preference even at that. Originally the scheme was that Quarme was to have New York; but as matters turned out the vacancy did not materialize, for the incumbent, Archibald Kennedy, kept going a few years yet. Not that Quarme had any intention of "a Temporal Transportation" to either New York or Boston, or even of actually becoming a collector of customs anywhere. It was sufficient that Rockingham get him the first refusal, which he would then exercise in consideration of the eventual appointee paying him an annuity — £300 was mentioned — "out of the profits of the Place." This annuity to Quarme would have been but a second charge on the emoluments of the collectorship, for Newcastle was adamant that he himself must have £200 a year "for a poor long disappointed Friend" in one letter, and "for Two Friends" in another. Rockingham had his eye on a young man named Crowle as the doubly encumbered appointee.[10]

In the outcome, however, the man who went to Boston was not a Rockingham client. And one hesitates to assume that Benjamin Barons took on the job under the same conditions as had been envisioned for Crowle; Barons was a bit above that, probably. It had taken some doing — through influential friends — to get the Treasury to pay out that condemnation money for the *George* in 1750. The secretaryship to the governor of New York was not without clout either; Thomas Pownall had risen from it to become lieutenant governor of New Jersey and then governor of Massachusetts. There is also the report that Barons was more or less in the running for the Massachusetts agency, a post important enough to have had attractions even for Thomas Hutchinson and Governor Pownall himself.

10. For Quarme, see W. R. Ward, "Some Eighteenth Century Civil Servants: The English Revenue Commissioners, 1754-9," reprinted from *English Historical Review,* January 1955 in Rosalind Mitchison, ed., *Essays in Eighteenth-Century History* (London, 1966), 214, 224. The correspondence between Newcastle and Rockingham is in Add. MSS 32873. *Cf.* also Barrow, *op. cit.,* 122-24.

For Kennedy, see M. M. Klein, "Archibald Kennedy: Imperial Pamphleteer," in L. H. Leder, ed., *The Colonial Legacy* (New York, 1971) II, 75-105. Kennedy died in 1763. Robert Temple, an intermittent member of the Boston custom house, was designated to succeed him temporarily, but sickness appears to have supervened: John Temple to customs commissioners, 25 July 1763, in "A Letter-book of Sir John Temple 1762-68," in MHS.

John Bindley's inquiries for Charles Townshend (chapter 9, n. 24) elicited that "At Boston . . . the Collector seldom made less than £3000 sterling per annum, but he was rode in England. New York, Philadelphia, and Hallifax are the next best collectorships."

Above all, Barons enjoyed the patronage of an even more substantial figure than the Marquis of Rockingham. The Earl of Halifax may have been a notch below Rockingham in the peerage, but unlike Rockingham he was a member of the ministry. In itself this might not have been enough to swing the Boston collectorship to Barons, but as president of the Board of Trade Halifax was in a position to offer quid pro quo.

It is apposite at this point to consider the present condition of a familiar figure from the Massachusetts past, former governor William Shirley. Shirley had fallen on evil times. Returning to Boston from his duties as commander-in-chief around the end of January 1756 Shirley had left behind him the seeds of disaster, not least to himself. His military dispositions had not gone as hoped, and the ill will of disaffected subordinates made itself felt in quarters where it mattered. In March 1756 the British government wrote him that the command was being changed, that he was to become governor of Jamaica, and that he must depart for Britain forthwith.[11] By the time he reached England in the fall his situation had worsened. The Earl of Loudon, now in command of the army, had done badly. Oswego was lost, and the insufficiency of Shirley's preparations for its defense made him a suitable scapegoat. The atmosphere at Westminster was heavy with recrimination; nothing came of the promised governorship of Jamaica, and the next year or so witnessed a piteous series of petitions and letters in which Shirley pleaded for a pension or another job.[12] His old patron, Newcastle, would do nothing for him however. Word had gotten around that Shirley had been instrumental in supplying the political opposition with information about military expenditure in America, which Charles Townshend used as ammunition against the ministry.[13] To Newcastle this could have

11. H. Fox (secretary of state, southern) to Shirley, 13 March 1756: Add. MSS 32874 ("Mr Pownal, Lieutenant Governor of New Jersey, has been thought of by the King, as a person proper to succeed you, as Governor of Massachusetts Bay"). In a more formal letter, dated 31 March, Fox said nothing of the Jamaica post but spoke only of Shirley's being urgently required in England for consultation. The same day Fox asked the Admiralty to prepare a frigate to transport Shirley "with all convenient Speed, as His Services are wanted here immediately": C05/212/2. Shirley seems not to have left Boston till September, however: see, *e.g.*, *BWNL* 23 September 1756, and his petition to the king in Add. MSS 32874, which tells of his getting orders to leave in June and arriving in England in October. *Cf.* chapter 11, n. 6.

12. See, *e.g.*, Shirley to Newcastle, 13 March, 24 and 27 September 1757: Add. MSS 32874.

13. Halifax to Newcastle, 15 February 1758: Add. MSS 32877. *Cf.* n. 14 below.

been a culminating infamy sufficient to destroy Shirley's chances entirely.

For his eventual deliverance Shirley had to thank Lord Halifax. In February 1758 Halifax wrote to Newcastle with the object of absolving Shirley from responsibility for the Townshend attack: Shirley's "Behaviour in that affair turns out very differently from what your Grace & I imagined it," he said.[14] But Newcastle was unmoved, and Shirley remained unprovided for. Some months later Halifax took an initiative of his own. One respect in which he had been able to augment the influence of the Board of Trade was that this department now had the appointment of colonial governors in its gift. Halifax wrote Newcastle on 14 September: "Poor Shirley is indeed miserable to a great degree for want of some mark of his Majesty's Favor; and hopes that your Grace will obtain a Pension for him soon. Considering his services, My dear Lord, & considering that no one Tittle of Charge has been attempted to be made out against him, it is hard a poor old Servant of the Crown who has filled such important Stations should be reduced to Want." Pensions, Halifax realized, were what Newcastle least chose to provide; however, the governor of the Bahamas had recently died. Here, perhaps, Halifax could help? Although applications enough had been made for the vacancy, "I shall be happy to give it to Shirley, if it will be any means of accommodating your Grace, & preserving you from further Sollicitations from the poor old man. The Government is worth about £1,200 per annum sterling . . . ."[15] And so Shirley became governor of the Bahamas.

While it would be unfair to discount the generosity of Halifax's action,[16] he could have appointed Shirley to the Bahamas governorship without reference to any ministerial colleague. Instead, he cast it

14. *Ibid.* Newcastle himself had been a special target of Townshend's attack (7 February 1757): see L. Namier and J. Brooke, *Charles Townshend* (London, 1964), 48. To judge by Townshend's own background papers, he went closely into the 6d per man/day currently spent on victualling from British suppliers in contrast to the 3½-4½d for local American produce when Shirley was in command; and Newcastle could be forgiven for suspecting that the detailed data had come from Shirley. But the true source of Townshend's information seems to have been Charles Paxton (with the involvement of John Huske, expatriate New Englander turned Westminster politician): Huske to Townshend, n.d., Scottish Record Office, Townshend bundle in Buccleuch (Bowhill) muniments. For the Townshend-Paxton connection see chapter 7, n. 6, and the references there cited.

15. Add. MSS 32883.

16. *Cf.* Halifax to Newcastle, 13 June 1746, imploring Newcastle's intercession with the king for a soldier under sentence of death: Add. MSS 32707.

in the form of a favor to Newcastle. One remembers that Halifax had a man of his own he wanted to see placed, the former secretary of the governor of New York, Benjamin Barons. As will become evident, and as Halifax would have realized from personal knowledge, Barons — unlike his secretarial predecessor, Thomas Pownall — was not gubernatorial material. But a berth in the customs might be all right for him. The power of appointment to the vacant Boston collectorship belonged to Newcastle as first lord of the Treasury. If Halifax gave Shirley a job, so that Shirley was gotten off Newcastle's back in a manner that carried no overt implication that Newcastle had restored his patronage to Shirley, might not a reciprocal favor be due from Newcastle to Halifax?

Barons's warrant of appointment as collector of customs was dated 2 May 1759. He arrived in Boston from England on 21 September. In less than four months he was on his way back again, having been suspended by Surveyor General Thomas Lechmere. Of what the trouble was, not a scrap of direct evidence has been found. But it cannot have impressed the customs commissioners too much, for they reinstated Barons (and, according to him, rebuked Lechmere). In August 1760 — a week or so after Francis Bernard came as governor — Barons made his second start in the custom house.[17]

It was not long before he lighted upon another adversary there. This time it was Charles Paxton, the surveyor and searcher. Exactly what inflamed Barons against Paxton is uncertain. It was said that Barons believed Paxton was aware of harsh things that Governor Pownall had been writing home about him, and considered it unfriendly of Paxton not to have let him know.[18] Or it may have been

17. Appointment: T11/26. Arrival: *BEP* 24 September 1759. Suspension: Charles Paxton to George Townshend, 21 January 1760 ("Mr Lechmere the Surveyor General . . . and Mr Barons the Collector of this Port, have fallen out, and Mr Barons, who is suspended from his Office by the Surveyor General, goes home in this Ship with Compliants to his Friend Lord Halifax, of the Arbitrary Proceedings of the Surveyor General." And Paxton to the life — "Should this Dispute Occasion the removal of either of those Gentlemen from their Posts, may I Sir, presume to take the Liberty to beg of you to get the Lords of the Treasury to appoint me to fill up the Vacancy . . ."): MHS, Paxton Papers. Reinstatement, etc.: memorial by Barons to Lord Bute, 23 March 1763: Bodleian Library, MS North (photo in MHS); and *BNL* 22 May 1760. Rearrival in Boston: *BNL* 21 August ("Last week came to Town, Benjamin Barons, Esq . . . who lately arrived at New-York from England . . .").

18. Writing to Thomas Pownall on 28 August 1761, Governor Bernard said that Barons had been told that when he went to England under suspension, "you wrote to advise that his friends should provide for him there & not send him back again, for he was so very silly that he would certainly disgrace his recommenders if he returned here": Bernard Papers II.

more that Paxton was so closely connected with the vice-admiralty court, the court that a few years ago had cost Barons the loss of a ship. "My dear Paxton," he is reported as having once said, "I would give five hundred pounds Sterling you were not an Officer of the Admiralty I am sure you would join with me to demolish that devilish or Confounded Court."[19]

Materials on Barons's activities in this second phase of his Boston career exist in abundance. In large measure they are the documentation of certain "Articles of Complaint against Benjamin Barons Esqr Collector of . . . Customs for the port of Boston, exhibited by Charles Paxton Surveyor of . . . Customs for the said Port." These "Articles of Complaint," and various persons' testimony in support of them, much of it sworn, are an important source of information on the "confederacy" that shook the custom house, the vice-admiralty court, and Governor Francis Bernard in the fall and winter of 1760-61. The "Articles of Complaint" are not dated, but the overall time frame strongly indicates that Paxton put them to Thomas Lechmere, surveyor general of customs, early in February 1761. They were not the first occasion of trouble for the reinstated Barons, but because the story of his disruptions depends largely on the mass of evidentiary material produced in support of them it is necessary to disregard chronological sequence and say something of them right now.

By February 1761 everything was set for Charles Paxton to be sued for payments he had received out of the province's shares in Molasses Act forfeitures; and he identified Barons as a principal architect of this. Various other improprieties were alleged as well. Barons, Paxton recited in his articles, had "formed the following Designs

I To prevent the laws against illegal trade being executed within the Port aforesaid [Boston] , and for that purpose

II To abolish or render inactive the Court of Admiralty

Perhaps another angle is discernible in Anne Rowe Cunningham, ed., *Letters and Diary of John Rowe* (Boston, 1903), 377: "Mr P- has inflamed the Collector by telling him you wrote home Letters against him & by what I can find Mr Barrons has wrote to know how it stands — this I thought Convenient to advise you" (Rowe — a leading Boston merchant — to an unidentified correspondent, possibly Thomas Pownall, 29 September 1760).

Paxton had been well regarded by Governors Belcher and Shirley, and was to become something of an intimate of Governor Bernard; but no evidence has appeared of Governor Pownall reposing special confidence in him.

19. Deposition of Paxton, 18 February 1761: T1/408 (the bundle for practically all the Barons materials; a little more is in Adm. 1/3883).

III   To intimidate and prevent the Custom-House Officers in doing their
        Duty

IV   To prevent and controll the Governor in his Duty of Supporting the
        Court of Admiralty and the Custom House.

For which purposes he hath entered into a confederacy with divers fit
persons and by himself and confederates hath acted as follows . . . ."[20]

And then came two and a half pages of specific charges under each
of the four main heads.

Barons was not to be judged by Lechmere alone, however. Governor Bernard related: "Soon after the prorogation of the Assembly,
which was the last day of January, Mr Paxton the Surveyor of the
Customs delivered unto the Surveyor General a charge against Mr
Barons consisting of 20 Articles. The Surveyor General by letter
desired that I and the Judge of the Admiralty would assist him in
making an enquiry into Mr Barons Conduct therein. To this I agreed
on condition that the Judge of the Admiralty would accede thereto:
& the Judge of the Admiralty acceded thereto."[21] The tribunal thus
formed − Bernard, Lechmere, and Chambers Russell − were "desir-
ous to render the proceedings unexceptionable," Bernard said; and
while they did not go so far as to give Barons a hearing (or even to
send him a copy of Paxton's allegations against him − he would only
bruit them about, and "the Town was still in ferment" as it was),
they remained faithful to a certain punctilio throughout the two
months, mid-February to mid-April, over which their proceedings
stretched.

The proceedings consisted mainly of the receipt and examination
of sworn testimony, oral and written, from persons able to speak to

20. T1/408. The "Articles" were reproduced in *BG* 18 September 1769. (And see text
at n. 30 below.)

None of the supporting testimony was included in the *BG* piece. Probably, the exact
terms of it never got out to the Bostonians. The gist of it seems to have reached them,
however. On 31 August 1765 Governor Bernard told Lord Halifax (C05/755) how Briggs
Hallowell "of this Town, who was in London about two years ago, had got a sight of the
depositions . . . . Upon his return to Boston He took upon him to report the Substance of
these with additions of his own, & concluded with an assertion that the whole Body of
Merchants had been represented as Smuglers."

A postscript said Briggs Hallowell "is of no significance & has a brother who is a very
faithful officer of the kings." The brother was Benjamin Hallowell junior, who had been
master of the province warship, was now comptroller of customs at Boston, and would
become one of the American commissioners of customs; reference is made to him in
chapters 18, 19, and 20. The brothers' father, Benjamin Hallowell senior, mentioned later in
the present chapter, was a merchant and more to Briggs's way of thinking.

21. To ? 21 February 1761: Bernard Papers I.

particular points in Paxton's list of charges. A considerable amount of documentary evidence, including a long factual "narrative" by Governor Bernard himself, was forwarded to London, and has survived in the Public Record Office there. From these materials it is possible to attempt an analysis or reconstruction of what Benjamin Barons got up to after his return to duty — if it can be called that — in August 1760.

First there was Barons's part in the instigation of *Province v. Paxton.*

Paxton himself deposed: "That when Mr Barons first set about raising a Clamor against him ... he the said Barons went to the Register of the Court of Admiralty and took out Copys of divers bills of Costs which had been allowed by the said Court ... many of which were before the said Mr Barons came into his office and carried the same Copys all over the Town Shewing them to the merchants of the Town with his remarks upon them to inflame the Minds of the people against the deponent."[22] Something similar was sworn to by Benjamin Pemberton, the naval officer. Pemberton referred to a meeting of merchants from which resulted the petition to the Assembly and thence the province's lawsuit against Paxton, and affirmed that this fateful meeting "had its rise by Mr Barons publishing the Copys of the bills of Costs he took out of the Admiralty Office." Pemberton had "frequently heard Several of the Merchants of the Town take Notice of some of the Charges in said bills as being extravagant and impositions and that the Province had been very much wronged thereby . . . ."[23]

As collector of customs with a responsibility to see that the king's share in forfeitures (other than those under the Molasses Act) was properly accounted for and remitted to London, Barons could scarcely be denied access to the information he sought out and went

22. 18 February 1761: T1/408. The "Register" was in fact the deputy register, William Story, whose deposition of 24 March 1761, also in T1/408, supported Paxton.

23. Deposition of 27 February 1761: T1/408. Although an establishment man *ex officio,* Pemberton cannot have felt a total commitment at this time. His George II appointment having lapsed, he was under pressure from Governor Bernard to share the naval officership with one of Bernard's sons. See, *e.g.,* Bernard to John Pownall, 2 March 1761: Bernard Papers I. It was pressure in vain, however: Bernard to John Pownall, 6 June 1761, *ibid.;* Pownall to Bernard, 22 July 1761, and Barrington to Bernard, 14 January 1762, Bernard Papers IX. Pemberton had suffered, and weathered, this sort of trouble before, under Governors Belcher and Shirley: Shirley to Newcastle, 2 January 1737: C05/899; and 23 August 1741, 4 December 1741, 23 January 1742, and 4 May 1742: C05/900.

on to broadcast around. That he was motivated not so much to protect the exchequer interest as to make trouble for Paxton and the vice-admiralty court is clear enough; but how far he was responsible for actually spotting the full significance of the bills of costs is problematical. It could be that when he first obtained them he did not wholly appreciate the mischief-making potential of those that related to Molasses Act cases. Governor Bernard relates in his "Narrative" how he himself had tried to persuade Barons to behave:[24] in a private conversation, early in November apparently, he sought to calm Barons down on the "objections" that seemed to be bothering him most. Notable among these were "the Allowances made to Mr Paxton for procuring private intelligence." Bernard pointed out to Barons that such allowances had been made as long as anyone could remember. Governor Shirley had "greatly encouraged the enlarging the allowance," and both Governor Shirley and Governor Pownall had agreed to specially large allowances in particular cases. "That for himself, the present Governor, He observed that he paid as much to every such Allowance, as the King did; and tho the King's Exchequer and the Governors private purse differed beyond all degrees of comparison, yet in these instances, he should always be ready to contribute his full Share of the Necessary Allowances for preventing illicit trade." It could be inferred that Barons's concern at this stage was to safeguard the interests of the British exchequer; in other words, that he was thinking of the king's shares which for most forfeitures were sent to London, rather than of those that arose from the Molasses Act and belonged to the province.

Of course, it was over the latter that local opinion would bridle most at deductions for informers. Whatever Barons's first intentions may have been, it was not long before this promising seam of mischief was gotten on to. Bernard's private admonitions having had no effect (his "narrative" went on) he called upon Surveyor General Lechmere and Vice-Admiralty Judge Russell to join him in "a formal expostulation with Mr Barons." This second attempt to get Barons to mend his ways took place around the middle of November 1760. [25] But it only made matters worse. Bernard says,

24. 16 March 1761: T1/408.
25. Though the presiding triumvirate was the same this "formal expostulation" in November is not, of course, to be confused with the proceedings on Charles Paxton's "Articles of Complaint" some three months later. Paxton attended throughout the November business, however; and, according to Bernard's narrative, "occasionally exprest himself too hastily against Mr Barons which the Governor put a stop to & reprimanded him for."

A few days after the conference, the Governor was informed that Mr Gray the provincial Treasurer had been at the Court of Admiralty to demand an account of the Seizures in which the Province was concerned. As this was done without the Governors privity, He sent for the treasurer & asked him how he came to take this step without consulting him and askt him who set him about it. The Treasurer told the Governor that Mr Hallowell came to him & told him that Mr Barons had such bills of Costs allowed by the Court of Admiralty to show us would amaze him; said he sought, as provincial treasurer, to see that the province was not injured; and desired he would go immediately to Mr Barons, who would give him proper information. That two days after he went to Mr Barons' house who showed him the Statute of 6 Geo 2^d [the Molasses Act] & a number of bills of Costs taxed by the Court of Admiralty . . . .

Clearly, Barons was now well aware of the Molasses Act and the opportunity for mischief it afforded.

The developments that led to *Province v. Paxton* were taking shape. Benjamin Hallowell senior was a leading adversary of the vice-admiralty court. And the deputy register of the court, William Story, deposed that "sometime after" he had dispatched certain copy bills of costs which Barons had requisitioned on 3 November, "John Rowe Esqr applied to him for Copys of Sundry Accounts of Charges on Seizures made by Mr Paxton and others and that afterwards he delivered Copys of the same Accounts of Charges to James Otis Junior Esqr. at the request of Mr Rowe."[26] John Rowe was a prominent merchant and a signer of the petition of the "sundry Inhabitants" from which *Province v. Paxton* resulted. James Otis junior was the lawyer who would be arguing the petitioners' case before the House of Representatives. Presumably it was thought advisable, if only for the sake of appearances, for the petitioners to be able to ascribe "the Schedules and Evidence presented with this Petition" to a direct sight of the vice-admiralty records; it would look rather lame if on being challenged as to the authenticity of their evidence they had only Barons's copies to go on.

Next, Barons and *Erving v. Cradock*. This was the action in which John Erving sought damages from George Cradock, in respect of the seizure in April 1760 (when Cradock was acting collector in place of Barons, under suspension and away in England) of the brigantine *Sarah* and her cargo, which seizure had been compounded between Erving and Cradock in the vice-admiralty court shortly afterward.

26. N. 22 above.

However, it was not until March 1761 that Erving issued his writ, in active repentance of his bargain. The reason for the delay appears to have been that it was not until the fall, when Barons had gotten into stride against the vice-admiralty court and all its works, that Erving formed the intention. Or had it suggested to him, as would appear from two depositions on Charles Paxton's articles of complaint against Barons. These were in fact supplementary depositions, put in to the Bernard-Russell-Lechmere tribunal on 30 March 1761, when its deliberations were almost complete; and evidently they had been prompted by the issuance of Erving's writ a few days before.[27]

One of the depositions was by Paxton himself, recalling a conversation in early November in which Erving had said to him "what is the meaning of all this bustle that Mr Barons makes about Admiralty proceedings he . . . tells me that in the Seizure of my Briganteen made by Mr Cradock that I was greatly imposed upon and that he wondred I would submit to such ill Treatment and that there were Several most unreasonable Charges and he . . . would give him any assistance to redress himself . . . ." The other supplementary deposition was by William Story, the deputy register of the vice-admiralty court, who thought he could remember Erving telling him "that Mr Barons had more than once applied to the said Erving for the Copy of the bill of Costs which he paid Occasioned by the Seizure," and "Erving was unwise to Submit to such unreasonable Charges"; Erving had repeatedly told Story "that he intended to get the whole money he paid on the Seizure aforesaid back again . . . ."

In face of this sworn testimony, not to mention common-sense probability, it is entirely credible that it was from Benjamin Barons that Erving first got the idea of suing Cradock.

The mischief that Paxton's "Articles of Complaint" imputed to Barons ranged wider than *Province v. Paxton* and *Erving v. Cradock.* Of particular interest is this:

> He hath declared that the Superior Courts granting Writs of Assistance is against Law and hath encourag'd a Representation from the meeting of Merchants hereafter mentioned to the Superior Court against granting such Writs.

Elaborating in a deposition, Paxton affirmed that "in conversation with . . . Mr Barons in presence of Robert Temple Esqr Controller of

27. T1/408.

his Majesty's customs for this port he the said Mr Barons said that the standing writs of assistance which had been usually granted by the Superior Court of Judicature &c in quality of the Court of Exchequer to the Custom house Officers to enable them to enter Warehouses &c to make Seizures of prohibited goods were against Law and made use of many Arguments to Support his Opinion."[28]

Robert Temple, mentioned as a witness of Barons's denunciation of "the standing writs of assistance," was the elder brother of the man shortly to become surveyor general, John Temple. They were sons of Captain Robert Temple who had come to New England earlier in the century and settled down to a life of agriculture. Through family connections with the Grenvilles John went to England as a youngster and was raised there. Robert, married to a daughter of Governor Shirley, stayed home on the farm. (He seems to have been a kind of Esau all long: when the succession to a baronetcy came up he was no longer alive, and John got it.) Possibly by the anticipatory influence of the future surveyor general he took over the acting comptrollership of customs around the turn of 1760-61, and in this period his name was often coupled with Paxton's in the making and prosecution of seizures. Not surprisingly, he gave testimony backing up his partner's charges against their errant colleague. Robert Temple deposed — among much else besides — that he had heard "Mr Barons declare that in his Opinion the Customs house Officers were not intitled to the writs of assistance that had been usually granted to them and that Mr Gridley his Lawyer was of the same Opinion."[29]

It is in point to recall from chapter 9 the "address" that the Society for Encouraging Trade and Commerce sent to the Treasury at Westminster in February 1762. Although this communication

28. Deposition of 18 February 1761: T1/408. Paxton added, however, "That he doth not know that the said Barons encouraged the petition to the Superior Court Against Granting writs of assistance to the Custom house officers any otherways than that the Meeting of the Merchants who preferred said petition was brought about by him and his Confederates and he was as this deponent Credibly informed Consulted and advised with relating to their proceedings from time to time."

On 27 August 1761 Vice-admiralty Judge Russell wrote the Admiralty how his court had been beset: Adm. 1/3883. But he seems to have imputed the merchants' "Several Meetings" to Barons' "associates" rather than to Barons himself. (Russell endorsed statements by Paxton, Nathaniel Hatch, and the substantive register of the court, Andrew Belcher.)

The memorandum by William Bollan in Appendix H says that the merchants were "encouraged by the collector." Bollan did not speak from direct knowledge, however: cf. chapter 9, n. 62.

29. 25 February 1761: T1/408. More of Gridley later, notably in chapter 13.

consisted in substance of a detailed denunciation of racketeering in the Boston vice-admiralty court, notably by Charles Paxton, it was also a follow-up to a protest sent by the society to the customs commissioners in August 1761 against the severities which had by then been served out to Collector Barons. The address said that the Boston merchants had "lately obtained" a sight of Paxton's articles of complaint against Barons, and they were now concerned "to vindicate, not Mr. Barons only, but themselves, from the unjust Aspersions, which are therein cast upon them." Accordingly, appropriate passages in the articles were utilized for what the address had to say about, for example, the merchants referring their ordinary maritime business to private arbitration rather than incur the inflated expense of vice-admiralty process. Here is how the address responded to the articles' charge about Barons's part in the petition against writs of assistance:

> A Number of the Merchants and Inhabitants petitioned that a Hearing might be had upon the Subject, concluding no Doubt, that the Superior Court would not assume the Powers of the Exchequer, in order to grant this Writt, but the Court has determined otherwise. It is certain that Mr Barons did not influence, nor attempt to influence the Merchants to any Step for preventing this Writt being issued, as is alledged against him; so far from it, that he was the only one, as we are well informed, of all the Officers of the Customs, who advanced Money for Council to support it, and to our Knowledge steadily pursued it, and contended for it, against the united Voice of the People, to the End.[30]

Whatever credibility this testimonial might deserve is not strengthened by the reflection that payment for custom house representation in the writs of assistance case naturally was made by the official whose function it was to have the custom house's money in his keeping: the collector.

On the merchants' own part in the writs of assistance controversy the society expressed itself less equivocally. "We together with the rest of the Inhabitants desired to be heard upon the Subject of Writts of Assistance, in the manner in which they were proposed to be granted, as an unwarrantable stretch of Power, and an Attack on our Liberty; And we presume that a legal Enquiry into such Attempts,

---

30. It seems from the address (18 February 1762: T1/415) that John Temple, who had succeeded Lechmere as surveyor general in November 1761, showed a copy of the articles to Barons, who showed it to the merchants.

The society's representation to the customs commissioners, 14 August 1761, is in T1/408. It bore 96 signatures.

will never be charged to us as a Crime, which is the distinguishing and darling Virtue of English People; From them we sprang and like them we hate Tyranny."

"I can truly say with Lear," lamented Governor Francis Bernard in March 1761, "I am a Man / More sinn'd against than sinning."[31] He was writing of the personal vendetta that Barons was now waging against him — or, it is more accurate to say, had been waging some months past. One entire head of Charles Paxton's "Articles of Complaint" had as its subject a variety of means whereby Barons had sought to undermine the position of the governor.

This animus of Barons toward Governor Bernard was all one with his hostility toward the vice-admiralty court and Paxton. Not least among the accidental human factors lacing the explosive politico-economic mix in Boston in 1760-61 was Bernard's lack of private wealth and the worrisome impecuniousness which his large family and domestic commitment reduced him to. Quite aside from his formal identification with the vice-admiralty court (being himself the vice-admiral), Bernard had a lively concern of a more subjective kind in that part of its jurisdiction which yielded him a one-third share in all customs forfeitures; to a man in his strained financial condition this perquisite represented sorely needed income. It was equally natural that he struck up a relationship with the star practitioner of customs seizure and forfeiture in the province's main port. Charles Paxton had been well regarded by Governor Shirley, and his usefulness to the chronically hard-up Governor Bernard was no less great.

Barons's designs against the governor became apparent soon after the "conference" in mid-November, when Barons received a "formal expostulation" from the assembled governor, surveyor general, and judge of vice-admiralty. It has been seen how, according to Bernard's "narrative," Barons had suggested to the province treasurer, Harrison Gray, that the province was being milked of its dues by illegal or excessive costs in Molasses Act condemnations. Among the bills of costs shown to Gray was a very recent one, relating to thirteen hogsheads of spirits seized by Nathaniel Hatch, the then acting comptroller of customs at Boston, on 3 November 1760 and condemned by the vice-admiralty court on 17 November. This particular bill of costs had not yet been settled by the court, on which account Barons advised Gray "to make no Stir at present." For if it tran-

31. To John Pownall, 30 March: Bernard Papers I.

spired that the province's share of the forfeiture had been unlawfully charged with prosecutor's costs Bernard could be implicated in any recovery proceedings, since his own share was the greater for the wrongdoing. As Bernard himself put it: "The Governor . . . had not received any money on account of any Seizure in which the Province was interested; but when the Seizure made by Mr Hatch should be settled, if the costs were allowed as usual, the Governor might be chargeable with having his share increased at the expense of the Province. From hence it plainly Appeared to him that, by Mr Barons desiring the Treasurer to make no Stir till Mr Hatch's costs were settled; he waited for an Opportunity to involve the Governor in the dispute, by making him Subject to a Claim from the Province." Of course, Bernard did not let himself be caught so easily. The vice-admiralty court's account book (another chance survival from the general destruction of the court's records in 1765) shows that Hatch's bill of costs was not settled until 4 April 1761. The costs included £24 for information, but "it being signified to the Court from the Governor that he Desired that the aforementioned sum of twenty four pounds Charged by the prosecutor for private information might not be made a Charge upon the King's [i.e., the province's] thirds but might be placed to the account of him the Governor and the prosecutor joyntly and the prosecutor consenting thereto," the court ordered that the province's share be immune from this £24 charge.[32] So Barons's scheme for trapping Bernard came to nothing.

By early December Barons was openly at war against Bernard: Ebenezer Richardson, the notorious informer, told the Bernard-Russell-Lechmere tribunal how on 4 December Barons had tried to persuade him to abandon Charles Paxton, his regular custom house employer, and to enter Barons's own service. Barons, said Richardson, had declared that "the Governor, The Judge of the Admiralty, and Paxton are all of a Club, but I will make the Governor know his driver, and that I am his driver . . . . I will make the Judge, Paxton, and the Governor ashamed and lap their Ears like Doggs, and I have friends that will carry it through." Barons went so far as to allege that Paxton's charges for information in the vice-admiralty bills of costs were spurious and that in fact Paxton shared the money with the governor and the vice-admiralty judge.[33] What with this and his

32. Cf. C05/854, p. 7.
33. Deposition of Richardson 27 February 1761: T1/408. It witnesses to Richardson's dubious character that Attorney General Edmund Trowbridge told of Governor Bernard

suspicion of improper augmentation of the governor's share in the Hatch seizure, Barons plainly had it in for Governor Bernard from fairly early on.

It was specially hard on Bernard that Barons should turn out this way, for there was also the dread of offending the collector's influential friends in England: not least Lord Halifax, who was both the patron of Barons and Bernard's own political chief at the Board of Trade. Signs of discomfiture are to be seen in some of the governor's letters back home. It was not only Halifax that he had somehow to square. His own patron, Lord Barrington, had specifically recommended Barons to him (and Bernard claimed that his first, informal, admonition to Barons had been motivated by Barrington's interest).[34] Perhaps Governor Bernard was entitled to feel a little sorry for himself.

"There never existed such mischeivous [sic] folly in all my acquaintance of mankind as in this Gentleman," he said.[35] But Barons was not the only activating element in the "confederacy" that came to plague Bernard so grievously. Indeed, Barons was not the half of it.

---

having required him to vet what Richardson had said, and to give "my Sentiments concerning the Truth of his deposition from the knowledge I have of the man or otherwise": deposition of Trowbridge 18 March 1761. Charles Paxton also was "desired to . . . give his opinion concerning the Credibility of the Deponent Richardson": deposition of Paxton 18 March 1761.

34. Bernard to Barrington, 10 August 1761: Bernard Papers II.
35. To ? 19 January 1761: Bernard Papers I.

11

Hutchinson and the Otises

W ITHIN barely more than a month of Governor Francis Bernard's arrival in Boston in August 1760 the chief justice of the province, Stephen Sewall, took sick and died. Ordinarily the nomination of a successor might have been a useful piece of patronage (with which Massachusetts governors were none too well endowed), but in this instance and through little fault of Bernard's own it brought him a further packet of trouble. The affair of the chief justiceship helped thrust a formidable recruit into the "confederacy" that smote the custom house and vice-admiralty court in the winter of 1760-61.

Given a plurality of candidates, as proved to be the case, there was a special element in the problem from the start. It was a reflection of the fact that in terms of monetary reward a seat on the Superior Court bench was not worth having. Salaries were miserably low: £150 each for the four puisne judges, with £40 extra for the chief justice; and even these pittances were subject to the hazard of an annual vote in the House of Representatives. With the expense of circuit travel it must have been all but impossible for the members of the Superior Court bench to make do on this sort of money:[1] indeed, Chief Justice Sewall, a bachelor and not at all given to high living, died insolvent. Certainly a man did not seek to become a Superior Court judge for the sake of the pay.

A corollary is that the motivation of an aspirant to the Superior

---

1. The salary figures are from the Massachusetts accounts of 1755-60 in C05/853; though they seem to have been the norm, there is no record of an extra £40 for the chief justice in 1757-58. In 1766 Governor Bernard (to Charles Lowndes, Treasury secretary, 31 December: T1/452) wrote of £150 as the chief justice's salary, and £120 the puisne judges': "one would conclude that the fees of their Offices would make up the deficiency of the Salary. But it is no such thing: the fees . . . wont near pay for the Expence of their Journeys in which they are constantly employed for the greater part of the year. One of the judges lately told the House, that having kept an exact account of the income & expences of the Office, He found he had not £70 p.an. left for his trouble. But it signified nothing . . . ."

Court bench might be something specially sensitive to disappointment. It could be genuine and disinterested attraction to useful public service, of course, or the prospect of work which by its nature would keep a man's abilities at full stretch. But appetite for status was probably as constant an element as any. Though social stratification in Massachusetts was never comparable to that in Europe, the province was not without its pecking order. Appointment to the Superior Court meant arrival in a big way. Accordingly, someone who thought himself up to that sort of mark might well be a person of too much substance and self-esteem to take kindly to a put-down.

Waiting in the wings in September 1760 was a candidate whose failure to win a place on the Superior Court was to be taken very badly indeed. He was Colonel James Otis.

Of a piece with a status-conscious provincial society was a tendency for men in the public eye to trick themselves out in military nomenclature.[2] However, it is convenient that this James Otis was styled colonel, for thereby he can be distinguished from his celebrated son of the same name. Colonel Otis was a leading resident of Barnstable, some seventy miles south of Boston. His basic livelihood was in commerce, but as could happen in those days he had somewhere along the line picked up enough law to engage in the practice of it. Otis's ambition for a Superior Court judgeship stemmed, however, less from his standing in the legal profession than from his career in province politics.

His earlier career, it is more accurate to say. Although Colonel Otis was currently speaker of the House of Representatives this was only a recent advance. The last few years had not been fruitful for him politically. After blossoming handsomely in the heyday of the Shirley administration Otis's political fortunes declined toward the end, and he had never gotten back on the inside track. But such had once been his closeness to Shirley that, to quote Thomas Hutchinson's *History of Massachusets-Bay*, the governor had "encouraged, if not promised him that, upon a vacancy in the superior court, he should have a seat there."[3] It was upon this that Otis was now pinning his hopes of a permanent place among the province élite.

2. "King's Governors . . . grant all commissions in the militia, which gives the Governors a great influence; people in the Plantations are readily bribed by distinguishing titles": W. Douglass, *A Summary History . . . of the British Settlements in North-America* I (London, 1755), 472.

3. Page 63.

The colonel was showing quite remarkable persistence, for he had already missed out once at the hands of Shirley himself. "A vacancy happened," Hutchinson's *History* records, "and Mr Shirley, from a prior engagement, or for some other reason, disappointed him."[4] The vacancy occurred in September 1756, when Judge Richard Saltonstall fell mortally sick. The preferred appointee was Peter Oliver, a well-heeled ironmaster, farmer, judge of the Plymouth court of common pleas, and Shirleian adherent. Years afterward, in loyalist exile in England, Oliver wrote up the history of revolutionary Massachusetts as he himself had experienced it. In this vigorous polemic Oliver told of Colonel Otis in 1760 "pleading . . . repeated Promises of a former Governor."[5] It could be, then, that when he gave Oliver the judgeship Governor Shirley had excused himself to Otis with assurances of better luck next time. If so the colonel perhaps should have known better than to take him seriously: Shirley was on the point of embarking for England, under notice to quit, and in no position to make good his word.[6] It is conceivable that the governor immediately following, Thomas Pownall, who became friendly with James Otis junior, would have appointed Colonel Otis if a vacancy had occurred in his short governorship; and Pownall may have said

4. *Ibid.*
5. D. Adair and J. A. Schutz, eds., *Peter Oliver's Origin and Progress of the American Rebellion: A Tory View* (Stanford, 1961), 27.
   Oliver, though on the Superior Court bench at the 1761 writs of assistance hearings, says nothing on the subject. However, on page 52 he tells how in 1765

> Seizure had been made by breaking open a Store, agreeable to act of Parliament; it was contested in the supreme Court, where Mr. *Hutchinson* praesided. The Seizure was adjudged legal by the whole Court.
> This raised Resentment against the Judges. Mr. *Hutchinson* was the only Judge who resided in *Boston*, & he only, of the Judges, was the Victim; for in a short Time after, the Mob of *Otis* & his clients plundered Mr. *Hutchinsons* House of its full Contents, destroyed his Papers, unroofed his House . . . .

The present writer has discovered nothing corroborative of Oliver's story of a search-seizure case in the Superior Court in 1765. It could well be a confused reference to the writs of assistance case, regard being had to Chief Justice Hutchinson's unpopularity on this account (see, *e.g.*, p. 437 below) and to contemporary opinion ascribing the destruction of his house in the Stamp Act disturbance to his championship of the writ of assistance.
6. However, Otis may well not have realized that Shirley was going for good. On 9 August 1756 his son James wrote him from Boston that Shirley was "like to remain Govr as long as he pleaseth": Otis Papers I (New York: Butler Library, Columbia University). And see BWNL 23 September 1756, where the terms on which Shirley and the Boston merchants exchanged good wishes on his embarkation strongly indicate that Shirley had not let it be known that his departure was final. (Departure as governor, that is: years later he was to return to Boston to spend his retirement.) This lack of openness perhaps connects in some way with Shirley's curious dilatoriness in removing himself, observed in chapter 10, n. 11.

something which kept the colonel's hopes alive. How far the colonel was entitled to stretch his expectations to obligate not only the next governor after Shirley, but the next but one, is hard to say.[7]

The way things went wrong for Colonel Otis at the end of the Shirley administration is illuminated by an unhappy note that he jotted down a few months later. Thomas Hutchinson, it had been reported to him, "had said that I never Did Carry things . . . By any merit But only By Doing Little Low Dirty things for Governor Shirley such as Persons of worth Refused to medle with and that Shirley made use of me only as a Tool . . . ."[8] This was written in the wake of another failed ambition: election to the province council. But it might also have given the colonel another perspective on his let-down over the 1756 vacancy on the Superior Court; when the vacancy happened Governor Shirley was at the end of his time, and must have known full well that his old henchman could be of no further service to him.

Hearing of Thomas Hutchinson's disdainful utterances must have been all the more bitter for the reason that in the old days Otis had worked closely with him in Shirley's political camp. Indeed, when Hutchinson lost his seat in the House of Representatives for his part in an unpopular currency reform in 1748-49, it had been largely through Otis's political management that he obtained a place in the Council instead.[9] Nor was it only Hutchinson who had turned against him. The brothers Oliver, Andrew and Peter, also had been fellow-laborers with him in the Shirleian vineyard. But, again according to the unflattering report that Otis noted down, Andrew Oliver — who in 1756 had become secretary of the province — as well as Hutchinson "had a Bad opinion of my Conduct." Still more gall: Peter Oliver had not scrupled to accept the Superior Court judgeship that would have placed Colonel Otis once and for all in the establishment top drawer.

The aspirant's situation on the next Superior Court vacancy can be

---

7. John Adams believed that both Shirley and Pownall had promised Colonel Otis a Superior Court judgeship; also, however, that "Bernard was not bound by the promises of Shirley and Pownall": *LWJA* X, 183-84. Note too the plural in Hutchinson's relating of "the promise . . . in former administrations", at p. 216 below.

8. Otis Papers I (n. 6 above), cited in J. J. Waters and J. A. Schutz, "Patterns of Massachusetts Colonial Politics; The Writs of Assistance and the Rivalry between the Otis and Hutchinson Families," *William and Mary Quarterly* (1967): 555; and in J. J. Waters, *The Otis Family in Provincial and Revolutionary Massachusetts* (Chapel Hill, 1968), 105.

9. Waters and Schutz, *op. cit.*, 549-51.

gauged from Peter Oliver's *Origin and Progress of the American Rebellion,* quoted briefly a few paragraphs back:

> Towards the latter End of the Year 1760, *Stephen Sewall,* Esqr., Chief Justice of the Province of *Massachusetts Bay,* died. As there are generally Candidates for such Posts, so one in particular vizt. *James Otis Esqr.* claimed the Palm; pleading the Merit of Age, long Practice at the Bar, & repeated Promises of a former Governor. Mr. *Otis* was one, who in the early Part of his Life, was by Trade a Cordwainer. But as the People of the Province seem to be born with litigious Constitutions, so he had Shrewdness enough to take Advantage of the general Foible, & work'd himself into a Pettifogger; which Profession he practised in, to the End of his Life. He had a certain Adroitness to captivate the Ear of Country Jurors, who were too commonly Drovers, Horse Jockies, & of other Lower Classes in Life. He also, for many Years, had been a Member of the lower House of Assembly, too great an Ingredient of which Composition consisted of Innkeepers, Retailers, & yet more inferior Orders of Men. These he had a great Command of, & he ever took Care to mix the Chicane of the Lawyer with the busy Importance of the Assembly Man; by which Methods he acquired a considerable Fortune. Thus circumstanced, he put in his Claim to a Seat upon the Bench . . . .

In fact, the "Palm" that Colonel Otis claimed was not the chief justiceship but the puisne judgeship which would become vacant if, as he expected, one of the surviving judges was promoted. And it also has to be said that Oliver's monograph, written as it was in 1781 (the year of lost hope for loyalists), made little pretense to historical objectivity; though not without engaging touches of the humor characteristic of its author, it was for the most part a rollicking denunciation of "New England perfidy" and the politicians principally responsible. Oliver himself had been through the mill of revolutionary hostility, and no doubt his judgment was coarsened by disagreeable personal memories.[10] But his latter-day ruderies about Colonel Otis may have mirrored contemporary establishment opinion faithfully enough. Certainly they accorded with the disparaging assessment the colonel had smarted under in 1757.

10. One of them might have been of a letter which Colonel Otis had addressed to him, 18 August 1772: "Sir: I cant be Easy in my own mind to Let the Obligation I have against you & Jeremiah Gridley Decsd for Two Hundred Pounds Lawfull Money (wherein you were bound Joyntly & Severally) Ley any Longer unsettled I have spoke to you Sundry Times about it But have been Put off as I think in a slightly Manner . . . ." Otis wanted only an "Equitable" settlement; "and if nothing else will Induce you to one Gratitude ought all Circumstances considered . . .": Otis Papers II (n. 6 above). He cannot be thought impatient; the debt presumably went back to a partnership between Oliver and Jeremiah Gridley (a leading performer in the writs of assistance case — see, in particular, chapter 13) in an iron works at Middleboro. The partnership had been dissolved in 1758. (Gridley died in 1767.)

Oliver made plain his view that however popular Colonel Otis might be with the ragtag and bobtail, persons of quality had no time for him. These, from a belief "that Integrity was an essential Qualification of a Judge, expressed a jealous Fear of such an Appointment; the surviving Judges of the Bench also, not willing to have an Associate of such a Character to seat with them, applied to Mr. Bernard . . . asking the Favor to have such a Colleague with them, that the Harmony of the Bench might not be interrupted . . . ." Colonel Otis's hopes of a seat on the Superior Court in 1760 were, if anything, even less realistic than in 1756.

The morning after Chief Justice Stephen Sewall's death, Thomas Hutchinson recorded in his diary, "Mr Gridley, the first lawyer at the Bar met the Lt. Gov. . . . in the street, and said to him he must be the successor. This was unexpected, but it caused the Lt. Gov. to think seriously upon it, for it was an employment which nothing but a diffidence of his qualification for it would render unwelcome to him."[11] As in his *History* so in his diary, Hutchinson was given to cloaking his own identity in the third person. The lieutenant governor to whom Jeremiah Gridley paid this remarkable compliment was Hutchinson himself.

His elevated rank notwithstanding, Hutchinson had not been doing well lately. The Pownall administration, from August of 1757 to three months ago, had seen him in political eclipse. He had made the acquaintance of Pownall at the Albany conference in 1754, himself long established as a leading man of affairs in Massachusetts and Pownall as the thirty-two-year-old secretary to the governor of New York. Evidence that Hutchinson had hopes of the Massachusetts governorship after the departure of William Shirley in 1756 suggests that he was not best pleased to learn that Pownall (now lieutenant governor of New Jersey), visiting England in that year, had landed it for himself.[12] However, Massachusetts was also without a lieutenant governor, the aged Spencer Phips having died. In 1758, soon after his own installation, Governor Pownall bestowed the post on Hutchinson. Neither man gained much continuing satisfaction from the appointment. The situation under Pownall was pictured in one of the

11. P. O. Hutchinson, ed., *Diary and Letters of Thomas Hutchinson* I (London, 1883), 65.

12. See M. Freiberg, "How to become a Colonial Governor" (reference chapter 7 above, n. 5); and *cf.* chapter 9, n. 2 above.

lampoons so much in vogue at this time: *Proposals for Printing by Subscription the History of the Publick Life and distinguished Actions of Vice-Admiral Sir Thomas Brazen, Commander of an American Squadron in the last Age* .... This rumbustious critique of Pownall spoke of how "Sir Thomas Brazen,"[13] as he was dubbed, "us'd to creep out on the main deck disguis'd, and talk with the *Sentries* and other common people about ship-affairs .... How he countenanced and distinguished the dirtiest, most lubberly, mutinous, and despised part of the people — avoiding, as much as possible the company and conversation of the second in command." It is not hard to envision a governor with populist impulses finding himself at a distance from a lieutenant governor whose effectual hostility to depreciating paper currency had not been to the interest of the debtor class. And perhaps an incompatibility of style and temperament worked against comfortable rapport between Governor Pownall and Lieutenant Governor Hutchinson. Hutchinson was a model of decorum in demeanor and address. "Brazen," on the other hand, "used to go sculling about the yard, from ship to ship himself ... unconscious neglect of ceremony and character in some things ... often tripping it about on the main deck in *frock* and trowsers, and *little rattan switch* ...."[14] It seems that as time passed Hutchinson moved more and more toward the periphery of politics, and let Pownall get on with it. "I have no Schemes in Politicks," he wrote in 1758, "but am of the same Principles in Civil Affairs that the Quietists are in Religious matters ...."[15] By 1759, a year in which Pownall lost valuable political support by death and electoral failure, Hutchinson was contemplating overt opposition; and it may be that Pownall, who had become much at odds with the British military, suspected him of stirring up trouble in that influential quarter. At one stage, when William Bollan seemed on the brink of dismissal from the province agency in London, Pownall asked Hutchinson to

---

13. *Cf.* chapter 9, n. 30.

14. Pownall was not one of the boys at all times, however. "A few Days ago a Gentleman was standing on the Stairs going to the Council Chamber, to speak with some Body: and the Governor was coming down: But the Gentleman, not knowing Him, did not pull off his Hat to Him: wherefore he, the Governor, it is said, gave him a good Box in the Ear which struck off his Hat": letter from Samuel Mather to Samuel Mather junior, 26 April 1760, in Mr. Malcolm Freiberg's introduction to the MHS edition of the Journals of the House of Representatives 1760-61.

15. To Israel Williams, 17 July 1758: MHS, Williams Papers II. Writing to Williams, 5 June 1758, *ibid.*, Hutchinson said he had "a good many times wished the Commission in some other hands ...."

take the job (which would have been a way of getting rid of him). But Hutchinson stayed and bided his time, perhaps sensing that this raffish and offbeat character, whom the military did not think well of, would not last long.[16]

The weeks between Thomas Pownall's departure and Francis Bernard's arrival would have had a bittersweet quality for Hutchinson. As acting governor he had a brief taste of what might have been. But the moment the new governor set foot in the province the pleasures of being top man and of doing all that satisfying work instantly dissolved, and Hutchinson was at a comparatively loose end again. It is important to remember that the lieutenant governorship was a non-job most of the time. The post amounted to little more than its name implied: when the governor was absent from the province the lieutenant governor took his place. In normal circumstances it was purely titular. Hutchinson was not entirely without active employment, it is true. He held an appointment that carried responsibilities for the military establishment at Castle William. He was a member of the province Council. Though he had given up his common pleas judgeship at the time of his appointment as lieutenant governor he retained the probate judgeship of Suffolk County. And if past experience was anything to go by, there would be the occasional special job that the government wanted doing. (The province accounts show him as having been paid amounts of £80 for "important" or "extraordinary" services.)[17] But there was not enough in all of this to keep a man like Hutchinson busy. He had handed over his business affairs to his sons; and, wifeless, he did not have much by way of domestic commitment to occupy him. No doubt his scholarly interests helped fill the time, but these were no more than a hobby. Especially with the uncongenial Pownall gone there clearly was more to life for a man of Hutchinson's energy and capacities than cultivation of his garden.

It is not surprising, then, that Hutchinson felt some quickening of

16. Sir William Pepperell and Samuel Waldo both died suddenly in 1759; and Pownall was "unable to keep [Thomas]Hancock in the Council . . . he failed to make the elder Otis a councillor while the Hutchinson faction had the votes to nominate Peter Oliver and Chambers Russell as councillors": Waters and Schutz, *op. cit.* (n. 8 above), 557. To Israel Williams, 10 February 1759 Hutchinson spoke of opposing the governor; also of Pownall's request that he become agent: Williams Papers I. For Pownall and the military *cf.* chapter 9, n. 33.

17. CO5/854, where it also appears that Hutchinson was paid £500 for his acting governorship. (Emoluments of the governor and lieutenant governor were tax-exempt: *cf* Hutchinson to Lord Hillsborough, 20 December 1769, in CO5/759.)

interest when Jeremiah Gridley suggested him as the new chief justice. Quite aside from its prestige, the office offered work of as high a quality as anyone could wish, and plenty of it. But here one remembers Hutchinson's hesitation. The duties of the office might be too much for a man who was not a lawyer by training. Of course, lay judges were nothing uncommon in colonial America. Three of the four surviving Superior Court judges — John Cushing, Chambers Russell, and Peter Oliver — were cases in point. (Benjamin Lynde, whose father had been chief justice, had had some systematic tuition in legal studies.) Hutchinson was by no means without experience as a judge. There was his probate judgeship, and formerly his common pleas judgeship. He had even sat on the Superior Court as a "special justice" when one of the regular judges was absent.[18]   But what held good for run-of-the-mill judgeships did not necessarily hold good for the highest judicial appointment of them all. Chief Justice Sewall had been a legal scholar before going on the Superior Court bench. His predecessor, Paul Dudley, had studied at the Inns of Court in London; likewise the chief justice before Dudley, Benjamin Lynde senior. Tradition thus suggested that the chief justice, the head of the province judiciary, should be a person learned in the law. So, attracted to the post though he was, Hutchinson really would have been a bit of a fool if he had not felt some misgiving about his fitness for it. Besides, others might see it the same way. Instant positive response to Gridley's flattering overture could appear presumptuous; and Hutchinson had suffered too much mortification under Governor Pownall to court a snub from Governor Bernard.

Hutchinson's will to action was still in suspense at the end of September. Andrew Oliver, secretary of the province, wrote to Israel Williams, a frontier magnate and a close friend of Hutchinson:

> The Death of the late Chief Justice is a very great Loss to the Public. I am intirely in sentiment with you as to supplying the Vacancy . . . . If his Excellency & the Lieut. Governor were to confer together on the Subject the matter might be accomodated. The Lieut. Govr is so diffident of his own fitness, that if he could be brought to accept of the place yet I am persuaded he would never move in it. And on the other hand it might be a difficulty with the Governor to bestow it unasked, and pass by those who

18. MA Council Records 12: "His Excellency nominated Thomas Hutchinson Esq to be a Special Justice of the Superior Court of Judicature in the Cause depending between William Vassall & William Fletcher in the Room of John Cushing Esq. To which Nomination the Council advised and Consented" (21 February 1755). *Cf.* chapter 6, n. 47.

have applied for it. But as the Govr does not appear to be in a hurry about the Affair, I can't but hope it will turn out right at last.[19]

To the extent that Hutchinson for all his genuine diffidence nevertheless hankered for the chief justiceship and adopted a tactic toward it, the tactic consisted in leaving others to move on his behalf. (Part of it seems to have been to avoid actually asking Governor Bernard for the appointment while there was still a possibility of a humiliating refusal.) Hutchinson was well enough placed in this regard. Among the first to mention him as a candidate had been the doyen of the Boston bar, Jeremiah Gridley; and the secretary of the province, Andrew Oliver, together with the politically substantial Israel Williams, also was beating the drum for him. Another powerful advocate in the Hutchinson cause was the attorney general, Edmund Trowbridge.[20] Also rooting for Hutchinson were no lesser personages than Superior Court judges themselves.

His *History of Massachusets-Bay* relates: "Upon the death of the chief justice, the first surviving judge, and two other judges, together with several principal gentlemen of the bar, signified their desire to the governor, that he would appoint the lieutenant-governor to be the successor."[21] (The one Superior Court judge who did not join in may have been John Cushing — not the most outgiving of men, it would seem from what John Adams said of him[22] — who, as next senior judge to Benjamin Lynde, perhaps considered himself best entitled to the chief justiceship if Lynde did not want it.) Nor is this on Hutchinson's word alone. Peter Oliver's *Origin and Progress of the American Rebellion* followed up its account of the judges' representations to Governor Bernard against the candidacy of Colonel James Otis by telling how they "accordingly proposed Mr. *Hutchinson* . . . ." Bernard, Oliver went on, "most readily acquiesced, & had already, before requested, determined on the Appointment." But not even the judges could persuade Hutchinson to declare himself. "Mr. *Hutchinson* was also applied to, by the Judges, to take a Seat with them," Oliver said, "but he refused, 'till he could be informed of the general Sentiment . . . ."

It would seem from Peter Oliver's account that the judges' spon-

19. 30 September 1760: Williams Papers I.
20. See pp. 225-26, 509-10 below.
21. Page 63.
22. "Cushing has the sly, artful, cunning — Artiface and Cunning is the reigning Characteristic in his face. The sly Sneer . . .": *DAJA* I, 335-36.

sorship of Hutchinson did no more than confirm Bernard in a decision he was already resolved upon. Hutchinson's unwillingness to move precipitately or prematurely worked out well. That in the end he acquiesced in the governor's insistence upon a formal application he nowhere wholly denies; but even then Bernard came quite a way to meet him. "A month had passed," Hutchinson recorded in his diary, "when the Govr observed to one of the Lt. Govrs friends, that many people had pressed him to appoint the Lt. Gov. Chief Justice, but he had never said a word about it himself. This caused the Lt. Gov. to say to the Gov. that he had been silent because he wished to leave the Governor free to do what appeared to him most proper and not from disdain of asking any favour."[23] In his *History* Hutchinson put it thus:

> Several weeks elapsed, before any nomination was made, or any thing had passed between the governor and lieutenant-governor, upon the subject. At length it was intimated to the lieutenant-governor, that the governor, when he had been applied to by many persons in his behalf, was at a loss to account for his silence upon the subject. This caused a conversation, in which the lieutenant-governor signified that he had desired no persons to apply in his behalf, and had avoided applying himself, that the governor might the more freely use his own judgment, in appointing such person as should appear to him most fit.

A third Hutchinson account adds a fragment more:

> A month or more had passed before I had any conversation with the Governor upon the subject: I then told His Excellency I had designedly avoided saying any thing to him concerning it; I knew the importance of the trust, I knew the peculiar disadvantages I should be under, as I should succeed a gentleman of such distinguished merit, whose virtures had been so conspicuous. The Governor was pleased to say that the major voice seemed to be in my favour, that he had not determined upon the person, and that after full consideration he would do what he should think most agreeable to the people of the Province, and most for their interest.[24]

According to Hutchinson's *History* it was "soon after" that he was told that the chief justiceship was indeed to be his; but he can have been in no real doubt of Bernard's intentions before he at last approached the governor and, however obliquely, made due submission for the job.

23. *Diary and Letters* I, 65.
24. *Massachusetts Gazette and Boston News-Letter* 7 April 1763.

Meanwhile a storm was brewing. Hutchinson's stalling over the chief justiceship may have proved a good way of getting it, but the ambiguity of his position was not all advantage. Whatever the satisfaction over his appointment in some quarters, to the thwarted Colonel Otis of Barnstable it stank of betrayal and bad faith. And more significantly for the course of history, the colonel's eldest son, James Otis junior, also smarted under the supposed Hutchinsonian double-cross.

What happened has to be pieced together from various sources, but the substance of it is in an exchange of newspaper articles between James Otis junior and Thomas Hutchinson some two and a half years afterward, in April 1763. It is relevant to explain how this newspaper duel came about. Whereas at the beginning of the decade Otis had little or no part in public affairs, by 1763 he had become the province's leading anti-establishment activist. Politics of Otis's virulence naturally brought him enemies, and it was freely put about that his onslaught on the Bernard administration and its adherents was motivated not by principle or genuine conviction but by personal bitterness over his father's disappointment in 1760. A supporting tale that gained much currency was that at this time Otis had "declared publickly, with oaths, that if his father was not appointed Judge, he would set the whole Province in a flame, tho' he perished in the attempt."[25] In the spring of 1763 Otis felt driven to try to scotch these damaging calumnies. Accordingly, in the *Boston Gazette* for 4 April 1763 he related the events of 1760 as he knew them and had participated in them. This piece, which touched unpleasantly upon the man who did get the Superior Court appointment, Thomas Hutchinson, drew a reply from him in the *Massachusetts Gazette and Boston News-Letter* for 7 April. Otis rounded off the exchange with another piece in the *Gazette* for 11 April. These circumstantial accounts by Otis and Hutchinson supply most of the material for what follows.

James Otis junior, himself a barrister and resident in Boston, was visiting his father at Barnstable when the news of Chief Justice Sewall's death encouraged the colonel to hope once again for a seat on the Superior Court. Colonel Otis wrote two letters, one to Thomas Hutchinson and the other to Andrew Oliver, asking them, as

25. This version was by Governor Bernard (to Board of Trade, 22 December 1766: C05/756).

his political colleagues of a bygone time, to put in a word for him with Governor Bernard. James Otis junior was to deliver the letters on his return to Boston. "These Letters I bro't to Town over Night," recalled Otis junior, "but before I had Opportunity to deliver them, I heard that it was a settled Point that his Honor [Hutchinson] was to be Chief Justice." Nevertheless, "I waited upon him . . . next Morning, and communicated the Substance of the Letter to him, . . . telling him that if he was determined to accept the Office of Chief Justice it would be needless to leave the Letter, and in vain to expect his Honor's Assistance." Here now was where misunderstanding came in. "Upon which," Otis continued, "he assured me he had no Thoughts or Desire of the Office, told me that some of his Friends had indeed mentioned such a Thing to him, but he had already Engagements enough upon his Hands, expressly declared he tho't Col *Otis* had the best Pretensions to be Judge of that Court, promised his Interest, and took the Letter . . . ." On this basis, as he supposed it to be, Otis went off to deliver the letter for Andrew Oliver, who gave him "much the same Encouragement." Oliver counseled him to call upon Charles Paxton also. "I confess I was a little surprized at this, wondering what Influence that Gentleman could have in an Affair of that Importance." (Oliver presumably had in mind that Paxton was already well in with Governor Bernard on account of their common interest in the profits of customs forfeitures, and that Otis had a family connection with Paxton.)[26] Anyway, Otis did go and see Paxton, who "paid my Father a great many Compliments, and promised his Interest, assuring me that he had not the least Reason to think his Honor had made any Interest to be Chief Justice, and finally advised me to wait on his Excellency, telling me that the Governor was determined not to fill the Vacancy in Favor of his Honor or any other Gentleman, without a personal Application."

26. Otis was married to Ruth Cunningham, stepdaughter of Paxton's sister: *cf.* p. 313. In chapter 6, n. 39, it was suggested that the Cunningham connection may have helped ease merchant pressure against Paxton (and the vice-admiralty court) in the 1730s. Paxton perhaps found it a shield against Otis also. In his *BG* article 11 April 1763 Otis referred to the merchants' 1760-61 campaign against Paxton's questionabe fees (*Province v. Paxton*: chapter 9 above, and *passim*), "in which, by reason of my old acquaintance with Mr. Paxton, I would not engage until I had his express consent and advice on it, however angry he grew against me afterwards . . . ." One wonders too whether Otis's sworn disclaimer of authorship of the "Charles Froth" lampoon in *BG* 2 March 1761 (see pp. 173-74 above and 391 below) may not have been motivated, in part, by family considerations (if not a sharp word from his wife, who — no Abigail Adams — seems to have had little time for his politicking).

This advice was sound, for Governor Bernard did indeed expect candidates for the Superior Court bench to come forward and make personal application to him. However, Colonel Otis was slow. Not until "about six Weeks after, in the ordinary Course of his Business," did he come up to Boston from Barnstable and present himself to the governor. It was hopelessly late. His chances of success had never been good, and through delay he had reduced them to nothing. By now Thomas Hutchinson had at last put in his bid for the chief justiceship, and, apparently, Bernard had told him that he would be appointed. Bernard thus had the perfect answer to Colonel Otis: the chief justiceship had already been filled, and there was no vacancy. The colonel did not take it well, declaring, as Bernard later recounted, "that if [Hutchinson] was appointed, we should both repent it."[27] Bernard sought to deflect some of the colonel's wrath, by saying to him — according to James Otis junior — "that he might be appointed as the youngest Judge of the Superior Court if the Lieutenant Governor would relinquish his Pretensions." The colonel went to see Hutchinson, and found him "extremely fond of the Place of Chief Justice, and set upon having it." It is perhaps to be supposed that the object of the colonel's visit was not so much to persuade Hutchinson to step down as to give him a verbal roasting. At all events Governor Bernard tells of Hutchinson as well as himself having been warned by the colonel that if the Hutchinson appointment went through they would both repent it.[28]

What upset the Otises as much as anything was Hutchinson's lack of straightforwardness when James Otis junior delivered the colonel's letter asking for help toward the expected vacancy. Otis junior had taken leave of Hutchinson with, as he believed, a promise of support and an assurance that the rumor that Hutchinson himself was to become chief justice (so precluding the vacancy for a puisne judgeship) was without foundation. Asked Otis:

Should he have accepted or even solicited the Place for himself, when he had promised to give his Interest in Favour of another? Should he have promised that Interest to his Friend, and kept him in Dependence upon it after he had determined to use it for himself? If his Honor forgot his Promise, nay suppose it is certain he never made any, as certain as I am that he did; surely he can't have forgot that he took the Letter, which alone but especially with his Declaration of his having no Tho'ts of the

27. In the letter at n. 25 above.
28. *Ibid.*

Place etc, would seem to imply a Promise. I grant his Honor had a Right to change his Mind upon what he tho't good Reasons, and if it appeared to him either from the flattery of his Friends, or his Opinion of his own Importance, that the Superior Court could not be tolerably filled by any Gentleman from the Barr, or elsewhere, without he would condescend to take upon him the Office of Chief Justice, in addition to the Rest of his lucrative Places, he is highly to be praised for his disinterested Benevolence to an otherwise sinking Province. But then it would have been but consentaneous . . . if he had sooner intimated this Change of Sentiments to his old Friend, that he might either chearfully have given up his own personal Advantage for the good of the Commonwealth, or have sought to other Friends to support his Pretensions.

To which sarcastic recriminations Hutchinson addressed himself in the *Massachusetts Gazette*:

The next day after the death of the late Chief Justice several gentlemen spake to me and told me they hoped the Governor would nominate me for his successor. It was some surprize to me, and I answered them in no other way than by thanking them for their favourable opinion of me, and expressing a diffidence of my own abilities. I was not determined in my own mind that it would be adviseable for me to undertake so great a trust; nor did I know the Governor's mind concerning it. Before the Chief Justice was buried Mr OTIS came to be with a letter from his father desiring me, whom he had always looked upon as his friend, to use my interest with the Governor that he might be one of the Justices of the Superior Court. While I was reading the letter Mr OTIS said to me, that he had heard one proposed for the place of Chief Justice, and if I had any thoughts of it, neither he nor his father had a word more to say, no person in the Province would be more agreeable to them; but if I had not, he thought his father had a better pretence to a place in the Court than anybody else, having been longer at the bar than any other gentlemen and having had the promise of the place in former administrations, to which facts I was knowing. I told Mr OTIS the proposal to me was new and what I had not time to consider of, and expressed my doubts of my abilities to give the Country satisfaction. I said many civil things of his father, as I had done before and have since, and of the friendship there had been between us; but I must deny that I gave him any reason to suppose that I was determined to refuse the place; or that I promised to use my interest with the Governor that his father should be appointed.

As for the failure to answer Colonel Otis's letter:

A few days after I received it I was informed by Gentlemen of undoubted veracity, that Mr OTIS the Son had declared that neither he nor his father would give up their pretensions to the Lieutenant Governor nor any other person, that he uttered many revengeful threats; particularly, that he would do all the mischief he could to the Government, and would set the

Province in a flame, &c. if his father should not be appointed (the town was full of the talk of it) and I soon after had reason to suspect that these threats were carrying into execution. Under these circumstances I thought it most prudent to say nothing to Mr OTIS or his father upon the subject.

James Otis did not fail to make plain in his counterblast that Hutchinson's reason for not replying to Colonel Otis's letter left out some of the facts. The reason as stated was that within a few days of receiving the letter Hutchinson heard that Otis junior, "uttering many revengeful threats," had declared that his father would not give up his "pretensions" in favor of Hutchinson or anyone else. From the way Hutchinson had put it the reader might get the impression that almost immediately after his interview with Hutchinson Otis junior proclaimed open rivalry between Colonel Otis and Hutchinson, and that his own professed belief that Hutchinson had agreed to support the colonel was just so much eyewash. Otis now sought to put the record straight. His making it known that his father was still in the field had been occasioned by rumors that the colonel had given up.

What seems to have happened is that, just as Otis himself had wrongly interpreted Hutchinson's expressions of hesitation and diffidence as signifying noncandidacy for the chief justiceship, so Hutchinson — or perhaps Andrew Oliver or Charles Paxton, whom also Otis had called upon — had read too much into Otis's assurances that the colonel would not give the judgeship another thought if Hutchinson were running. It could well be that Otis's suspicions about Hutchinsonian maneuverings against his father began only a few days after the interview. Having had his meetings with Hutchinson, Oliver, and Paxton, he next made to call upon Governor Bernard. Riding horseback toward Castle William (some distance out of Boston, where the governor was in residence) one afternoon he was overtaken by a coach with Hutchinson and Paxton in it. Before reaching the castle he met them coming back, the governor accompanying them. With rumors of Hutchinson becoming chief justice still persisting Otis may have put two and two together. Certainly in retrospect he saw this meeting between the governor and Hutchinson as the occasion when the chief justiceship issue was settled. (Hutchinson flatly denied this in his *Massachusetts Gazette* piece; and on the evidence already considered it does seem most unlikely that Hutchinson was at this stage — mid-September — ready to declare his candidacy.) However that may have been, James Otis affirmed that in no more than a fortnight after his interview with Hutchinson he heard that "the Governor had been persuaded that Colonel Otis had given up his pretensions." Whether or not Otis had already formed suspicions of a Hutchinson candidacy he could scarcely fail to have them now; and he made off to see Governor Bernard — this time successfully — to tell him that the report of the colonel having withdrawn was false "and that the only colour for such a story was, my having said to the Lieutenant Governor and Secretary, that I believed his Honor would be more agreeable to Col. Otis than any man, if his own pretensions were rejected."[29]

Nor was James Otis willing to pass unchallenged that other element in Hutchinson's excuse for not replying to Colonel Otis's letter, namely, that "Mr OTIS the son . . . uttered many revengeful threats; particularly, that he would do all the mischief he could to the Government, and would set the Province in a flame, &c. if his father should not be appointed, (the town was full of the talk of it) . . . ." Most probably, indeed, this allusion was of special offense to Otis, since the object of his breaking into print in the first place had been to disclaim every such thing: "As it has been very industriously reported in the House of Representatives, as well as abroad," he protested in the *Boston Gazette* for 4 April 1763, "that upon the Lieutenant Governor's being appointed Chief Justice, I threatened to *set the Province in a Flame*; I think myself obliged in my own Vindication thus publickly to declare, that I have not the least Remembrance of having used such Expressions in my Life; nor do I believe I ever did." That Hutchinson should have replied by giving still further currency to the story must have been — and perhaps was intended to be — all the more infuriating to Otis. However, in his comeback on 11 April it was not to his purpose merely to repeat the

29. This interview with the governor took place, Otis's 11 April article indicates, somewhat more than a fortnight after he saw Hutchinson. Presumably, it also served to make up for the abortive attempt to see the governor "the Monday after Judge SEWALL's death" (when Otis met Bernard coming away from Castle William in the company of Hutchinson and Paxton: BG 11 April 1763).

There seems no evidence or reason to suppose that the meeting was at all explosive. These were early days (probably in September still); whatever suspicions of a Hutchinson candidacy Otis junior might already have formed and were voicing abroad, in the nature of the situation he had not abandoned hope for his father and would hardly have been so foolish as to imperil it by offending the governor to his face.

On page 43 of his *Life of Sir Francis Bernard* . . . (London, 1790), Thomas Bernard confuses his father's preliminary interview with Otis junior and the later interview with Colonel Otis, when, upon the colonel being told of Hutchinson's appointment, hard things were indeed said. (According to Governor Bernard, anyway: letter to Board of Trade, 22 December 1766: C05/756.)

disavowal of the week before. The object now was to disprove Hutchinson's stated reason for not replying to the colonel's letter, that because of Otis junior's "revengeful threats," it was "most prudent to say nothing." The story about setting the province aflame, said Otis in effect, did not get around until long after his waiting upon Hutchinson with the letter. That was early in September, but this "most cruel and inhuman charge . . . was never tho't of till the late prosecution of some of the officers of the admiralty set on foot by a number of worthy merchants . . . ." The reference obviously was to *Province v. Paxton,* which took its rise in December (and in which Otis had been prominent as counsel).[30]

Whatever the exact truth of the matter, it is not likely that these protestations of Otis carried much conviction. The very fact that he engaged so energetically in the merchants' cause, and the further fact that he had resigned his post as acting advocate general, were clear evidence that something had happened which upset him badly; and it would have been more in character than not for the notoriously uninhibited man to have allowed himself some pretty free language at the first whisper of a Hutchinson candidacy. And contemporary Boston newspaper readers, schooled as they needed to be in the legalistic cast of controversialist writing, would have noticed that Otis did not categorically disown having threatened to set the province in a flame. He limited himself to saying that he could not remember using those words and that he did not believe he had done so. Probably he knew himself too well to be absolutely sure of what he might or might not have said — and promptly forgotten — in the heat of the moment.

It may have been somewhat the same with the interview with Thomas Hutchinson, except that the recollection of neither side can be confidently relied upon. One has only to picture the excruciating embarrassment of the scene. On the one side, Otis soliciting on behalf of his father the good offices of a man whom only three years previously the elder Otis had the bitterness to find a false friend — and who, he had just heard it rumored, was interested in a Superior Court appointment for himself.[31] On the other, Hutchinson, attracted

30. The *BEP* lampoon quoted at pp. 502-3 below may have some relevance to Otis's claim that talk of his threatening to set the province aflame did not begin till well after the Superior Court appointment was decided.

For another illustration of the persistence of the "flame" story see p. 509 below.

31. What made Colonel Otis swallow his pride may have been that Hutchinson — and Andrew Oliver, to whom also he applied for help — were the only persons able to testify to Governor Shirley's promise.

by the chief justiceship but not yet willing to declare himself (least of all to the likes of the Otises), forced to observe common politeness but silently cursing those flummoxing importunities of the roughneck colonel and his son. Obviously, the atmosphere of the interview could not have made either for clarity of statement or for perfect recollection of just what had been said. The substantial differences between the two participants' accounts do not mean that either man was deliberately lying: rather it was that both were so flustered by the tensions and artificialities of the occasion that amid all the murmured civilities and the ceremonious professions of esteem some of the ifs and buts got muffled and lost. Hutchinson was temperamentally a cooler customer than Otis, and perhaps his account wins by a nose; but one could not put it higher than that.[32]

In terms of plain dealing neither side comes out particularly well. Colonel Otis's ambition must have been pretty ripe for him to solicit the help of a man of whose disdain he was aware and resentful. Thomas Hutchinson, for all his understandable disinclination to show his hand, ought to have been able to manage the Otises with better grace and style. The failure to reply to the colonel's letter was perhaps made too much of in Otis junior's recriminations, but neither it nor the implausible excuse for it said much for Hutchinson's upper-crust pretensions.

How did Governor Francis Bernard stand in relation to the scuffling and jockeying?

Assuredly he took his time. It was not until 13 November 1760 — more than two months after the death of Chief Justice Sewall — that he formally nominated Thomas Hutchinson to the succession. Writing four days later to Lord Halifax, head of the Board of Trade, Bernard said that his "motives . . . for this proceeding" would be explained in a later letter "as this letter must soon go to the Post Office";[33] there is no sign of his ever having carried out this undertaking, however.

It could be that recent experience had engendered a certain cautiousness in Bernard. His last months in New Jersey had been vexed by rivalries for the chief justiceship there. (Only in March

---

32. And see B. Bailyn, *The Ordeal of Thomas Hutchinson* (Cambridge, Mass., 1974), 275-78, for a striking instance — an interview with George III in 1774 — of Hutchinson again being misunderstood for not speaking directly enough.

33. MA Council Records February 1759-May 1765; and Bernard Papers I.

HUTCHINSON AND THE OTISES

1760 he had written to Lord Halifax about this, "which I can't consider as a mere contest for an Office, but think it looks more like a Commencement of Hostilities against the Government".)[34] Despite Bernard's receptiveness toward Hutchinson as a candidate, and Peter Oliver's assertion that he had fixed upon Hutchinson even before the canvassing was complete, there is some reason to believe that his mind was not dogmatically closed to other possibilities and even that some other candidate might have been agreeable to him.

Common report had it that the polymath adjutant general, William Brattle, was an aspirant to the chief justiceship.[35] Governor Bernard would hardly have turned him down out of hand. He was a man of learning in the law, and he had sufficient private resources to supplement the meager pay. Above all, perhaps, Brattle's Pownallite associations might have rated in his favor with a governor who was aiming to ground his administration upon coalition and political harmony. But there was another side to Brattle. As the modern idiom might put it, he had personality problems. He was in fact a bit of an oddity. "I really think my far distant Kinsman to be a queer fellow," was Governor Jonathan Belcher's assessment of him.[36] And a man who had been called out in a tavern as "a Damned Villin," suffering his nose to be wrung in the process — even though it had been years ago[37] — was not ideal material for the province's highest court of law. Anyhow, it does seem that Brattle had hopes. "There is no question that after Hutchinson's appointment he plunged into politics with new vigor and headed the anti-government party in the Council . . . ."[38] And to the extent that personal disappointment over a Superior Court appointment contributed to Brattle's political opposition Governor Bernard may have had moments of repentance. This is suggested by an entry in John Adams's diary years later, in 1774: "Returned from Charlestown with Coll. Tyng of Dunstable who told me some Anecdotes of Bernard and Brattle, Otis, Hutchinson,

34. 31 March 1760, *ibid.*

35. C. K. Shipton, *Sibley's Harvard Graduates* VII (Boston, 1945), 17. *Cf.* p. 161 above.

36. *Ibid.,* 14.

37. *Ibid.,* 12. Brattle won £35 damages and costs: *Brattle v. Tidmarsh* (Suffolk, October 1734; SCR 1733-36).

38. Shipton, *op. cit.,* 17. Andrew Oliver's reference (p. 210 above) to it being difficult for the governor to give the chief justiceship to Hutchinson unasked "and pass by those who have applied for it" implies a plurality of candidates, which could have included Brattle. See also *DAJA* I, 168, n. 2, to 5 November 1760, citing Edmund Trowbridge to William Bollan, 15 July 1762; on Hutchinson's appointment Otis and Brattle were "very angry with him and every one else they knew or suspected had not favoured their Respective Claims."

&C. Bernard said 'he never thought of Pratt' — he would find a Place for him now upon that Bench. Brattle shall be Colonel and Brigadier, &c — Bernard said — Afterwards this Miff broke out into a Blaze."[39] Colonel Tyng of Dunstable was the Pownallite John Tyng who had fallen victim to the opposition in the election of 1760; and from the references to Bernard, Brattle, Otis, Hutchinson, a seat on the bench, and a miff that subsequently broke out into a blaze, it seems pretty clear that this anecdote harked back to the chief justiceship controversy of that same year. The "Pratt" whom Bernard said he had not thought of was Benjamin Prat, leading Boston barrister and former leader of the Pownallites, who had lost his seat in the House of Representatives and currently was out of public employment altogether. Of his ability to do the work as a chief justice there is no doubt, for in 1761 he was to be appointed — through the good offices of his former boss, Thomas Pownall, now in London — chief justice of New York. (In the course of his newspaper attack on Thomas Hutchinson in 1763 James Otis jibed at the pro-Hutchinson lobby which had seen Hutchinson as the only man fitted for the chief justiceship of Massachusetts, and drew attention to Prat.) But it is also possible to discern in the anecdote an inclination in Governor Bernard to propitiate William Brattle.

According to Hutchinson's *History*, after he had at last spoken to the governor for the chief justiceship, and apparently after Bernard had told him that it was his, "he gave his opinion, that a refusal to comply with the solicitations which had been made to the governor by the other person [Otis], would cause a strong opposition to his administration, and, at the same time, assured the governor, that he would not take amiss the compliance, but would support his administration with the same zeal as if he had been appointed himself." (A revealing sidelight on Hutchinson's political attitude to judicial office.) But Bernard would not have it: "The governor declared that, if the lieutenant-governor should finally refuse the place, the other person would not be nominated." "Thereupon," says Hutchinson in his *History*, and "soon after" in his diary, he himself was appointed. One wonders whether Hutchinson might not have been taken at his word if Bernard could have lighted upon a compromise candidate (more suitable than the eccentric Brattle) or had thought of Benjamin Prat.

It is not hard to see why Bernard was not going to appoint Colonel

Otis at any price. For one thing, there was the declared opposition of the Superior Court judges (as testified to by Judge Peter Oliver). For another, no governor with a shred of self-respect could appear as yielding to the threats of revenge that, publicly or in private, the Otises had been uttering. Quite aside from anything his fire-eating son may have said, and quite aside too from Bernard's view that "there was no ballancing between the candidates,"[40] Colonel Otis cooked his goose when he told the governor that if Hutchinson was appointed both of them would repent it. The governor may have sought to soften the rebuff by placatory words; but, his surface amiability notwithstanding, he could not be expected to respond submissively to that sort of talk.

To John Adams the American Revolution started "in the minds and hearts of the people" long before any military conflict broke out. It started in February 1761, when "the great cause of writs of assistance was argued before the supreme judicature of the province, in the council chamber in Boston." However, "this important question was tainted from the beginning with an odious and corrupt intrigue."[41] Here one takes up a thread in the Adams story of events left over from chapter 8. According to Adams, James Cockle, the newly appointed collector of customs at Salem, applied for a writ of assistance when the Superior Court was on circuit in that town in the fall of 1760; and it transpired that, although the aged former president (writing in the second decade of the nineteenth century) had not remembered every detail to perfection, his attribution of the origin of the writs of assistance case to this application by Cockle was right. Doubt as to the legal authenticity of the writs of assistance that the Superior Court had been authorizing since 1755 had been deepened by the appearance in the summer of 1760 of an article in the London Magazine strongly suggesting the inference that the writ in Massachusetts was materially at variance with current English practice. The hypothesis was ventured in chapter 8 that, disquieted by the London Magazine article and preferring not to commit themselves to a definitive position on it, the judges of the Superior Court — bereft of leadership by the death of Chief Justice Sewall — postponed Cockle's application for hearing in Boston. There they would have better facilities for study and consideration and any

40. Letter to Board of Trade, 22 December 1766: C05/756.
41. Letter to J. Morse, 29 November 1815: LWJA X 182-83.

necessary assistance from the bar. And by that time they could hope to have a new chief justice presiding over them. Governor Bernard, John Adams reminisced, "appointed Hutchinson, for the very purpose of deciding the fate of the writs of assistance, and all other causes in which the claims of Great Britain might be directly or indirectly implicated . . . ."[42] "Every observing and thinking man," Adams wrote again, "knew that this appointment was made for the direct purpose of deciding this question in favor of the crown, and all others in which it should be interested."[43] Here too there may well have been something in what Adams said.

Central to the situation was Bernard's chronic impecuniousness. Anything that might swell the emoluments of his office was of interest to the hard-pressed governor. The writ of assistance answered to this, of course. By means of it the customs organization was the better able to effect seizure of illicit importations which, having eluded interception on the waterfront, might otherwise remain safely stored away in a merchant's warehouse. The power of entry and search signified by a writ of assistance meant more seizures; and more seizures meant greater profit to the governor in the form of his statutory one-third share of the proceeds.

That Bernard soon got to know of the new-found precariousness of the writ of assistance caused by the *London Magazine* article is not attested by direct positive evidence, but it is all but certain just the same. Aside from the likelihood that his instant familiar in the Boston custom house, Charles Paxton, lost no time in telling him of this disquieting development, there is an even stronger probability that the recently appointed collector of customs at Salem talked it over with him. Bernard and Cockle happened to be old acquaintances. They had known each other in the English city of Lincoln (and in course of time their association in America became so close that when Cockle fell to be dismissed for corruption there was a real possibility that Bernard might also depart in disgrace). The relationship between the new governor and the new customs collector, begun as it was before either of them even set foot in America, makes it an entirely safe guess that Bernard was kept well in touch with the fate of Cockle's application for a writ of assistance.

It is not impossible, even, that Bernard, already having learnt of

---

42. *Ibid.*, 183.

43. To W. Tudor, 29 March 1817: *LWJA* X, 247. Nor was it in advanced old age that Adams first spoke in this way: *cf.* chapter 8, n. 18 above.

the *London Magazine* article and the doubts it had aroused (for example, in the mind of the late Chief Justice Sewall), actually prompted Cockle to try his luck with a writ of assistance when the surviving Superior Court judges called at Salem in the earlier part of October, and see how they reacted.[44] Be that too as it may: what matters is the proposition that, long before he decided upon the chief justice appointment, Governor Bernard was fully able to see a question mark on the future of the Massachusetts writ of assistance. What happened to the Cockle application at Salem can only have intensified the governor's fears. Presided over by the timid Benjamin Lynde ("little matters as well as great, frighten Lynde," Thomas Hutchinson once observed),[45] the four puisne judges had ducked a decision. Given the unpopularity of customs search, when they resumed in Boston these bemused haverers — who would still have the majority voice on the court — might all too easily opt for peace and quiet and a final negative to a general writ of assistance for Cockle. If that happened Paxton's and all the other extant writs of assistance could not but lapse into illegality at the same time. The governor's best chance of averting a turn of events so ominous in its various implications, not least for his own personal stake in the profits of customs seizure, lay in finding a new chief justice with sufficient character and will power to infuse into his doubting brethren a suitably robust and affirmative attitude toward the general writ of assistance.

Among those who urged the governor to appoint Thomas Hutchinson was the attorney general, Edmund Trowbridge. By reason both of his office and of his reputation as the most learned lawyer in the province, Trowbridge ranked naturally as one of Governor Bernard's leading advisers in the matter of the chief justiceship. Moreover, as the originating draftsman of the writ of assistance whose legal authenticity the *London Magazine* had now cast into doubt, he had a distinct concern in the outcome of the impending deliberations. A repudiation of his professional handiwork would be an uncomfortable experience, perhaps damaging to his ordinary law practice.

To develop another rumination: about Hutchinson's role in the

44. Thomas Hutchinson referred to Cockle as "the Governor's creature": *Diary and Letters* I, 67.

45. Letter 28 August 1770, quoted in E. Washburn, *Sketches of the Judicial History of Massachusetts* (Boston, 1840), 165. See also *MHSP* XLIV (1911), 524. It is conceivable that apprehensiveness over the writs of assistance issue influenced Lynde against seeking promotion to the chief justiceship (which he in fact got in 1771, after Hutchinson).

genesis of the Massachusetts writ of assistance back in 1755. What occasioned that piece of Trowbridgian virtuosity was Hutchinson challenging the legality of the customs search warrant currently in use under the signature of Governor Shirley. Might there not have been an element of liaison between Hutchinson and the attorney general behind that rather pat encounter with Charles Paxton at the Hutchinson warehouse? On first impression this hardly makes sense. What possible interest could Thomas Hutchinson have had in some convoluted design to improve the techniques of customs law enforcement? Especially if, as some people alleged, his family business was as deep as the rest in unlawful trade? Yet there could be another way of looking at it. It would have been entirely in character for Hutchinson to have lined up with that wing of Boston merchant opinion which, when a revitalized vice-admiralty condemnation jurisdiction in the early and middle 1750s had put an end to free and open violation of the British staple, decided on the one hand to play safe and on the other to protect the "fair trader" against undercutting competition from the less timorous by urging tough action on smuggling. In this perspective it becomes more credible that Hutchinson consciously set the scene for Attorney General Trowbridge's writ of assistance in 1755. So that, five years later, Trowbridge had reason for confidence that the prospective chief justice most likely to fight for the survival of the writ of assistance was his old collaborator, Thomas Hutchinson.

The thought may also have crossed Trowbridge's mind that, as a new chief justice with no training in the law and with very little experience of judicial work at Superior Court level, Hutchinson would feel in need of backstairs tuition and coaching. Who better to give it than his friend the attorney general? And it would scarcely be prudent for Chief Justice Hutchinson to alienate so valuable a mentor by allowing his professional competence to suffer a humiliating tumble on the writs of assistance question.

All the same, John Adams put it a little too high when he characterized Thomas Hutchinson's appointment to the chief justiceship as "an odious and corrupt intrigue." There does not appear to have been anything specially reprehensible in the conduct of the Hutchinson lobbyists. It may be that Andrew Oliver, who was said by James Otis junior to have given "much the same Encouragement"[46] to the colonel's cause as Hutchinson had done, but who in fact was an active supporter of the Hutchinson candidacy, did not behave as straightforwardly as he might have done. Attorney General Trowbridge probably had an ax of his own to grind, over the writ of assistance. The canvassing engaged in by the surviving Superior Court judges perhaps was not entirely seemly. But nothing points to ever-lasting infamy in any of this. And the support of Israel Williams probably was motivated by nothing other than sincere regard for Hutchinson. Equally, the commendation expressed by Jeremiah Gridley, doyen of the bar, does not seem to have been tainted by ulterior or collateral purpose.

Another of the objections to Hutchinson's appointment was that it tended toward too much concentration of public authority in one man or family. John Adams commented: "Hutchinson was then lieutenant-governor, judge of probate, Oliver, judge of the Supreme Court."[47] Here too, perhaps, the criticism was a little overdone. Both Andrew Oliver and Judge Peter Oliver had been political associates of Hutchinson in Governor Shirley's time, but his family connections with them were not all that close. Hutchinson's relationship with Andrew Oliver was that their wives had been sisters; and his son had recently married Peter Oliver's daughter. Whatever might be said about the pervasiveness of the Hutchinson-Oliver family axis in later years, in 1760 it was not so conspicuously in evidence.[48]

Hutchinson's multiplicity of public offices also attracted unfavorable comment. "Summa Potestas," was what one antagonist dubbed him. In the *Boston Gazette* in March 1761 Hutchinson was lampooned as "Sir Thomas Graspall, who was dictator general . . . not satisfied with being general of the horse, propraetor & military tribune . . . even wanted to be created justice twice in the same county . . . to give his worship more weight and honor . . . ." James Otis made much of Hutchinson's pluralities in the exchanges with him in 1763. He had in fact done the same in 1762, in an earlier newspaper battle with Hutchinson (on currency questions, in which

46. *BG* 4 April 1763.
47. *LWJA* X, 183.
48. It could be said that the Hutchinson family itself had established something like an hereditary principle on the Suffolk inferior court. Thomas followed his uncle Edward in 1754, and was followed by his brother Foster in 1758. Another Hutchinson, Eliakim, had been appointed to it in Edward's time: W. H. Whitmore, *The Massachusetts Civil List 1630-1774* (Albany, 1870), 78.

Hutchinson was something of an expert): "Instances may be found, where a man of abilities, shall monopolize a power proportionate to all those of lord chief baron of the exchequer, lord chief justice of both benches, and lord chancellor of Great Britain, united in one single person."[49] All this newspaper stuff was good knockabout, but not much more than that. It was no very serious breach of principle that Hutchinson did not give up his judgeship of probate upon becoming chief justice. His doubling-up as chief justice and county judge of probate was a good deal less open to objection than Chambers Russell's combination of Superior Court judge and judge of vice-admiralty. On being commissioned lieutenant governor Hutchinson had resigned his judgeship in the Suffolk court of common pleas, and there might have been a case in logic for resigning as lieutenant governor on his appointment as chief justice of the province. But the lieutenant governorship was void of functional content most of the time, and in practice it meant very little. Still less was Hutchinson's captaincy-general of the military installation at Castle William likely to impair his performance as chief justice. As for Otis's grumble about one man occupying a position equivalent in England to those of the chief baron of the Exchequer, the chief justice of the King's Bench, the chief justice of the Court of Common Pleas, and the lord chancellor, the answer simply is that in Massachusetts the Superior Court did duty for all three courts and was the highest tribunal in the province, so that it necessarily followed that the man who presided over the Superior Court was in a manner of speaking three chief justices in one, and also the counterpart of the lord chancellor as head of the whole judicial system.

There remains the objection that Chief Justice Hutchinson stayed on the province Council — in effect the executive government. However, Stephen Sewall, Hutchinson's immediate predecessor, had been on the Council throughout his chief justiceship; moreover, all four of the other Superior Court judges were councilors. In itself, then, Hutchinson's retaining his seat in the Council was anything but unusual. What *was* new, perhaps, was the thinking behind the criticism. The principle of the separation of powers had attracted atten-

49. *BG* 11 January 1762. Otis may have been stimulated into this controversy by recollection of his father having helped in Hutchinson's currency reform of 1749-50. See H. F. Bell: " 'A Personal Challenge': The Otis-Hutchinson Controversy, 1761-1762" (Salem, 1970), reprinted from *Essex Institute Historical Collections* CVI: "In return for this and other political chores, Shirley is purported to have promised Colonel Otis the first vacancy on the Superior Court . . . ."

tion in recent years, with the publication in 1748-1750 in English translation — of Montesquieu's *L'Esprit des Lois*: the passage from James Otis's 1762 newspaper article quoted in the foregoing paragraph was followed by a reference to Montesquieu.[50] Hutchinson seems to have been an early target of one of revolutionary America's favorite ideologies.

Hutchinson's own behavior in the weeks that passed before his nomination to the chief justiceship does not show up too badly, save that his handling of the Otises left him open to imputations of false-facedness. Ambition was by no means alien to him; but it is hard to see the chief justiceship episode as a particularly striking illustration of this. The doubts and hesitations he displayed appear to have been genuine: most men of Hutchinson's intelligence would have had them. Almost certainly the originating initiative was not his; and if his sponsors had once relaxed their efforts he probably would have let the whole thing go.[51]

Governor Bernard's position also has to be seen in the round. Pressure from the Hutchinson lobbyists practically preempted such choice as he had. He would have needed an outstandingly good alternative candidate — and no little nerve even at that — to disregard the explicit representations of the Superior Court judges themselves. And then there were the pro-Hutchinson sentiments of senior members of the bar, such as Jeremiah Gridley. Of course, none of this is to deny that Bernard had positive reasons of his own for appointing Hutchinson. Almost certainly there was truth in John Adams's statement that Hutchinson was made chief justice "for the very purpose of deciding the fate of the writs of assistance." Bernard may well have had an eye on this worrisome matter when he decided that Hutchinson was the man. If James Cockle did not get his writ of assistance, with the consequence that all the existing writs had to go too, the fewer seizures for the hard-up governor to get his one-third shares from. But this is not to go all the way with Adams's characterization of the Hutchinson appointment as "odious and corrupt." It

---

50. *Cf.* M. J. C. Vile, *Constitutionalism and the Separation of Powers* (Oxford, 1967), 128-29.

An extract from *L'Esprit des Lois*, on combination of legislative and executive powers being inimical to liberty was in *BG* 2 January 1758.

Entries in John Adams's diary beginning 26 June 1760 (*DAJA* I, 142) speak of him studying "the Spirit of Laws."

51. Hutchinson "was never fully confident of his abilities": Bailyn, *op. cit.* (n. 32 above), 26.

was not a major venality in Governor Bernard to guard against the writ being lost for want of someone on the Superior Court whose mind was not already half made up against it.

The Hutchinson appointment was just one more element in the situation that blew up in Francis Bernard's face before he had been in the province six months. By any reckoning, fate was not kind to the new governor.

Bernard's professed hopes for political harmony with one and all were vain from the start. Aside from the generations of discord between crown authority and Massachusetts localism, it was inevitable that sooner or later the governor would find himself seriously at odds with the merchant interest. He might proffer placatory gestures; he might fulminate with the best against the disadvantage suffered by Massachusetts from the unbridled illicit trading in the charter colonies alongside; but when it came to issue and the merchants moved against the agencies of all their woes, the vice-admiralty court and the custom house, there was only one side the royal governor could be on. And in Bernard's case the call of duty was coupled with exigent self-interest: if the merchants succeeded in disabling the institutions of customs law enforcement, so much for the penurious governor's one-third shares in forfeitures.

It was Governor Bernard's misfortune that sheer chance intervened to hasten the showdown. He arrived in Massachusetts just when the *London Magazine* had cast the legality of "general" writs of assistance into doubt. Hardly had he set foot in the province when that most extraordinary of customs collectors, Benjamin Barons, returned from England full of splenetic resolution to wreck the vice-admiralty court. And then there was the death of Chief Justice Sewall, within only a few weeks. This was the direst stroke of them all (even allowing that, had he lived, Sewall might have been so disturbed by the *London Magazine* as to junk the writ of assistance). The disposal of the resultant vacancy on the Superior Court earned Bernard a mountain of trouble.

For the wrath of the Otises not only gave to the merchants' "confederacy" a highly adroit and articulate steersman, in the person of James Otis junior. Its blight persisted, in varying degrees of virulence and in one manifestation or another, through Bernard's nine-year administration.

12

〜〜〜〜〜〜〜〜〜〜〜〜

Materials and Setting

〜〜〜〜〜〜〜〜〜〜〜〜

A QUEST for evidentiary material with which to put together a picture of the writs of assistance case as it actually took place starts from a frustrating paradox.

What is perhaps the most celebrated court case in the history of Massachusetts, if not of America, went almost completely unrecorded in the books of the Superior Court. The paradox is that "that legal and historical treasure which, largely unexplored by lawyers and historians alike, rests in the office of the Clerk of the Massachusetts Supreme Judicial Court for Suffolk County"[1] yields very little about the writ of assistance. One thinks in particular of the immense series of large volumes that comprise, more or less year by year, the official record of the Superior Court's work throughout the provincial period (and beyond). The record follows the court on circuit from county to country, telling in greater or lesser detail of cases decided and other business transacted. These volumes give an impression of the completeness that a record of this importance ought to have (for it was the actual record appertaining to that distinctively common law forum, a court of record); it is all the more disappointing, therefore, to see how reticent they are on the court's deliberations on the writ of assistance.

Although the volume for 1755-56 recites the order for Charles Paxton's original writ of assistance given by the court in Boston in August 1755, the corresponding entry for when he actually applied, at York the previous June, is a blank: that is to say, instead of writing something to the effect that Paxton's application had been received and postponed to Boston, the clerk, Samuel Winthrop, left an empty space of almost a whole page between the last recorded business and the customary formal statement of the court having

---

1. See *LPJA* I, xxxiii.

entered up judgments and adjourned. Subsequent issuances of a writ of assistance to named customs officers are duly entered, but at no time does anything indicating a substantive discussion appear. In the record of the court's sitting at Salem in October 1760 there is not even so much as a gap to signify that the new collector of customs there, James Cockle, had made an approach for a writ. The hearing on writs of assistance at Boston in February 1761 must have ranked among the most important business of the term; but the only sign of it in the record is a blank space of nearly a page between two ordinary cases of private litigation. It is much the same with the next Boston term, when the writs of assistance case was resumed and argued to finality. Here, however, the blank space is sidenoted "Greene & others Petition . . .," which plainly is a reference to the petition headed by Thomas Greene that asked for the hearing in the first place; but, the sidenote goes on (in a different and presumably later hand), "No papers are on file." And there is another incompleteness in the Superior Court's archives. In addition to its formal record the court kept paper-backed quarto minute books for each of the counties it visited on circuit. A good many of these minute books have survived, but not the one for Suffolk county over the period September 1759-August 1762.[2]

Other volumes in the Suffolk county court office consist of miscellaneous documents pertaining to particular cases dealt with by the Superior Court in provincial times. (Edmund Trowbridge's draft of the original Massachusetts writ of assistance is in one of these volumes.) As to the writs of assistance case, this series of "Suffolk Files" is much of a piece with the official record of the court. Just as the blanks left in the record were never filled out, so the surviving documentation of the case is exceedingly meager. This fact was noted in the discussion in chapter 8 of the onset of the case; and the two documents there reproduced, the Greene petition and Surveyor General Lechmere's memorial in response, appear to be the only original documents of the case to have escaped whatever fate befell the rest.

Why the court record of the writs of assistance case should be all but nonexistent is quite a question. A guess can be ventured, however. Thomas Hutchinson, it was suggested in chapter 8, was unwilling to have it believed that he had been made chief justice in November 1760 for the sake of a decision favoring the writ of assistance. It was further speculated that his *History of Massachu-sets-Bay* omitted to name the originating applicant, James Cockle, the new collector at Salem, the better to conceal the fact that the Superior Court had had a writ of assistance application on file since its circuit visit to Salem in October 1760. If an account of Cockle's application were to appear in the official public record of the court, Hutchinson the historian would need to provide his readers with a persuasive explanation that, contrary to the suspicions of the ill-disposed, his appointment as chief justice had had nothing to do with the pending problem of Cockle's writ of assistance. As chief justice, the topmost man in the Superior Court, he was well placed to see that the court's record remained suitably uncommunicative.

Law reports of the conventional kind, meticulous write-ups of court proceedings and judgments for publication in authoritative books of precedents, were not a feature of the judicial system of provincial Massachusetts. Individual lawyers might take notes for future use in their own professional practice, but that was as far as it went. However, a collection of such notes, the work of Josiah Quincy junior over the years 1761 to 1772, did eventually get into print.[3] One of these notes was of the second and concluding phase of the writs of assistance case, in November 1761. More of this will be seen in a later chapter, when the November hearing is dealt with. For the moment it is sufficient to say that the real meat of the writs of assistance case, the arguments in February 1761, were not touched upon by Quincy at all.

The prime chronicler of the February arguments was John Adams. Some of Adams's contributions to historical knowledge of the writs of assistance case have already been drawn upon in this book. Though not always reliable in detail, and in parts downright puzzling, the Adams materials are nevertheless the work of a man actually present at the hearing in February 1761. The evidence of Thomas Hutchinson, the only other known eyewitness to have written of the February debate, naturally is of considerable value; but there is not much of it. Despite the winnowing it has to be put through in the

---

3. *Quincy's Reports* (see chapter 1, n. 1), 51-57.

interests of factual accuracy, and notwithstanding some mystifying gaps in it, the variegated Adams testimony has to be accepted as including much of the best there is.

At the time of the writs of assistance case Adams was twenty-five. In 1756, after graduation from Harvard he had left his parental home at Braintree, some ten or so miles south of Boston, to take up work as a schoolmaster in the inland town of Worcester. Soon after arriving at Worcester he entered however upon the study of law as a pupil of James Putnam, the leading attorney there. He returned to Braintree in 1758, and began practicing as a country lawyer. One of the numerous attorneys who attended the writs of assistance hearing, Adams fell to jotting down notes of what the contending advocates were saying.

These contemporaneous notes have been preserved among the Adams Papers in the Massachusetts Historical Society. Adams used a single sheet of paper doubled over three times to convenient pocket size, and of the sixteen segments thus produced nine are written on. The whole is set forth in Appendix I. It includes not only the notes proper but an obvious addition: excerpts from relevant legislation; a copy of Charles Paxton's first application for a writ of assistance, in 1755; and the text of the writ that was issued to Paxton. The notes themselves begin with a fragment of Jeremiah Gridley for the crown, go on (more amply) to Oxenbridge Thacher and James Otis on the other side, and finish with more from Gridley.

Uniquely valuable though they are, John Adams's on-the-spot notes leave much to be guessed at and speculated upon. Manifestly they are not a complete record: for instance, not a word do they show the judges uttering; and Jeremiah Gridley's opening speech surely consisted of more than three brief sentences. They do not even bear a date. Adams himself looked back on them with no great satisfaction: "Those despicable Notes," he called them once.[4] And on another occasion he excused his poor workmanship: "I took a few minutes . . . [but] was much more attentive for the Information and the Eloquence of the Speakers, than to my minutes, and too much alarmed at the prospect that was opened before us, to care much about writing a report of the Controversy."[5]

4. See the excerpt from the original Adams papers, *LPJA* II, 106-7. In *LWJA* X, 246, "poor" is substituted for "despicable." The context indicates that Adams, writing in 1817, was thinking of the Abstract write-up rather than of the notes themselves. See also n. 65 below.

5. *DAJA* III, 276.

Whatever his intentions or state of mind when the arguments were actually going on, John Adams soon formed the idea that "a report of the Controversy" was worth attempting. Thus the genesis of the "Abstract," an amplified version of his contemporaneous notes that has been cited in previous chapters and which, particularly for its rendition of the speech of James Otis, is probably more familiar than the notes as a basic document of the writs of assistance case. The term "Abstract" seems odd as applied to something enlarged rather than reduced, but it presumably was meant to convey that even this expanded write-up did not include everything that had been said. Anyway, the Abstract was down on paper within no more than a few weeks of the February hearing, as Adams makes apparent in a diary entry in April 1761. This diary entry did not relate to the Abstract or to the writs of assistance case as such; it had to do with young Adams's furious mortification over a leg-pulling session he had had to endure from a Braintree neighbor, Colonel Josiah Quincy (father of the November notetaker). It seems that Quincy had set out to embarrass Adams by obviously overdone expressions of praise and esteem. As an illustration of the colonel's "Deceit and Insincerity" the diary includes this:

> He saw an Abstract of the Argument for and against Writts of Assistants — and crys did you take this from those Gentlemen as they delivered it? You can do any Thing! You can do as you please! Gridley did not use that Language. He never was Master of such a style. It is not in him — &c . . . .[6]

Plainly it was the write-up that Quincy had seen; however laden with irony, this extravagance could not possibly have been applied to Adams's very sketchy on-the-spot notes. Another indication of the origins of the Abstract is in a letter from John Adams to Mercy Otis Warren, 20 July 1807:

> I heard your brother James Otis, and Mr. Thacher, in the Council Chamber before the Superior Court against the legality of these writs, and Mr. Gridley in their favor; took minutes of the argument, made a short sketch of a report of it, which was afterwards surreptitiously printed, though garbled . . . .[7]

6. *DAJA* I, 209-210.

7. *MHSC* Fifth series IV (1878): "Correspondence between John Adams and Mercy Warren," 340. Mrs. Warren's recent *History of the . . . American Revolution* (Boston, 1805) had displeased Adams. On 27 July 1807 he bade her remember that "I made the only report of her brother's argument in the great question of writs of assistance in 1761, which would have been forgotten, but is now recorded in history as the first appearance of a controversy which terminated only with the American Revolution" (p. 355).

A text of the Abstract is in Appendix J. Some explanation of it is necessary.

Unlike the notes he took at the hearing, John Adams's manuscript of the Abstract has long since disappeared. Moreover, as far as is known, there exists no copy of the Abstract that is absolutely reliable in every point of detail. The text in Appendix J is a compilation, borrowed from the work of several contemporaries of Adams who appear to have had access to the original.

The last trace of the original manuscript of the Abstract is in George Richards Minot's *Continuation of the History of the Province of Massachusetts Bay,* published in 1803.[8] Minot gave an account of the writs of assistance case (more particularly the first phase of it, in February 1761) which consisted for the most part in an account of the arguments by Jeremiah Gridley on behalf of the crown, partly in reported and partly in direct speech; a paragraph, in reported speech, on the contribution of Oxenbridge Thacher on the opposing side; and the oration of James Otis. As to this last, "we shall insert more at large such minutes as we possess; lamenting that we cannot recover at this day many elegant rhetorical touches and weighty arguments, which were unavoidably omitted." The whole of the extensive Otis passage was rendered in direct speech; and a marginal note alongside acknowledged Minot's source to have been "M.S. minutes taken at the bar." This can mean only that the "minutes" which in the text Minot said he had in his possession were in fact John Adams's original manuscript of the Abstract.

Adams probably was thinking of William Gordon's *History of the . . . Independence of the United States . . .* I (London, 1788), 141, on the political advent of James Otis: "He signalized himself, by pleading in a most masterly manner, against granting *writs of assistance . . . .* The custom-house officers had received letters from home, directing them to a more strenuous exertion in collecting the duties, and to procure writs of assistance. The idea of these writs excited a general alarm . . . . From this period may be dated, the fixed, uniform, and growing opposition, which was made to the ministerial plans of encroaching upon the original rights and long established customs of the colony . . . ." Equally probably it had been on conversations with Adams himself that Gordon drew. Gordon, a clergyman at Roxbury, Mass., had no direct knowledge of the writs case, for he arrived from England only in 1770; but he and Adams became well acquainted (*cf. DAJA* II, 174, 176). His brief account shows little sign of borrowing from Adams's Abstract (even though he may have seen something of this: *LPJA* II, 123, n. 52), which in any case — and naturally enough — said nothing about the Revolution, still years ahead. *Cf.* n. 45, n. 59 below.

8. Vol. II (Boston, 1803), 91-99. Apparently it was from Minot, and hence, derivatively, from John Adams, that Mercy Warren (n. 7 above) took her own book's quotation (pp. 48-49) of James Otis's famous speech. "Continuation" in Minot's title had reference to Thomas Hutchinson's *History* which for want of its final volume — not published until 1828: *cf.* chapter 7, n. 4 above — seemingly had left the tale incomplete.

Evidence for this was supplied by Adams himself. In his auto-biography, written at much the same time as Minot's book came out, Adams said this: "I took a few minutes . . . which by some means fell into the hands of Mr. Minot who has inserted them in his history." [9] And in a letter in 1817 to his old associate William Tudor he wrote of having sat in court "minuting those despicable Notes which you know that Jonathan Williams Austin your fellow student in my office, stole from my desk, and printed in the Massachusetts Spy, with two or three bombastic expressions interpolated by himself; and which your pupil, Judge Minot has printed in his history." [10]

In one central respect neither Minot's marginal note ("M.S. min-utes taken at the bar") nor this supporting testimony from Adams is as clear as it might have been. At first glance, it could have been not the Abstract but Adams's on-the-spot notes that was meant. But it is just as immediately obvious that what Minot quoted "at large" of Otis (and the same applies to his less extensive renditions of Gridley and Thacher) must be identified not as those scrappy con-temporaneous jottings but as the much fuller Abstract that Adams wrote up from them soon after. If proof were needed it might be seen in the *Life and Works of John Adams*, where the editor, Charles Francis Adams, sets forth Minot's text of the Otis speech after having excised the passages which the old statesman had underlined as interpolations (presumably the same interpolations as he mentioned to William Tudor) in his own copy of Minot's book. [11]

How Minot got hold of John Adams's Abstract is as obscure as what happened to it afterward. Some thirty years had passed since any of it previously appeared in print. This was in the *Massachusetts Spy* for 29 April 1773. The *Massachusetts Spy* was a paper founded in Boston in 1770 by Isaiah Thomas, catering to radicalism in the artisan class. The issue for 29 April 1773 carried an unsigned piece which began

For the MASSACHUSETTS SPY.
Mr THOMAS,
AS the public have been lately alarmed with the evil and wicked effects of the power lodged in custom-house officers, by virtue of that most execra-ble of all precepts, a Writ of Assistance: And as I conceive it to be more immediately destructive of the liberties of the subject, than any other

9. *LWJA* II, 107. Possibly, of course, Adams was merely going by Minot's own statement.
10. See n. 4 above.
11. *LWJA* II, 523; X, 246; and see *LPJA* II, 142, note 138.

innovation of power: The following is offered to the public, being taken from the mouth of that great American oracle of law, JAMES OTIS, Esq; in the meridian of his life.

The piece went on to a further introductory paragraph,[12] which recited that "On the second Tuesday of the court's sitting, appointed by the rule of the court for argument of special matters, came on the dispute of Mr Cockle and others on the one side, and the inhabitants of Boston on the other, concerning Writs of Assistance"; and continued with brief mention of Jeremiah Gridley's having "endeavoured to support the legality of Writs of Assistance by force of several statutes and precedents in England, but his chief stay he acknowledged was *the necessity of the case*, and in the course of his arguments he discovered himself to be an ingenious lawyer." Save for a word here and there the remainder of the piece was devoted to a rendition of the speech of James Otis practically indistinguishable from Minot's.

From Adams's account of how he lost possession of the Abstract it would seem that the contributor to the *Massachusetts Spy* may have been one of his law pupils, Jonathan Williams Austin, who allegedly took it from his desk.[13] The manner of the reference to Gridley ("he discovered himself an ingenious lawyer") strengthens this impression. None but a youngster without personal memory of Gridley — who had died in 1767 — could have written in such a way about a man who in his day had been one of the leading lawyers in the province. And an immediate reason for the piece in the *Spy* is not far to seek. On the page opposite was an indignant report of one "R. Parker, big with a writ of assistance" having forcibly searched warehouses on the Long Wharf.[14]

The Long Wharf searches were not the only cause of heightened interest in the writ of assistance in the spring of 1773. Whether or

---

12. Under an obviously erroneous heading: "*Boston Superior Court, February term, 1771.*"

13. A letter from John Adams to General Washington in June 1775 may be of some relevance (*LWJA* IX, 360): "There is another gentleman of liberal education and real genius, as well as great activity, who, I find, is a major in the army. His name is Jonathan Williams Austin. I mention him, Sir, not so much for the sake of recommending him to any particular favor, as to give the General an opportunity of observing a youth of great abilities, and of reclaiming him from certain follies which have hitherto, in other departments of life, obscured him."

14. The report also appeared in *BG* 26 April 1773. Further reference to it is in chapter 19.

not young Austin had more motivations than one, herein may lie a clue to another transcript of Adams's Abstract (though not, alas, to the fate of the original).

The Townshend legislation of 1767 had sought to establish writ of assistance search in all the American colonies, mostly in vain. An instance of how tough the going could be had recently occurred in Connecticut, where customs officers at New London, vexed by the rescue of a seizure, had made the latest of a long succession of endeavors to obtain the writ from the Superior Court of the colony. Local newspapers sprang into action with denunciations of the writ, and warned the judges off granting it; and soon afterward the Connecticut Committee of Correspondence wrote around to its counterparts elsewhere for support in the stand against the writ. [15] The journal of the Massachusetts Committee of Correspondence recorded that on 26 August 1773

> Mr Cushing Communicated a Letter which he had received from the Committee of Correspondence in Connecticut, requesting that they may [be] Informed what has been Done by the Judges of the Superior Court of this Province, on the requisition made for a writ of assistance. — where upon the sub Committee procured the minutes of the arguments made by Mr Thacher and Mr Otis before the Judges of the Superior Court of this Province against such a writ being Granted here, which together with a Letter were forwarded to the Committee of Correspondence in Connecticut. [16]

It seems almost certain that the Thacher and Otis arguments thus sent to Connecticut were from John Adams's Abstract. If the document was still in the hands of Jonathan Williams Austin the committee would have had no difficulty in tracking it down to him, through Isaiah Thomas at the *Massachusetts Spy*. [17]

One of the members of the Massachusetts Committee of Correspondence was the whig lawyer, Joseph Hawley. Among Hawley's papers in the New York Public Library is a "Common Place Book," which included a rendition of the speeches of Jeremiah Gridley and James Otis on writs of assistance that clearly emanated from the

---

15. See O. Zeichner, *Connecticut's Years of Controversy 1750-1776* (Chapel Hill, 1949), 133-34; also Horace Gray, in *Quincy's Reports*, 501-4.

16. *MHSP* second series IV (1887-88), 88.

17. Just possibly, their contact with Austin may have been more direct, as a leading member of the Chelmsford Committee of Correspondence. The *Massachusetts Spy* for 2 June 1774 reproduced a letter which he signed as chairman of the Chelmsford committee.

same master text as those in Minot and the *Massachusetts Spy*. It is not impossible that Hawley borrowed the original Abstract from John Adams, for the two men knew each other (at any rate from 1768 on); but there is no hint of this in Adams's writings. A likelier explanation of how Hawley was able to copy the Abstract perhaps lies in the Connecticut inquiry on writs of assistance and the Massachusetts Committee of Correspondence's manner of responding to it. Though not on the subcommittee that obtained the Abstract, or for that matter regular in his attendance on the committee proper (he lived at Northampton, quite a distance from Boston), Hawley probably knew of this business; and he could have seen it as an opportunity to get hold of the document and copy out such passages as particularly interested him.

What an established lawyer in middle age should have wanted with a record of young John Adams's reconstruction of the Gridley and Otis arguments back in 1761 is far from obvious. However, Hawley was an odd character, given to intensive zeal in controversy. For example, at one time he "entered upon a religious Altercation" with the renowned divine Jonathan Edwards — and drove him to resign his pulpit.[18] On the secular front he developed an animus against Thomas Hutchinson so ferocious as to betray him into misbehavior toward the Superior Court where Hutchinson presided as chief justice, and from October 1767 he was in effect disbarred for two years. In 1773 Hutchinson, now governor of the province, was more unpopular than ever. Hawley's interest in a record of the writs of assistance case, the disappointing outcome of which had owed everything to Hutchinson, conceivably signifies a germinating intention to promote some kind of propaganda drive against the New England-born adjutant of British knavery; Hutchinson's departure for England not long after, in 1774, could account for Hawley making no use of the Abstract after all. This is guesswork, however.

In its treatment of Jeremiah Gridley the Hawley text, which is actually headed "Substance of Mr Gridley's Argument before the Superior Court in favor of Writs of Assistance," is an advance on both Minot and the *Spy*. Minot gives only a condensed version of Gridley's arguments, partly in reported speech, and in the *Spy* they get barely a mention. The Hawley version is wholly in direct speech, and is a great deal fuller. But, going as it does straight into Gridley, it

18. See D. Adair and J. A. Schutz, eds., *Peter Oliver's Origin and Progress of the American Rebellion* (Stanford, 1967), 38.

omits the introductory material about the writs of assistance case taking place on a day set aside for "special matters" and the originating role of James Cockle. A larger omission — and in this Hawley is one with the *Spy* — is all reference to Oxenbridge Thacher's contribution to the debate. The speech of James Otis fared better, though not without editorial doctoring and pruning. Or, for that matter, without editorial interpolation.

The most audacious of Hawley's liberties is worth a moment's pause. Where Minot and the *Massachusetts Spy* show Otis ending his speech with a reaffirmation that the writ of assistance should be granted only on probable suspicion specifically sworn to, Hawley has this instead:

> It is the business of this court to demolish this monster of oppression, and to tear into rags this remnant of Starchamber tyranny.

Stirring stuff; but it was not Otis's. Or even Hawley's own. The words were those of Serjeant John Glynn, arguing against general warrants in the leading English case of *Entick v. Carrington*. Such warrants, Glynn is reported as saying,

> are not by custom; they go no further back than 80 years and most amazing it is they have never before this time been opposed or controverted, considering the great men that have presided in the King's Bench since that time; but it was reserved for the honour of this Court, which has ever been the protector of the liberty and property of the subject, to demolish this monster of oppression, and to tear into rags this remnant of Star-Chamber tyranny.[19]

Entick v. Carrington was decided four years after the writs of assistance case. As a kind of bonus, one can deduce from Hawley's bit of plagiarism that it could not have been earlier than 1770, the year in which the report of *Entick v. Carrington* was published, that he took his copy of Adams's Abstract.

Something else that appears in Hawley but not in the *Massachusetts Spy* is a tailpiece, after the Otis speech: "The court suspended the absolute determination of this matter. I have omitted many authorities; also many fine touches in the order of reasoning, and numberless Rhetorical and popular flourishes." Here Hawley does not seem to have been inventing. The first sentence occurs in another version of the Abstract that has yet to be discussed. And the second

---

19. (1765) 2 Wils. K.B. 275, 278. Glynn, a political associate of John Wilkes, was well regarded in America. See, for illustration, his inclusion in the toasts proposed at a gathering of the Boston Sons of Liberty on 14 August 1769: *BG* 21 August 1769.

has an echo in George Richards Minot's apology on his own rendition: "we cannot recover at this day many elegant rhetorical
touches . . . ." The other element in Hawley's second tailpiece sentence is likely to have been authentic Adams, too. If it had been
Hawley admitting to omissions of his own (and why should he have
done this, anyway, in a document privy to himself?), he surely would
not have regarded the speech of Oxenbridge Thacher, the whole of
which he left out, as appropriately and adequately signified by the
words, "many authorities . . . many fine touches in the order of
reasoning." Much more probably the entire tailpiece was in the
Adams original. That the Abstract did indeed miss out a great deal —
a fact that Adams could not have failed to be conscious of — will
emerge in chapters that follow.

Another transcription of the Abstract is known to have been
made. The papers are lost, but an account of it, and of the man
whose work it was, is given in Horace Gray's treatise on writs of
assistance written in the early 1860s.[20] The arguments of all three
advocates in the writs of assistance case, Gridley, Thacher, and Otis,
headed by an introductory paragraph, were found set forth in a
commonplace book of Israel Keith. Not much is known of Keith,
and he seems to have taken little or no part in public life. After
graduating from Harvard in 1771 he took to the law; and, says Gray
(who had been allowed to use it), his commonplace book contained
"sufficient evidence that Mr. Keith . . . had access to some of *John
Adams's* materials." What made this possible nowhere appears. It
does not seem probable that Keith was a pupil of Adams, for Adams
had a conscientious misgiving about taking on more than one pupil
or "clerk" at a time, and he already had two, Jonathan Williams
Austin and William Tudor, when Keith left Harvard.[21] A guess might
be that Keith was sufficiently acquainted with Austin — young men
in the same line of work but in different offices or firms commonly
get to know one another — to obtain a sight of any interesting or
instructive papers that came Austin's way. At any rate, Gray was
given to understand that Keith's transcript of the Abstract dated
from when "he was studying his profession."

Though he makes it clear that the Keith Abstract had the speeches
of all three advocates, Gray did not reproduce that of Otis. "The

20. *Quincy's Reports,* 478-82.
21. *DAJA* I, 338.

extended sketch of *Otis's* argument," he explained, "... has been twice printed already," in Minot and in John Adams's *Life and Works* (the *Massachusetts Spy* perhaps did not count in this context) and the variations were trifling. When Gray was writing nothing had appeared of the Hawley version of Gridley; and all that was in print of Gridley's argument was the truncated piece in Minot. Gray reproduced Keith's version of Gridley, for all practical purposes in full.[22] It was much the same with the speech of Oxenbridge Thacher: till Gray published the Keith text the attenuated Minot version was all that existed in print. The value of the Keith material is as great today as when Gray published it, for, with Hawley having omitted Thacher altogether, it still seems to be the only entire text of Thacher to have come down.

There is another respect in which Keith, thanks to Gray, is helpful. It will be recalled that the *Massachusetts Spy* version of the Otis speech carried an introductory paragraph which included the following: "On the second Tuesday of the court's sitting, appointed by the rule of the court for argument of special matters, came on the dispute of Mr Cockle and others on the one side, and the inhabitants of Boston on the other, concerning Writs of Assistance." Of course, one might suspect from the reference to a rather recondite rule of court that this was not something souped up for journalism's sake, but was taken straight from the Adams original; but it is convenient to find Keith corroborating this informative item of detail, which appears neither in Minot nor in Hawley. Keith gives a bit extra, in fact. To the sentence reproduced in the *Spy* he adds this: "*Mr. Gridley* appeared for the former, *Mr. Otis* for the latter. *Mr. Thacher* was joined with him at the desire of the Court." How Oxenbridge Thacher came into the writs of assistance case, and exactly what may have been his status — in relation to the protesting merchants, for example, whose accredited spokesman was James Otis — are questions for later in the book. But it can be said that they would have been considerably more difficult without this additional fragment in Keith.

According to Horace Gray, Keith ended his rendition of the Abstract with "The Court suspended the absolute determination of the matter." The Hawley rendition, on the other hand, has a further sentence, about the omission of authorities, finer points of reasoning,

22. Although Keith showed Gridley reciting the text of Charles Paxton's 1755-56 writ *in extenso*, Gray, who had given it elsewhere in his treatise, left it out.

and rhetoric; which confession seems to have been in the Abstract as John Adams penned it. Cutting this off, as far as one can tell, was the only indulgence Keith permitted himself.

Appendix J presents a composite rendition of John Adams's Abstract, not in terms of detailed comparison of the various texts one with another (where that might have been possible), but chiefly on a judgment of which text (where there is a choice) appears most reliable for which speech.

For Jeremiah Gridley's opening speech on behalf of the crown, Keith has been preferred to Hawley. (Minot gave only a shortened version of Gridley; and the brief reference to Gridley in the *Massachusetts Spy* is just not in the running.) Although Hawley's heading to his manuscript, "Substance of Mr Gridley's Argument before the Superior Court in favor of Writs of Assistance," might imply some special interest in what Gridley had said, there is also the indication that Hawley rendered the argument down so as to leave merely the "Substance"; and it is a fact that his version does not include all that Keith's includes (notably, the text of the writ of assistance ordered for Charles Paxton in 1755 and a quotation from the Act of Frauds of 1662). Wherever Keith has no counterpart in Hawley it is much more likely to have been Hawley omitting than Keith inventing. Likewise one opts for Keith on the other — few and small — differences from Hawley. Keith, a young law student whose purpose in copying the Abstract consisted, presumably, in what it could teach him, was less likely to tamper with it than was the politically minded oldster Hawley (who demonstrably did tamper with it, anyway: witness his insertion from *Entick v. Carrington*).

For the speech of Oxenbridge Thacher there is no alternative to Keith. Minot gives only a truncated rendition, in indirect speech; and Hawley and the *Spy* do not so much as mention it.

With James Otis's speech it is rather the other way about. The Keith version is unavailable, Horace Gray having decided not to reproduce it (because it was virtually identical with other versions already in print). However, Hawley, Minot, and the *Massachusetts Spy* all offer candidates.

Hawley misses out as the favorite, for his known embellishment of the original text.

Inasmuch as Minot alone actually cited the original of the Abstract, and John Adams himself attested that Minot had been in possession of that document, the Minot version plainly has a claim.

Nor does it greatly matter that Adams disowned some "bombastic" or "fantastical" expressions. Very possibly he could not believe himself capable of ever having augmented the revered oration with stuff like "the trump of the arch-angel" and "the curse of Canaan" (two supposed interpolations struck out from Charles Francis Adams's reproduction of the Minot version of Otis). However, these flatulencies appear in Hawley too; and Horace Gray gives no indication that the Keith text was without them. When Minot's book came out John Adams had not seen the Abstract manuscript in thirty years; his memory — not always at its most reliable on the writs of assistance case — seems to have been enriched by imagination in these points of textual detail.

Nevertheless, Minot's version of Otis does not win the palm. This has little to do with occasional signs of editorial license (though the omission of a not entirely unimportant sentence, "I was sollicited to engage on the other side," is a blackish mark). More difficult to indulge is Minot's unimpressive handling of evidence. For a lawyer, and a judge at that, he is distinctly amiss in this department. His citation of the Abstract could have been clearer; and there is something even more unsatisfactory about another of his marginal notes, this one alongside the paragraph immediately following the Otis speech. "Notwithstanding these and many more arguments were enforced with a zeal peculiar to the spirit and manner of the pleaders," the paragraph runs, "the writ of assistance was granted." The marginal note is this: "Supr. Court Records." The Superior Court's surviving documentation of the writs of assistance case is unlikely to have been much ampler in Minot's time than it is today; and assuredly there was nothing he could have seen either of how the arguments went or of their outcome in the blank pages that are practically the only sign of the case in the court's formal record.

The version of Otis chosen for Appendix J is that which appeared in the *Massachusetts Spy* on 29 April 1773. John Adams's objection that it had interpolations has already been countered (in relation to the Minot version). There is no evidence that the *Spy* gave other than a straight rendition of what the original Abstract actually said. On the contrary, there are positive probabilities that the text was not interfered with. Aside from any alteration or gloss risking immediate denunciation by Adams, James Otis himself was still on the scene (even though past "the meridian of his life," through bouts of mental disorder) to challenge any falsification.

Not that the textual variations among any of the speeches in any of the versions are reason enough to arouse suspicion of serious misrepresentation by any of the copyists. The most flagrant of the liberties taken was Joseph Hawley's insertion of a purple passage from an argument by counsel in *Entick v. Carrington*, but even this did not affect the pattern of argument in any degree. Likewise, a sentence omitted by Minot could be thought repetitious and unnecessary to the argument. Indeed, the only differences of substance between Minot, the *Spy*, Hawley, and Keith are in the treatment of the Abstract's introductory and concluding paragraphs; variations in the speeches proper are so trivial that choice of a version (of the Otis speech) for the composite Abstract in Appendix J might almost as well have been decided by the toss of a coin.[23]

Even with allowance made for the "many authorities" and the "many fine touches in the order of reasoning" that it admitted to leaving out, John Adams's Abstract fell well short of a perfect record of the proceedings in February 1761. Most conspicuously, it said nothing of the recent *London Magazine* article but for which the writs of assistance case probably would not have happened at all, and which even Hutchinson's *History of Massachusets-Bay*, in its insufficiently accented way, pinpointed as the source of the opposition's principal argument. Further instances of the Abstract's incompleteness will fall to be noticed as the book goes on.

The Abstract is in no danger, however, of standing revealed as a tissue of wholesale fabrication. Aside from any other consideration, it corresponds too closely to Adams's on-the-spot notes. For the most part, that is. One doubts, indeed, that those courtroom jottings were not too sketchy to have been capable of expansion, wholly from within themselves, into a full and exact record. It will be to the point, as occasion presents itself, to speculate how it became possible for John Adams to take these skeletal fragments and fill them out in the Abstract, at times to almost unrecognizable transfiguration.

It is a most puzzling thing that, having put himself to the labor of preparing and writing the Abstract (not to mention the recent impact of the oratory he was to find so memorable in years to come), John Adams immediately lost interest in the writs of assistance case.

After the entry in April 1761 telling of the incident when Colonel Josiah Quincy "saw an Abstract of the Argument for and against

23. For a detailed concordance of the various versions of the Abstract texts, see *LPJA* II, 134-44.

Writts of Assistants," Adams's diary is totally silent on the case. Of the resumed hearing in November there is not so much as a hint. The signs are, indeed, that Adams was quite unaware of its having taken place, and so remained to the end of his long life. In March 1817 he believed the sequel to the Superior Court's adjournment for advice about the writ of assistance in England to have been this:

> In six months the next term arrived, but no judgment was pronounced, no letters from England were produced, and nothing more was ever said in Court concerning writs of assistance; but it was generally reported and understood that the Court clandestinely granted them . . . .[24]

This blank in John Adams's knowledge is all the more mystifying because he in fact attended the Superior Court in November 1761. On Saturday 14 November, as his diary states,[25] he and Samuel Quincy (also from Braintree, and a son of Colonel Josiah Quincy) were sworn attorneys for practice in the Superior Court. That same day the court "entered up Judgment according to the verdicts and then adjourned to Wednesday next,"[26] says the record. This supplementary sitting on Wednesday 18 November was to be the occasion for the resumed hearing on writs of assistance. It may well be that Adams went straight back to Braintree on the Saturday and was busy through the following week with preparations for a new law office he was opening there.[27] All the same, it is surprising that he should not have heard that the writs of assistance case was coming on again. Even if he had left the court before the concluding announcement of the adjournment and of the sitting scheduled for Wednesday, the

24. *LWJA* X, 248. See also *ibid.*, 233 (18 December 1816): "The public never was informed of the judgment of the Court. No judge ever gave his opinion, or discussed the question in public. After six or nine months, we heard enough of custom-house officers breaking houses . . . by virtue of writs of assistance."

Adams wrote H. Calkoen, 4 October 1780 (*LWJA* VII, 266): "the question, whether such writs were legal and constitutional, was solemnly and repeatedly argued before the supreme court . . . ." The "repeatedly" possibly was meant in relation to the November hearing; but Adams's statements quoted above make this unlikely. See *Quincy's Reports*, 50.

25. *DAJA* I, 224. SCR (1760-62), 239. For Quincy at the February writs of assistance hearing see p. 267 below.

26. Page 239.

27. See *DAJA* I, 225; entry headed "Novr. 20th. 1761. Monday." Editorial note 1 says: "This entry fixes the date of JA's fitting out and establishing himself in his law office in the house now known as the John Quincy Adams Birthplace." However, 20 November was a Friday. Since Adams was less likely to have mistaken the day of the week, the correct date presumably was 24 November (though, of course, 16 November cannot be ruled out absolutely).

resumption of the writs of assistance hearing surely might have come up in conversation with Jeremiah Gridley, who would again be appearing for the crown, and upon whose motion Adams had just been admitted to a Superior Court attorneyship.

Nor did the November hearing and determination on writs of assistance go unremarked in the Boston press. The *Gazette* for the following Monday, 23 November, carried a sizable report of it; and adverse comments on the fact that writs of assistance were now being issued were to be seen in the editions of 7 and 21 December. On 4 January 1762 the paper printed a long and ferocious attack on the result of the case. Yet John Adams must have missed all this. Living out at Braintree he may not have had regular access to the Boston newspapers.

It is possible that pressure of affairs in Braintree distracted Adams from a continuing interest in the writs of assistance case. In May 1761 — soon after his work on the Abstract — his parents, with whom he lived, fell seriously ill; and his father died. The house in which he set up office in November 1761 had been willed to him, and there was a farm as well. A public concern that much engaged him at this time was his campaign to reduce the number of licensed houses in the Braintree locality. And then of course he had his profession to see to. Nor was this exclusively a matter of ordinary legal work. Having gotten himself qualified as an attorney proper (he was admitted to practice in the inferior court of Suffolk County in November 1758), he quickly turned to sorting out the competition, in the form of "Deputy Sheriffs, Pettyfoggers and even Constables, who filled all the Writts upon Bonds, promissory notes and Accounts, received the Fees established for Lawyers and stirred up many unnecessary Suits."[28] In one way and another, young Adams had plenty to occupy him in the middle and later months of 1761.

John Adams's remembered experience of the writs of assistance case was not dead, however, but sleeping. Again and again it came back to him in later life. In his last twenty years or so, after a term as president of the United States, Adams's thinking turned much to events of the revolutionary period; and he became a kind of public remembrancer. Aside from his own direct contributions to the Boston press he seems to have been always responsive to requests for information, and ready to dash off pages of reminiscence for others

28. *DAJA* III, 274.

to make use of. It was in such correspondence as this that most of his latter-day material on the writs of assistance case came to be produced.[29]

Specially notable was a series of letters in 1818 to his former pupil, William Tudor, whose son of the same name was planning a biography of James Otis. Adams wrote Tudor more than a dozen letters, some very long, devoted to Otis's writs of assistance speech.[30] These letters were a kind of culmination, for the writs of assistance case had been cropping up in Adams's writings to various persons some three years past. However, it cannot be said that the volume of testimony in all these letters adds proportionately to the corpus of reliable knowledge on the writs of assistance case. Of the speeches of Jeremiah Gridley and Oxenbridge Thacher there is virtually nothing. The reconstructed Otis speech in the 1818 letters has little counterpart in either Adams's contemporaneous notes or the Abstract (though he had both available — the former in the original, and the latter as published in Minot's *History*), and its credibility is therefore at a discount. Its principal source is obviously imagination and afterthought. In the various earlier letters Adams treats not only of Otis, but also of the onset of the case — Cockle's application at Salem and so forth; and among these accounts there are elements of factual error.

None of this is to discount entirely the value of Adams's long-distance testimony; the imaginative rendition of Otis's speech is not totally without a touch of authenticity, as will be seen when the speech is examined in a later chapter; and use has already been made of the Cockle material despite its mistakes. It is only fair, in any case, to include in this commentary the caution administered by Adams himself at the beginning of the first letter of his series to William Tudor: "No man could have written from memory Mr. Otis's argument of four or five hours . . . . How awkward, then, would be an attempt to do it after a lapse of fifty-seven years!"[31] In the other

29. See L. H. Butterfield, "John Adams: What Do We Mean by the American Revolution," in D. J. Boorstin, ed., *An American Primer* I (Chicago, 1966). Adams's correspondence, edited by C. F. Adams, may be found in *LWJA*; volume X is particularly in point. Other compilations include J. A. Schutz and D. Adair, eds., *The Spur of Fame. Dialogues of John Adams and Benjamin Rush, 1805-13* (San Marino, 1966); W. C. Ford, ed., *Statesman and Friend — Correspondence of John Adams and Benjamin Waterhouse 1784-1820* (Boston, 1927).

30. These are in *LWJA* X. Tudor junior's *Sketches of the Life and Writings of James Otis of Boston* (Boston, 1823) relied heavily on the former president's letters. It incurred severe censure by Horace Gray, in *Quincy's Reports*, 417-18.

31. 1 June 1818: *LWJA* X, 314.

letters too he repeatedly spoke of the imperfection and fallibility of memory. Adams's old-age contributions to the lore of the writs of assistance case have sometimes been adversely commented upon. But criticism would have been the better balanced for an acknowledgment of his own quiet admissions that they were not to be taken wholly as straight history. A footnote to the Tudor series by Charles Francis Adams in his edition of the *Life and Works of John Adams* is somewhat off-target, too:

> By comparison of this sketch of Mr. Otis' speech with that taken at the time . . . it is difficult to resist the belief that Mr. Adams insensibly infused into this work much of the learning and of the breadth of views belonging to himself. It looks a little as Raphael's labor might be supposed to look, if he had undertaken to show how Perugino painted. It has a historical value independently of the generous endeavor to do justice to a man who had, at the moment, fallen into discredit and oblivion, most undeservedly.[32]

Infusion of John Adams's own thinking there undeniably was, but he was not insensible of it.

Charles Francis Adams's comment is worth noticing for the reason it indicates for his grandfather's departure from strict historicity: a "generous endeavor" to rescue the memory of James Otis from "discredit and oblivion." More of that shortly, after another motivating factor has been observed. This was that John Adams was "jealous, very jealous, of the honor of Massachusetts." He expressed himself thus in January 1818 to William Wirt, the author of a recent and hugely popular book, *Sketches of the Life and Character of Patrick Henry.*[33] Wirt's hagiographic account of the Virginian orator and patriot might have let it be supposed that Henry — as it might be, with his "If this be treason, make the most of it" in 1765 — was first in the field in the pre-revolutionary war of words. Adams could not allow this. James Otis of Massachusetts had gotten in well before, with his speech on writs of assistance. "The resistance to the British system for subjugating the colonies, began in 1760," he told Wirt (not erring on the side of understatement), "and in . . . February, 1761, James Otis electrified the town of Boston, the province of Massachusetts, and the whole continent, more than Patrick Henry did in the whole course of his life."

It was not only "the honor of Massachusetts," and establishing his native state's precedence in the origins of the Revolution, that John

32. *Ibid.*, 362.
33. 5 January 1818: *ibid.*, 272.

Adams was concerned with. As Charles Francis Adams indicated, there was also a vindication of the personal character of Otis. Although, as his career as a political figure went on, Otis became the American perhaps best known and most resented in Great Britain, there had been an element of inconstancy in his attitudes that brought him into considerable if intermittent unpopularity in Boston. This was still remembered thirty years and more after Otis's death; and his posthumous detractors were bruiting about the same allegation which he had been so anxious to rebut in his newspaper controversy with Thomas Hutchinson in 1763, that his motivation in political life was not patriotic conviction but vengefulness over the chief justiceship affair. John Adams himself had been critical of Otis at the time,[34] but it was probably as much in sorrow as in anger, and in old age only the affection remained. He had cause to remember Otis kindly, if only because Otis had thought well of him. Otis, he had heard from others, "often said . . . that John Adams would one day be the greatest man in North America"; disclaim such "extravagant hyperboles" though he might,[35] Adams would have been less than human not to be pleased to listen to them. But, of course, there would have been more to Adams's regard for Otis than that. Probably of far greater consequence was a grateful remembrance that Otis had been one of the established Boston lawyers who encouraged and helped him to make a start in his profession.

In William Tudor junior's biography of Otis, John Adams perhaps saw a book that he himself would have liked to write. To Wirt, author of the Patrick Henry book, he said: "If I could go back to the age of thirty-five . . . I would endeavour to become your rival . . . I would adopt . . . your title, 'Sketches of the Life and Writings of James Otis, of Boston.' "[36] His "forces fail," he told Benjamin Waterhouse in March 1817, or he "could write you a Volume of Commentaries . . . [on the "great Question"] . . . historical, political, phylosophical and moral."[37] As it turned out Adams did not forbear from going into print on the writs of assistance case; his failing forces and Tudor's book notwithstanding, he afterward published various of his writings for himself.[38] And it must not be supposed, either, that

34. See, *e.g.*, *ibid.*, 295-96.
35. Adams to Mercy Warren, 27 July 1807: *MHSC* fifth series IV (1878), 357. Mrs Warren denied ever having heard the prediction: *ibid.*, 365.
36. 5 January 1818: *LWJA* X, 271. Adams actually wrote "adapt," perhaps.
37. *Statesman and Friend* . . . (n. 29 above), 128.
38. *Novanglus and Massachusettensis* (Boston, 1819).

it was only through the Tudor book that Adams sought to set the record straight (or at any rate bent another way) on the primacy of Massachusetts and James Otis in the movement toward revolution. When Wirt's book on Patrick Henry reached him Adams was in correspondence with Hezekiah Niles of Baltimore, the owner of the *Weekly Register* ("the first American news magazine," it has been called).[39] Niles had approached him for material on the revolutionary period, and Adams did not neglect the opportunity to promote his cherished cause. He wrote to Niles telling of "an awakening and a revival of American principles and feelings" in Massachusetts as early as 1760 and 1761, and of the heroes of that time. Of these, "first and foremost, before all and above all, James Otis";[40] and pre-eminent among Otis's services to the future United States was his speech on writs of assistance:

> Who, at the distance of fifty-seven years, would attempt, upon memory, to give even a sketch of it? Some of the heads are remembered, out of which Livy or Sallust would not scruple to compose an oration for history. I shall not essay an analysis or a sketch of it at present. I shall only say, and I do say in the most solemn manner, that Mr. Otis's oration against *writs of assistance* breathed into this nation the breath of life.[41]

Powerful vindication, indeed, of "the honor of Massachusetts" and the memory of a traduced friend.

A clue, moreover, to the spirit in which Adams in due time reconstructed the Otis speech for William Tudor. If historians in the ancient classics could play posthumous speech-writer to their departed heroes, why should not John Adams do likewise for James Otis? Adams belonged to an age before the writing of history had acquired its modern professional standards. That what he served up to Tudor was more literary than historical in character is nothing surprising. Indeed (and not unlike his obliquely acknowledged exemplar, Sallust),[42] he gave explicit warning of it.

---

39. Butterfield, *op. cit.* (n. 29 above), 227.
40. 13 February 1818: *LWJA* X, 284.
41. 14 January 1818: *ibid.*, 276.
42. "The addresses in Sallust's works are introduced by such phrases as 'hoc modo disservit', 'huiuscemodi orationem habuit' . . . , and hence do not purport to give the exact words of the speakers. They are carefully composed and their sentiments adapted to those who are represented as delivering them, but the language is that of Sallust himself": J. C. Rolfe, ed., *Sallust* (London and New York, 1920), xiv.

The beginning of 1818 saw John Adams concerned to publicize the priority of Massachusetts and James Otis over Virginia and Patrick Henry in early revolutionary stirrings; but this was not the start of his insistence upon the historical significance of the writs of assistance case. And the most famous and vivid of his depictions not only was written before the Wirt book on Henry came into his hands, but seems unrelated to any calculated prospect of publication. It was in a letter to William Tudor on 29 March 1817, more than a twelvemonth before his series of letters for the Otis biography:

> Otis was a flame of Fire! With the promptitude of Classical Allusions, a depth of Research, a rapid Summary of Historical Events and dates, a profusion of legal Authorities, a prophetic glare of his eyes into futurity, and a rapid Torrent of impetuous Eloquence, he hurried away all before him; American Independence was then and there born. The seeds of Patriots and Heroes to defend the non sine Diis animosus infans, to defend the vigorous Youth, were then and there sown. Every man of an crowded Audience appeared to me to go away, as I did, ready to take up Arms against Writs of Assistants. Then and there was the first scene of the first Act of Opposition to the arbitrary Claims of Great Britain. Then and there the child Independence was born. In fifteen years, i.e. in 1776, he grew up to manhood, declared himself free.[43]

And more than a year still earlier Adams was ruminating to Dr. Jedidiah Morse that the American Revolution was "in the minds and hearts of the people" long before it got to the point of actual fighting:

> When, where, by what means, and in what manner was this great intellectual, moral and political change accomplished? Undoubtedly it was begun in the towns of Boston and Salem . . . .

43. Tudor's *Life of Otis*, 61, ascribes the "non sine Diis animosus infans" figure "to the Alliance Medal, struck in Paris. One side of which contains the head of Liberty, with the words *Libertas Americana*, 4th July 1776, and on the reverse a robust infant struggling with the serpent, attacked by a Lion (England) defended by Minerva (France) who interposes a shield with the *fleurs de lis*, and on which the Lion fastens: the motto furnished by Sir William Jones, *Non sine die animosus infans,* and underneath the dates $\frac{17}{19}$ Oct. $\frac{1771}{1781}$."

See also *Statesman and Friend* (n. 29 above), 132. ("Non sine dis animosus infans": Horace, *Odes* III, 4, line 20.) Adams may also have been remembering an allegory that went the rounds at the time of the Stamp Act, about the death of "Lady North American Liberty." Her dowry from her father, John Bull, had been that she and her children should enjoy traditional English rights and liberties. She left a son "prophetically named Independence and on him the hopes of all her disconsolate servants are placed for relief of their afflictions, when he shall come of age." See M. Jensen, *The Founding of a Nation* (New York, 1969), 130, quoting the *New York Gazette* 5 September 1765, and citing the *Georgia Gazette* 31 October 1765 and *BEP* 19 August 1765.

> In the month of February, 1761, the great cause of writs of assistance was argued before the supreme judicature of the province . . . .

In particular, James Otis

> displayed so comprehensive a knowledge of the subject . . . . with such a profusion of learning, such convincing argument, and such a torrent of sublime and pathetic eloquence, that a great crowd of spectators and auditors went away absolutely electrified.[44]

Nor was this the start of it. Whatever ulterior polemical purposes influenced John Adams's writings on the writs of assistance case in the last dozen years of his life, his conviction that in February 1761 he had witnessed the first significant wrench against the British connection went much farther back.

To Mercy Otis Warren in 1807 Adams described how, as a young man in the time of the French and Indian war, he had been so displeased by the attitudes of the British military that even then his thoughts had turned toward American independence. However,

> Wolfe and Amherst succeeded, affairs went well, and all my revries about independence vanished.
>
> But they were not allowed to sleep long. As early as 1760 orders came to Paxton and Cockle to demand Writs of Assistance to break open houses, cellars, shops, and ships, to search for uncustomed goods. Judge Sewall died: Hutchinson was appointed Chief Justice on purpose, as I believed, to give judgment in favor of these writs.
>
> I heard your brother James Otis, and Mr Thacher, in the Council Chamber before the Superior Court in February, 1761, against the legality of these writs . . . . The cause opened to my view a nearer prospect of a revolution than I had ever seen before. I saw a haughty, powerful nation, who held us in great contempt, bent upon extending the authority of Parliament over our purses and all our internal concerns as well as external. I saw, on the other hand, the people of America cordially and conscientiously averse to these pretensions, and such was my opinion of their resolution that I believed they would oppose them to the last extremity. I saw no possible way in which these opposite opinions and determinations could be reconciled, and therefore concluded the controversy would be long continued, productive in time of a civil war, and actually terminate in a separation of the Colonies from the mother country.[45]

44. 29 November 1815, LWJA X, 182-83.
45. 20 July 1807, op. cit. n. 7 above, 339-40.
Here was another instance, apparently — cf. pp. 134, 135, 139 above — of Adams mistakenly associating the writs case with William Pitt's August 1760 directive against trading with the enemy. The passage from William Gordon's History at n. 7 above has something similar: further supporting the suggestion in n. 7 that Gordon's information on the case derived from his acquaintance with Adams. See also, however, n. 59 below.

Four or five years before this comparatively sobersided affirmation to Mrs. Warren (whose own historical work he was purporting to set right) Adams had written a no less graphic account in his autobiography:

> I was much more attentive to the Information and the Eloquence of the Speakers, than to my minutes, and too much allarmed at the prospect that was opened before me, to care much about writing a report of the Controversy. The Views of the English Government towards the Collonies and the Views of the Collonies towards the English Government, from the first of our History to that time, appeared to me to have been directly in Opposition to each other, and were now by the Imprudence of Administration, brought to a Collision. England proud of its power and holding Us in Contempt would never give up its pretentions. The Americans devoutly attached to their Liberties, would never submit, at least without an entire devastation of the Country and a general destruction of their Lives. A Contest appeared to me to be opened, to which I could foresee no End, and which would render my Life a Burden and Property, Industry, and every Thing insecure. There was no Alternative left, but to take the Side, which appeared to be just, to march intrepidly forward in the right path, to trust in providence for the Protection of Truth and right, and to die with a good Conscience and a decent grace, if that Tryal should become indispensible.[46]

All this was piling it on good and thick. In 1761 young Adams had other things to occupy him than thoughts of revolutionary struggle. Most of his time was spent out at Braintree building up a law practice, denouncing pettifoggers, campaigning against the proliferation of taverns, and looking after the farm. Every indication is that well before the year was over the writs of assistance case had faded from his mind.[47]

However, that is not quite to the point. The object has been to demonstrate that Otis's speech on writs of assistance meant something to Adams well before the last decade of his life. And the demonstration can be pushed back farther still. In October 1780 Adams wrote to the Dutch lawyer, Hendrik Calkoen, about the writs of assistance case:

> the arguments advanced upon that occasion . . . opened to the people such a view of the designs of the British government against their liberties and

46. *DAJA* III, 276.

47. *Cf.*, however, a memoir of John Adams by C. F. Adams in April 1827 (*MHSP* I 1791-1835): "It appears to have been the argument of James Otis, on the legality of . . . 'writs of assistance' which first opened his mind to the practical consequences of investing arbitrary authority in . . . officers of the crown. From this date he became more and more engaged in political controversy . . . ."

of the danger they were in, as made a deep impression upon the public, which never wore out.

From this moment, every measure of the British court and parliament and of the king's governors and other servants confirmed the people in an opinion of a settled design to overturn those constitutions under which their ancestors had emigrated from the old world, and with infinite toil, danger, and expense, planted a new one.[48]

This has the ring of a more considered assessment. The British had not driven the French out of Canada without an idea of how a vastly extended North American dominion might have to be governed; and established colonies were not unaware that plans to restructure them were never far below the surface of British thinking at this time. Inasmuch as British intentions for after the war were already the subject of colonial misgiving and watchfulness, the writs of assistance case may have been interpreted by some as a sign of the menacing new order having begun.

John Adams's lapse of interest in the writs of assistance case seems to have lasted from the middle months of 1761 till well into the 1770s.. That his interest still had not revived in the spring of 1773 is suggested by his apparently doing nothing to retrieve the Abstract manuscript when it was purloined at that time (for use in the *Massachusetts Spy*).[49] Of course, there is an obvious logic in Adams's full-scale reaction to the case being so long delayed, and his vision of it as the start of the movement toward independence taking on a quality of back-projection. For the case to be seen in that perspective, time had to pass. Even as late as 1773 the ultimate was three years away. But when the moment came he was quick to bring the whole picture into focus:

Yesterday the greatest Question was decided, which ever was debated in America, and a greater perhaps, never was or will be decided among Men. A Resolution was passed without one dissenting Colony 'that these united Colonies, are, and of right ought to be free and independent States, and as such, they have, and of Right ought to have full Power to make War,

48. Note 24 above.

49. However, in the spring and summer of 1773 Adams was fairly heavily occupied politically and professionally: see *DAJA* II, 82; and *LPJA* III, 345. The year following he argued the case of Richard King, of Falmouth, whose house in 1766 had been rifled by a mob: "An Englishmans dwelling House is his Castle. The Law has erected a Fortification round it . . .": *King v. Stewart*, *LPJA* I, 137. Adams could hardly have failed to recall the writs of assistance case at this time (for particular words of echo see, *e.g.*, p. 344 below); and *cf.* P. Shaw, *The Character of John Adams* (Chapel Hill, 1976), 77-78; also chapter 19, n. 1.

conclude Peace, establish Commerce, and to do all the other Acts and Things, which other States may rightfully do.' You will see in a few days a Declaration setting forth the Causes, which have impell'd us to this mighty Revolution, and the Reasons which will justify it, in the Sight of God and Man. A Plan of Confederation will be taken up in a few days.

When I look back to the Year 1761, and recollect the Argument concerning Writs of Assistance, in the Superior Court, which I had hitherto considered as the Commencement of the Controversy, between Great Britain and America . . . .[50]

Thus John Adams writing from Philadelphia to his wife Abigail on 3 July 1776. On the following day the declaration of which he spoke was duly promulgated.

The writs of assistance case began on Tuesday 24 February 1761. This much can be deduced from the introductory words of John Adams's Abstract, which identified the day as that "appointed by the rule of the Court for argument of special matters." While the admission at the end of the Abstract, that "many authorities; also many fine touches in the order of reasoning, and numberless Rhetorical flourishes" had been omitted, might be an indication to the contrary, it would be easy to infer from the Abstract that the proceedings were all over in the one day. But this was not so. In the opening letter of his series to William Tudor in 1818 Adams told of the Otis speech alone having lasted "four or five hours." In 1816 he wrote of the court announcing its decision "after many days" and "after some days."[51] His autobiography recalls that "The Argument continued several days in the Council Chamber . . . ."[52]

Nor does the next ranking source of evidence add anything. The value of the account of the writs of assistance case and its background in Thomas Hutchinson's *History of Massachusets-Bay* has already become apparent in this book and there will be occasion to acknowledge it again; but the paragraphs which Hutchinson gives to this subject do not extend to even a hint as to just how many days he and his fellow judges spent on it. For supplementary material on the time frame of the writs of assistance hearing it is necessary to range wider. By chance, on this particular topic the Superior Court records are not wholly useless. And another repository of official

50. L. H. Butterfield *et al.*, eds., *Adams Family Correspondence* II (Boston, 1963), 27-28.

51. *LWJA* X, 233, 248.

52. *DAJA* III, 276.

documentation, the Public Record Office in London, affords a few useful scraps besides. But the most direct evidence, and first in line for notation, is to be found in the letter books of Governor Francis Bernard in the Houghton Library at Harvard. Writing in 1765, Bernard recollected that the granting of writs of assistance four years before had been "so strongly opposed by the Merchants that the Arguments in Court from the Bar and upon the Bench lasted three days." [53]   In 1768 he again harked back to the opposition having been "prosecuted with such earnestness, that the hearing lasted three days successively." [54]

That the three days of the hearing were successive is consistent with the rule of the court under which it took place; and it seems safe to conclude that the writs of assistance hearing that began on Tuesday 24 February 1761 occupied the Superior Court throughout Wednesday and into if not through Thursday. The court record states that the court adjourned "without day" on the Monday following, 2 March; and the entry of further business after the blank for the writs of assistance hearing goes to confirm that after the judges' quite long session on this contentious question they still had other work to get through.

Although it seems likely enough that the court took no other business than the writs of assistance case on the opening day (which was, after all, given over to "special pleadings"), the day may not have been of normal working length. The sources of information here are the minutes of the province Council transmitted to the Board of Trade and now in the Public Record Office. [55] The minutes show that there was a meeting of the Council on Tuesday 24 February, and that among those present were all five members of the Superior Court (of course, in their independent capacities as elected members of the Council): Thomas Hutchinson, Benjamin Lynde, John Cushing, Chambers Russell, and Peter Oliver. The writs of assistance hearing took place in the same room as Council meetings. Unless the Council meeting took place in the evening, the working day of the Superior Court must have been the shorter for it.

Something else may have affected the length of time that the

53. To Board of Trade, 30 November 1765: Bernard Papers IV (reproduced in *Quincy's Reports*, 416). The actual letter is in C05/891.

54. To William Franklin, 24 March 1768: Bernard Papers V. Bernard was not referring to the November hearing (*cf. LPJA* II, 114), which from the SCR and *BG* 23 November 1761 plainly lasted only one day.

55. C05/823.

court actually sat in the course of the three days. It so happened that in that week of February the tribunal considering Charles Paxton's articles of complaint against the troublesome collector of customs, Benjamin Barons, was meeting to examine witnesses. One member of the tribunal was Chambers Russell, judge of vice-admiralty and also of the Superior Court. It does not appear in the closely detailed documentation of the tribunal's activities (in the Public Record Office) that Russell was absent from any of these sessions. On the contrary, it was he who, when the witnesses swore to their depositions, administered the oaths.[56] It would seem then that either the Superior Court carried on its writs of assistance hearing without Judge Russell or it did not sit while he was away attending to the Barons affair. Such positive evidence as there is favors the latter alternative: John Adams's long-distance recollection was of five judges sitting on the bench.[57] Common sense probability comes down on the same side. While it was not strictly necessary for all five judges to attend the Superior Court, good form and the dignity of the court might have suggested that if Judge Russell could not be spared from the Barons tribunal — which had no legal standing — the highest court in the province should not be expected to do without his services either (especially in such an important case). And for Russell to have slipped out of court for an hour or two and yet joined in the eventual decision might have been open to even graver objection than participating in the Barons proceedings only part time.

The opening day of the writs of assistance case, then, probably found the Superior Court short of time on two accounts: a meeting of the province Council, and the Barons tribunal. How much time was thus taken up, and when in the day, are impossible to tell with confidence. The only recorded business of the Council had to do with the issuance of warrants for soldiers' pay; if that was indeed all the meeting would not have been a long one. The Barons tribunal occupied itself with examining evidence from George Cradock, custom house sidekick and deputy judge of vice-admiralty; Cradock's testimony against the delinquent collector was fairly extensive, and can hardly have been gotten through in a matter of minutes. One might guess, perhaps, that it would have suited Governor Bernard's

56. T1/408, passim.
57. To Tudor, 29 March 1817, LWJA X, 245; and to Waterhouse, 19 March 1817 — Statesman and Friend (n. 29 above), 127.

convenience, when he had Judge Russell already with him, to get on to the Barons business immediately after the Council meeting. If that was the way things went, the probabilities point to the first part of the day taken up by the Council and the Barons tribunal, so that the Superior Court was not at full strength and ready to start until the afternoon.

The next day, too, the court's time on the writs of assistance case would have been similarly the shorter by reason of Judge Russell's absence. On this Wednesday the Barons tribunal took evidence, and again there seems to have been plenty of it, from Robert Temple (another member of the custom house). As on Tuesday, such evidence as there is suggests that the Wednesday session of the tribunal preceded the Superior Court's sitting. The record shows the tribunal, after examining Temple, adjourning to Thursday.

For Thursday, however, the record says simply, "The meeting was adjourned till tomorrow." Even though there were witnesses yet to be examined the tribunal postponed seeing them to Friday. Might not the explanation be that Judge Russell, hopeful that work on the writs of assistance case would again permit, agreed on the Wednesday morning to attend the tribunal's Thursday session, only to find, after Wednesday's sitting of the Superior Court, that the writs of assistance issue was still so far from settled that it looked like requiring the whole of a third day as well? If this was the position and on Thursday Judge Russell found that the Superior Court was too heavily occupied with writs of assistance for him to attend the Barons tribunal, the tribunal had no choice but to postpone its business.

It cannot be assumed that the third day of the writs of assistance hearing was taken up wholly, or even mainly, by one or other of the advocates addressing the court. Governor Bernard's testimony is that the three days' argumentation was not only "from the Bar" but "upon the Bench." Corroboration is supplied by the chief justice himself. In his *History* Hutchinson puts it like this:

> Some of the judges . . . from a doubt whether such writs were still in use in England, seemed to favour the exception, and, if judgment had been then given, it is uncertain on which side it would have been. The chief justice was, therefore, desired, by the first opportunity in his power, to obtain information of the practice in England, and judgment was suspended.[58]

58. Page 68.

Writing to England of his losses in the Stamp Act riots he was more specific. The Massachusetts Archives show a letter to Henry Seymour Conway, secretary of state, in which Hutchinson drew attention to his services in the matter of writs of assistance: "the court seemed inclined to refuse to grant them but I prevailed with my brethren to continue the cause until the next term . . . ."[59]

Even allowing that Hutchinson's concern was to impress the British government with the justice of his claim for compensation, it is not hard to imagine that the new chief justice (mindful perhaps of the understandings behind his appointment) had to tussle hard and long to give the "general" writ of assistance a fighting chance. His fellow judges came to the hearing still infected by the doubts, implanted by the London Magazine, that had caused them to draw back from granting such an instrument to James Cockle at Salem in the fall. Besides, there was always the disquieting fact that the text of the writ they had issued in the past did not fit the actualities of the smuggling problem in Massachusetts. Nor can the crown's arguments in court have done much to convince the hesitant bench (that they were not designed for maximum impact will become clear in chapter 13). And this quite apart from the formidable oratory on the other side. Plainly, unless Hutchinson himself redressed the balance the cause of the custom house was hopeless. He cannot have found it easy. Not a lawyer, he had no reserves of superior learning to argue from; and glad as his colleagues may have been to have him sitting with them — rather than the disdained Colonel Otis — it nevertheless required no little nerve in a newcomer, chief justice or not, to shove them even half-way off the negative stance they evidently preferred. If Hutchinson used the whole of the third day in getting his way (the judicial tug-of-war presumably took place in private session), it probably was a fair indicator of the size of his task.

"After many days," John Adams recalled in December 1816, "the Chief Justice arose, and with that gravity and subtility, that artless

---

59. 1 October 1765: MA 26; C05/755; *Quincy's Reports*, 415. Compare with this, and the slightly ampler excerpt at p. 386 below, the further element in William Gordon's account of the writs of assistance case (n. 7 above): "The great opposition that was made . . . , and the arguments of Mr. *Otis*, disposed the court to a refusal; but Mr. *Hutchinson*, who had obtained the place of chief justice, prevailed with his brethren to continue the cause till next term; and in the mean time, wrote to England, and procured a copy of the writ, and sufficient evidence of the practice of the exchequer there, after which like writs were granted . . . ." Gordon claimed to have read "near thirty folio manuscript volumes" of Massachusetts records; here, plainly was a product of that labor: cf. M. C. Tyler, *The Literary History of the American Revolution* II (New York, 1897), 423, n. 4.

design of face, which will never fade in my memory, said, 'the Court could not, at present, see any foundation for the writ of assistance, but thought proper to continue the consideration of it till next term, and, in the mean time, to write to England, and inquire what was the practice and what were the grounds of it there.' "[60] Soon afterward Adams wrote of this again. Now he was specific that "The Court adjourned for consideration, and after some days, at the close of the term," Chief Justice Hutchinson announced the decision to defer a decision until word had been obtained from England.[61] The "close of the term" was on Monday 2 March.[62] It would seem from this that the judges may still have been brooding upon the writs of assistance case over the weekend.

John Adams's reference to Chief Justice Hutchinson's "artless design of face, which will never fade in my memory," may have meant no more than that Adams remembered Hutchinson as always looking like that, not that he was actually present on that last day of the February term when Hutchinson announced the deferment of a determination upon the writ of assistance. Adams was at this time a tenderfoot lawyer hoping to build up a country practice in and around his home town of Braintree, and as yet he had been sworn attorney only in the Inferior Court. Boston was two or three hours' ride from Braintree; and although Adams claimed to have attended every Superior Court in Boston from 1758 to 1765, ordinarily there would have been nothing to bring him in for the final bits of business at the very end of the term. But it chanced that the Superior Court's February 1761 term at Boston was something rather special for John Adams; and it is not at all improbable that he actually saw and heard Chief Justice Hutchinson's announcement on Monday 2 March.

For one thing, there was the impact of what he had heard the previous week. After the speech of James Otis, Adams was to recall in old age, "Every man of a crowded audience appeared to me to go away, as I did, ready to take arms against writs of assistance." Eagerness to know the result of oratory that had excited him so much could have had young Adams galloping in from Braintree on the Monday morning. But there may have been another and more solid motivation. According to an editorial note in the *Legal Papers of John Adams*, Adams's "first appearance in the Superior Court was

60. To Tudor, 18 December 1816, *LWJA* X, 253.
61. To Tudor, 29 March 1817, *ibid.*, 248.
62. SCR 1760-62.

in Feb. 1761, when he filed a prayer for affirmation, a privilege apparently allowed to Inferior Court attorneys."[63] This, one imagines, was the sort of item that gravitated naturally to the bottom of the court's list. In other words, Adams had to attend the Superior Court on that last day of term for it was not until then that his little bit of business was called.

Perhaps it is not too far-fetched a speculation, either, that Adams's "prayer for affirmation" accounted for his being around in the previous week when the writs of assistance case was being argued. Just as this small stuff might be left until more important matters had been disposed of, so it may have been the kind of thing that the judges were apt to call for and deal with any time they had a few minutes to spare — for example, while waiting for a jury to come back with its verdict. A youngster in Adams's position might have to kick his heels for quite a time.

This is not to say, however, that Adams was in the Superior Court from the moment the writs of assistance case first came on, on Tuesday 24 February. Given over as it was to "special pleadings," that day was on the face of it a *dies non* for all other business, including such odds and ends as Adams's "prayer for affirmation." Moreover, the rule of the court was not only that the second Tuesday in the term should be set aside for special pleadings, but also that there should be no sitting the day before (so that the attorneys could prepare their arguments). All in all there was really nothing to bring Adams in from Braintree, where he would have spent the weekend, until Wednesday morning at the earliest (when, for all he could have known to the contrary, the special pleadings of Tuesday would be finished and the court's normal business resumed). At this stage in his career he had no money to waste on unnecessary lodging expenses.

John Adams's attendance at the hearing he was to make famous was perhaps in a sense accidental. For all he knew when he showed up at the Superior Court on Wednesday 25 February, the "special pleadings" of the previous day had been disposed of and the court was back to normal business (including, it was to be hoped, his own). As it turned out, however, Tuesday had been a short working day for the court; and the argumentation on writs of assistance was still going on. Adams's first reaction to the writs of assistance case may

63. Vol. I, lviii, n. 98.

have been nothing more elevated than that he might as well stay around until it were over.

In his autobiography Adams wrote of having taken "a few minutes, in a very careless manner." It is not obvious what first motivated him, for when he first set pen to paper the great oration by James Otis was still two speeches away. As it was, Adams began his notes when Jeremiah Gridley was still delivering his opening speech for the crown, and all he got of it was this:

> The Constables distraining for Rates. more inconsistent with Eng. Rts. & Liberties than Writts of assistance. And Necessity, authorizes both.

Not much here, one would have thought, to inspire gratuitous reportage.

The notes afford no direct evidence on the chronology of the hearing. They show no dates or any other explicit indication of time. What little there is has to be extracted by inference and by way of comparison with materials from other sources. The Gridley fragment in the last paragraph is a case in point. Those staccato sentences are distinctly echoed in the Abstract rendition of Gridley's opening speech, the two concluding paragraphs.

In the Abstract Gridley speaks of the writ of assistance taking away "the common privileges of Englishmen"; and, " 'Tis the necessity of the Case and the benefit of the Revenue that justifies this Writ." Distraint by local tax collectors was a parallel; and the speech comes to an end with the affirmation that "the necessity of having public taxes effectually and speedily collected is of infinitely more moment to the whole, than the Liberty of any Individual." The noticeably close correspondence between Gridley's peroration in the Abstract and what John Adams recorded at the time strongly suggests that barely had Adams begun writing when Gridley sat down. Here another possibility comes into view. It is that Adams could not have gotten the whole of the speech in any event, for the reason that what Gridley said on the Wednesday was by way of completion of what he had started the day before. If, what with the province Council meeting and Judge Russell's absence at the Barons tribunal, the Superior Court had not been able to sit till quite late on Tuesday Gridley's opening speech might have had to be interrupted by the adjournment and resumed on the morrow.

Despite what he later said about writing "in a very careless manner," once started Adams appears to have worked reasonably diligently on his notes. He used a large single sheet of paper folded into sixteen segmented pages; the Gridley tailpiece is on the first page, naturally, and immediately below, with no dividing line and no change of writing, is Oxenbridge Thacher's speech against the writ. A comparison with the Abstract rendition of the Thacher speech suggests that Adams did not miss much here. (Of course, he was still fresh to his work.) Thacher's speech goes on to the second page, across which a line is drawn at the end. And then follows the Otis speech, through the third page and on to the fourth. Not far down the third page, however, the handwriting begins to lose shape; and the notes themselves become scrappier and scrappier, and on the fourth segment they not so much come to an end as peter out.[64]

Presumably it was the inadequate treatment of Otis that Adams had foremost in mind when years later he wrote so disparagingly of "those despicable Notes."[65] Given the historic significance that he came to see in the Otis speech it was back luck that Otis had not spoken before Thacher, for Adams would have been better able to do it justice. As it was, his energies had given out. His autobiography might claim that he had been "more attentive to the Information and Eloquence of the Speakers" than to his note-taking, and "too much allarmed at the prospect that was opened . . . to care much about writing a report of the Controversy"; but a sight of what he actually wrote at that time presents a different explanation. A quill pen is not the most convenient writing instrument ever to have been invented; and when Otis got into his "rapid Torrent of impetuous Eloquence" (difficult enough to take down at the best of times) Adams had already been scratching away — with all that dipping, too — several hours. His hand was stiff and aching, and the notes had to go by the board. Had Adams been still fresh enough to make as good a job of Otis's speech as he had made of Thacher's, he would have had less regret to vex him in later years (when the full historic significance of the Otis speech had become apparent to him), and perhaps less need to get that elaborate reconstruction out of his system in 1818.

It is reasonable to suppose that the second day of the hearing closed when Otis ended his speech. In large part of course this is a matter of common sense: Otis had spoken "four or five hours"

64. According to the "Journal of the Times" (for which see p. 470 below) in *BEP* 27 March 1769, "one or two o'clock has been the hours for dining in this town, time out of mind." It seems likely enough that the whole of the postprandial sitting was given over to Otis.

65. "The minutes of Mr. Otis' argument are no better a representation of it than the gleam of a glow-worm to the meridian blaze of the sun": Adams to Tudor, 29 March 1817, *LWJA* X, 248-249.

(according to John Adams's recollection) and he was the third speaker of the day; there simply would not have been time for any more. However, there is corroboration in Adams's notes. At the end of the note of the Otis speech a thin and broken line is drawn across the page, looking much of a piece with the weary scrawl in which the last fragments of Otis were jotted down. The writing next below this line is altogether livelier. By now Adams was using a different pen, or at any rate had sharpened the old one; and the text, which is of more argument by Jeremiah Gridley for the crown, is more coherent and better articulated than any preceding it. It is obvious that Adams left off after Otis finished speaking, and that this sprightly resumption was at a comfortable interval after — next morning, perhaps. The appearance presented by John Adams's notes bears out the proposition that the court adjourned the second day of its hearing at the conclusion of the Otis speech. And there is one more small thing that can be adduced. Writing in 1817 of the effect of the Otis speech, Adams said: "Every man of a crowded audience appeared to me to go away, as I did, ready to take arms against writs of assistance." The picture is one of people thronging out of the courtroom with Otis's oration still ringing in their ears, no further speechifying or anything else having yet dulled its force.

If it is almost certain that John Adams left off writing at the end of Otis's speech and resumed with more from Gridley only after an interval (at least long enough to get his hand rested), it is beyond question that the remainder of his work on that segmented sheet of paper — the "Extracts from the Acts of Parliament" (plus the province enactment on the jurisdiction of the Superior Court), and the texts of Charles Paxton's 1755 petition for a writ of assistance and of the writ actually issued — was added later. This leads to one further thought about the chronology of the writs of assistance hearing. The likelihood that Adams obtained at least some of these additional materials from his mentor, Jeremiah Gridley, who naturally had to have them when preparing the case for the crown, suggests a possibility that the note of further arguments from Gridley, as it were in reply to Thacher and Otis, is not what it seems, and that it too was written outside the courtroom after the hearing was over. This will be discussed further in the next chapter; it is mentioned here because, if there is anything in it, it means that the third day of the writs of assistance case — Thursday 26 February — was spent wholly behind closed doors in argument among the judges themselves — or, rather, in Chief Justice Hutchinson persuading his reluctant colleagues not to find against the crown there and then but to agree to his sending to England for authentic particulars of the writ of assistance. Even at that, however, it seems not to have been until the Monday following that the bench was ready to announce Hutchinson's victory.

For a visual image of the writs of assistance hearing resort may be had to three letters by John Adams, to Benjamin Waterhouse on 19 and 25 March 1817 and to William Tudor on 29 March 1817.[66] How seriously it is impossible to say, but Adams was purporting to describe the scene in sufficient detail for a picture to be painted of it: "Would not Copely have made a great Painting of that Counsell Chamber and its Contents?" he asked Waterhouse. It was to Tudor however that he gave the ampler account:

> The scene is the Council Chamber in the old Town House in Boston. The date is in the month of February, 1761 . . . .
>
> That Council Chamber was as respectable an apartment as the House of Commons or the House of Lords in Great Britain, in proportion, or that in the State House in Philadelphia, in which the declaration of independence was signed, in 1776. In this chamber, round a great fire, were seated five Judges, with Lieutenant-Governor Hutchinson at their head, as Chief Justice, all arrayed in their new, fresh, rich robes of scarlet English broadcloth; in their large cambric bands, and immense judicial wigs. In this chamber were seated at a long table all the barristers at law of Boston, and of the neighboring county of Middlesex, in gowns, bands, and tie wigs. They were not seated on ivory chairs, but their dress was more solemn and more pompous than that of the Roman Senate, when the Gauls broke in upon them.
>
> In a corner of the room must be placed as a spectator and an auditor, wit, sense, imagination, genius, pathos, reason, prudence, eloquence, learning, and immense reading, hanging by the shoulders on two crutches, covered with a great cloth coat, in the person of Mr Pratt, who had been solicited on both sides, but would engage on neither, being, as Chief Justice of New York, about to leave Boston forever. Two portraits, at more than full length, of King Charles the Second and of King James the Second, in splendid golden frames, were hung up on the most conspicuous sides of the apartment . . . .
>
> One circumstance more. Samuel Quincy and John Adams had been admitted barristers at that term. John was the youngest; he should be painted looking like a short thick archbishop of Canterbury, seated at the table with a pen in his hand, lost in admiration, now and then minuting those poor notes . . . .

66. *Statesman and Friend,* n. 29 above, 126-28; *LWJA* X, 244-45.

Whatever its usefulness to a painter, this passage calls for a few lines of historical commentary.

The Council chamber is still there, on the upper floor of the building now known as the Old State House; and it is a handsome enough room, to be sure. It may well have been true that the writs of assistance hearing attracted spectators from the legal profession, but Adams's artistic license got the better of his memory when he described the way they were dressed, for barristers formally attired in "gowns, bands, and tie wigs" had yet to be seen in the courts of Massachusetts.[67]   Benjamin Prat, the former Pownallite politician, may have been expecting to become chief justice of New York, through Thomas Pownall's influence in England; but he had not been appointed yet, and in fact was still in law practice in Boston. The recollection of the crutches is reliable enough, however: in his youth Prat had lost a leg through falling off a horse. And Adams can be assumed to have remembered his companion accurately (though he was wrong in saying that he and Samuel Quincy "had been admitted barristers that term": it was not until the following November that they were admitted to practice in the Superior Court).

Adams's description of the scene resumed:

> Now for the actors and performers. Mr Gridley argued with his characteristic learning, ingenuity, and dignity, and said every thing that could be said in favor of Cockle's petition . . . . Mr Thacher followed him on the other side, and argued with the softness of manners, the ingenuity and cool reasoning, which were remarkable in his amiable character.

Then came the encomium, which perhaps more than anything else scored the writs of assistance case indelibly into American history: how Otis was "a flame of fire"; how his audience appeared "to go away . . . ready to take arms against writs of assistance"; and how "Then and there the child Independence was born."

67. *LPJA* I, lviii.

13

~~~~~~~

Gridley

~~~~~~~

J EREMIAH GRIDLEY was neither the first nor the most obvious choice as the advocate to conduct the case for the crown. The brief might have been expected to go to one of the lawyers with a standing connection with crown causes. Why it did not go to — or was not accepted by — Attorney General Edmund Trowbridge, nowhere appears. Possibly it would have been a little awkward to have the draftsman of the writ of assistance arguing its legality before a court presided over by one of his friends; and Chief Justice Thomas Hutchinson himself had played a part in the advent of the writ to Massachusetts. James Otis junior claimed to have been "sollicited to argue this cause as Advocate-General," but resigned the office. The man who stood in as advocate general after Otis's resignation, Benjamin Prat, apparently preferred to sit the writs of assistance case out:[1] perhaps the whiggishness of Governor Pownall's administration, of which he had been a principal supporter, had rubbed off on to him. Another possibility, which could have influenced most Boston lawyers, is that the task of upholding the "general," openended, writ of assistance in face of the recent *London Magazine* article, which implied that in England such a writ would be illegal, was too unpromising. There were no reported cases — the lawyer's staple source of argument — by which the *London Magazine* might be refuted; besides, most of the Superior Court judges (those who had favored postponement of the Cockle application at Salem) were half persuaded against the writ already. And what would be the fruits of the custom house brief, anyway? Public hostility, redounding perhaps upon the foolhardy fellow's ordinary law practice: there

---

1. "The Merchants of Salem and Boston . . . applied to Mr. Pratt, but he had been solicited by Mr. Paxton, and refused to engage on either Side . . .": John Adams to Benjamin Waterhouse, 25 March 1817, in W. C. Ford, ed., *Statesman and Friend . . .* (Boston, 1927), 130. See also chapter 15, n. 16.

would be lawyers who remembered the costly professional fate of Robert Auchmuty in the 1740s, after his services to customs law enforcement had affronted the merchant interest.

With Jeremiah Gridley it may have been different. Now fifty-nine, he was long established as the doyen of the Boston bar — on the opposition side of the writs of assistance case, James Otis, and possibly Oxenbridge Thacher too, had numbered among his pupils. Gridley's sympathies had always been broadly whig. Back in the 1740s he had allowed the House of Representatives to go through the motions of making him attorney general of the province, a gesture of defiance to the governor who claimed (successfully as it turned out) the right of appointment himself. Latterly his affiliations had been rendered suspect by his being "the chief supporter of Loudon's war measures."[2] However, as a colonel in the militia he perhaps had an excusable commitment in this regard; and he seems to have scotched any incipient unpopularity by promoting a scheme whereby soldiers were billeted in Castle William rather than (as Lord Loudon had wished) on private property. Gridley was a sophisticated operator in law as well as in politics: for many years after his death lawyers "related his grand stratagems as classics of practice." As a test of all-round virtuosity the crown brief on writs of assistance, compounded as it was of political sensitivity and difficult law, could have held attraction for such a man.

That Gridley knew what he would be up against, in the shape of the *London Magazine* article, cannot be doubted. As well as everything else he was an accomplished man of letters, and had in the past turned his hand to literary journalism. In fact, one of his publications, the *American Magazine*, had been "an imitation of the *London Magazine* so dear to educated colonials." Gridley, as a literary man, could have been among the first to read the *London Magazine* for March 1760, and, as a lawyer, to apprehend the significance of its comments on the writ of assistance.

It added piquancy to Gridley's acceptance of the custom house brief that he did not believe in it. In the sworn testimony on Charles Paxton's articles of complaint against the turbulent collector of customs, Benjamin Barons, is the following from Robert Temple: "This deponent saith that he has heard Mr. Barons declare that in his Opinion the Custom house officers were not entitled to the writs of

2. For materials in this paragraph and the next see C. K. Shipton, *Sibley's Harvard Graduates* VII (Boston, 1945), 518-29.

assistance that had been usually granted to them and that Mr. Gridley his Lawyer was of the same Opinion."[3] (The reference presumably was to the general writ of assistance that the Superior Court had been issuing since 1755, as distinct from the specific writ propounded in the *London Magazine*; Gridley could be identified as Barons's lawyer in the sense that it would be Barons, as custodian of the custom house cash, who paid him his fee on the writs of assistance brief.) Of course, the advocate's function is not to pre-judge a case but to present it. To that extent a personal opinion that the general writ of assistance was wrong did not bar Gridley from accepting a brief to argue the opposite. But it called for still greater artistry in his footwork.

How Jeremiah Gridley coped with the brief for the crown is not the least interesting aspect of the writs of assistance case.

First, however, it is necessary to try to account for a strange discrepancy in the evidentiary materials — John Adams's original notes and the Abstract he wrote up from them. The notes open with Gridley, follow with his opponents, Oxenbridge Thacher and James Otis, and return to Gridley. The Abstract on the other hand has Gridley speaking only once, at the beginning of the proceedings. In the notes Gridley's opening speech is a mere fragment of four short sentences, but the Abstract expands it into a quite long and elegant oration; the second Gridley note is perhaps the most coherent and lucid of all four, yet in the Abstract it has no place whatever. Inasmuch as the Abstract was conceived as a filled-out version of the skeletal jottings that Adams made at the time, that a whole speech should appear to have been omitted obviously needs explanation.

In fact, the one Gridley speech in the Abstract includes all the points and arguments (plus others besides) made in the two Gridley speeches in the notes. The assumption at once suggests itself that for reasons of presentation or style John Adams simply gathered to-gether all that Gridley said and fashioned it into a single composite speech. If to Adams the significance of the writs of assistance case lay in the oratory of James Otis, and the Otis speech was what the labor of writing the Abstract was really all about, it may have been a natural temptation to the young man to rig the record a little and show his hero as having the last splendid word. After all, he was not

3. T1/408: 25 February 1761.

writing a formal law report. If he chose to allow himself a measure of license, who was to deny it to him?

But closer scrutiny of the actual texts discloses a number of problems which this rather simplistic theory does not answer. In chapter 12 it was noticed that both the fragment of Gridley's opening speech in the notes and the theme of his peroration in the Abstract had to do with comparison of writ of assistance search with distress for local taxes, and justification for both in "necessity." The point then made was that Adams caught only the end of the opening speech. The point now is to observe a similarity between the final paragraphs of the second Gridley speech in the notes and the lead-in to his Abstract peroration. Thus the Abstract:

> It is true the common privileges of Englishmen are taken away in this Case, but even their privileges are not so in Cases of Crime and fine. . . .

> In fine the power now under consideration is the same with that given by the Law of this Province to Treasurers towards Collectors, & to them towards the subject. A Collector may when he pleases distrain my goods Chattels . . .

Thus the notes:

> And the Power given in this Writ is no greater Infringement of our Liberty than the Method of collecting Taxes in this Province. —
> Every Body knows that the Subject has the Priviledge of House only against his fellow Subjects, not vs the K. either in matters of Crime or fine.

Of course, this reference to existing infringements of the "privilege" of hearth and home for certain constabulary and fiscal purposes could be reaffirmation of what Gridley had said at an earlier stage in the proceedings. To some extent the fragment of Gridley's opening speech in the notes suggests that this was so:

> The Constables distraining for Rates. more inconsistent with Eng. Rts. & liberties than Writts of assistance. And Necessity, authorizes both.

Yet one cannot help wondering whether there may not have been more to this element of duplication than Gridley getting to his feet a second time and repeating himself.

The second Gridley note seems more introductory than re-affirmative:

> By the 7. & 8 of Wm. C. 22. § 6th. — This authority, of breaking and entering Ships, Warehouses Cellars &c given to the Custom House officers in England by the Statutes of the 12th. and 14th of Charl. 2d, is extended to the Custom House officers in the Plantations: — and by the Statute of

the 6th of Anne, Writts of Assistance are continued, in Company with all other legal Proscesses for 6 months after the Demise of the Crown. — Now what this Writ of assistance is, we can know only by Books of Precedents. — And we have produced, in a Book intituld the modern Practice of the Court of Exchequer, a form of such a Writ of assistance to the officers of the Customs. The Book has the Imprimatur of Wright C.J. of the K.'s B. wh is as great a sanction as any Books of Precedents ever have. altho Books of Reports are usually approved by all the Judges — and I take Brown the author of this Book to have been a very good Collector of Precedents. — I have two Volumes of Precedents of his Collection, wh I look upon as good as any, except Coke & Rastal.

And the Power given in this Writ . . . .

Surely such basic points as the originating legislation and what the writ of assistance was would have been expounded long before the fourth speech in the proceedings?

Moreover, this second Gridley note does not read as if it were replying to arguments that had occurred in the speeches of Oxenbridge Thacher and James Otis. The contrary, if anything. To help demonstrate the respectability of the writ of assistance the Gridley note cites the fact that an instrument of that name was included in the list of documents which an act of Parliament in 1702 saved from automatic expiry immediately on the death of the monarch.[4] Here is what the note of Otis's speech has to say on this subject: "Continuance of Writts and Proscesses, proves no more nor so much as I grant a special Writ of ass. on special oath, for specl Purpose." This has the tone of a retort. Possibly, Otis was anticipating Gridley. But why should Gridley have omitted to make this point, for whatever it were worth, in his opening speech? Or, if he in fact made it then, why should he have repeated it in a second speech? After all, Otis had demolished it pretty thoroughly (as having no bearing on the substantive proposition at issue, that the writ of assistance should not be general but should be granted only for the special occasion duly sworn to). A similar impression of wrong sequence is given by Gridley's attempt to make something of the book used for the Massachusetts writ of assistance bearing a judicial imprimatur. Otis had already said: "The authority of this Modern Practice of the Court of Exchequer. — it has an Imprimatur — But wt may not have? — It may be owing to some ignorant Clerk of the Exchequer."

4. This was 1 Ann., stat. 1, c. 8. As is stated in *LPJA* II, 129, n. 85, "the Statute of the 6th Anne" as recorded by Adams was probably a confusion with 6 Ann., c. 7, which prescribed a like six-month extension for Parliament, etc.

Again the Otis note reads as if in response to an argument from Gridley earlier.

What appears in John Adams's notes as a second speech by Gridley now takes on the aspect mentioned briefly in chapter 12: that it in truth represents not contemporaneous reporting but an effort after the event, with Adams seeking to reconstruct the speech with which Gridley had opened the proceedings and of which he had taken down only the concluding fragment. Thus it may be that the last paragraphs of the second Gridley note — about existing legal exceptions to the inviolability of hearth and home — not so much duplicate the fragmentary note at the end of Gridley's opening speech as overlap it or dovetail into it. This hypothesis is also consistent with facts apparent from the document actually bearing the notes as Adams wrote them (which still survives): the second Gridley note was written with a fresh pen and a rested hand, and it is markedly the least scrappy and disjointed note of them all. Facts which compel the inference that the second Gridley note was written not under pressure of the immediate spoken word but at leisure afterward.

Above all, of course, the hypothesis that the second Gridley note represents not a second speech but a *post factum* attempt to reconstruct Gridley's opening speech eliminates the puzzle of two Gridley speeches in Adams's notes but only one in the Abstract. In this perspective it is evident that the last address to the court came not from Jeremiah Gridley but — as Adams's long-distance reminiscences so powerfully suggest — from James Otis.

The Abstract did more than join the two parts of Gridley's presentation into a single speech. To the bare and incomplete material attributed to Gridley in John Adams's original notes it added volume, shape, and even art.

In the Abstract Gridley begins by declaring that he appeared "on the behalf of Mr. Cockle & others," and proceeds to recite what seems to have been a formal request for writs of assistance in virtually the same terms as Charles Paxton had used when applying for the first writ, in 1755. This introduction out of the way, argument begins.

It does so from the proposition that both the Court of Exchequer in England and the Superior Court in Massachusetts had been issuing writs of assistance, a matter of plain historical fact. Less unquestionable, however, was one of the supplementary assertions. "Such

Writs," said Gridley, "are mentioned in several Acts of Parliament, in several Books of Reports . . . ." It was true that writs of assistance were mentioned in the act of 1702 for preserving the force of certain legal instruments six months beyond the death of the monarch, and also that acts around the turn of the century for regulating the importation into England of certain textiles ("alamodes and lustrings")[5] spoke of the writ of assistance; but Gridley must have been hard put to it to find "several Books of Reports" in which the writ was mentioned. Even today the number of reported English cases featuring the customs writ of assistance could be counted on the fingers of one hand; in 1761 there probably was only one — a 1733 case in a book of reports by Sir John Strange.[6]

Gridley next says "in a Book called the Modern Practice of the Court of Exchequer, We have a Precedent, a form of a Writ, called a Writ of Assistance for Custom house Officers, of which the following a few years past to Mr. Paxton under the Seal of this Court, & tested by the late Chief Justice is a literal Translation." Clearly the precedent referred to was the *Breve Assisten' pro Officiar' Custum'* in William Brown's book on exchequer practice (indeed, later in the speech Gridley is explicit on Brown as the author). But Brown's book — revised edition — had the title *The Practice of his Majesties Court of Exchequer at Westminster.* The slip may be trivial and of no importance, but it is worth noticing. A book known as *The Modern Practice of the Court of Exchequer*, angled at customs matters specifically, did exist at this time;[7] and numerous precedents and model legal formulae were set forth in it. These precedents did not include the *Breve Assisten' pro Officiar Custum'*; but it may have added confusion that — since when the book appeared the common law still shrank from the English language — many of them were in the same peculiar near-Latin that the *breve* in Brown's book had had to be translated from for the Massachusetts writ of assistance. A curious thing is that in John Adams's original notes all three advocates

5. (1698) 9 and 10 Gul. 3, c. 43 (which envisioned search either with writ of assistance or by warrant on sworn information); (1706) 5 Ann., c. 20. See also (1700) 11 and 12 Gul. 3, c. 10.

6. See pp. 296-97.

7. The book's full title is indicative: *A Sure Guide to Merchants, Custom-House Officers, &c. or the Modern Practice of the Court of Exchequer in Prosecutions relating to his Majesty's Revenue of the Customs.* The dedication is initialed "B.Y.," but on title page the author is wholly anonymous (simply "an Officer of the Customs"). Publication was in London, 1730.

are shown speaking of "a Book, intituled the Modern Practice of the Court of Exchequer" (Thacher); "this Modern Practice of the Court of Exchequer" (Otis); and "a Book intituld the modern Practice of the Court of Exchequer" (Gridley, second note), as the source of the solitary precedent for the writ of assistance. A guess might be that the three agreed to economize on basic research and shared the same material: the researcher had made a mistake with the title of Brown's book, and they all fell into it.

The next phase of Gridley's argument illustrates the extent to which the Abstract filled out Adams's original notes. "The Ground of Mr Gridley's argt. is this," say the notes on Oxenbridge Thacher, "that this Court has the Power of the Court of Exchequer." One would never have thought it from any of the notes on Gridley. What Thacher identified as a central theme of Gridley's speech — that because the Superior Court could sit as a court of exchequer, it could issue writs of assistance like the Court of Exchequer in England — is not so much as hinted at. The Abstract makes good the lack, however; in it Gridley says: "The first Question . . . is, whether this practice of the Court of Exchequer in England . . . is legal or illegal. And the second is, whether the practice of the Exchequer (admitting it to be legal) can warrant this Court in the same practice." Not that the questions so robustly propounded were very satisfactorily answered.

"In answer to the first," said Abstract-Gridley, "I cannot indeed find the Original of this Writ of Assistance. It may be of very antient, to which I am inclined, or it may be of modern date. This however is certain, that the Stat. of the 14th. Char. 2nd. has established this Writ almost in the words of the Writ itself." And then he went on to quote — not altogether accurately — the words he had in mind (from section 5 of the Act of Frauds of 1662):

> And it shall be lawful to & for any person or persons *authorised by Writ of Assistance under the seal of his Majesty's Court of Exchequer* to take a Constable, Headborough, or other public Officer, inhabiting near unto the place, & in the day time to enter & go into any house, Shop, Cellar, Warehouse, room or any other place, and in case of Resistance, to break open doors, Chests, Trunks & other Package, & there to seize any kind of Goods or Merchandize whatever prohibited, and to put the same into his Majesty's Warehouse in the Port where Seisure is made.

Comments such as those that fell from Gridley betray the fact that the customs writ of assistance was not really understood. Gridley speaks as if the writ was already in existence when the legislation of 1662 ("the Stat. of the 14th. Char. 2nd.") was enacted, and its text in some sense the model for the new statutory provision for customs entry into houses and so forth. This was not the case, of course. Far from being "very antient," the writ was no older than the 1662 act itself: it was a product of that "secret in law" disclosed in Coke's *Institutes*, by which the common law permitted the invention of new writs for facilitating the provisions of a statute. And certainly the element of similarity between the text of the writ and the statutory provision in which the writ was mentioned did not mean that the statute had borrowed its wording from the writ. Quite the reverse: the writ was merely reciting the statutory purpose it had been designed to serve.[8]

Failing to see its true origin Gridley sought to locate the writ, and thus establish its respectability, in legal treatises and elsewhere. However, "the Books in which we should expect to find these Writs, & all that relates to them are Books of Precedents, & Reports in the Exchequer, which are extremely scarce in this Country." On its own terms, not a bad point; but Gridley went on to overdo it a little. Of the books in question, "we have one, & but one that treats of Exchequer matters, and that is called the 'Modern practice of the Court of Exchequer.' " If the book of that title was on hand, as well it may have been, Gridley was wrong in his arithmetic: there must have been at least two books an "Exchequer matters," the *Modern Practice* and William Brown's *Practice*, since it was this latter that provided the precedent for the Massachusetts writ of assistance. Be that as it may, however, it was Brown's book that Gridley meant. Having vouched its authenticity by pointing out that it had been published with the appropriate imprimatur (for there was still a regime of censorship in England in 1688),[9] Gridley proceeded to

8. Not forgetting, of course, section 32 of the 1662 act, which, by placing an almost limitless generality of naval, military, and civic officers, and private persons under obligation to assist the customs officer, was the substantive statutory foundation of the writ of assistance: see pp. 33-34.

9. See *LPJA* II, 130, n. 87. "The Book has the Imprimatur of Wright C. J. of the K.'s B." the notes have Gridley saying (and the Abstract has a similar reference).

Holdsworth, *HEL* VI, 507-8, says Wright "was not only a notoriously incompetent lawyer and a man of immoral life, but also guilty of perjury." In Campbell, *Lives of the Chief Justices of England* II (London, 1849), 95, Wright is "the last of the profligate Chief Justices of England . . . if excelled by some of his predecessors in bold crimes, yields to none in ignorance of his profession, and beats them all in the fraudulent and sordid vices." See also *Quincy's Reports*, 477.

make up for his inability to produce any other work in which the writ of assistance appeared by saying what a sound fellow Brown was: "the best Collector of Precedents; I have Two Volumes of them by him, which I esteem the best except Rastall & Coke."[10]   And, aside from published precedent: "we have a further proof of the legality of these Writs, & of the settled practice at home of allowing them; because by the Stat. 6th Anne which continues all Processes & Writs after the Demise of the Crown, *Writs of Assistance are continued among the rest.*" As to this, Gridley might have done rather better. The context in which "the Stat. 6th Anne"[11]   mentioned writs of assistance left it open to argument that it was not customs writs of assistance that were meant but quite different instruments of the same name (those used in the Court of Chancery, for example). The textile acts mentioned on page 275, in which the references to writs of assistance clearly intended the customs type, would have been more to Gridley's purpose.

Anyway, there it was: on the strength of Brown's precedent and the mention of writs of assistance in the Queen Anne act of 1702 Gridley argued the legality of the writ in England. He had missed the real doctrinal source of the writ, Coke's "secret in law," but as far as it went his argument was not ill conceived. The Abstract now shows him passing to the question whether, given that the Court of Exchequer rightfully issued writs of assistance, the Superior Court of Massachusetts "as a Court of Exchequer for this Province" could not do likewise. There could be little doubt of it, he said. By the Act of Frauds of 1696,

> it is enacted 'that all the Officers for collecting and managing his Majesty's Revenue, and inspecting the Plantation Trade in any of the said Plantations, shall have the same powers &c. as are provided for the Officers of the Revenue in England; also to enter Houses, or Warehouses, to search for and seize any such Goods, & that the *like Assistance* shall be given to the said Officers as is the Custom in England.'
>
> Now what is the Assistance which the Officers of the Revenue are to have here, which is like that they have in England? Writs of Assistance

10. *LPJA* II, 130, note 88, identifies the Brown books as probably *Formula bene placitandi; a Book of Entries, containing Precedents* (London, 1671), and *Methodus Novissima intrandi Placita Generalia* (London, 1699); the Coke book as his *Booke of Entries; containing perfect and approved Presidents of Counts, Declarations, etc.* (London, 1614); and William Rastell's as *Colleccion of entrees, of declarations, of barres, replicacions, rejoinders, issues, verdits, and divers other matters and fyrst an Epistle, with certayne instructions* (London, 1566).

11. As was seen at n. 4 above, the statute was not of "6th Anne," but the first of 1 Ann.

under the Seal of his Majesty's Court of Exchequer at home will not run here. They must therefore be under the Seal of this Court.

(And then Gridley cited the province act that gave the Superior Court an English-style exchequer jurisdiction.) Again Gridley's quotation from statute was inexact. What purports to be a simple extract from the 1696 act, section 6, is in reality a series of extracts strung together, with no indication of the intervals between them and even with an element of paraphrasing. But one must not be too censorious, having regard to what this book itself has said (in chapter 7) on section 6's submerging customs search, together with assistance to customs officers and miscellaneous other bits of enforcement machinery, in a single unreadable sentence hundreds of words long. To fault Jeremiah Gridley for selecting what he needed and compressing it into shape would not be altogether fair. No outrageous violence was done. And the argument he conjured forth was not without neatness: the 1696 act said that customs officers in America were entitled to "the like Assistance" to that enjoyed by customs officers in England; *ergo,* customs officers in America were entitled to the writ of assistance. (In fact it did not quite follow that a right to assistance implied a right to a document facilitating assistance; but the legislative text was incapable of being read straight anyhow.)

Gridley's arguments thus far, aside from where he spoke of the Superior Court of Massachusetts having the powers of the Court of Exchequer at Westminster, can be glimpsed in the original Adams notes (though not in the same order as in the Abstract). Something now to be noticed is that both from the notes and from the Abstract it transpires that Gridley, whatever his misunderstanding of what the writ of assistance was, did not fall into the error of supposing that the power of entry associated with the writ was actually given or transmitted by it. The notes:

> By the 7. & 8 of Wm. C. 22. § 6th — This authority, of breaking and entering Ships, Warehouses Cellars &c given to the Customs House officers in England by the Statutes of the 12th. and 14th of Charl. 2d, is extended to the Custom House officers in the Plantations . . . .

And the Abstract (Gridley having just spoken of the Act of Frauds of 1662):

> By this act & that of 12 Char. 2nd. all the powers in the Writ of Assistance mentioned are given . . . .

It is plain that Gridley recognized that the power of entry was given directly by statute.

Something else has to be observed, however. In both renditions Gridley saw the statutory power of entry as derived not only from the *Act for preventing Frauds, and regulating Abuses in his Majesty's Customs* of 1662, but also from the *Act to prevent Frauds and Concealments of his Majesty's Customs* of 1660. It will be recalled from chapter 4 that the act of 1660 was concerned to authorize the issuance, on sworn application, of specific warrants for the entry into places where undutied goods were suspected to be concealed. A reason for the fairly detailed study in chapter 4 of the relation between the 1660 act and the 1662 provision for customs power of entry was that the 1660 act and its specific search warrants were brought into the American writs of assistance arguments in 1761. Horace Gray saw it in these terms:

> As general warrants were not authorized by the common law, *Otis* argued that the writ of assistance mentioned in St. 13 & 14. Car. 2 [the 1662 act], must be special, according to St. 12 Car. 2 [the 1660 act]. This seems to have been considered . . . the most important point; and upon the ordinary rules of interpreting statutes *in pari materia* together, and according to the rule and reason of the common law, the conclusion of *Otis* seems inevitable.[12]

This line of argument in James Otis's speech is something to be looked at in a later chapter. One is surprised, however, to find material for it embodied in the case for the crown. In the first place, to relate the writ of assistance to the act of 1660 was wrong in both law and history. Secondly, and more important, this proposition could do nothing but confound the cause that Gridley was supposed to be representing. For him to imply that the new-style power of entry introduced in 1662 was somehow of a piece with the oaths and specific search warrants of 1660 was not at all what the custom house interest required. Perspective on this will sharpen when the two concluding paragraphs of Gridley's Abstract argument have been examined.

These rank among the most intriguing passages in the entire Abstract. Having thus far adhered to an ordered and systematic exposition of the law on writs of assistance as he conceived it to be, Gridley changed key and ended in a manner as much declamatory as jurisprudential. Here are his last two paragraphs in full:

12. *Quincy's Reports*, 531-32.

It is true the common privileges of Englishmen are taken away in this Case, but even their privileges are not so in cases of Crime and fine. 'Tis the necessity of the Case and the benefit of the Revenue that justifies this Writ. Is not the Revenue the sole support of Fleets & Armies abroad, & Ministers at home? without which the Nation could neither be preserved from the Invasions of her foes, nor the Tumults of her own Subjects. Is not this I say infinitely more important, than the imprisonment of Thieves, or even Murderers? yet in these Cases 'tis agreed Houses may be broke open.

In fine the power now under consideration is the same with that given by the Law of this Province to Treasurers towards Collectors & to them towards the subject. A Collector may when he pleases distrain my goods and Chattels, and in want of them arrest my person, and throw me instantly into Goal. What! shall my property be wrested from me! — shall my Liberty be destroyed by a Collector, for a debt, unadjudged, without the common Indulgence and Lenity of the Law? So it is established, and the necessity of having public taxes effectually and speedily collected is of infinitely greater moment to the whole, than the Liberty of any Individual.

Fairly purple, by any standard.

Argument of a legal kind was not entirely absent from these curious apologetics. Neither the Abstract nor John Adams's original notes abound in citation of common law authority, but it is a safe guess that the fifth volume of Sir Edward Coke's law reports was resorted to by the participant lawyers in the writs of assistance case. Included in this work was a leading case on common law powers of entry and search. *Semayne's Case*,[13] decided by the Court of King's Bench in 1604, could not have been regarded as a complete and up-to-date statement of the law in the middle of the eighteenth century, but certainly there was enough in it to support Gridley's statement in the opening sentence in the text just quoted, "It is true the common privileges of Englishmen are taken away in this Case, but even their privileges are not so in cases of Crime and fine." [14]

---

13. 5 Co. Rep. 91.

14. The original Adams note, "Every Body knows that the Subject has the Priviledge of House only against his fellow Subjects, not vs. the K. either in matters of Crime or fine." focuses better than these Abstract-Gridley words on the point (which, admittedly, the latter goes on to bring out) that in some matters the common law allowed public exigency to override private right.

Contemporary practice on entry and search of private premises then probably reflected Sir Matthew Hale more than Sir Edward Coke. (It was expressly in contradiction of Coke's view that no such thing existed that Hale acknowledged the common law search warrant for stolen goods: *cf* chapter 3, n. 36.) More of Hale on this subject in chapter 16.

This old authority stated the basic common law principle, "the house of every one is to him as his castle" — a turn of phrase that James Otis was to borrow — and went on to discuss occasions upon which the principle might give way, even to the extent that forcible entry were permissible. The apprehending of felons was given a mention, as also was the execution of certain court processes that could bear the designation "fine" (a term not limited to its modern meaning, a monetary penalty). To illustrate the first exception — "Crime" — Gridley lighted upon the common law power of forcible entry for arrest of thieves and murderers. To illustrate "fine," however, he went to an enactment of the province legislature, passed in 1730, under which local constables and collectors of taxes were authorized to levy distress upon the belongings of defaulters, and in some cases where distress did not answer commit the defaulter to prison.[15] Entry with writ of assistance and this more or less peremptory power of distress alike were justified by the "necessity" attendant upon the public revenue — a necessity to which even "the common privileges of Englishmen" must be subordinated. If Gridley turned to Coke's fifth volume of reports for the fundamental common law on hearth and home in *Semayne's Case,* it may well have been in that same compilation that this notion of an overriding power in "necessity" was suggested to him. Earlier in the book is *Dormer's Case,* where it was stated that "necessity has often overborne the common law, and that which is necessary is lawful."[16]

Of course, "necessity" was not in fact a constituent of the little known common law doctrine on which the writ of assistance was founded; still less did the statute which the writ subserved owe any of its force to "necessity." Again the nature of the writ was not being properly understood. And even by reference to the dialectical situation actually confronting him, Gridley's mode of rationalizing the writ's legitimacy did not measure up. It cannot be too strongly emphasized that the key issue in the hearing was not so much whether the writ had any legal right to exist — James Otis, Gridley's principal opponent, accepted that it had — as whether the Superior

15. 3 October 1730, c. 1. This example, taken from legislation, perhaps had reference to a line of ratiocination by James Otis (to be examined in chapter 16) involving propositions about acts of parliament being adjudged void.

16. 5 Co. Rep. 40b. In fact, "necessity" came up in *Semayne's Case,* too. The court explicitly did not accept that a wider right of forcible entry (into a house, by a sheriff) at the suit of a private judgment creditor should be acknowledged on ground of "necessity."

See also *Manby v. Scott* (1672) 1 Lev. 4: "The law of necessity dispenses with things which otherwise are not lawful to be done" (*per cur.*).

Court should continue to grant it in its general and open-ended form or should in future limit it to a single occasion duly particularized and sworn to. Part of Gridley's object in citing the "Crime and fine" exceptions to the inviolability of private dwellings presumably was to illustrate that a statement on oath was not always an indispensable preliminary to a lawful intrusion: neither the common law entry in pursuit of a felon nor the province act's distress for unpaid taxes depended on a prior oath. As far as it went the analogy was plausible; but it did not go the whole way. As the speech of Otis was to indicate, an objection to the "general" writ of assistance was (rightly or wrongly) that it facilitated entries and searches of a promiscuous or even frivolous character, regardless of whether the harboring of contraband were seriously suspected or not. There was nothing random about the search for a felon, or distress upon the goods and chattels of a particular defaulter. To that extent Gridley's rationalization fell short. In other words, the existing powers of entry related to "Crime and fine" had an inbuilt specificity to which the customs power of entry with writ of assistance did not correspond, and by comparison with which it was therefore still open to objection.

No more in the concluding paragraphs than elsewhere in his speech did Gridley come up with a square reply to the opposition's claim that entry with writ of assistance should be limited to the one specific occasion only. Aligning this omission with Gridley's erroneous association of writ of assistance entry with entry by specific warrant under the *Act to prevent Frauds and Concealments of his Majesty's Customs* of 1660, one begins to see that the case for the crown was not being presented too effectively.

Uncertainty as to Jeremiah Gridley's attitude is further deepened by a few moments' reflective observation of the less legal, or more rhetorical, content of his two concluding paragraphs. Take, as a cue, the very last words the Abstract attributes to him: "the necessity of having public taxes effectually and speedily collected is of infinitely greater moment to the whole, than the Liberty of any Individual." A strange sentiment, one would think, from a man of Gridley's whiggish orientation. Anxiety over the prosecution of the war may have edged him toward the right, but surely not into high toryism of this gross order. Then there was all that extravagant thunder about the writ of assistance being justified by necessity, and benefit to the revenue:

> Is not the Revenue the sole support of Fleets & Armies abroad, & Ministers at home? without which the Nation could neither be preserved

from the Invasions of her foes, nor the Tumults of her own Subjects. Is
not this I say infinitely more important, than the imprisonment of
Thieves, or even Murderers?

Somewhat far-fetched as well as overblown, especially in relation to
New England where the only revenue upon which writ of assistance
search had a bearing (of dubious legality even at that) was the
Molasses Act duties, which were openly and notoriously evaded
anyway.

Yet these puzzlements cannot be dismissed as so much hot air. For
all their difference in key from the ordered sobriety of what had
gone before, Gridley's two concluding paragraphs were not just
thrown together. For example, the reference to houses being "broke
open" for the arrest of felons is not permitted to extend to the
subject immediately following in the final paragraph, which had to
do with a different subject (the powers of distress and arrest for
nonpayment of local taxes: here the province legislation made no
provision for entry by force). With a man like Gridley, indeed, it is
especially prudent to remember how carefully the documentation of
colonial American controversy has to be watched. Litterateur as well
as lawyer, Gridley would have been doubly mindful of the words he
was using. The assumption has to be that those out-of-character,
excited, and seemingly off-target utterances were by design, and
intended for some sort of effect.

Irony suggests itself as the spirit of Gridley's odd commendations
of the writ of assistance and the revenue it supposedly safeguarded.
The revenue as "the sole support of Fleets & Armies abroad . . . .
without which the Nation could . . . [not] be preserved from . . . the
Tumults of her own Subjects" might have seemed a doubtful benefit
to colonists already apprehensive that British armed force would
remain a presence in America after the war was over. As for the
revenue being the support of "Ministers at home," the picture of
political fat-cats at Westminster lining their pockets at the taxpayers'
expense was likely to evoke nothing so much as an early New
England archetype of the Bronx cheer. The powers of distraint and
arrest possessed by local tax collectors were not for too straight a
face, either. As any Boston contemporary would have known, they
were hardly ever exercised. Collectorships of taxes were political jobs
in more senses than one; their holders tended to go easy on public
debtors in return for votes and support,[17] in which situation powers

---

17. See G. B. Warden, *Boston 1689-1776* (Boston, 1970), 115. It may be that Sam
Adams did not disdain to cultivate his constituency this way.

of distraint and arrest might in practice be little other than an *in terrorem* political device. Nor was Gridley's repeated invocation of "necessity" free of ambiguous overtone. What comes to mind is Milton's "So spake the fiend, and with necessity, / The tyrant's plea, excused his devilish deeds."[18] Much more probably than not these well-known lines were equally present in the mind of the literary Gridley. Many another Bostonian, long used to hearing the puritan poet brought into sermons of congregationalist divines, could have caught the echo too.

These various elements of double-speak in Gridley's peroration come into view without strain; in any case it would be a very large proposition that they all happened by accident. Even before discussion of them was entered upon, the impression had begun to form that Gridley's failure to come to grips with the Otis position (rejection of the general writ of assistance but acceptance of the special) had more behind it than mere error as to what the writ really was. A look at the verbal figures he employed has added to the likelihood of conscious equivocation in his attitude to the custom house brief.

The question naturally arises, however, whether the foregoing commentary, some of which subjected the Abstract version of Gridley's speech to exegesis of almost scriptural refinement, may not have made too much of words and phrases that came more from the pen of John Adams than from the lips of Gridley himself. It is a question prompting a further hypothesis.

Or, rather, embellishment of a hypothesis that has already been advanced. Earlier in the chapter, when the conundrum of two Gridley speeches in Adams's original notes but only one in the Abstract was being pondered, the suggestion was offered that in fact there had been just the one speech, and that what appeared in Adams's notes as Gridley on his feet a second time was in reality an attempt by Adams, whose contemporaneous note of what Gridley had said was a mere fragment, to reconstruct it afterward. He may have gotten some help from Gridley himself.

Following the second Gridley entry in the notes, and undoubtedly after the hearing was finished, Adams copied out certain relevant legal materials: extracts from the Acts of Frauds of 1662 and 1696 and the province act vesting the Superior Court with exchequer jurisdiction, and the respective texts of the original petition for a writ of assistance by Charles Paxton in 1755 and of the writ that was

18. *Paradise Lost*, book 4, 393.

subsequently granted. Here a pertinent question arises. The legislative extracts were easily come by; but how did young Adams manage to lay hold of such out-of-the-way documents as Paxton's 1755 petition and the first writ of assistance? It cannot be assumed that he got them from the files of the Superior Court, for in all probability this was no richer a source of documents on the writs of assistance case than it is today. In any case, detailed comparison between Adams's text of the writ and the original Trowbridge draft still extant in the Superior Court records indicates that it was not this draft that he used. Nor is it an unreasonable speculation that Paxton's 1755 petition, which has been in the possession of the Massachusetts Historical Society for generations, was already absent from the court files when Adams was writing his notes. The petition was the sort of document that would have been needed in the preparation of the writs of assistance case in the opening weeks of 1761. Indeed, as has been seen, the Abstract actually shows Jeremiah Gridley drawing upon it practically word for word. It is relevant also that the Abstract shows Gridley as reciting the text of what is explicitly stated to have been the writ issued to Paxton "a few years past" (i.e., in 1755 or 1756). What all this points to is obvious. For the purposes of his brief for the crown Gridley had obtained, as part of his basic working material, the first of the succession of writ of assistance petitions over the period 1755-60 and the first of the writs issued in response, and had let John Adams have a sight of them.

Adams was something of a protégé of Gridley. The relationship had begun in the fall of 1758, when Adams approached Gridley for advice on how to start in law practice in Suffolk County. Gridley not only advised him that he must "get sworn," but instantly volunteered to make this possible.[19]   Three years later, when Adams sought admission to practice in the Superior Court, it again was Gridley who sponsored him.[20]   In the meantime, as Adams gratefully recorded in his autobiography, Gridley gave him practically the run of his library (for at this time the young man "suffered very much for Want of Books"), and a measure of sage counsel.[21]   It was in this period of Adams's quasi-tutelage to Gridley that the writs of assistance case happened. Their relationship being what it was, there

19. *DAJA* I, 54; III, 272.
20. SCR (1760-62), 239.
21. *DAJA* III, 271-74.

would have been nothing strange in Adams, wishing to make a fair write-up of the scrappy notes he had taken, borrowing documents — such as Paxton's 1755 petition and the writ issued in consequence — that Gridley had used.

By much the same token Adams might have prevailed upon Gridley to repeat in outline the main points in his opening speech, of which Adams had taken down only the very last words. (The theory in chapter 12 will be recalled: Gridley had all but completed his speech the day before Adams showed up at the hearing, and Adams therefore missed everything except the tail-end pieces remaining for the morrow.) The scenario: Adams goes to Gridley soon after the February hearing ended; shows him the notes he has taken; says he hopes to write them up into better shape; expresses regret for having caught so little of Gridley's own arguments, and asks if Gridley would be so kind as to repeat the gist of them for him to jot down (and also to lend him Paxton's petition and writ for copying out at leisure). This goes far to explain the second Gridley entry on the paper bearing Adams's original notes, and why it is so much better ordered and written than the notes already there and sets forth material markedly more appropriate to an opening speech than to counterargument in reply and conclusion. (And similarly: Gridley's helpful dictation having finished, Adams took away the Paxton documents and copied them, together with extracts from relevant legislation, where he had left off from Gridley.) When Adams came to the actual writing-up of the Abstract he of course transposed the *post factum* Gridleiana into proper sequence: to the earlier and main part of the speech with which Gridley had begun the proceedings — the only speech Gridley in fact made.

John Adams was to become a prolific newspaper polemicist: his "Novanglus" broadsides in 1775 are historically famous. An editorial comment in his *Diary and Autobiography* suggests that it was something of a habit with him to write on public topics as if anticipating an occasion for his work to be put into print.[22] Indeed, several drafts of articles or essays among his papers of the early 1760s plainly seem to have been composed with an eye toward the local press.[23] In this light it may be possible to see the answer to a

22. III, 283, note 6.
23. See, *e.g.*, *DAJA* I, 167, 190, 204, 212.

question that has not yet been tackled: what was Adams's purpose in
going to the trouble of writing up his Abstract of the writs of
assistance arguments in February 1761?

It can hardly have been that such a document might prove useful
to him in his profession. Quite commonly lawyers would note down
points and arguments which they heard deployed in court; thus they
added to their store of useful precedent for the future. But Adams's
work on the writs of assistance case cannot be rationalized in this
way, for much of the very interest in the case lay in the probability
that nothing like it would happen again (in the lifetime of the
twenty-year-old George III, anyway). Nor does Adams's Abstract
resemble a conventional law report. Certainly it is much less like a
law report than Josiah Quincy junior's rendition of the second writs
of assistance hearing, in November 1761. Aside from the scant
citation of precedents (not that there were all that many to cite), it
would be a peculiar law report that concentrated exclusively upon
arguments from the bar and recorded absolutely nothing of what was
said from the bench. The editors of the *Legal Papers of John Adams*
see the Abstract as "a minor work of political propaganda."[24] And
so indeed it may have been conceived.

For one thing, Adams had the habit of writing as if for the press.
For another, to perceptive opponents of the writ of assistance the
February hearing had ended encouragingly. Indeed, it may have
seemed that victory against the writ — at any rate in its obnoxious
general form — was practically assured. The *London Magazine* article
looked well enough informed, and that Chief Justice Hutchinson's
check with the practice in England would confirm it was a by no
means unreasonable expectation; so that the court's definitive decision, when it came, would rid Boston and the province of the general
writ of assistance once and for all. John Adams may therefore have
calculated that before long Boston would be celebrating a forensic
triumph in the vindication and recovery of a valued civil liberty —
not to mention the removal of a piece of custom house weaponry
that had added to the misfortunes of the Boston trader by comparison with his competitors in Rhode Island. Members of the legal
profession were not particularly high in public esteem; nor had they
yet been especially active in the political life of the province. Here, in
a resounding conquest of the writ of assistance, the lawyer would
have done his stuff with a vengeance. By his learning and skill the

24. *LPJA* II, 123.

lawyer had frustrated, and even beaten back (for the writ of assistance that had existed these five years past would henceforth be no more), an encroachment of governmental power directed from without the province. So signal a victory, gained for the Massachusetts merchants and public by practitioners at the Boston bar, surely would not pass without due notice, if not tribute, in the newspapers of the town? Adams's other private attempts at journalism might have come to nothing, but a unique eyewitness record of how the great court battle against the writ of assistance had been fought and won, suitably pointed up with touches of drama and flourishes of oratory, could hardly fail to find a place in the *Gazette* or the *Evening-Post.*

Such may have been the aspirations in which the "Abstract of the Argument for and against Writts of Assistants" came to be written.

If John Adams purposed to write the Abstract for publication (anticipating a defeat for the general writ of assistance), he would hardly have failed to mention the fact when approaching Jeremiah Gridley for help. In that case Gridley's interest would have been more than friendly willingness to help a young protégé. Inevitably he himself would appear as the loser, which was bad enough; but also, insofar as there were a villain of the piece, the role would fall to him. His whig image had already been dented, and it would not do for him to appear in the public prints as a wholehearted champion of the ill-famed writ. On a subject of such sensitivity he could not have young Adams putting words into his mouth. The subtleties of his position could not be left to the raw perceptions of a near-apprentice. If anything, the opportunity might be taken to improve upon them. Accordingly, Gridley's part in the preparation of the Abstract may have gone beyond lending Adams various documents and repeating to him the main points of the argument. Possibly it reached a point where the Abstract rendition of the Gridley speech was closely vetted, if not actually written, by the man himself. The suggestion that a piece so elegantly arranged and paragraphed, its peroration suffused with sophisticated irony, and its whole purport capable of being read as conceding the opposition's case, did not proceed unaided from the pen of young John Adams is not offered in a belittling spirit. It is merely to say that no one — Adams or any person else — could have so thoroughly gotten the feel of Gridley's peculiar situation without a generous measure of collaboration.

Something that might be recalled at this point is Adams' diary entry, soon after the writs of assistance hearing, in which he brooded upon the leg-pulling of Colonel Josiah Quincy:

> The same Evening, I shew him, my Draught of our Licensed Houses and the Remarks upon it. Oh he was transported! he was ravished! He would introduce that Plan at the sessions, and read the Remarks, and say they were made as well as the Plan by a Gentleman to whom there could be no Exception — &c. He saw an Abstract of the Argument for and against Writts of Assistants — and crys did you take this from those Gentlemen as they delivered it? You can do any Thing! You can do as you please! Gridley did not use that Language. He never was Master of such a style. It is not in him — &c . . . .
>
> These are the bold, gross, barefaced Flatteries that I hear every Time I see that Man. Can he think me such a Ninny as to be allured and deceived by such gross Arts? . . . .[25]

In contrast to "my Draught of our Licensed Houses," Adams writes unpossessively of "an Abstract of the Argument for and against Writts of Assistants." The average man does not write in his diary with the accuracy of statement appropriate to a conveyance, and the difference between "my Draught" and "an Abstract" may have been a mere accident of wording. On the other hand, Adams was a lawyer and consciousness of property was very much a feature of his time and place. The better assumption is that his abstention from a possessive pronoun in relation to the Abstract did in fact signify something: namely, that the Abstract was not wholly his work.

Part of Colonel Quincy's offense to Adams seems to have been that he professed to believe otherwise, and even that the true begetter of the handsome presentation of the Gridley speech was Adams himself. Like most effective leg-pulls, this had a grain of truth in it. Gridley's oral delivery was poor: "At the bar his speech was rough, his manner hesitating . . . . "[26] But if the Abstract rendition of Gridley was too good to be true, Adams was not such a simpleton as to suppose that Colonel Quincy genuinely attributed the improvement to him. Gridley's own written style befitted a former literary publicist. "He was an easy and graceful writer," one commentator has said, "being imbued with the spirit of classical literature."[27] The colonel must have realized perfectly well that the Abstract was an

---

25. See p. 235 above.
26. J. T. Buckingham, *Specimens of Newspaper Literature* (Boston, 1850), 127, citing Eliot's *Biographical Dictionary*.
27. E. Washburn, *Sketches in the Judicial History of Massachusetts* (Boston, 1840), 211.

idealized rather than a verbatim account of the writs of assistance arguments, and that, despite the writing being that of Adams, the cosmetic quality of the opening speech had been supplied by Gridley's own practiced hand. Quincy's praise of Adams, suspect anyway by its very extravagance, was a transparent pretense; and like many a victim of teasing that smacks as much of malice as of humor, Adams was upset by it.

Without overmuch convolution of thinking, Adams's diary entry on the writs of assistance case is consistent with and even supports the theory that the Abstract was not the composition of Adams alone and that its rendition of the Gridley speech owed a lot to the intervention of Gridley himself. Something else seems worth a mention. Again not too much should be made of it — possibly nothing at all — but the version of the Abstract texts of Gridley and Otis in Joseph Hawley's commonplace book happens to be headed "Substance of Mr Gridley's Argument Before the Superior Court in favor of Writs of Assistance." Why the accentuation of Gridley? Was it simply that Gridley's argument came first? Or might it have been that Hawley had heard Adams, who was a friend of his, speak of how the Abstract came to be written, and of Gridley having taken a leading hand?

To whatever degree a calculated lack of impact in his argument caused Gridley a twinge of professional conscience he could always comfort himself with the reflection that, with Thomas Hutchinson presiding on the bench, the case for the crown would be looked after. Aside from any other obligation Hutchinson might have toward the writ of assistance, had it not been Gridley who first put him in mind of the chief justiceship? And Judge Peter Oliver, too, might feel promptings of old acquaintance: he and Gridley had been business partners (in an iron-making enterprise).[28] In one way and another, Gridley may have thought to himself, the custom house brief did not require him to pull out all the stops. If he chose to treat it as a whimsical *jeu d'esprit,* a vehicle for a clever line in literary-legal doubletalk, no real harm was done. Chief Justice Hutchinson would see to it that King George was not shortchanged.

Though Gridley may have supervised the Abstract rendition of his speech, so that if it were published he could point to all those pulled punches and ingenious ambiguities and show he had really been on

28. See chapter 11, n. 10.

the right side all the time, the precaution proved unnecessary. When at length the Abstract material did get into print it was as history, not contemporary reportage. A question remains, nevertheless. How came it, the popular side in the writs of assistance case having been defeated, the advocate responsible seems to have suffered no ill consequences? "The next year the town of Boston bought his bull and appointed him to the committee to visit the schools, unrelated actions showing faith in him. He continued to pass pleasant evenings in the coffeehouses with James Otis and the other radicals . . . ." [29] Among the numerous spectators at the writs of assistance hearing there may have been some who perceived the tongue in Gridley's cheek, and spread the word. John Adams for one reminisced, apropos of the speech of James Otis, that "Mr. Gridley himself seemed . . . to exult inwardly at the glory and triumph of his pupil." [30]   Gridley himself could have put it around in private conversation that his advocacy of the writ of assistance was not all that it might seem: if he told Benjamin Barons that he disbelieved in the legality of the general writ, he probably told others as well.

"Mr. Gridley was incapable of prevarication or duplicity," wrote John Adams in 1818. [31]   How was that again?

---

29. Shipton, *op. cit.* (n. 2 above), 527. Gridley was given a high masonic funeral in 1767, but too much should not be read into this. He was grand master of America; and freemasonry in Boston — which in the pre-revolutionary period had divisions of its own — was not politically oriented. (An illustration, possibly: the provincial grand mastership held by Joseph Warren, the patriot leader who fell at Bunker Hill, arguably might not have existed but for the good offices of military lodges in the British garrison.)

30. *LWJA* X, 343.

31. *Ibid.,* 327.

Thacher

O<small>XENBRIDGE THACHER</small> followed Jeremiah Gridley in the order of speaking.

Somewhat as Gridley had not been the custom house's first choice, so Thacher's position in relation to the petitioners against the writ of assistance is not entirely clear. According to the preamble to John Adams's Abstract, it was James Otis who appeared for "the Inhabitants of Boston"; "Mr *Thacher* was joined with him at the desire of the Court." And Thacher began his speech: "In obedience to the Order of this Court I have searched . . . all the antient Reports . . . ." The impression is that Thacher was not so much spokesman for the petitioners as *amicus curiae,* whose function was less to argue on one side or the other than to help the court with his learning. The presence of such a figure would have been consistent with a lay bench, embarrassed by doubt, wishing to have the writ of assistance researched by a professional.

Present-day knowledge of Oxenbridge Thacher draws fairly heavily on the testimony of John Adams; and in general Adams was well disposed. It had been Thacher upon whom, next after Gridley, he had called as a young man hoping to make a start at the bar. Adams's diary account of this initial meeting shows something of Thacher's cast of mind: "Drank Tea and spent the whole Evening, upon original sin, Origin of Evil, the Plan of the Universe, and at last, upon Law."[1]

Thacher was really a clergyman *manqué.* In his youth — he was forty when Adams met him — he read for the ministry; unable to

---

1. *DAJA* I, 55.

John Adams to Mercy Otis Warren, 27 July 1807, in *MHSC* fifth series IV (Boston, 1878): "I was sworn at the bar in Boston in 1758; and from that time I became intimately acquainted with your brother and Mr Thacher, both of whom treated me to the hour of their deaths like a brother . . . ." Thacher's "amiable character": *LWJA* X, 247. And, "There was not a citizen . . . more universally beloved for his learning, ingenuity, every social and domestic virtue, and conscientious conduct in every relation of life": *ibid.,* 285.

make a go of this he at length turned for his livelihood to the law (possibly under the tutelage of Jeremiah Gridley).[2] Though well thought of as a practicing lawyer Thacher's true interest in the subject of his profession seems to have tended toward the philosophical; and, as the piece from Adams's diary illustrates, his thinking remained impregnated with theology. Nevertheless he was not a bookish recluse. Adams records him in 1759 as wishing himself a soldier; or, perhaps it might be more accurate to say, wishing himself a soldier still, for he had taken part in the Crown Point expedition in 1756.[3] As the 1760s advanced, and until his death in 1765 Thacher became a figure of some prominence in whig politics. A disposition toward "wild, extravagant, loose Opinions and Expressions" was noted against him as early as 1759.[4] However, he was not yet the pamphleteering activist he later became: under the whiggish administration of Governor Pownall there had been little to excite him politically. Possibly Thacher's quietness in that period misled establishmentarians into believing him favorable to the government. At any rate, the Superior Court would have been unlikely to look to him for help in the writs of assistance case if he was already vocal against the tory-oriented regime of Governor Bernard (and notably the pluralizing chief justice, Thomas Hutchinson).[5]

Not that the recruitment of Oxenbridge Thacher should have caused the opponents of the writ of assistance any anxiety. Whether the court wanted him as a lawyer given to exploration into the remoter areas of jurisprudence or as a counterweight to the noisy and turbulent Otis, or for any other special reason, he produced a line of argument against the writ a good deal more sweeping than that of his rumbustious colleague.

Of the three advocates Thacher spoke the least length of time. His speech appears to have been sandwiched between Gridley's opening

2. C. K. Shipton, *Sibley's Harvard Graduates* X (Boston, 1958), 323 and *passim*.

3. *DAJA* I, 110.

The "Minutes of Assembly" in C05/821 include an entry for 7 June 1759 about Thacher having lost his gun on the Crown Point expedition, for which £4 had been stopped from his pay. Now having bought a gun and sent it into the commissary he prayed — successfully — "that the said Stoppage may be taken off."

4. *DAJA* I, 110.

5. Establishment predisposition toward Thacher may have been conditioned by his superior family connections: his mother was the sister of Sir Charles Hobby (Shipton, *op. cit.*, 322). Significant also is John Adams's recollection, "Hutchinson often said, 'Thacher was not born a plebeian, but he was determined to die one.' "

speech (or the concluding part of it) in the morning and the famous oration of James Otis in the afternoon, on Wednesday 25 February 1761. The notes that John Adams took down while the advocates were on their feet that day do better by Thacher than by either of the other two. All that Adams got of Gridley were a few brief final sentences, and his hand began to give out with fatigue before Otis had been speaking long. But the notes of Thacher's speech show no sign of inattentiveness or waning energy. It is unlikely that Adams stopped writing before Thacher finished. So Thacher's speech really was as short as the notes — and the Abstract, too — make it appear.

Possibly it was because Adams got most of it down at first go that the Thacher speech received comparatively little editorial emendation in the Abstract. Certainly there is nothing like the massive restructuring accorded to Gridley, or the rhetoric added to Otis. However, the Abstract rendition of Thacher is not totally innocent of improvement upon the notes. For example, the notes have Thacher saying that he had searched for a precedent of the customs writ of assistance

> in the Register (Q, wt the Reg. is) and have found no such Writt of assistance as this Petition prays. — I have found two Writts of ass. in the Reg. but they are very difft, from the Writt prayed for. —
>
> In a Book, intituled the Modern Practice of the Court of Exchequer there is indeed one such Writt, and but one.

By when he came to write up the Abstract John Adams evidently had found out that "the Reg." was the *Registrum Brevium tam Originalium quam Judicialium* (a collection of standard forms of writs dating from medieval times), for he was now able to specify that the writs of assistance that Thacher had found were "only to give possession of Houses &c. in cases of Injunctions and Sequestration in Chancery."[6] And the Abstract did not repeat the mistake of attributing the one known precedent of the customs writ of assistance, in William Brown's book on the Court of Exchequer, to the later and anonymous *Modern Practice of the Court of Exchequer.*

It is evident that Adams had done some checking around, and not only among his own books. He clearly did not have the *Registrum Brevium,* if only because when Thacher alluded to it in the speech Adams had to remind himself to ascertain what it was. Possibly this was another point on which he went to Jeremiah Gridley — or at any rate to Gridley's library. For the speech at large, however, he seems

6. See *LPJA* II, 124, note 56.

to have relied wholly on his notes. At any rate it would be hard to suppose that he sought the assistance of Thacher himself. Evidence for this is at the end of the first paragraph of the Abstract rendition of Thacher's speech. Thacher having said he could find nothing of the customs writ of assistance in the old precedent books, the Abstract continues:

> By the Act of Parliament any private Person as well as Custom House Officer may take a Sheriff or Constable & go into any Shop &c. & seize &c. (here Mr. Thacher quoted an Authority from Strange which intended to shew that Writs of Assistance were only temporary things.)
> The most material question is . . . .

The piece in parenthesis is the clue. Adams would not have resorted to this makeshift manner of statement if Thacher had been on hand for consultation. It may be that while Adams would have shown Thacher the Abstract if publication had looked like materializing (common politeness apart, the two men were on good terms), he believed his notes, written as they had been when he was still fresh to his task, to be complete and reliable enough.

So they were, probably.

The transcription from notes to Abstract was not absolutely flawless. In fact, Adams went somewhat adrift in the Abstract passage last quoted. The corresponding notes were these:

> By the Act of Palt. any other private Person, may as well as a Custom House Officer, take an officer, a Sheriff, or Constable, &c and go into any Shop, Store &c & seize: any Person authorized by such a Writt, under the Seal of the Court of Exchequer, may, not Custom House Officers only. — Strange. — Only a temporary thing.
> The most material Question is . . . .

As the Abstract text makes plain, Thacher had cited a case in the law reports of Sir John Strange (published in England in 1755, and thus fairly new). And it is not difficult to identify the case as *Horne v. Boosey,* decided in 1733, since this is the only one in which the writ of assistance is mentioned. *Horne v. Boosey* was a successful action for damages in the Court of Common Pleas at Westminster, in respect of some casks of brandy which the defendant, a tidesman (a subordinate customs functionary), had seized and brought to forfeiture in the Court of Exchequer. The report is not entirely clear, but the essence of the plaintiff's grievance seems to have been that the casks of brandy had not in fact been in violation of the law and had been forfeited merely by default of his having shown up in the Court of Exchequer to contest the condemnation process. His action in the Court of Common Pleas was in trover, which implied that his title in the casks of brandy had been impugned and lost wrongfully. The decision turned upon the defendant having exceeded his authority. Had he been "the proper officer" the action against him would have failed: the plaintiff would have had no ground upon which to ask the Court of Common Pleas to consider the rights and wrongs of a title which the Court of Exchequer had adjudged forfeit.[7] As it was, however, the defendant had not been "the proper officer." He was only a tidesman, whose authorization by the commissioners of customs to make seizures appeared limited to instances where he entered with "a writ of assistance and a peace officer." Such was not the case here, and the jury were directed in favor of the plaintiff. Actually, *Horne v. Boosey* was authority for little or nothing on writ of assistance law. That the defendant did not have a writ of assistance was partly why the decision went against him; but all this says about the writ is that, as a tidesman, he could have had one. It is clear from John Adams's original notes that Thacher was invoking the tidesman's writ of assistance to illustrate his statement that "any . . . private person . . . not Custom House Officers only" could use the writ. But in writing up the Abstract Adams associated the "Authority from Strange" not with what Thacher had just been saying about the writ being usable by anybody, but with what he afterward went on to say: "Only a temporary thing." Certainly there is nothing in *Horne v. Boosey* "which intended to shew that Writs of Assistance were only temporary things."[8]

But it is only in this small respect that John Adams's Abstract write-up of the Thacher speech is substantially at variance with his original notes. On the assumption that the notes (taken when Adams's hand and mind were at their liveliest) included the gist of

7. *Cf.* Blackstone J. in *Scott v. Shearman* (1775) 2 W. Black. 977 (as it happens, a case which arose from a writ of assistance search and seizure). However, "A judgment *in rem* is evidence to the whole world, that the goods have been properly seized, but it is not evidence . . . of the facts constituting the cause of forfeiture": *A-G v. Feeny* (1831) Hayes's Exchequer Reports [Ireland] 135.

For uncertainties of doctrine on the correct form of action see Holdsworth *HEL* III, 286 and n. 9; also XII, 137. n. 6.

8. Conceivably, "only a temporary thing" did not relate to the writ of assistance at all; but was a reference — in a context that Adams wholly failed to record — to the old customs search warrant act of 1660, which was expressed to "continue in Force unto the End of the first Session of the next Parliament, and no longer" (*cf.* pp. 42-43 above).

the whole of Thacher's arguments, the Abstract can be accepted as reasonably faithful to what Thacher actually said.

Oxenbridge Thacher did not use the hortatory style of Gridley and Otis. In private conversation he may have been inclined to take off into the blue on points of high philosophical or theological abstraction; but his performance before the Superior Court was practical enough in its orientation. What he identified as the "most material question" went for the jugular, so to speak. He denied the court's right to issue the writ of assistance at all. In this, as will appear later in the book, Thacher came closer than anyone to the view of the law eventually arrived at in England (and which led to the Townshend legislation of 1767 for American writs of assistance). If for no other reason, the position from which he argued deserves attention.

Rather curiously, Adams's notes on this are fuller than his Abstract rendition:

> The most material Question is, whether the Practice of the Exchequer, will warrant this Court in granting the same.
> The Act impowers all the officers of the Revenue to enter and seise in the Plantations, as well as in England. 7. & 8 Wm. 3, C.22, §6, gives the same as 13. & 14. of C. gives in England. The Ground of Mr Gridleys argt. is this, that this Court has the Power of the Court of Exchequer. – But This Court has renounced the Chancery Jurisdiction, wh the Exchequer has in Cases where either Party, is the Kings Debtor. – Q. into tht Case.

Thacher was taking up Gridley's point that under the Act of Frauds of 1696 customs officers in America had powers of entry and seizure similar to those that the Act of Frauds of 1662 gave to customs officers in England: "And it shall be lawful," said section 5(2) of the act of 1662, "to or for any Person or Persons, authorized by Writ of Assistance under the Seal of his Majesty's Court of Exchequer, to take a Constable . . . [and enter and seize]." Thacher's argument was that in America as in England the writ of assistance appertained to a court of exchequer; but in Massachusetts there was in effect no such court, since the Superior Court had disavowed exchequer jurisdiction. This particular point comes out slightly more fully in the Abstract:

> The most material question is whether the practice of the Exchequer is good ground for this Court. But this Court has upon a solemn Argument, which lasted a whole day, renounc'd the Chance of [Chancery?] Jurisdiction which the Exchequer has in Cases where either party is the King's Debtor.

But the best presentation of all is in Thacher's repetition of his argument, at the resumed hearing of the writs of assistance case in November 1761. According to the report by Josiah Quincy junior,[9] Thacher

> moved further that such a Writ is granted and must issue from the Exchequer Court, and no other can grant it.... That this Court is not such a one ... This Court has in the most solemn Manner disclaimed the Authority of the Exchequer; this they did in the Case of McNeal of Ireland & McNeal of Boston. This they cannot do in Part; if the Province Law gives them any, it gives them all the Power of the Exchequer Court; nor can they chuse and refuse to act at Pleasure.

A short excursion into remoter history is necessary to make Thacher's argument clear.

The Court of Exchequer in England can conveniently be thought of as the judicial organ of the fiscal department of government.[10] The jurisdiction of the court was primarily in matters concerning the king's revenue. Basically it partook of the common law — as, for instance, in condemnations of customs seizures, where all might depend upon the verdict of a jury — but there was an equitable component also. Equity is usually associated with the Court of Chancery, where, from the fourteenth century onward the lord chancellor, sitting without a jury, drew upon a residual *gubernaculum*[11] in the king to promote justice. Somewhat as the insufficiency of the common law to put down social disorders necessitated the auxiliary criminal processes of the Court of Star Chamber, manifestly intolerable injustices resulting from hardening formalism on the civil side of the common law led to the emergence not only of the Star Chamber but also of the Court of Chancery to provide remedies which suited the particular need. (Including, for example, inhibition upon unconscionable exploitation of rights whose only merit was their strict legality: the "equity of redemption," by which a mortgagor might get back his land after the agreed date for repayment of the loan, is a familiar case in point.)

9. *Quincy's Reports*, 54 (Appendix K in the present book).

10. "To speak Exactly, There are Seven Courts in the Court of Exchequer, (*viz.*) The Court of Pleas or of Common Law, the Court of Equity, the Court of Accounts, the Court of Receipt, the Court of the Exchequer-Chamber (being the Assembly of all the Judges of *England* to Debate Difficult Matters of Law) The Court of Exchequer-Chamber upon Errors in the Court of Exchequer, the Court of Exchequer upon Errors in the Court of Kings Bench": as cited from Coke's Fourth Institute, 119, in T. Wood, *An Institute of the Laws of England, etc.* II (London, 1720).

11. See p. 21 above.

Unlike the Star Chamber, the Court of Chancery managed to
survive the onslaughts of the common lawyers and their parliamentary allies in the time of Charles I. Though it was not long before the
equity jurisdiction of the Court of Chancery became as formalized
and as leathery of texture as the common law itself (witness the
interminable processes depicted in Dickens's *Bleak House*), in principle it remained based in conscience and judicial discretion. The
equity jurisdiction of the Court of Exchequer probably had existed
from the beginnings of the court, back in the middle ages. There was
a discretionary element at work in all courts of common law orientation in those early times. However, whereas the King's Bench and
Common Pleas came to prefer hard and fast legalism, abandoning
discretionary amelioration of the hard case to collateral remedy
institutionalized elsewhere, the Court of Exchequer retained the old
duality. Even so, the discretionary component of the Court of
Exchequer's jurisprudence answered to the same name — equity — as
the regime of conscience in the Court of Chancery, and came to be
administered as near as might be in the same way.

The Court of Exchequer was a court of both common law and
equity in a manner that masked its true nature. Throughout its
history (it was abolished in the nineteenth century) it remained at
bottom a court of revenue. Its revenue jurisprudence was *sui generis*,
an amalgam of common law and equity peculiar to itself. It was only
at the edges, so to speak, that the Court of Exchequer operated as an
ordinary court of common law and an ordinary court of equity. [12]
This peripheral business was considerable, nevertheless. Business was
the word; and it is relevant to see how. Competition for work — for
the fees that went with it, that is to say — caused the various
jurisdictions at Westminster to practice a kind of refined cannibalism
upon one another. The principal sufferer was the Court of Common
Pleas, whose right to handle civil litigation fell prey to the King's
Bench (the natural jurisdiction of which looked more to criminality
than to civil wrongdoing) and to the Court of Exchequer both. Legal
fictions were the key to this filching of business. The King's Bench
made believe that the defendant was in its custody, exploiting an
authentic rule that gave it jurisdiction over civil actions against
persons thus placed. The Court of Exchequer's fiction focused more

---

12. On the Court of Exchequer's jurisdiction in the round, see the judgment of Pollock
C.B. in *A-G v. Halling* (1846) 15 M. & W. 687. Not to the exclusion however of W. H.
Bryson, *The Equity Side of the Exchequer* (Cambridge, 1975).

on the plaintiff. The court had a rule that gave it jurisdiction over claims by persons who were in debt to the king and who were the less able to pay the king by reason of their own claim against the defendant being unsettled; and it made its process (which could offer a plaintiff valuable practical advantages)[13] available to all by permitting anyone to pretend that he was in debt to the king. It was to this wangle process of *quo minus* (from the words of the writ, *quo minus sufficiens existit*) in its application to private litigation of a Court of Chancery sort that Oxenbridge Thacher was referring when he spoke of the Superior Court of Massachusetts having "renounced the Chancery Jurisdiction wh the Exchequer has in Cases where either Party, is the Kings Debtor."

Examination of Thacher's argument can now be brought into a more specifically American context. In chapter 5 it was noticed how, before the Act of Frauds of 1696 set up English-style customs enforcement law in America, its principal architect, Edward Randolph, sought to have courts of exchequer authorized there. The act of 1696 settled for vice-admiralty jurisdiction instead. Various reasons for the decision not to legislate for colonial exchequer courts were suggested in chapter 5, among them the practical difficulty of transplanting so specialized and arcane a jurisdiction to regions where legal learning was pretty scarce anyway. Nevertheless, in 1699 the province act which established the Superior Court of Massachusetts included a provision that the court should possess the same authority "as the Courts of Kings Bench, Common Pleas and Exchequer within his Majesty's Kingdom of England, have, or ought to have." Why the Massachusetts legislature should have wanted the Superior Court to have exchequer powers is a matter for speculation. Possibly it was to anticipate further efforts by Randolph to get Westminster legislation for colonial exchequer courts (presided over, as he conceived them, by judges sent from England). Or it may have been to make available a proper common law process for the condemnation of customs seizures,[14] so as to allow the custom houses that much less excuse for invoking the condemnation jurisdiction of the obnoxious vice-admiralty court which sat without a jury. Whatever the reason, it was on the province statute book that the Superior Court could act as a court of exchequer; and the court had issued writs of assistance in

13. See T. F. T. Plucknett, *Concise History of the Common Law*, 5th ed. (London, 1956), 160.

14. The information *in rem* (see chapter 2), that is, a process natural and peculiar to exchequer jurisdiction, for adjudicating things into the king's ownership.

this capacity. Thacher was now arguing that the Superior Court could not in fact assert an exchequer jurisdiction, for the reason that in a recent case it had refused to acknowledge that it had such a jurisdiction; that refusal, he maintained, was comprehensive and definitive, and the court could not trim it or go back on it.

As Thacher indicated, the case in which the Superior Court had declined exchequer jurisdiction had arisen by way of *quo minus.* The reason for this mode of proceeding was that the remedy being sought sounded in equity. The full factual content of the case does not appear in the records of the court, but the essentials are given clearly enough:

> Ann McNeal Widow and Mary Brideoak Spinster both of the City of Dublin in the Kingdom of Ireland Debtors and accountants to his Majesty Complts against Sarah Brideoak of Boston in the County of Suffolk. . . . Defendant on a Bill in Equity filed in Court Decembr the 20th 1752 . . . .[15]

The bill was "dismist" in February 1754;[16] and although the complainants were given permission to appeal to the Privy Council there is no sign of their having done so. *McNeal v. Brideoak* was of the nature of a lawyerlike device to get round the circumstance that there was no court of chancery in Massachusetts. There being no court of chancery, the McNeals' only hope for their "Bill in Equity" lay in the Superior Court's exchequer jurisdiction: on English precedent this jurisdiction should have included equitable remedies, similar to those in a chancery court invocable by *quo minus.* The hope was vain, however. The Superior Court balked. The reasons are not stated in the records, but there can be little doubt that they stemmed from a complex inhibition against equitable jurisdiction.

Part of it may have had to do with the attitude, or supposed attitude, of the English government in the 1690s when Massachusetts was legislating for a system of courts under its new province charter. Notwithstanding that the charter gave the General Court apparently unlimited power to set up courts, a province act for a court of chancery was disallowed. The reasoning at Westminster seems to have been that such an act trenched upon the royal prerogative. Commenting in 1704 on the relevant clause in the Massachusetts charter, the English attorney general, Sir Edward Northey, had this to say:

15. SCR (1753-54), 150.
16. SCM, Suffolk (1752-56), 26.

On consideration of this clause, if there be no other clauses that exclude the power of the crown, I am of opinion her majesty may, by her prerogative, erect a court of equity in the said province, as by her royal authority they are erected in other her majesty's plantations, and it seems to me that the general assembly cannot, by virtue of this clause, erect a court of equity.[17]

On the other hand, Westminster did not disallow province acts that enabled the ordinary courts, somewhat as if they were courts of equity, to soften hardships following from insistence upon the strict letter of, say, a mortgage deed or a bond; and the province act of 1699 which envisaged the Superior Court operating as a court of exchequer (with, for all that it expressed to the contrary, an equitable as well as a common law jurisdiction) was not disallowed either.[18]

In renouncing equitable or exchequer jurisdiction in *McNeal v. Brideoak* the Superior Court may have been vaguely influenced by the refusal of Westminster to countenance a provincial court of chancery back in the 1690s; but this is unlikely to have been the whole of it. There were other considerations, nearer home. Judicial courts of equity were not wished for in mid-eighteenth century

17. In G. Chalmers, *Opinions of Eminent Lawyers on Various Points of English Jurisprudence* . . . II (London, 1814), 183. However, it became firm law that only common law courts could be created by prerogative: *In re Lord Bishop of Natal* (1864-65) 3 Moo. P.C.C. (N.S.) 115, citing Coke's Fourth Institute, 87. The Cokeian position was known in eighteenth-century America, of course; and made use of. Adverting to Governor Bernard's tribunal on Benjamin Barons in 1761, *BG* 26 January 1767: "a high court of justiciary erected without law, and held in conjunction with the late surveyor-general and the late judge of admiralty. We all know that new courts cannot be established but by act of Parliament, or of assembly. The King alone cannot erect a new court . . . ."

18. Unspoken though it may have been, an objection to courts such as the Superior Court of Massachusetts having full chancery jurisdiction may have related less to constitutionalities about authority to create courts of equity (of what practical consequence could it have been to Westminster whether private litigation among distant colonists might sound in equity?) than to the danger of politically dominated colonial judicatures asserting a common law jurisdiction comparable to that of the Court of Chancery in England. This jurisdiction was small, but in a colonial context it had hazardous potential. It included the process of *scire facias*, which could be invoked for the annulment of legal instruments of certain kinds: a royal grant of office, as it might be, because of wrongdoing by the appointee; and it happens to have been by *scire facias* that Massachusetts lost its colony charter in 1684. If this process were to be available in a colony with a royal governor, someone might try it on as a means of invalidating his document of appointment and thus of effectively removing him.

But whatever system there may have been in British policy toward chancery jurisdiction in America, it had to live with wide institutional differences among the various colonies: see L. M. Friedman, *A History of American Law* (New York, 1973), 47-48.

Massachusetts. In fact they had become the subject of an opposing tradition. Why this should have been so is not immediately evident. One of the earliest acts of the newly constituted province legislature had been that vain endeavor to establish a court of chancery.[19] Also, the last judicial tribunals created under the previous colonial charter had been of magistrates elected to exercise a jurisdiction *"secundum aequum et bonum"* in a manner strongly reminiscent of a court of chancery. In 1706 the lack of equitable remedies was a matter of complaint by one aggrieved inhabitant to the British government.[20] The apparent reason for the disallowance of the province act for a court of chancery — concern for the royal prerogative — caused feelings to harden, perhaps: if only in reaction against an unpopular governmental upper crust who saw possible advantage in the British attitude. For certainly there were persons who saw the possible establishment of a prerogative court of chancery in a light which would not have been popularly favored. In 1704 Paul Dudley, son of Governor Joseph Dudley, wrote to a kinsman in England:

> This Country will never be worth Living in, for Lawyers and gentlemen, till the CHARTER IS TAKEN AWAY. My Father and I sometimes Talk of the Queen's Establishing a COURT OF CHANCERY in this Country; I have Writ about it, to Mr Blathwayt: If the Matter should Succeed, you might get some Place with your Return.[21]

Populists would have remembered, too, that courts of equity sat without juries.

What developed from the absence of a judicial court of equity probably explains much. It is described in former Governor Thomas Pownall's book on colonial government:

> There is no court of chancery in the charter governments of New England, nor any court vested with power to determine causes in equity, save only that the justices of the inferior court, and the justices of the

19. E. Washburn, *Judicial History of Massachusetts* (Boston, 1840). 34-35.

20. G. A. Washburne, "Imperial Control of the Administration of Justice in the Thirteen American Colonies 1684-1776": *Studies in History, Economics and Public Law*, vol. 105 (Chicago, 1923). C05/864 is cited.

21. Paul Dudley's letter is in Sir Henry Ashurst's *The Deplorable State of New-England* (London, 1708), 9-10. Ashurst was agent for the province and an enemy of Governor Dudley. The governor had inimical designs on the new province charter, Ashurst believed, and Dudley junior's letter was reproduced as indicative of this. Paul Dudley (for whom as chief justice of Massachusetts from 1745 to 1751, see references in chapters 6 and 11 above) was himself attorney general of Massachusetts and advocate general at this time.

William Blathwayt ran the Board of Trade (and had been closely involved in the transatlantic activities of Edward Randolph).

superior court respectively, have power to give relief on mortgages, bonds, and other penalties contained in deeds: in all other chancery and equitable matters, both the crown and the subject are without redress. This introduced a practice of petitioning the legislative courts for relief, and prompted those courts to interpose their authority. These petitions becoming numerous, in order to give greater dispatch to such business, the legislative courts transacted such business by orders or resolves, without the solemnity of passing acts for such purposes; and have further extended their power by resolves and orders, beyond what a court of chancery ever attempted to decree, even to the suspending of public laws: which orders or resolves are not sent home for the royal assent. The tendency of these measures is too obvious to need any observations thereon.[22]

In other words, denial of equity jurisdiction in the judicial courts tended to increase the power and independence of the provincial politicians in Council or House of Representatives assembled. Those persons also controlled the salaries of the judges of the Superior Court. In *McNeal v. Brideoak* the judges might have thought it unwise to assert a jurisdiction that would not only earn popular disesteem through the novelty (outside the court of vice-admiralty) of trial without jury, but trench upon a valuable privilege of the assemblymen. Besides, the *quo minus* device itself was none too respectable from the whig point of view. A plaintiff suing in the Court of Exchequer was regarded as "participant of the prerogative," as any Boston lawyer familiar with his Plowden's *Commentaries* would have known.[23]

On another plane of ratiocination, influences of an almost atavistic kind also may have been at work. "Equity has never been popular in

22. *The Administration of the British Colonies* I (1764: reprint ed., London, 1774), 114. For this material Pownall cites Benjamin Prat, the Boston lawyer for whom he obtained the chief justiceship of New York (see p. 222 above).

Wrote Governor William Shirley to the Duke of Bedford, 27 February 1749 (CO5/886), apropos a scheme of government for Nova Scotia: "The Assemblies of the Northern Colonies seem to have an aversion to Erecting Courts of Equity and are fond of taking the Administration of that part of Justice into their own hands, which frequently occasions great Irregularities & Encroachments upon the Courts of Judicature . . . ."

Rhode Island had had an equity court (of a sort) from 1741 to 1744: see Z. Chafee, Jr., "Records of the Rhode Island Court of Equity 1741-1743," *Colonial Society of Massachusetts Publications,* XXXV (Boston, 1951), 91-118. According to the Hardwicke Papers: Privy Council Cases 1759-63 (Add. MSS 36218), "The Courts of Justice in *New Hampshire* are a mixt Jurisdiction, not only exercising the Powers of Courts of Law, but, as the Parties, or Occasion requires, they moderate the Rigour of the Law, and judge according to the Equity of the Case."

23. At page 322. And on page 14 of the 1699 edition of William Brown's book on exchequer practice (whence derived the first Massachusetts writ of assistance): "the Debtor of the King is participant of the Prerogative of the King."

America," said the late Dean Roscoe Pound.[24] Certainly the puritan antecedents of the Commonwealth of Massachusetts did not favor it. Law was one thing; and the common law in particular, with its accent on rigidity of form and rule (conditioned by the severe logic of property in land that was the common law's major concern), well suited the puritan mind. Equity, a discretionary regime informed by nothing so much as the imperfect conscience of a mortal man inevitably far gone in sin, was different. Opposition to equity in seventeenth-century England (and the Court of Chancery came within a hairsbreadth of abolition in the mid-century revolution) was not wholly a matter of the common lawyers' professional resentments. Men were genuinely troubled by the uncertainties and imponderables of so wobbly a jurisprudence. There was John Selden's well-worn jibe about equity and the length of the lord chancellor's foot. More solemnly expressive of the mood was the grumble of the parliamentarian Bulstrode Whitelocke in 1648, about being a commissioner of the great seal:

> the judges of the Common Law have certain fixed rules to guide them; a Keeper of the Seal has nothing but his own conscience to guide him and that is oftentimes deceitful. The proceedings in Chancery are "secundum arbitrium boni viri" and this *arbitrium* differs as much in several men as their countenances differ.[25]

It may be that by the 1750s pilgrim modes of thought had undergone considerable secularization in Massachusetts; but equity, suggestive as it often was of a broken bargain, could still have stuck in the craw of covenanting New England saint turned Boston businessman and votary of the social contract.

Thacher's root-and-branch line of argument, which went to the jurisdiction of the Superior Court and would have denied special

---

24. *The Formative Era of American Law* (Boston, 1938), 155: "nor did the courts of Massachusetts have complete equity jurisdiction till the last quarter of the nineteenth century." (Federal equity jurisdiction applied, nevertheless: *United States v. Howland and Allen* (1819) 4 Wheaton 108; and *cf. Payne v. Hook* (1869) 7 Wallace 425.)

25. Whitelocke, *Memorials of the English Affairs* (London, 1732), 379.

The Selden jibe in full: "Equity is A Roguish thing, for Law wee have a measure of what to trust too. Equity is according to the conscience of him tht is Chancellor, and as tht is larger or narrower soe is equity. Tis all one as if they should make the Standard for the measure wee call A foot, to be the Chancellors foot; what an uncertain measure would this be; One Chancellor ha's a long foot another A short foot a third an indifferent foot; tis the same thing in the Chancellors Conscience." See F. Pollock, ed., *Table Talk of John Selden* (London, 1927), 43.

writs of assistance no less than general, did not succeed. Indeed, what he identified as "the most material question" seems to have cut no ice at all: on the evidence of Chief Justice Hutchinson's *History,* the issue addressed by the court was whether the writ should be of one kind or of the other, not whether it should be repudiated altogether. That the Superior Court did not regard itself as having totally disowned exchequer jurisdiction in *McNeal v. Brideoak* is evident not only from this but also from what Governor Francis Bernard told the Board of Trade some time afterward: "About two years ago great Endeavours were made to disable the Officers ... and a public opposition was made in open Court (which is here vested with the Powers of the Court of Exchequer) granting writs of assistance except in special Cases, but the Judges overruled the exceptions . . . ."[26] Moreover, it appears that Thacher's interpretation of *McNeal v. Brideoak* was not subscribed to even by his colleague James Otis, who, according to John Adams's notes, said merely that "this Court confined their Chancery Power to Revenue &c" (which was well short of total abandonment: and Otis in fact centered his own argument upon the acceptability of "special" writs of assistance from the Superior Court).

And there was a further respect in which Thacher's "most material question" was misplaced. He spoke as if issuance of the customs writ of assistance belonged peculiarly and exclusively to an exchequer court. This·was not so. The writ, it will be recalled, rested on a little-known common law doctrine which authorized the invention of new writs for the better execution of the public purposes of an act of Parliament "according to the force and effect of the act." The statutory foundation of the customs writ of assistance in the Act of Frauds of 1662 was not so much section 5(2), which made the writ a precondition of entry and search, as section 32, which obligated practically all the king's subjects to assist customs officers. A writ of assistance could have been founded upon section 32 even if section 5(2) had not positively required it. Such a writ would have been issued in the ordinary way, under the great seal of England by the clerks in the lord chancellor's office (the chancery). This is the background against which to read the reference to the seal of the Court of Exchequer in section 5(2):

> And it shall be lawful to or for any Person or Persons, authorized by Writ of Assistance under the Seal of his Majesty's Court of Exchequer, to take a Constable . . . .

26. To Board of Trade 5 September 1763, in British Library, King's MSS 205.

Section 5(2) was stipulating that the writ of assistance used in customs search should be under the exchequer seal, rather than under the great seal — as would have been the case if it had spoken of a "Writ of Assistance" without qualification. The words "under the Seal of his Majesty's Court of Exchequer" were prescriptive, not descriptive. The fact that statutes do not normally use words to no purpose is a double check; if the writ of assistance pertained to the Court of Exchequer anyway, there would have been no need for section 5(2) to say so. Reasons why the draftsman opted for the Court of Exchequer are not far to seek. The Court of Exchequer had a traditional connection with customs law enforcement, and thus a kind of preemptive right to this new bit of business. (Though there was nothing in it for the court as a judicial body: the issuance of the writ was a purely administrative process, and the fees went to the official who did the work, the king's remembrancer.) Of greater practical importance is the historical circumstance that writs under the exchequer seal were free from the territorial limitations of the great seal. Writs under the great seal did not run in Wales or in all the English counties palatine, but the king had revenue interests everywhere and his exchequer process reached out accordingly. By requiring the writ of assistance to be issued from the Court of Exchequer the draftsman of the act of 1662 made sure that it held good all over the country.[27]

But the Court of Exchequer's process did not extend to the colonies, and the reasons for its adoption for the writ of assistance in 1662 had no application there. What with this, and the unreadable text of the Act of Frauds of 1696 which seemed to extend writ of assistance search to America without actually saying as much, Oxenbridge Thacher might have made more than he did out of the problematical standing of the Superior Court as a court of exchequer. As will be seen when the events that led up to the Townshend legislation of 1767 are discussed in a later chapter, it was by reference to this sort of question that 1662-style writ of assistance search in the colonies came to be found legally deficient.[28] In concentrating upon the Superior Court's exchequer jurisdiction as

27. See L. A. Harper, *The English Navigation Laws* (New York, 1939), 110. And *cf.* "A Discourse against the Jurisdiction of the King's-Bench over Wales by Process of Latitat" (anonymous, but written by Charles Pratt, later Lord Camden) in F. Hargrave ed., *Law Tracts* (Dublin, 1757).

28. Pages 442, 463-64.

the weakness in the case for the crown Thacher was in the right area; but he did not put his finger on the exact spot.

Of course, Thacher was not alone in missing the true significance of the 1662 act's requirement that the writ of assistance be under the seal of the Court of Exchequer. His opponent, Jeremiah Gridley, also made the mistake of seeing the writ of assistance as linked naturally to exchequer jurisdiction. Nor for that matter did Thacher's colleague, James Otis, get on to the point. It is possible, indeed, that the confusion existed long before the great debate on writs of assistance in 1761. Edward Randolph's eager (though unsuccessful) sponsorship of colonial exchequer courts for inclusion in the Act of Frauds of 1696 perhaps owed something to the notion that the assured existence of such courts would facilitate the establishment of writ of assistance search.

Thacher's argument that the Superior Court did not have the power to grant writs of assistance was so sweeping and absolute that it did not leave much room for any further mode of attack; the remainder of what he said did little more than supplement this blockbusting jurisdictional issue. Here it is, from the Abstract (which does not differ significantly from Adams's original notes):

> In England all Informations of uncustomed or prohibited Goods are in the Exchequer, so that the Custom House Officers are the Officers of that Court under the Eye & Direction of the Barons & so accountable for any wanton exercise of power.
>
> The Writ now prayed for is not returnable. If the Seizures were so, before your Honors, and this Court should enquire into them you'd often find a wanton exercise of power. At home they seize at their peril, even with probable Cause.

Thacher was rounding off his argument rather cleverly. He was saying, in effect, that even if the Superior Court were to affirm its power as a court of exchequer, and grant writs of assistance, it would still be unable to match the role of the Court of Exchequer in England. In England the Court of Exchequer could, as it were, see the whole job through. Having issued the writ of assistance by dint of which the customs officer made his seizure, the Court of Exchequer would be the forum in which he had to make good his right to seize, for in no other court was the necessary condemnation process available. The court was thus in a position to see that he had not engaged in "any wanton exercise of power." In Massachusetts, however, the condemnation process took place in the court of vice-admiralty. There, Thacher hinted, the custom house often got away with "wanton exercise of power," and it was wrong that the Superior Court should contribute to that power by granting writs of assistance. The writ was not returnable — that is to say, the issuing authority received no information as to how it might be used (or abused). If seizures in which it had been instrumental were brought to the Superior Court for condemnation the court would be able to inquire into them, and give a remedy. But even this amelioration was nonexistent (thanks, as the whiggish Thacher undoubtedly would have felt, to the unconstitutional condemnation jurisdiction of the vice-admiralty court).[29] As an argument, it was pretty well integrated.

But Thacher's view of the way things were done in England was somewhat out of focus. That the Court of Exchequer was the proper court for suits against revenue officers was settled law.[30] There was authority, also, that an otherwise lawful seizure would render the officer liable in trespass if he abused it.[31] It could not be said, however, that customs officers in England were "under the Eye and Direction of the Barons" ("baron," it will be recalled, was the name for a judge in the Court of Exchequer) in the sense of administrative supervision. That sort of control belonged to the commissioners of customs. Such discipline as the Court of Exchequer exercised was according to the standard forms and categories of the ordinary law. And although Thacher's perusal of Strange's reports evidently took in *Leglise v. Champante*, a case in 1728 where "it was held, that . . . the officer seizes at his peril, and that a probable cause is no defence," he had been less assiduous with the statutes, for since 1746 legislation had in effect given exemption from liability for a seizure which, though wrongful, had been made with probable cause.[32]

Oxenbridge Thacher's standing in the writs of assistance case, particularly *vis-à-vis* James Otis, will be touched upon further in

29. See, *e.g.*, Thacher's draft of an address to the king and parliament, in "The Thacher Papers": MHSP first series 20 (1884), 46-56.

30. *Bereholt v. Candy* (1718) Bunbury 34. For the reputation of Bunbury's reports see Holdsworth *HEL* XII, 137-38.

31. *Gibson's Case* (1606) Lane 90.

32. *Cf.* chapter 2, n. 9. The same oversight occurred in Thacher's pamphlet, "The Sentiments of a British American" (1764), reproduced in B. Bailyn, *Pamphlets of the American Revolution 1750-1776* I (Cambridge, Mass., 1965): criticizing the Sugar Act 1764 Thacher referred to section 46, which extended "probable cause" justification to America, as "peculiarly confined to America."

chapter 15, when Otis's entry on to the scene has been looked over. It does seem that the two men, whatever their respective formal positions may have been (hired partisan advocate?; *amicus curiae?*), struck up a working relationship. Each pursued a distinctive line of argument and by and large kept clear of the other's.

The extremely radical approach of Thacher, a challenge to the very jurisdiction, produced something of a payoff in the longer term. To all appearances ignored by the court in February, it could be brought out again later in the year.

15

~~~~~~~~
~~~~~~~~

Otis (I)

~~~~~~~~
~~~~~~~~

J AMES OTIS was the third speaker and the man but for whom the writs of assistance case would have been remembered only by the specialist historian, as one of the several scuffles that broke out between the Boston merchants and the customs enforcement regime in the winter of 1760-61.

Aside from his published pamphlets and newspaper pieces, there is little by way of personal documentation to speak for Otis: in a fit of the mental disorder that overtook him in middle age he burnt all of his letters and papers he could lay hands on.[1] History's view of Otis is largely what others saw of him. However, the basic framework of his life is known.

He was born in 1725 at West Barnstable, in the spur of Massachusetts that bounded Cape Cod Bay, the first child of James Otis, of whom something was seen in chapter 11, and Mary Allyne Otis. As a boy James Otis junior was put to study with the minister of the parish, and in 1739-43 he attended Harvard College. At Harvard and for a year or two after his interests were mostly classical and literary. Otis senior apprenticed him in the law to Jeremiah Gridley in Boston; and in 1748 he began practice at Plymouth. That southern area of the province was his father's stamping-ground as a lawyer, and no doubt the influence of Otis senior helped him get started. He seems to have made reasonable progress, for as early as May 1751 the

---

1. John Adams (to William Tudor, 5 June 1817: *LWJA* X, 265) recalled asking whether Otis's unpublished work on Greek prosody had been found among his papers. His daughter "answered me with a countenance of woe . . . that she 'had not a line from her father's pen; that he had spent much time, and taken great pains, to collect together all his letters and other papers, and, in one of his unhappy moments, committed them all to the flames.' I have used her own expressions." Tudor junior in his *Life of James Otis of Massachusetts* (Boston, 1823), xviii: "His papers have all perished." This was an overstatement. For instance, a few of Otis's intrafamily letters are in the Butler Library of Columbia University. That numerous items are missing from the bound volume, "Otis Legal Memoranda," in the Suffolk court office in Boston, encourages the hope that more Otis materials may become accessible some day.

Superior Court on circuit in Bristol appointed him "attorney for the Lord the King at this Term, the Attorney General being absent."[2] It is possible that Otis himself was by now riding circuit from Boston, for it was around this time that pursuit of better professional opportunities caused him to set up office there. In 1755 he married Ruth Cunningham, daughter of the substantial merchant and long-time foe of the vice-admiralty court Nathaniel Cunningham (and hence into a sort of kinship with that supreme custom house operator Charles Paxton, whose sister was Cunningham's second wife). It was not a case of marriage for money, if only because Otis was earning enough of his own. "He was soon generally known in many of the other colonies," says William Tudor's biography, "and often consulted from a distance; at one time he yielded to the urgent solicitations that were made to him to proceed to Halifax in the middle of winter, to plead the cause of three men accused of piracy" (and got them off).[3] Another instance of Otis's more distant out-of-town operations was his representation (with John Andrews) of Governor Stephen Hopkins in a protracted lawsuit with Samuel Ward, in Rhode Island.

Throughout the first nine or ten years of his Boston-based practice Otis took little part in public affairs. He was made a justice of the peace for Suffolk County in 1756; but this was largely an honorific mark of social advance. Politically he was a sideliner at most. In 1755 he joined in a petition against inequitably high taxation of towns, but that signified little. In July 1756 he was deploring the military disaster that had lately befallen British arms in America ("our most shameful Defeat . . . a very scandalous Expedition . . ."); this, however, might have been the reaction of a good many people. He seems to have moved slightly nearer the active center of things after Thomas Pownall's accession to the governorship of the province in 1757, as a kind of contact man between Pownall, who angled for country support, and Otis senior, the Barnstable baron who could deliver it. Otis may have been a link between Pownall and the merchants also.[4] But none of this amounted to much in terms of

---

2. SCR 1750-51. Such *pro hac vice* appointments were common: *cf.* chapter 8, n. 29.

The SCR volume of 1746-47 (Plymouth, July 1747) has a reference to "James Otis junr. Dept. Sherife of the County of Barnstable."

3. Tudor, *Otis,* 15. See also H. F. Bell, " 'A Melancholy Affair' — James Otis and the Pirates," in *The American Neptune* XXXI, no. 1. (1971).

4. See J. J. Waters, *The Otis Family in Provincial and Revolutionary Massachusetts* (Chapel Hill, 1968), chap. VI, *passim;* and Otis to James Otis, senior, 24 July 1756, in Butler Library, Columbia University: Otis Papers, box 1.

partisan politics. If Otis had been a pronounced Pownallite politico the fact surely would have been brought out in Samuel Waterhouse's lampoon on Pownall, *Proposals for . . . the History of . . . Vice-Admiral Sir Thomas Brazen, Commander of an American Squadron in the last Age . . . .*[5] Waterhouse did not spare Benjamin Prat, William Brattle, and other henchmen of the now (1760) departed governor, but of Otis there is not a word. Otis's apolitical stance during Pownall's governorship is evidenced, though again in a negative way, by another Waterhouse lampoon a little later. This one, *Proposals for . . . the History of Adjutant Trowel and Bluster,* was an attack specifically on Brattle and Otis.[6] Pownall naturally came into the picture (now as "the General") because of Brattle's association with him; and if the former governor's relationship with Otis had likewise been significantly political Waterhouse undoubtedly would have made something of it. As it was, the lampoon's savaging of "Bluster" shows Otis emerging as a politician in the wake of the chief justiceship affair, which of course was after Pownall had gone.

Otis's good relations with Governor Pownall possibly meant nothing so much as a shared interest in the classics. This early taste had never left Otis. As late as 1760 he published *The Rudiments of Latin Prosody with a Dissertation on Letters and the Principles of Harmony in Poetic and Prosaic Composition* —

> a book of minute and precise textual scholarship — a book which shows that its author's natural aptitude for eloquence, oral and written, had been developed in connection with the most careful technical study of details. No one would guess . . . that it was written by perhaps the busiest lawyer in New England.[7]

He also wrote a treatise — presumably companion to this — on the rudiments of Greek prosody; it remained unpublished, however, because of supposed printing difficulties with Greek type, and it perished with the rest of his papers.[8] The literary historian of the

5. See chapter 9, n. 30.

6. See chapter 9, n. 35. And *cf.* L. H. Butterfield, ed., *The Earliest Diary of John Adams* (Cambridge, Mass., 1966), 89.

7. M. C. Tyler, *The Literary History of the American Revolution 1763-1783* I (New York, 1897), 37. BPBA 24 November 1760 carried an advertisement for the book, as published "this day"; the author was not named, however.

8. *Cf.* n. 1 above. According to Tudor (p. 15), Otis replied to a suggestion that it be published: "there were no Greek types in the country, or if there were . . . no printer knew how to set them."

Isaiah Thomas, *The History of Printing in America* I (Albany, American Antiquarian Society, 1874), says that in 1718 Thomas Hollis gave sets of Hebrew and Greek type to

American Revolution, from whom the comments just quoted were taken, was less complimentary about Otis as an original writer; on paper he was too much the orator.[9] Another opinion, suggested by how his newspaper pieces could change in tone and temper as he warmed to his work, might be that a bottle was not always far from his elbow. Conviviality of disposition may have been another reason why he got on so well with the unceremonious Pownall.

Possibly it was as a farewell gift from Governor Pownall that Otis was made acting advocate general (William Bollan, the province's agent in Britain, still held the substantive appointment). This was as close as he ever got to substantial governmental office. "I never asked a Court Favour . . . ," he declared in the *Boston Gazette* on 4 April 1763. "Before I belonged to the General Court, I had the Office of Advocate General *unasked* and *unexpectedly,* by the Recommendation of the late Chief Justice PRATT, and the unmerited Good Will of Governor POWNALL . . . ." Benjamin Prat was himself still acting advocate general in May 1760.[10] Why he should have stepped down in favor of Otis is not apparent: perhaps he did not care to continue in office after the departure of his patron Pownall, since, until Governor Bernard arrived, it would have been by courtesy of his political opponent, the anti-Pownallite lieutenant governor, Thomas Hutchinson.[11] But step down he did, and for Pownall to have appointed James Otis it must have been before 5 June, that being the day Pownall left for England. There was of course nothing to inhibit Otis serving in the period of Hutchinson's caretaker administration. As yet there was no antipathy between the two men: Otis was not in politics, and his family quarrel with Hutchinson over the chief justiceship was several months in the future.

Harvard, and that before being destroyed in a fire in 1764 the Greek had been used only once, in 1761. Hebrew and Greek type occurred in a theological article in *BNL* 27 January 1763.

9. Tyler, *op. cit.,* 37-38: "Yet with all Otis's soundness of taste as a student of literature, he often seemed wholly lacking in taste when he himself came to the act of literary composition. He was a powerful writer, and he wrote much; but in the structure and form of what he wrote there are few traces of that enthusiasm for classical literature which we know him to have possessed . . . . He was, above all things, an orator."

However, "It sometimes seems as if he *thought* in Latin, often quoting from memory, with an oral text of his own making": R. M. Gummere, *The American Colonial Mind & the Classical Tradition* (Cambridge, Mass., 1963), 101.

10. See *Quincy's Reports*, 534.

11. On the other hand, Prat and Hutchinson "though never warm friends . . . were much together," possibly through a shared interest in Massachusetts history: C. K. Shipton, *Sibley's Harvard Graduates* X (Boston, 1958), 231.

The principal concern of this chapter is with Otis's personal position at the time of his celebrated performance on writs of assistance in February 1761, as reflected in John Adams's Abstract. No less than one-third of the text attributed to Otis, a solid block of oratory at the beginning of his speech, relates rather to Otis himself than to the legalities of the writ:

> I was desired by one of the court to look into the books, and consider the question now before the court, concerning Writs of Assistance. I have accordingly considered it, and now appear not only in obedience to your order, but also in behalf of the inhabitants of this town, who have presented another petition, and out of regard to the liberties of the subject. And I take this opportunity to declare, that whether under a fee or not, (for in such a cause as this I despise a fee) I will to my dying day oppose, with all the powers and faculties God has given me, all such instruments of slavery on the one hand, and villainy on the other, as this writ of assistance is. It appears to me (may it please your honours) the worst instrument of arbitrary power, the most destructive of English liberty, and the fundamental principles of the constitution, that ever was found in an English law-book. I must therefore beg your honours patience and attention to the whole range of an argument, that may perhaps appear uncommon in many things, as well as points of learning, that are more remote and unusual, that the whole tendency of my design may the more easily be perceived, the conclusions better descend [discerned?] and the force of them better felt.
>
> I shall not think much of my pains in this cause as I engaged in it from principle. I was sollicited to engage on the other side. I was sollicited to argue this cause as Advocate-General, and because I would not, I have been charged with a desertion of my office; to this charge I can give a very sufficient answer, I renounced that office, and I argue this cause from the same principle; and I argue it with the greater pleasure as it is in favour of British liberty, at a time, when we hear the greatest monarch upon earth declaring from his throne, that he glories in the name of Briton, and that the privileges of his people are dearer to him than the most valuable prerogatives of his crown. And as it is in opposition to a kind of power, the exercise of which in former periods of English history, cost one King of England his head and another his throne. I have taken more pains in this cause, than I ever will take again: Although my engaging in this and another popular cause has raised much resentment; but I think I can sincerely declare, that I cheerfully submit myself to every odious name for conscience sake: and from my soul I despise all those whose guilt, malice or folly has made my foes. Let the consequences be what they will, I am determined to proceed. The only principles of public conduct that are worthy a gentleman, or a man are, to sacrifice estate, ease, health and applause, and even life itself to the sacred calls of his country. These manly sentiments in private life make the good citizen, in public life, the patriot and the hero. — I do not say, when brought to the test, I shall be

invincible; I pray GOD I may never be brought to the melancholy trial; but if ever I should, it would then be known, how far I can reduce to practice principles I know founded in truth. In the mean time I will proceed to the subject of the writ . . . .

Altogether, a remarkably personalized way to begin a speech in court.

In fact, there is little or no trace of any of this in John Adams's on-the-spot notes. The notes themselves begin:

This Writ is against the fundamental Principles of Law. — The Priviledge of House. A Man, who is quiet, is as secure in his House, as a Prince in his Castle . . . .

True, the reference to "the fundamental Principles of Law" could tie in with the flourish in the Abstract, which spoke of "the fundamental principles of the constitution." But it could equally belong down toward the middle of the Abstract, yet to be examined, where other bits — such as houses being like castles — are mirrored. Not that it matters much. Obviously the Abstract's opening mass of fustian was not verbatim reportage but constructed afterward.

Constructed, not reconstructed. There is no reason to suppose that Adams's note-taking was at fault here. As the day wore on his hand became tired and his notes scrappy, but at this stage his writing was still reasonably firm. Nor, on the chronology of the hearing suggested in chapter 12, is it likely that Adams was absent when Otis began speaking; this seems to have been around the middle of the day (Wednesday 25 February), after Oxenbridge Thacher, whose speech Adams certainly heard, had sat down. Above all, perhaps, there is an intrinsic unlikelihood that an advocate of Otis's experience and standing would in real life have engaged in so unprofessional display of self-centeredness. The opening blast of the Otis speech in the Abstract was probably an early instance of what was to be so much in evidence in Adams's old-age reminiscence of the great occasion: a disposition, in keeping with literary and classical tradition, to compose oratory for the printed page after the event.

Yet, however fictional in the ordinary sense, the Abstract's windy exordium may nevertheless be authentic Otis.

In essence it resembles the transfiguration of Jeremiah Gridley's performance. Just as Gridley seems to have participated in the Abstract's radical rearrangement and refurbishment of his argument, a great deal of the Abstract rendition of the Otis speech may have been afterthought from the horse's mouth. Young John Adams stood in somewhat the same relationship to both Gridley and Otis. Gridley had sponsored him for practice at the Suffolk County bar, and Otis had lent support; and in a way they remained his mentors still. It might well have been as a matter of course as much as in hope of help·that Adams revealed to Otis as well as to Gridley his plan to write up the writs of assistance hearing. Assuredly Otis would have been no less cooperative than Gridley. For one thing, there was his sheer approachability. "Attended Court all Day," John Adams wrote in his diary at the time of his hopes of a start at the bar, "and at night waited on Otis at his office where I conversed with him and he, with great Ease and familiarity, promised to join the Bar in recommending me to the Court." [12] Ferocious in enmity though he was, in everyday disposition Otis seems to have been affability itself. But there was something else besides. If Gridley was mindful that the Abstract might get into print, such a possibility would have impinged upon Otis even more. Placed as he was when the Abstract was being prepared, Otis had a special interest of his own in what it reported him as saying.

By now Otis was moving toward the forefront of province politics. In the fall of 1760 he was still holding a government appointment as acting advocate general, the lawyer most identified with the custom house interest in the vice-admiralty court; before the spring of 1761 ended he had swung into opposition to the governor and the custom house, and was in the thick of the roughest common law assault the vice-admiralty court had undergone in thirty years. In the elections of May 1761 the previously apolitical government lawyer had become one of the representatives for Boston in the House of Representatives and leader of an incipient anti-court party. Certain public-image problems attended the transformation. It was not just that vexation at his father's disappointed hopes of a Superior Court judgeship had betrayed him into wild statements that his enemies would not allow people to forget; rather it was allegations that his entry into political life, and his conduct thereafter, were motivated not by sincere conviction but by personal spleen. How worried he could be by these was manifested in his recriminatory newspaper exchange with Thomas Hutchinson in 1763, noted in chapter 11. If he was troubled two years after, when for all his ups and downs in public esteem he was an established force on the political scene,

12. *DAJA* I, 56.

anxiety to cleanse his credentials of so damaging a calumny would certainly have been present at the time he was just beginning.

The hypothesis will be recalled that young John Adams conceived the Abstract in anticipation of a victory against the writ of assistance, for the celebration of which a publishable account of the great forensic struggle might be a useful thing to have ready and waiting. The final result of the case, which depended upon word from England as to issuance of the writ there, could not be delayed more than a few months. In the meantime the slurs on Otis's motivation in entering politics were not abating. Might not the epic dimension of his part in the triumph over the hated writ of assistance appear in print as including an explicit avowal of the purity of his position? The dry legalities of his actual argument had to be prettied up for the lay readership in any case. Why not, then, lead into them with a little imaginative oratorical flourish, telling of his concern for "the liberties of the subject," his indifference to monetary reward, his sacrifice of office as advocate general, his regard for "the greatest monarch upon earth" — perish any thought of disaffection toward the crown (though without forgetting that some previous monarchs had come to grief for exercising this kind of power), and the quite exceptional pains he had taken? And why not use the opportunity to discourage his detractors by a cheerful submission "to every odious name," and for "conscience sake"? What with sacrifice of "estate, ease, health and applause, and even life itself to the sacred calls of . . . country" making for "the good citizen, . . . the patriot and the hero," and the breast-beating prayer about never being "bought to the melancholy trial," the Abstract has Otis's superadded opening apologetics pretty far gone in staginess. Even so, the whole was consistent with a design to convince the Boston public that their deliverance — should they get it — from "the worst instrument of arbitrary power, the most destructive of English liberty . . . that ever was found in an English law-book," the general writ of assistance, was the work of a man of principle and grit, not an exercise in private spite.

As with Gridley's reconstituted speech, it is not probable that so much that fitted Otis's personal situation got into the Abstract by accident, or even by the unguided artistry of John Adams. The likelihood rather is that the opening one-third of the Abstract rendition of Otis's speech was inspired by Otis himself, though not so much in court as in conversation with Adams afterward.

The opening passages of Otis's speech, Abstract version, may be valueless as a record of what he actually said at the hearing; and as legal argument they do not amount to anything. Their general design seems to have been to refute the imputations that this rocketing political star was powered by nothing worthier than personal rancor. But to the extent that Otis himself participated in the writing of them they have a sort of authenticity. They were not all bravura bombast: here and there they afford or suggest useful fill-in material for the background scene.

The very first words are a case in point. "I was desired by one of the court," Otis appears as saying, "to look into the books, and consider the question now before the court, concerning Writs of Assistance." It could be that this call for help was made quite a long time back; in fact, to shortly after the four puisne judges of the Superior Court returned to Boston from circuit the previous fall. At Salem the new collector of customs, James Cockle, had asked the judges for a writ of assistance. Embarrassed by a recent article in the *London Magazine* which indicated strongly that the general writ they had become accustomed to issue was wrong, and not having enough learning of their own, they ducked a decision till they got back to Boston and could more conveniently inquire into the true law. Abstract-Otis, be it observed, spoke not of having been asked "to look into the books" by the court as a whole, but by "one of the court": in other words, by just one of the judges he was now addressing. (His going on to say that he appeared "in obedience to your order" could have been directed — with a bow, perhaps — to that particular judge.) Here may be a useful clue to events.

For it is no problem to spot the Superior Court judge likeliest to have made the request. Chambers Russell was not only one of the Superior Court judges, he was also judge of the vice-admiralty court, in which capacity he enjoyed the advantage, not shared by his colleagues on the Superior Court, of a standing relationship with one of the leading lawyers in the province: the advocate general. If the Superior Court judges on their return to Boston[13] wanted learned advice on the unresolved Cockle application, what better than that Judge Russell, wearing his vice-admiralty hat, be left to take soundings of the current incumbent, Acting Advocate General James Otis?

13. SCR 1760-62 shows the court (Lynde, Cushing, Russell, and Oliver, JJ) adjourning at Salem on 23 October 1760. The next entry is dated 27 January 1761, at Charlestown (when Hutchinson C. J. took his seat).

It would seem, however, that the judges did not plan to dispose of Cockle's application in a wholly informal manner. Otis's statements, a little way down the Abstract text, "I was sollicited to engage on the other side," and "I was sollicited to argue this cause as Advocate-General," imply an appointed occasion. Nor is the projected occasion to be identified as the hearing that actually took place, in February 1761. Hutchinson's *History of Massachusets-Bay* indicates that Otis presented the merchants' petition that asked for the February hearing,[14] by which time he could no longer have been advocate general. (Exactly when he resigned is not known, but it can hardly have been later than 24 December 1760, for on that day he was spokesman for the petition to the Assembly against unlawful fees in the vice-admiralty;[15] he surely would not have spearheaded such an attack if he had still been accredited to that same court.) That in 1761 Otis could say he had been "sollicited to engage on the other side" does not necessarily mean that at the time to which he was looking back, the fall of 1760, there were more sides than one. Similarly, "to argue this cause" was not necessarily to debate it against an opponent. What the judges had in mind may have been that, although past practice had been to grant general writs of assistance for the asking, in the atmosphere of uncertainty generated by the recent *London Magazine* article Cockle's application for a general writ should be the subject of a researched and reasoned oral presentation. They would listen, perhaps behind closed doors, to whatever case might be made out for the legality of the writ and decide the application accordingly.

Naturally it would be for the customs authorities, who wanted the writ, to appoint counsel to perform this task; and to whom else should they turn in so important a matter than the advocate general — the king's advocate, as he was sometimes called — especially if he was thought to be researching the subject anyway (for Judge Russell)? At that time, of course, the customs authorities were not "the other side." Issuance of a general writ of assistance had not yet ceased to be simply a matter on which they hoped to dispel the court's doubt. It did not become the subject of an adversary process, with the customs authorities and the merchants as contending parties,

14. Page 68: "Upon application . . . by one of the custom-house officers, an exception was taken to the application; and Mr. Otis desired a time might be assigned for an argument upon it."

15. JHR, 238.

until Otis was no longer advocate general. Indeed, it was Otis himself who transformed the occasion into a kind of *lis inter partes*,
when, now spokesman for the merchants, he asked the court to give
them a hearing. The emergence of two sides, thus brought about,
meant abandonment of the different mode of proceeding, less
overtly and publicly judicial, that had been in prospect when Otis
was invited to speak in the custom house interest.

Another small essay in speculative deduction concerns Oxenbridge
Thacher. That at the February hearing Otis and Thacher were not
colleagues in the ordinary sense — two men working for the same
employer — is indicated in the preamble to the Abstract, which states
that Thacher was joined with Otis "at the desire of the Court." It
also seems possible that Thacher was less Otis's colleague than his
successor.

If, back in the fall, Otis had been approached as advocate general
to "look into the books" and to speak for Cockle's postponed
application, presumably some other lawyer had to be found when he
resigned. The natural choice would be the man who took over as
advocate general. There is evidence that Benjamin Prat, Otis's predecessor, resumed the office temporarily (pending departure to New
York, as chief justice there);[16] and it may also be a pointer that
John Adams believed that Prat had declined the crown brief[17] when
the writs of assistance issue came to be debated in open court. But
no regular occupant of the vacancy was appointed till toward the end
of 1761, when Robert Auchmuty junior got the job. It is not
improbable that Otis's departure as acting advocate general was
followed by a hiatus, and perhaps it was in this period that the
Superior Court judges, still in need of learned guidance on the writ of
assistance, turned to Oxenbridge Thacher. The result of Thacher's

16. Report in *BG* 8 June 1761: "*Benjamin Pratt,* Esq;, His Majesty's Advocate-General
of this Province, is appointed to be Chief Justice of New York . . . ." Similarly in *BWNL*
4 June.

James Cockle, 24 November 1764: "When I came first into my office, I soon made a
seizure, and advising with Mr. Prat the then advocate general . . ." (copy attested by John
Temple; acknowledgments to Huntington Library, STG Box 13(4)). Cockle arrived as
customs collector at Salem in the summer of 1760 (p. 139 above), well after Prat's original
resignation in favor of Otis.

Robert Auchmuty junior became regular acting advocate general in 1761. His petition
for a salary, referred to in chapter 9, n. 52 (undated, but probably October 1766), spoke of
"the late Honourable Benjn. Prat Esqr. your Petitioner's immediate Predecessor."

17. *LWJA* X, 245.

researches, that the court had no jurisdiction to issue any kind of writ of assistance, certainly would have demolished any possibility of Thacher being expected to follow up with a formal presentation in support of the Cockle application (as might have been the case with Otis). Thacher may have remained on the scene in an *amicus curiae* role; but assuredly he was no friend of the custom house.

Relating how he had been asked to argue in favor of the writ of assistance, the Abstract shows Otis going on to speak of his resignation as acting advocate general:

> I was sollicited to argue this cause as Advocate-General, and because I would not, I have been charged with a desertion of my office; to this charge I can give a very sufficient answer, I renounced that office, and I argue this cause from the same principle; and I argue it with the greater pleasure as it is in favour of British liberty . . . .

Otis's concern to rebut ill report is plainly visible here.

He had not run away from the advocate general's obligation to espouse the custom house cause; he had given up the post. The words of the Abstract convey the impression that it had been on account of the writ of assistance that he quit: even that he quit specifically in order to argue against it. If this were truly so it would enhance the historical importance of the writs of assistance controversy still more, for when James Otis moved out of the establishment circle and into opposition politics a force of unique impact was loosed upon the pre-revolutionary American scene. But *was* it truly so? The question is posed even by the words of the Abstract themselves. There is something out of focus about them. They fall well short of asserting an exclusive cause-and-effect link between the writs of assistance issue and Otis's resignation. If Otis really did sacrifice his job solely because he objected to arguing for the writ of assistance and in order to speak out against it, one wonders why he did not say so more clearly and positively. So telling a point for his public image surely could have been delivered with greater force. By the look of things, there was more to Otis's resignation than writs of assistance.

The proposition is that Otis's resignation was precipitated by hostile influence bearing down from on high. From the man, that is to say, whom Otis probably had in mind when denying that refusal to argue for the writ of assistance constituted a desertion of office, namely, Governor Francis Bernard. Years later Bernard recalled how, on his arrival in the province in August 1760, "immediately began the confederacy against the Custom house & Admiralty, which was attended by much popular Commotion. At the beginning of this the then acting advocate general deserted his post & put himself at the head of the attack ...." [18] That Bernard was Otis's active enemy at the time of the writs of assistance case is apparent from Thomas Hutchinson, an insider well placed to know. In his *History* Hutchinson recounts how in January 1761 the Assembly resolved to initiate the legal action that became the case of *Province v. Paxton,* for the recovery of allegedly unlawful deductions from the king's — in effect, the province's — share of Molasses Act forfeitures, and how Governor Bernard tried to insist that the brief be given to the attorney-general of the province, Edmund Trowbridge:

> The governor, at first, declined his assent, and, in a message to the house, gave as the only reason, their appointing the province treasurer to bring the action; whereas, the money sued for being granted to the king, the king's attorney was the person in whose name the action should be brought.
> This objection from a governor was really of no weight, because the money was granted to the king for the use of the province; and all money belonging to the province had always been sued for by the province treasurer .... But he hoped to prevent Mr. Otis from carrying on the suit. [19]

Otis, the spokesman for the "sundry Inhabitants of the Province" whose petition to the Assembly had started the whole business, was the natural choice to present the case in the courts. On the assumption, that is, that the action were on behalf of the province treasurer, who would need an attorney to represent him. If however the action were brought in the name of the attorney general, Trowbridge would conduct it himself. It may have occurred to Governor Bernard that Trowbridge, at this time a keen government man and somewhat of a friend of the prospective defendant, Charles Paxton, would perhaps pull his punches so that the action failed. But the reason given by Hutchinson was probably uppermost: the hope (vain as it turned out) to dish the objectionable Otis of an assignment so manifestly of a piece with his move into opposition politics. The gubernatorial ill will thus evinced in January 1761, after Otis had ceased to officiate as advocate general, probably went far enough back to have played some part in his resignation.

18. To Lord Halifax, 17 May 1765: Bernard Papers III, and C05/755. Similarly to Board of Trade, same date: C05/891.
19. Page 66.

Also involved was Benjamin Barons, the disaffected customs collector. To Governor Bernard, Otis and Barons were joint authors of all the mischiefs that were so soon to mock his hopes of an easy administration: "Mr Otis Junr ... has been Mr Barrons faithfull Councellor from the first beginning of these Commotions ...," he wrote in July 1761.[20] It is important to notice, however, that there had been a prior period in which the Otis-Barons relationship was anything but matey. Evidence of this is in one of the depositions sworn by Charles Paxton in support of his "articles of complaint" about Barons. After the meeting at which the merchants decided on the petition that culminated in the province's lawsuit against Paxton, "the said Mr Otis having been appointed Solicitor to the Com^tee of said Merchants was by the Deponent very frequently seen in Consultation with Mr Barons altho before this Meeting they were at so great a varience as not to speak to one another."[21] The cause of that previous "varience" can be surmised. When Barons first trained his guns on the vice-admiralty court Otis stood right in the line of fire. As acting advocate general he was a leading member of the vice-admiralty establishment. And insofar as the unlawful payments that Barons began shouting about included excessive fees to lawyers Otis might have felt himself a special target. Far from "faithfull Councellor," at this embryonic stage he was the rampaging collector's discomfited quarry.

Into an already sour situation Governor Bernard injected a subtle poison of his own. The occasion was the interview in November 1760 when Bernard tried to persuade Barons into a more moderate attitude toward the vice-admiralty court. Writing of this interview, Bernard told how Barons suspected chicanery in a recent vice-admiralty condemnation of certain foreign spirits seized by his custom house colleague, Nathaniel Hatch. According to Barons, these spirits, though they perhaps had been shipped from the West Indies, were of European origin. Nevertheless, condemnation had been under the Molasses Act, which applied only to actual produce of the (foreign) West Indies. Barons saw this as a fraudulent abuse. Had the spirits been condemned under the Staple Act, the legislation truly in point, the prosecution costs would have been deducted before the

---

20. To ? 2 July 1761: Bernard Papers I.

21. This, and another reference in the deposition to how Otis and Barons "became very intimate tho before that time they were not upon Speaking Terms," are included in extracts from the deposition published by Otis in *BG* 4 September 1769.

proceeds were divided among the three statutory recipients, the king, the governor, and the customs officer, so that each of the three bore the costs equally. As it was, the governor's and the customs officer's shares in the Hatch condemnation would not be subject to this deduction; they would benefit by a peculiarity of the Molasses Act which made the costs of prosecution a charge on the king's (in practice, the province's) share alone. In the result Bernard and Hatch averted the trouble that Barons was brewing by taking the most contentious element in the costs — payment to the informer — wholly on to their own shares, leaving the king's share free of it.[22] However, there was a more immediate move by Bernard to defuse the situation in which Barons was hoping to see him hurt. It was to deflect prime responsibility for any chicanery in the Hatch condemnation from himself to James Otis. Bernard's account of the Barons interview:

> In regard to Mr. Barons Objections to Mr. Hatch . . . libelling some foreign Spirits, supposed to be European brandy, under the Statute of the 6th Geo. 2, by which the Kings third is Subjected to the payment of Costs, The Governor observed to Mr. Barons, that he, the Governor had not directed that manner of proceeding; but upon Mr Hatchs applying to him he had ordered that the Advocate generals Opinion should be taken and followed. That, indeed, The Governor approved of the Advocate generals bringing the suit on the 6 Geo. 2, as it would assure the Condemnation, which otherwise might be precarious . . . .[23]

The governor certainly made a job of it. Two swipes at Otis are visible here. It was not only that the onus of the decision to invoke the Molasses Act should be swung on to him, as advocate general. The concluding sentence insinuated a further damaging barb. The approval of Otis's action was a reminder that though in the ordinary way the condemnation might have failed, it was the practice of Judge Chambers Russell's vice-admiralty court never to refuse a condemnation favored by the advocate general.[24] Otis could thus be seen as doubly culpable. If the spirits were indeed European the falsehood involved in their condemnation had been his, a falsehood compounded by the knowledge that, coming from himself as advocate general, it would not be questioned. Francis Bernard may have

22. As set forth by Judge Russell on 4 April 1761, in Admiralty Book of Accounts. And *cf.* C05/854. See also pp. 199-200 above.
23. T1/408; memorial by Bernard 18 March 1761.
24. See pp. 168-69 above.

been a bit of a chucklehead in some ways, but his footwork against Otis over the Hatch condemnation undeniably showed style. Not for nothing was the *Boston Gazette* to lampoon him "Sir Wm. Slygripe." [25]

It was all rather hard on Otis. Whatever ruderies he had uttered since 13 November, when his father's hopes of becoming a Superior Court judge were definitely ended by the appointment of Thomas Hutchinson as chief justice, at the time of the Hatch seizure ten days previously he was still doing his duty by the custom house and the governor, not to say playing their game; and however aggrieved he felt in the latter stages of the case — the decree was not pronounced till 17 November [26] — he had seen the condemnation through (though, to be sure, by then he may have felt too committed to do anything else). This is not to say that Otis suffered the judgeship issue to pass in silence. Justly or not, word was going round of his having threatened dire consequences if his father should not be appointed, [27] hardly the proper spirit for a man in the government circle, and perhaps this is the light in which Governor Bernard's disclosures to Barons need to be seen. If Otis was still in office at the time of the Bernard/Barons interview, and there is no evidence or likelihood that he was not, it could not be long before his position became intolerably uncomfortable. Barons had only to run true to form, retailing his scandals as industriously as he gathered them, and Otis would soon be on public view as a venal hack, who despite his noisy talk against the establishment ("Bluster" was his lampoon name, after all) was nevertheless content to pick up a few guineas by doing the government's dirty work in the vice-admiralty court. Nor was the Hatch condemnation the whole of it. There was that other custom house chore now pending, the defense and justification of the writ of assistance. Everything considered, Otis was in an impossible situation. No man with a scrap of self-respect could at the same time have loudly criticized the government establishment, endured personal mortification at their hands, while yet continuing under a uniquely special obligation of service to them. Otis had no choice but to quit.

Since it is at least possible that he had been pressured out of office

25. In the "Charles Froth" lampoon on Charles Paxton, 2 March 1761 (see pp. 172-73 above).

26. Admiralty Book of Accounts.

27. Thomas Hutchinson in *Massachusetts Gazette* 7 April 1763. *Cf.* pp. 216-17 above.

by Governor Bernard, Otis's resentment at having been charged with
deserting it, reflected in the Abstract rendition of his writs of
assistance speech, may have been all the more bitter. And, though it
set him free for politics and to make his mark on history, his
resignation seems to have left something that always rankled. In
1765, when his popularity and political fortunes were in a down-
swing, he addressed this reproachful lament to the Boston public:

> I am, ever have been, and expect ever to be, a poor man. I tell you a
> melancholly truth, yet I have taken more pains for an honest quiet living
> than many who ride in their coaches and six. − I have given up £200 a
> year sterling, that I might have honestly made, besides what are called
> good decent perquisites. − I know not where to go for any part of this
> money. Should my children want it, and their daily bread, I hope it will be
> some consolation to them, that their father lost part of it in a vain attempt
> to serve his country.[28]

Ten years after the event he was still reminiscing on his sacrifice.
John Adams relates how, in response to a catalogue of unrewarded
virtues which one of the members of a "club" was inflicting on the
company, Otis told how he had resigned as advocate general, by the
emoluments of which he would by now have been £2,000 the
richer.[29]

At no time does he appear as ascribing his resignation clearly and
specifically to opposition to the writ of assistance. The reference in
the 1765 piece to "a vain attempt to serve his country" could
perhaps connect with the fact that his advocacy against the writ
proved unsuccessful. An explanation he gave two years earlier was
even less communicative on this point. In the *Boston Gazette* for
4 April 1763, after telling how he had been appointed by Governor
Pownall, he continued: "I soon found the Place did not suit with my
Way of thinking & resigned it after clearing by my Office about Two
Guineas instead of a Hundred Pounds Sterling per Annum that may
be made of it by those who understand & can conform to all the
Ways of the World."[30] Not a great deal can be made out of this

---

28. *BG* 13 May 1765.

29. *LWJA* X, 289-90.

30. The Admiralty Book of Accounts of Sales, in the Suffolk county court offices,
shows £2. 8s. as advocate general's fees in the condemnation on 19 August 1760 of four
chests of tea seized by Charles Paxton. This is near enough to Otis's "about Two Guineas."
The entry for the Hatch condemnation in November 1760 shows an "Advocates fee" of
12s., which presumably went to Otis; there is also a miscellaneous deduction of £31. 9s. 6d.
in which he may have shared. But that is all. If Otis earned anything else as advocate general
it was not included in this accounts book.

negative evidence, of course; but it does seem consistent with that curiously loose-jointed allusion to Otis' resignation in the writs of assistance speech, which conveys the impression that he resigned on account of the writ but falls short of actually saying so.

In any case there would have been an inherent implausibility in Otis claiming to have given up as advocate general purely out of nausea at the thought of arguing for the writ of assistance. After all, this obnoxious instrument was not new in the province; and Otis must have been aware of its existence when only a few months previously he agreed to be acting advocate general, an office that meant close identification with the enforcement regime of the custom house, part of whose weaponry the writ was.

The obligation to argue for the writ may have contributed to the embarrassment that drove Otis out of office. It could even be that his then tormentor, Benjamin Barons, deepened Otis's discomfiture still further by personally — as collector and head of the Boston custom house — requesting him to take on the writ of assistance work. But, to repeat, it was not the writ that the whole of the heat came from. Quite a lot had been stoked up by Governor Bernard. For all his protestation about Otis having deserted his post, Bernard's behavior toward him in the fall and winter of 1760-61 scarcely implies anxiety to retain him in the government network. The governor had in fact proved himself a fairly ugly operator. It is possible to feel some sympathy for him in the tempest of sheer bad luck that hit him almost the moment he arrived in Massachusetts; but the beginning of his troubles with James Otis was partly of his own making.

With other pressures driving him from office anyway, Otis might have welcomed the writs of assistance issue as a providential accident. A vow to raise hell if he could not prevail in heaven is part of the Otis legend.[31] So, having cut the painter with government and

---

Interestingly, in the tea condemnation £60 was allowed for "procuring Information"; and Paxton also collected (in addition to his one-third share of the new proceeds) about £80 in charges of various kinds. As advocate general Otis presumably concurred in all this. Yet, within months, he was promoting the province's action against Paxton for excessive and wrongful charges. There was the difference, of course, that *Province v. Paxton* related to Molasses Act condemnations, the king's share in which, after deduction of all charges, went to the province, whereas in Staple Act condemnations — of tea, for example — the king's share, after a proportionate deduction for charges, went to London.

31. *Cf.* Gummere, *op. cit.* (n. 9 above), 101-2. *Flectere si nequeo superos, Acheronta movebo* was how Otis put it, apparently (drawing upon Virgil, *Aenid*, vii, 312).

about to switch to opposition politics he needed an eye-catching public controversy the better to project himself. The province's lawsuit over excessive fees in the vice-admiralty court was all right, as far as it went; but what tribune of the people ever made his name by arguing an *indebitatus assumpsit*? Forcible search into people's houses, though: that was something else. If the writs of assistance issue could somehow be worked up into a full-scale public debate in the Superior Court, what wonders of oratory might he not perform? What more telling a curtain-raiser to political stardom in the populist-libertarian interest than a resounding vindication of the rights of home and property?

Perhaps this helps explain Otis's unprofessional attitude toward remuneration: "And I take this opportunity to declare, that whether under a fee or not, (for in such a cause as this I despise a fee) I will to my dying day . . . oppose all such instruments of slavery . . . and villainy as this writ of assistance is." It may be that not all the sixty-odd persons who had obliged with their signature on the petition for a court hearing on writs of assistance saw themselves committed to putting their hand in their pocket for attorney's charges. But even aside from the likelihood that no one thought to pay him anyway, Otis's writs of assistance assignment represented an opportunity that a person limbering up for entry into politics might almost have laid out money to get.

There could have been an element of pleasurable irony, too. Back in the fall, when Thomas Hutchinson was edging gingerly toward the chief justiceship, the assumption probably was that the awkward question left pending from Collector James Cockle's writ of assistance application at Salem would be gone into and disposed of in private session of the Superior Court. As things actually happened, not only was this abstruse legal conundrum to be debated in open court, but the tyro chief justice was to experience a baptism of fire at the hands of one of the ablest lawyers in the province; a man, moreover, to whom Hutchinson's very presence on the bench was a bitter affront. For all his display of shock and anguish at the general writ of assistance and the enormities it stood for, Otis must have rather enjoyed putting Chief Justice Hutchinson through the hoops.

16

Otis (II)

THE ARTS of the publicist were not abandoned when the Abstract at last got away from Otis the trumpeter of true principle and personal righteousness and on to Otis the legal dialectician. If anything, the intermittent noise and flash in the remaining two-thirds of the text outdo in impact the actual argument.

Nevertheless, and although it soon takes off into rhetoric again, the Abstract does show Otis coming straight to the point once the long and windy exordium is over. His basic position is visible in the text next following: .

> In the mean time I will proceed to the subject of the writ. In the first, may it please your Honours, I will admit, that writs of one kind, may be legal, that is, *special writs, directed to special officers,* and to search *certain houses,* &c. *especially set forth in the writ,* may be granted by the Court of Exchequer at home, *upon oath made before* the Lord Treasurer by the person, who asks, *that he suspects such goods to be concealed in* THOSE VERY PLACES HE DESIRES TO SEARCH. The Act of 14th Car. II. which Mr. Gridley mentions proves this. And in this light the writ appears like a warrant from a justice of peace to search for stolen goods. Your Honours will find in the old book, concerning the office of a justice of peace, precedents of general warrants to search suspected houses. But in more modern books you will find only special warrants to search such and such houses specially named, in which the complainant has before sworn he suspects his goods are concealed; and you will find it adjudged *that special warrants only are legal.* In the same manner I rely on it, that the writ prayed for in this petition being general is illegal. It is a power that places the liberty of every man in the hands of every petty officer. I say I admit that *special* writs of assistance to search *special* houses, may be granted to certain persons on oath; but I deny that the writ now prayed for can be granted . . . .

Then came a lapse into verbal fireworks; but, as will be seen later on, even these were angled to the focal proposition in the piece just quoted: that although generality and open-endedness could not be tolerated, a form of writ of assistance "special" to the occasion would be acceptable.

If only because of the Abstract's presentational imbalance and blur a check reference is convenient. Otis's centering upon this notion of a one-time-only writ of assistance is attested by no less a witness than the man who presided over the hearing. In his *History of Massachusets-Bay* Thomas Hutchinson recorded:

> It was objected to the writs, that they were of the nature of general warrants; that, although formerly it was the practice to issue general warrants to search for stolen goods, yet, for many years, this practice had been altered, and special warrants only were issued by justices of the peace, to search in places set forth in the warrants; that it was equally reasonable to alter these writs, to which there would be no objection, if the place where the search was to be made should be specifically mentioned, and information given upon oath. The form of a writ of assistance was, it is true, to be found in some registers, which was general, but it was affirmed, without proof, that the late practice in England was otherwise, and that such writs issued upon special information only.[1]

The correspondence between Hutchinson's *History* and the Abstract piece is obvious.

No other argument was mentioned in the Hutchinson account. Oxenbridge Thacher's challenge, that having once renounced an exchequer jurisdiction the Superior Court had no jurisdiction to grant any sort of writ of assistance, had not so much as a hint of recognition. What registered with the judges was the more moderate argument, put forward only by Otis, that the essential thing wrong with their writ of assistance was its generality.[2]

One would not think it from a first glance at the Abstract — "instruments of slavery . . . . and villainy," "the worst instrument of arbitrary power," "every one with this writ may be a tyrant," "terror and desolation," typify the epithets that spring to the eye — but Otis was really a soft-liner.

Not that his willingness to settle for a modified writ of assistance derogates from his performance. On the contrary, it denotes a shrewd appreciation of certain important realities.

1. Page 68.
2. Governor Bernard wrote to the Board of Trade, 5 September 1763 (C05/891): "About 2 years ago Great endeavours were made to disable the Officers in carrying the laws into execution, & a public opposition was made in open Court against the Superior Court (which is here Vested with the Powers of the Court of Exchequer) granting writs of Assistance except in special cases . . . ."

For one thing, a writ of assistance so cumbersome in issuance and so restricted in scope as to require a sworn application every time was practically as good as no writ of assistance at all.[3] For another, and Otis must have been well aware of this from his experience as advocate general, there was already considerable unease on the Superior Court bench about the general writ of assistance.

As has been suggested in earlier chapters, the first moves toward getting the true legal position of the writ researched and argued out could well have come from the four puisne judges themselves, embarrassed by an application for the usual general writ (by James Cockle at Salem, in October 1760) at the very time when the legality of the writ was buffeted by doubt. "As to a writ of assistance from the Exchequer, in pursuance of the act of the 13th and 14th of Charles II," a writer in a recent *London Magazine* had said, "I believe, it was never granted without an information upon oath, that the person applying for it has reason to suspect that prohibited or uncustomed goods are concealed in the house or place which he desires a power to search." Disquieting reading, this, for judges whose court had been issuing general writs of assistance for the asking these five years past. And those same men were now up there on the bench, still in their quandary. Otis made it his business to harden their doubts into firm decision.

But, useful as this head start was, he nevertheless had a job of advocacy to do. He could not simply get to his feet, read out the *London Magazine* piece, and sit down again. The Superior Court could not be on public view as changing their practice on the authority of Grub Street. More technically — and as Hutchinson's *History* put it — there was no proof on hand that what the *London Magazine* had said about writs of assistance in England was true. It was for Otis to put up a respectable argument with the tacit objective of underpinning the legal position as the *London Magazine* had stated it. Total disavowal of the writ of assistance, as contended for

3. According to Hutchinson's *History* (p. 68), "The court was convinced that a writ, or warrant, to be issued only in cases where special information was given upon oath, would rarely, if ever, be applied for, as no informer would expose himself to the rage of the people." However that might have been (and *cf.* p. 388 below), certainly it would have hampered such a regime that the duly issuing authority, the Superior Court, might be scores of miles distant (even from Boston, when on circuit).

An influence on the court might have been a suggestion in the *London Magazine* article (see Appendix G) that in the event of a special writ proving to have been granted "without any reasonable or solid ground of suspicion ... an action would lie against the grantors ...."

by Oxenbridge Thacher, would have meant the Superior Court back-tracking absolutely — in effect admitting that their former issuances of writs of assistance had been entirely erroneous. The *London Magazine* line, which allowed the writ to continue even though in severely attenuated form, was less abject. It meant not rout, but merely a measure of retreat. Otis would provide decent cover.

Otis's acknowledging the legality of customs entry and search with a one-time-only writ of assistance implied acceptance that section 6 of the Act of Frauds of 1696, despite its baffling obscurity, some-how brought the originating English writs of assistance enactment into play in America, section 5(2) of the Act of Frauds of 1662:

> And it shall be lawful to or for any Person or Persons, authorized by Writ of Assistance . . . to take a Constable, Headborough or other publick Officer inhabiting near unto the Place, and in the Day-time to enter, and go into any House, Shop, Cellar, Warehouse or Room, or other Place, and in Case of Resistance, to break open Doors, Chests, Trunks and other Package, there to seize, and from thence to bring, any Kind of Goods or Merchandize whatsoever, prohibited and uncustomed . . . .

The actual terms of the writ of assistance, a directive to a wide miscellany of public and private persons to assist the customs officer, depended for their legal validity upon a little-known common law doctrine which authorized the invention of writs for the better implementation of a public statute; the acts of 1662 and 1696 each laid down a generalized obligation to assist, by reference to which this doctrine could apply and the writ of assistance eventuate. James Otis nowhere appears as addressing himself to these particular fun-damentals. However, though he missed out on what the writ of assistance really was, he did not make the mistake of identifying the writ as the substantive source of the customs officer's power of entry and search. Like his opponent Gridley, he well saw that the customs officer's power emanated directly from statute. In fact, the essence of the problem he set himself was how this statutory power of entry and search — identified with section 5(2) of the Act of Frauds of 1662 — should be interpreted. His key objective was to establish that on a proper reading of the statute the power was available for the one sworn and specific occasion only, by dint of suitably regulated issuance of the writ of assistance it was contingent upon.

Otis signals his central theme in the Abstract:

I will admit, that writs of one kind, may be legal, that is, *special writs, directed to special officers,* and to search *certain houses,* &c. *especially set forth in the writ,* may be granted by the Court of Exchequer at home, *upon oath made before* the Lord Treasurer by the person, who asks, *that he suspects such goods to be concealed in* THOSE VERY PLACES HE DESIRES TO SEARCH. The Act of 14th Car. II. which Mr. Gridley mentions proves this.

It was to be an important part of Otis's position that section 5(2) of the Act of Frauds of 1662, which introduced entry and search with writ of assistance, should be regarded as one with the customs search warrant act of 1660: in particular, that the 1660 regime of issuance of warrants on sworn statements as to specific place and occasion should be fastened on to the 1662 writs of assistance. Here was an early glimpse of this. The 1662 act ("The Act of 14th Car. II") said nothing about an oath before the Lord Treasurer or anyone else; but that dignitary undeniably was one of the personages fastened upon by the 1660 act as authorized to issue its search warrants and to administer the oath accordingly. The Abstract passage just recited clearly represents Otis superimposing the issuing procedure for the 1660 search warrant on to the 1662 writ of assistance.

This remarkable essay in statutory manipulation will be considered later on, when other aspects of it have come into view. Right now there is something else to notice. In chapter 13 it was seen how Otis's opponent, Jeremiah Gridley, ascribed writ of assistance search to the 1660 and 1662 acts both (and how this was of a piece with a certain ambiguity, not to say equivocation, in his handling of the custom house brief). Gridley thus contributed useful material for Otis to exploit on the other side, and according to the Abstract Otis indeed utilized the benefaction. His "The Act of 14th Car. II. which Mr. Gridley mentions proves this," related as it was to the supposed identity between the acts of 1660 and 1662, delivered a highly disputable proposition as a closed package. If the Abstract is a reliable record of this phase of the speech, possibly it was for maximum advantage in debate — taking up Gridley's gift while it was still fresh — that Otis plunged in so early with his 1660-1662 fusion, expressly citing Gridley's own recognition of it.

However that may have been, it was not until this next passage that the Abstract shows Otis getting down to doctrinal foundations, marking out the basics of his position in materials from the common law:

> And in this light the writ appears like a warrant from a justice of peace to search for stolen goods. Yours Honours will find in the old book, concerning the office of a justice of peace, precedents of general warrants to search suspected houses. But in more modern books you will find only special warrants to search such and such houses specially named, in which the complainant has before sworn he suspects his goods are concealed; and you will find it adjudged *that special warrants only are legal.* In the same manner I rely on it, that the writ prayed for in this petition being general is illegal.

This is perhaps the most important passage in the entire Abstract text. At any rate, it embodies the argument that Thomas Hutchinson, presiding judge and subsequent historian, identifies as the one that weighed with the court.

Hutchinson's own digest of the argument will itself bear repeating:

> although formerly it was the practice to issue general warrants to search for stolen goods, yet, for many years, this practice had been altered, and special warrants only were issued by justices of the peace, to search in places set forth in the warrants; that it was equally reasonable to alter these writs, to which there would be no objection, if the place where the search was to be made should be specifically mentioned, and information given upon oath.

Footnoted to its reference to the former practice of issuing general warrants the Hutchinson *History* has this: *"Dalton's Justice." The Countrey Justice* by Matthew Dalton, which dated back to 1618, was a manual of practice for justices of the peace still widely used in America. In it was a specimen search warrant for stolen goods that was general in scope, enjoining the constable to "make diligent search in all suspected houses you . . . shall thinke convenient." Clearly, this was "the old book, concerning the office of a justice of peace" that Abstract-Otis speaks of as containing "precedents of general warrants to search suspected houses."

Abstract-Otis gets further useful amplification in Hutchinson's *History.* Whereas in the Abstract Otis speaks merely in terms of books — "the old book" of Dalton having been displaced by "more modern books" — Hutchinson shows the argument extending to what had actually happened right there in Massachusetts: "formerly it was the practice to issue general warrants to search for stolen goods, yet, for many years, this practice had been altered, and special warrants only were issued . . . ." It is of interest, moreover, that evidence of the earlier practice exists in the Superior Court records: a warrant dated in 1728 which tells of the theft of "a brown Horse with a Sprigg Tail About fourteen hands high" reported by the owner to a justice of the peace for Middlesex county, and which ordered that the sheriff or a constable "Search for the said Horse in all suspected Places within your respective Precincts where you are informed or may reasonably suppose the said Horse is . . . ."[4] Part of the interest lies in the circumstance that the owner of the horse, at whose behest this more or less Daltonian directive was issued, was Edmund Trowbridge (then using the name Edmund Goffe), who, twenty-seven years later and as attorney general of the province, was to draft the first Massachusetts writ of assistance.[5]

In keeping with a journalistic purpose the Abstract does not weigh down its prospective readership with detailed legal citations. On the "more modern books" invoked by Otis for the supervening special warrants it is as inexplicit as on "the old book" that had sanctioned general warrants. But, just as Dalton's *Countrey Justice* can be identified, so it is possible to spot the less superannuated authorities Otis had in mind, where only special warrants were approved and where indeed they exclusively had been "adjudged" lawful. For the Dalton reference Hutchinson's *History* is a check. For the "more modern books" John Adams's contemporaneous notes afford evidence and a clue.

"Genl. Warrant to search for Felonies, Hawk. Pleas Crown" has nothing connecting in the notes immediately before or immediately after. These isolated fragments were all that Adams managed to catch of a saliently important part of Otis's speech. Nevertheless, they are distinctly better than nothing. They point to the books upon which Otis founded his argument that inasmuch as search warrants for stolen goods had been reduced from general to sworn and special, writ of assistance search should be similarly moderated in relation to smuggled goods. "Hawk." denotes the English legal writer William Hawkins. And Hawkins had disapproved of "a general Warrant to search for Felons or stolen Goods"[6] in his *Treatise of the Pleas of the Crown.*

4. SF 164478.

5. John Adams's diary entry for 14 December 1760 speaks of "a Warrant to search for stolen goods" issued on oath (*DAJA* I, 180); presumably it was special.

For early practice, under the colony "Burglary and Theft" law of 1652, see J. H. Smith, ed., *Colonial Justice in Western Massachusetts (1639-1702)* (Cambridge, Mass., 1961), 142.

6. Vol. II, 1788 edition, 132. See also *LPJA* II, 126, n. 65.

That Otis should have cited this well-known book is not remarkable. Also, first published in 1716, it might well have ranked among
the "more modern books" which Abstract-Otis contrasted with Dalton's general warrant for stolen goods. But reflection shows up
something else. Aside from the fact that Hawkins was not particularly expansive on the supersession of general warrants by special
ones, there is evidence — in the the case of Trowbridge's horse — that
Massachusetts still had general warrants for stolen goods in 1728,
when Hawkins's *Pleas of the Crown* was already twelve years old and
in a second edition. Then one remembers (from chapter 3) that a lot
had been said about powers of search in a quite different *Pleas of the
Crown,* namely, *History of the Pleas of the Crown,* by Sir Matthew
Hale. Included in Hale's comments was this:

> In case of a complaint and oath of goods stolen, and that he suspects the
> goods are in such a house, and shows the cause of his suspicion, the justice
> of peace may grant a warrant to search in those suspected places men-
> tioned in the warrant . . . .
>
> But the general warrant to search all places, whereof the party and
> officer have suspicion, tho it be usual, yet it is not so safe upon the reason
> of justice Swallow's case . . .; and yet see precedents of such general
> warrants, *Dalt,* p. 353, 354.[7]

These words of a revered master of the common law did not get into
general currency till 1736, for only then — sixty years after his
death — was Hale's *History of the Pleas of the Crown* published.
What with the Trowbridge general warrant in 1728, it looks to have
been Hale's much more than Hawkins's *Pleas of the Crown* that
caused the Massachusetts change of practice expressly mentioned in
Hutchinson's *History.* Almost certainly, therefore, Abstract-Otis was
referring to Hale's *History of the Pleas of the Crown* when he spoke
of "more modern books" having displaced Dalton's general warrant.[8]

Corroborative signs exist in plenty. Might it not have been in
deference to the key text of the great Hale that Abstract-Otis
dropped the usual "justice of the peace" in favor of the outdated
"justice of peace"? Again, "warrants to search such and such houses"
carries an idiomatic echo of Hale's "he suspects the goods are in such
a house." More significantly still, Abstract-Otis, having referred the

7. Vol. II (London, 1736), 113. For *Swallow's Case* see *ibid.,* 111.

8. Granted the obvious, that the scrappy Adams notes omitted much here, it is
conceivable that "Pleas Crown" in fact was Hale's *History* and not Hawkins's *Treatise,* the
immediately preceding "Hawk." notwithstanding. Adams owned a copy of the Hale book at
this time: *Catalogue of the John Adams Library* (Boston, 1917), 113.

court to the "more modern books," winds up by saying, "you will find it adjudged that special warrants only are legal." What else would he have meant than the judgment cited by Hale, that is, in "justice Swallow's case"? Hale particularizes it as follows:

> A justice of peace may make his warrant to apprehend a person suspected by name upon a complaint made to him; but where upon a complaint to a justice of a robbery he made a warrant to apprehend all persons suspected, and bring them before him, this was ruled a void warrant, P. 24 *Car.* 1 in the case of justice *Swallowe,* and was not a sufficient justification in false imprisonment.

Authoritative doctrine against general warrants was not abundant in 1761. The Wilkesian litigation that definitively outlawed them in England was several years in the future. *Swallow's Case* as recounted by Hale was the handiest, if not the only, precedent for Otis to cite. And inasmuch as *Swallow's Case* motivated Sir Matthew Hale against general warrants in the seventeeth century, the likelihood is that James Otis adopted it as the doctrinal justification for his opposition to the general writ of assistance in the eighteenth.

The opening oratory which accounted for no less than a third of the entire Abstract rendition of Otis's speech had little warrant in John Adams's contemporaneous notes. Much the same can be said of the Abstract material that followed, which has just been discussed. Here are the first paragraphs, so to call them, of the Adams notes:

> This Writ is against the fundamental Principles of Law. — The Priviledge of House. A Man, who is quiet, is as secure in his House, as a Prince in his Castle — notwithstanding all his Debts, & civil processes of any Kind. — But
>
> For flagrant Crimes, and in Cases of great public Necessity, the Priviledge may be [encroached?] on. — For Felonies an Officer may break upon Proscess, and oath. — i.e. by a Special Warrant to search such an House, sworn to be suspected, and good Grounds of suspicion appearing.
>
> Make oath corm. Ld. Treaer., or Exchequer, in Engd., or a Magistrate here, and get a Special Warrant, for the public good, to infringe the Priviledge of House.
>
> Genl. Warrant to search for Felonies, Hawk. Pleas Crown — every petty officer from the highest to the lowest . . . .

The first sentence, "This Writ is against the fundamental Principles of Law," perhaps corresponds to a like piece of declamation in the opening oratory (and the rest of that opening paragraph, about a man's house being his castle, is transplanted into a purple passage farther down the Abstract text). "Make oath corm.[9] Ld. Treaer., or Exchequer, in Engd., or a Magistrate here . . . ." in the third paragraph clearly has some connection with the oath-taking for a 1660 act warrant that the Abstract shows Otis wishing on the writ of assistance. "General Warrant to search for Felonies, Hawk. Pleas Crown," in the fourth paragraph, has already been used to identify the "more modern books" alluded to in the Abstract. The words "such an House" in the second paragraph perhaps match up with the comparable turn of phrase already noticed in the Abstract for its probable derivation from Hale's *History of the Pleas of the Crown* (and hence augment the evidence of Otis's reliance on that work). For the most part, however, these first four paragraphs of the Adams notes bear no relation to the Abstract presentation so far discussed in this chapter. Some of the material is taken into the Abstract later on, but not all.

The second paragraph of Adams's notes, where Otis is on record as admitting the existence of exceptions to the principle of inviolability of hearth and home, shows that the Abstract's liberties with the on-the-spot notes involved subtraction as well as addition. Very little of this is visible in the Abstract:

> For flagrant Crimes, and in Cases of great public Necessity, the Priviledge may be encroached upon. – For felonies an Officer may break upon Proscess, and oath. – i.e. by a Special Warrant to search such an House, sworn to be suspected, and good Grounds of suspicion appearing.

Fairly meaty stuff to be simply discarded, one would have thought. And certainly it would not be right to follow the Abstract's example and leave this solid evidence of what Otis actually did say in a limbo of silence, without an attempt to understand what it was all about.

This is not too difficult. Immediately recognizable is an echo of Jeremiah Gridley's argument, from Adams's notes: "Every Body knows that the Subject has the Priviledge of House only against his fellow Subjects, not vs the K. either in . . . Crime or fine." And Otis's talk of "Cases of great public Necessity" chimes in with Gridley's big point about "necessity" justifying violation of hearth and home. These two straws in the wind suffice to show the drift. As might be expected at this early stage in his speech, Otis had not yet begun to develop his own argument but was responding to his opponent's.

9. Presumably *coram* ("in the presence of").

And it was to vigorous positive effect that Otis took Gridley up. He could not deny that the "privilege of house" was subject to peremptory violation when there was crime to be dealt with, so he stressed how grave and urgent the situation must be before the exception applied: the crime must be "flagrant," the necessity "great" and "public." True it was too that the common law sometimes facilitated prosecution of wrongdoing by allowing search warrants (for stolen goods, as it might be); but Otis turned this to good account as well, for did not the warrant have to be special and an oath taken as to the particular house suspected — exactly the principle in which he wished to corset the writ of assistance? Finally, the man who procured a search warrant might be at risk of a lawsuit if his suspicions proved unfounded.[10]

Otis's response to Gridley had its limitations, however. He might make hay with Gridley's point that "Open in the name of the King" could be a lawful command in matters of felony. But Gridley had included "fine" in the principle — meaning not a pecuniary penalty but the execution of certain court processes of a civil kind. Here there was no contradicting him. There was *Semayne's Case* from the early seventeenth century (seen in chapter 13, and upon which Otis himself probably drew for a man's house being his castle), which clearly recognized this further area where the common law countenanced intrusion on to private property, even by force. The notes on Otis do not show him saying anything about the king's officers entering in a civil cause, or, in Gridley's parlance, "in matters of . . . fine." An exception to the "privilege of house" in a civil cause might have seemed too close to writ of assistance entry and search to be of service in a speech critical of that process.

Possibly, then, it was because Otis's reply to Gridley was only half a reply, and therefore not good enough for the write-up of the speech, that the Abstract left out all reference to it. The omission looked the starker for the Abstract rendition of Gridley making quite some play of "Crime and fine" and "necessity"; but there it was. Or perhaps the reason was altogether different. The sheer technicality of this part of the debate may have made it unsuitable for journalistic presentation. The Abstract is noticeably short on particularized legal references; witness how lightly it handled Otis's crucial argument from Hale, Hawkins, and Dalton. To judge by all the theology, philosophy, and other subjects of learned discourse their newspapers

---

10. Otis probably got this from Hale (*History of the Pleas of the Crown* II, 151).

served up, contemporary New Englanders were persons of austere reading habits; but turgidities from seventeenth-century law reports might have been too much even for them. Refined debating points professionally incumbent on Otis in the courtroom did not make good copy for the public prints.

Sufficient, for the moment, of what the Abstract did not include; and to revert to what it did. It is a reversion in more senses than one. Next following in the Abstract is a farrago of rhetoric, dubious law, and apocryphal anecdote, reminiscent of nothing so much as the personalized harangue at the beginning. True, this part of the Abstract text has more elements of resemblance to John Adams's original notes than could be claimed for that earlier effusion; bafflingly, however, they occur mostly in the wrong places. The piece overall is plainly a major reshaping of the argument Otis actually delivered, with an injection of new or reconstituted thinking as well.

To take up, then, where the Abstract has Otis declaring:

> the writ prayed for in this petition is illegal. It is a power that places the liberty of every man in the hands of every petty officer. I say I admit that *special* writs of assistance to search *special* houses, may be granted to certain persons on oath; but I deny that the writ now prayed for can be granted, for I beg leave to make some observations on the writ itself before I proceed to other Acts of Parliament.

The writ "prayed for in this petition" and "now prayed for" and "the writ itself" were all of course the writ of assistance general in form. And with "the liberty of every man" being placed "in the hands of every petty officer," hyperbole has already begun to take over.

But this is nothing to what comes after, when Otis moves into an enumerated series of denunciations, with an anecdote and further particularized animadversions trailing behind. At length the pyrotechnics die down, and the argument resumes more soberly; but they are vivid enough while they last. For a start:

> In the first place the writ is UNIVERSAL, being directed "to all and singular justices, sheriffs, constables and all other officers and subjects, &c." so that in short it is directed to every subject in the king's dominions; every one with this writ may be a tyrant: If this commission is legal, a tyrant may, in a legal manner also, controul, imprison or murder any one within the realm.

High-flying rhetoric, not to be taken seriously as legal argument. The notion that if the general writ of assistance could call upon all and sundry to help in customs search it could likewise serve the furtherance of tyrannical imprisonment and murder was far adrift from the writ's legal anchorage; it could apply only on the improbable hypothesis that one day Parliament might legislate for promiscuous governmental mayhem and for everyone to cooperate in it.

Otis' second head of objection does not strip down too well either:

> In the next place, IT IS PERPETUAL; there's no return, a man is accountable to no person for his doings, every man may reign secure in his petty tyranny, and spread terror and desolation around him, until the trump of the arch-angel shall excite different emotions in his soul.

Even with the manifest flatulencies discounted,[11] this is little more than expostulation. The writ lasted indefinitely, true enough, and it could be used again and again; and to someone who wished to see customs entry and search subjected to a prior process of authorization on each individual occasion these characteristics obviously were objectionable, but nothing followed from a statement of that fact. It is much the same with "there's no return." A document such as a search warrant, which ordered an identifiable person to a certain course of action, usually obligated him to report back to the issuing authority — a bench of justices, as it might be — saying how the job had turned out; but such an obligation was impossible in the case of a writ of assistance, whose order to render assistance was addressed to an anonymous range of public personages, civic functionaries, and "all other our officers and subjects." On which particular individual in this indeterminate multitude could responsibility for making the return be fixed?

Next in Otis's list of anathemas:

> In the third place, a person with this writ, IN THE DAY TIME may enter all houses, shops &c. AT WILL, and command all to assist.

The source for this was the Superior Court's 1755-type writ, which spoke of the customs officer and his men searching "at his or their Will" and "in the day Time . . . ." But the accentuation is odd. That the power of entry and search with writ of assistance was available only in the daytime and not round the clock was a point in its favor, one would have thought. Otis would have done better to confine his emphasis to "AT WILL," for the message he was trying to put across

---

11. For passages here and under the fourth head which Adams disowned as interpolations (by Jonathan Williams Austin: p. 237 above) see *LPJA* II, 142, n. 138.

was presumably that entry of houses and so forth with the general writ of assistance was entirely at the discretion and pleasure of the holder. On the other hand, there was a gain in impact from what he omitted to say: for instance, that the power of entry and search required not only a writ of assistance but the attendance of a local peace officer; and for there to be no possibility of misapprehension Otis should have mentioned the 1662 act's inhibition on the use of force, which was permissible only "in case of Resistance." Here the Abstract has Otis coming out not quite straight. And, after that:

> Fourthly, by this not only deputies &c but even THEIR MENIAL SERVANTS ARE ALLOWED TO LORD IT OVER US — What is this but to have the curse of Canaan with a witness on us, to be the servant of servants, the most despicable of GOD'S creation.

This too was drawing on the text of the writ of assistance that the Superior Court had been issuing since 1755, which, following the archaic and peculiar precedent in William Brown's book on exchequer practice, enjoined assistance not only to the customs officer to whom it had been issued but to "his Deputies and servants" as well. The legal authenticity of so wide a spread may indeed have been questionable; but Otis's point seems to sound less in law than in affronted social sense. Another illustration, perhaps, of Abstract material designed not so much for the courtroom as for the coffee house.

A broadening of constitutional perspectives followed:

> Now one of the most essential branches of English liberty, is the freedom of one's house. A man's house is his castle; and while he is quiet, he is as well guarded as a prince in his castle. — This writ, if it should be declared legal, would totally annihilate this privilege. Custom house officers may enter our houses when they please — we are commanded to permit their entry — their menial servants may enter — may break locks, bars and every thing in their way — and whether they break through malice or revenge, no man, no court can inquire — bare suspicion without oath is sufficient.

The effect was a recapitulation of some of the points just taken against the general writ of assistance, placed in the context of violation of the rights of hearth and home. One point however was singled out for development and illustration: so free-ranging a power of entry and search was dangerously open to abuse. And thus to an anecdote:

> This wanton exercise of this power is no chimerical suggestion of a heated Brain. — I will mention some facts. Mr. Pew had one of these writs, and

when Mr. Ware succeeded him, he endorsed this writ over to Mr. Ware, so that THESE WRITS ARE NEGOTIABLE from one officer to another, and so your Honours have no opportunity of judging the persons to whom this vast power is delegated. Another instance is this. — Mr. Justice Wally had called this same Mr. Ware before him by a constable, to answer for a breach of the Sabbath-day acts, or that of profane swearing. As soon as he had done, Mr. Ware asked him if he had done, he replied, yes. Well then, says he, I will shew you a little of my power — I command you to permit me to search your house for unaccustomed goods; and went on to search his house from the garret to the cellar, and then served the constable in the same manner.

A colorful illustration, well of a piece with the brightly painted commentary that preceded it.

In fact, the anecdote was apocryphal in practically every material particular. Jonathan Pue and Nathaniel Ware were not predecessor and successor in the customs service; in the period 1750 to 1752 they had been colleagues at Boston, Pue as surveyor and searcher and Ware as comptroller; and when Pue left to become surveyor and searcher at Salem in 1752 his post at Boston was taken not by Ware but by Charles Paxton. If Pue made over any document to Ware it could not have been a writ of assistance, for no such thing existed in Massachusetts before Paxton got one in 1755 or 1756. If at any time Ware had the use of a writ of assistance, it can only have been Paxton's, for by when he sailed for England in 1756, never to return, no other had been issued. Abiel Walley was a justice of the peace for Suffolk county from 1740 to his death in 1759, so to that extent the incident described by Otis could have happened in the few months between the issuance of Paxton's writ and Ware's departure; but there is no evidence of its having done so, or, for that matter, any inherent likelihood that Paxton, that most indefatigable of operators on his own private account, would have parted with his writ even temporarily.[12]

12. See *LPJA* II, 143, n. 144. It would seem from *Homans v. Paxton* (SF 81403 and 82115) that Paxton, surveyor and searcher at Salem before exchanging ports with Pue, was to have paid £250 sterling for the deal, but somehow fell short.

Ware was something of a commentator on American affairs (*MHSC* I [1792; reprint ed., Boston, 1968, 66-84). The "extreme severity of that climate" was too much for him, however, and he hoped for a different appointment (letter to Duke of Newcastle, 26 June 1758: Add. MSS 32881). He hoped in vain. Eventually, policy having hardened against absentee officials, Ware was ordered to "repair forthwith to his Duty"; he refused, and lost his job: customs board to Treasury, 3 January 1764: T1/426. He was succeeded by Benjamin Hallowell junior.

For the death of Walley see *BEP* 3 September 1759.

Otis's "negotiability" objection is commented on in n. 45 below.

Altogether, this was a strange story to tell the Superior Court. It is not impossible that Otis genuinely felt entitled to take the point that it purported to illustrate, that a general writ of assistance could be misused with impunity; for there was as yet no firm precedent in the English law reports for holding writ of assistance entry and search justifiable by the event (that is, trespassorial unless offending goods were actually found).[13]   Yet it is hard to envision Otis seriously hoping to influence the court by the Pue-Ware-Walley story as related in the Abstract. The population of Boston and thereabouts was not a vast metropolitan mass and the judges of the Superior Court a group of distant mandarins to whom one name meant no more than the next. If there was any truth at all in the story, which was the sort of thing certain to have gone the rounds in a milieu of small-town gossip, the men on the bench, who were also men of wider public affairs, were as well placed as any to know what it was. Even as a human-interest condiment for popular newspaper material the Pue-Ware-Walley anecdote would have been dangerously prodigal of journalistic license: there were too many people able to check from their own knowledge.[14]

"I have taken more pains in this case, than I ever will take again," is one of the statements in the opening declamation of Abstract-Otis; and there is evidence enough in his drawings upon Hale, Hawkins, Dalton, and so forth — not to mention his preparatory exertions on his actual argument — to show that he really must have labored. He would hardly risk spoiling the effect of so much good work by regaling the Superior Court with something so vulnerably unresearched as the tale of Pue, Ware and Walley — at any rate, the way the Abstract told it. As a literal record of what Otis said in the

---

13. Cf. p. 424 below.
14. The slightly odd figure employed as introduction to the anecdote — "chimerical suggestion of a heated Brain" — seems to echo S. Pufendorf: *The Law of Nature and Nations,* trans. B. Kennet (London, 1749), bk. II, chap. III, sec. XIII, p. 131: "we need not fear that any one shall be able to foist upon us for natural law, either the freakish Notions of his ill-purg'd Brain, or the irregular Designs of his misguided Mind . . . ." (Of course, Otis could have preferred to do his own translating from Pufendorf's Latin.) The Pufendorf book is quoted in Otis's 1764 *Rights* pamphlet (for which cf. n. 42 below, and text).

John Adams surely would not have risked offending Otis by including this turn of phrase, if whispers of mental instability in Otis were already being heard; so its appearance in the Abstract perhaps strengthens the likelihood that Otis helped guide young Adams's hand. See p. 418 below for where the same figure occurs in a newspaper piece almost certainly written by Otis.

Cf. p. 363 below for evidence of Otis drawing upon a foreign writer on natural law (Vattel) in his writs of assistance speech.

speech he actually delivered, the Abstract anecdote seems very far gone in improbability.

After the Pue-Ware-Walley anecdote, Otis winds up his free-swinging attack on the general writ of assistance and all its horrendous tendencies:

> But to shew another absurdity in this writ, if it should be established, I insist upon it EVERY PERSON by 14th of Car. II. HAS THIS POWER as well as Custom-house officers; the words are, "it shall be lawful for any person or persons authorized, &c." What a scene does this open! Every man prompted by revenge, ill humour or wantonness to inspect the inside of his neighbour's house, may get a writ of assistance; others will ask it from self defence; one arbitrary exertion will provoke another, until society will be involved in tumult and in blood. — Again these writs ARE NOT RETURNED. Writs in their nature are temporary things; when the purposes for which they are issued are answered, they exist no more; but these monsters in the law live forever, no one can be called to account. Thus reason and the constitution are both against this writ.[15]

The aim seems to have been to underline, to some extent by repetition of arguments already used, the message of the anecdote: the irresponsible excesses to which the general writ of assistance lent itself. On the whole the effect is not impressive. It was true that the Act of Frauds of 1662 explicitly spoke of writ of assistance entry and search by "any Person or Persons"; but elsewhere in the legislation were provisions that in effect limited the use of this power to customs officers.[16] The extended fantasy which envisioned "society . . . involved in tumult and in blood" was just as insubstantial as the earlier imprecations about tyranny, terror, desolation, and so forth. Here as elsewhere the Abstract declamations ignored the essential fact that, far from exemplifying promiscuous license, entry and search with writ of assistance was explicitly conditional upon the presence of a local peace officer. As for the writ not being returnable, the point has already been made that such inevitably was the nature of a document addressed to everyone at large and no one in particular.

To much in this Abstract-Otis series of fulminations — enumerated, anecdotal, recapitulatory — Adams's notes afford no authenticating counterpart whatever; and even where a glimpse of something from

15. Otis's quotation from section 5(2) of the 1662 act was wrong. The actual text reads: "it shall be lawful to or for . . . ."

16. Section 15. In terms the limitation related to the making of seizures; impliedly, however, it related to search also, since seizure was the purpose of search. For more on this, and for the position in America, see pp. 366-67 below.

the notes does seem possible it is likely to be out of sequence or context. The lead-in reference to power being "in the hands of every petty officer" may have drawn upon a reference in a note to "every petty officer from the highest to the lowest"; but it would have been for turn of phrase only, for there is no other point of resemblance. The blast about a man's house being no longer his castle may have been inspired by the note "A Man, who is quiet, is as secure in his House, as a Prince in his Castle"; but the respective positionings in the Abstract and the notes are widely different. In due course it will be seen that the rhetoric about the general writ being perpetual and irreturnable has a counterpart of sorts down toward the end of the notes; and the very last note but one shows — fragmentarily — that Otis really did recount an anecdote about Jonathan Pue, Nathaniel Ware, and Justice Abiel Walley.[17] Beyond these few echoes and borrowings, neglectful as even these were of the original order of argument, the Abstract eloquence had little or no warrant in the notes.

Imperfect in its law, careless of its facts, and from start to finish the product of wholesale doctoring and invention, this lower middle part of the Abstract appears less concerned with genuine chronicle than with impact and effect. It may have been legitimate in a critique of the general writ of assistance to draw attention to the unusual scale of the power which it signified; and there are indications in John Adams's notes that Otis did do this in some degree. But the Abstract shows him interrupting himself to dwell upon the enormities of the writ in a manner and at a length that on the evidence of the notes cannot be accepted as historically true. With this oratorical extravaganza the Abstract again smacks of composition for a lay readership, whose interest might flag if the legal material were not enlivened with a bit of knockabout.

Returning to Adams's notes at a place roughly corresponding to where the Abstract takes off into high fervor against the awfulness of the general writ of assistance, one notices another instance of the Abstract subtracting as well as adding. After their reference to Hawkins's (or was it Hale's?) book on the *Pleas of the Crown* the notes go on:

— every petty officer from the highest to the lowest, And if some of 'em are uncom others are uncomm. Gouvt Justices used to issue such perpetual Edicts. (Q. with wt particular Reference?)

17. See p. 373 below.

The blank space signifies a crossing-out of what Adams originally put, "com, others." Not that the correction helped much. What with this and the question at the end, Adams evidently had lost track of the argument. All that the Abstract has of these notes is "every petty officer," and out of context at that. Once more, the Abstract was simply using odds and ends from the notes for the better fabrication of its blockbuster against the general writ.

If the mysterious "uncom" and "uncomm," together with the words Adams crossed out, signify a reference to subordinate customs men engaging in antismuggling enterprise, perhaps Otis was adverting to the case mentioned by Oxenbridge Thacher earlier in the proceedings, *Horne v. Boosey.* This was about a seizure by a tidesman, a lowly employee of the customs, whose authorization to make seizures — probably it did not rate as a commission — appeared to be conditional upon his having a writ of assistance. The Abstract rendition of Thacher invoked *Horne v. Boosey* ("an Authority from Strange") for the proposition that writs of assistance were "only temporary things," which was a misunderstanding of the case. If Adams got *Horne v. Boosey* wrong when writing up the Thacher speech, equally he might have been confused by Otis's citation of it. Hence, conceivably, the muddle in his notes, and his puzzled "Q. with wt particular Reference?"

Adams's reminiscences in old age told of Otis delivering a "rapid summary of Historical Events . . . ."[18] Accordingly, Otis might in some sense have been recounting the history of customs search in Massachusetts. If, as seems possible, the garbled note "And if some of 'em are   uncom others are uncomm" was about customs men of various degree, some commissioned and others not, it perhaps could relate to the first phase of customs search described in Hutchinson's *History of Massachusets-Bay,* when "collectors and inferior officers of the customs, merely by the authority derived from their commissions, had forcibly entered warehouses . . . ."[19] Likewise the next note, "Gouvt. Justices used to issue such perpetual Edicts," could tie in with the second phase, when Governor Shirley "as the civil magistrate, gave out his warrants to the officers of the customs to enter."[20] There is something else to notice, besides. It was suggested in chapter 7 that Shirley's warrants were to much the same effect as the Superior Court's "general" writs of assistance that

18. *LWJA* X, 247.
19. Page 67.
20. *Ibid.*

displaced them after the incident at the Hutchinson warehouse in 1755. Otis's words "such perpetual Edicts" square with this, in the "such" and in the allusion to indefinite continuance.

But there was more to the cryptic "Gouvt. Justices used to issue such perpetual Edicts." The Adams reminiscences had Otis encompassing other things besides history, "Classical Allusions" among them. Quite aside from his literary interests, Otis would have been something of a classicist in his legal learning. "A Lawyer in this Country must study common Law and civil Law, and natural Law, and Admiralty Law," the experienced Jeremiah Gridley is on record as saying.[21] So when a lawyer of James Otis's known interest in the ancient world speaks of "perpetual Edicts," one remembers that "edict" belongs much more in Roman law than in English; and notices that the general writ of assistance, a document valid throughout the king's reign, had a sort of affinity with the *edictum perpetuum*, in which the urban praetor laid down the law for his period of office. Young John Adams was by no means unacquainted with Roman jurisprudence,[22] but this rather *recherché* whimsicality of Otis's seems not to have registered.

It is regrettable that the flavor of Otis's witty analogy relating the general writ of assistance to the legal practice of ancient Rome (where the principles of government were never conspicuously libertarian) nowhere comes out in full. However, enough is discernible in the Adams notes to illustrate once again the contrast between Otis's styles of delivery in court and in the Abstract write-up. The astute lawyer-turning-politician did not disdain all oratorical flourish in his courtroom work; but he seems to have pitched it on a more scholarly level than was afterward thought suitable for a prospective newspaper readership.

Correspondence between Adams's original notes and the Abstract now takes a turn for the better. The next notes read:

> But one Precedent, and tht in the Reign of C.2 when Star Chamber Powers, and all Powers but lawful & useful Powers were pushed to Extremity. —
> The authority of this Modern Practice of the Court of Exchequer. — it has an Imprimatur. — But wt may not have? — It may be owing to some ignorant Clerk of the Exchequer.

21. *DAJA* I, 55
22. See, in particular, L. H. Butterfield, ed., *The Earliest Diary of John Adams* (Cambridge, Mass., 1966), 101-2, for some of Adams's civil law studies touching the praetor.

The Abstract, its tirade against the enormities of the general writ of assistance having come to an end, changes key as follows:

> Let us see what authority there is for it. No more than one instance can be found of it in all our law books, and that was in the zenith of arbitrary power, viz. In the reign of Car. II. when star-chamber powers were pushed to extremity by some ignorant clerk of the Exchequer.

Not a perfect match, but a reasonably close one.

Had the writs of assistance case been about issuance of a writ for the first time, Otis might have gone straight in to argue that the writ should be like common law search warrants and the statutory customs search warrant of 1660, and valid for the one sworn occasion only. But this was not the situation. The general writ of assistance had actually existed in Massachusetts these five years past, and with a seemingly authoritative precedent backing it up. These incommoding facts were not to be shamed into oblivion by indignant rhetoric (vividly though they might be denounced in a popularized write-up such as the Abstract). In a court of law something more sophisticated and professional was required. Even without any mention of it by his opponent Otis would have had to tackle the circumstance that the general writ of assistance issued by the Superior Court since 1755 was taken, virtually word for word, from a precedent in a respectable English law book, William Brown's *Practice of his Majesties Court of Exchequer at Westminster*. The excerpts in the foregoing paragraph show him setting about the task of playing down Brown's awkward *Breve Assisten' pro Officiar' Custum'* in point of weight and authority.

It was not too hard a task, one might have thought. On the plain words of its text – or of the Massachusetts writ that so faithfully followed it – Brown's *breve* simply did not answer to the sort of smuggling that went on in America. The goods to which it related were such as had been imported for re-exportation. It had been something of a freak even in England.[23] Yet evidence that Otis attacked it from this point of view is hard to see. His approach seems to have been less direct.

Inauspicious history, rather than the Brown precedent's intrinsic inaptness, was what Otis focused upon. Not only was this *breve* the sole exemplar of a customs writ of assistance, it dated from "the Reign of C.2 when Star Chamber Powers, and all Powers but lawful

23. See pp. 106-7 above.

& useful Powers were pushed to Extremity," and which, according to the Abstract, was "the zenith of arbitrary power." The words themselves were more denunciation than argument – and pretty wild denunciation, too, on first impression. The Court of Star Chamber had ceased to exist long before Charles II's time. Even taken figuratively, a reference to "Star Chamber Powers . . . pushed to Extremity" under Charles II would have been extravagant: Restoration standards of government and judicial administration were low, but not as bad as that. It may be that Otis's meaning did not get through properly.

John Adams's reminiscences of the Otis speech spoke not only of classical and historical allusions but of "a depth of Research." Both in Adams's contemporaneous notes and in the Abstract write-up the research was kept well below the surface; and Otis's overdone metaphor about Star Chamber powers in the time of Charles II may be another instance of muted homework and muffled message. A clue, if not the key, is in the more particularized reportage of the resumed hearing in November 1761, by Josiah Quincy junior.[24] Quincy was not present for the whole of Otis's November speech, but he did note several citations by Otis of Rapin-Thoyras's *History of England* (a treatise well suited to whiggish sentiment). One of these references was to a page[25] telling of the order made by Privy Council in 1629 for search of houses and other places for goods which had evaded Charles I's tunnage and poundage. This Privy Council order of 1629 has been identified as a forerunner – conceivably even the inspiration – of the statutory regime of entry and search with writ of assistance introduced in 1662.[26] For his material on the Privy Council order Rapin had drawn upon the *Historical Collections* of John Rushworth;[27] and it is not improbable that Otis too went back to Rushworth, for further and better particulars. If Otis knew of the writ of assistance's conciliar antecedent at the November hearing the chances are that he already knew of it in February. It could be, then, that the reference in Adams's notes to Brown's *breve* having originated "in the Reign of C.2 when Star Chamber Powers, and all Powers but lawful & useful Powers were pushed to Extremity" was garbled; and that in reality Otis was pointing to Brown's *breve* as

24. See Appendix K.
25. P. Rapin-Thoyras, *History of England*, trans. N. Tindal (London, 1733) II, 285; *cf.* chapter 17 below, n. 29 and text.
26. See pp. 30-31 above.
27. Vol. II (London, 1721), 9.

something not so much invented in the Restoration period as resurrected from the bad old days of Star Chamber.

Having attacked Brown's *breve* for having been born at a bad time, Otis moved on to Brown's book itself, "this Modern Practice of the Court of Exchequer," as he called it. It will be recalled from chapter 13 that all three advocates, Gridley and Thacher as well as Otis, somehow confused the (second edition) title of Brown's book, *The Practice of his Majesties Court of Exchequer at Westminster,* with an anonymous work, *The Modern Practice of the Court of Exchequer,* published in 1730. Another point taken in chapter 13 was that Otis's disdainful comment on the Brown book, "it has an Imprimatur. — But wt may not have?" seems to have been by way of retort to Gridley's commendation of the imprimatur. Otis did not go so far as to impugn the judge whose imprimatur it was, Wright C.J. (though well he might have done, for Wright was classically a man of the rock-bottom judicial standards under the two last Stuart kings[28]). It sufficed, apparently, to flick the imprimatur aside. By whomsoever given it testified nothing to the worth of the book's contents; its significance had never been more than that the book had complied with contemporary censorship requirements.

"It may be owing to some ignorant Clerk of the Exchequer," Otis continues in the notes. In the Abstract the "ignorant clerk of the Exchequer" is made responsible for Star Chamber powers having been pushed to extremity in the reign of Charles II; but there is little doubt that Otis had meant the person who penned the *Breve Assisten' pro Officiar' Custum'* which Brown had procured for transcription into his book. Here Otis possibly did intend an allusion to the inaptness of the Brown *breve* to the New England scene, if not to its questionable legality even on its home ground.

Much of Otis's attack on the Brown *breve* seems to have been more oratorical than legal. For example, it was not really conclusive of anything that the *breve* had originated in a murky period of English legal history. But not everything was sound effects. In particular, there may have been a good deal more than abusive scorn to the slighting of the *breve* as the work of "some ignorant clerk of the Exchequer." The real point of this rudery may have had to do with that fundamental principle of the common law which insisted that a writ was not valid merely by virtue of having been issued. The invocation of the name of the king, the teste, the mumbo-jumbo

28. *Cf.* chapter 13, n. 9.

language, even the fact that it had been sealed and handed out by the chancery or other agency whence writs usually came: nothing signified if the substantive content of the writ could not pass as lawful on challenge by judicial process.[29] The distinction between administrative issuance of a writ and judicial assessment of the writ's legal validity applied in Massachusetts no less than in England. That the *breve* had been reproduced in a precedent book might mean no more than that it had never been subjected to challenge by judicial process but had acquired a kind of provisional acceptance through passage of time. There was nothing — not even the fact that a Massachusetts version of it had been issued under the Superior Court's own administrative process — to inhibit the court now scrutinizing this undeniably strange piece of draftsmanship and throwing it out.

However, the Superior Court's power to disown the general writ of assistance was one thing; that it should use the power was something else. And so Otis essayed a further, and culminating, heave against the inconvenient circumstance that a general writ of assistance already existed in the province on the strength of a precedent in Brown's book:

> But had this writ been in any book whatever it would have been illegal. ALL PRECEDENTS ARE UNDER THE CONTROUL OF THE PRINCIPLES OF THE LAW. Lord Talbot says, it is better to observe these than any precedents though in the House of Lords, the last resort of the subject.

In Adams's on-the-spot notes:

> But all Precedents and this am'g the Rest are under the Control of the Principles of Law. Ld. Talbot. better to observe the known Principles of Law thn any one Precedent, tho in the House of Lords.

An echo — more distinct in the Abstract than in the notes — of the originating theme of Otis's argument: notwithstanding that a widely used manual of practice, Dalton's *Countrey Justice,* had long since sanctioned a general search warrant for stolen goods, Sir Matthew Hale had adduced authority and principle for repudiating this and substituting a warrant good for the one sworn occasion only.

Otis was now back to main-line argument. Disposal of the general writ that actually existed, and of the English precedent it was based

29. See pp. 31-32 above.

upon, had been a necessary part of his task. Even so, it had delayed resumption of the essential and positive thrust of his speech: absolute supremacy to be yielded to "the principles of law," particularly — following the precept of the old master of the common law, Sir Matthew Hale, and simultaneously demonstrating how right the judges had been to heed what they had read in the *London Magazine* — the principle that outlawed general search.

Ultimately Otis purposed to show that "the principles of law" went so far as to regulate statute itself. But before they were pitted against section 5(2) of the Act of Frauds of 1662 — the enactment in which writ of assistance search first began — it was desirable to be in no doubt they applied to that other but lower source of law: precedent.

There is an ambiguity in Otis's "all Precedents . . . are under the Control of the Principles of Law." This statement had application both to precedents of the kind he had just been talking about, specimen writs in manuals of legal practice that attorneys might copy and adapt, and to precedents in the sense of judicial determinations of law as set forth in law reports. Apparently Otis used it as a bridge across which he might pass to the second kind of precedent and argue that this too, while an authoritative source of law beyond compare with specimen writs such as the *Breve Assisten'pro Officiar' Custum'*, was nevertheless liable to be subordinated to whatever higher "principles of law" were in point. This was bold stuff. That a writ drafted by an "ignorant clerk" might be overruled by the judicial process was little more than a common-sense axiom of the law; but a challenge to the binding authority of decided cases went to the very root of English-style jurisprudence. Necessary though he may have believed it to be as a link in the chain that vindicated the "principles of law" at the expense even of statute, Otis cannot be said to have succeeded here.

The doctrine of *stare decisis* occupies a position of the highest importance in the English legal system. "Decided cases are the anchors of the laws, as laws are of the state," Francis Bacon said.[30] Certainly it would not have done, in a jurisprudence so strongly property oriented as the common law, with sureness of title the copestone of the society it served, for judges to jump whichever way they pleased. A judge-made jurisprudence implied judicial solidarity, in which not only judges of the present but their brethren of the past

30. See Holdsworth, *HEL* XII, 148, for this and other references, and commentary.

were partakers. Of course, even in England *stare decisis* took time to develop to the full; and in the mid-eighteenth century it may have looked less formidably unaccommodating than in years to come.[31] But Otis's assertion that "all precedents" were "under the principles of law," if it meant that judges were at liberty not to recognize a precedent as embodying the "principles of law," went much too far.

Aptly, the extravagance of Otis's statement is illustrated by his misreading of the precedent that he himself drew upon. This was *Clare v. Clare*, decided by Lord Chancellor Talbot in the Court of Chancery in 1734.[32] *Clare v. Clare* had to do with a will under challenge for a perpetuity. Perpetuities were a prime hobgoblin in English jurisprudence. Time out of mind the courts of law and equity alike had nurtured an obsessive determination that landed property should not remain tied up indefinitely by a dead hand. There existed a mass of subtle and highly technical doctrine all dedicated to the principle — of great economic and social consequence — that within no more than a few years of the present generation having passed on the use of land should be free of all inhibition from the graveyard, and fully available to answer the needs of the living. Let a real property disposition betray the faintest tendency to a perpetuity and the courts would strike it down. The question in *Clare v. Clare* was whether the testator's intentions for his land should be given effect or whether the vice of a perpetuity could not be read into them. Lord Talbot thought he saw this fatal element, a precedent to the contrary notwithstanding. The precedent was imperfectly reported, he said; and it was "much better to stick to the known general rules, than to follow any one particular precedent, which may be founded on reasons unknown to us: such a proceeding would confound all property." He opted instead for another case, decided in the House of Lords (the topmost jurisdiction in England). It was, he considered, "the strongest authority that can be; and even, had it not been in the House of Lords, I should have thought myself bound to go according to the general and known rules of law."

Otis's "better to observe the known Principles of Law than any one Precedent" was an accurate enough rendition of Talbot as far as it went, but it omitted to say that Talbot was referring to a particular precedent that he had special reason for regarding as unreliable. Not in the least was Lord Talbot saying that it were "better to observe

31. *Ibid.*, 152-53.
32. Talb. 21.

the known Principles of Law than any one Precedent, tho in the House of Lords"; rather it was that he would have preferred the case he followed even if it had been in a court lower than the House of Lords. Above all, Otis was short on perspective. The "known general rules" and "general and known rules of law" that Lord Talbot had been so concerned to uphold were the expression of a specific principle — freedom of land use for the future — which ranked as high as any in the English tradition. Talbot was not generalizing. Otis, on the other hand, talked of "the known Principles of Law" having priority over precedent, as if to adumbrate a catch-all doctrine that entitled a court to subordinate *stare decisis* to whatever philosophical abstraction next attracted its fancy.[33]

Ironically, there was in fact no decided case that Otis needed to overturn: in 1761 the writ of assistance had received barely so much as a mention in the law reports. The purpose of this unsatisfactory endeavor against definitiveness in judicial precedent can only have been a theoretical or dialectical one; a beachhead from which to move forward and proclaim the "principles of law" — in particular, the principle against general search — supreme at even the topmost level of man-made legal authority, statutory enactment.

The series of propositions next to appear in the Adams notes make as if to scale that ultimate height:

> As to Acts of Parliament. an Act against the Constitution is void: an Act against natural Equity is void: and if an Act of Parliament should be made, in the very Words of this Petition, it would be void. The Executive Courts must pass such Acts into disuse — 8. Rep. 118. from Viner. — Reason of the Com^n Law to control an Act of Parliament.

A great deal of the fame of the writs of assistance case derives from these jottings; and more than a little of Otis's key argument can be teased out of them.

It is important to recognize that Otis's low-pitched purpose — to hamstring writ of assistance search with specificity and sworn information more than to eliminate it altogether — was not catered to by the farther reaching of these pronouncements, that characterized certain reprehensible classes of parliamentary enactment as altogether void. The enactment that might have seemed in point is section 5(2) of the Act of Frauds of 1662, which said:

---

33. Or, as it is put in *LPJA* II, 127, n. 70, "principles variously described as those of common law, natural law, and common sense."

and it shall be lawful to or for any Person or Persons authorized by Writ of Assistance under the Seal of his Majesty's Court of Exchequer, to take a Constable . . . and in the Day-time to enter . . . .

Perhaps not the most obvious of candidates for judicial anathema in any case. Assuredly it was not an attack on section 5(2) that Otis intended in his celebrated declamation, "if an Act of Parliament should be made, in the very Words of this Petition, it would be void." [34] (How could it have been: given his willingness to see section 5(2) operate as before, save only that the writ of assistance should be specifically sworn for?) The opposite was nearer the truth. Section 5(2), exactly as it stood, was crucial to Otis's developing argument. Those words of his just quoted cannot be understood otherwise than in reference to the fact that section 5(2) said nothing about its power of search being general. Their meaning was governed by the opener "if," and they evidently served as oratorical emphasis on the utter unthinkability of writ of assistance search being general: putting the hypothesis that even had generality been expressly written into section 5(2) such a monstrosity could not be acknowledged as law. Equally to Otis's purpose, of course, was the amenability of section 5(2)'s neutral text to benign construction, allowing of a writ of assistance in the severely hobbled form he was contending for.

Much more sharply directed to Otis's substantive theme are the jottings that follow his drumbeat about acts of Parliament being void: "8. Rep. 118. from Viner. — Reason of the Com^n Law to control an Act of Parliament." The reference here was to the common law's *locus classicus* on judicial review of statute: a dictum by Coke C.J. in *Dr Bonham's Case*, decided in 1610, reported in the eighth volume of Coke's own reports and retailed in the more recent *General Abridgment of Law and Equity* by Charles Viner:

And it appears in our books, that in many cases, the common law will controul Acts of Parliament, and sometimes adjudge them to be utterly void: for when an Act of Parliament is against common right and reason, or repugnant, or impossible to be performed, the common law will controul it, and adjudge such Act to be void . . . . [35]

34. By "the very words of this Petition" is meant, undoubtedly, the words of the general writ of assistance; it is likely enough that any documentation of the Cockle petition at Salem in October 1760 included, if it did not mostly consist of, the writ in draft ready for signing and sealing by the court clerk.

35. The Viner *Abridgment* (23 vols., Aldershot, 1741-53) varies Coke's text slightly: e.g., for "many" it substitutes "several" (vol. 19, 512-13). See *LPJA* II, 128, n. 73. *Bonham's Case* is reported not only in 8 Rep. but also, *sub nom. College of Physicians' Case*, in 2 Brownl. at 255.

There is a duality in this dictum that is of the utmost relevance. Coke's words, "in many cases, the common law will controul Acts of Parliament, and sometimes adjudge them to be utterly void," speak of two situations: acts of Parliament being subjected to "controul" in "many cases," the full treatment — being adjudged void — applying only "sometimes." This differentiation is mirrored in the Adams jottings on Otis. And it was "controul" rather than avoidance that Otis went to *Bonham* for.[36]

The less sweeping of the two *Bonham* canons, by which a statute could be toned down according to "common right and reason," suited Otis's purpose exactly. For, of course, the task he had set himself — to prove that what the *London Magazine* had said about specifically sworn writs of assistance was legally sound — was not yet accomplished. The textual neutrality of section 5(2) of the Act of Frauds of 1662 was well enough so far as it went, but it cut both ways. Just as the statute's words did not expressly require writ of assistance search to be general so it afforded no positive warrant for the alternative being urged by Otis. Here was where *Bonham*-style "controul" by "common right and reason" came in.

It fits that Otis did not use the actual words from *Bonham's Case*. Though clearly his "Reason of the Com̄ Law to control an Act of Parliament" corresponds to Coke C.J.'s "when an Act of Parliament is against common right and reason . . . the common law will controul it," it is not quite the same. It suggests a sharpening of focus, by which something else from Coke is brought into view: his report of *Prohibitions del Roy,* in 1607. In this classic of English constitutionalism, which Otis cannot conceivably have been unaware of, Coke relates how James I, having been rebuffed by the judges for adjudicating in person a "controversy of land between parties" which "did belong to the common law," protested "that he thought the law

---

36. Coke's report of *Bonham's Case* shows him citing authority fairly copiously and at length for the voiding of statute, but not for "controul" short of avoidance. *Cf.,* however, his note to Littleton's section 464, in 1 *Inst.* 272b: "The surest construction of a statute is by the rule and reason of the common law" (see also *Quincy's Reports,* 56, 523). In *Bonham* Coke perhaps thought the principle too incontrovertible to need authentication. Commentary on *Bonham* has likewise tended to say little on the lesser theme. However, Professor S. E. Thorne, in his edition of *A Discourse upon the Exposicion & Understandinge of Statutes* . . . . (San Marino, 1942), 88–89, affirms that "Coke must be understood to say that 'in many cases the common law will control acts of parliament' — that is, will restrict their words in order to reach sound results; and 'sometimes it will adjudge them to be completely void' — that is, will reject them completely if modification cannot serve."

For Otis in relation to Coke's Littleton note *cf.* n. 39 below.

was founded upon reason, and that he and others had reason, as well as the Judges"; to which Coke C.J. had replied that the king, while bright enough in a general way, was not learned in the law, and that cases involving people's lives and property were "not to be decided by natural reason but by the artificial reason and judgment of law."[37] James Otis in the writs of assistance case had an example of the "Reason of the Com^n Law" immediately to hand and in point. His staple source material, the *History of the Pleas of the Crown* by Sir Matthew Hale, having affirmed that search warrants for stolen goods had a place in the common law, went on to prescribe certain "moderations and temperaments" the effect of which was to discountenance generality from those warrants and to subject their issuance to sworn specificity.[38] This was the "Reason of the Com^n Law" actually at work, and very relevantly. Why should not those same "moderations and temperaments," so perfectly expressive of the reason of the common law as to have been brought in to regulate a document of the common law itself, control an act of Parliament in essentially like case? Furthermore, was not the power of search in section 5(2) of the Act of Frauds of 1662 contingent upon a writ of assistance, a document whose issuance surely could be regulated to similar result? Thus might Otis have argued that the "Reason of the Com^n Law," as exemplified by Hale in relation to common law search for stolen goods, applied equally to statutory search for smuggled goods by dint of an appropriately disciplined writ of assistance.[39]

And what of those other items in Otis's celebrated descant, "an Act against the Constitution is void: an Act against natural Equity is void"? The thought that they may have had more to them than hot air repays pursuing. In particular, they spark a few useful insights into Otis on the *Bonham* tack.

37. 12 Co. Rep. 63.
38. Vol. II, 149.
39. Possibly, Otis's "Reason of the Com^n Law to control Acts of Parliament" brought in not only *Bonham, Prohibitions del Roy*, and Hale, but also Coke's Littleton note quoted in n. 36 above (which however, speaks of the "construction" of statutes: a milder word than "control"). Otis appears to have made use of the note in the resumed hearing in November: see chapter 17, n. 30 and text.

The Superior Court bench may not have been entirely unreceptive to a suggestion that what went for the common law should go for an act of parliament equally. John Cushing, one of the judges in the writs of assistance case, wrote to his son William (later of the U.S. Supreme Court) on 25 March 1762, counseling study of Coke's common law works: "But the Acts of Parlt. wch make Great part of what is Called Comon Law ought to be well understood also": MHS, Robert Treat Paine papers.

Bonham's Case was an action for damages against the College of Physicians which arose from the college's supervisory powers over the practice of medicine in the city of London. The powers originated in the charter of Henry VIII by which the college had been founded; they included direct imposition of fines and imprisonment for specified classes of violations, fines to be shared by the king and the college itself. The charter was confirmed after some four years by act of Parliament (possibly, one speculates, because of common law objection to penal regimes in a prerogative instrument of that kind); and again, with an added enforcement provision, in the reign of Mary.[40] Dr. Thomas Bonham had practiced in London without the approval of the officials of the College of Physicians, and in defiance of them; and they had fined and imprisoned him. Wrongfully, as he considered; hence his action. The action succeeded. One of the points taken by Coke C.J. was that the officials of the college could not be "judges to give sentence or judgment; ministers to make summons; and parties to the moiety of the forfeiture, *quia aliquis non debet esse judex in propria causa . . .*"; and it was to this that Coke linked his statements about common law authority over acts of Parliament.

There was relevance to the dialectical position of James Otis not only in Coke's doctrinal dictum about common law reason controlling statute, but also in the more particularized content of *Bonham's Case.* On Otis's argument that writ of assistance search should be preceded by a specific court determination, a general writ, which by its nature precluded such process, could be protested as making the customs officer *"judex in propria causa."*

The reference to "natural equity" indicates that Otis actually did extend his thinking along these lines. Not so much from *Bonham,* however, as from a case that followed soon after (though without citing it, apparently): *Day v. Savadge,* decided in 1614. Hobart C.J. said this:

> An Act of Parliament made against natural equity, as to make a man judge in his own cause, would be void, for *jura naturae sunt immutabilia* and they are *leges legum.*[41]

40. 14 & 15 Hen. 8, c.5; 1 Mar. c.9.

41. Hob. 85. Hobart C. J.'s *"jura naturae sunt immutabilia"* presumably came from the 16th-century work by Christopher St German, *Doctor and Student* (see the Selden Society edition, by T. F. T. Plucknett and J. L. Barton [1974], 14). As earlier set forth, in Bracton, the tag was tempered by allowable departures *ad hoc: cf.* T. F. T. Plucknett, "Bonham's

The *Bonham* disapproval of a man judge in his own cause was elevated by *Day v. Savadge* into a canon of "natural equity," and "natural equity" into a standard by which even an act of Parliament might be weighed and if found wanting struck down. A perceptible advance on *Bonham,* in other words; and if *judex in propria causa* featured in Otis's rhetoric, Hobart's "natural equity" perhaps was the preferred citation, because of its sharper pertinence.

On the evidence, indeed, *Bonham's Case* may have played no direct part in Otis's talk about acts of Parliament being void. His "an Act against natural Equity is void" came from *Day v. Savadge.* But whereas *Day v. Savadge* at least was a derivative of *Bonham,* Otis's accompanying "an Act against the Constitution is void" had no traceable foundation in *Bonham* at all. Exploration continues, nevertheless.

In John Adams's notes, "an Act against the Constitution is void: an Act against natural Equity is void" occur together. There happens to be quite another context where Otis made much the same juxtaposition, and which probably affords an informative glimpse into his cast of thinking in the writs of assistance case. The year 1764 produced a barrage of American protest against the new British revenue measures then introduced or soon to come (notably the Stamp Act). James Otis's contribution was a pamphlet, *The Rights of the British Colonies Asserted and Proved.* He made no mention of the writ of assistance, but he did say this:

> The Parliament of *Great Britain* is circumscribed by certain bounds which if exceeded their acts become those of mere *power* without *right,* and consequently void. The judges of England have declared in favor of these sentiments when they expressly declare that *acts of Parliament against natural equity are void.* That *acts against the fundamental principles of the British constitution are void.* This doctrine is agreeable to the law of nature . . . .[42]

Case and Judicial Review," *Harvard Law Review* 40 (1926), 49, for criticism of Hobart's "rather serious misquotation of Bracton"; also Horace Gray in *Quincy's Reports,* 525.

Hobart was "a thorough believer in Coke's doctrine": Plucknett, *op. cit.,* 50, referring to *Lord Sheffield v. Ratcliffe* (1615) Hob. 334a. Coke himself had spoken of natural law as part of the law of England, and, citing *Doctor and Student,* as immutable, in *Calvin's Case,* 7 Rep.: see R. Berger, "*Doctor Bonham's Case:* Statutory Construction or Constitutional Theory?" in *University of Pennsylvania Law Review* (1969), 521-45, and *Congress and the Supreme Court* (Cambridge, Mass., 1969).

42. For the text of this pamphlet, and a commentary, see B. Bailyn, *Pamphlets of the American Revolution . . .* I (Cambridge, Mass., 1965), 408-482. The present quotation is at pp. 476-77, from an appendix to the pamphlet which embodied a memorial earlier prepared for adoption and use by the province Assembly.

The *Rights,* and *Bonham,* will be returned to in chapter 19.

Among quotations cited in a long footnote were Hobart C.J.'s dictum in *Day v. Savadge* and an extract from the contemporary Swiss jurist, Emmerich de Vattel, in *Le Droit des Gens ou Principes de la Loi Naturelle . . .* (which had appeared in English translation in 1760). The subject of the Vattel extract was a denial that legislators could ever go against the constitution of their country. As the title of his book indicates, Vattel was writing in the natural law tradition. Natural law was explicitly invoked in the Hobart dictum. Otis's *Rights* text fixes upon this shared natural law orientation, and as it were syllogizes itself into the position that what Hobart said about acts of Parliament void for offense against natural equity extended to unconstitutional legislation as outlawed by Vattel.

Consistency of utterance was sometimes lacking in James Otis. His attitude to parliamentary authority is not altogether easy to interpret as a flawless whole even within the bounds of the *Rights* pamphlet. Yet, and while it is by no means axiomatic that what he wrote in 1764 corresponded exactly to what he had said in 1761, it seems a fair presumption that the reasoning behind his "an Act against the Constitution is void: an Act against natural Equity is void" in the writs of assistance case was much the same as later went into the *Rights*.

But why should Otis have brought Vattel and natural law into the writs of assistance case at all? Aside, that is, from rhetorical descant on the innocent neutrality of the statutory text on writ of assistance search? For his substantive theme, that the common law aversion from general search should be superimposed on the noncommittal section 5(2) of the 1662 Act of Frauds by means of appropriately regulated issuance of the writ of assistance, the *Bonham's Case* doctrine about acts of Parliament being controllable surely was authority enough?

This may have been the very question in Otis's mind. Practically speaking, *Bonham* had ceased to mean much in the shadow of the parliamentary absolutism that had set hard as supreme constitutional canon in eighteenth-century England. The case was still getting into the books, even so; and Otis's citation not only of the original Coke report but also the rendition in the comparatively modern Viner's *Abridgment* may have been to demonstrate that there was life in the old doctrine yet. All the same, in the middle of the eighteenth century those Cokeian pronouncements from the reign of the earliest of the Stuart kings had the look of times come and gone. Otis cannot have been unaware that, massage it as he might, the *Bonham* line of authority was none too robust for the weight his argument required it to bear. Therefore, he underpinned the whole thing by contriving a foundation for it in the immutabilities of natural law.

What young John Adams made of it all is hard to tell. But what he took down in his notes, manifestly incomplete though it was, is of immeasurably greater value than its counterpart in the Abstract. The Abstract rendition of Otis's famous subordination of acts of Parliament to the claims of superior legal principle gives scarcely a glimpse of his reasoning:

> No Acts of Parliament can establish such a writ: Though it should be made in the very words of the petition it would be void, "AN ACT AGAINST THE CONSTITUTION IS VOID." Vid. Viner.

Not a hint even of Otis's truly crucial point from *Bonham*, about acts of Parliament being subject to judicial moderation ("controul," short of outright avoidance), and silence on general writ of assistance search violating "natural equity" by making the customs officer judge in his own cause. There is an element of positive garbling, in fact: legislation void for unconstitutionality was a concept from Vattel's treatise on natural law, not from Viner's *Abridgment* or any version of *Bonham's Case*. The Abstract is all but worthless here. One single thing deserving notice is that, in the Abstract as well as in the notes, Otis does not denounce the writ of assistance legislation as void. In both he limits himself to the rhetorical hypothesis that even if (though perish the thought) Parliament should ever be so wrong-headed as to pass an act corresponding in generality to the writ now being sought, the act would be void.

Obviously it is a pity that the Abstract should have done so poor a transcription job on this centrally important part of Otis's argument. Again, the reason may be that the Abstract was written not with an eye to historical analysis but for the contemporary Boston public at large; this phase of the great oration was altogether too technical and sophisticated for popularized rendition to be possible.

By now John Adams's notes were becoming more fragmentary still, with the handwriting badly misshapen by fatigue. Valuable as they are for elicitation of Otis's stance on the *Bonham's Case* authorities, they nevertheless did not get beyond "Reason of the Com Law to control an Act of Parliament" and left completion of the argument to be conjured forth as best it might. What came next,

> — Iron Manufacture. nobel Lord's Proposal, tht we should send our
> Horses to Eng. to be shod. —

perhaps did so after Adams had taken a respite, for it does not follow
on too well. This fragment is the only sign, in either the notes or the
Abstract, of what Adams in later years was to magnify into a quite
massive block of oratory on the acts of trade. It had to do with the
passage of the act of 1750 which restricted iron and steel manufacture in America; and here is how Adams expanded upon them in
1818:

> Mr Otis . . . said one member of Parliament had said, that a hobnail
> should not be manufactured in America; and another had moved that
> Americans should be compelled by act of Parliament to send their horses
> to England to be shod. He believed, however, that this last was a man of
> sense, and meant, by this admirable irony, to cast a ridicule on the whole
> selfish, partial, arbitrary, and contracted system of parliamentary regula-
> tions in America.[43]

It could be, of course, that this was indeed a part of Otis's speech
where he took time out from argument proper to grumble about the
imperial system at large. Just possibly, however, it connected back
with what he had been saying about acts of Parliament, reason, and
so forth. Whatever was said in debate, the act of 1750 had not gone
to the absurd length of prohibiting American manufacture of nails;
Otis may have been pointing to it as an illustration of legislation
conforming to what was reasonable and just.

The Abstract is no help. In contrast to the long declamation
against the acts of trade that Adams was to put into Otis's mouth
fifty-odd years afterward, this near-contemporaneous account shows
nothing. Even the unquestionably authentic reference to the act of
1750 is totally discarded.

---

43. *LWJA* X, 350. Horace Gray (*Quincy's Reports*, 474) implies that this was a
mistaken transcription of "a threat of *Chatham*'s in 1766, in case Americans should deny
the power of Parliament over their trade." But an article in *BEP* 5 August 1754 (on the
Massachusetts excise bill: *cf.* chapter 7) has this: "If it should ever be the unhappy fate of
the plantations to be restrained from manufacturing so much as an horse-shoe nail, as has
formerly been proposed by a bill in parliament, will not the most effectual way of enforcing
such an act be to oblige every inhabitant who keeps an horse, to swear every six months,
that all the nails which have been used in his shoes were the manufacture of *Great Britain*?"
(Governor Bernard to Lord Shelburne on Massachusetts manufactures, 24 March 1768:
"There has been an attempt to make nails; it is found they cannot be brought within a
saleable price": British Library, King's MSS, 206.)
 As the text implies, this 1818 passage is probably indicative of Adams having his
contemporaneous notes before him and occasionally using them: the Abstract has nothing
corresponding to the "Iron Manufacture . . ." fragment. *Cf.* pp. 381-82.

A rag-bag attitude to the notes seems to have set in. Whereas the snippets on iron manufacture and sending horses to England to be shod were junked for the Abstract write-up, the notes next following — if following is the word for something so fragmented and inconsequential — were not so much omitted as plundered:

If an officer will justify under a Writ he must return it. 12th Mod. 396 — perpetual Writ

occurs in the midst of the postfabricated rhetoric with which the Abstract depicts Otis slamming the general writ of assistance all over the field: "IT IS PERPETUAL; there's no return, a man is accountable to no person for his doings, every man may reign secure in his petty tyranny . . . ." Likewise the notes

Stat. C.2. We have all as good Rt to inform as Custom House officers — & every Man may have a general, irreturnable Commission to break Houses. —

clearly were used as base material for the Abstract tirade which had Otis insisting that "EVERY PERSON by 14th of Car. II. HAS THIS POWER as well as Custom-house officers . . . . Every man prompted by revenge, ill humour or wantonness to inspect the inside of his neighbour's house, may get a writ of assistance; others will ask it from self defence; one arbitrary exertion will provoke another, until society will be involved in tumult and in blood. — Again these writs ARE NOT RETURNED . . . ." Why the products of Adams's on-the-spot labors should have been so misused in the Abstract is hard to say: perhaps by now they were so scrappy as to be thought fit for nothing better. However, they are not without value as indicators of Otis's developing dialectic.

"If an officer will justify under a Writ he must return it. 12th. Mod. 396" is taken from *Freeman v. Bluet,* decided in 1700 to the broad effect that execution of a court process was a defense to an action (in trespass, for example) only if there had been a report back to the court on completion of the assignment. By going on to speak of a "perpetual Writ" Otis may have accentuated the incompatibility between the *Freeman v. Bluet* doctrine and a writ of assistance that could be used repeatedly; but he can hardly have overlooked the extensive reach of a more fundamental dissonance. It was axiomatic that the writ of assistance that bade an anonymous miscellany of persons to aid the customs man could not be returned, because the responsibility could not be pinned down to one identifiable individual. But if the special writ of assistance that Otis was urging on the court differed from the general writ only in being valid for the one sworn occasion, the same objection would apply. It would be just as impracticable that this special writ, similarly addressed to a nameless multitude, should be the subject of a return. Yet the notes record Otis as saying: "If an officer will justify under a Writ he must return it." Evidently the writ of assistance he had in mind must be susceptible of a return, which implies that it could not be simply the old-style writ tailored for one-time-only use.

It would also tie in that the Otisian special writ of assistance should reflect the sentiment in the other note, "Stat. C.2. We have all as good Rt. to inform as Custom House officers — & every Man may have a general, irreturnable Commission to break Houses." This was extravagantly put: one of the few authentic touches of rhetoric to come through in the notes. Otis seems to have been asserting the common law position that it was open to anyone, private persons as well as customs officers, to make and prosecute customs seizures, from which it followed (since seizure was the object of writ of assistance entry and search) that the words of the 1662 act which allowed writ of assistance search "to any Person or Persons" meant literally what they said. He was wrong in this, for, in the first place, the 1662 act in effect limited its search power to customs officers by overriding the common law on seizures broadly to this same degree; and, secondly, the provision in the Act of Frauds of 1696 which supposedly extended the 1662 mode of search to America was clear — however obscure it may have been in other respects — that it applied to customs officers only. It was also a slip that the notes spoke of everyone having a (customs officer's) "Commission": obviously the word should have been "writ." However, the point is not that Otis's complaint of the writ of assistance being available to every Tom, Dick, or Harry was misconceived. It is that the new-style writ he advocated would need to be manifestly free not only from the vice of irreturnability but from this objection too.

Despite their cavalier treatment in the Abstract these two paragraphs of notes afford a glimpse of an important element in the position Otis was taking. And it was as if the weary hand of John Adams was activated again, even though only momentarily, by the apprehension of something really significant now being said. Otis was making it clear that his commitment was not to a writ of assistance on the model of Brown's *breve,* rendered down to one-time-only use.

Consistently with the drubbing he gave that unsatisfactory document earlier in his speech, he was breaking away from it altogether. The new-style writ would be substantially different.

But what should actually be the form and terms of the new, special, writ of assistance? Otis could not simply argue at large for a new-style writ, offering no positive specifications for it. The business before the court was not an exercise in academic jurisprudence. The customs were asking to be issued with the usual kind of general writ, good for the reign of George III; Otis was arguing that they should have special writs instead, and as a matter of plain practicality he needed to be ready with a reasonably precise description of the document he wished the court to approve for issuance.

Otis was in a peculiar difficulty. It was not a matter of sitting down and drafting something of his own invention and hoping it would do. His entire argument had been based on the proposition, suggested by the *London Magazine* article, that in England the writ of assistance was special and not general. A separate writ for each and every customs search implied a document so common that its text must be well settled and established. Inasmuch as the special writ of assistance Otis hoped to see introduced in Massachusetts were warranted by English practice the drafting of it could not be left to local invention. He needed to know what the English writ said, in order that the new Massachusetts writ might conform. The lay journalism of the *London Magazine* had nothing of such technicality, of course; and, as both Otis and Thacher had discovered, information on the writ was not plentiful in legal writings either.

It so happens that the final sentences of the Abstract illuminate, in a rather opaque way, how Otis tackled this culminating problem. Having declared that "No Acts of Parliament can establish such a writ" (as the general writ of assistance), he proceeded thus:

> But these prove no more than what I before observed, that *special* writs may be granted *on oath* and *probable suspicion*. The Act of 7th, and 8th of William III. that the officers of the plantations shall have the same powers, &c. is confined to this sense, that an officer should show probable grounds, should take his oath on it, should do this before a magistrate, and that such magistrate, if he thinks proper should issue a *special warrant* to a constable to search the places. That of 6th of Anne can prove no more.

By "these" acts Otis presumably meant all those he identified as having a bearing on the writ of assistance: the 1660 search warrant act, perhaps, and the Act of Frauds of 1662 with which writ of assistance search originated in England, as well as the two he specifically mentioned, namely, the Act of Frauds of 1696 (for a replica English-style customs enforcement regime in America) and the act of 1702 (for giving a six-month reprieve to various legal instruments, writ of assistance among them, from automatic expiry on the death of the monarch). Having explicitly affirmed that none of these acts was inconsistent with his contention that the writ should be *"special"* and *"granted on oath and probable suspicion,"* he proceeded to spell out a more itemized discipline for superimposition upon entry and search under, in particular, the Act of Frauds of 1696: "an officer should show probable grounds, should take his oath on it, should do this before a magistrate, and . . . such magistrate, if he thinks proper should issue a *special warrant* to a constable to search the places." In these words lies the key to where Otis turned for the precedent he needed.

One remembers the specimen English customs search warrant set forth in *Conductor Generalis,* the manual for justices of the peace widely used in America. This warrant was mentioned in chapter 4 in connection with the customs search warrant act of 1660, and again in chapter 7 as the likely inspiration for Governor William Shirley's customs search warrants in the earlier 1750s; a reproduction of it is in Appendix D. Here was Otis's precedent. The Abstract speaks of Otis's "special warrant" as directed to a constable; the *Conductor Generalis* warrant was addressed "To the Constables of . . . ." Otis spoke of the customs officer taking the oath for the warrant, and so it was in *Conductor Generalis.* Otis's customs officer must "show probable grounds" for issuance of the warrant; the *Conductor Generalis* warrant recited various factual circumstances, "all which being considered, there is good Reason to suspect that the said *John Badblood* hath concealed Liquors . . . ." Under the Otis warrant it would be for the constable "to search the places": this was probably a misreading of the unsatisfactorily worded *Conductor Generalis* warrant, which at first sight implied that the constable rather than the customs man was in charge of the search operation and that another house besides Badblood's was to be gone through.

In the perspective that Otis envisioned the *Conductor Generalis* warrant as the model for his special writ of assistance quite a lot of other material falls into place. Obviously, an instrument of this kind, addressed not to an anonymous miscellany of persons but to a particular constable, would be susceptible of a return, which immunized it from one of the most strident of Otis's objections to the previous writ of asssistance. And since it would be inconsistent with the nature of a returnable warrant that the constable to whom the warrant was directed should be free to transfer its obligations to someone else, the disagreeable possibility of all manner of lowly or nondescript persons intruding on to private property would effectively disappear. A warrant or writ on *Conductor Generalis* lines would not place "the liberty of every man in the hands of every petty officer"; it would not be "UNIVERSAL . . . directed 'to all and singular justices, sheriffs, constables and all other officers and subjects &c' "; or "PERPETUAL"; or signify a power of entry and search exercisable "AT WILL." In sum, the document which Otis described at the end of the Abstract would avoid all the vices of the general writ of assistance he had catalogued in the course of it.

However, adoption of the *Conductor Generalis* warrant was not without its own problems. It might be the nearest to a special writ of assistance that could be found in available published sources, but a man of Otis's perspicacity would not have felt entirely comfortable about it. Aside from anything else, it obviously partook more of the old 1660 customs search warrant act than of the provision for writ of assistance search in the Act of Frauds of 1662. Although the Abstract is silent on this awkward circumstance, how Otis coped is discernible in John Adams's next notes. Again, perhaps, a sense of the importance of what Otis was now saying overcame the fatigue in Adams's hand:

> By 12. of C. on oath before Ld Treasurer, Barons of Exchequer, or Chief Magistrate to break with an officer. – 14th. C. to issue a Warrant requiring sheriffs &c to assist the officers to search for Goods not entrd, or prohibitd; 7 & 8th. W. & M. gives Officers in Plantations same Powers with officers in England. –
>
> Continuance of Writts and Proscesses, proves no more nor so much as I grant a special Writ of ass. on special oath, for specl Purpose. –
>
> Pew indorsd Warrant to Ware . . . .

Unlike the corresponding piece at the end of the Abstract, these notes show little of the text of the *Conductor Generalis* warrant coming through. What they do show, though, is how Otis rationalized the *Conductor Generalis* warrant into an acceptable instrument for customs search under the Act of Frauds of 1662. The notes begin with a reference to the customs search warrant act of 1660, which authorized the Lord Treasurer, a baron of the exchequer, or the local chief magistrate to administer oaths for the issuance of warrants "thereby enabling... [the holder] ... with the Assistance of a Sheriff, Justice of Peace, or Constable, ... to enter into any House ... and in Case of Resistance to break open such Houses ..." in search of dutiable goods "landed or conveyed away without due Entry ...." Next the notes speak of the Act of Frauds of 1662. But it is not the 1662 act's writ of assistance, attendant local "Constable, Headborough or other publick Officer," and pursuit of "prohibited and uncustomed" goods, that they proceed to spell out. Instead it is a "Warrant," "sheriffs &c," and "Goods not entrd, or prohibitd." This was mostly the vocabulary of the 1660 act, with only the "prohibitd" category of pursuable goods to keep the 1662 act with a foot in its own camp. Otis's frame of thinking seems plain enough. He was reading the two enactments as one, so as to be able to contend that the *Conductor Generalis* warrant which may have proceeded originally from the 1660 act served the purpose of the 1662 act also.

Horace Gray approved of Otis having "argued that the writ of assistance mentioned in St. 13 & 14 Car.,2 [the 1662 act] must be special, according to St. 12 Car. 2 [the 1660 act] ...'"; as Gray saw it, "upon the ordinary rules of interpreting statutes *in pari materia* together, and according to the rule and reason of the common law, the conclusion of *Otis* seems inevitable."[44] As for the "rule and reason of the common law," it perhaps was a fair guess that Otis brought his *Bonham's Case* line of argument into play again: inasmuch as the "Reason of the Comn Law to control an Act of Parliament" was manifested in the search warrant provisions of 1660 and ought to apply equally to the 1662 power, the same apparatus of control — centering upon a sworn statement — might serve here too. But the other factor in Gray's analysis, that the enactments of 1660 and 1662 were *in pari materia*, is less plausible. As chapter 4 labored to demonstrate, the 1660 search warrant act and the writ of assistance power of search in the Act of Frauds of 1662 were very far from being in like case.

Otis himself appears to have had second thoughts about the 1660-1662 assimilation. When the Abstract came to be written it was no longer the enactment of 1662 that fell to be governed by the 1660 disciplines as woven into the *Conductor Generalis* warrant, but

44. See p. 280 above.

"The Act of 7th, and 8th of William III," namely, the Act of Frauds of 1696. The general objective of the 1696 act was to set up in America a replica of the customs enforcement regime that existed in England under the Act of Frauds of 1662, and when it came to power of search on land generalization was all that the 1696 act expressed. Section 6 neither repeated the specifics of 1662 nor incorporated them by reference. The loose wording it employed to convey the impression that customs officers in America were to have writ of assistance search 1662-style was more accommodating to Otis's purpose than the explicit prescriptions of 1662 had been. The 1696 text's very meaninglessness rendered it capable of being "confined" to the sense of the 1660 act and the *Conductor Generalis* warrant, whereas the 1662 provision was too sharply and too differently drawn for this. Besides, it was a point of legitimate dialectical advantage that, although its principal object was little more than to extend the 1662 act to America, the 1696 act was the one that had direct application there. It could be that Otis shifted his ground from 1662 to 1696 with a fall-back purpose in mind. If after he had won and the *Conductor Generalis* precedent was in use it somehow transpired that the authentic English writ of assistance was in fact different, he could retort that this did not matter, for the 1696 law for America and the 1662 law for England were not the same.

Possibly, Otis's shift of ground went wider. The counterpart in the notes to the Abstract's concluding sentence, "That of 6th of Anne can prove no more," has him saying, "Continuance of Writts and Proscesses, proves no more nor so much as I grant special Writ of ass. on special oath, for specl Purpose." The argument here is of course that all references in statute — in this case the act of 1702 postponing the expiry of "Writs and Proscesses" — to the writ of assistance were consistent with the writ being special rather than general; but the present point of interest is that Otis spoke of a "writ" of assistance. In the corresponding place in the Abstract he speaks of a "warrant." On the face of it, this change could suggest that just as Otis was now identifying the 1696 act rather than the 1662 act with the search warrant act of 1660, he had also abandoned all pretense that the *Conductor Generalis* warrant was an acceptable form of writ of assistance; in other words, he had dropped the writ of assistance along with the act that bespoke it, so that the *Conductor Generalis* document could be seen and spoken of for what it was, a warrant associated with the act of 1660 and equally applicable, as a manifestation of the "reason of the common law," to the specifically American orientation of the act of 1696.

Although the Abstract rendition of Otis's speech was now concluded, John Adams's notes give a little more.

> Pew indorsd Warrant to Ware. — Justice Walley searc'd House. Law Prov. Bill in Chancery. — this Court confined their Chancery Power to Revenue &c.

With these fragments the notes themselves come to an end.

The first sentence obviously corresponds to the Abstract's apocryphal anecdote about Nathaniel Ware of the Boston custom house, having obtained a writ of assistance originally issued to Jonathan Pue, misusing it to search the house of Justice Abiel Walley for reasons of personal pique. It represents yet another example of the Abstract (where the anecdote occurred not at the end but somewhere in the middle) raiding the notes for oddments of fill-in material. Adams's jottings are by now so scrappy that conjecture on how the tale of Pue, Ware, and Walley fitted into the argument as actually delivered gets to be pretty desperate. A possibility is suggested, however, by Otis's speaking about a warrant, not a writ of assistance. Conceivably there had been a search of Walley's house in the early 1750s under one of the gubernatorial customs search warrants then in use: the original holder, Pue (perhaps on his move from Boston to Salem), having made it over to Ware. On the evidence of Thomas Hutchinson's *History of Massachusets-Bay* it was on account of the illegality of such warrants the writ of assistance had been introduced. Otis's intention may have been to underline to the court that the warrant or writ he was arguing for should not be a throwback to the old gubernatorial warrant, and its obnoxious generality.[45]

---

45. *Cf.* p. 345 above.

This fragment's Abstract counterpart (p. 000) shows Otis protesting endorsement and negotiability from one customs officer to another, in relation to a writ of assistance. In that the Massachusetts writ specified the customs officer entitled to the assistance, the protest had a superficial validity. But it was not the customs officer to whom the writ actually addressed itself: the writ looked for its execution to the anonymous miscellany of his putative "assistants." There was no statutory requirement that the writ specify the customs officer to be assisted; and the true logic of the matter was better served by current English practice, under which (*cf.* Appendix C) this was not in fact done and questions of endorsement and negotiability therefore could not arise. Similar observations would apply if, as the notes fragment indicates, Otis had in reality been talking about a warrant, and if the warrant was addressed to a collectivity of constables, on the *Conductor Generalis* model. (*Cf.* pp. 119-20 also, however, 369-70.)

The other fragment is not reflected anywhere in the Abstract. It is of interest nevertheless. Clearly it had to do with that jurisdictional point upon which Oxenbridge Thacher had founded his argument against writs of assistance of any kind, special as well as general. According to Thacher, only an exchequer court had authority to issue the writ; under an act of the province the Superior Court was entitled to sit as an exchequer court, but in the case of *McNeal v. Brideoak* (1754) it had declined to allow a private litigant to invoke the equitable jurisdiction that went with exchequer court status. This meant, Thacher had argued, that the court had disqualified itself for issuance of writs of assistance, for refusal of exchequer jurisdiction in the one case meant total renunciation of it in all. Otis's willingness to settle for a special writ of assistance was altogether less radical, his noisy oratorical fireworks notwithstanding, and this last fragment of his speech shows him as positively on the side of moderation. It was not to echo Thacher that he said that "this Court confined their Chancery Power to Revenue &c." Rather he was affirming that the Superior Court had not renounced its status as a court of exchequer in *McNeal v. Brideoak;* and, moreover, that it still possessed "Chancery Power" at any rate in matters of revenue. Later on, when both men were members of the House of Representatives, Otis tended to treat Thacher "in so overbearing and indecent a manner that he was obliged at times to call upon the speaker to interpose and protect him."[46] It could be that an element of upstaging crept into Otis's attitude to Thacher in the writs of assistance hearing. Victory against the custom house was bound to do him good politically; all the same he could not afford to share too much of the credit. While his comparatively soft line for a modified writ of assistance might stand a better chance, success for Thacher's more all-out attack could not be discounted altogether; and it was not entirely in Otis's interest to help that possibility along.

Suspicion of impure motive must not be carried too far. Behind Otis's conservative interpretation of *McNeal v. Brideoak* there may have been another, and more respectable, concern. The point has to do with custom house bonds, an everyday feature of maritime commerce. Against the event that some specified requirement of customs law were not complied with, a merchant (or whoever) would bind himself to the king to pay a certain sum of money if evidence of compliance were not produced within a stated period. However,

---

46. C. K. Shipton, *Sibley's Harvard Graduates* X (Boston, 1958), 324.

equity doctrine frowned upon penalties unrelated to the injury actually suffered, and a court of equity jurisdiction would "chancer" them down accordingly. In the ordinary way there was no problem here. Although Massachusetts did not have a court of chancery, the normal forum for equity process, legislation had empowered the common law courts to allow certain equity-type remedies, including the chancering of bonds. There was a peculiar snag, however, which a lawyer as acute as Otis would have been conscious of. According to contemporary opinion in England, equitable relief against the crown was available nowhere but in a court of exchequer jurisdiction;[47] and the only such court in Massachusetts was the Superior Court. If, as Oxenbridge Thacher contended, *McNeal v. Brideoak* meant that the Superior Court had relinquished the whole of its exchequer jurisdiction, sooner or later customs officers, claiming bond penalties on the king's behalf, would assert immunity from chancering and insist on payment in full. Otis had his merchant clientele to think of. Hence, probably, his correction of Thacher, in terms (*sc.*, "Revenue &c") indicative of a continuing exchequer jurisdiction over custom house bond penalties in the Superior Court.

Why Otis's shrewd handling of the implications of *McNeal v. Brideoak* received no mention in the Abstract can only be guessed at. Possibly it was considered too technical. And, by when the Abstract was written up it may well have been clear that the Thacher argument had cut no ice anyway (if the judges had been persuaded by it they surely would have come down against the customs absolutely and at once; as it was they postponed a decision pending information from England). The Superior Court thus having indicated that it had not abandoned the whole of its exchequer jurisdiction, Otis's argument on the subject no longer had any practical relevance.

John Adams's notes peter out on a technical point about equity jurisdiction in the Superior Court, and the Abstract stops dead with a reference to Queen Anne's legislation for postponing the automatic expiry of writs and so forth on the demise of the crown. In neither is there the remotest trace of a culminating storm of eloquence to account for Adams's old-age recollection of a crowded audience inspired to go away, as he himself claimed to have done, "ready to take up Arms against Writs of Assistants." With the notes this is

---

47. Holdsworth, *HEL* IX, 30, citing *Reeve v. A-G* (1741) 2 Atkyns 33; *Burgess v. Wheate* 1 Eden at 255-56; and Blackstone's *Commentaries* III.

understandable: Adams was by now too weary to keep on writing. But he was under no such strain with the Abstract; if he grew tired he had only to stop, and start up again later. Instead, he simply signed off.

At the end of the Abstract rendition of the Otis speech the tailpiece is added (in Joseph Hawley's transcript):

> The court suspended the absolute determination of this matter. I have omitted many authorities; also many fine touches in the order of reasoning, and numberless Rhetorical and popular flourishes.

Full marks for candor anyway. Even the few authorities that did get into the Abstract tended to be out of focus: Oxenbridge Thacher's reference to "an Authority from Strange" (*Horne v. Boosey*), for example, and Otis's "Vid. Viner," an inexact citation of *Bonham's Case;* then too the all-important *Swallow's Case* from Hale's *History of the Pleas of the Crown* was blurred almost to invisibility. The "order of reasoning," Gridley's and Otis's both, lost not merely "fine touches" but much of its articulation and true sequence: there was the puzzle of one speech by Gridley in the Abstract when from the notes there appear to have been two; and important passages of Otis's argument are either exceedingly difficult to follow or — as in the case of his attempt to link the writ of assistance enactment of 1662 to the search warrant act of 1660 — are left out altogether.

It is harder, however, to know what to make of the third element in Adams's litany of omissions, "numberless Rhetorical and popular flourishes." On Thacher the Abstract is terse, but so are the notes. Gridley was reckoned a poor speaker, and the substantial reconstruction that his contribution indisputably underwent may have meant not a loss in color and flourish but net gain. Adams presumably had Otis in mind. And this despite all the declamatory barnstorming of which there is scarcely any sign in the contemporaneous notes. The suggestion is, then, that if the Abstract rendition of Otis went easy on the rhetoric it can have been only at the end. Again relevant is Adams's recollection of going away at the end of the hearing exultant at what he had just been listening to from Otis. It is a recollection that rings true. However fitfully and imperfectly, Adams had the Otis speech in his head for the rest of his long and eventful life; at the actual time there surely was something about it that hit him hard. It is not to be believed that Otis was so unaware of the effect his speech was having as to spoil it by sitting down without any sort of peroration. Abstract-Otis ends abruptly, on a minor point

of technical argument: "That of 6th of Anne can prove no more."
Not much peroration in that. The conclusion seems reasonable that
the omission of "Rhetorical and popular flourishes" related to Otis,
and principally if not solely to a final volley of vibrant oratory.

The hypothesis throughout this chapter and the last has been that
although the actual penmanship of the Abstract rendition of the Otis
speech probably was John Adams's own, Otis himself may well have
supplied the mass of supplementary material which had no place in
Adams's original notes. Anticipation of the Abstract getting into
print in celebration of victory might equally have moved Otis to a
measure of superintendence over how the young man actually
presented the great debate. After all, a publicity-conscious politician
of Otis's sharp intelligence would not have failed to see problems of
projection, focus, and emphasis if his own contribution to the
triumph were to appear in suitably advantageous perspective. The
line of argument that Otis adopted was not really the stuff of which
heroic postures of defiance were made. While it was true that the
one-time-only writ of assistance he had urged upon the court would
have been of little use to the customs authorities (since in the time
needed to obtain a writ the things to be searched for would probably
be moved elsewhere), it was also too subtle. To the man in the street
(or the average newspaper reader) with no special interest in the less
obvious aspects of customs enforcement practice, a mode of opposition that countenanced a writ of assistance of any kind might look
soft and wanting in thrust. The writs of assistance case, with the
scope it afforded for populist and libertarian excitations, may have
been ideal for a lawyer out to make a quick political name; but, at
any rate the way Otis played it, it could easily have gone sour. His
essentially moderate position, shrewdly attuned to the temper of the
court though it was, and for all the professionalism it evidenced, was
not what the lay public would expect to see from a man of real fire.
Otis's concern to avoid the image of a trimmer could explain quite a
lot about the Abstract.

The Abstract obviously could not, and in fact did not, suppress all
reference to Otis's commendation of the special writ of assistance,
the true substance of his speech. But this politically delicate material
was not conspicuously on view. If anything, it almost has to be
looked for. Various factors come into this. Omission of "many
authorities; also many fine touches in the order of reasoning" necessarily meant that passages of argument were shorter than they would

otherwise have been. And they also lost vertical dimension, as it were: had the Abstract spoken out about Hale's *History of the Pleas of the Crown, Swallow's Case,* and so forth, there would have been a highlighting effect. The actual effect was just the opposite. Such allusions to the special writ of assistance as did come through − they were only two, and widely spaced at that − were cast in shadow. In terms of gripping the reader's attention they were far too feeble to compete with those vivid set pieces of oratory which occupied so much more space, and whose flash and dazzle so filled the eye. It could be conjectured, moreover, that the camouflage was not limited to the rendition of Otis's own speech. How meagerly the Abstract treats of the speech of Oxenbridge Thacher may signify more than just fidelity to the record in John Adams's notes. Sandwiched between Gridley and Otis, both of whom are accorded oratorical frills and furbelows − lavishly in the case of Otis − Thacher gets markedly the least space of the three, and his contribution to the debate comes through almost as colorlessly as the Otis text's muted references to special writs. On the evidence considered in chapter 14 it may truly have been that way. All the same, one cannot help wondering whether Otis's superintendence of the Abstract would not have made quite sure that the Thacher challenge to writs of assistance of whatever kind, in appearance so much more full-blooded than his own willingness to settle for a scaled-down writ, received suitably low-key treatment. As with the equivocal ambiguities in the Abstract's write-up of Jeremiah Gridley, the signs of accentuation to the advantage of Otis seem too pronounced to have been entirely accidental.

A loose end remaining, and the more obtrusively if Otis took a hand with the Abstract, is the peroration that was left out. This is not much of a problem, however. The Abstract was prepared when the ultimate outcome of the writs of assistance case was not yet known. Written in anticipation of victory over the custom house the Abstract may have been; but victory in what terms? Otis's terms − the spavined one-time-only writ − probably enough, but there was no absolute certainty: for instance, and however unexpectedly, the decision might partake of the more root-and-branch attack of Oxenbridge Thacher. Otis may therefore have withheld his counsel from John Adams at the end of the argument proper, preferring that the construction of the final phase of his more or less postfabricated speech be postponed for tailoring according to the event.

In a refracted way, a sidelight falls on a far more difficult riddle: how the writs of assistance case that impressed John Adams so strongly in February 1761, and which he was to extol so fervently late in life, should have totally failed to register with him when it came up again in November. Preoccupation with affairs at Braintree was a guess in chapter 12, and this second shot will not venture much deeper: the old saw of lawyers, "the Devil himself knoweth not the mind of man,"[48] packs a lot of sense still. Yet it does seem possible to see Adams's strange mental foul-up in some sort of context, if not pattern. In later years he repeatedly appears as thinking poorly of the Abstract: "those despicable Notes," he once called them (not bothering, even, to differentiate the Abstract and his contemporaneous jottings); when it was stolen — or so he alleged — for use in the *Massachusetts Spy* in 1773 he seemingly made no attempt to get it back. Altogether, it is as though he never quite rehabilitated the Abstract after the episode with Colonel Josiah Quincy in the spring of 1761, when (as shown by the longish quotation from his diary on page 290) he was provoked into a savage and brooding resentment by Quincy's pretending to believe, with expressions of transparently bogus praise, that, alone and unaided, he had worked a miracle of stylistic restatement. John Adams was not one of nature's dissemblers, and perhaps his consciousness of invention — not to say falsification — carried beyond reasonable journalistic license sharpened the sting of the colonel's raillery all the more. Long afterward Adams was to disown some of Abstract-Otis's purpler patches, declaring them to be interpolations; but it may be the truth that, as a lawyer, he had at no time felt wholly at peace with the Abstract's representation of a court proceeding. In this perspective there may be something more to see in the missing Abstract-Otis peroration. Otis's guidance having paused at the end of the argument proper, Adams possibly welcomed the respite from further creative writing. After the Quincy trauma he may have been only too ready to let the entire business go, and forget it — at any rate until the passage of years had made recollection of it less uncomfortable.

So much for the Otis speech according to John Adams's notes and Abstract, with additional perspective supplied by Thomas Hutchinson's *History of Massachusets-Bay*. It remains to look at that version of the speech which, fifty-seven years afterward, the aged former

48. (1477) Y.B. 17 Edw. 4, Pasch. f. 2, pl. 2, *per* Brian C. J.

president of the United States set forth in a series of letters, for incorporation in William Tudor's biography of Otis. Not a great deal is to be expected. This long-distance reconstruction was largely factitious — though factitious in a different way from the Abstract. The Abstract smacked of journalism, written with an eye to the immediate political situation. The letters of 1818 show Adams more or ˙less confessedly in the posture of those authors of classical antiquity who acted as *post factum* speechwriters for their historical characters. His aim now was to get the memory of Otis scored into the national consciousness: of all states of the Union and of all patriot prophets anywhere, none had been quicker off the mark toward revolution than Massachusetts and James Otis. However uneasy Adams may have felt about the Abstract and its extravagances, this new relation to his subject enabled him in good conscience to make fairly free with literal fact and to put into Otis's mouth as eloquent and impressive a discourse as could be thought up. Precedent and justification in the classics were easily come by. "As to the speeches of particular persons . . . whether such as I heard myself or such as were repeated to me by others, I will not pretend to recite them in all their exactness," said Thucydides, "It hath been my method to consider principally what might be pertinently said upon every occasion to the points in debate, and to keep as near as possible to what would pass for genuine by universal consent." [49] If the great historian of ancient Greece did not handle Pericles' funeral oration as a straight reporting job, John Adams (who claimed to have read him over and over to the point of weariness) [50] could equally legitimately romanticize Otis's writs of assistance speech for the annals of revolutionary America.

According to the several "heads of discourse" with which Adams prefaced his reminiscences, Otis began with "an exordium, containing an apology for his resignation of the office of Advocate-General . . . ." [51] To that extent Adams followed the Abstract, if not his notes. But the other heads had not a particle of warrant in either: a "dissertation on the rights of man in a state of nature" and in

49. W. Smith's translation (London, 1781), in W. O. Clough, *Intellectual Origins of American National Thought* (New York, 1961), 25.

50. "I have read Thucidides and Tacitus, so often, and at such distant Periods of my Life, that elegant, profound and enchanting as is their Style, I am weary of them . . .": Adams to Thomas Jefferson, 3 February 1812, in L. J. Cappon, ed., *The Adams-Jefferson Letters* (New York, 1971), 295.

51. *LWJA* X, 314, 1 June 1818.

society; how these rights had been enshrined in "the old Saxon laws" and in Magna Carta and were not to be subverted "by any phantom of 'virtual representation' "; and how the acts of trade, grounded in "necessity" (an echo of Jeremiah Gridley's argument here), were now being enforced as revenue laws, in plain confutation of the theoretical distinction between external and internal taxes. Adams was pressing into service points of argument not yet heard of in 1761.

Through a dozen long letters Adams had Otis elaborating on the acts of trade, with further anachronistic borrowings from controversies yet to happen. Copious extracts from this legislation were painstakingly retailed, among them the 1662 provision for writ of assistance search. What, Adams asked, were writs of assistance:

> Where were they to be found? When, where and by what authority had they been invented, created, and established? Nobody could answer any of these questions. Neither Chief Justice Hutchinson, nor any one of his four associate judges, pretended to have ever read or seen in any book any such writ, or to know anything about it. The court had ordered or requested the bar to search for precedents and authorities for it, but none were found. Otis pronounced boldly that there were none, and neither judge nor lawyer, bench or bar, pretended to confute him. He asserted farther, that there was no color of authority for it, but one produced by Mr. Gridley in a statute of the 13th and 14th of Charles II, which Mr. Otis said was neither authority, precedent or color of either in America. Mr. Thacher said he had diligently searched all the books, but could find no such writ. He had indeed found in Rastall's Entries a thing which in some of its features resembled this, but so little like it on the whole, that it was not worth while to read it.

In the Act of Frauds of 1662 was "all the color for 'writs of assistance' which the officers of the crown, aided by the researches of their learned counsel, Mr. Gridley, could produce"; and

> Where, exclaimed Otis, is your seal of his Majesty's court of exchequer? And what has the court of exchequer to do here?[52]

Again on exchequer jurisdiction, in another letter:

> Could it be pretended, that the superior court of judicature . . . had all the powers of the court of exchequer in England . . . ? No custom-house officer dared to say this, or to instruct his counsel to say it.[53]

It is apparent from these pieces that Adams paid scant regard even to his own contemporary sources of evidence, the notes and the Abstract

52. *Ibid.*, 322-23, 17 June 1818.
53. *Ibid.*, 341-42, 6 August 1818.

(the former still in his possession and the latter sufficiently reproduced in Minot's *History*). For example, those sources show all three
advocates commenting upon the precedent of a customs writ of
assistance in William Brown's book on exchequer practice, but who
would have thought it from what Adams was now saying? Rastell's
Entries was mentioned in both notes and Abstract; but by Gridley,
not by Thacher. And Otis is on view more as adopting Thacher's
total denial of exchequer jurisdiction in the Superior Court than as
tempering it. And, far from the custom house not daring to invoke
such jurisdiction, the Abstract shows their spokesman, Gridley, doing
that very thing.

   The letters to Tudor reflect considerable diligence by the old
statesman in fields outside the law as well as within. Otis is depicted
as dilating, usually in implausible detail, on various nonlegal treatises
on the mercantilist philosophy and theories that went with the acts
of trade: works of Josiah Child and Charles Davenant, for example,
which included decidedly uncomplimentary references to the sorts of
people who became colonials. A miscellany of writers, monarchs, and
others received critical mention for "conspiring to make the people
of North America hewers of wood and drawers of water to plantation governors, custom-house officers, judges of admiralty, common
informers, West India planters, naval commanders . . . ." [54] References were made to bits and pieces of legislation with some sort of
bearing on the subject in hand. The Molasses Act of 1733 had the
better part of two letters to itself, yet its contribution to the writ of
assistance trouble in 1760-61 cannot have been more than peripheral.

   Little of this ranging material is to be seen in Adams's contemporaneous notes or near-contemporaneous Abstract. An extract
from one of the letters to Tudor was quoted earlier for illumination
of the notes' brief reference to the 1750 act which restricted iron
manufacture in America. And conceivably it could have been the
Bonham's Case line of ratiocination that accounted for:

> Mr. Otis roundly asserted this whole system of parliamentary regula-
> tions, and every act of Parliament before quoted, to be illegal, unconsti-
> tutional, tyrannical, null, and void. [55]

On the other hand, accompanying text suggests that the inspiration
for this was not authentic writs of assistance case material, but Otis's
1764 paper against revenue legislation from Westminster, in which he

54. *Ibid.*, 349, 21 August 1818.
55. *Ibid.*, 351.

included *Bonham's Case* as part of his armament. Besides, it had not been Otis's purpose in 1761 to argue that even so much as the legislation on writs of assistance was void, let alone the "whole system" of imperial trade regulation.

Though most of the story of the Otis speech as told by Adams in 1818 was imagination on the loose, not everything without a counterpart in the 1761 documentation was invention, or memory playing tricks. And while it is true that Adams's knowledge of the writs of assistance case remained extraordinarily imperfect over the years it does not follow that no absolutely genuine memories of the case lodged in his mind, which for some reason had not been noted down or put into the Abstract. A possible instance is in a letter where Tudor was told of Otis causing much amusement on the subject of search powers in an act of 1660, for the regulation of baize manufacture in the English town of Colchester.[56] If, as was suggested earlier, Otis consulted the *Historical Collections* of John Rushworth he could have read a quaint story of how, back in a time when Colchester baize-making was controlled by conciliar process, the punishment of a violator of the regime, one Thomas Jupp, included a spell in the pillory "with a Paper on his Head, wherein shall be described Words declaring the nature of his Offence," to the discouragement, it was hoped, of "other like lewd Persons."[57] Not specially high grade comedy, perhaps, but the sort of thing Otis might have lighted upon to jolly things along a little. John Adams's recollection of goings-on at the Colchester Bay hall making "sport for Otis and his audience" has a ring of truth about it. A man raising a laugh out of material on the writs of assistance case would have been something to remember.

In general, though, the letters to Tudor are all but valueless as additional evidence to Adams's on-the-spot notes and the Abstract. The foregoing sketch of the Adams reminiscences obviously is not exhaustive, but nowhere in them is to be found even a trace of Otis's central theme: the acceptability of a writ of assistance limited to the one sworn and specified occasion. The discursiveness attributed to Otis in the letters — the lengthy sorties into mercantilist theory, for instance — prompts the same comment as the breast-beating fustian at the beginning of the Abstract rendition: this was not the kind of thing that an advocate of Otis's professional standing would have

56. *Ibid.,* 323-24, 24 June 1818.
57. Vol. III (London, 1721), 102-5.

spouted forth in the highest court in the province; hot air on such a scale would have evoked nothing so much as drumming of fingers on the table and swiveling of eyes to the ceiling.

But to complain that what John Adams wrote in 1818 was not history would be to miss the point. The ordinary standards of modern scholarship do not apply. A classical or literary form was legitimate for a man of Adams's time. More particularly, it was appropriate to his purpose: that Tudor's book should secure for Massachusetts and James Otis the honors due to them in the hagiology of the American Revolution.

Just how sound in law was the central theme of Otis's argument? This fairly exhaustive scrutiny of the materials on his speech has not forborne from critical evaluation, more or less in passing, of various bits that seemed the wrong shape or to stick out at the wrong angle. Much of the Abstract invective against the writ of assistance general in form has been seen as extravagant or misconceived. But Otis's positive proposition, that writs of assistance should be issued for the one occasion and place specifically sworn to, has yet to be judged.

In terms of the practice in England Otis was wide of the mark, as evidence from there was shortly to show. The writ of assistance currently in use was general; and while its resemblance to the *Breve Assisten' pro Officiar' Custum'* in Brown's book was not close, it bore no resemblance whatever to the *Conductor Generalis* warrant which Otis seems to have favored.

That Otis was wrong on the empirical level does not demolish his position conclusively. Although the *Conductor Generalis* warrant must be discounted as a species of special writ of assistance by which the customs officer's statutory power of entry and search were limited to one occasion and place specifically sworn to, the principle is not necessarily contradicted. The point taken by Otis remains: the Act of Frauds of 1662 did not explicitly require the writ of assistance to be general. Again, section 5(2):

> And it shall be lawful to or for any Person or Persons, authorized by Writ of Assistance under the Seal of his Majesty's Court of Exchequer, to take a Constable, Headborough or other publick Officer inhabiting near unto the Place, and in the Day-time to enter, and go into any House . . . .

For all that this text said to the contrary the writ of assistance could be good for the one sworn occasion only.

There can be no doubt, however, that the 1662 act's power of entry and search was intended to be general. Nor is this just because authoritative opinion in England was to say so (in response to American intransigence over the writs of assistance legislation of 1767). Basically it is common sense. The 1662 act required that the writ of assistance should issue from the Court of Exchequer. The location of the Court of Exchequer — in actual practice, of the office of the king's remembrancer — was London and nowhere else. England is not a large country, but it is not so small that in the seventeenth century London would have been within easy reach of every port on the coastline where search for smuggled goods might need to be made. From a northern port it might be several days' ride; twice as many there and back. One reason for the unsatisfactoriness of the customs search warrant act of 1660 probably was that the "Chief Magistrate of the Port or Place" authorized to issue the warrant might reside at an inconvenient distance. It would have been absurd if this defect, far from being eliminated, were made vastly worse by the act of 1662. Outside London, successful searches would have been few and far between if a separate writ of assistance had to be obtained for each one: the offending goods could not be relied upon to stay put till the customs officer had completed a round trip to the capital. Besides, so elaborate was the seventeenth-century writ of assistance — a portrait of the king, highly stylized Latin script, and so forth — that physical production alone took days, if not weeks. Obviously, all this could not possibly have been part of the design for a new-style customs search in 1662.

Unpracticality in special writs of assistance disfigured Otis's position as to doctrine also. The writ of assistance derived from a common law canon that permitted the invention of writs for the better implementation of a public act of Parliament. In the words of Coke, by whom the canon was formulated, a writ thus invented must be "according to the force and effect of the act." Otis's conception of the writ of assistance, an instrument for the "Reason of the Com Law to control an Act of Parliament," was an impossibility. A writ that balked rather than facilitated the statutory power of entry and search for which it was required would have conflicted with the law of its own existence.

From what has just been said it is clear that Otis did not really know what the customs writ of assistance was. Another sign was his failure to respect the wide juridical difference between the writ and a warrant. Not that Otis was alone in the dark. Chief Justice Hutchinson used writ and warrant interchangeably, and it is evident that the other judges, whose doubts about the general writ of assistance Otis made it his business to confirm, remained as uncomprehending as before. Otis's brethren at the bar betrayed nothing of having lighted upon the "secret in law" upon which the writ of assistance was founded. But fair play all round. One recalls that no less a personage of the common law than Lord Mansfield C.J., with all the best legal materials in England at his disposal, years later was uncertain enough about the writ of assistance to send off a barrister to research it (and not to appreciable result).[58]

Inasmuch as James Otis saw his task as giving color of law to the special and sworn writ of assistance spoken of in the *London Magazine* his performance was remarkable, in terms of resourceful ingenuity alone.

And, on the word of the presiding judge himself, it nearly came off. "Some of the judges . . . seemed to favour the exception" (*i.e.,* Otis's protest against the general writ), stated Thomas Hutchinson in his *History of Massachusets-Bay,* "and if judgment had been then given, it is uncertain on which side it would have been."[59] In a private letter Hutchinson put it more strongly:

> In the year 1761 application was made by the Officers of the customs to the superior court of which I was then chief justice for writs of assistance. Great opposition was made . . . and the court seemed inclined to refuse to grant them but I prevailed with my brethren to continue the cause until the next term & in the mean time wrote to England & procured a copy of the writ & sufficient evidence of the practice of Exchequer there . . . .[60]

On this testimony, Otis's speech sustained and perhaps fortified the doubt about the general writ of assistance that the puisne judges had felt all along.

That Otis did not then and there win the day owed less to the flaws in his argument (not that his opponent, Jeremiah Gridley, worked specially hard on them anyway) than to the unwillingness of Chief Justice Hutchinson to be overwhelmed.

58. See chapter 3, n. 32 and text.
59. Page 68.
60. To H. S. Conway, 1 October 1765: CO5/755; *Quincy's Reports,* 415.

17

Interval, November, and After

T HE ONLY first-hand recorder of the Superior Court's reaction to the February arguments was Chief Justice Hutchinson himself.

One version is in his *History of Massachusets-Bay.* Here Hutchinson tells how a special writ of assistance would have been acceptable to the objectors, and continues:

> The court was convinced that a writ, or warrant, to be issued only in cases where special information was given upon oath, would rarely, if ever, be applied for, as no informer would expose himself to the rage of the people. The statute of the 14th of Charles II. authorized issuing writs of assistance from the court of exchequer in England. The statutes of the 7th and 8th of William III. required all that aid to be given to the officers of the customs in the plantations, which was required by law to be given in England. Some of the judges, notwithstanding, from a doubt whether such writs were still in use in England, seemed to favour the exception, and, if judgment had been then given, it is uncertain on which side it would have been. The chief justice was, therefore, desired, by the first opportunity in his power, to obtain information of the practice in England, and judgment was suspended.[1]

Informative, though muddled. "The statutes of the 7th and 8th of William III" is a mistake for the one statute of William III, the Act of Frauds of 1696. A triviality, of course. But there is confusion, too, in what the Superior Court is said to have been "convinced" by; namely, that special writs of assistance issued on sworn information would be useless, because "no informer would expose himself to the rage of the people." Ratiocination such as this might have had something in it if the "informer" were of the Ebenezer Richardson sort, who made an income from tipping off the custom house on the whereabouts of potential seizures; probably enough the likes of Richardson would have incurred even worse unpopularity had a spotlight fallen on him every time the custom house wished to make

1. Page 68.

a search. In actuality, however, the "informer" who testified for a writ of assistance would have been the applicant customs officer who purposed to search for and seize the offending goods and get them condemned as forfeited by the legal process known as an information. The informer in this sense — a man whose initiation of a condemnation process was in no way secret or *sub rosa* — was just as identifiable by the populace whether the writ of assistance by dint of which he had made his seizure were special or general. The Superior Court judges may not have been fully trained in the law, but it is hard to believe that they knew so little, after years of experience on the bench, as not to perceive and differentiate the two meanings of "informer." Historian Hutchinson was not at his clearest here.

Despite the unpracticality of special writs of assistance, Hutchinson's *History* goes on, the court forbore from immediately reaffirming the general writ out of doubt (fortified, one supposes, by the arguments of James Otis) whether general writs continued in use in England. The impression next conveyed by the *History* is of Chief Justice Hutchinson's perplexed colleagues asking him to send to England for what really was the practice there. This perspective is a little at odds with Hutchinson's account in the private letter quoted at the end of chapter 16: "the court seemed inclined to refuse . . . [general writs] . . . but I prevailed with my brethren to continue the cause until the next term, and in the mean time wrote to England . . . ."[2] Here the picture is of an embattled chief justice in a minority of one struggling to persuade the other judges into a stay of execution for the general writ so as to allow him a chance of rescuing it.

The man to whom Hutchinson wrote was William Bollan, still nominally advocate general in the Boston vice-admiralty court, lately displaced absentee collector of customs at Salem and Marblehead, and since 1746 resident in Great Britain as the Massachusetts agent. A memorandum by Agent Bollan records:

> Mr Hutchinson the chief justice wrote . . . desiring to know whether . . . writs of assistance ever issue from the exchequer, except upon special information, and confined either to particular houses or to particular goods of which information is made.[3]

2. Chapter 16, n. 60, for reference.
3. See G. G. Wolkins, "Bollan on Writs of Assistance," in *MHSP* 59 (1925-26), 414, quoting Add. MSS, 32974. Another Bollan memorandum, touching both the writs of assistance controversy and *Province v. Paxton*, is in Appendix H.

The accent seems to have been more on probing into what Boston had read and heard about the special writ of assistance than on merely verifying the general one.

From what Hutchinson wrote privately and from Bollan's memorandum, and for all the cold water poured on it in Hutchinson's *History*, the idea of a special writ of assistance plainly caught on among the puisne judges. What this may have owed to the *London Magazine*, to James Otis's arguments, or even to its appeal as a compromise between the general writ and Oxenbridge Thacher's root-and-branch claim that the court lacked jurisdiction to grant any kind of customs writ of assistance at all, cannot be known. But however the puisne judges' attitude came to be formed, the length of time spent in discussion — a whole day perhaps, according to the estimate in chapter 12 — indicates that Chief Justice Hutchinson did not find it easy to talk them out of it.

Hutchinson's letter to Bollan for information about the writ of assistance in England was dated 5 March 1761,[4] and there the case rested for the time being. The background situation in Boston was not uneventful, however.

The province's common law action against Charles Paxton for allegedly excessive expenses in Molasses Act condemnations and John Erving's against George Cradock to negate a composition agreement over the forfeiture of a brigantine, scored success in the court of first instance. Both actions had an ulterior purpose, to weaken the vice-admiralty court. In mid-1761 the vice-admiralty court's companion object of merchant resentment, the custom house, also found itself in common law trouble. This was the doing, characteristically, of the pandemoniac collector, Benjamin Barons. Anything but chastened by admonition, gubernatorial and other, or scared by the inquisitional process on Charles Paxton's "articles of complaint," Barons was running wilder than ever. A "violent and prophane" outburst in the street against various "damned Rascalls," Governor Francis Bernard included, who had engineered the seizure of a ship contrary to his authority as collector resulted in Barons being taken before Justice Richard Dana, fined, and bound over to be of good behavior. The incident also finally decided Surveyor General Lechmere to put the delinquent collector under suspension. About the

4. *Cf.* n. 3 above.

fine and binding over there was little Barons could do but pay up and take it. To ⁸Lechmere's move, however, he reacted instantly and fiercely, with a battery of writs: against Lechmere for suspending him, this time — June 1761 — and in December 1759 both (he even went so far as to have the elderly surveyor general arrested pending bail); against Charles Paxton for procuring the 1761 suspension, and for defaming him; and against George Cradock for taking over his job, as acting collector.⁵

These various developments were duly reported to Westminster by Governor Bernard (with a suggestion, in which the Board of Trade was to concur, that the establishment would be safe if its assailants were warned that they would be resisted or challenged, in court after court, at crown expense).⁶ And in the meantime something else was being borne upon the governor: that James Otis junior was a man not to make an enemy of.

Bernard was not quick to sense what he had let loose by his treatment of Otis. For several months, indeed, he may have imagined himself well on top. First there had been the put-down of the Otises, father and son, over the Superior Court judgeship; next the heat on Otis junior to resign as acting advocate general, which handily left him open to the charge of deserting his post. Bernard's determined maneuverings to prevent Otis representing the province in its action against Charles Paxton misfired; but there was a compensating satisfaction a few weeks after. On 3 March the *Boston Gazette* had come out with the lampoon "History of CHARLES FROTH, Esq."⁷ The

5. Materials on the Barons episode are in T1/408. Governor Bernard recounted it to John Pownall 15 June 1761 and to an unidentified correspondent 28 June: Bernard Papers I. The 28 June letter refers to Lechmere having been held to bail: "The writ was served on the public Exchange on the afternoon of the last day for the return of writs. So that he must have gone to Goal, if he had not got bail in a few hours. But Mr Flucker a Gentleman of the Council of large fortune immediately relieved him by becoming Bail for him."

6. 6 August 1761, T1/408; and J. Pownall to J. West, 20 November 1761, C05/920. See also *Quincy's Reports*, 545, 553-56. Of the inferior court proceedings against Paxton and Cradock Bernard wrote: "the chief Subject of the Harangues of the Council for the Plaintiff (and some of the Judges too) were on the Expediency of discouraging a Court immediately subject to the King and independent of the Province, and which determined Property without a Jury, and on a necessity of putting a Stop to the Practices of the Custom House Officers, for that the People would no longer bear having their Trade kept under restrictions, which their Neighbours (meaning Rhode Island) were entirely free from. And one gentleman, who has had a considerable hand in promoting these disturbances, has been so candid as to own to me, that it was their Intention to work them up to such a pitch, as should make it necessary for the Ministry to interpose and procure them Justice (as they call it) in repealing or qualifying the Molasses Act, and in obliging the Neighbouring Provinces to observe the same restraints . . . ."

7. See p. 172 above.

principal subject of this rancorous skit was Charles Paxton; but the description of Paxton's connections in high places included a reference to "Sir Wm. Slygripe . . . steward of the manner . . . a facetious merry man, of an easy temper, and naturally well dispos'd," whose "stumbling gate" required him to be constantly supported by "Sir Thomas Graspall, who was dictator general . . . ." A week later Otis published a sworn denial of responsibility for the Froth piece. It was possible to read this as from a man nervous of publicly mocking the governor and lieutenant governor of the province; and Bernard might have reckoned that Otis was more noise than fight. In May Otis was elected to the House of Representatives. "Out of this election will arise a damned faction, which will shake this Province to its foundations," was the comment of one observer;[8] but Governor Bernard still did not know his man. He wrote at the end of June: "The New Assembly has proved a very good one and business goes on very well. The Commotions that were heretofore raised are subsided in general, tho' there is some small remains of the Ill humour that Mr Barrons friends created last Winter."[9] However, early July brought a slightly less cheery tone into Bernard's correspondence, and another name to the fore: "The Assembly keeps in very good temper; all necessary business is properly done notwithstanding an opposition is kept up (seldom raising the minority to one third) by Mr Otis Junr. who has been Mr Barrons faithfull Councellour from the first beginning of these commotions . . . ."[10] In August, longer shadows and positive identification of Otis as the chief enemy: "Mr Otis Jun. is at the head of the Confederacy," Bernard wrote to former Governor Pownall. He went on (possibly not realizing that Pownall and Otis had been friendly), "If you are acquainted with the natural Violence of his temper, suppose it to be augmented beyond all bounds of Common decency inflamed by & inflaming the general Clamour of Illicit traders, who think they now have the Custom house at their Mercy, & seem determined to show none."[11] As a political force, James Otis had arrived.

Agent Bollan wrote from England to Chief Justice Hutchinson on 13 June, sending him

a copy of the writ of assistance taken out of the exchequer, with a note thereon, setting forth the manner of its issuing. This writ is directed to the

8. Timothy Ruggles, in the presence of John Adams: *LWJA* X. 248.
9. To ? 28 June 1761: Bernard Papers I.
10. To ? 6 July 1761: *ibid.*
11. 28 August 1761: *ibid.*

officers of the admiralty, justices of peace, mayors, sheriffs, constables, and all other his majestys officers, ministers and subjects in England, requiring them to permit the commiss'rs of the customs and their officers by night or day to enter on board any vessel, to search etc., and in the day time to enter the vaults, cellars, warehouses, shops and other places, where any goods etc. lye concealed, or are suspected to lye concealed, for which the customs are not paid, to inspect and search for the said goods etc. and to do all things which according to the laws shou'd be done, and commanding them to be aiding and assisting to the said commiss'rs and their officers in the execution of the premises.

"On the copy," Bollan continued,

> this endorsement was made. N.B. These writs upon any application of the commiss'rs of the customs to the proper officer of the court of exchequer are made out of course by him, without any affidavit or order of the court.[12]

Hutchinson must have felt well vindicated in having held out against his brother judges' inclination toward a writ of assistance good for the one place and time specially sworn to. The writ undoubtedly was still in use in contemporary England; it bore reassuringly sufficient resemblance to the *Breve Assisten' pro Officiar' Custum'* that had served as the model for the Massachusetts writ of assistance, without however embodying the *breve*'s outdated and inapt idiosyncrasies of detail. Most important of all, it was not specific to place or occasion and could be obtained from "the proper officer of the court of exchequer" for the unsworn asking.

It may be relevant that on 12 November, a week or so before the Superior Court went back to the writs of assistance case, several letters and accompanying papers from Agent Bollan were considered in the Council and the House of Representatives. What these were about is not stated in the records;[13] but it is not impossible that one of them, which bore the date 13 June, was Bollan's letter to Hutchinson on the English writ of assistance.

Even though the letter was addressed to him personally, Hutchinson might have felt it prudent to put it on view in this way. By any standards it had been pretty unorthodox, not to say irregular, for the Superior Court to adjourn a fully argued case while the chief justice obtained, privately and out of the sight of the disputants, crucial evidentiary material upon which the ultimate decision would depend. Hutchinson may have hoped to anticipate criticism, and in some

12. Wolkins, *op. cit.*, n. 3 above; and *cf.* Appendix H.
13. *JHR* vol. 38, pt. 1 (MHS edn., Boston, 1966).

degree to disarm it, by coming clean and freely disclosing his correspondence with Bollan. Too, the Superior Court's next Boston term after February began on 18 August; Bollan's letter could have reached Hutchinson by then. If it did, why else should the resumed writs of assistance hearing have been postponed to November — to a date in November, in fact, some days after the Assembly's consideration of the Bollan papers — than that Chief Justice Hutchinson wished those papers to include what he himself had received from Bollan on the potentially explosive writs of assistance question?

As on the February hearing so on the November, the records of the Superior Court are silent. Worse, in one respect their silence is positively misleading. Although it was in November that the writs of assistance case came up for final decision, the court was still in its August term. Several cases had been dealt with in August, among them the appeals of George Cradock and Charles Paxton in the litigation attacking the conclusiveness of vice-admiralty decrees. Before the record gets to these, however, there is a blank space — a whole page — sidenoted "Greene & Others Petition. No Papers are on file." Thomas Greene headed the signers of the merchants' petition for a hearing on writs of assistance, back in January or thereabouts; this blank space plainly had to do with the resumption of the writs of assistance case after the February adjournment. What happened to the missing papers might be a question, obviously; but what signifies at the moment is that the occurrence of the blank space before entries undoubtedly belonging to August might convey the false impression that the resumed writs of assistance hearing also took place in August.

Nor does the truth come out too clearly when the record actually gets to November. The transition to November is itself indistinct, for straightway after an entry about the Paxton case, which certainly was in August, is an undated note on the swearing-in of John Adams and Samuel Quincy as attorneys qualified to practice in the Superior Court. Immediately following the note come these entries:

Saturday Novr 14th 1761 The Court entrd up Judgment according to the verdicts and then adjourned to Wednesday next.
Thursday November 19. the Court Adjourned without Day.

For all that the court records show, the swearing-in of Adams and Quincy could have been in either August or November. John Adams's diary, however, indicates that it was in November. On

Saturday 14 November, in fact;[14] the day on which the court "entrd
up Judgment according to the verdicts and then adjourned to
Wednesday next." By the look of it, 14 November was the day when
the court reconvened in Boston for the unfinished August term; with
the swearing-in of new attorneys the only thing done on that day and
the real business of the unfinished term deferred until the Wednesday
following, 18 November. The records have no entry for 18 November, and they nowhere so much as hint what the business of that day
consisted of. Let, then, the *Boston Gazette* for Monday 23 November speak:

> Wednesday last, a Hearing was had before the Hon. the Superior Court . . .
> upon a Petition of the Officers of the Customs for a Writ of
> Assistance . . . .

Moreover, the completion of the writs of assistance case seems to have
been all there was for the court on 18 November. At any rate the
record shows no sign of further substantive items at the November
sitting: the next day, Thursday 19 November, "the Court Adjourned
without Day," which meant that the August term's work was over.

Of course, there was more to the opaqueness of the records than
the papers on "Greene & Others Petition" having somehow chanced
to go astray. There are pointers discernible even in the dim light of
the August term entries. The words with which the records customarily denoted the conclusion of a court term were that the court
"entered up judgment according to the verdicts and then adjourned
without day": the first phrase an attestation of the results of the
various cases dealt with, and the second a way of stating that no
work remained on hand. With the August 1761 term at Boston it was
different. As has just been seen, judgment was entered up on Saturday 14 November, prior to adjournment "to Wednesday next." The
final adjournment "without day" was on the day after the business
of Wednesday had been disposed of. The business of Wednesday, the
writs of assistance case, evidently was regarded as something out of
the ordinary run of the Superior Court's judicial activity.

So far out of the ordinary, in fact, that what the records should
say of it seems to have been a matter of some perplexity. The court's
handling of the writs of assistance case perhaps was felt to be too
unusual, not to say too heterodox, for routine inclusion in the
formal archive. Space might be left in case something suitable for

14. *DAJA* I, 224.

insertion were thought of later; but right now the whole thing was excessively problematical. A prime inhibiting factor can be guessed readily enough.

Chief Justice Hutchinson's behind-the-scenes contact with Agent Bollan may have been vulnerable to political censure, or it may not; but assuredly it could have been thought too improper in point of law for the Superior Court record to tell of it.

One can only continue to marvel that the enthusiastic reporter of the February hearing, the man who would make the writs of assistance case into history, was totally unaware of the November hearing. John Adams attended the Superior Court to be sworn in as an attorney on the day it convened, Saturday 14 November. The single other item on the calendar, and for which the court adjourned to the following Wednesday, was the writs of assistance case. Indeed, the writs of assistance case was the only item of any consequence; without it the Superior Court might well not have convened at all at that time (with admission of novice attorneys stood over indefinitely). One of the leading participants in the writs of assistance case, Jeremiah Gridley, was also Adams's sponsor at the swearing-in. Yet, and despite the near-certainty that Gridley knew of the young man's intense interest in the case in its earlier phase, not a word seems to have passed between them, even in casual talk before the swearing-in, to alert Adams to what the November sitting of the court was really scheduled for.[15]

Thomas Hutchinson, though as knowledgable on the November hearing as Adams was ignorant, was almost as uncommunicative. Nothing illuminating it has been found in his correspondence; and his *History of Massachusets-Bay* is laconic:

> The chief justice was . . . desired . . . to obtain information of the practice in England, and judgment was suspended. At the next term, it appeared that such writs issued from the exchequer, of course, when applied for; and this was judged sufficient to warrant the like practice in the province.[16]

On that showing (by comparison with which the *History*'s treatment of the February hearing is just this side of garrulous) the November hearing might never have happened.

15. See pp. 247-48 and 379 for speculative explanations; also n. 18 below.
16. Page 68. Bollan materials cited at notes 3 and 12 above state that the copy of the English writ sent by Bollan (pp. 391-92 above) was "produced to court." Bollan's informant was Hutchinson, presumably.

Not all is silence, however. In particular, the November hearing, unlike that of February, got into the press. The report in the *Boston Gazette* for 23 November 1761 has already been drawn upon for supporting evidence of Wednesday 18 November as the actual day the hearing took place. It went on to say more: "As this was a Matter in which the Liberty of the People was most nearly interested the whole Day and Evening was spent in the Argument." As to the debate itself:

> The Gentlemen in favour of the Petition alledged, that such Writs by Law issued from the Court of Exchequer at home; and that by an Act of this Province, the Superior Court is vested with the whole Power and Jurisdiction of the Exchequer; and from thence it was inferr'd, that the Superior Court might lawfully grant the Petition.
> The Arguments on the other Side were enforced with such Strength of Reason, as did great Honour to the Gentlemen concerned; and nothing could have induced one to believe they were not conclusive, but the Judgment of the Court *immediately* given in Favour of the Petition.
> It is probable that the very *urgent* Necessity for this Writ was set forth in the Petition . . . .

The *Gazette* report is useful, but if it constituted the sum total of evidence on the November arguments knowledge of them would not amount to much.

Fortunately, the November hearing had another reporter. He was Josiah Quincy junior, a son of the Colonel Josiah Quincy to whom John Adams had shown the Abstract rendition of the February hearing and brother of Samuel Quincy who had sat with Adams in court. Perhaps prompted by interesting talk at home of the writs of assistance case, young Quincy turned up at the November renewal of the great debate, and, luckily for history, took notes of what he heard. These notes, or a write-up of them, appeared on public view more than a hundred years later, in 1864, as an item (to which Horace Gray appended a diligently researched commentary on the writs of assistance case) in a compilation of Quincy's legal papers published by his grandson, General Samuel Quincy, under the title *Reports of Cases Argued and Adjudged in the Superior Court of Judicature of the Province of Massachusetts Bay between 1761 and 1772.* Josiah Quincy junior ("the Patriot," as he came to be known for his services to the cause) packed a lot into his short life; and his report of the November hearing of the writs of assistance case shows him to have been a youngster of some precocity. In 1761 he was a seventeen-year-old undergraduate at Harvard College, and his admission as an attorney was still five years ahead. Yet there he was in the courtroom, already interesting himself in the practicalities of his future career. And he did not make a bad job of his note-taking. There were blemishes. Quincy mistakenly attributed the writs of assistance case to an application by Charles Paxton (perhaps because, the prior application of Cockle of Salem notwithstanding, it was Paxton to whom the first writ of the George III series was actually issued).[17] A particularly regrettable imperfection is that the speech of James Otis appears only in part, for, as Quincy put it, "I was absent while he was speaking, most of the Time, and so have but few Notes." However, the Paxton slip is unimportant, and Quincy's candor on the Otis omission encourages confidence in what he did get down. That the report as a whole — it is reproduced in full in Appendix K — is taken up much more by arguments at the bar than by utterances from the bench in no way renders it suspect. It is not even an instance, probably, of an aspirant lawyer seeing greater instructional value in the learning deployed by professional advocates than in what might fall from the lips of a lay judiciary. On the testimony of the *Gazette* that the court found in favor of the general writ *"immediately,"* the absence of a reasoned and articulated judgment in Quincy's report means simply what it appears to mean, that no such exposition was delivered. Altogether, Josiah Quincy junior handled this youthful venture into lawyerly craftsmanship pretty well. The arguments are readily intelligible as he set them forth; and he was a lot more successful with notations and references than John Adams had been in February. One could go so far as to wish that Josiah Quincy as well as John Adams had been on hand to take notes of the previous hearing. The February arguments had really signified, for at that stage there was genuine uncertainty as to how the case might go (whereas the November hearing, its outcome predetermined by the Hutchinson-Bollan correspondence, was little else than a matter of form).[18]

Oxenbridge Thacher was the first speaker, and not only in sequence. James Otis dominated the February hearing, to the point of

17. On 2 December 1761: *Quincy's Reports,* 418. Cockle's was the second writ issued, apparently not until 5 February 1762: *ibid.,* 422.

18. That the result was a foregone conclusion might have been a plausible guess why the November hearing was a blank for John Adams: he just did not bother about it. However, the evidence is practically solid that he did not so much as know about it — ever: *cf.* chapter 12, n. 24 and text.

upstaging Thacher; but now it was Thacher's turn to head the opposition to the custom house. Although Otis's speech did not get fully reported in Quincy, there can be little doubt that most of the wind had gone from his sails. His great theme of February, that the Massachusetts writ of assistance should be special and sworn because that was how it was with the writ in England, was destroyed beyond all possibility of salvage. The intelligence from Agent Bollan in London that the English writ was general had ruined it utterly. In fact, after Bollan's blockbuster only one hope remained to the opposition: that the legal position in Massachusetts might somehow be differentiated from that in England, so that what Bollan had told Chief Justice Hutchinson arguably did not apply. This put Thacher at an advantage (over Otis). Thacher's principal February argument — that the Superior Court lacked authority to issue any kind of writ of assistance because it had irretrievably renounced exchequer jurisdiction — depended not at all upon what might or might not be the practice in England. It was inevitable that Thacher should now move to the number one spot.

And, as one would expect, his jurisdictional argument was at the center again. As Quincy reported it:

> He moved further that such a Writ is granted and must issue from the Exchequer Court, and no other can grant it; 4 Inst. 103; and that no other Officers but such as constitute the Court can grant it. 2 Inst. 551. That this Court is not such a one, vid. Prov. Law. This Court has in the most solemn Manner disclaimed the Authority of the Exchequer; this they did in the Case of McNeal of Ireland & McNeal of Boston. This they cannot do in Part; if the Province Law gives them any, it gives them all the Power of the Exchequer Court; nor can they chuse and refuse to act at Pleasure.

Of course, this was no sounder in November than in February, despite all those researches into Coke's *Institutes*. Thacher still had not found out that the customs writ of assistance in England issued from the exchequer rather than from the chancery — the natural office for a common law writ of that sort — only because the Act of Frauds of 1662 so stipulated. But there was a difficulty that he would not have been unconscious of. Back in February his argument had not found favor with the court. It may not have been positively rejected so much as ignored (Hutchinson, in his *History of Massachu-sets-Bay*, said nothing of it); in all common sense, however, there was no hope of the judges changing their minds nakedly in public. If they did, the reason would have to look respectably different from the one that failed to move them previously. The realistics of the situation demanded that Thacher wrap up his February argument in something new.

So there is a second sense in which Thacher's February theme was at the center of his November speech too. Both before it and after it are layers of ancillary material. The lower layer will be taken first. This is how Thacher followed on from his restated argument against the Superior Court's jurisdiction, and concluded his speech:

> But supposing this Court has the Power of the Exchequer, yet there are many Circumstances which render that Court in this Case an improper Precedent; for there the Officers are sworn in that Court, and are accountable to it, are obliged there to pass their Accounts weekly; which is not the Case here. In that Court, there Cases are tried, and there finally; which is another Diversity. Besides, the Officers of the Customs are their Officers, and under their Check, and that so much, that for Misbehaviour they may punish with corporal Punishment. 3 & 4 Car.2, §8. 7 & 8 W. & M. does not give the Authority.

In February Thacher had tried to make something of the point that whereas in England seizures that resulted from writ of assistance search underwent condemnation proceedings in the same Court of Exchequer whose seal was on the writ, "so that," as John Adams's Abstract put it, "the Custom House Officers are the Officers of that Court under the Eye and Direction of the Barons and so accountable for any wanton exercise of power." It had not been a point well taken. Issuance of the writ of assistance was an administrative routine, nothing to do with the judicial work of the Court of Exchequer. Customs officers were under the commissioners of customs; the Court of Exchequer was the appropriate forum for redress against customs officers,[19] but the judicial barons operated only according to standard legal form and remedy, and in no way as managerial supervisors. These November elaborations were no better in focus. Customs officers in England were required, by section 33 of the Act of Frauds of 1662, to swear "for the true and faithful Execution and Discharge . . . of their several Trusts and Imployments" — but before their departmental superiors, not in the Court of Exchequer. Section 8 of the 1662 act provided for them to be imprisoned, as Thacher stated; but it was only for the specific offense of granting false certificates of landing, not for "Misbehaviour" at large. And Thacher was wrong in suggesting that nothing of the kind applied in

19. See p. 310 above.

America under the Act of Frauds of 1696: section 6 of that act was clear that customs officers there were subject to the same 1662-style regime of offenses and penalties as their colleagues in England. Very wide of the mark was his notion of customs officers in England "accountable" to the Court of Exchequer in the sense of being "obliged there to pass their Accounts weekly." Thacher seems to have picked up a confused idea of the practice whereby a customs headquarters official, the receiver general, to whom collectors at the various ports remitted their takings, prepared a weekly certificate and account for the exchequer (not the judicial Court of Exchequer either, but the government accounts office).[20]   It was another instance of a lawyer long on learning but short on workaday nous. A moment's reflection on the practicalities surely would have persuaded Thacher of the unlikelihood of a system whereby the Court of Exchequer suffered a weekly inundation of paper from every customs officer in the kingdom.

So much for how Thacher went on to end his speech. Now for two arguments, unrelated both to each other and to the central challenge to the court's jurisdiction that they prefaced. These seem to be wholly new, and not in any degree an extrapolation or a variant of things he had said in February.

The first, at the very outset of the speech, started with a reading of the two Acts of Frauds, of 1662 and 1696, "upon which the Request for this Writ is founded." What this led into was as thoroughgoing in its way as the attack on the court's jurisdiction. It also bears some slight surface resemblance to the doctrinal propositions in the February speech of James Otis, that acts of Parliament should in some circumstances be adjudged void:

> Though this Act of Parliament has existed 60 Years, yet it was never applied for, nor ever granted, till 1756; which is a great Argument against granting it; not that an Act of Parliament can be antiquated, but Non-user is a great Presumption that the Law will not bear it . . . . Moreover, when an Act of Parliament is not express, but even doubtfull, and then has been neglected and not executed, in such a Case the Presumption is more violent.

Here Thacher was invoking a line of authority, less familiar than the *Bonham's Case* tradition but at least as legitimate and certainly more

20. *Cf.* E. E. Hoon, *The Organization of the English Customs System 1696-1786* (New York, 1938), 99-101; and E. Carson, *The Ancient and Rightful Customs* (London, 1972), 51.

durable (English courts were still applying it in the nineteenth century), that a statute which after a period had never been put into effect could be lawfully ignored.[21]   The supplementary point, about the Act of Frauds of 1696 being "not express, but even doubtfull" on writ of assistance search, was fair enough: the obscure draftsmanship of that provision will be recalled from chapter 7. All the same, and whatever merit Thacher's argument may have had in the abstract, the facts were against him. Chief Justice Hutchinson interrupted: "The Custom House Officers have frequently applied to the Governour for this Writ, and have had it granted them by him, and therefore, though he had no Power to grant it, yet that removes the Argument of Non-user." Hutchinson would have had in mind the encounter with Charles Paxton in 1755, when his own denial that Governor Shirley's customs search warrants were legal had led to the invention of the Superior Court's first writ of assistance. He was saying that Shirley's use of the 1696 act had been wrongful, but use it was nevertheless, so "the Argument of Non-user" — whatever might have been said for or against its doctrinal soundness — simply could not bite. The tyro chief justice did rather nicely here. Thacher did not persist with "Non-user."

He passed instead to this:

> If this Court have a Right to grant this Writ, it must be either *ex debita Justitia* or discretionary. If *ex debita Justitia,* it cannot in any Case be refused; which from the Act itself and its Consequences . . . could not be intended. It can't be discretionary; for it can't be in the Power of any Judge at discretion to determine that I shall have my House broken open or not . . . .

It could be that, remembering the writs of assistance for chancery injunctions and sequestrations turned up in his February researches, Thacher assumed that the customs writ of assistance was in the same family, that is, the family of writs issued by a court in furtherance or determination of business before it. Some such writs — prohibition, for example, and *habeas corpus* — the court had no choice but to issue once the pertinent circumstances were duly established; others — like those having to do with assistance in the executive

---

21. See T. F. T. Plucknett, *Concise History of the Common Law* (London, 1956), 338-39; *Stewart v. Lawton* (1823) 1 Bing. 374 cited. Otis's "The Executive Courts must pass such Acts into disuse," in John Adams's notes of the February hearing, almost smacks of this doctrine, but not quite (disuse was a condition, not a consequence, of the court's jurisdiction).

duties of sheriffs — were issued or not as the court thought fit. The customs writ of assistance was not in this family of writs at all, either the prescriptive or the discretionary branch. Its affinity was rather with writs for the commencement of a lawsuit, which were available, with no judicial interposition whatever, simply on application to the appropriate administrative officer (the clerk of the court, as it might be). Conceivably it was this type of nondiscretionary writ — the writ of routine issuance — that Thacher had in mind: his claim that a thing so indeterminate in its "Consequences" as a general writ of assistance was not to be inferred from "the act itself" perhaps resting on the proposition — again reminiscent of James Otis's argument in February — that the legislation on customs search, which did not specify whether the writ of assistance was general or special, ought to be construed conservatively. But there is no knowing for certain what Thacher was driving at in this argument about discretionary and nondiscretionary writs. If argument it can be called, indeed; for in truth what Thacher said amounted to no more than the propounding of a kind of dilemma. Having postulated that the customs writ of assistance must of necessity be either discretionary or nondiscretionary, he seems to have been concerned to demonstrate that in fact it answered neither category satisfactorily. The puzzle thus posed he makes no attempt to work out. Perhaps realizing that he was up a blind alley (for assuredly there was no possibility of resolving such a tangle of confusion and error), he just drops the subject.

It was at this point that Thacher brought in his argument against the Superior Court's exchequer jurisdiction, the February meat in the November sandwich. The theory that the new November dialectics were concocted as something for the bench to hide behind while changing its mind loses nothing from the inspection of them that has now taken place. Thacher cannot have entertained much serious hope of scoring with them in a substantive way, on their intrinsic force. Obviously he put some thought into them; yet they seem slapdash, showing some professional application but not really up to standard. They served as garnish for the jurisdiction argument, and that was about all.

The only argument specifically mentioned in the *Boston Gazette* on 23 November [22] affords confirmatory evidence of where the emphasis in the November debate lay: "that such Writs by Law issued from the Court of Exchequer at home; and that by an Act of this

22. See p. 396 above.

Province, the Superior Court is vested with the whole Power and Jurisdiction of the Exchequer; and from thence it was inferr'd, that the Superior Court might lawfully grant the Petition." A few weeks later, the Society for Encouraging Trade and Commerce included a reference to the writs of assistance case in an address to the Treasury: "Merchants and Inhabitants" had petitioned to be heard against the writ, "concluding no Doubt, that the Superior Court would not assume the Powers of the Exchequer, in order to grant this Writt, but the Court has determined otherwise."[23] As between Oxenbridge Thacher and James Otis the tables had turned with a vengeance. Not only had the leadership of the struggle — such struggle as remained possible — passed to Thacher, it was Thacher's argument against exchequer jurisdiction that contemporary notice fixed upon.

Even though the remaining hopes of the merchant opponents of the writ of assistance must in November have centered upon Thacher, his position in relation to them presumably was as indeterminate as it seems to have been in February. He was not so much their spokesman (this accreditation belonged to Otis) as *amicus curiae*, enlisted by the judges to help lighten their darkness. Some support for this perhaps is given by a note with which Quincy prefaced his report of the November hearing "the Court desired the Opinion of the Bar, whether they had a Right and ought to grant . . . [the writ]." The truth could be that Thacher was speaking more for himself than on anyone else's behalf, for the whiggish satisfactions of confounding the custom house *Apparat* and not giving Chief Justice Hutchinson an easy run.

A newcomer to the writs of assistance case must now be introduced. A hint of his existence is to be seen in one of the excerpts from the *Boston Gazette* for 23 November, which spoke of the "Gentlemen" who argued in favor of the writ. Jeremiah Gridley, the leader of the Boston bar who in February had been the custom house's sole spokesman, now had a partner.[24] He was Robert Auchmuty junior, son of the late vice-admiralty judge. The younger Auchmuty was himself destined to occupy that office — to fill it, indeed, for he was a lawyer of ability — but in 1761 he was still making his way. It is nowhere stated, but he probably appeared in the capacity of acting advocate general. After Otis's resignation,

---

23. T1/415. This address was referred to in chapters 9 and 10.
24. "It was usual for two lawyers to argue on each side of a case": *LPJA* I, lxv.

Benjamin Prat stood in for a while; in October 1761, however, he departed the province to become chief justice of New York, and it seems likely enough that Auchmuty, who some years later actually claimed to have been appointed acting advocate general in 1761 as successor to Prat, took over at that time.[25] Just as Otis had been asked to help the custom house when the writ of assistance first became a question and he was still in the acting advocate generalship, so the rounding off of it might have seemed a proper perquisite for the new holder of the post. The fees were not the problem they might have been if Benjamin Barons, no friend to the writ of assistance, still had the keeping of the custom house's money. And it was only sensible for the crown to have a second string. Chief Justice Hutchinson's news from Bollan was encouraging, but who could tell what that crafty old operator Gridley might not get up to, if left on his own? There had been talk, after all, of his privately believing that the general writ of assistance was not lawful,[26] and the equivocation in his February utterances hardly made for confidence. Besides, with both Thacher and Otis again showing up it looked a better balance to have a twosome for the crown as well. In the result, though, there was as much polarization as balance. The order of speaking was Thacher, Otis, Auchmuty, Gridley, but the pattern of debate discernible in Quincy's report unmistakably shows a pairing off: Auchmuty answering Thacher, and Gridley answering Otis. It makes sense, then, to break sequence and discuss Auchmuty's speech next after Thacher's.

Auchmuty went straight to Thacher's central argument, that because the Superior Court had once refused to use its exchequer status

25. *BG* 8 June 1761: "*Benjamin Pratt,* Esq., His Majesty's Advocate-General of this Province, is appointed to be Chief Justice of New York . . . ."

Governor Bernard wrote to the Board of Trade on 15 October 1766 enclosing (and supporting) a petition in which Auchmuty asked for a regular salary. Auchmuty said "That in 1761 he was appointed his Majesty's Advocate General . . . by his Excellency Francis Bernard, Esqr., which place was then vacant, by the absence of William Bollan, Esqr. . . . and by the appointment of Benjamin Prat Esqr., your Petitioners immediate Predecessor to the office of Chief Justice of the Province of New York . . . ." (CO5/892 and CO5/755, respectively.)

In fact, Bollan was still substantive advocate general at this time. In 1767 he was superseded by Jonathan Sewall (Auchmuty was now vice-admiralty judge) by a mistake in the admiralty department, and, according to a petition by Bollan to the king in 1773 (CO5/894), through "the Misrepresentation of others." Bollan's petition also alluded to that other mistake, in 1760, by which he was superseded as customs collector at Salem by James Cockle. (*Cf.* chapter 8, n. 23, and text.)

26. See pp. 197, 271 above.

to conjure forth an otherwise impermissible equity jurisdiction it was barred from acting as an exchequer court for writs of assistance:

> From the Words of the Law, this Court may have the Power of the Exchequer

The "Law" here obviously was the province act that gave the Superior Court the competence of the three common law courts at Westminster, King's Bench, Common Pleas, and Exchequer; Auchmuty seems to have insisted flatly that the law was to be found in what the act said, not in the court's having shrunk from stretching it to a dubious extreme.

What Quincy has him going on to say,

> Now the Exchequer always had that Power; the Court cannot regard Consequences, but must follow Law,

is less easily sized up, and was less soundly based. If "that Power" was the power to issue the customs writ of assistance — and it is hard to imagine what else might have been meant — Auchmuty had fallen into the common mistake of seeing exchequer jurisdiction as the natural and the only conceivable source of such a writ; so that, like his opponent, Thacher, he failed to realize that when the Act of Frauds of 1662 spoke of a "Writ of Assistance under the Seal of his Majesty's Court of Exchequer" it was prescribing exchequer issuance in place of issuance under the great seal (which would have been the norm for a common law writ such as this), not superfluously spelling out a mode of issuance that would have applied anyway.[27] And "the Exchequer always had that Power," seems to betray a concomitant error, that the customs writ of assistance was by some providential dispensation ready and waiting among the antiquities of the exchequer to be summoned into active use by the Act of Frauds of 1662; whereas in fact the writ was no older than the act of 1662, having been invented at that time under a little known doctrine of the common law which authorized creation of new writs for the better implementation of a public statute. So if by what he went on to argue, "the Court cannot regard Consequences, but must follow Law," Robert Auchmuty meant that generality had to be accepted as one of the natural features of the writ of assistance that had come down with it through the ages, be the "Consequences" what they might and however unthinkable to the custom house's opponents,

27. See pp. 307-8 above.

the real juridical provenance of the writ plainly had proved as elusive to him as to everyone else in the Boston debate.

The Auchmuty speech occupies only a single paragraph in Quincy's report. The rest of it was by way of reply to Oxenbridge Thacher's invocation of the doctrine that a statute never enforced became legally defunct:

> As for the Argument of Non-user, that ends whenever the Law is once executed; and this Law has been executed in this Country, and this Writ granted, not only by the Governor, but also from this Court in Ch. Justice Sewall's Time.

This seems to have been in supplementation of Chief Justice Hutchinson's interruption of Thacher with the objection that "the Argument of Non-user" did not hold because "this Writ" had been granted years ago by Governor Shirley (and even "though he had no Power to grant it"). Auchmuty now followed up with the writ having since been issued by the Superior Court itself. He may have supposed that Hutchinson had not ventured this clinching point for fear of premature and prejudicial entanglement in the very question under debate: the question whether the court could properly assert jurisdiction. It was a work of supererogation, nevertheless. The practical fact was that the Hutchinson interruption had stopped Thacher's "Argument of Non-user" dead in its tracks. The winding-sheet supplied by Auchmuty may have been warranted in point of lawyerlike logic, but it could have been done without.

Auchmuty appears to have said nothing further. Noticeably he was silent on Thacher's attempts to capitalize on an imagined contrast between the Court of Exchequer at Westminster and the Superior Court of Massachusetts in terms of a continuing supervision of customs officers equipped with a writ of assistance. It could be that he considered them too insubstantial to be worth the research of contradicting. Or he may have recognized them for what they most probably were — a mere smokescreen behind which the court might retreat if by some chance it should now accept the antijurisdiction argument it had spurned in February.

After all, what really mattered from Auchmuty's point of view was that the antijurisdiction argument be scotched. That accomplished, no local disparity with the English situation signified. Given the authenticity of what had been received from Agent Bollan on the writ of assistance and its issuance in England, "the Court . . . must follow Law." It is of a piece that the thrust of everything reported of

Auchmuty's argument was toward vindication of the Superior Court's jurisdiction.

James Otis's February speech on the writ of assistance is famous. His November speech is forgotten. The position he had taken in February, that in England and hence in Massachusetts the only valid writ of assistance was one specifically sworn to by reference to occasion and place had been completely shot away by the evidence from Agent Bollan that the English writ was general.

The *Boston Gazette* report on 23 November that "the whole Day and Evening was spent in the Argument" has to be understood on the footing that the court's day had not begun early. Before the hearing all the judges save Chambers Russell attended a meeting of the Council. This was scheduled for ten o'clock, and the agenda was fairly heavy.[28] There cannot have been much of the morning left when the court at last assembled (and with four speeches to be delivered well might the hearing have lasted into the evening). Time enough for the opening speech by Oxenbridge Thacher, perhaps, and then the midday meal break. On the showing of Josiah Quincy's report, Otis spoke next after Thacher. One surmises that he did so when the hearing was resumed following lunch (or dinner, in contemporary usage). And it also seems reasonable to suppose that young Quincy's confession to having missed most of what Otis said means that he himself arrived back from lunch rather late, when Otis was already more than halfway through.

Of the two paragraphs of Otis that Quincy did manage to record this is the first:

> 12 Car.2, 19. 13 & 14 Car.2, p. 56. Let a Warrant come from whence it will improperly, it is to be refused, and the higher the Power granting it, the more dangerous. The Exchequer itself was thought a Hardship in the first

28. C05/824, "Minutes of the Council in Assembly." Russell had resigned from the Council 18 April 1761, ostensibly because "it was very inconvenient for him to attend the Duty of a Councellor": C05/823; MA 12. However, a currently circulating pamphlet strongly critical of dual membership of the Council and the Superior Court may have been a factor. Although all the Superior Court judges were in the line of fire, Russell may have felt specially vulnerable by reason of his additional judgeship in the vice-admiralty court. The pamphlet's author was probably Oxenbridge Thacher: see E. E. Brennan, *Plural Office-Holding in Massachusetts 1760-1780* (Chapel Hill, 1945), 41. And *cf.* p. 87 above.

Russell was elected to the House of Representatives barely more than a month after his resignation from the Council (C05/824). Possibly this helped stimulate moves in 1762 — vain as they turned out — to legislate Superior Court judges out of *both* houses of legislature. See JHR February-August 1762, *passim*; and, for a disappointed comment, *BG* 24 May 1762.

Constitution. Vid. Rapin, Vol. 1st, p. 178, 386, 403, 404. Vol. 2, 285, 375.

It looks as if Otis, by citing the 1660 act for customs search warrants in conjunction with the Act of Frauds of 1662, and still talking of warrants rather than of writs, may have been trying to salvage something from the wreck of his February argument. Mostly, however, he was having recourse to history.

Not that the references to Rapin-Thoyras's *History of England*[29] — some of them were in fact to Rapin's translator, Tindal — added much punch to what Otis was putting over. In the first, far from making the Court of Exchequer a "Hardship," Rapin applauded it as an exception among the Normanizing legal institutions supposedly introduced by William the Conqueror to subvert the good old indigenous English laws; it "became very advantageous to the People," Rapin said. The second reference apparently was to a note in which Tindal writes that the exchequer "before the end of Henry III's Reign . . . fell in great Measure from its ancient Grandeur, and from thenceforward continued in a State of Declension . . . . The Exchequer was a Court greatly concerned in the conservation of the Prerogatives, as well as the Revenue of the Crown." The third and fourth references are to a long and uncontentious note by Tindal on the exchequer and its work (with nothing, however, about the customs writ of assistance). The fifth is where Rapin, drawing upon Rushworth's *Historical Collections,* describes customs search by conciliar directive on account of Charles I's irregular exaction of tunnage and poundage. And in the sixth Rapin quotes one of the articles of impeachment against the Earl of Strafford in 1640, for signing a general warrant of arrest in Ireland. Obviously, none of this was much to the point. Indeed, to Jeremiah Gridley's schoolmasterish admonition, "Quoting History is not speaking like a Lawyer," the comment might be added that on this occasion Otis's history was no great shakes either.

The other paragraph of the Otis speech also shows how little was left to Otis by the news that the general writ of assistance was in use in England:

> It is worthy Consideration whether this Writ was constitutional even in England; and I think it plainly appears it was not; much less here, since it was not there invented till after our Constitution and Settlement. Such a

29. Second edition (1732) by N. Tindal, vol. I; *cf.* chapter 16 above, n. 25 and n. 27 and texts.

Writ is generally illegal. Hawkins B.2. ch. 1. Of Crim. Jr. Viner, Tit. Commission, A. 1 Inst. 464. 29 M.

In February it had been more or less for form's sake that Otis brought unconstitutionality into his argument; if the courts could invalidate an act of Parliament logic required a justifying principle, and unconstitutionality — borrowed from contemporary natural law theory — answered the purpose. Not that there had been any compelling need for such philosophizing, since the argument Otis was then constructing could have stood up well enough without it. In November, however, with his earlier position in ruins, unconstitutionality took on the dimension of a major theme. Never mind that they had the general writ in England, they ought not to: the thing was unconstitutional. For the proposition that it was even more unconstitutional in Massachusetts, Otis apparently sought to bend into service the accepted doctrine that while pre-existing acts of Parliament were binding on a new colony, a later act had effect there only if it said so. This might have been a nice point. The customs writ of assistance subserved an act — the Act of Frauds of 1662 — which was later than the Pilgrims (though not the province charter) and which said nothing apposite about America. But the writ itself was a product of the common law. Was it or was it not infected by the territorial limitation on its parent act? Logic suggests yes; but beyond that the beguiling fancy of new Otisian virtuosity does not go. It is indeed shattered by what came next, the statement that "such a Writ is generally illegal," which only goes to confirm that Otis still had not, after all, tumbled to what the customs writ of assistance really was. And, significantly, the citations with which he ended did not include Coke's Third *Institute,* where the doctrinal source of the writ was actually to be found. They were a mere jumble from Hawkins's *Pleas of the Crown,* Viner's *Abridgement,* Coke's First *Institute,* and the twenty-ninth article of Magna Carta, variously relating to the unlawfulness of general warrants and arrests without due process and to interpretation of statutes according to common law principle.[30]

Incomplete though the evidentiary materials are, Otis's contribution to the November hearing seems unimpressive. The hand he had

30. Otis's "1 Inst. 464" is identifiable as the Coke note on Littleton cited in chapter 16, n. 36; it echoes his February position (*cf.* chapter 16, n. 39). For Otis's interest in article 29 of Magna Carta ("No free man shall be taken, imprisoned ... except by the law of the land") see *Quincy's Reports,* 483-85.

played so skillfully in February, that in England and therefore in Massachusetts the writ of assistance had to be good for the one sworn occasion only, was a busted flush. What little hope remained of defeating the custom house lay in somehow differentiating Massachusetts from England, and this had been preempted by Oxenbridge Thacher. Possibly there was something of it in Otis's reference to the writ not having been invented when Massachusetts was settled, but that is all. For the most part there was little left to him but to beat the air with rhetoric about history and constitutionalism.

"Quoting History is not speaking like a Lawyer," was Jeremiah Gridley's reply; and

> If it is Law in England, it is Law here; it is extended to this Country by Act of Parliament. 7 & 8 Wm. & M. ch. 18. By Act of Parliament they are entitled to like Assistants; now how can they have like Assistants, if the Court cannot grant them it; and how can the Court grant them like Assistance, if they cannot grant this Writ. Pity it would be, they should have like Right, and not like Remedy; the Law abhors Right without Remedy. But the General Court has given this Court Authority to grant it, and so has every other Plantation Court given their Superiour Court.

This was much the same as one of the arguments Gridley had deployed in February: under the Act of Frauds of 1696 customs officers in America were entitled to "the like Assistance in the Execution of their Office as . . . the Officers in England" under the Act of Frauds of 1662; therefore they were entitled to the writ of assistance.

The statement at the end, that legislatures in all other colonies had given their superior courts authority to grant the writ of assistance — exchequer jurisdiction, Gridley evidently meant — presumably was intended as emphasis; whether factually true or not,[31] the emphasis was more rhetorical than logical (given that the colonial customs officer's entitlement to the writ did not follow from the act of 1696

---

31. The fact almost certainly is that the writ of assistance was peculiar to Massachusetts in America: witness the researches of Horace Gray in *Quincy's Reports*, 500-511; and see B. Knollenberg, *Growth of the American Revolution 1766-1775* (New York, 1975), 212. New Hampshire got them in 1762: cf. chapter 19, n. 23, below.

In 1764 preparations for the Stamp Act required governors to send to Westminster lists of legal documents that would attract the new duty. (See, e.g., Lord Halifax to Governor Bernard, 11 August 1764: Bernard Papers X.) The Massachusetts list (Bernard to Halifax, 12 November 1764: C05/755) included "Writ of Assistance to Custom House Officers"; but others that have been discovered (C05/390, C05/1280, T1/430, T1/442) did not. The writ of assistance bore a stamp in England.

as a matter of necessity but depended upon an accident of local legislation). Of more significance, possibly, is Gridley's reference to "the Writ." If he was speaking of the English-style writ commended by Agent Bollan, to that extent he had moved away from his February position of equivocal noncommitment to writs of assistance general in form. Even so, one would hesitate to conclude that he had at last come off the fence. What he was now saying was by no means as positive as it might have been, hanging as it did upon a mere hypothesis — "If it is Law in England . . . ." Hardly the language of a man eagerly seizing on the Bollan materials. Of course, Gridley had no need to urge the Bollan materials on the court. Chief Justice Hutchinson had swung the February hearing, and assuredly he would follow through and insist that what he had received from Agent Bollan meant a decision in favor of the custom house. With the president of the court a kind of *de facto* ally, Gridley was free to soft-pedal even to the point of suggesting that Bollan might have gotten the story wrong. All considered, Gridley in November was simply an extension of Gridley in February: whiggish in sympathy, and careful not to antagonize his ordinary merchant clientele by all-out espousal of the custom house cause.

It remains to comment on the beginning of Gridley's speech. His reply to Otis's appeal to history and constitutionalism ("Quoting History is not speaking like a Lawyer . . .") occurs as his second argument. What came first was this:

> This is properly a Writ of Assist*ants*, not Assistance; not to give the Officers a greater Power, but as a Check upon them. For by this they cannot enter into any House, without the Presence of the Sheriff or civil Officer, who will be always supposed to have an Eye over and be a Check upon them.

Gridley's point, that the writ of assistance signified limitation upon a power that otherwise would have been wider still, was more or less well taken. But it is of interest for another reason. If Gridley's second argument was by way of reply to Otis, perhaps this first one was too. When Josiah Quincy came back from lunch to find Otis already in full flight about history and constitutionalism, what he had missed in the opening of Otis's speech was something to which Gridley's opening, about the moderating aspect of the writ of assistance, had reference. What that something was may be guessed at. In the November hearing Otis had blasted off with the same sort of expostulation he had employed in February, against the enormity of the discretionary powers available to a customs officer with a general writ of assistance.

The court's finding in favor of the general writ of assistance was announced "immediately," according to the *Boston Gazette*. "*The Justices* were unanimously of opinion that this Writ might be granted; and some Time after, out of Term, it was granted," was how Josiah Quincy junior signed off his report.[32]

In all likelihood, the judges had been of a mind to grant the writ not only at the end of the November hearing but at the beginning. Certainly, if Quincy is a reliable indicator, there can have been little in what they heard from the four attorneys to influence their thinking one way or the other. Oxenbridge Thacher's refurbishment of his February challenge to the jurisdiction added little to its cogency. James Otis was a spent force. Robert Auchmuty's answer to Thacher was skimpy; and Jeremiah Gridley again straddled the fence. Although Thacher seems to have put some genuine effort into his November speech even he cannot have seriously expected to win. There might have been a chance that the puisne judges who had doubted the general writ at the February hearing would dig in, the Bollan evidence notwithstanding. On the other hand, the men who had allowed themselves to be overborne by Chief Justice Hutchinson in February, when he had really nothing in the way of hard law or reliable factual information to sustain him, were not likely to hold out against him now that he was armed with the daunting material from Agent Bollan in England. The conclusion is hard to resist that for most of the barristers the November hearing was largely a matter of putting up a show, for appearances as much as anything. The judges had in elementary decency to hear the barristers out; but, going on as it did into the evening, listening to this mere speechifying, with more than its natural proportion of slipshod argument, must have been one big yawn.

It was remarked earlier that for all that Thomas Hutchinson told of it in his *History* the November hearing might not have happened at all; he was almost as uncommunicative as John Adams. Perhaps this was too ungenerous, for there was a sort of eloquence in how Hutchinson said nothing. Here are his words again:

---

32. Governor Bernard to Governor Wm. Franklin, New Jersey, 24 March 1768: "The Court was unanimous for granting them as the Laws then stood": Bernard Papers V.

The chief justice was . . . desired, by the first opportunity in his power, to obtain information of the practice in England, and judgment was suspended. At the next term, it appeared that such writs issued from the exchequer, of course, when applied for; and this was judged sufficient to warrant the like practice in the province.

Given Hutchinson's habitual low-key style, he could hardly have made it plainer that the November decision in favor of the general writ of assistance was founded on what he had received from William Bollan, on nothing else, and regardless of any articulated opposition that remained. Small wonder that he did not rate the hearing as deserving even so much as a mention. To him the whole performance had been a waste of time.

Hutchinson's *History of Massachusets-Bay* ended its brief account of the writs of assistance case with a sentence on how the Massachusetts writ, hitherto based on an archaic and inapt curio, was now remodeled on modern English lines, and how it would be issued in the future:

A form was settled, as agreeable to the form in England as the circumstances of the colony would admit, and the writs were ordered to be issued to custom-house officers, for whom application should be made to the chief justice by the surveyor-general of the customs.[33]

An illustration of the new-style writ of assistance — issued on 3 June 1762 for Nathaniel Hatch, acting comptroller of customs at Boston — is in Appendix L.[34] In *Quincy's Reports*[35] Horace Gray reproduced, with indicators of erasures and alterations, the draft by Chief Justice Hutchinson from which the Hatch writ evidently was taken.

If Hutchinson had the text of the current English writ[36] to guide him he did not allow himself to be overawed by it. His own handiwork, though scarcely terse, eliminated much of the tedious prolixity of the transatlantic original (for example, a recital of details from the commission of the board of customs). Adaptation was inevitable, of course, especially in the citation of the relevant statutes on customs search. Some of the adaptation was bold. The originating

33. Pages 68-69.
34. This is still in the Superior Court archives: SF 100515.
35. Pages 418-21. The first writ was issued 2 December 1761, to Charles Paxton.
36. The text of the George III English writ, first issued 14 April 1761, is in T1/465. See Appendix C.

enactment for writ of assistance search, in the Act of Frauds of 1662, could apply in America only insofar as the Act of Frauds of 1696 were read as making it do so. That the wording of the 1696 act was impossibly obscure on this point did not prevent Hutchinson from drafting as if it were crystal clear. Less audaciously, Hutchinson met the difficulty that the 1662 act required the writ of assistance to be under the exchequer seal by inserting a reference to the province act that gave the Superior Court exchequer jurisdiction. If one were looking for positive faults the point could be taken that the Hatch writ ought not to have been worded so as to suggest that Hatch got his search power not only from the acts of 1662 and 1696 but also from the surveyor general who appointed him. It is noticeable too that these new-style Massachusetts writs were issued to named customs officers, whereas the English prototype was not.[37] All that said, however, the Hutchinson writ of assistance was an enormous improvement upon its predecessor, taken from the almost non-sensically inappropriate *Breve Assisten' Pro Officiar' Custum'* in an old manual of exchequer practice.

Along with the revised Massachusetts writ came a procedural innovation. Formerly there had been no special drill for obtaining a writ of assistance — by the look of things, the customs officer simply went to the clerk of the Superior Court and asked — but in future all applications would go through the surveyor general and up to the chief justice. (And so it transpired: the researches of Horace Gray show applications in the form of a "certificate" by the surveyor general to the chief justice, who would endorse the certificate with a directive to the clerk to issue the writ.)[38] This new ceremoniousness may have been suggested by Agent Bollan having told Hutchinson that in England it was the customs commissioners who applied for writs: it perhaps seemed proper, therefore, that in Massachusetts application should be by the highest-ranking customs man available, the surveyor general. And it probably suited the man who now held that post, successor to the superannuated Thomas Lechmere. John Temple had only just arrived, but he was not a man slow to show regard for his importance. Why the application should have had to be to the chief justice is harder to speculate. It too perhaps had to do with the intelligence that in England application was to "the proper officer of the court of exchequer." The idea may have been to

37. *Cf.* chapter 16, n. 45.
38. *Quincy's Reports*, 418-434.

minimize risk of contentiousness as to just who that "proper officer" was in Massachusetts: the topmost man in the judicial system was as safe a selection as any.

Prior to the final result in November press comment on the writs of assistance case had been nonexistent, and even allusion to it almost imperceptible. There was the *Boston Evening-Post*'s deadpan reproduction, in January 1761, of the *London Magazine* article that quietly lay behind the whole commotion. The *Boston Gazette* for 2 March lampooned Charles Paxton ("Charles Froth") unsparingly, but of his activities with the writ of assistance it said not a word. In December 1760 two successive issues of the *Gazette* carried pieces which, drawing respectively on a Chinese allegory about a rat destructively chewing its way through a wooden statue, and a German story of a man being devoured by an army of rats, had unmistakable if oblique reference to custom house forays in pursuit of smuggled merchandise; and the *Evening-Post* for 9 February contributed a comic verse on the rat theme, with Paxton explicitly identified.[39] But in none of these quaintly circumlocutory attacks was there mention of the prime instrument of the unpopular surveyor's activities, the writ of assistance. So it was too with the February court hearing. This historic display of forensic fireworks occupied the Superior Court several days solid, yet it received not so much as a passing word in the contemporary press. But the November decision, which meant that the likes of Paxton would once again be making their way on to private premises, signaled a change. Newspaper reference to the writ of assistance had been at most muted and indirect; now it burst forth with head-on vehemence.

The *Boston Gazette* for 23 November was drawn upon earlier for fragments of factual detail about the proceedings in court, but the purpose of the piece was less to report the proceedings than to sound off about their result and the state of things it signified. Thus:

> It is probable that the very *urgent* Necessity for this Writ was set forth in the Petition, as some *private* Hints had been given that the King's Officers were set at Defiance — An Assertion which no *unbiassed* man will believe to be true, who is either acquainted with the Character of the Body of Merchants in this Town, or knows the *powerful* influence under which the King's Officers are *protected.*

39. See chapter 9, pp. 172-73 above. Another "rat" theme appeared in *BG* 2 February 1761.

It is worth observing, that the Power of the Exchequer had never been exercised by the Superior Court, for near Sixty Years after the Act of this Province investing them with such Power had been in Force — The Writ, which was the first Instance of their exercising that Power now granted, was never asked for, or if asked, was constantly deny'd for this long Course of Years, until *Charles Paxton,* Esq; whose Regard for the Liberty and *Property* of the Subject, as well as the *Revenue of the King,* is well known, apply'd for it in 1754 — It was granted by the Court in 1756, *sub silentio,* and continued till the Demise of the late King — Upon this new Application, it is now revived, and no doubt will be of *eminent* use to the present Generation at least; otherwise it is not to be presumed the Court would have allowed it — it will never be looked upon in an *indifferent* Light; and therefore if it lives to Posterity, it will afford to them one striking Characteristic, at least of the *present Times,* according as *they* shall find the *Effects* of it to be, when it may arrive to *more perfect maturity,* whether good or bad.

The anonymous writer, whoever he was, was not short on political awareness: his testimony to "the Character of the Body of Merchants in this Town" probably had some sort of reference to the growing suspicion that in correspondence with Westminster Governor Francis Bernard was damning the Boston merchants as a company of smugglers. The writer's knowledge of the history of the writ of assistance in Massachusetts was not perfect, but it was fairly sound; possibly he got it from listening to Oxenbridge Thacher on the subject in court. And perhaps he had been present at the February hearing too: "Necessity" as the justification asserted for the writ of assistance does not appear in the November arguments (as reported by Quincy), but in February it had been the crown's main and culminating theme.

On 7 December the *Gazette* carried a piece by "A FAIR TRADER," which reiterated in a tone as much pained as angry the chronic gripe of the Bostonians, that whereas they were hammered into the ground by the law enforcement activities of the custom house their "Neighbours" and rival traders in Rhode Island could get away with practically anything. So it was superadded injustice that "WRITS OF ASSISTANCE are now established . . . ." A fortnight later the same paper came out with a long leader, heavy with mock irony, about the state of trade in the province, and "the *Writ of Assistance,* lately established as an expedient of the greatest *utility."* For example:

Let every informer have a writ of assistance in his pocket, for you had as goods [sic] have no writs at all, as confine them in a few hands in the

trading towns — break open doors, trunks, chests and boxes — alms houses
bridwells, jails or churches — never be affraid of a dwelling house — no,
not a colonels, a justices, a representatives, or even a ministers — the writ
will bear you out — O — this *wholesome severity*! this merciful thing called
rigor!

(This fierce blast has an echo of James Otis's February tale about
the house of a justice of the peace being rifled under cover of writ of
assistance.) And on 4 January 1762 the *Gazette* published the most
thunderous broadside of the lot.

One way of viewing this long and vigorous polemic is by contrasting it to what the *Boston Gazette* might have blazoned forth if the
Superior Court's decision had been different, with the hesitations of
February resolved in favor of the one-time-only writ of assistance
urged by James Otis. In that gladsome event what more suited to the
occasion than the depiction of how the orator had wrought his
triumph, conveniently to hand in John Adams's Abstract? With
things as they actually were, however, what went into print was a
piece that catered to, if it did not designedly stimulate, a public
mood of resentful disappointment (while Adams's Abstract was left
to gather dust in his law office). There is parallel as well as contrast,
however. In the Abstract's treatment of Otis, Otis himself probably
took a hand. The *Gazette* article bore no signature, but, in the words
of Horace Gray, it repeated "with such clearness and power the very
grounds taken by the counsel against the writ, as almost to compel
the inference that it was from the pen of one of them; and at that
time *James Otis* was a frequent contributor."[40] The article is reproduced in full in Appendix M.

Ample cause to accept Gray's identification of Otis as the author
of the 4 January article will soon emerge, but it is no problem to
show some cause right now. In Otis's February speech, Abstract
version, the anecdote about the customs comptroller misusing a writ
of assistance to search the house of a justice of the peace was
introduced as follows:

> This wanton exercise of this Power is no chimerical suggestion of a
> heated Brain . . .

The *Gazette* article also told how "a late comptroller of this port,
by virtue of his *writ of assistance,* FORCEABLY enter'd into and

40. *Quincy's Reports,* 488.

rummag'd the house of a *magistrate* of this town." To this too there was a defensive preface:

> I expect that some *little leering* tool of power will tell us, that the publick is now amus'd with *mere chimeras* of an overheated brain . . . .

In all common sense, that idiosyncratic turn of phrase came from one and the same person, James Otis.[41]

However, to take the Gray position is not to imply that the 4 January article was exclusively and wholly a rehash of Otis in the courtroom. For one thing, the article was by no means all law. Politics was what people looked for in newspaper commentary on public affairs; and Otis, himself quite a star in the political firmament by now, mixed the dish accordingly. Both start and finish of the article, in fact, glimpsed the contemporary political scene. The very opening was a sarcastic dig at the layman lately appointed to preside over the Superior Court (to the intense mortification of the Otis family): "SINCE the advancement of so great a lawyer as the Hon. Mr. H-TCH-NS-N to the *first J-st-s* seat . . . ." And at the other end, the province's tussle with Charles Paxton over his profits in the vice-admiralty court: a man who refused "to account to *any power* in the province, for monies receiv'd by him *by virtue of his office,* belonging to the province" certainly should not be trusted with the "uncontroul'd power" signified by the writ of assistance. In between, a muted protest at Governor Bernard's spreading the word in England that the Boston merchants were just a bunch of smugglers; (inevitably) the Bostonians' chronic complaint against the *de facto* free port status of Rhode Island; "PECULATION" in customs forfeitures, which, facilitated by the writ of assistance, afforded no benefit to the public but "PUT FORTUNES INTO PRIVATE POCKETS"; and so forth. Nor was the article's presentational or journalistic art employed only on light political knockabout. Appeal went out to historical and patriotic sentiment:

> — THE people of this province formerly upon a *particular occasion* asserted the rights of *englishmen*; and they did it with a *sober, manly* spirit: they were *then* in an insulting manner asked 'whether english rights were to follow them to the ends of the earth' — we are *now* told, that the rights we contend for 'do not belong to the English' — these writs, it is said, 'are frequently issued from the exchequer at home, and executed, and the people do not complain of it — and why should we desire more freedom than they have in the mother country' — such is the *palliating*

41. *Cf.* chapter 16, n. 14.

language of the great *patrons* of this writ — and who claims more liberty
than belongs to us as *British* subjects? we desire no securities but such as
are deriv'd to us from the *british* constitution, which is our glory — no
laws but what are agreeable to the *true spirit* of the *british* laws, to which
we always have, and I hope always shall yield a chearful obedience — these
rights and securities, we have with other *british* subjects gloriously defended against *foreign* invasions, and I hope in God we shall always have
spirit enough to defend them against all *other* invasions.

The "particular occasion" of which the *Gazette* readers were reminded went back to 1687 and the bad old days of the Dominion of
New England, when a fiscal expedient adopted by Governor Andros
(of execrated memory) met with a Hampden-like opposition from
certain inhabitants of Ipswich, who accordingly were brought to
trial: "Judge Dudley in answer to some who pleaded 'the Rights of
Englishmen' — said 'You must not expect the Privileges of Englishmen to follow you to the Ends of the Earth.' ""[42] *Plus ça change,
plus c'est là même chose,* the message seems to have been. Only
worse, for it now appeared — from Agent Bollan — that the rights of
Englishmen were not safe from the writ of assistance even in
England.

The next phase of the article also was new, more or less:

Is there then any *express* act of parliament authorizing the exchequer to
issue such writs? for if there is not *plain law* for such a power, the practice
of one court *against law,* or which is the same thing, *without law,* can
never be deem'd a *good* precedent for another, allowing there is no reason
to doubt, the one is *legally* vested with all the power and jursidiction of
the other: but if ALL this be matter of *uncertainty,* ought it not then
forever to be determin'd in favor of common right and liberty? and would
not every wise man so determine it?

To repeat: this was new, but only more or less. It can be seen as an
ingenious adaptation of one of the main themes in Otis's February
argument, when he contended for the writ of assistance to be special
on the grounds that the relevant statute was not explicit that writ of
assistance search should be general and that the common law traditionally discountenanced general search. That position had been
destroyed by the advice from Agent Bollan that in England, its home
territory, the writ of assistance was general. In this *Gazette* piece he
returned to it, but with a different twist. Thus: lawfulness for the

42. Exactly these words were woven into a piece in *BEP* 25 January 1733, in which "A
Lover of Liberty" identified current goings-on with "those detested Principles, which
actuated *Sir Edmund Andros* and his abandoned Minions." *Cf.* also *Quincy's Reports,* 491,
and the works there cited.

general writ of assistance still could not be positively asserted, for nowhere was there express legislative authority for such a writ; and never mind, either, that it had been sanctioned by the Court of Exchequer at Westminster — bad precedent was not to be followed ("better to observe the known Principles of Law than any one Precedent tho in the House of Lords," Otis had said in February) and all the less so when, as in the writs of assistance case, the jurisdiction of the court was not beyond challenge. With such an abundance of uncertainty the benefit of the doubt surely belonged to "common right and liberty."

What the *Gazette* article next went on to again smacked of Otis in February:

> BUT admitting *there is such* a practice at home, and that it is not disputed, even at this time, when there is so warm a sense of liberty there; it may nevertheless be an Infringement upon the constitution: and let it be observ'd, there may be at some times a necessity of conceeding to measures there, which *bear hard* upon liberty; which measures ought not to be drawn into precedent here, because there is not, nor can be such necessity for them here; and to take such measures, without any necessity at all, would be as violent an infraction on our liberties, as if there was no pretence at all to law or precedent. It is idle then, to tell us we ought to be content under the same restrictions which they are under at home, even to the *weakning of our best securities,* when it is tolerated then only *thro' necessity,* and there is no necessity for it here. — In *England* something may be said for granting these writs, tho' I am far from saying that anything can justify it. In *England* the revenue and the support of government, in some measure, depend upon the customs; but is this the case here? are any remittances made from the officers here? has the king's revenue, or the revenue of the province ever received the addition of a farthing, from all the collections . . . , excepting what has been remitted by the late worthy collector *Mr. B-r-ns?*[43]

43. Customs of duties, possibly featured in a memorial to Lord Bute dated 23 March 1763 (MS North b.6, Bodleian Library; copy in MHS) in which Barons spoke of "having Remitted a very considerable Sum Collected by him in the Port [Boston], which never had been done by any of his Predecessors." Since the only customs duties exigible in Boston were the Molasses Act duties, whose yield was negligible (see pp. 59-61 above), and the plantation duties which had little application so far north, Barons's remittances perhaps related to importations of Staple Act commodities that had bypassed the proper revenue mechanisms in Great Britain. Rather than seize such importations, and thus augment business in the abominated vice-admiralty court, he collected duty on them. (The hesitation of the customs officer, Sheaffe, when John Erving asked to pay duty on the offending goods in the *Sarah* — p. 179 above — indicates that this unofficial option was not unheard of.)

This could explain the merchants' liking for Barons: it eliminated the risk in Staple Act violations if the worst that could happen was a revenue charge that the goods should have borne anyway, at a port in Great Britain. (The merchants' numerous references to Barons's

The theme here, that whatever "necessity" might exist for writ of assistance search in England there was none in Massachusetts, goes straight back to the Adams materials on the February hearing: in particular to the prominence they give to "necessity" as the justification for the writ, in Jeremiah Gridley's arguments on behalf of the crown. Adams's notes show some sign of Otis having responded to this, on the lines that whenever the common law countenanced peremptory violation of hearth and home the exigency had to be very compelling indeed. But nowhere is there any trace of Otis responding to the Gridley argument as rounded out in the Abstract:

> 'Tis the necessity of the Case and the benefit of the Revenue that justifies this Writ. Is not the Revenue the sole support of Fleets & Armies abroad, & Ministers at home?

Otis may have gone back to "necessity" in his *Gazette* article on 4 January because of the reference to it in that newspaper's report of the writs of assistance case on 23 November ("It is probable that very *urgent* Necessity for this Writ was set forth in the Petition . . ."): he perhaps felt the 4 January article would be too uncomfortably incomplete unless he included a counter reference on this point. But whatever his motivation, he set about "necessity" with considerable dialectical force. Gridley himself had loaded his "necessity" argument with ironical commendation of revenue for the permanent stationing of British armed forces in America, and for topping-up the Westminster pork barrel. Otis now took the idea, turned it upside down, and played it straight. In England, he allowed, there possibly might be a case in "necessity" for the writ of assistance as a piece of custom house weaponry. The government needed the money the custom houses collected there, and techniques of securing it perhaps needed to be tough. But customs enforcement in the northern colonies of America had mostly to do with the import restrictions associated with the British staple, and scarcely at all with revenue collection. The "necessity" that might warrant the enormity of writ of assistance search in England therefore had no place in Massachusetts. This line of argument was not without weaknesses

---

honesty perhaps were meant comparatively — in relation to, say, so notorious a racketeer as Charles Paxton.) And a practice so accommodating to illicit trade might also account for Surveyor General Lechmere's otherwise unexplained first suspension of Barons, in 1759. It would have been awkward, however, for the customs commissioners to impose further punishment on a man whose offense had consisted in collecting revenue, the primary purpose of their own existence; hence, possibly, Barons's reinstatement.

(for example, if staple goods came unhindered into American ports direct from continental Europe the imperial revenue mechanism, which was centered in Great Britain, would not collect on them); but it probably served the turn well enough.

That the 4 January article repeated "the very grounds taken by the counsel against the writ" was Horace Gray's reason for identifying Otis as the author. He seems, however, to have intended "the counsel" in the plural. The next excerpt shows why:

> I desire it may be further consider'd, that the custom house officers at home, are under certain *checks* and *restrictions,* which they cannot be under here; and therefore the writ of assistance ought to be look'd upon as a *different thing* there, from what it is here. In *England* the exchequer has the power of controuling them in *every respect;* and even of *inflicting corporal punishment upon them for mal-conduct* . . .; they are the proper officers of that court, and are accountable to it as often as it shall call them to account, and they do in fact account to it for money receiv'd, and for their BEHAVIOR, once every week — so that the people there have a short and easy method of redress, in case of injury receiv'd from them: but is it so here? Do the officers of the customs here account with the Superior Court . . .; or are they as officers under any sort of check from it?

The notion that customs officers in England were under managerial supervision by the judicial Court of Exchequer was lifted straight from the November speech of Oxenbridge Thacher. It was not plagiarism, exactly; Otis added a twist of his own. Thacher had argued that because nothing comparable to the Court of Exchequer's (erroneously) supposed control over the use of the writ of assistance was possible in Massachusetts, the writ itself could not rightfully exist there. Otis preferred a different corollary, a sort of challenge to the Massachusetts judiciary:

> does this court, notwithstanding *these* are powers *belonging* to the exchequer — notwithstanding it is *said to be vested with* ALL THE POWERS *belonging to the exchequer* — and, further, notwithstanding this *very writ of assistance* is to be granted AS a power belonging to the exchequer, will the Superior Court itself, assume the power of calling these officers to account, and punish them for misbehavior?

With that, the article moved to its conclusion, about the danger of the "uncontroul'd power" represented by the writ of assistance being entrusted to men like Charles Paxton.

What is to be made of these successive gobbets of lawyerlike argument? Toward the beginning of the article, amid the less lawyerlike political sarcasms, Otis told of having been "inform'd that this writ is not yet given out." "I heartily wish it never may," he added.

As it happened his information was wrong (a writ had been issued to Charles Paxton on 2 December);[44] but could it be that he had not abandoned all hope of victory even now, and that his reason for cramming so much lawyers' law into this newspaper piece was a hope that, just possibly, those Superior Court judges who had earlier resisted the general writ might change their minds back again? This conjecture seems worth ventilating, but only just. For all their lawyers' law content Otis's slabs of apparently hard argument did not point to a clear practical conclusion. No judge, however well disposed, could have known for sure whether the article was proposing outlawry for the writ of assistance in whatever shape or form, or for just the general writ. The likeliest conclusion is a lame one: Otis infused so much law into his *Gazette* article on the writ of assistance merely because it came naturally to him; he had been thinking about the writ in a severely legal framework for the past year and could not kick the habit.

Of the lawyers' law segments in the 4 January article one more remains to be looked at. It came fairly early on in the article, between the anecdotes about the search of a magistrate's house and the judicial refutation of "english rights" in the dark days of Governor Andros. Discussion of it has been deferred the better to highlight a point of special interest. First the text:

> IT is granted that upon *some occasions*, even a *brittish* freeholder's house may be forceably opened; but as this violence is done upon a presumption of his having forfeited his security, it ought never to be done, and it never is done, but in cases of the most urgent necessity and importance; and this necessity and importance always is, and always ought to be determin'd by *adequate* and *proper* judges: Shall so tender a point as this is, be left to the discretion of ANY person, to whomsoever this writ may be given! shall the *jealousies* and mere *imaginations* of a custom house officer, as *imperious* perhaps as injudicious, be accounted a sufficient reason for his breaking into a freeman's house! what if it shall appear, after he has put a family which has a right to the King's peace, to the utmost confusion and terror; what, if it should appear, that there was no just grounds of suspicion; what reparation will he make? is it enough to say, that damages may be recover'd against him in the law? I hope indeed this will always be the case; — but are we *perpetually* to be expos'd to outrages of this kind, & to be told for our *only* consolation, that we must be *perpetually* seeking to the courts of law for redress?

The opening sentences are of a piece with much other of the legalism in the article; a restatement of courtroom argument. Otis's own, in

44. *Quincy's Reports*, 418.

fact, where (according to John Adams's notes) he had to acknowledge that "For flagrant Crimes, and in Cases of great public Necessity," the common law allowed the "Priviledge of House" to be violated; and there is also a possible whiff of his February insistence that the writ of assistance ought not to make the searching customs officer judge in his own cause. But what these opening sentences led into was something new. New, and directed to an interesting practical objective.

In February, when Otis was striving to persuade the Superior Court to disown the general writ of assistance, it had been to his purpose to hold forth as emphatically as might be on the excesses made possible by "the worst instrument of arbitrary power, the most destructive of English liberty, and the fundamental principles of the constitution, that ever was found in an English law-book." To depict the writ as an open-ended license for ransacking people's houses with complete impunity had been part of the business. And if the business had succeeded, well and good. In fact, however, it had not succeeded. On the contrary, the general writ of assistance was about to be entrenched more firmly than ever. A disconcerting logic followed. If the custom house were to claim for it all the immunity that Otis himself had said attached to writ of assistance search, who could say them nay? Although no authority yet existed in the books, an action for damages where the search proved vain (by extension of the established common law on search warrants for stolen goods) was not unthinkable. In his February speech James Otis had put this meliorating possibility at serious risk. The *Gazette* article gave him a chance to recover it. And so, years ahead of any authenticating law report yet for all the world as if it were already accepted doctrine, the law was propounded in the *Boston Gazette* that where "there was no just grounds of suspicion . . ." — in other words, where the customs officer's entry and search with writ of assistance produced nothing forfeitable — "damages may be recover'd against him in the law."[45] It could have been because of this reclamation job that the *Gazette* article was anonymous. A piece which spoke as if justification by the event were settled law in writ of assistance cases would have lost force over the signature of a man notorious for having propounded exactly the opposite. If he was to neutralize the embarrassment liable to spill over from his previous position Otis must unperson himself.

---

45. *Cf.* chapter 8, n. 5; also chapter 16, n. 3, in which a garbled notion about liability for unjustified search is cited from the *London Magazine*.

Otis's 4 January article was not the last of the grumbles about writs of assistance to appear in the Boston press, but it was by far the strongest denunciation to reach the contemporary public.

Political dissatisfaction with the result of the writs of assistance case found expression a few weeks later in the province legislature.

On 20 February 1762 the Council sent down a bill for the concurrence of the House of Representatives, "for the better enabling the Officers of his Majesty's Customs to carry the Acts of Trade into Execution."[46] Among legislative titles this must rank as a humorous classic. Far from "better enabling" customs officers, the bill was designed to promote the very sort of frustration urged for them by James Otis a twelvemonth before. The general writ of assistance recently affirmed and issued by the Superior Court would be displaced by a "Writ or Warrant of Assistance" good for the one sworn occasion only. All common law courts and individual judges and justices of the peace were to be empowered, upon a customs officer giving them a sworn written statement that he had credible "Information of the Breach of any of the Acts of Trade," and which specified the informer and the person and place informed against ("and not otherwise"), to issue a "Writ or Warrant of Assistance" to the constables and other peace officers of a particular locality, reciting what the customs officer had sworn, bidding them assist the customs officer "relating to the Information aforesaid," and calling for a return within seven days. Distinctly reminiscent, this, of the curious *Conductor Generalis* warrant as commended to the Superior Court in Otis's February speech. From the Abstract:

> an officer should show probable grounds, should take his oath on it, should do this before a magistrate, and that such magistrate . . . should issue a *special warrant* to a constable to search the places.

Having provided for the issuance and wording of this one-time-only "Writ or Warrant" (terms also used as alternatives in Otis's February speech), the bill went on to the substantive power of entry and search. The constable, or whoever, "authorized . . . in manner and Form as aforesaid, and not otherwise" might in the day time "enter . . . any Place; and in Case of Resistance, . . . break open Doors, Chests, . . . and other Packages, them [*sic*] to seize and from thence to bring any Kind of Goods or Merchandize whatsoever prohibited and unaccustomed . . . ." This last formula was taken

---

46. See Appendix N.

practically straight out of the original English writ of assistance enactment, section 5 of the Act of Frauds of 1662. Similarly with the final words of the bill: "And all his Majesty's good Subjects are required to be aiding and assisting in the due Execution of said Writ or Warrant of Assistance, and all such shall hereby be defended and saved harmless." Both points, the statutory obligation to give assistance and the exemption from trespassorial or other liability, were inspired by section 32 of the 1662 act.

Again it is observable that Massachusetts legal thinking did not make the mistake of identifying the substantive power of entry and search with the writ of assistance itself: the bill correctly made the power the subject of direct statutory provision. However, while the bill's indeterminately named "Writ or Warrant of Assistance" assuredly did no more than command assistance to the customs officer, which was orthodox enough so far as it went, one doubts the logic of the rest of it. There surely was something confused in a situation where the entry and search for which the customs officer had obtained a writ of assistance were carried out not by him but by the constable whose obligation — according to the writ — was merely to assist him. Evidently the Bay province lawyers, for all their understanding of the statutory basis of entry and search with writ of assistance, still had not lighted upon the Cokeian "secret in law" which would have enabled them to get the writ right too.

The writs of assistance bill did not pass into law. Governor Bernard vetoed it, on 6 March, the day on which the province Assembly stood prorogued. In his prorogation speech the governor declared the bill to have been "so plainly repugnant and contrary to the Laws of England . . . that if I could overlook it, it is impossible it should escape the penetration of the Lords of Trade . . . ."[47] That the bill indeed was off-center legally has been noticed, though whether Bernard took exactly those points of criticism perhaps is doubtful. His objection, as recounted to the Board of Trade on 13 April, had more to do with the purely practical consideration that a writ of assistance that had to be sworn for on every separate occasion meant the end of effective customs search:

> I shall in this acquaint your Lordships with my rejection a Bill of a very popular Construction & my reasons for and manner of doing it.
> The Bill . . . was the last Effort of the confederacy against the Custom-

47. C05/824: "Minutes of the Council in Assembly," 24 May 1761 to 24 April 1762; *Quincy's Reports*, 498.

house & Laws of trade. The intention of it was to take away from the
Officers the writ of assistance granted in pursuance of the Act of Will 3.; &
substitute . . . another Writt which would have been wholly inefficacious.
This was covered with all the Art which the thing was capable of; but I was
too well acquainted with the Subject to be deceived in it. I had not the
least doubt upon the first reading of it, of rejecting the bill. Nevertheless as
it was very popular; I knew the negativing of it would occasion a clamour,
I gave it a more solemn condemnation than it deserved . . . .[48]

That Governor Bernard associated the bill with the merchants' war
on the customs is not to be wondered at, or quarreled with. But
there was more to his delay in killing the bill than his report to the
Board of Trade could have respectably disclosed.

Francis Bernard was even harder up than usual. For a start, the
size of his family had put him to the expense of extending his
residences in Boston and on Castle William.[49] But something that
particularly oppressed him was outlay on gubernatorial commissions:
he had had to have a commission for New Jersey in 1758, another
when he went to Massachusetts in August 1760, and yet a third on
the accession of George III; and the fees on each had come to
upwards of £400 sterling.[50] Those crippling commission fees were
almost certainly a root factor in Bernard's foot-dragging over the
writs of assistance bill veto. In January 1761, losing no time after the
news of the old king's death and its expensive corollary, he had
besought his patron, Viscount Barrington, for help toward the fees
from public funds. Not a chance, replied Barrington (notwithstanding that he himself was now chancellor of the exchequer and
the executive head of the Treasury); but why not try the province
Assembly?[51] The extremity of the governor's plight was such that he
plucked up the gall to do just that. No less remarkably, he got a
favorable response. Although a grant of money would be difficult,
the local politicians replied, how about a nice plot of land? So it was
settled; and the House of Representatives accordingly voted that
Governor Bernard be granted the island of Mount Desert, in
Maine.[52] The scenario is obvious. Political attitudes to the Mount

48. Bernard Papers II; *Quincy's Reports*, 498-99. CO391/65 has the receipt of Bernard's
letter, of a copy of the bill, of an extract from the Council minutes for 6 March, and of
other (unrelated) papers, entered under date 19 November 1762.

49. Bernard Papers X, 216.

50. To W. Bollan, 12 January 1761: Bernard Papers IX.

51. Bernard to Barrington, 6 June 1761: Bernard Papers IX. Bernard attempted self-
help, too, with the naval officership: *cf.* chapter 10, n. 23.

52. Bernard Papers X, 216: "The Grant accordingly passed the House on the 27th of
February 1762 and tho', to make it appear more honorable, it is said to be in consideration

INTERVAL

Desert benefaction might have been much less accommodating if, only a few days previously, instead of allowing the "very popular" writ of assistance bill to pass in the Council and down to the House of Representatives, the governor had come straight out and blocked it. Nor indeed was Bernard the man to overlook a more positive possibility. Inasmuch as the progressing of the bill on 20 February seemed to have his blessing, dispositions in the house toward the Mount Desert grant might become that much the sweeter.

Bernard's statement to the Board of Trade that he had all along intended to destroy the writs of assistance bill is entirely credible, of course. There is no question of a change of heart between 20 February when he let the bill through the Council and 6 March when he vetoed it. For one thing, even if he signed the bill, the British government almost certainly would have quashed it (and told him off). For another, and probably more important, his chronic money problems gave him a special interest in maximizing the efficiency of customs law enforcement. The wider the liberty of customs officers to search out seizures the greater the personal profit to the governor, from his entitlement to one-third of the proceeds. Whether or not Bernard had had a hand in his friend Cockle's application for a writ of assistance in October 1760, and to whatever extent his appointment of Thomas Hutchinson to the Superior Court had been aimed at a satisfactory decision on this, the writ of assistance at last affirmed by the Superior Court was rich in promise of gubernatorial gravy. A legislative bill to displace this invaluable instrument by something that rendered effective customs search impossible and extinguished Bernard's rosy expectations of augmented income was doomed from the start.

By when the House of Representatives passed the Mount Desert grant on 27 February they had already given the writs of assistance bill its first and second readings. On 5 March, after amending it somewhat, they gave it a third reading and sent it back to the Council.[53] The following day, say the Council minutes, "James Otis Esq. from the House of Representatives came up to the Board with a Message to inquire if they had passed on the engrossed Bill sent up from the House for the better enabling the Officers of his Majesty's

---

of the extraordinary Services of the Governor, yet the real Consideration was to reimburse him the forementioned expences . . . ." Cf. C05/824, minute for 27 February 1762.

53. Horace Gray (Quincy's Reports, 496) gives the date as 6 March. But see Appendix N.

Customs to carry the Acts of Trade into execution."[54] Messages of this kind between house and Council were not uncommon. One wonders, nevertheless, whether the message borne by Otis may not have proceeded from an uneasy feeling among the sponsors of the bill in the house that all might not be well upstairs. Whatever understanding had been reached with Governor Bernard in return for the Mount Desert grant, and however encouraging his earlier willingness to let the writs of assistance move forward, no one with a particle of insight could be sure that he would deliver in the end. If the inhibitions working on him are visible at more than two hundred years' distance, they surely would have been plain enough to his contemporaries. Yet the way Bernard in fact handled the bill on 6 March might have surprised the deepest of his doubters. The bill had actually gone through its remaining stage in the Council, and the Council's concurrence notified to the house, before the governor moved against it. And even that blow was not immediate and direct. The Council minutes tell blandly how the bill, having been laid before the governor for his consent, "appeared to him to be repugnant and contrary to the Laws of the Realm of England . . ."; "wherefore," the minutes continue, "he thought proper in Council to take the opinion of the Judges . . . ." Three of the Superior Court judges were present as members of the Council: Thomas Hutchinson, John Cushing, and Peter Oliver; and presumably it was they who "retired into the Lobby, and soon after returned declaring

> That if this Bill should pass into a Law the Superior Court would be restrained from granting a Writ of Assistance in the manner such Writs of Assistance are granted by the Court of Exchequer in England.[55]

With that, Governor Bernard at last did what he had all along intended to do, and imposed his veto. The House of Representatives, who earlier that day had been told of the Council's concurrence in the bill, and presumably were expecting to see the obnoxious general writ of assistance duly legislated into perdition, learned of the death of the legislation instead. And since it was in the governor's prorogation speech that this disappointing intelligence was delivered the house had no means of protest or reply.

Nor could there be any clawing back on the Mount Desert grant, be the house's disappointment over the writs of assistance bill what it

---

54. C05/824.

55. C05/823; Massachusetts Archives, "Council Records February 1759-May 1765"; *Quincy's Reports*, 497.

might. However, this may not have rankled too much. If the bill had been a *quid pro quo* for the politicians it was not the only one. There was another, as it were built into the Mount Desert grant. The grant was in fact somewhat notional. Essential to an understanding of the province politicians' remarkable generosity toward Governor Bernard[56] is the fact that the territory of which Mount Desert was a part, between the Penobscot and St. Croix rivers, did not really belong to Massachusetts. It had been acquired by Great Britain, from the French, long after the boundaries of Massachusetts were established; and the province's rights over it were still subject to determination by the British government. Nevertheless, this uncertainty of title had not prevented Massachusetts from creating a number of townships in the region. The true meaning of the Mount Desert grant to Governor Bernard is plain enough. With a proprietary interest of his own he would press Westminster that much harder to come up with confirmation of the Massachusetts claim. In fact, the grant of 27 February was followed by an express request that he get busy[57] (though, as things turned out, the question still had not been settled when Bernard's governorship ended seven years later).

As between the Mount Desert grant by the province politicians and the handling of the writs of assistance bill by the governor, honors — if that is what they were — seem to have been about even.

On 13 February 1762, barely three weeks before his veto of the writs of assistance bill, Governor Bernard had been exceedingly downcast: "The Flame that Barons & his People lighted this time twelve months still continues . . . a violent Spirit of disunion still prevails."[58] Soon after the veto all had changed. On 13 April, writing to his masters at Westminster, he was positively chipper: his report to the Board of Trade on rejection of the writs of assistance bill had marked "a total end to this troublesome Altercation about the Custom house officers." Likewise on 25 April in a letter to John Pownall: "All the disputes concerning the Admiralty & Custom house are ended & in every instance are determined on the side of the Kings Authority. The last and finishing stroke was my negativing a Bill for substituting another writ in lieu of the writ of assistance

---

56. *Cf.* chapter 9, n. 22.
57. Journal of the House of Representatives, 282, as in C05/842.
58. The letters quoted in this paragraph are all in Bernard Papers I.

granted by the Act of 7 & 8 of Will 3 . . . ." As Bernard implied, the killing of the writ of assistance bill was a culmination. Other deliverances had contributed to the upswing in his morale.

For example, the political détente signified by the Mount Desert grant. Whatever self-service lay behind that ambiguous benefaction, clearly neither the grant nor Bernard's originating approach for help with his commission fees would have been possible if governor and politicians had been openly at loggerheads. Yet the animus against the governor that had somehow to be swept under the rug had been very considerable. Largely this flowed from the widespread suspicion, already mentioned, that Bernard's despatches to England had included ruderies about the Boston merchants. In that disconsolate letter of 13 February Bernard showed himself aware of the atmosphere: "Barons's party among the merchants are very angry with me at this time, upon some advices they have received of my representations against Barons . . . ." Evidence from other sources is plentiful. Some has been noticed already, in the 23 November *Boston Gazette* report on the writs of assistance case, and in James Otis's *Gazette* article on 4 January. An item of particular relevance is a letter from the collector of customs at Newbury, Massachusetts, who happened to be in London when the papers on the misconduct and suspension of his obstreperous colleague at Boston, Benjamin Barons, arrived on the desks of the departmental chiefs, the board of commissioners of customs. James Nevin wrote to Theodore Atkinson, himself a customs official at Portsmouth, New Hampshire, in November 1761: "Mr Baron's affair is not yet done. A Petition from many Gentlemen in Boston is just come to hand. The Gov Barnet in his Letr to the Board says that all the Petitioners are Rascals & Smuglers. This has occasioned the Board to send for the Marchts of reputation here to know the truth of the Govrs assertion. The Board has been a day on this affair & had scenes of iniquity opened to their view."[59] This letter from Nevin to Atkinson may have been one of the "advices" that Bernard spoke of. Direct testimony also exists from a member of the calumniated body of merchants, John Rowe, who checked back with his own London contacts: "Wee find the merchts here have been pretty Roughly handled in a Representation from our

---

59. Theodore Atkinson Papers (photostats in Massachusetts Historical Society). The "Petition" presumably was an appeal for Barons's restoration which the "Society for Encouraging Trade and Commerce, and others, Inhabitants of the Town of Boston" addressed to the customs commissioners on 14 August 1761 (in T1/408).

Governour . . . . I shall Esteem it a favour you'l do what's necessary to Support our Reputation & Lett me add to get a Copy of the Governors Representations."[60] The political management by which these resentments were contained sufficiently to make possible the Mount Desert project may have been specially pleasing to Governor Bernard. Prominent among the managers were, of all people, the James Otises, father and son. At the beginning of 1762 Bernard had come to apprehend the afflictions he had let loose upon himself by his treatment of the Otises in the fall and winter a year ago, and set forth upon a process of fence-mending and propitiation. In January he appointed Joseph Otis, a younger son of the colonel, sheriff of Barnstable county. In May the colonel at last attained his ambition for a seat on the province Council; less than two years later he was to become chief justice of the Barnstable court of common pleas, and judge of probate. The Otises did not say bought indefinitely,[61] any more than their help with the Mount Desert grant was untainted by equivocal intention; but in the early spring of 1762 it was not unreasonable for Governor Bernard to suppose that, on balance, the political front had brightened.

There was something else — fringe-political might be a term for it — that lifted Governor Bernard's spirits at this time. When Bernard wrote on 13 February about the persistence of the "Flame that Barons & his People lighted this time twelve months," the suspended collector of customs, though of diminished political consequence (as far back as May 1761 Bernard had written him down as "a tool of . . . the Merchants"),[62] was still around and making a considerable nuisance of himself. Barons's three lawsuits against his former custom house colleagues were awaiting trial; and his campaign against the governor personally, which already ranged in threat from a duel to removal from office, now included written obloquy (which, however, no printer could be persuaded to publish).[63] Although much of this clearly could not be taken very seriously, Bernard was never able to rid himself of a nagging nervousness about Barons. Under suspension though he was, and however justified the strictures upon him transmitted to England, the man had powerful connections there

60. To Messrs. Lane and Booth, 24 February 1762, in Anne Rowe Cunningham, ed., *Letters and Diary of John Rowe 1759-1762, 1764-1779* (Boston, 1903), 415.

61. See L. J. Thomas, *Partisan Politics in Massachusetts during Governor Bernard's Administration 1760-1770* (Ph.D. diss., University of Wisconsin, 1960), 113-17.

62. To A. Colden, 11 May 1761: Bernard Papers I.

63. Bernard to ? 28 June 1761, and 13 February 1762: Bernard Papers I and II.

who might save him yet. Bernard told Lord Barrington how, when the new surveyor general, John Temple, showed up in November 1761 "he brought with him the most favorable intentions toward Mr Barons" and seemed "predetermined . . . to restore him." The governor naturally did not neglect to tell Temple the other side of the story, and succeeded in modifying the surveyor general's embarrassing inclination; he admitted, even so, that if Temple had insisted on a reinstatement he would have gone along with it.[64] And Bernard was mindful that Barrington himself had been moved to commend the wayward collector after his first suspension.[65] True, on 22 July 1761 Barrington had acknowledged that "The Indiscretion of Barons has been amazing — his friends all condemn him";[66] but this was far short of an undertaking that Barons would not get away with it again. To Bernard the possibility must have seemed real enough that this implacable adversary, hell-bent not only on personal vengeance but on wrecking the entire enforcement apparatus of the acts of trade, might have clout enough in high places to withstand the sheaf of testimony supporting Charles Paxton's "Articles of Complaint" against him, and even now to regain his post as head of the Boston custom house. Therefore it must have been with great relief that, probably in the third week of February 1762, Bernard received word from Barrington: "I have the pleasure to acquaint you that Mr Baron is turn'd out with the entire approbation of the Treasury, Board of Trade & Customs."[67] One of Barons's friends among the merchants, John Rowe, saw the situation differently: "it gives great Uneasiness to See the Usage & art, has been made use off to destroy, I must say, a honest man . . . ."[68] But rightly or wrongly, the game was up for Benjamin Barons. On 20 February he was reported as having withdrawn two of his actions and having been nonsuited on the third.[69] Exactly when he left Boston seems nowhere recorded, but life in the town must have become a lot quieter, not least for Governor Bernard.

To repeat Bernard's exultant affirmation in April 1762: "All the disputes concerning the Admiralty & Custom house are ended & in every instance are determined on the side of the Kings Authority."

64. 12 January 1762: Bernard Papers II.
65. Bernard to Barrington, 10 August 1761: *ibid.*
66. Bernard Papers IX.
67. Letter dated 12 December 1761: *ibid.*
68. Letter cited at n. 60 above.
69. Bernard to Barrington, 20 February 1762: Bernard Papers II.

Barons's three actions were dead. In the term that began at Boston on 16 February the Superior Court prevailed upon a jury to find in favor of Charles Paxton in the last and definitive hearing of the province's action against him for his ill-gotten gains in the vice-admiralty court.[70] For the action in which John Erving sought to renege on the deal whereby he had recovered his seized brigantine from George Cradock of the Boston custom house, Bernard's affirmation was not strictly true: what did happen was that Erving, whom no jury could be persuaded to find against, threw in his hand when faced with the enormous expense of resisting an appeal to the Privy Council in England (financed, as Bernard had recommended it should be, by the British government).[71] And, perhaps most important from Bernard's personal point of view, the writs of assistance case had come out right.

So it was not just that the general political surface of things had improved for Governor Bernard in the spring of 1762. The judicial system — taken broadly — had worked to satisfactory effect. Wherein was a bonus reason for the governor to feel pleased with himself: under the guidance of his appointee, Chief Justice Thomas Hutchinson, the highest court in the province had proved its reliability.

That the executive orientation of the Superior Court begun by Governor Shirley was now perfected to such splendid effect may have pleased Governor Bernard, but reaction elsewhere was different. Thomas Hutchinson wrote on 6 March 1762, shortly after the province finally lost its action against Charles Paxton: "A cause of great expectation . . . has been determined against the Province . . . . This trial, the Writ of Assistance, and my pernicious principles about the

70. SCR 1760-62.

After initial success, in the Inferior Court, the recovery action went off the rails. In August 1761 the Superior Court upheld a plea in abatement to the effect that Harrison Gray, the province treasurer in whose name the action had been taken, in fact had no standing. (Cf. texts at chapter 9, n. 67; and chapter 15, n. 19.) Having failed as *Gray v. Paxton*, the action now entered the lists as *Province v. Paxton*. In January 1762 an Inferior Court jury found against Paxton; in February, on appeal, a Superior Court jury reversed this.

The province's counsel, James Otis junior, cannot be said to have distinguished himself. (And one wonders whether, in the last phase, the Otises' compact with the establishment — see p. 432 above — perhaps did not cause him to lessen his effort.)

For a full and documented account of *Gray v. Paxton* and *Province v. Paxton* see *Quincy's Reports*, 541-52 (cf. chapter 9, n. 70).

71. *Quincy's Reports*, 553-57, tells of *Erving v. Cradock*.

currency have taken away a great number of friends."[72] As Hutchinson went on to indicate, it was not only friends who registered disapproval, or only he who suffered: the House of Representatives had refused to pay him more than the puisne judges, and had reduced their salaries to boot.[73]

There is no sign of Governor Bernard having lifted a finger to shield the judges from the hostile politicians. (Rather the reverse: if, as he claimed, Bernard recognized the writs of assistance bill as impossible from the start, his calling in the judges to advise against it served no other purpose than to deflect on to them some of the anger its rejection was certain to arouse.) The principal target of the politicians' wrath was of course Thomas Hutchinson, the man whose appointment as chief justice had so stiffened the Superior Court. Hutchinson's letter of 6 March, written, he said, at the end of a "troublesome session of the General Court," showed him distinctly put out with Governor Bernard. "The G for the sake of peace complied, I think, further than [he] would otherwise have inclined to have done with the opposers of government & found by experience the truth of S R Walpoles saying that one expedient makes necessary a great many more . . . ." In another letter, at the end of March, Hutchinson's bitterness was even more apparent. There was nothing that certain persons would stick at "to feed their malignity," he said. "It has been levelled at me all the past year & I tell the Gov. I have kept it off from him . . . ."[74] Not that the governor needed to

72. To W. Bollan: MA 26.

73. The province accounts in C05/853, 854 indicate that the norm was £750 for division among the five judges, with £40 extra for the chief. On 23 February 1762 only £700 was voted. The following year it was back to £750, and £40 was entered separately to Hutchinson "for sundry Services to the Province." The year after that the bulk sum went up to £800 for the judges' "very eminent Services" and with £40 to Hutchinson "in Consideration of his faithfull Discharge of the Trust reposed in him as Chief Justice."

Political fire had been trained on the Superior Court judges since the spring of 1761, with agitation for them to be disqualified from membership of the Council: see n. 28 above; also BEP 1 December 1766.

74. To W. Bollan (?), 31 March 1762: MA 26.

The Mount Desert grant to Governor Bernard (pp. 427-30 above) perhaps contributed to Hutchinson's vexation, inasmuch as the Kennebec company may have encouraged it behind the scenes. Hutchinson was on bad terms with the company, having some five years previously produced documentation inimical to certain land claims it had in legal dispute (cf. chapter 7, n. 18). That the new governor might be edging toward the company (who were in fact to grant him some land in 1763) would not have pleased Hutchinson. Also it may be in point that James Otis junior, who sponsored the Mount Desert grant in the house, was often engaged by the company as counsel. For most of this see G. E. Kershaw, The Kennebeck Proprietors 1749-1775 (Portland, Me., 1975), passim.

be told, probably. It was his professional business to have things work out that way.

The vengeful politicians did not forget the collaborative element in the result of the writs of assistance case. Without the explorations of William Bollan in London not even the dedication of Chief Justice Hutchinson could have won through.

Bollan's position as agent for the province was already precarious. Reasons for this ranged wide, from the high cost of his services to tardiness in his communications with the province;[75] and his history as a charter member of the unlamented regime of Governor Shirley did not help. In 1760 the houses of Assembly had actually voted his dismissal; only the efforts of Hutchinson, a friend from Shirleian times, reprieved him.[76] In 1762 there was no hope of shielding him from the wrath of his enemies, least of all by Hutchinson. Bollan had his fate explained to him in a personal letter from another solid government man, Attorney General Edmund Trowbridge. James Otis junior "togeathere with a Number of Other firebrands" in the Assembly.

> were determined to remove You, and for that End privately Insinuated to the Members of the house that our Dissenting Churches were in danger, that You being a Church man were a Very Unsuitable Person to represent us in Time of Danger. . . . That You favoured the Officers of the Customs, Spent your Time in Solliciting their Affairs in England . . . .[77]

How far Bollan's episcopalianism might have worked against the interests of the province's old-time religion is hard to say;[78] but his service to the customs spoke for itself, in the perpetuation of the general writ of assistance. Anyway, he was fired.

Hutchinson's slate was not wiped clean by the salary cut in 1762. A high point in the Stamp Act disturbances in 1765 was the systematic demolition of his Boston home; the building and its contents were almost totally destroyed, overnight, by the rioting populace.

75. See, e.g., Thomas Hutchinson to Israel Williams, 28 October 1759, in MHS, Williams Papers II; *BPBA* 23 June 1760; and C05/820, *passim*.

76. See Thomas, *op. cit.*, n. 61 above, 69-70.

77. 15 July 1761: MHS, Dana MSS.

78. It can have done Bollan no good that the establishment of an American bishopric was rumored at this time: C. W. Akers, *Called unto Liberty: A Life of Jonathan Mayhew 1720-1766* (Cambridge, Mass., 1964), 172. And in October 1760 a proseletyzing episcopalian church had opened in Cambridge — "fountainhead of the Congregational ministry of eastern New England": B. Knollenberg, *Origin of the American Revolution 1759-1766* (New York, 1965), 78.

Governor Bernard reported the spoliation of the "(Lieut Gov) Chief Justices" house thus:

> I mention him as Chief Justice, as it was in that Character he suffered: for this connecting him with the Admiralty & Custom house was occasioned by his granting writs of assistance to the Custom house Officers, upon the accession of his present Majesty: The Chief Justice took the lead in the Judgment for granting Writs, & now he has paid for it.[79]

On this showing, the writs of assistance case was already a lively piece of history.

---

79. To Board of Trade, 12 October 1765: Bernard Papers IV.

There has long been suspicion that destruction of papers relating to land titles gave the Kennebec company an interest in the attack on Hutchinson's house: cf. n. 74 above and the work there cited, p. 181. As a chronic litigant the company had been disturbed by Hutchinson's appointment as chief justice, moreover: *ibid.*, 180.

18

Scenario for the Townshend Writ

THE AUTHORITIES in Great Britain learned something of the writs of assistance case, if only from references to it in papers on the delinquencies of Collector Barons. How much more may have reached the customs commissioners is unknowable, for most of their records were lost in a fire early in the nineteenth century. What is certain, when some years later they did concern themselves with customs search in the American colonies it was to discover that search with writ of assistance had no lawful place there. From which it followed — indeed, high legal counsels in England were explicit — that the writs that Chief Justice Hutchinson and his brethren on the Superior Court of Massachusetts had braved so much to uphold were without proper effect.

This ungrateful and embarrassing intelligence seems not to have been transmitted to Boston. The preferred corrective lay in legislation.

What led to these developments began in Connecticut. In the spring of 1766 the custom house at New London was at odds with the local merchant community and having special trouble with smuggling.[1] Part of the problem had to do with customs officers' powers of entry and search on private premises, and it was included in a Case — a request for a considered statement of the law on a specified matter — which the customs commissioners, to whom the New London difficulties had been reported, addressed to the attorney

---

1. See, *e.g.*, collector and comptroller, New London, to customs commissioners, 24 May 1766, copied to Treasury in T1/453 (*cf.* n. 2 below). Also, *ibid.*, copy letter, 14 August 1766 from Capt. Durell, HMS *Cygnet*, to customs commissioners. (Royal Navy involvement in customs enforcement had been stepped up in 1763, under the stimulus of 3 Geo. 3, c. 22; Durell's letter spoke of his "bearing a Deputation from your Board." For the situation generally, see O. Zeichner, *Connecticut's Years of Controversy 1750-1776* (Chapel Hill, 1949), 82 *et seq*.

general of England. From the facts recounted by the commissioners[2] it appears that the collector at New London, Duncan Stewart, had been less fortunate with the Superior Court of Connecticut than his colleagues to the north had been with the Superior Court of Massachusetts a few years previously:

> some doubts having lately arisen at New London the Collector applyed for advice to the Kings Attorney there who returned him the following answer, Vizt. "I carried your Papers to Newhaven, and mentioned the Affair to the Judges relative to the Writ of Assistants, they considered it as a matter of Importance, but were at a great Loss with Regard to the Affair — As the Act of Parliament has made express Provision that it shall issue under the Seal of the Court of Exchequer, and we have no Statute here relative to it, the Judges therefore made no determination about it."

In short, whatever may have occasioned the New London custom house's wish for a writ of assistance, the Superior Court of the colony would not play along.[3]

The report from Connecticut in May 1766 at last confronted the authorities in England with the deeply unsatisfactory state of the law on customs search in the colonies. This law, it may be recalled from chapter 7, was set forth in the Act of Frauds of 1696, a statute whose broad purpose was to introduce into America a regime of customs enforcement law as closely similar as possible to that which already existed in England under the Act of Frauds of 1662. It may also be remembered that however well the 1696 transplantation succeeded in other respects, its provision for customs search on land was exceedingly obscure. Customs officers in the colonies were to have

> the same Powers and Authorities, for visiting and searching of Ships . . . as are provided for Officers of the Customs in *England* by the . . . Act made in the fourteenth Year of the Reign of King Charles the Second [the Act of Frauds of 1662], and also to enter Houses or Warehouses, to search . . . .

A little farther on the act prescribed that "the like Assistance" should be given to customs officers in the colonies as the 1662 act

---

2. The Case, with supporting documents, and the attorney general's Opinion, were copied with a letter from the customs commissioners to the Treasury, 31 October 1766: T1/453. (The letter was drafted by Henry Hulton, then plantation clerk to the commissioners but soon to be one of the American customs commissioners constituted in 1767.) The originating directive is in a Treasury minute, 2 October 1766: T29/38.

3. Possibly the writ of assistance was envisioned, and objected to, as an innovation enabling entry and search to be by force: *cf.* chapter 7, n. 33 and text.

gave to their colleagues in England, which added to the impression that customs search in the colonies was to be just like that in England, writ of assistance and all. But it could be no more than an impression. The 1696 text was anything but explicit. That the English law on shipboard search would extend to the colonies was stated clearly enough; but the words "and also to enter Houses or Warehouses" might at first sight seem deliberately disconnected from the English prototype, and to give customs officers in the colonies an unqualified *ex officio* power to enter and search "Houses or Warehouses." Yet they could not quite bear this meaning, for did they not relate back, as the reference to shipboard search had done, to "the same Powers and Authorities . . . as are provided for the Officers of the Customs in England" under the act of 1662? To repeat: when it came to customs search on land the Act of Frauds of 1696 was very difficult to understand.

How the commissions or deputations of customs officers in the colonies were phrased so as to skirt round the embarrassing unintelligibility of the search provision in the Act of Frauds of 1696 was described in chapter 7.[4] How the customs commissioners faced the necessity of an explanation to the crown's principal legal adviser appears in the Case as follows:

> In the Deputations granted to the Officers of the Customs in England there is the following Clause, Vizt. "He hath Power to enter into any Ship, Bottom, Boat or other Vessel & also in the day Time with a Writ of Assistants under the Seal of his Majestys Court of Exchequer & taking with him a Constable, Headborough or other public Officer next inhabiting to enter into any House, Shop, Cellar, Warehouse or other Places whatsoever there to make diligent Search &c" but there never having been any Writ of Assistants granted by the Court of Exchequer in England for the use of the Officers in the Plantations, the Deputations granted for such Officers have been as follows Vizt. "he hath Power to enter into any Ship, Bottom, Boat or other Vessel; as also to enter into any Shop, House, Warehouse, Hostery or other Place whatsoever to make diligent search &ca."

That is, a writ of assistance under the seal of the Court of Exchequer was available to customs officers in England, whose deputations accordingly specified possession of a writ of assistance and the attendance of a local peace officer as a precondition of power of entry and search; but no such requirement was included in deputa-

---

4. Pages 116-118. The two different words for a customs officer's document of appointment do not reflect any difference of substance.

tions of officers in the colonies because the Court of Exchequer had never granted writs of assistance for use there. No doubt conscious that the writ of assistance and the attendant peace officer were enjoined in England by the Act of Frauds of 1662, the customs commissioners went on to suggest a statutory justification for doing without the writ and the peace officer in America. It was that the Act of Frauds of 1696 was different:

> And It has been understood that such Writ of Assistants was not required by the 7 & 8 Wm. 3d. the Power given by that Law — vizt. "And also to enter Houses or Warehouses to search for and seize any such Goods" not expressly mentioning a Writ of Assistants, or even in this Particular referring to the Act of the 14th Car. 2d, as it does in every other Instance in the Clause where either any Powers are given to Officers, or Restrictions prescribed this Power to enter Houses &c. therefore seems to have been inserted after the Reference to the 14th. Car. 2d. with design to make the Writ of Assistants unnecessary, as no particular Court had any Power to grant One.

This was not entirely satisfactory. Aside from the fact that the act of 1696 did not read so straightforwardly, the colonial deputations the commissioners themselves had quoted went wider than the act in terms of the locations to which the power of entry and search purportedly applied. The deputations spoke of "any Shop, House, Warehouse, Hostery or other Place whatsoever"; the act spoke only of "Houses or Warehouses."[5] Preparation of the Case for the attorney general cannot have been an easy task for the commissioners.

Again, their next paragraph:

> However in the subsequent Part of the same Clause of 7th. & 8th. Wm. 3d, It is enacted that the like Assistance shall be given to the said Officers in the Execution of their Office as by the said last mentioned Act 14 Car. 2d Ch 11 is provided for the Officers in England upon which Words the Collector of Boston in New England a few Years since obtained a Writ of Assistants from the Chief Justice for that Colony & frequently entered Houses without any Objection . . . .

This was another half-somersault. Having just questioned the need for customs search in the colonies to be under writ of assistance and even whether the writ could be lawfully granted for use there, the commissioners now were affirming that writ of assistance search did in fact take place in America and suggesting a legal basis for it.

5. Apparently, the customs commissioners' standard administrative instructions to their officials in America made no express reference to a writ of assistance when touching upon search and spoke only of "Houses and Warehouses": *Quincy's Reports*, 433-34.

From this they went on to tell of the contrasting unhelpfulness of the Superior Court of Connecticut, and to crystallize the problem. Attorney General William De Grey was asked:

> Does the Act 7th & 8th. Wm. 3d. empower the Officers of the Customs in the Plantations to enter Houses & Warehouses to search for & seize any prohibited or run Goods without a Writ of Assistants & if you are of Opinion it does not, can such Writ of Assistants issue under Seal of the Court of Exchequer in England, or from any and what Court in the Plantations.

The reply was given on 17 October 1766. It could not have been more negative. Said De Grey:

> I think the Words of the Act will not admit of the Construction put upon them in this Case, for the Words "and also to enter" &ca. must be connected with the preceding Words "the same Powers and Authorities" so as to run in this manner, Vizt. "the Officers of the Revenue shall have the same Powers and Authorities as they have in England for visiting Shops &c. and also to enter Houses &ca." which Words give only a relative and not an absolute Power; and the Court of Exchequer in England do not send their Process into the Plantations, nor is there any Process in the Plantations that corresponds, with the description in the Act of K.W.

The chain of reasoning was none too tidily expressed, but it comes through. The power of entry and search contemplated by the 1696 act for "Houses or Warehouses" in the colonies partook of the corresponding power that existed in England under the 1662 act. But the 1662 power was conditional upon a writ of assistance under the seal of the Court of Exchequer, and the processes of the Court of Exchequer did not extend to the colonies (which accounted for the fact related in the Case, of "there never having been any Writ of Assistants granted by the Court of Exchequer in England for the use of the Officers in the Plantations"). From this it followed that the 1696 power depended upon a condition that was incapable of fulfilment. The textual hocus-pocus that the draftsman of 1696 had resorted to had at last tripped itself up.[6]

The customs commissioners' reference — not strictly accurate, but near enough — to a writ of assistance having been issued in Massachusetts cut no ice with Attorney General De Grey. An occasion to check this out was shortly to present itself.

---

6. See pp. 108-111 above. The point that a writ of assistance from the Court of Exchequer would not run in America had been taken in Jeremiah Gridley's February 1761 argument: p. 279 above.

Around the end of 1766 the authorities in Great Britain received a welter of paper from Boston, telling of an episode in which a writ of assistance had featured prominently.[7]

Harmony among the various accounts was far from perfect at every point, but the sequence of events seems to have started with information given to the Boston custom house (by, it was suspected, the notorious Ebenezer Richardson) that illegally imported wines and spirits had been taken to the house of Captain Daniel Malcom, a former seafarer and now a small-time merchant, in the early hours of 23 September 1766. They belonged to "one Simenton of Casco Bay," with whom Malcom and his partner William Mackay were known to have had dealings. Benjamin Hallowell, comptroller of customs, and William Sheaffe, deputy collector,[8] laid plans to search Malcom's house the following morning, 24 September. They determined to use a writ of assistance in Hallowell's possession, and presumably it was in relation to this that they wrote to Stephen Greenleaf, sheriff of Suffolk County, asking him to meet with them at 8 A.M. However, Greenleaf was out of town; and a deputy sheriff, Benjamin Cudworth, "ready at Call by Virtue of a Writ of Assistance legally granted" (as Hallowell and Sheaffe related), was enlisted instead. Two custom house understrappers attended in addition.

The party arriving at Malcom's dwelling, he admitted them, and

7. Except as indicated by separate notes, evidentiary materials in the next thirteen paragraphs are variously from T1/446, 452, 453, and C05/755. See also G. G. Wolkins, "Daniel Malcom and Writs of Assistance": *MHSP* LVIII (1924-25).

8. For Sheaffe's periods deputizing for collectors, see *LPJA* II, 158. The 1766 period occurred between the departure of Roger Hale and the arrival of Joseph Harrison. Hale had succeeded the obstreperous Benjamin Barons in 1762; the fact that he was already in the customs service in England, and the probability that he did not have the influential connections of his predecessors, perhaps is an early indication of the British authorities' toughening-up policy on customs enforcement in America. Harrison's appointment smacks of reversion to old ways; he had been private secretary to the Marquis of Rockingham: W. J. Smith, ed., *The Grenville Papers* IV (London, 1853), 12. On the other hand, he too had had customs experience, at New Haven, Connecticut: T. C. Barrow, *Trade and Empire* (Cambridge, Mass., 1967), 124.

For Hale's stay at Boston, abbreviated by serious differences with Surveyor General John Temple, see Barrow, *op. cit.*, 194-95. References to Hale's "suffering" and to his being "so anxious to exchange his Office for one in England" are in the Rockingham Papers in the Sheffield City Libraries, Wentworth Woodhouse muniments: respectively, Benjamin Hallowell to customs commissioners, 17 December 1765 (copy: R/24), and Joseph Harrison to Lord Rockingham, 1 November 1767 (R/63). Hale is commemorated in the given names of Lieut. General Sir Roger Hale Sheaffe, baronet, born 1763 son of William Sheaffe. (Benjamin Hallowell, that other Boston custom house regular — more of him in n. 9 below — also fathered a warrior of distinction, Admiral Sir Benjamin Hallowell Carew, G.C.B.)

allowed Hallowell and Sheaffe to look round the outbuildings and kitchen, and into a cellar. But when they asked to inspect a partitioned-off area of the cellar Malcom told them that this was in the tenancy of Mackay, and that he himself did not have the key. Sheaffe thereupon went off and asked for the key from Mackay, who protested that "it was very extraordinary Proceedings to search private Dwelling Houses," and instead accompanied Sheaffe back to Malcom's house. Outside he saw Deputy Sheriff Cudworth and the supporting customs men who had been posted there while the leaders of the party took stock of the interior. On going into the house Mackay commented on this scene to Malcom: it was, he said, "beset by the whole Possey of the Custom House Officers and Mr. Cudworth the Deputy Sheriff." Malcom, who seems to have been fairly amiable up to now, reacted with an appropriate display of spirit. Or perhaps it was because the possibility of a forcible break-in was beginning to emerge. Hallowell and Sheaffe having, as they deposed, "insisted upon having the said Cellar Door opened . . . Malcom solemly swore that it should not be & if any Man attempted it he would blow his Brains out." By now the atmosphere was pretty electric, and word was sent for Cudworth and the custom house factotums to step in and help.

At this, Malcom put on a sword, took up a brace of pistols, and· repeated his intention (as he himself put it) that "the first Man that would break open my House without having Legal Authority for the same, I would kill him on the Spot." An attempt to persuade him of the customs officers' "Legal Authority" availed nothing. "We assur'd him we had Power to search his Cellar," they said, "& shew'd him a Writ of Assistance for that purpose, & told him we had brought a Civil Officer with us, whom he saw." But "Malcom Replied he did not care for any Officer & that none should search his House . . . ." It was a convincing show (although Malcom afterward claimed that the pistols were not loaded). Even Hallowell, no poltroon himself, [9] was disconcerted: "Mr Hallowell called me aside," William Mackay testified, "and begged I would advise Malcom to open the Doors and

9. Henry Hulton (see chapter 5, n. 18) tells of an incident at Cambridge in 1774 when Hallowell, then a customs commissioner, defied a mob "galloping as fast as he could with a pistol in each hand." And Thomas Hutchinson retailed a story of Hallowell, who had been master of the province's warship, falling out with a British admiral (Graves) over naval dispositions at the time of Bunker Hill; some time afterward "the Admiral drew his sword, though the Commissioner had none, and that he disarmed him, and then the blows followed": to Earl of Hardwicke, 22 September 1775. Add. MSS 35427.

if there was anything there . . . he would endeavour to make it as easy as possible and that for Peace sake he would give up his Part [his share in the seizure] and Mr. Sheaffe would do the same . . . ." Deputy Sheriff Cudworth, who stood to gain nothing anyway, understandably was no readier to breach the defenses of the irate householder. Indeed, he seems to have balked at the summons to come into the house; for Malcom testified to Cudworth speaking to him from the yard, saying "Capt. Malcom I hope you are not angry with me," and professing not to understand what the business was all about.

After "near two Hours" expostulating with Malcom, and "the Deputy Sheriff Benjamin Cudworth not being willing to enter the said Cellar by Force," Hallowell and Sheaffe "quitted the House of sd. Malcom leaving several under Officers in the Customs to watch sd. House" and went off to report the morning's frustrations to Surveyor General John Temple. Temple was not to be found; but at the custom house they met up with Sheriff Stephen Greenleaf, now returned to Boston. The discomfited pair told Greenleaf of the Malcom fracas, and Hallowell showed him the writ of assistance "and desired him to go with him & the said Collector to aid and assist them in making proper Search . . . ." Such is Greenleaf's testimony anyway. The Hallowell-Sheaffe account says nothing of the meeting with Greenleaf. According to this the two customs chiefs waited "immediately . . . on the Governor then sitting in Council" after their failure to contact the surveyor general. It could be that Sheriff Greenleaf was not entirely sure of the power of entry and search that the writ of assistance was claimed to signify, or convinced of his own obligations in that regard. His testimony goes on to read as if the meeting with Hallowell and Sheaffe ended on the footing that the legality of the renewed visitation upon Malcom's house should somehow be verified: "he readily offered to do his Duty & to attend them at any Time they should fix, and that he would wait at the Court House for their further Direction." He further says that "about 12 OClock the same Day he was called before the Governor & Council & told by his Excy that it was expected that he . . . should attend the Officers of the Customs & assist them in the Execution of their Office of searching . . . ." One surmises that in the meantime Hallowell and Sheaffe had themselves gotten into the council chamber and persuaded Governor Bernard to back up the writ of assistance by sending for Sheriff Greenleaf and reminding him of the duty it put upon him.

It may be a sign that Greenleaf was still unconvinced about the writ of assistance that when he met with Hallowell and Sheaffe after lunch they presented him with not only the writ but with a warrant they had procured from Justice Foster Hutchinson (a brother of Lieutenant Governor and Chief Justice Thomas Hutchinson, and himself a reliable establishmentarian). This warrant, which seems to have smacked of the old search warrant act of 1660 that so heavily infected the argument about the writ of assistance back in 1761, had been issued upon Hallowell and Sheaffe swearing to having received information of an illegal importation concealed in Malcom's house; it ordered "the Civil Officers . . . to be aiding & assisting" Hallowell and Sheaffe "to Enter the House & Cellar of . . . Daniel Malcom." The possibility cannot be excluded, of course, that this warrant from a justice of the peace was conceived as something that might succeed in impressing the intransigent Malcom where the writ of assistance had failed.

However, the warrant proved as useless as the writ, in terms of inducing Malcom to open up. In fact, the afternoon expedition made even less headway than the morning. This time Malcom had shuttered his windows and locked his doors; and not only were the search party thus barred from the house itself, a fastened gate kept them out of the curtilage as well. While Malcom sat indoors with Mackay and a few other cronies the invaders fretted in the street outside, where the demeanor of bystanders was not such as to encourage heroic assault on the invested dwelling.

The possibility of public commotion had not gone unanticipated. At the Council meeting there had been talk of the sheriff raising the *posse comitatus,* an ancient institution of the common law whereby the "force of the county," consisting of practically all able-bodied men in the neighborhood, might be called out to quell tumultuous disorder. It was talk that accorded with the position taken by most of the councilors: the sheriff had powers enough of his own, and "any Aid from his Excellency and the Board does not appear, at present, to be needful."[10] This was not steadiness of nerve, exactly. Rather it was the hesitation of councilors, whose concern for the government interest stopped well short of foolhardiness, to associate themselves with so unpopular a cause as customs search: under the stimulus of the Stamp Act experience the previous year a powerful

10. C05/823. Minutes of Council; entry for 24 September 1766.

patriot spirit was both in the air and on the streets. Governor Bernard finally managed to sell the idea of bringing in the local magistrates if the going got rough. Justice John Ruddock, in particular, who was also a captain of militia, might perhaps be prevailed upon to put his company under arms.

According to Sheriff Greenleaf and the customs men, the total failure that befell their afternoon expedition was explained and excused by the ugly rhubarbing of a hostile street mob whose numbers would be augmented in the event of an actual forcing of Malcom's house, by a ringing of the bell of the Old North meeting house. Nor had the idea of enlisting the magistrates been of any use. Writ of assistance notwithstanding, Justice Ruddock would not turn out. He had disbanded his company of soldiers, he said; anyway, he was too fat to walk far and would have to be carried in a chaise. Besides, "he much doubted of the Propriety of a Justice of the Peace being called upon to give any other aid to the Executive Officers than by granting a warrant when applied for . . . ." (What sufficed for Justice Foster Hutchinson should suffice for him also, he may have thought.) The attitude of the onlookers/mobsters toward a call to assist was true to the local tradition of colorable legality: not so much outright refusal as insistence on that the name of the informer on Malcom first be made known and sworn to. Raising the *posse comitatus,* reported Sheriff Greenleaf rather needlessly, would have been "not only in vain, but highly imprudent." Time passed, darkness came on, and Greenleaf and the customs men called it a day: "The Warrant would not justify a forcible Entrance into any Dwelling House after sun set." The invaders thus routed, Malcom sent out some buckets of wine to his well-wishers in the street.

The sheriff and the customs men went straight to Governor Bernard to tell of the failure of their mission to search Malcom's house. They had been "obliged to quit it," they said, "having been assured that an Attempt to force it would cost some of them their Lives."[11] Bernard had them return the following morning, to repeat their story before the Council. What he purposed — to gather attested descriptions of the Malcom affair that would remind Westminster yet again of Boston's incorrigible turbulence — naturally met with resistance from councilors of patriot sympathy. He was allowed to have his way, but apparently at the price of postponing actual

11. Bernard to Lord Shelburne and Board of Trade, 10 October 1766: Bernard Papers IV (also C05/755).

despatch of the incriminating depositions. In the time thus gained a
town meeting was convened, which set up a committee whose first
task was to obtain copies of the tale as told by Sheriff Greenleaf and
the custom house. This done, a batch of counterdepositions —
orchestrated, probably, by James Otis[12] — was collected, also for
transmission to England.

Malcom himself disputed much that Hallowell and Sheaffe had
said; he protested innocence of anything smuggled being under his
roof, denied having seen (presumably in the afternoon, when he was
barricaded indoors) "any Writ of Assistance nor any other Power or
Authority whatsoever to break open my House," and asserted an
intention to thwart or pursue the invaders only "in Law as far as
Justice would go." One of his postmeridian companions inside the
house, Benjamin Goodwin, spoke of the bystanders he saw outside:
"People that was passing by about their Business seeing the Officers
in the Street askt what the Matter was and stood and talk't five 5 or
6 or so, and I never saw People that was going to a Funeral behave
more solemn and concern'd than they did, not the least noisome nor
disturbance no more than if Mr Whitefield had been preaching . . . ."
Other deponents testified to their being about fifty onlookers, all
well-behaved. To William Mackay, for instance, they "seemed to be
standing in different Parties and seemed very quiet and looked with
melancholly countenances." As for a reported plan to ring the bell of
the Old North, Paul Revere swore he had heard nothing of it; and
someone else thought it was just a tale put around by boys from the
nearby Latin school who, as they broke up, added to the
gathering.[13]

The burden of the Boston town meeting's material was that the
Malcom incident had been exaggerated out of all proportion to its
true significance. "The Dispute that has arisen between the Custom

---

12. Ms diary of John Rowe in MHS, vol. 3, 425: "10 Oct. This afternoon I met the
Committee on Capt. Danl. Malcoms Affair — James Otis, Sam Adams — myself Edm Quincy
Tertius John Hancock Joshua Henshaw and Edw Payne." Also Governor Bernard to Board
of Trade, 22 December 1766: "the Man who opposed the Officers, sent for Otis, & he went
thither as his Councellor": C05/756.

13. John Rowe's diary (n. 12 above), 417, has this: "24 Sept Wednesday A fine
Morning . . . . The custom house attempted to seize some wine out of Malcoms Cellar, but
were hindred from it by about two hundred people making their appearance in the Street."
Rowe's company at the coffee house that evening included Harrison Gray, a member of the
Council present at the day's deliberations on the Malcom affair (C05/823); presumably it
was from Gray that he learned that "The Governour & Council . . . could make nothing of
it."

House Officers at Boston and Mr. Malcolm, is of too little Importance to trouble the Ministry with, had not the Officers drawn up a partial Account & sundry Affidavits & sent them to England, insinuating that, that Dispute was an open & notorious contempt of Publick Authority": the words of Dennis De Berdt, London agent for the town meeting, putting the Bostonians' case to the British government. Also, "The sole design of the first Affidavits & sending them to England was to cast a Reflection on Capt. Malcolm, and thro' him on the whole Town, as if they were contemners of publick Authority & Encouragers of Tumults & Riot." Probably De Berdt's constituents were concerned lest the Malcom affair intensify British pressure for compensation of persons — Comptroller Hallowell among them — whose property had been despoiled in the Stamp Act riots. The radical *Boston Gazette* saw the town meeting's *démarche* this way:

> The Metropolis has shared largely in the so vile and false Representations, from the Days of that worthy and conscencious C---r Mr B---n's, to the Affair of Capt. M-lc-b's, and they have, and are taking proper Measures to ward off the Evils they have been threatened with.[14]

A telling echo from the past, back to the days of Benjamin Barons, when the popular belief first took hold that Governor Bernard neglected no occasion to tell the British government what a dreadful breed of people he was bravely presiding over.

Counterdepositions playing down the Malcom incident were still being collected when Governor Bernard dispatched the originals, together with his own story, to the Earl of Shelburne and the Board of Trade on 10 October.[15] But John Temple, surveyor general of customs, got in still earlier. Temple's report to the customs commissioners in London, with which he enclosed the Hallowell-Sheaffe account, was dated 1 October. His turn of speed may have had something to do with an implacable hatred (not too strong a word) that had developed between him and Governor Bernard. Though the foot-dragging decision to leave Sheriff Greenleaf to his own resources in the afternoon expedition was less the governor's fault than the Council's, it would have been Bernard whom the authorities in

14. 24 November 1766. *BEP* 20 March 1769, referring to tittle-tattle: "Such were the methods taken against a late worthy Collector M- B-s which *caused* his removal — such methods were taken against the town of Boston, in the well known affair of Capt Malcomb."

15. See n. 11 above.

London identified in the animadversion in Temple's covering letter: "had the Civil Authority proceeded with the firmness (I think) their Duty requires, there is no reason to doubt that a Seizure would have been made . . . ." It was all rather hard on Bernard. Not only was he belabored in the Boston press for letting on about the Malcom incident to the government in England: the man who got in first with the story, and whose own fealty to the crown interest was to become more and more ambiguous, was blaming him for the incident ever having happened.[16]

The customs commissioners' reaction to the Temple report was not specially galvanic. For one thing, whatever general spirit of lawlessness the Malcom episode might have been thought to exemplify was not the responsibility or concern of their department. For another, the writ of assistance element had been overtaken by the Opinion of Attorney General De Grey on the question from New London, Connecticut, and the comments they had already passed upon it. Writing to the Treasury on 31 October 1766, the commissioners had simply accepted De Grey's view that writ of assistance search had no lawful place in America and made the obvious recommendation, that it was "expedient to have the interposition of Parliament for granting the proper power to the Officers of the Revenue in America . . .": in other words, the situation following from the De Grey Opinion needed to be put right by legislation. Surveyor General Temple's news of the Malcom affair merely served, by convenient coincidence, to underline the position thus taken. Forwarding the Temple material to the Treasury on 22 November the commissioners pinpointed the Hallowell-Sheaffe reference to Hallowell's writ of assistance having been "legally granted," but only to discount it in the manner of Attorney General De Grey: "In the Case now laid before Your Lordships, it is stated that the Officers had a Writ of Assistants legally granted. The Writ of Assistants directed by the Act of the 14th of King Charles 2nd is to be under

16. The antagonism between John Temple and Governor Bernard may have begun soon after Temple's arrival in November 1761. On 19 February 1762 the governor recounted to the Board of Trade (Bernard Papers II) how he had refused to swear in Temple's brother Robert as deputy surveyor general, claiming that under his instructions any such deputizing was for himself as governor. (Robert Temple was sworn in nevertheless, by the governor of New Hampshire where John Temple was lieutenant governor.) See also chapter 9, n. 75.

More recently Surveyor General Temple had procured the dismissal of James Cockle from the Salem collectorship, for corruption; he had implicated Bernard, as Cockle's collaborator, but without success. Cf. chapter 8, n. 21.

For how John Temple spent the period of the revolutionary war as a kind of double agent, see L. Einstein, Divided Loyalties (London, 1933).

the Seal of the Court of Exchequer, but the Court of Exchequer do not issue their Writs into the Plantations." And so, the commissioners went on in effect, there really was nothing for it but to act upon their recommendation of 31 October and bring in legislation.

The Treasury made no overt move until 14 January 1767. By this time Governor Bernard's collection of depositions had arrived in England; and the Board of Trade, no doubt aware that the Treasury already had papers on the same subject and glad enough of a reason to drop this hot potato some place else, passed the entire batch over. Stimulated, perhaps, by Board of Trade agitation over the general law and order aspect, the Treasury took a bolder line than that recommended by the customs commissioners. It was not enough just to accept the De Grey Opinion and look for better things in the future; something ought to be done to punish that roughneck contumaciousness visited upon the agents of crown authority by the likes of Daniel Malcom. The crown's legal advisers must be asked to think again. Causing all the Malcom papers to be sent to the attorney general and solicitor general, the Treasury made no bones about "the violent Resistance made by . . . [Malcom] . . . and others to the Execution of a legal Writ commanding Aid and Assistance to be given to the Officers of his Majesty's Customs . . .", and squarely demanded "what proceedings may be fit to be carried on against the sd. Daniel Malcom for his Offences mentioned in the said Affidavits."[17]

But there was no budging De Grey and his colleague. The Treasury minutes for 6 February speak of an "Opinion of the Attorney and Sollicitor General on the case of Mr Malcom of Boston in New England," that

no Civil Action or Criminal Prosecution can be brought against any of the Parties complained of, for obstructing the Officers of the Customs in the execution of their office, inasmuch as the Writ of Assistance by virtue of

17. C. Lowndes to T. Nuthall, 14 January 1767: T27/29.

A letter dated 13 December from "one — in London to another — in Boston" was excerpted in *BG* 2 March 1767: "The rioting against the custom house officers in your province, was mentioned in the house of Commons early in the Session, when the chancellor of the Ex declared in the strongest terms that so long as he was in office, he would not suffer the authority of the King's laws to be trampled upon, and that he thought it the highest injury to the nation to suffer the acts of the British Parliament to be broken with impunity. And the whole house seemed animated with the same spirit, so that if your assembly will suffer themselves to be led by that very absurd ignorant *Firebrand* he may bring them into a worse scrape than they can imagine." Harbottle Dorr (for whom see p. 499 below) annotated "The rioting . . ." "vide the affair at Cap Malcombs"; and the "Firebrand," "Supposed to be spoke with reference to J Otis junr Esqre." The chancellor of the exchequer was Charles Townshend, of course.

which they entered the House and Cellar was not in this case a legal Authority.[18]

The Treasury were not without a touch of obstinacy either. On 14 February they tried again, in terms reminiscent, in a converse sort of way, of one of the arguments in the writs of assistance case in Boston six years before:

> It has occurred to their Lordships that an Act of Assembly of the province of Massachsets Bay had passed & been confirmed by the King in the 11th year of Wm. the 3d. intitled an Act for establishing a Superior Court of Judicature within that province by which Act Jurisdiction and cognizance is given to that Superior Court of all matters as fully and amply to all Intents and purposes whatsoever as the Courts of King's Bench Common Pleas & Excheqr. within his Majestys Kingdom of England have or ought to have and it also appearing to my Lords upon a search made by their order amongst the papers and Documents of the Plantation Office that Writts of Assistance have been by constant usage since the period of passing that Act issued out of the Superior Court at Boston as a Court of Exchequer. My Lords direct me to desire you forthwith to lay this matter before Mr. Attorney and Mr. Sollr. Genl, together with the case and their opinion for their reconsideration whether as this Act of Assembly duly passed into a Law of the province is made supplementary to and in aid of the Act of the 7 & 8 of King William [the Act of Frauds, 1696], and as in fact & by constant usage the superior Court of the Province has exercised the Jurisdiction as a Court of Exchequer of Granting Writts of Assistance such Writt of Assistance do not give a legal Authority to the Officers of the Customs to search &c. And whether the resistance made by Mr. Malcolm to Mr. Hallowell the Officer of the Customs armed with such a Writt does not subject him to the punishments directed by the 13th. & 14th. of Ch 2d [the Act of Frauds, 1662] to be inflicted on persons forcibly hindering the Offrs. of the Customs in the execution of their Office.[19]

Standards of historical research and reporting were none too high here: the Superior Court of Massachusetts, far from having issued writs of assistance from when it was first set up, took to the practice only in 1755; besides, any records of issuances were likelier to be with the customs commissioners than in the Plantation Office. However, this does not greatly affect the Treasury's main point: to remind the law officers of the Superior Court of Massachusetts' full exchequer jurisdiction; on which basis, perhaps, De Grey's unhelpful Opinion on the writ of assistance in Connecticut need not apply to

18. T29/38.
19. T27/29.

Massachusetts after all. The Treasury's letter skirted around the error of explicitly identifying the writ of assistance predicated in customs enforcement legislation as peculiar to the inherent jurisdiction of an exchequer court. (It will be recalled from chapter 14 that when the Act of Frauds of 1662 spoke of a "writ of assistance, under the seal of his Majesty's Court of Exchequer" it was not wasting words: issuance from the exchequer was something distinctively prescribed, as affording certain practical advantages over issuance in the normal course from the chancery.) But, careful though it may have been in this rather technical respect, the Treasury's second attempt fared no better than the first.

Worse, perhaps — there is no record of the law officers having replied to the second attempt at all. Of course, for a working department, even the mighty Treasury, to bandy points of law with the law officers of the crown was to court a snub. All the same, it was not necessarily a case of the law officers merely standing on their dignity. A sense of the practical probabilities could have come into it. Aside altogether from the point of law, the factual evidence was by no means unanimous in the custom house's favor. The law officers could not ignore the sheaf of pro-Malcom testimony gathered by the Boston town meeting, and the strong likelihood that a local jury would prefer it and acquit Malcom in triumph.

Anyway, and boggle as the Treasury might, there it was: solid confirmation that when Attorney General De Grey advised on the Case which arose in Connecticut, but which made mention of Massachusetts too, to the effect that customs entry and search in the American colonies depended upon a writ of assistance impossible of lawful issuance or force, he meant what he said.

And so in 1767 the British government decided to do what the customs commissioners had been recommending since the previous fall. The chancellor of the exchequer, Charles Townshend, included in his legislation for a new American import duty revenue a clause designed to establish writ of assistance search in all the colonies. Section 10 of the Revenue Act of 1767 (as the clause became) was in its way a remarkable piece of work. It ought to be reproduced in full, even if not actually read:

> 'And whereas by an Act of Parliament made in the thirteenth and four-teenth Year of the Reign of King *Charles* the Second, intituled, *An Act for preventing Frauds, and regulating Abuses, in his Majesty's Customs*, and

several other Acts now in Force, it is lawful for any Officer of his
Majesty's Customs authorised by Writ of Assistants under the Seal of his
Majesty's Court of Exchequer, to take a Constable, Headborough, or other
Publick Officer inhabiting near unto the Place, and in the Day-time to
enter and go into any House, Shop, Cellar, Warehouse, or Room or other
Place, and, in case of Resistance, to break open Doors, Chests, Trunks, and
other Package there, to seize, and from thence to bring, any Kind of
Goods or Merchandize whatsoever prohibited or uncustomed, and to put
and secure the same in his Majesty's Storehouse next to the Place where
such Seizure shall be made: And whereas by an Act made in the seventh
and eighth Years of the Reign of King *William* the Third, intituled, *An Act
for preventing Frauds, and regulating Abuses, in the Plantation Trade,* it is,
amongst other Things, enacted, that the Officers for collecting and managing his Majesty's Revenue, and inspecting the Plantation Trade, in *America,* shall have the same Powers and Authorities to enter Houses or
Warehouses, to search for and seize Goods prohibited to be imported or
exported into or out of any of the said Plantations, or for which any
Duties are payable, or ought to have been paid; and that the like Assistance shall be given to the said Officers in the Execution of their Office,
as, by the said recited Act of the fourteenth Year of King *Charles* the
Second, is provided for the Officers in *England*: But, no Authority being
expressly given by the said Act, made in the seventh and eighth Year of
the Reign of King *William* the Third, to any particular Court to grant such
Writs of Assistants for the Officers of the Customs in the said Plantations,
it is doubted whether such Officers can legally enter Houses and other
Places on Land, to search for and seize Goods, in the Manner directed by
the said recited Acts:' To obviate which Doubts for the future, and in
order to carry the Intention of the said recited Acts into effectual
Execution, be it enacted, and it is hereby enacted by the Authority
aforesaid, That from and after the said twentieth Day of *November,* one
thousand seven hundred and sixty-seven, such Writs of Assistants, to
authorise and impower the Officers of his Majesty's Customs to enter and
go into any House, Warehouse, Shop, Cellar, or other Place, in the *British*
Colonies or Plantations in *America,* to search for and seize prohibited or
uncustomed Goods, in the Manner directed by the said recited Acts, shall
and may be granted by the said Superior, or Supreme Court of Justice
having Jurisdiction within such Colony or Plantation respectively.

Remembering how anaesthetizing verbiage enabled the meaningless
piece about customs search of "Houses or Warehouses" in the Act of
Frauds of 1696 to get by on one sort of nod or another, the reader
will not be surprised by elements of politico-legal artifice, not to say
calculated bambozzlement, in this scarcely less enervating text of
1767.[20]

20. Section 10's recital of the 1662 provision on writ of assistance search substituted
"or" for "and" in the 1662 act's unsatisfactory "Goods . . . prohibited and uncustomed"

Prominent among the draftsman's problems was that his phraseology could not allow it to appear, much less say outright, that customs search in the colonies was illegal. The law officers of the crown were free to say so in private exchanges with the Treasury and the customs commissioners; and of course it had been the attorney general's Opinion of October 1766 that started the whole thing. But when it came to the actual job of writing this inconvenient situation out of the law, and setting forth just how a power of customs search was to operate from then on, care had to be taken that those notoriously litigious colonials were not given ideas. In Massachusetts searches with writ of assistance had been known for years; if the new legislation were so worded as to imply that every one of them had been unlawful, and therefore actionable as a trespass, the customs officers responsible would face ruinous liability in damages. Thus it was that section 10's recital of the pre-existing law, while initially faithful to the Opinion of Attorney General De Grey — spelling out the 1662 enactment for writ of assistance search and bracketing the obscure 1696 text on to it — eased itself toward an altogether less hard-nosed position than De Grey's. In contrast to the law officers' unequivocal repudiation of colonial writs of assistance, section 10 did not close the door on all possibility of such writs having been valid. What appeared in intradepartmental files as a firm denial was presented to the public as a mere doubt. To the innocent reader section 10 would signify not a headlong rush to panic stations but rather a helpful, though not strictly necessary, clarification of the' law as it already was. And to Bostonians and others who might otherwise have moved in on customs officers with writs for trespass it would mean nothing doing.

Legislation ostensibly "To obviate . . . Doubts" but in truth to head off certainty of trouble in the courts is an old trick of the lawsmith's trade. Section 10 of the Revenue Act of 1767 is a prize specimen.

A spark-back now to the writs of assistance case.

Section 10 of the Revenue Act 1767 did not simply assert the doubt it purportedly set out to resolve; it employed a process of ratiocination. The first element in this was the bracketing, in the manner of Attorney General De Grey, of the text on customs search

---

formula (see pp. 46-50 and 109-110 above). The justification presumably was in one of the "several other Acts now in Force," which also section 10 invoked; namely, the *Act for preventing Frauds and Abuses in the Publick Revenues*, 1719 (see chapter 21, n. 3 below).

in the Act of Frauds of 1696 to the basic text on writ of assistance search in the Act of Frauds of 1662. A further element was the 1696 act's prescription that customs officers in America should have "the like Assistance . . . in the Execution of their Office, as by the said recited Act of the fourteenth Year of King Charles the Second [the Act of Frauds of 1662] is provided for the Officers in England." And so, section 10 flanneled on, with "no Authority being expressly given by the said act [of 1696] . . . . to any particular Court to grant such Writs of Assistants . . . it is doubted whether such Officers can legally enter Houses and other Places on Land, in the Manner directed by the said recited Acts."

The "like Assistance" argument had been utilized in the customs commissioners' Case that evoked the October 1766 Opinion of Attorney General De Grey (though in fact the Opinion made no response to it). The commissioners, whose concern was with negative attitudes to the writ of assistance in Connecticut, rounded out the Case with a description of how different things were in Massachusetts. Their words again:

> However in the subsequent Part of the same Clause of the 7th. & 8th. Wm. 3d, It is enacted that the like Assistance shall be given to the said Officers in the Execution of their Office as by the said last mentioned Act 14 Car. 2d Ch. 11 is provided for the Officers in England. upon which Words the Collector of Boston in New England a few Years since obtained a Writ of Assistants from the Chief Justice for that Colony & frequently entered Houses without any Objection.

To be sure, it would have been perfectly possible for the draftsman of the 1767 act to see the "like Assistance" point for himself; a statutory text that might serve as a foundation for the obligations propounded in a writ of assistance was fairly obvious material for his sort of problem. Even so, inasmuch as the De Grey Opinion must have been included among his working papers, he would almost certainly have seen the Case to which it related and hence this account of the "like Assistance" argument actually in use. The customs commissioners' story of the Massachusetts writ of assistance having been founded upon the "like Assistance" words in the Act of Frauds of 1696 played at least a supporting role in the draftsmanship of 1767.

When speaking of how the Massachusetts writ came to be granted the commissioners had in mind the 1761 court decision, pretty evidently. But it was not the "Collector of Boston," the disaffected

Benjamin Barons, who had set this process in motion; it was the collector of Salem, James Cockle. And while the writ that was at length issued to Cockle had been the subject of an application to the chief justice of the province, the applicant was not Cockle himself but the surveyor general. What signifies about these trivialities is that the commissioners of customs were not drawing their information from any first-hand reports of the writs of assistance case received at the time. A contemporary despatch from subordinate officials to their chiefs would not have confused the collectors of two different ports, compounding the error by misdescribing the surveyor general as a mere collector. A twofold departmental solecism of this sort, in the status-conscious eighteenth century, is almost unthinkable.

But the centerpiece of the commissioners' story was authentic enough. John Adams's Abstract of the February 1761 hearing and Josiah Quincy's report of the November hearing show Jeremiah Gridley on both occasions invoking the "like Assistance" text in the 1696 Act of Frauds. And that it entered into the thinking of the court itself is attested by none other than the presiding judge: Thomas Hutchinson's *History of Massachusets-Bay* says

> The statute of the 14th of Charles II. authorized issuing writs of assistance from the court of exchequer in England. The statutes of the 7th and 8th of William III. required all that aid to be given to the officers of the customs in the plantations, which was required by law to be given in England.[21]

If the customs commissioners did not have detailed official archives to draw upon, how were they so accurate on a matter of such particular technicality?

Enter, once again, Charles Paxton. Few men were better able to advise on all aspects of the Massachusetts writ of assistance than the egregious surveyor and searcher of the Boston custom house. When on 26 September 1766 the customs commissioners set forth their Case for the attorney general's advice on (among other things) writ of assistance issuance in America, Paxton had recently arrived in England. He made the trip "for the Recovery of his Health," apparently;[22] and well it may have been that stresses of the previous year

---

21. Page 68.

22. Surveyor General Temple to Boston customs collector, 10 June 1766: Winthrop MSS 26, MHS. In Bernard Papers XI a letter from Lord Barrington to Governor Bernard, 11 September 1766, tells of Barrington and Paxton having conversed ("He is very much your friend").

left him feeling in need of a break, for Boston in the Stamp Act period was no place for a man so thoroughly execrated. The house he occupied certainly would have been among those wrecked, had not the landlord bought off the invading mob with drink.[23]   Besides, there was now very little of his speciality business to detain him in Boston. Seizures were too hard to come by in these times of direct popular action; his friend Thomas Hutchinson wrote to former Governor Pownall on 11 May 1766 that "P— had information of a vessel unloading dutch goods from Statia a few days ago, but he did not think it safe to go himself, nor could he find anybody else who would venture to seize her."[24]   In the round, though, fate was kind to Paxton. Socially, he had the distinction of a town being named for him.[25]   And it happened that an old connection that he had assiduously cultivated with the Townshend family in England[26] was about to pay off handsomely. Paxton had sailed from Boston in July 1766, the month in which Charles Townshend became chancellor of the exchequer and hence the political controller of the customs department. This coincidence was to give Paxton considerable influence over the new-modeling of the American customs that Townshend set in train, and, on his return to Boston in November 1767, a seat on the American board of customs commissioners now installed there. More immediately, so inveterate a courtier was sure to have made his presence known to the English board, who were still his chiefs. His friendship with the chancellor of the exchequer no doubt countervailed any ill report from Surveyor General Temple (Paxton's alle-

---

23. See *Quincy's Reports*, 422.

24. *Ibid.*, 445. See also pp. 468-69 below.

25. An act of the General Court brought Paxton, in Worcester county, into existence on 12 February 1765. According to Ledyard Bill, *The History of Paxton, Massachusetts* (Worcester, Mass., 1889), 7: "When the bill for incorporating this town passed the House of Representatives no name was inserted; the blank was filled in by the Council by the word Paxton in honor of Charles Paxton . . . a friend of Francis Bernard, the Governor, and of Thomas Hutchinson, the Deputy-Governor. It is said that Paxton promised the town a church-bell if it was named for him: this promise was never fulfilled." Such was Charles Paxton's unpopularity, says Bill (page 8), that "among the earlier public acts of the citizens was to petition for a change of name, and why the Legislature did not grant this reasonable request is a marvel. It should be attempted even at this late day . . . ." But Paxton the town remains still.

26. See chapter 7, notes 6 and 8. Also Paxton Papers, MHS, *passim*: Charles Townshend's brother, George, when on military service in America in the 1750s appears to have borrowed money from Paxton. *BG* 13 February 1769 carried a rumor that Paxton gave Charles Townshend the reversion of a £50,000 estate (Townshend died in September 1767, however.).

giance to Governor Bernard was enough to earn him Temple's hostility), and ensured him a polite audience with the commissioners. What more natural than that, faced with that awkward question of the writ of assistance in Connecticut, they should consult a most experienced officer from practically the same neck of the woods? And who better than the very man with whom the writ of assistance in New England had begun?

More probably than not, Paxton knew of the Connecticut question before he left America. Aside from the fact that Boston was not all that far from New London, it was the headquarters of the customs district to which New London belonged; matters sufficiently important to reach the principal law officer of the crown in England were not likely to have bypassed Boston. And certainly there was time for word to get to Paxton: the New London affair was already being written about in May; Paxton did not set sail until 27 July.[27] There would also have been time for him to brush up on his understanding of the legal issues behind the Superior Court of Massachusetts' decision in favor of the writ of assistance in 1761, in anticipation of the customs commissioners quizzing him on the problem now posed by the less helpful attitude of the Superior Court of Connecticut. The best man to prime Paxton about the legal reasoning for the Massachusetts writ of assistance was his old friend, Chief Justice Hutchinson. Hence, perhaps, the close correspondence between the reasoning behind the Massachusetts writ of assistance as recounted by the commissioners to Attorney General De Grey, and Hutchinson's own account in his *History*. As for the commissioners' inaccuracy on points of circumstantial detail, when was anything written from recollections or notes of a conversation ever free from all possibility of error?

It is piquant to think that the consecration of the American writ of assistance by section 10 of the Revenue Act of 1767 not only carried an echo of the forensic battle in the Boston town house in 1761, but owed something to the instrumentality, however indirect, of the same two men, Thomas Hutchinson and Charles Paxton, with whom the writ of assistance first began in Massachusetts back in 1755.[28]

---

27. *BEP* and *BG* 28 July 1766. A subsequent Harbottle Dorr (n. 17 above) annotation of *BG* illustrates the strength of feeling against Paxton: "Better he died in his passage, for it is supposed he was the Chief Contriver of the Tea Act, & Board of Commissioners."

28. *Cf.* p. 102 above.

Not that section 10 of the Revenue Act of 1767 proved of much use. It succeeded well enough in its "removal of doubt" contrivance, for there appears to have been no move whatever to mulct customs officers in damages over past searches that on the showing of Attorney General De Grey's Opinion had been illegal. But that was only a subsidiary objective. As was stated in the opening pages of this book, the main purpose of the 1767 provision — writs of assistance for a general power of customs search in all the American colonies — came to almost nothing, by reason of the unwillingness of American judges to play it the British way. In fact, there were features of the draftsmanship that positively facilitated defeat of section 10 at the hands of the unsubmissive colonial judicatures.

Insofar as genuine belief that such was the true law motivated the American courts' refusals to issue the Townshend writ of assistance otherwise than for a specifically sworn occasion, section 10 would have been the better for an explicit affirmation that the writ must be general. As it was, the legislative mandate to the colonial courts was simply that they issue writs of assistance; for all that section 10 said to the contrary they were free to superimpose upon the issuance process any regulatory usage they might consider proper. In August 1768 Attorney General De Grey delivered an Opinion which insisted that writs of assistance in America should be as general as in England,[29] and the customs commissioners at Boston circulated the American courts accordingly. But De Grey's attempt to educate the American judges was too late for any effect it might have had. The idea had already taken firm hold that the only lawful writ of assistance was one that had been specifically sworn to. Section 10's failure to anticipate and guard against this stultifying outcome is not wholly inexplicable, perhaps. One thinks of the De Grey Opinion of October 1766,[30] which signaled this legislative exercise in the first place and which presumably constituted the draftsman's principal working document. As far as appeared in the Opinion, the only difficulty about writ of assistance search in America was this: the Act of Frauds of 1696 being construed as extending to America the original 1662 English enactment on writ of assistance search, the writ needed to be under the seal of the Court of Exchequer at Westminster; issuance by a colonial court would not do, even though it transpired that Court of Exchequer writs could have no validity in

29. Appendix A.
30. Page 442 above.

the colonies. This seminal Opinion having centered upon points of jurisdiction, the draftsman of section 10 limited his substantive handiwork — all that presentational finesse was something different, of course — to a single and unelaborated provision that put writs of assistance for customs search within the competence of American courts. (No less useful to him would have been a transcript of James Otis's speech in February 1761, as a warning of what American attitudes to the Townshend writ would be.)

It was not only this fault of omission that left the wording of section 10 vulnerable to the crippling construction the American judges chose to apply. Scarcely less unfortunate was "Writs of Assistance, to authorise and impower the Officers of his Majesty's Customs to enter and go into any House, Warehouse, Shop, Cellar, or other Place . . . ." This read very much as if the writ of assistance itself did the authorizing and empowering, and it may have further encouraged a supposition that the writ was a species of search warrant and that the standard common law disciplines on the issuance of search warrants — notably the specific oath — were therefore appropriate to it. Here it is less possible to excuse the draftsman: the effect of his text was to cut the writ of assistance adrift from its historical and doctrinal moorings. In the original provision for writ of assistance search, section 5(2) of the Act of Frauds of 1662, the customs officer got his power of entry direct from statute; possession of a writ of assistance was a necessary precondition for exercise of the power, but no more than that. The 1767 act's distortion of the true juridical position was what Attorney General De Grey sought to correct in his 1768 Opinion. Having been told how the "General Writ of Assistance" was being denied by the American courts, to the serious detriment of "the true Intent of the Act," De Grey recommended that the colonial courts be given a specimen of the writ and an account of its issuance in England, in the belief that they would then see

> that the Power of the Custom House Officer is given by Act of Parliament, not by This Writ, wch. does nothing more than facilitate the Execution of the Power . . . ; The Writ only requiring all Subjects to permit the Exercise of it & to aid it. The Writ is a Notification of the Character of the Bearer . . . .

But, as has been indicated, the Americans continued to prefer their own views.

The wording of section 10 may also have contributed to the

situation in 1772 to which the next attorney general, Edward Thurlow, addressed himself.[31]   At the center of this was the old act of
1660 which allowed customs search by warrant on specific oath:

> The Supream Court of Virginia seems to have proceeded upon a meer
> mistake of the Law. They have issued an illegal warrant, founded on an
> expired Law, the 12 C.2 c.19; at the same time refusing to issue a lawful
> one, on 13th C. 2 2 c.11; not observing, as it should seem, that the first
> act has a different object, and proceeds by different means. These were
> found useless, and inconvenient; and, to remedy the mischief, the second
> act was made, on which the present writ of assistance in England is
> founded.

In its recital of existing statutes on customs search with writ of
assistance, section 10 spelt how doubt had arisen from the failure of
the respective texts of the Acts of Frauds of 1662 and 1696 to
engage satisfactorily. It was all rather wordy, but sharp-eyed colonial
lawyers would have observed that reference was made not only to
these two acts but to "several other Acts now in Force" — among
them, arguably, the 1660 act invoked by the Supreme Court of
Virginia for the "illegal warrant" criticized by Attorney General
Thurlow.

Again it might be said in the draftsman's defense that he was not
to know how firmly and astutely American judges would set their
faces against a writ of assistance general in form. Still, common sense
should have alerted him to the unwisdom of allowing the Americans
the slightest leverage. Only very recently there had been much debate
in England, centering on John Wilkes, about general powers of
search and seizure, and affirmations made both in Parliament and in
the courts that such transgressions against liberty were illegal. Fresh
from their successful resistance to the Stamp Act, the Americans
were not the men to overlook the relevance of these Wilkesian anti-
government triumphs in England to their own situation under section 10 of the Revenue Act of 1767.

All considered, so unguarded was section 10 on points of substantive importance (whatever its cleverness presentationally) that one
begins to wonder whether the draftsman himself properly understood the writ of assistance. That slip which contemplated that the
writ would "authorise and impower the Officers of his Majesty's
Customs to enter . . ." is very strange indeed. One remembers that Sir
Edward Coke's "secret in law," the doctrinal foundation of the

---

31. Appendix B.

customs writ of assistance, has never been made much use of. It could be that the research that in 1768 enabled Attorney General De Grey to explain the true nature of the writ (in the vain hope of enlightening the American judges) had not yet been done in 1767.

On the American side, an invigorating unity of defiance; on the British, futility and frustration. Such were the products of the attempt in Charles Townshend's Revenue Act of 1767 to fasten English-style writ of assistance search on to the American colonies. But there is another twist yet. The October 1766 Opinion of Attorney General De Grey, to which this ill-fated legislation owed its origin, does not stand up too well.

The essence of the Opinion was that what section 6 of the Act of Frauds of 1696 said on the subject of customs search on land in America was without practical effect: the power of search contemplated by section 6 depended upon a writ of assistance issued by the Court of Exchequer at Westminster; which, because Court of Exchequer process did not reach into the colonies, was an impossibility. It is true that section 6 was incapable of being understood on a straight reading; there is nothing remarkable in a book such as this pointing out the fact, trying to explain it, and perhaps seeing historical reasons to deplore it. However, for a closet commentator to tear into the draftsmanship of a bygone statute and pronounce it unintelligible gibberish is one thing; for a practicing lawyer, an attorney general at that, to interpret a statute still current so as to drain it of all operative power is quite another. It is hard to reconcile De Grey's vitiation of a statutory text with the common law attitude classically expressed as long ago as 1584, in *Haydon's Case*:[32]

> the office of all the judges is always to make such construction as shall suppress the mischief and advance the remedy . . . and to add force and life to the cure and remedy according to the true intent of the makers of the Act *pro bono publico*.

De Grey satisfied himself that the intention in section 6 had been to introduce English-style writ of assistance search into America. Having gone thus far — and it meant some liberty with the text — he then about-faced and wrecked the whole thing by insisting that only the impossible Court of Exchequer writ would do.

Superficially, this was not unlike the position Oxenbridge Thacher

32. 3 Co. Rep. 7a.

had tried to urge upon the Superior Court of Massachusetts in 1761. However, whereas Thacher's challenge to the jurisdiction had depended upon a purely local and accidental circumstance, De Grey committed himself to a devastating universality. Regardless of whatever status in point of exchequer jurisdiction it might or might not possess, no court anywhere in America could issue a writ of assistance sufficient to perfect a lawful power of customs search there. It is curious to reflect that, on De Grey's 1766 view of the law, Governor Francis Bernard would have done better not to veto the 1762 writs of assistance bill (since a power of customs search limited to the one sworn occasion surely was preferable to no such power at all). And the fact of the Massachusetts writ of assistance's introduction in 1755 and continuance in 1761 says something, too. By the yardstick of *Haydon's Case* — interpret a statute so as to suppress the mischief and advance the remedy — the lay judges of that distant province may very well have been closer to true doctrine than was the crown's principal legal adviser in England.

The comparison here is with De Grey's 1766 Opinion, as underlined shortly afterward by his (and the solicitor general's) denial of the legality of the Massachusetts writ of assistance in relation to the Malcom incident. But his 1768 Opinion (in Appendix A) also shows up rather oddly. Admonishing the unwillingness of American courts to implement section 10 of the Revenue Act of 1767 by issuing writs general in form, De Grey felt able to say that from "the General Import" of the Act of Frauds of 1696 the writ "ought to have been set on Foot from that Time in America," and that the purpose of section 10 was merely to "explain" the 1696 provision. And, De Grey's remarkable change of front went on, "it appears accordingly, that in Boston, where a very able Judge presides and some Experience had been had upon the Subject," granting the writ had made no difficulty. If De Grey heard the clatter as the scales fell from his eyes he perhaps took to thinking how different things might have been — no section 10, and no Townshend writ of assistance for the Americans to be so tiresome about — if only he had gotten the law right in 1766.

19

~~~~~~~~~~~~~~~~~~~~~~~~~~~~~

Perspectives at Large

~~~~~~~~~~~~~~~~~~~~~~~~~~~~~

I N PHILADELPHIA on the very eve of 4 July 1776 John Adams looked back to Boston in 1761 and wrote of "the Argument concerning Writs of Assistance, in the Superior Court . . . as the Commencement of the Controversy, between Great Britain and America." Yet the Declaration of Independence that he had helped prepare made no reference to the writs of assistance case, or even to the intercolonial stand against the writ of assistance projected in the Townshend legislation of 1767.

Explanations for the silence are not hard to conjecture. General search was something thoroughly objectionable, sure enough; and individual colonies were already putting proscriptions upon it into their new state constitutions. Even so, it was not a wholly satisfactory candidate for the Declaration's catalogue of grievances. For one thing, there was a war going on: a lofty protest about promiscuous violation of the rights of landed property would do little good for the impact of the Declaration — which, after all, had its public relations side — when the exigencies of the Congress's own military effort might at any time require prompt and unceremonious intelligence operations into the houses and papers of the disaffected. Again, it had not been so long ago that patriot bands went the rounds enforcing nonimportation agreements, not always with fastidiously principled regard for doors closed against them.[1] As for general customs search with writ of assistance, this could scarcely

---

1. In Massachusetts, anyway. William Jackson, shopkeeper, deposed 22 January 1770 how "Mr William Molineaux" with "a Committee of Merchants . . . wanted entrance into my House" asserting "a right to demand it": C05/759. Agitation about tea caused an incident at Richard Clarke's warehouse in Boston, also involving Molineaux and company: "As it was apprehended violence would be offered the doors of the warehouse were shut but in a moment were forced open and torn off their hinges & the Rabble entered with great violence . . .": copy "Narrative" by Joseph Green, 3 November 1773, signed by Thomas Hutchinson, C05/895.

count among the British liberties denied to America since England was where it began.[2] But what more than anything might have ruled the writ of assistance out of the Declaration of Independence was the fact that it did not represent a real grievance, a grievance actually felt. In the form intended for it by the Revenue Act of 1767, an instrument for general customs search, it practically did not exist. Almost every colonial judicature had refused to issue it.

Many years later John Adams again reminisced, and, anxious to establish the revolutionary primacy of his native state and to rescue the reputation of James Otis, went so far as to see the birth of "the child Independence" in the writs of assistance case. "In fifteen years," Adams continued, "i.e. in 1776, he grew up to manhood, declared himself free." Adams's vivid figure has scored itself into history. But at the time of the revolutionary struggle its lineaments would have been hard to make out, even in Massachusetts.

When Charles Paxton was in England from the summer of 1766 to the early fall of 1767, and counseling Charles Townshend on a restyled customs regime for America, he could not have failed to learn that the Massachusetts writ of assistance had been pronounced legally ineffective by the English law officers of the crown. However, this embarrassing knowledge seems to have been kept under wraps on Paxton's return to Boston as a member of the newly constituted American board of customs commissioners, for it was not until April 1769 that Massachusetts custom houses were fitted out with writs of assistance tailored to the post-Townshend regime. (In other colonies, where the writ was previously unknown, movement began — however fruitlessly — in the winter of 1767-68.) The April 1769 writs presumably were replacements for those of the 1761 dispensation. One

---

"These private Mobs, I do and will detest . . . these Tarrings and Featherings, these breaking open Houses by rude and insolent Rabbles . . . must be discountenanced, cannot be even excused upon any Principle": John Adams to Abigail Adams, 7 July 1774 (on the occasion related in chapter 12, n. 49), *Adams Family Correspondence* I, 131.

2. *Cf.* however chapter 21, *passim.*
General customs search did not pass in silence in all lesser statements of American grievances. The first Continental Congress included in its address to "the inhabitants of the British Colonies" (21 October 1774): "The officers of the customs are empowered to break open and enter houses without the authority of any civil magistrate founded on legal information." Virtually the same was in something sent to the king (25 October). But — significantly — not in an address to "the people of Great-Britain": W. C. Ford, ed., *Journals of the Continental Congress . . .* I (Washington D.C., 1904), 96-97, 104, 82-90.
See also *BG* 21 August 1769. *BEP* 17 December 1770 confusedly identified the writ of assistance with Walpole's abortive excise proposals of 1733 (*cf.* chapter 20, n. 13).

advantage from carrying on with the old-style writs in Massachusetts, the American customs commissioners may have calculated, was that if the post-Townshend atmosphere were given time to cool a little the likelihood of a troublesome courtroom confrontation such as that in 1761 would be lessened. Rather noticeably, too, when the replacement writs were at last applied for the venue of the Superior Court was not hotbed Boston, but Charlestown, at a convenient distance across the river. But it scarcely ranks as an accomplishment of custom house strategy that the April 1769 issuances passed with nothing worse than a grumble in the press.[3] Whatever the American customs commissioners' scheming to avert a rerun of the writs of assistance case, they need not have bothered.

In terms of a supercharged customs enforcement process the crown's success in the writs of assistance case had soon wilted. Though for a different reason, the situation in the late-middle 1760s was much the same as that which Governor Shirley had maneuvered to put right a decade or more before. The prime institution of customs enforcement, seizure of offending merchandise, was again deep in the doldrums. In Shirley's time there would have been little point in making seizures, much less searching for them, when there was still no hope of getting them condemned as forfeited. Now the discouragements were more positive and direct. Customs officers were not going after seizures because they were afraid to.

One consideration they would have been mindful of was on the inside of their own establishment. Throughout the 1760s it was as if the customs organization in Massachusetts had acquired some sort of resident devil, hell-bent on tearing it apart. Early in the decade there had been the disruptions wrought by the Boston collector, Benjamin Barons. Toward its close there would be schism and strife in the restructured outfit presided over by the American customs commissioners. Between times, other behavioral malaise again. Now it was at the very top, in the surveyor general himself, John Temple. Many of the later troubles in the American customs board were attributable to Temple and his patriot affiliations, but already in 1765 Governor Francis Bernard was reporting Temple to be "not very friendly to seizing and prosecuting."[4] (The ferocious hostility between the two

---

3. "Journal of the Times" for 28 April 1769: O. M. Dickerson, *Boston under Military Rule* (Boston, 1936). And see p. 470 below.

For the model post-Townshend writ, see Appendix O; and *cf.* chapter 20, n. 1 and text.

4. Bernard to Lord Halifax, 17 May 1765, Bernard Papers III; C05/755. See also Bernard to Lord Shelburne, 28 February 1766, Bernard Papers V; and to Board of Trade,

men, far from discounting Bernard's testimony, makes it the more credible: by dampening enforcement activity, Temple struck at his enemy's gubernatorial share in forfeitures.) In disposition Surveyor General Temple was a bit of a thug; his personal disinclinations were not something his subordinates could afford to ignore.[5]

But menace from their formidable superior was not all, or the worst, the customs officers had to reckon with. As the year 1765 moved on, an altogether different terror confronted them. The Stamp Act discontents produced daunting manifestations of mob muscle; fear of bodily violence, added to the frustrating apprehension that even if a seizure did somehow get made it would be rescued, brought customs enforcement work almost to a stop. Governor Bernard, writing on 17 March 1766: "People do not wonder at the Goods being rescued, but at an Officer being so hardy & foolish as to seize them & think he would be able to retain them. Under the present dominion of the People I have never expected that any goods, tho' ever so notoriously forfeited would be seized . . . ; an attempt being judged impracticable in every step by some of the most diligent and discrete Custom House Officers."[6] It was seen in chapter 18 that Charles Paxton's trip to England in 1766 took place against the background of no seizures and his not daring to make them.

Of course, not every one in the customs service was a Paxton, nor would it be true to say that if seizures were few searches were nil. In August 1766 a seizure was sought out under writ of assistance at Falmouth; and the following month witnessed Comptroller Hallowell's and Deputy Collector Sheaffe's excursion to the house of Daniel Malcom in Boston. Yet both these episodes only illustrated

---

1 July 1765, *ibid.*, where he tells of Capt. Allen RN (*cf.* p. 472 below and chapter 18, n. 1) having "said last winter he seized 3 or 4 Vessels at Casco Bay, for breaches of the Acts of Trade . . . ; that presently after the Surv. genl. sent an order that they should be delivered up to the Owners, & never acquainted him with the reasons why . . . nor pointed out what his mistake was . . . ." Similarly to Lord Halifax, 1 July 1765: C05/755.

Possible origins of the Bernard-Temple vendetta were mentioned in chapter 9, n. 75, and chapter 18, n. 16. *Cf.* also notes 5 and 8 below.

5. Temple's temperament is illustrated by how he "flew into a violent passion" with Comptroller Benjamin Hallowell (for consulting Governor Bernard about a seizure) and threatened to assign him to punishment duty: Bernard to Lord Halifax, 29 December 1764, C05/755. In 1773 Temple, then in England, was suspected of involvement in the theft and dispatch to Boston of letters exploited to the embarrassment of Thomas Hutchinson and others; he fought a duel in consequence. More on Temple's relations with his subordinates is in chapter 18, notes 8 and 16.

6. To H. S. Conway and Board of Trade, 17 March 1766: Bernard Papers IV.

the larger reality of the situation. The Falmouth seizure was rescued;[7] and Hallowell's writ of assistance did not open a way into
Malcom's cellar.

It could be argued that the writs of assistance case in 1761, by
reason of which writs were already in the hands of Massachusetts
customs officers when the Townshend legislation began, did something to spare the crown authorities an additional participant in the
intercolonial forensic backlash against general customs search; and in
the most turbulent of the American storm centers at that. Also
because of the writs of assistance case an attempt to raise the contest
anew probably could have been blocked as *res judicata*: having once
been judicially established (by the Superior Court in 1761), the
lawfulness of the general writ was not to be adjudicated again.
Equally, this negative influence of the writs of assistance case may
have been a factor in why the attempt was not made: in face of the
res judicata principle it might have looked rather green.

But the likeliest reason why Massachusetts had no repeat of the
writs of assistance case is somewhat of a piece with the reason
suggested for the omission of general customs search from the
complaints listed by the Declaration of Independence. People had
not been experiencing search in their homes and of their personal
belongings. What grievance the writ of assistance caused them was
more theoretical than actually felt. In terms of workaday public
nuisance the thing was not worth powder and shot.[8]

That no one contested the new-modeled writs of assistance at
Charlestown in April 1769 — or, for that matter, any of a number of

7. Governor Bernard wrote of this to the Board of Trade, 18 August 1766: "Formerly a
Rescue was an accidental or occasional affair; now, it is the natural & certain consequence
of a Seizure, & the Effect of a predetermined Resolution that the Laws of Trade shall not be
executed": Bernard Papers IV.

8. The last successful writ of assistance operation was perhaps in April 1765, when the
rescued cargo of a sloop seized by Collector John Robinson, of Newport, R.I. (where the
custom house was now showing signs of life), was removed into Bristol county, in
Massachusetts. Local magistrates were not too forthcoming in the matter of searching
premises for the missing goods. So, "I now send Mr Paxton with a Writ of Assistance to
co-operate with you . . .": Surveyor General Temple to Robinson, 14 April 1765, in an
entry, "Governor Bernard's Conduct Relating to the Riot & Robbery at Taunton . . . ," in
John Temple's letter book, MHS 26 Winthrop. Temple's keenness on this occasion perhaps
is explained by the circumstance that the gubernatorial share in the seizure would go not to
his enemy Bernard, but to the governor of Rhode Island. For materials on the Taunton
episode, including a disquisition by Hutchinson C. J. and Trowbridge A. G. on search
warrants and touching writs of assistance, see *Quincy's Reports,* 437-40.

writs issued individually (presumably with the pre-Townshend word-ing) earlier in that year and in 1768 — may be a sign that the writ had ceased to mean much to the man on the street, but it is not a sign that it meant nothing at all. The customs authorities did not go to the trouble of making those 1768 and 1769 applications merely out of bureaucratic habit and for the sake of empty form. Evidence exists that in Massachusetts writ of assistance activity made some-thing of a comeback.

It seems best to start with evidence that discourages visions of the writ of assistance restored in triumphant majesty. The source is the "Journal of the Times," an anonymously compiled diary which from September 1768 to August 1769 retailed to newspapers in all the American colonies dire accounts of life and its vexations in Boston as a military garrison. Prominent among the villains regularly depicted in the "Journal" were the American customs commissioners, whose scare-mongering had caused the troops to be sent in. Added grist to the propagandists' mill was the circumstance that the commissioners' arrival in November 1767 was soon followed by a marked upswing in customs enforcement. The seizure of John Hancock's sloop *Liberty* in June 1768 comes readily to mind, but there were numerous others. A surviving minute book of the vice-admiralty court records more than forty items of business in the post-Townshend period (till mid-March 1772, when the book ends) which, scant on detail though they are, plainly relate to customs violations.[9] The "Journal of the Times" gave seizure after seizure its portion of bitter notice. But — and this is the point — all that that beady-eyed and bileful propa-ganda sheet ever carried on the subject of writs of assistance was a generalized grumble prompted by the batch issuance in April 1769, and a brief piece on resistance in Connecticut. There is no escaping the inference. Granted that the first and last purpose of the "Journal of the Times" was to lash up indignation at the sufferings of beleaguered Boston, nothing is more certain than that a writ of assistance visitation upon an ordinary householder by minions of the execrated customs commissioners would have been scooped with delight and the utmost in lurid copy made of it. That no such visitations were shrieked about in the "Journal of the Times" is as near proof positive as evidence in the negative could ever be that none took place.

9. See also *LPJA* II, 210, and *cf. ibid.*, p. 102, n. 17; p. 103, n. 22; p. 104, n. 24 (for customs enforcement continuing until February 1776); and p. 151, n. 14.

The proposition remains to be demonstrated: the writ of assistance had a part in the revival of customs enforcement after 1767. Overmuch attention need not be paid to the reference to customs search of houses in a compendium of violated rights which the Boston town meeting saw fit to promulgate in November 1772: "Flagrant instances of the wanton exercise of this Power, have frequently happened in this and other seaport Towns."[10] One has only to remember that familiar constituent of contemporary polemics, *suppressio veri, suggestio falsi*, to perceive that the flagrant instances were not said to be recent; and to ponder whether this 1772 protest was not harking back to the early 1760s and before, when customs search of houses might indeed have been frequent enough. More deserving of notice is the report in the *Massachusetts Spy* for 29 April 1773, along with the first-ever print of James Otis's writs of assistance speech (Abstract rendition): "Last Friday, we had another Specimen of the Insolence of Office, when R. Parker, big with a Writ of Assistance, presumed to break open several warehouses on the Long Wharff . . . ."[11] On this showing, the writ of assistance was a practical reality in the province.

It is not necessary to suppose that the situation had changed since the epoch of the "Journal of the Times" and its eloquent silence on writ of assistance search. The Parker piece repays a closer look. For a start: a reference to Parker having "boasted that he had a Right to make as free with our Bed-Chambers" goes far to imply that the notion of writ of assistance search on domestic premises would come as news to people, or at least as something they needed to be jolted into remembering. Coupling this with Parker's searches having occurred in, specifically, "warehouses on the Long Wharff," one forms the impression that, while writ of assistance search undeniably took place, it did so only on nonresidential premises. Further, it emerges from the piece that Parker was a Royal Navy man. It had been not only the army that the American customs commissioners brought

---

10. *Boston Town Records, 1770 through 1777* (Boston, 1887), 95-108. Propagated in pamphlet form among other Massachusetts towns, this early product of the Boston committee of correspondence ranks as an historical document of some fame.

Customs search was little referred to in the towns' responding statements of protest; perhaps because most towns were inland and hence unaffected by it. Sheffield, however, complained of "domestic Security and Enjoyment" being rendered "insecure": *BEP* 15 February 1773.

And cf. p. 475, also n. 20 below.

11. *Cf.* p. 238 above. *BG* 26 April 1773 also carried the Parker report.

into Boston in 1768, and there was more to the revitalized enforcement activity than new verve among the hitherto demoralized customs officers: the commissioners made augmented use of the facility,
which had been in existence some years,[12] whereby naval personnel
might be employed on antismuggling work. When and how Parker
came by a writ of assistance is impossible to say; but that naval men
might be so equipped is corroborated by the Superior Court's having
issued a writ for Captain W. Reid (commander of HMS *Liberty*, the
sloop forfeited by John Hancock) in February 1769. Even if limited
to waterside commercial premises, might not writ of assistance search
have been too perilous an undertaking for civilian customs officers,
whose persons and dwellings were open targets for attack and re-
prisal? This kind of enforcement enterprise being therefore left to
sailors, whose professional business was combat and whose home was
safe on board ship.

And there is another sidelong light in which to see the writ of
assistance in post-Townshend Massachusetts. Ships and waterborne
craft in general were subject to a statutory power of customs search.
This power was markedly looser than its counterpart on land; in
particular, there was no question of it depending upon the presence
of a peace officer and a writ of assistance. All the same, in face of an
unwelcoming master and crew shipboard search could be an intimidating experience for a lone customs officer; and there was practical
good sense in having the writ of assistance available for such occasions, even though in law the search could take place without it. As
the specimen texts in Appendices L and O indicate, Massachusetts
writs were drafted widely enough to enable the customs officer to
drum up constabulary and other support not only for search of land
and buildings but in a variety of other circumstances as well —
including, specifically, shipboard search. To the point is a letter in
which Thomas Hutchinson discussed the legal position of a sheriff in
relation to a customs officer's writ of assistance:

> it is the especial business of the Civil Officers to whom the writ is directed
> to see that the Officers of the Customs are protected & aided & as-
> sisted . . . , but in the particular case that you refer to I do not see that
> you was obliged to furnish hands to unrig the Vessel . . . .[13]

"Journal of the Times" reports of seizures in 1768-69 give clear
signs — which are not contradicted by anything in the vice-admiralty

12. *Cf.* chapter 18, n. 1.
13. To William Tyng, 11 February 1770: *Quincy's Reports*, 465 (and MA 26).

minute book — that a great many were made on board vessels in the harbor, before the offending cargo had been put ashore.

Everything considered, it seems that while customs enforcement activity in Massachusetts recovered in the post-Townshend period, seizures tended to be on water, and some of these may have been facilitated by a writ of assistance; searches on land, however, tended not to reach beyond commercial premises on the quayside and were likelier to be undertaken by naval men than by regular custom house staff.

Many years were to pass before James Otis came into full public view as the hero of "the first scene of the first Act of Opposition to the arbitrary Claims of Great Britain"; in fact, he was long dead when former President John Adams gave him all those rave notices: "flame of Fire . . . promptitude of Classical Allusions . . . depth of Research . . . prophetic glare of his eyes into futurity . . . rapid Torrent of impetuous Eloquence . . . American Independence was then and there born," and so forth. Nearer the time it was different.

For upward of ten years after his part in the province legislature's abortive attempt to counteract the disappointing result of the writs of assistance case Otis did little or nothing to remind Bostonians of the strenuous debate before the Superior Court in February 1761. There was a small political fracas in the spring of 1765 that might have served as the occasion for a renewed blast against the general writ of assistance;[14] but Otis seems to have just sat it out. The writ of assistance in the expedition against Daniel Malcom's cellar was not made much of in the protracted political fuss that followed, though Otis was both a promoter of the fuss and the man whom Malcom engaged as "his Councellor."[15] And there is no reason to suppose that Otis was less tepid toward a post-Townshend rerun of the writs of assistance case than any other Massachusetts lawyer. These instances of the dog not barking in the nighttime are easily enough guessed at: they may have had to do with Otis's personal position or frame of mind at the particular time. In the spring of 1765 the détente between the Otis family and the government establishment may have still had a little life left in it.[16] Otis's low profile on the

14. Cf. n. 8 above.

15. Cf. chapter 18, n. 12.

16. See reference and text at chapter 17, n. 61. Also *DAJA* II, 66, diary entry for 27 October 1772 on Otis having taunted Adams with self-seeking (and other things): "I have never got [my] father chosen Speaker and Councillor . . . , my Brother in Law chosen into

Townshend writ of assistance accorded with a lapse into moderation after the Stamp Act excitements, which itself may not have been wholly unrelated to ominous utterances by high authority at Westminster to the effect that this dangerous troublemaker be sent to England and tried for treason (Lord North reportedly wanted him put to death).[17] But what was probably the chief reason for Otis's apparent quiescence on the writ of assistance has already been suggested: Otis, like other people, came to see the writ as a diminishing public nuisance, no longer all that explosive politically and not worth the effort of a second courtroom contest.

When Bostonians were at last put squarely in mind of Otis's 1761 oration the image imparted was not totally heroic. In the *Massachusetts Spy* for 29 April 1773 the Adams Abstract rendition of the speech was given a preface, which introduced its subject thus: "The following is offered to the public, being taken from the mouth of that great American oracle of law, JAMES OTIS, Esq; in the meridian of his life." These words pointed up a painful contrast. In 1773 Otis was not the man he once had been. For some years his more unfriendly contemporaries had professed to see something besides personal prudence or advantage in his vacillating political attitudes. For example, on 31 March 1766 the *Boston Evening-Post* carried a long lampoon dedicated to the theme that "Jangle Bluster" was off his head; "this *Mad Dictator*," it called him in another issue.[18] Cruelly, these barbs were poisoned with truth; and by the end of the

---

the House and chosen Speaker . . . , nor a Brother in Laws Brother in Law into the House and Council . . . Nor did I ever turn about in the House, betray my Friends and rant on the side of the Prerogative, for an whole Year, to get a father into a Probate Office, and a first Justice in a Court of Common Pleas, and a Brother into a Clerks Office."

17. Lord Mansfield said "that the Authors of the Riots and Seditious Pieces in America, should be sent for to England, and there tried for treason" – especially Otis, against whom "there is particular Evidence for his seditious and treasonable Speeches . . .": *BEP* 7 September 1767 and *Pennsylvania Gazette* 17 September, quoting a letter dated 13 June from London to Boston.

The *Providence Gazette* 4 March 1769 quoted a letter dated 18 November 1768 from London to Annapolis according to which Lord North had declared "that on the repeal of the stamp-act . . . he was determined never to consent to another repeal – or listen to any proposals for compromising matters, till he had brought America to his feet, and that he did not doubt, but if O-s, and some of the other principal persons, who had been active in enflaming the minds of the people, were executed – that it would effectually prevent the like attempts for the future – by intimidating others from their example . . . ."

18. 9 June 1766. A lampoon on patriot leaders in the *Boston Chronicle* 26 October 1769 featured Otis as "Counsellor Muddlehead." *Cf.* Nathaniel Coffin to Charles Steuart, 30 October 1769 in Steuart MSS National Library of Scotland, 5025; A. M. Schlesinger, *The Colonial Merchants and the American Revolution*, 169; L. J. Thomas, *op. cit.*, chapter 17 above, n. 61, at pp. 765, 827. See also pp. 502-3 below.

decade the mental instability that seems to have been discernible in Otis from boyhood[19] had overtaken him in a big way. Following a coffee-house brawl in September 1769, which saw him badly beaten about the head by one of the customs commissioners, he was never again free from the threat or the actuality of severe derangement.

Mention has been made of the law on customs search featuring in a protest on colonial rights, which the Boston town meeting put forth in November 1772. Here is an ampler excerpt:

> Thus our Houses, and even our Bed-Chambers, are exposed to be ransacked, our Boxes, Trunks and Chests broke open, ravaged and plundered, by Wretches, whom no prudent Man would venture to employ even as Menial Servants . . . . By this we are cut off from that domestic security which renders the Lives of the most unhappy in some measure agreeable. These Officers may under color of Law and the cloak of a general warrant, break through the sacred rights of the *Domicil,* ransack Mens Houses, destroy their Securities, carry off their Property, and with little Danger to themselves commit the most horrid Murders.

Otis was a member of the committee to whom preparation of the protest had been entrusted; and it was he who presented the committee's handiwork to the town meeting. These echoes of his February 1761 rhetoric against the writ of assistance suggest that he had also been well enough at this time to help with the drafting.[20]

Otis's services to the Boston town meeting in November 1772 are said to have been his "last public act."[21] The political obituary accorded him five months later in the *Massachusetts Spy,* with its reminder of how an attack on general customs search "in the meridian of his life" had signaled the opening of the career now at an end, had a neatness about it.

However, there was more to the *Massachusetts Spy* piece on 29 April 1773 than tribute to a lawyer-politician gone finally over the hill.

19. "James Otis," *American Law Review* 3 (1869), 663, citing a letter by Otis's brother Samuel in *MHSP* 1858-60, 53.

20. *Cf.* n. 10 above. Z. Haraszti, *John Adams and the Prophets of Progress* (Cambridge, Mass., 1952), 336-37, adverting to an extant draft in the handwriting of Sam Adams, refutes the belief fostered by John Adams that the whole thing was Otis's composition. And on the evidence of John Adams himself Otis was by no means totally recovered at this time: diary entry 27 October 1772 (n. 16 above), "his Eyes, fishy and fiery, looking and acting as wildly as ever he did." Even so, that Sam Adams may have been the penman of the final draft does not exclude the possibility of Otis having contributed: *cf.* n. 45 below and text.

21. *Quincy's Reports,* 446. Josiah Quincy junior, who recorded the resumed writs of assistance hearing in November 1761, was one of Otis's colleagues on the town meeting committee.

Nor was it only that the same issue of the *Spy* had the report of "R. Parker, big with a Writ of Assistance," breaking open warehouses on the Long Wharf and boasting of what else that fearsome instrument made possible. Also in the background was the circumstance that libertarians in neighboring Connecticut were conspicuously doing battle against the writ the customs authorities were still trying to foist on them. A report in the *Boston Gazette* for 12 April:

> We hear from Connecticut that application has been made to the Superior Court of that Colony, by the Officers of the Customs, for a Writ of Assistance; which is of the nature of General Warrants so justly clamour'd against by the people of England a few years ago.

Throughout the post-Townshend period Connecticut had been something of an orchestrater, almost a leader, of intercolonial opposition to the general writ of assistance (fittingly enough, since it was there, in 1766, that seeds of the Townshend writ legislation had been sown);[22] and one senses, if only from how commonly Boston press comment on developments on the writ elsewhere singled out Connecticut,[23] a persistent embarrassment at the contrast between so much brave pertinacity across the border and Massachusetts' own inaction and apparent submissiveness. The decision to put the riproaring Otis oration into the *Massachusetts Spy* had perhaps been influenced by a province-patriotic urge to demonstrate that it had not always been so, and that time was when Massachusetts too had fought the good fight.

22. See *Quincy's Reports*, 501-7. An early post-revolutionary instance of the Connecticut Superior Court outlawing a general search warrant on ground of legal principle occurred in *Frisbie v. Butler*, Connecticut Reports, 1 Kirby 213-15, cited in R. A. Rutland, *The Birth of the Bill of Rights* (London, 1969), 101.

23. For examples see pp. 498, 500 below. Another neighbor, however, had come into line: "Province of New Hampshire, July 15, 1762. At the Request of the Honourable JOHN TEMPLE, Esq., Surveyor-General of his Majesty's Customs, the Justices of the Superiour Court of Judicature of this Province have ordered Writs of Assistance to be issued to the Officers of the King's Customs here": *BEP* 26 July 1762. The going was much easier than in Massachusetts, seemingly. Aside from his own clout as lieutenant governor of New Hampshire (chapter 18, n. 16 above), Surveyor General Temple had recently given the chief justice's son, Theodore Atkinson junior, a job in the Portsmouth custom house: *BEP* 4 January 1762. And, as though for good measure, Governor Wentworth issued a proclamation in February 1762 ordering "all Officers both Civil and Military throughout this Province, as well as all other his Majesty's good Subjects, whom it may concern . . . to be aiding and assisting to . . . the Officers of the King's Customs . . .": *BPBA* 8 February 1762. However, like directives were issued elsewhere in Temple's district: Massachusetts (*ibid.*); Connecticut (*ibid.*, 1 March 1762); Nova Scotia (*ibid.*, 29 April 1762); New Jersey (*BEP* 12 April 1762).

There may have been another topical stimulus, to which also the *Gazette* piece contributed. The piece went on into a recital of the old customs search enactments of 1662 and 1696, and the Townshend legislation of 1767. Then:

> It is presumed that there is no Act of the Colony of Connecticut empowering their Superior Court to grant a Writ of Assistants. If then such Writ shall be issued from that Court, it must be by Virtue of the Authority of an Act of Parliament alone. Will not this, upon some future occasion, be urged by a pensioned Governor of another Colony, as an Instance of Submission to the Jurisdiction of the British Parliament in Connecticut? And what is still more, it will be giving the Sanction of the highest Court of Law, in the most popular and free Government in America, to an Act of Parliament made with the express Purpose of raising a Revenue in America without the consent of the people who pay it!

By now, in the spring of 1773, American freethinking on the legislative supremacy of Westminster was far advanced. This expression of it, in a writs of assistance context, could hardly have failed to react on the mind of a person who, with access in John Adams's office to the Abstract manuscript of the 1761 debate, had seen and remembered James Otis: "No Acts of Parliament can establish such a writ: Though it should be made in the very words of the petition it would be void, 'AN ACT AGAINST THE CONSITUTION IS VOID.' "

From this standpoint the historico-journalistic sense of Jonathan Williams Austin (assuming that Adams was right in identifying him as responsible for the Otis speech getting into the *Massachusetts Spy*)[24] worked not only for 1773 and its antiparliamentary temper but for the future history of the writs of assistance case, since nothing in Otis's speech has attracted more fame than those words about acts of parliament being void.

In the entrance lobby of the Massachusetts State House is a large wall painting of the writs of assistance hearing in February 1761, showing James Otis in full flight of oratory, arm aloft and forefinger pointed upward.

The appeal thus depicted to a higher law was not, in historical fact, a specially important element in Otis's argument. His central theme, that the statutory text on writ of assistance search should be construed so as to require the writ to be issued by reference to the one sworn and specific occasion only, was grounded in common law.

24. See pp. 237, 238 above.

Hale's *History of the Pleas of the Crown* evidenced that the common law had superimposed this principle upon its own regime of search for stolen goods; Otis contended that the same should apply to the statutory regime of search for smuggled goods, drawing also upon the common law doctrine propounded in 1610 by Coke C.J. in *Bonham's Case*:

> It appears in our books, that in many cases the common law will controul Acts of Parliament, and sometimes adjudge them to be utterly void: for when an Act of Parliament is against common right and reason, or repugnant, or impossible to be performed, the common law will controul it, and adjudge such Act to be void ....

From John Adams's courtroom notes (the Abstract write-up is practically valueless on this point) it can be seen that for his argument proper Otis invoked the lesser limb of this two-legged doctrine: judicial "controul" of an act of Parliament, in the sense of moderating it, according to "Common [*sc.,* common law] Right and Reason." The larger limb, about acts being adjudged void, was deployed merely as rhetoric. Otis's "if an Act of Parliament should be made, in the very Words of this Petition, it would be void" was a hypothesis which threw into sharper relief the proposition that the statutory text on writ of assistance search was in fact innocent of an express stipulation that the writ be general and should be given the benign construction he was urging. There was little enough metaphysical about this sort of thing. The declamation, "an act against natural Equity is void," smacks more of higher law; but even that was in fact from common law: *Day v. Savadge,* decided a few years after *Bonham.* Only "An Act against the Constitution is void" was higher law, deriving from some transcendent system of jurisprudence superior to the groundling rubrics of ordinary lawgivers: Otis got it from Vattel's *Le Droit des Gens ou Principes de la Loi Naturelle....* Again, neither "natural equity" nor unconstitutionality had much relation to the hard-nosed sophistications of Otis's substantive argument. They may have been intended as extra presentational rhetoric or perhaps Otis was stringing together a kind of higher law validity for his *Bonham* position, aware that common law attitudes toward parliamentary authority had solidified since 1610.

These recapitulations from chapter 16 carry a reminder that the writs of assistance case was not the only occasion when Otis descanted upon *Bonham, Day v. Savadge,* and Vattel. In 1764 he brought them into his pamphlet against the Sugar Act and the impending Stamp Act, *The Rights of the British Colonies Asserted and Proved.*[25] His purpose this time was different. According to the *Rights* pamphlet, the *Bonham* precedents were illustrative of judicial power to denounce as void an act of parliament that violated "the natural laws" of God.[26] And, on a less exalted plane, "the executive courts" could quash an act for demonstrable inconsistency with "natural equity"; indeed, wrote Otis, "I make no doubt of it, whether they are not obliged by their oaths to adjudge such act void."[27] Instant adjustment of focus is necessary here. Sentiments of this kind do not bulk large in the pamphlet, and nowhere do they translate into a call to action. Given the circumstances in which it was written, the *Rights* naturally had much to say about the wrongfulness of Westminster legislating money out of the pockets of unrepresented Americans, but disobedience was no part of its message. On the contrary: "The Power of Parliament is uncontrollable, but by themselves, and we must obey." And, "let the Parliament lay what burdens they please on us . . . it is our duty to submit and patiently bear them till they will be pleased to relieve us."[28] In none of this is there a sign of tongue in cheek.

James Otis's *Rights* pamphlet is not too close to the subject of this book; and how it squared *Bonham* with extravagant notions of the status of Parliament has little bearing on Otis's differently accented deployment of *Bonham* in the writs of assistance case. Nevertheless, if the tradition of Otis as a pioneer expositor of higher law is to be seen in the round, the pamphlet needs a little more study. Likewise, and to begin with, a look at the pamphleteer himself as a product of his place and time.

A striking thing about lawyers in eighteenth-century Boston is their appetite for academic philosophizing. (It is heard to imagine contemporary leaders of the English bar regularly forgathering to discuss remote topics of ancient and foreign law, yet exactly such a "sodality" was formed in Boston in 1765.)[29] Heritage had much to do with it, probably. Speculative jurisprudence certainly was nothing

---

25. Page references in notes below relate to B. Bailyn, *Pamphlets of the American Revolution 1750-1776* I (see chapter 16, n. 42, above).

26. Bailyn, *Pamphlets*, 454.

27. *Ibid.*, 449.

28. *Ibid.*, 448.

29. See *DAJA* I, 251 *et seq.* Jeremiah Gridley, the elderly doyen of the Boston bar, was the moving spirit. John Adams's "Dissertation on Canon and Feudal Law" flowed from his membership of the sodality.

new in America. Rather the opposite: it came with the territory. How to justify appropriation of lands hitherto available to the Indians had been a question for earnest consideration and debate ever since the earliest settlements.[30] Then again, though history in the British Isles afforded him some material, the colonial lawyer wishing to chart, *qua* lawyer, the constitutional orientation of the haphazard and variegated entity that was the British empire had comparatively little authoritative common law thinking to draw upon; exotica made up the lack.

And a more universal, and in time more proximate, intellectual climate was at work on Otis, no laggard in his reading. Eighteenth-century contemplation of political matters tended to interpret and project them, as it did in much else, in terms of nature. Natural law, in particular, was greatly in vogue. Of course, in one guise or another it had been wafting around in people's minds almost as long as workaday practical law had been constraining their deeds. But the Age of Reason, which came near to equating nature with perfection in all things (the evolutionist take-over, by which it became red in tooth and claw, was still a long way off), boosted natural law as never before. Not in a single formulation, though. The old phantom remained its protean and commodious self.

Otis's *Rights* pamphlet reflected something of the many-sidedness of natural law. It spoke of God's "natural law," as has been noticed. On a more secular plane it partook abundantly of the currently very modish natural law of John Locke for a bumper package of individual rights, liberties, and suchlike good things: indeed, it was largely to vindicate and preserve this inheritance of the Glorious Revolution that the pamphlet was written. And yet another sort of natural law came into play when Otis turned from propaganda to analysis. The *Rights* has been characterized by a modern commentator as the "bold and original if somewhat slapdash effort of a provincial American to define the limitations of Parliament's power over the colonies in terms of a comprehensive theory of the British constitution."[31] Otis's new schematic view of the imperial polity was framed in

---

30. See C. E. Eisinger, "The Puritans' Justification for Taking the Land," in *Essex Institute Historical Collections* LXXXIV (Salem, 1948). Also John Adams to William Tudor, 23 September 1818: *LWJA* X, 359-62. Robert Treat Paine included a legalistically argued essay on "Whether the Aboriginals of America are Proprietors by prior Possession" in a letter about rights over the Ohio territory to the Rev. T. Harrington in (n.d.) 1755: MHS, Robert Treat Paine papers.

31. Bailyn, *Pamphlets,* 410 (Introduction to *Rights.*)

natural law, but a natural law that had little in common either with religious ethics or with a subjectivist catalogue of civic desiderata. It belonged rather with Boyle's law, Ohm's law, the laws of thermodynamics, and the law of gravity: in short, with the laws of the physical universe. Toward the end of chapter 9 it was suggested that the chronic eighteenth-century apprehension of conspiracy, of inimical concert among apparently unconnected events, was a by-product of the Newtonian scientific vision. The idea that all creation operated like a gigantic piece of clockwork was just as apt to condition thinking on natural law. Natural law in this modern mechanistic mode was an ideal setting for the contemporary perception — identified most notably with Montesquieu — which admired the British constitution as a model of balance, counterbalance, and self-correction. The *Rights* pamphlet's explicit "analogy between the natural, or material . . . and the moral world" and talk of "gravitation and attraction . . . in the revolution of the planets"[32] shows James Otis well in the fashion. It could be, however, that Otis's modernism drew some nourishment from his other allegiance. At the heart of the English common law tradition lay real property jurisprudence, a closed calculus of concepts almost mathematical in its abstraction and its workings so dominated by their own unrelenting logic that the whole thing was something of a Keplerian firmament in itself.

It being the essence of government and law that people conduct themselves according to requirement and do as they are told, no constitutional or legal theory can very well accommodate a principle permitting disobedience. In the case of a constitution conceived as a mechanism it would be a nonsense: a component specifically designed to spoil the mechanism's performance. This seems to be the light in which to view Otis's rigorous stand on obedience of statute. As a mechanistic system the British constitution could not tolerate private autonomies contradicting its own lawgiving processes. Protest there might be: "if our hands are tied by the passing of an act of Parliament," says the *Rights,* "our mouths are not stopped"; similarly, "Reasons may be given why an act ought to be repealed, and yet obedience must be yielded to it till that repeal takes place."[33] Of

32. *Ibid.,* 428.
33. *Ibid.,* 449. Otis presumably was aware that the House of Commons would not listen to oral petitions against a money bill: *cf.* Cobbett's *Parliamentary History* IX (London, 1811), 1-6, 1060-63.

course, none of this was to deny the legitimacy — grounded in the law of nature, Lockeian version — of incorrigibly tyrannical regimes being *"deposed* by the people";[34] but, outrageous though such hints may have seemed to eyes at Westminster (and the *Rights* reportedly gave "great offence to the Ministry"),[35] Otis was far from trumpeting revolution. In fact, he was predicating the formal integrity of the British constitutional system as it actually and presently was, or at any rate as it ideally should be. And in an analysis such as his there had to be a *Grundnorm* (to borrow from positivistic theory of the twentieth century), the alpha and omega of validity in any legal order, where references back to remoter and remoter authority have to stop. In Otis's presentation of the British constitutional system this necessary final word was reposed in the legislation of Parliament.

The laws of the system were not incapable of injustice: indeed, it was from a belief that the recent and pending fiscal laws signified injustice to America that Otis had put pen to paper. But injustice caused by the laws was for correction within the law, within the system's own parameters. Parliament itself, the *Rights* pamphlet affirmed, might exercise the supreme legislative power in error, so as to conflict with God's natural laws. An act thus "contrary to eternal truth, equity, and justice" was void, "and so it would be adjudged by the Parliament itself when convinced of their mistake" and repealed accordingly. Furthermore, in cases where the mistake was "evident and palpable" (so as not to be susceptible of deliberative political debate), "the judges of the executive courts have declared the act 'of a whole Parliament' void."[36] Here, obviously, the *Bonham's Case* line of common law authority came in.

Essentially important, however, is the fact that whenever the *Rights* pamphlet made reference to acts of Parliament being void it did so — like Coke C. J. in *Bonham* — in terms of the act being pronounced void by a court. There was no suggestion that individual persons might privately decide that an act of Parliament violated some superior order of law and need not be obeyed. Insofar as the British constitution acknowledged that an act of Parliament might be

34. Bailyn, *Pamphlets*, 427.

35. Joseph Harrison to John Temple, 12 January 1765, "The Bowdoin-Temple Papers," *MHSC* Sixth series IX (Boston, 1897). Harrison had been customs collector at New Haven, Conn. (and would become collector at Boston), but was now in London. Though close to the Marquess of Rockingham, who was not yet in office, his official connection with Temple, a client of the Grenvilles, probably gave him access to the present administration.

36. Bailyn, *Pamphlets*, 454-55.

invalid, it entrusted the decision to its own accredited institutions, the courts. Unless and until adjudged void by due process an act of Parliament remained an act of Parliament and must be submitted to. Thus, on a properly narrow interpretation of *Bonham*, which made the doctrine of void statutes a matter for judicial determination, Otis's perception of the imperial British constitution as an integrated self-regulating whole stood up. In this light the *Bonham* doctrine appears as a piece of remedial machinery, auxiliary to Parliament's own procedures for setting legal injustices to rights. Only a modest flywheel, perhaps; but still part of the one great constitutional apparatus.

After citing the *Bonham* precedents and how "the judges of the executive courts" had declared legislation void, Otis cries:

> See here the grandeur of the British constitution! See the wisdom of our ancestors! The supreme *legislative* and the supreme *executive* are a perpetual check and balance to each other. If the supreme executive errs it is informed by the supreme legislative in Parliament. If the supreme legislative errs it is informed by the supreme executive in the King's courts of law. Here the King appears, as represented by his judges, in the highest luster and majesty, as supreme executor of the commonwealth; and he never shines brighter but on his throne, at the head of the supreme legislative. This is government! This is a constitution![37]

The thing to note is not so much the further evidence of Otis's Newtonianism (with even King George showing up as some sort of celestial body) as the high-flying sentiments themselves. These were not mere ebullience of the moment, caused by the excitements of literary composition or whatever having gone to the author's head. Elsewhere in the *Rights* pamphlet Otis sings of "the best natural constitution in the world,"[38] and avows that the "*British* constitution in theory and in the present administration of it in general comes nearest the idea of perfection of any . . . ."[39] One is again reminded of the times Otis was living in. Eighteenth-century admiration of symmetry and balance tended to ossify into static complacency: "Whatever is, is right."

This cosmic toryism, as it has been called,[40] may have infected James Otis's thinking too much for his immediate and local political

37. *Ibid.*, 455.
38. *Ibid.*, 442.
39. *Ibid.*, 428.
40. B. Willey, *The Eighteenth-Century Background* (London, 1940), chapter 3.

good. Certainly this exaltation of parliamentary authority — not only in *The Rights of the British Colonies Asserted and Proved* but in other mid-1760s writings besides — gave his political enemies something to move in on him with. Clear though Otis himself may have been that American submission to parliamentary legislation could be understood as a harmless item of constitutional theory, ordinary folk were not likely to have time and patience to trace through his convoluted subtleties to discover that he was not really saying what he seemed to be saying, and that his platform posture as a champion of American rights was true blue after all. How Otis's ambiguity was exploited by his enemies is illustrated by a piece, "MASANELLO, from the Shades below,[41] to JANGLE BLUSTER, Esq;" in the *Boston Evening-Post* 23 June 1766:

> Reflect, in how ample a manner you have *surrendered your country's rights to a superior power, and acquiesced in an hearty submission to their orders* ....

And it was not only in Massachusetts that the *Rights* pamphlet was seen in this unfriendly light — seen and remembered, in fact. In 1774 Roger Sherman, of Connecticut, remarked that it had "conceded away the rights of America."[42] Could Otis's contemporaries see that uplifted forefinger in the State House mural some of them would suppose that it had to do not with higher law but with the way the wind was blowing.

A few more thoughts on and around James Otis and *Bonham's Case.*
The fact that Westminster lawmaking for America became less and

41. Massanello, or Massaniello, was a fishmonger who in 1647 put Naples under a brief spell of mob rule; assassination by a follower ended his crazed tyranny. The nineteenth century accorded him heroic rehabilitation; but nearer his own time, and in the eighteenth century, he represented an awful warning against democratic excess. See D. S. Lovejoy, *The Glorious Revolution in America* (New York, 1972), chapter 16.

Otis, doubtless aware of the damage, may have sought to undo it in his public political oratory. Governor Bernard reported to Lord Shelburne how Otis (apropos the Stamp Act repeal, the Sugar Act, and — *cf.* p. 491 below — the Declaratory Act of 1766) "in a set speech told the People that the distinction between inland taxes & port duties was without foundation ... & therefore as the Parliament had given up the one (for he said the Act for securing the dependency had no relation to taxes) they had given up the other; & the Merchants were great fools, if they submitted any longer to the Laws restraining their Trade ...": 22 December 1766, C05/756, also *Quincy's Reports,* 445-46, from Bernard Papers IV. But even this stopped well short of total denial of parliamentary authority.

42. *DAJA* II, 100. And *cf.* n. 16 above.

less acceptable owed a great deal, naturally, to the climate of American public opinion. A piece by "Candidus" in the *Boston Gazette* for 27 January 1772 is relevant:

> 'The fundamental laws', says Vattel, 'are excepted from the legislators' commission, nothing leads us to think that the nation was willing to submit *the constitution itself* to their pleasure'. 'they derive their authority from the constitution, how can they change it without destroying the foundation of their own authority'? If then according to Lord *Coke, Magna Charta* is declaratory of the principal grounds of the *fundamental* laws and liberties of the people, and *Vattel* is right in his opinion, that the supreme legislature cannot change the constitution, I think it follows, whether Lord *Coke* has expressly asserted it or not, that an act of parliament made against *Magna Charta* in violation of its essential points, is void.

In chapter 16 and again in this chapter it has been observed that both in the writs of assistance case and in his *Rights of the British Colonies Asserted and Proved* James Otis resorted to Emmerich de Vattel's treatise on natural law as datum for the proposition that an act of Parliament contrary to the constitution was void. Another echo in the "Candidus" piece is with Otis's ratiocinated link between Vattel on the nullity of unconstitutional legislation and the dicta of Coke C. J. in *Bonham's Case*. It is an echo in more senses than one. That Coke in fact made no mention of unconstitutionality as a ground for striking down an act of Parliament appears to have inhibited "Candidus" as little as Otis from identifying him with it. And there was something else in "Candidus," as though to make good a further omission in Coke's *Bonham* dicta. To impute to the great master of the common law a principle that upheld the constitution might have been well enough so far as it went; but practical logic required to know, in more particularity, what Coke might have understood the constitution to consist in. Conveniently, Coke had been a strong promoter of Magna Carta as a muniment of English original liberties broadly of a piece with those the Americans were now striving for; and it fitted nicely that he had said of Magna Carta (in his institutional writings, not in *Bonham;* but no matter) that it was "the foundation of all the fundamental laws of this realm," and "for the most part declaratory of the principall grounds of the fundamental laws of England."[43] The "Candidus" article appeared at a time when American disenchantment with British parliamentary

---

43. Co. Litt., 81; and 2 *Inst.,* Proeme: J. W. Gough, *Fundamental Law in English Constitutional History* (Oxford, 1955), 40.

authority was already well under way; and it may be that by now —
1772 — it had sufficient momentum of its own, and was in no need
of displays of syllogistic juggling and legerdemain in newspapers.
However that may have been, there the "Candidus" piece was.

In fact, the idea articulated by "Candidus" had been around some
years. A letter by Thomas Hutchinson in September 1765, when
American antiparliamentarianism had scarcely gotten into stride,
affirmed the orthodoxy of "the Parliament being beyond dispute the
supreme legislature of the British dominions," yet

> our friends to liberty take the advantage of a maxim they find in Lord
> Coke that an Act of Parliament against magna charta or the peculiar rights
> of Englishmen is ipso facto void.[44]

Even in 1765 the "maxim . . . in Lord Coke" would not have come
entirely fresh to Hutchinson. Its overtones of *Bonham* went back to
February 1761, and the argument he had listened to from James Otis
in the writs of assistance case. More recently he could have caught
them in Otis's *Rights* pamphlet.

That "Candidus" in 1772 had been one of the "friends to liberty"
in 1765 is likely enough. But was he Otis? At first glance, no.
"Candidus" was a pseudonym used by Sam Adams. And in the
ordinary way it might not signify that a nonlawyer spattered his
journalism with legalities: eighteenth-century New Englanders were
like that. But there was a jurisprudential virtuosity about the "Candidus" piece that forces one to wonder whether the layman Adams
could have been wholly responsible for it. No doubt Adams might
have lifted the Vattel material from *The Rights of the British
Colonies Asserted and Proved*; likewise the *Bonham* doctrine. He
would have needed no little hardihood, however, to thread his way
through the none too readable institutional books of Sir Edward
Coke, select suitable fragments for subtly textured citation, and
come up with a confident guess at what the old master would have
said if only he had thought of it. One then calls to mind that Adams
sometimes worked in journalistic tandem with James Otis, in the
role of finisher or polisher of Otis's hasty drafts.[45] Otis's mental

---

44. MA 26, 153. The addressee was Richard Jackson: *Quincy's Reports*, 441.

45. John Adams to William Tudor, 7 March 1819: "meeting Mr. Otis one morning, I
asked him, 'How do you proceed with your petitions and letters?' He answered, 'I have
drawn them all up, and given them to Sam to *quieu whew* them'. Whether this word is
Arabic or Seminole, I know not. I believe it was an oddity of his own invention": *LWJA* X,
367.

health in 1772 was reasonably good (good enough, anyway, for him to resume active politics). All considered, it seems not improbable that the pen of Otis had been at work in the "Candidus" piece.

As to the "Candidus" line being bruited about upward of six years before, in 1765, the inconsistency so often charged against Otis may be of helpful relevance. Early in that year Otis's political stock was very low.[46] One contributory cause doubtless was the enthusiasm for parliamentary authority apparent in his *Rights* pamphlet. It seems a fair assumption that, in his parlous political position, he did what he could, over the coffeehouse table and elsewhere, to countervail the damaging impression he had created. His technique perhaps involved a glossed and garbled mixture of Cokeiana, including the judgment in *Bonham's Case,* presented as a "maxim" vindicating Magna Carta and "the peculiar rights of Englishmen" even against an act of Parliament. Of course, he had not treated *Bonham* this way in the *Rights.* But his treatment of *Bonham* in the *Rights* had been different from his invocation of it in the writs of assistance case. Having rung the changes once, this hard-pressed charter member of the "friends to liberty" may have felt free to do it again.

And if freebooting on *Bonham's Case* did have a part in American repudiation of the parliamentary yoke, why not?

Somewhat as the very early common law tempered itself with common sense justice, so its judges felt free to implement a legislative enactment as much in the spirit as to the letter; in time, equity lost out as a constituent of the common law to begin as a separately administered gloss, and judicial attitudes to legislation stiffened also.

The evolutionary process toward stricter regard to statutory text owed something to extraneous influences; like any other social phenomenon it did not take place in a vacuum. One thinks, in particular, of the Tudor monarchs' massive utilization of statute (though the hardening had begun long before their time). Royal business important enough to require the parliamentary treatment was too important to be knocked off course by any judge: it is a reasonable surmise, for example, that the new ecclesiastical dispositions of Henry VIII — many of them involving title to landed property — were not to be left vulnerable to unregenerate or crackpot

---

46. It is said that his seat in the House of Representatives was saved by public reaction against the immoderation of a lampoon verse attack, "Jemmibulero," that appeared shortly before the election (in *BEP* 13 May 1765).

theology from the bench.[47] In a sentence, it was necessary as a matter of essential practicality that the highest instrument of state policy, parliamentary enactment, should be certain and final beyond all question.

Revamped medievalism had a large place in the great constitutional struggles of the seventeenth century, and *Bonham's Case* perhaps partook of it a little. But the success that attended the repackaged promotion of Magna Carta eluded *Bonham*. Judicial supremacy was not on, in either the short term or the long and whether *versus* king or *versus* Parliament. One factor in the dismissal of Coke C. J. in 1616 was governmental displeasure with his doctrine in *Bonham*. (The paradox by which the future champion of Parliament appeared at odds with prerogativists for his seeming to deny Parliament the last word may have a solvent in the fact that, even though passed with the advice and consent of lords and commons, legislation was in form "enacted by the king's most excellent majesty": James I was not a monarch to have anyone tinker with this ultimate and extra-special expression of the royal will.) With the decisive victory of Parliament and the return of the king as it were on sufferance *Bonham* still stood little chance. True it was that the common law was now more than ever cock of the jurisdictional walk; also that, with the conciliar courts abolished beyond recall, executive government must henceforth arrange and conduct its domestic business in accordance with laws and lawmaking cognizable in courts of common law. But the legislative institution to which executive government had become so heavily beholden happened also to have the common law courts under obligation; for was it not Parliament that, by enacting the destruction of the collateral system of conciliar courts in 1641, elevated the common law to its present unique eminence? The interrelated monopolies of ultimate legislative and judicial power that emerged from the constitutional convulsions of the middle seventeenth century did not signify a partnership of equals. Who held the reins and who must ride pillion was conclusively underscored in 1701. The provision in the Act of Settlement

---

47. As the Act of Supremacy was going through, Cuthbert Tunstall, Bishop of Durham, canvassed a clause to limit its operation to the extent permitted by the law of Christ. This got nowhere. Tunstall, a learned civilian, may have been influenced by a Roman practice whereby saving clauses were inserted into legislation to inhibit violation of superior principle. On these *adscriptiones* see E. S. Corwin, *The "Higher Law" Background of American Constitutional Law* (Ithaca, 1955), 12-13. And see generally G. R. Elton, *The Tudor Constitution* (Cambridge, 1960), 233-34.

that foreclosed upon the royal option to appoint judges during pleasure did not so much preclude vulnerability to political dismissal as restructure it. Although under this new law judges would always hold their appointments during good behavior, and so without fear of removal by simple executive fiat, the act did not stop there. It added a qualification. The judges' good-behavior tenure notwithstanding, "upon the Address of both Houses of Parliament it may be lawful to remove them." What the houses of Parliament took away from the king they took unto themselves. Where once it had been the king at whose pleasure the judges remained in office, in future it would be the politicians. And there was another twist, conceivably, as if to screw down the judges still tighter: dismissal of a judge by the king "upon the Address of both Houses of Parliament" was a mode of tripartite action by king, lords, and commons different from the normal — statutory enactment, that is to say — and it did not allow of even the hypothetical possibility of judges rescuing one another from political dismissal by dint of a developing doctrine on judicial annulment of legislation. Of course, this may be an excessively fanciful guess into the parliamentary intention. Yet the seed of such a doctrine could have been thought germinating at that time. A judgment in 1701 by the learned and eminent Holt C. J. included this:

> What my Lord *Coke* says in *Dr. Bonham's case* . . . is far from any extravagancy, for it is a very reasonable and true saying, That if an Act of Parliament should ordain that the same person should be party and judge, or what is the same thing, judge in his own cause, it would be a void Act of Parliament.[48]

However, this judicial hurrah for *Bonham's Case* was to prove the last. Despite Holt's high standing, echo and amplification in other courts came there none. The posterity of the lesser partner in the old alliance of parliamentarians and common lawyers saw through to the reality of things and adjusted accordingly; judges knew their place, and kept it. How much their silent shrink from *Bonham* may have owed to the restructuring of the dismissal power by the Act of Settlement is impossible to tell; but one notices that 1701 was the year not only of the final flicker of *Bonham* but also of that problematic reform.[49]

48. *City of London v. Wood* 12 Mod., 687.
49. The Act of Settlement provision (12 and 13 Gul. 3, c. 2., s. 3) was of delayed effect, to the accession of George I in 1714. Even though judicial appointments during pleasure had

These historical glimpses indicate that the eclipse of *Bonham's Case* was much less genetic common law than outside politico-constitutional climate. Climate in England, though. The conditioning circumstances that stifled *Bonham* in England were peculiar to that country. There was no principle of logic or anything else to dictate that they somehow break loose, cross the Atlantic, and operate to like effect in America. The common law as administered in the colonies responded to locally enacted legislation (as well as to Westminster's); and colonial judicatures sometimes experienced political pressures of an extralegislative kind. But the common law in America — such as it had been in the mid-seventeenth century — was at a great distance from the tremendous boost that abolition of the Star Chamber had given it in England,[50] and it accordingly owed less to the political institution and process that had brought this about. And assuredly America did not have that hybrid form of judicial tenure by which the Act of Settlement tightened the politico-legislative grip on judges: good behavior during pleasure of king, lords, and commons. (The British repeatedly set their face against appointment of colonial judges on the simple good behavior formula, which, as distinguished from appointment during pleasure, meant permanence subject only to misconduct established by judicial process; a formula providing for dismissal at the initiative of local politicians would have been disfavored even more.)

Common law development in America, out of range of the political influences toward parliamentary absolutism that exerted powerful formative pressures in England, may have been less resistant to the survival or resuscitation of *Bonham.* After all, *Bonham* was still in the books, neither explicitly overruled by superior judicial authority nor formally legislated into oblivion. That it had become something of a fossil in England did not necessarily signify for America. Its fate in England had been determined not by anything in its doctrinal genes but by external forces of a wholly nonjuridical kind.

---

continued legally possible under William III and Anne, the practice of those monarchs had been to use the good behavior formula exclusively, which meant that the appointee could be removed only by a court process (*scire facias*: *cf.* chapter 14, n. 18). In this light, the Act of Settlement looks still less a charter for judicial independence. It did not so much displace one form of political removability by another as bring back political removability anew. (Leaving the all-purpose blunderbuss of impeachment aside, that is.) Neither good behavior tenure nor anything in the Act of Settlement exempted judges from the general principle (*cf.* pp. 130, 427 above) by which the death of the monarch caused such instruments as patents of appointment to lapse.

50. *Cf.* chapter 7, n. 3.

In America, where those forces were not felt, it was at least equally legitimate to approach *Bonham* in an organic way. Inductively, as when Otis in the writs of assistance case and his *Rights* pamphlet looked through *Bonham* and saw the law of nature. Or by way of extrapolation, as when "Candidus" applied *Bonham* to acts of Parliament which violated Magna Carta.

It tickles the fancy that *Bonham's Case,* adapted and stretched as might be, rose up in America to avenge itself upon the parliamentary absolutism that had thrust it into limbo in England.

But the decline of parliamentary authority in the restive colonies had something inevitable about it. The orthodoxy that acts of Parliament merited obedience no matter what had heavy loads wished upon it in the 1760s. In the case of the first of the major fiscal innovations, the Sugar Act of 1764, an act of Parliament still had what it took: the Americans grumbled, but buckled under. The following year brought the Stamp Act débacle; demonstrably, whatever magic there once might have been in an act of Parliament precious little remained of it now. The British were slow to read the situation, however. For all the world as if it enshrined some timeless transcendent verity, parliamentary absolutism had them hooked. The Declaratory Act of 1766,[51] with its shrill affirmation that the British Parliament "had, hath, and of right ought to have, full power and authority to make laws and statutes . . . to bind the colonies and people of America . . . in all cases whatsoever," smacked of a delusion that the logical postulates of current constitutional theory were somehow transmuted by the Westminster legislative process into moral imperatives of real life. The governing mind of empire thus stupefied on its own hokum, events took over and soon showed "the colonies and people of America" reducing first, second, and third readings in lords and commons to much the same case as the insistence of the Bellman in *The Hunting of the Snark* that what he said three times was true. The Americans went far beyond arguing, by reference to anything teased out of *Bonham's Case,* that an act of Parliament might be struck down for violating some specific principle. They did not stop even at a blanket denial of Westminster's right to tax them. They pushed on to far-out positions where, at any rate as regards their internal polities, Westminster had no proper authority to legislate whatever.

51. 6 Geo. 3, c. 12, modeled on a similar act for Ireland, 6 Geo. 1, c. 5 (1719).

Individual motivations for conforming to laws are many and various, from high civic principle to fear of being found out; and what makes for law-abidingness among a population at large is more imponderable still. A feeling of identification with the law-making process is as likely a factor as any, perhaps. At all events, it was something of this sort — the idea of representation, of vicarious say in the legislative debate — that was most fixed upon by the American colonists; and as its impossibility of attainment became more and more apparent (the spatchcock sophistry of "virtual representation" never stood a chance), American disenchantment with the Westminster obedience gathered pace. *Bonham's Case* had no such radical overtones. Propositions which would have circumscribed parliamentary authority in this or that particular impliedly acknowledged it good for the indefinite remainder. Nonrepresentation, on the other hand, pierced the jugular. In the advanced position the Americans came to occupy on Westminster legislation *Bonham* was redundant.

So, in different ways, *Bonham* became dead wood on both sides of the Atlantic. All the same, it had been of some use to the Americans on their way. As in 1765, for instance, in the reported utterances of the Massachusetts "friends to liberty." And although in 1772 American alienation from the British parliamentary process was already far gone, "Candidus" evidently thought *Bonham* could still serve a turn in warming things up: old timber fueling new fires.

Massachusetts was not conspicuous in the intercolonial defeat of the 1767 legislation for writ of assistance search. Yet, just as an echo from the 1761 writs of assistance case could be detected in the scuffles behind the Townshend enactment, so it is possible to catch reverberations of that bygone Massachusetts experience in the agitations that were to do the Townshend design practically to death. All of them, as it happens, touch upon the man for whom the writs of assistance case is remembered.

The full Townshend package, with its import duties and its reconstituted regime of customs administration and law enforcement, was ill received. Within weeks it had evoked that great original of American syndicated journalism, John Dickinson's letters by "a Farmer in Pennsylvania." Dickinson was no artless rustic, but an accomplished lawyer and Philadelphia man of affairs; and his series of learned and sophisticated essays on constitutional right and wrong were speedily taken up in colonial newspapers everywhere, for affronted American opinion to feed upon.

The ninth of the Farmer's Letters concerned itself with a component of the Townshend scheme under which judges in American courts would cease to be paid by vote of their colonial assembly and get instead a salary from the imperial revenue. Among the "considerations relating to this head that deserve the most serious attention" was writ of assistance search:

> By the late act, the officers of the customs are impowered to enter into any HOUSE, warehouse, shop, cellar, or other place, in the *British* colonies or plantations in *America,* to search for or seize prohibited or unaccustomed goods, &c; on "writs granted by the superior or supreme court of justice having jurisdiction within such colony or plantation respectively."
>
> If we only reflect, that the judges of these courts are to be *during pleasure,* — that they are to have *"adequate provision"* made for them, which is to continue *during their complaisant behavior* — that they may be *strangers* to these colonies — what an engine of oppression may this authority be in their hands?
>
> I am well aware, that writs of this kind may be granted at home, under the seal of the court of exchequer: But I know also, that the greatest asserters of the rights of *Englishmen* have always strenuously contended, that *such a power* was dangerous to freedom, and expressly contrary to the common law, which ever regarded a man's *house* as his castle, or a place of perfect security.
>
> If such a power was in the least degree dangerous *there,* it must be utterly destructive to liberty *here.* For the people there have two securities against the undue exercise of this power by the crown, which are wanting with us, if the late act takes place. In the first place, if any injustice is done *there,* the person injured may bring his action against the offender, and have it tried before INDEPENDENT JUDGES, who are NO PARTIES IN COMMITTING THE INJURY. *Here* he must have it tried before DEPENDENT JUDGES, being the men who GRANTED THE WRIT. . . .
>
> If this power is abused *there*, the parliament, the grand resource of the oppressed people, is ready to afford relief . . . . But what regard can *we* expect to have paid to our assemblies . . . .[52]

This appeared in the Philadelphia press in the last week of January 1768. By the spring it was available everywhere in a complete pamphlet set of the Farmer's Letters. It was around this time that customs officers in the various colonies were applying to their respective courts for Townshend writs of assistance. That the discouraging response owed something to the ninth Farmer's Letter goes without saying.

52. Writing to James Otis, 25 January 1768 ("The Warren-Adams Letters, I, 1743-1777," *MHSC* LXXII, 5), Dickinson stated that the letters were more accurately reproduced in the *Pennsylvania Gazette* than in the *Pennsylvania Chronicle.* The ninth letter appeared in the *Gazette* 28 January and in the *Chronicle* 18-26 January.

But how came it that John Dickinson, for all his learning as a lawyer, felt able to hold forth with such assurance on writ of assistance search? What he wrote was clearly on the footing that the writ was general and its use discretionary, yet how did he know this? Published materials on writ of assistance search were few and uninformative. Neither the Townshend act nor any other relevant legislation was in the least explicit that the writ possessed the objectionable features Dickinson (correctly) imputed to it. Even the Philadelphia custom house could not have helped him; that institution was in saucy correspondence with the customs commissioners at Boston, who had directed that writs of assistance be applied for, to the effect that no one had any idea what such things were.[53] Passing reference to the writ of assistance and its generality had been made in one of the recent Wilkesite general warrant cases in England;[54] and Dickinson, who doubtless shared in the widespread American approval of those classic vindications of domestic privacy, may have lighted upon this fragment. But even so it would not have been much from which to build so robust and confident a structure of denunciation as that set forth in his ninth Letter.

A clue to the source of Dickinson's material is discernible in the Letter itself. The argument that abuses of the writ of assistance could not be satisfactorily dealt with by the judges who had granted it looks something like a variant of what was being said in Boston in 1761, to the effect that because seizures resulting from writ of assistance search were adjudicated in another court (the vice-admiralty), the court that issued the writ had no way of seeing that it was used properly.[55] The clue becomes more telling when certain collateral circumstances are brought into view. One of these is that at the Stamp Act congress at New York in 1765 Dickinson had made the acquaintance of James Otis. That he formed a good opinion of Otis[56] indicates that their conversation amounted to more than passing the time of day. Probably it was from Otis, a fellow-lawyer

53. Historical Society of Pennsylvania, Custom House Papers VII, 863, 864, 916, 938. Wrote the American customs board to the Philadelphia custom house, 31 March 1768, "we are surprised to find any one of our Officers so ignorant of the Nature of a Writ of Assistants as you appear to be" — giving a distinct impression, however, that they did not know too much about it either.

54. Leach v. Money 19 St. Tr. 1002.

55. See pp. 309-10, 399-400, 422 above.

56. "I have a pleasing recollection of his candour, spirit, patriotism and philosophy": Dickinson to Mercy Otis Warren, 25 September 1805, quoted in W. Tudor, The Life of James Otis of Massachusetts (Boston, 1823), 234.

reminiscing over high or unusual experiences in his practice, that Dickinson first heard of the writ of assistance. Equally it could be that he kept in his mind scraps of the arguments that Otis had retailed from the great debate of 1761. Another significant circumstance is that Otis had seen the ninth Farmer's Letter before publication. Dickinson wrote to him on 5 December 1767 enclosing the Farmer's Letters, only one of which had yet been printed: "to be dispos'd of as you think proper . . . ."[57] He wrote again on 25 January 1768, evidently in acknowledgment of Otis's response: "I . . . am particularly oblig'd to you for the attention you have been pleas'd to bestow on the Papers, I ventur'd to trouble You with. I have made several Alterations in the Copy, from which, that I sent to you, was taken . . . ."[58] This reads very much as if Otis not only read the Farmer's Letters in draft but actually vetted them before they were finalized. One can imagine him giving the ninth a special going-over. Thus it may be that through the immense influence of the Farmer's Letters the writs of assistance thinking of James Otis, first formulated for the Massachusetts controversy in 1761, percolated into the intercolonial opposition to the Townshend writs seven years and more later.

About fifteen months after the ninth Farmer's Letter appeared in print, history in a manner repeated itself. The "Journal of the Times," the propaganda diary in which the Bostonians broadcast tales of their suffering under military occupation, could have been inspired by the success of the Farmer's Letters. If so, it was doubly the case with the entry for 28 April 1769, the piece prompted by the issuance of a batch of new, Townshend-style, writs of assistance at Charlestown.[59] Tacked on to a brief factual report was a fairly protracted disquisition on the infamies of the writ of assistance and all it stood for. The point of interest about the piece arises from the fact that practically none of its jeremiad was original. It consisted almost entirely of slabs of word-for-word text, sandwiched together with greater or less editorial skill, excerpted from, in the one instance, the ninth Farmer's Letter, and, in the other, the *Boston Gazette* for 4 January 1762, which issue will be remembered from chapter 17. What the "Journal" pirated in 1769 was that recriminatory and lengthily argued article, almost certainly written by James

57. "Warren-Adams Letters," n. 52 above.
58. *Ibid.*
59. See p. 467 above.

Otis, on the writ of assistance lately consecrated by the Superior Court. Anonymity was the rule among the contributors to the "Journal of the Times," and the crib has not been definitively cracked to this day. But, one thing taken with another, the chances surely are that Otis, who in April 1769 was still in reasonably good shape mentally, had a hand in the scissors and paste work that put the "Journal" piece together. The "Journal of the Times" achieved a wide circulation, as the Farmer's Letters had done; but somehow there seems little likelihood that the rather stale hash it served up on 28 April 1769 did much to nourish the laborers against general writs of assistance in colonies elsewhere. Resistance had now been in progress a year or more, and opinion was mostly settled and the lines of opposition firmly marked out.

Lastly, in August 1773, there was the Massachusetts Committee of Correspondence's dispatch, to its Connecticut counterpart, of "the minutes of the arguments made by Mr Thacher and Mr Otis," the Connecticut committee having asked "that they may [be] Informed what has been done by the Judges of the Superior Court of this Province, on the requisition for a writ of assistance." This episode has already been spoken of, in chapter 12.[60] It is true that customs officers in Connecticut were still persevering with attempts to get writs of assistance there. But by this time, after more than five years of almost total frustration and futility, the Townshend concept of general writ of assistance search in all America was virtually a write-off; and no more in Connecticut than in any other colony could the forces of opposition have been in real need of encouragement or support from outside. The Connecticut Committee of Correspondence was perhaps a little busy, and in the letter to Massachusetts there perhaps was an element of something else. It must have been well known in Connecticut that in point of intercolonial solidarity against the Townshend writ of assistance the large neighbor to the north, usually so forward and noisy in matters of confrontation with British authority, had not put up much of a show: the Connecticut committee's innocent request for information may have had a needle in it. But whatever might be made of the Connecticut-Massachusetts exchange in 1773, it is unimaginable that dissemination at that late time of the Thacher and Otis materials of 1761 contributed anything to the near-universal defeat of the Townshend writ.

60. Page 239 above.

It would also be unrealistic to suppose that even the ninth Farmer's Letter, the knowledge and thinking in which probably owed a good deal to James Otis, diffused more than a faint overtone of Boston 1761 into the all-America debate that did for the Townshend writ: a far stronger influence was the common law anathema on general warrants lately pronounced in England, in the Wilkes cases. Yet, all but invisible though they may have been, filaments did exist that could be traced back from the intercolonial stand in the post-Townshend period to Boston in the early 1760s. It is also a fact, however little known at the time, that the principle vindicated by the Wilkesite triumphs had been canvassed in America long before. (Not, indeed, that the Otis anticipation went wholly unnoticed: one remembers Joseph Hawley, the Massachusetts radical, slipping a turn of phrase from the climactic Wilkesite case, *Entick v. Carrington,* into his transcription of Otis's speech from John Adams's Abstract.)[61]

The story told in this book has not been without touches of irony. The present chapter has seen how James Otis's political career, signaled by the writs of assistance case, terminated some twelve years later with a denunciation extending to general customs search. In May 1783, on what proved to be his last visit to Boston (a few days after, he was killed by a bolt of lightning), Otis attended a dinner party given by Governor John Hancock. It seems to have been too much for him, and he was shortly packed off back into the country at the hands of two sheriff's deputies. He complained to Hancock:

> The villains seized me in my shirt and I demanded their Warrants. I was told they had authority but would show no warrant.[62]

Quite a curtain for the authentic American prophet of Fourth Amendment constitutionalism.

---

61. See p. 241 above.

62. Letter of 12 May 1783 in Harvard College Library, quoted by C. K. Shipton, *Sibley's Harvard Graduates* XI (Cambridge, Mass., 1960), 285. But see also W. Tudor, *Life of James Otis* (Boston, 1823), 482-83.

Otis "expired without a groan" on 23 May 1783, having been "leaning on his cane at the front door" of Isaac Osgood's house at Andover when the lightning struck; his remains were brought to Boston for interment. Source: *Historical Sketch and matters appertaining to the Granary Burial-Ground* (Boston, 1902), 16-17. See *ibid.,* how a Boston resident (who died in 1841) reported seeing "that the tomb was open in which I knew were the remains of James Otis, and with the help of the sexton, I opened the lid of Otis' coffin, and behold! the coffin was full of the fibrous roots of the elm, especially thick and matted about the skull; and, going out, I looked at the noble elm, and there, in transfigured glory, I saw all that was material of James Otis."

Otis is reputed to have wished to die by lightning.

20

Contemporary Retrospects

THAT "the first scene of the first Act of Opposition to the arbitrary Claims of Great Britain" had no immediately recognizable hero is understandable: the popular side lost. A villain was spotted much sooner, in the person of the chief justice of the province, but for whose pertinacity in stalling a decision till check were made in London the Massachusetts general writ of assistance would have been no more.

Newspaper fire on Thomas Hutchinson over writs of assistance opened up quickly enough, in James Otis's recriminatory and argumentative blast in the *Boston Gazette* for 4 January 1762. It was at its hottest, however, in the post-Townshend period. The *Gazette*, 15 August 1768:

> It is said the grand Pensioner, always ready with his Council, has advised the C-m-rs to remonstrate Home against the Civil Authority of Connecticut, for declining to issue Writs of Assistance for a General Search of contraband Goods, in the base unconstitutional Manner they have been granted in another Province . . . .

Hutchinson had been given the "Pensioner" sobriquet in reference to the Townshend dispensation under which judges were to be paid from British rather than from colonial funds. In the *Gazette* for 11 September 1769 an older lampoon style was favored:

> To the everlasting Honor of the great and worthy *Squire Graspall*, that Man of *Truth and Justice,* we are well informed that every Province in America, except Massachusetts-Bay and Halifax, have refused to grant General Warrants or Writs of Assistants . . . ; even the little Colonies of Georgia and the Florida's have absolutely refused it.

In the last years of the 1760s, when customs officers had for some time been staying clear of people's private dwellings, the writ of assistance represented not very much in terms of public nuisance actually experienced. As far as newspaper agitation went, the writ had dropped almost out of sight until noise from other colonies about the Townshend innovation attracted attention to it. For a while after the court hearing in 1761 it featured in indignant squibs, but by the middle of the decade these had sputtered out. The content and tone of what little comment did appear was indicative of the practical insignificance into which the writ had lapsed. The *Boston Evening-Post* had a piece, "Of the *Writ* called a *Writ of Assistance*," on 9 December 1765; talk of "despotic power . . . in revenue matters" was fairly strong stuff, but the follow-up recommendation that writ of assistance seizures be brought for condemnation to a common law court and not to the vice-admiralty was more representative of the detached, almost academic, style of the piece overall. Press commentary on the Malcom affair in September 1766 was voluminous and protracted; but it was mostly on the subject of Governor Bernard's supposed complaints to Westminster about Boston insurrectionism at it again. Comptroller Hallowell's writ of assistance received scarcely a mention. (Explicit non-mention might be nearer the mark, indeed, in the *Gazette* for 11 May 1767: "I shall not employ myself at present in a disquisition concerning the legality or necessity of certain w--ts of assistance lately foisted into being . . . .") Given that searches of residential premises were probably as infrequent after the Townshend legislation as before, when the writ of assistance was brought back into newspaper polemics in 1768 and 1769 the true purpose had less to do with the writ itself, or even with the resented Townshend package as a whole, than with the purely local political scene. By now, Lieutenant Governor and Chief Justice Hutchinson was deeper than ever in popular disesteem. The writ of assistance served as a good enough stick to beat him with.

That "the grand Pensioner" did lend "his Council" to the American customs commissioners on questions about the writ of assistance is true enough.[1] But the post-Townshend press gibes put Bostonians in mind of more than Hutchinson's current involvements with the writ. Evidence for this is provided in the annotated newspaper collections of a contemporary observer of the Boston scene, Harbottle Dorr. Little is known about Dorr outside his bequest to history of

1. See *Quincy's Reports*, 455, and the note to Appendix O below.

several bound files of Boston newspapers and other prints of the revolutionary period, and his sharply whiggish opinions as expressed in marginal commentary.[2] In point is his copy of the *Boston Evening-Post* for 26 June 1769, which carried a series of entries from the "Journal of the Times." The "Journal" entry for 29 April (the day after the announcement about the writs issued at Charlestown, with its appended amalgam from Otis and the ninth Farmer's Letter) had this:

> the c-l-r of the port of New London in Connecticut, has lately applied a second time to the superiour court there for such writs; at the same time laying a letter before them, which he had received from one of the crown lawyers in England . . . , in which letter, a great compliment was paid to the chief justice of the Massachusetts, for the proof he had given of a right understanding of the law, and of his zeal for his Majesty's service, by so readily granting those writs . . . ; and his example was recommended as worthy of their imitation. The court did not however, think proper to show a like complaisance . . . .

Harbottle Dorr annotated "those writs": "Judge Hutchinson was the first who granted 'em in this Province, wch made him obnoxious." In fact it was in the time of Stephen Sewall, Hutchinson's predecessor as chief justice, that the writ of assistance was first granted. But obviously Hutchinson's decisive role in the 1761 reaffirmation of the writ was remembered years afterward.

However empty of effective meaning it was to become later on, the writ of assistance probably was put into operation too often for comfort in the opening years of the 1760 decade. There is no reason to suppose that the sixty-odd merchants who petitioned for the writs of assistance hearing were motivated by a merely theoretical possibility of invasion by custom house explorers; or that when in 1762 the merchants' society spoke of "Tyranny"[3] in reference to the writ of assistance it was extravagance of language and nothing else. "We have seizures every day," wrote Thomas Hutchinson in November 1763;[4] common sense insists that the writ was instrumental in some of

---

2. See B. Bailyn, "The Index and Commentaries of Harbottle Dorr," *MHSP* 85 (1973), 21-35; *idem, The Ordeal of Thomas Hutchinson* (Cambridge, Mass., 1974), 5-6. Also, for (not specially vivid) examples of Dorr's annotations, *Quincy's Reports*, 271-78.

3. See p. 199 above.

4. To Israel Williams, 17 November 1763: MHS Williams papers. For implicit corroboration by John Adams see chapter 12, n. 24. But on 29 March 1817 (*LWJA* X, 248) his story was different: writs having been granted following the 1761 hearing, "the custom-house officers had them in their pockets, though I never knew that they dared to produce them or execute them in any one instance."

them. In the early 1760s, before Surveyor General Temple had taken to discouraging seizures to spite Governor Bernard, and before the frightening force of the mob was unloosed by the Stamp Act, people may well have had real cause to resent the writ of assistance.

People of the commercial interest, anyway. "About three years ago," Thomas Hutchinson wrote in 1765, ". . . writs of assistance were granted in aid of the officers of the customs, which were complained of as grievous by the illicit traders, and by them a notion was put into the heads of the common people that these writs were contrary to their liberties as Englishmen."[5] In the devastating commotions of 1765, sparked off by the Stamp Act, Governor Bernard ascribed the destruction of Hutchinson's house to the lead he had taken in the writs of assistance case.[6] Hutchinson himself commented (as if pre-echoing Harbottle Dorr): "The change of the currency, writs of assistance, & letters in favour of the stamp act are said to be the reasons of my being particularly obnoxious."[7] Comptroller Benjamin Hallowell, another of those whose homes had suffered attack, put it down to "Vigilance in Office, and for having writ of assistance."[8] And at a dinner to celebrate the uniting of the north and south Boston street factions word reportedly went round: "let us see now, who will seize Merchants Goods, what Judge will condemn them, what Court will dare to grant Writs of Assistance now."[9] An artisan's small dwelling afforded little scope for the harboring of smuggled cargo, one would suppose; and it seems unlikely that the generality of persons who turned out on the streets had had their own houses broken into by customs officers. But it is not hard to imagine men who did have experience of disturbance or loss through customs search, and who were also of a class directly affected by the Stamp Act; exploiting the writ of assistance as something else with which to prod popular opinion into disruptive action.

The way things were after the Stamp Act (custom house morale never recovered fully), no one in Boston, merchant or artisan, had all that much reason, spontaneous or stimulated, to get steamed up about the writ of assistance. The scars left by Thomas Hutchinson's masterful début as chief justice in 1761 still did not heal over,

5. To H. S. Conway, 1 October 1765: MA 26, and C05/755.
6. See p. 437 above.
7. To H. S. Conway, n. 5 above.
8. Hallowell to customs commissioners, 14 November 1766: T1/452.
9. Governor Bernard to John Pownall, 26 November 1765: copy extract in BL Stowe MSS 264.

however. As Harbottle Dorr indicated, it remained possible for later propagandists like those in the *Gazette* and the "Journal of the Times" in 1768 and 1769 to scratch them and make them sore again.

In the years approaching the Revolution the Boston press repeatedly harked back to 1760-61. Long after his departure Benjamin Barons, the disaffected customs collector, was still being held in honor: "that worthy and conscencious C...r Mr B...n's," in the *Gazette* for 24 November 1766; "honest Barons" two weeks later; and the *Evening-Post* for 11 June 1770 unearthed a petition of his to the House of Representatives in January 1762 (though perhaps less in pious memory of Barons than as occasion for strictures on Francis Bernard and "the P----r" for "their avarice and ambition").[10]   John Erving's lawsuit against Deputy Collector Cradock over the seizure of his ship was aired again ten years after, in the summer of 1770, in several issues of the *Evening-Post*. Then there was the newspaper exchange in 1763 when Thomas Hutchinson and James Otis set each other to rights about the Superior Court vacancy in the fall of 1760,[11] which Otis's father had striven for and Hutchinson had won. That noisome affair was never laid to rest for good, and a pervasive and enduring legend from it was familiar enough to be lampooned. The *Evening-Post* for 31 March 1766, a time when the paper was savagely critical of Otis, told how *"Bluster"* had "had always some oddities in his behavior, which gave apprehensions that his head was not as it should be"; however,

> He had . . . some lucid intervals, till the twenty-ninth day of December 1760, when he happened to dream that his father was made *Lord-Chancellor*, and himself Master of the Rolls. This dream made such an impression on his mind that, when he awaked, he really believed the thing true; and it was some days before those about him could persuade him it was only a dream. Upon this he fell into a most violent rage; he foamed at

10. Barons showed up in America again, as a deputy postmaster general: *cf*. L. W. Labaree, ed., *The Papers of Benjamin Franklin* 12 (New Haven, 1968), 121. And still with a propensity to get into authority's hair, apparently. An undated "Copy of some further observations of the Chief Justice of South Carolina" in C05/390 indicates that Barons was in Charleston in the Stamp Act period, and that he had lost the good opinion of Chief Justice Charles Shinner (who had at first favored him through their common patron, Lord Halifax) for opposing secret reporting on a critic of the act.

A piece from Boston in the *Newport Mercury* 9 November 1767 told of that other dismissed customs collector, James Cockle, having returned to America, as "harbinger to his friend C-l-s P-x-n." Paxton arrived in Boston on 5 November, as one of the new American customs commissioners; but the present writer has seen no further sign of Cockle.

11. See pp. 213-19 above.

the mouth, cursed and called names, and swore by G-- *he would burn the Town down.*

Another lampoon souvenir of 1760-61, though of a slightly different kind, was "Squire Graspall" — Thomas Hutchinson — whom the *Gazette* admonished in 1769 for Massachusetts being almost alone in not refusing writs of assistance, and whose original appearance, as "Sir Thomas Graspall," had been in the *Gazette*'s "short Sketch of the History of CHARLES FROTH, Esq;" on 2 March 1761.[12] Nor had the eponymous antihero of the sketch by any means been left to oblivion: the press in later years had countless references to Charles Paxton as "Froth," and even "Sir Charles Froth" (marking, presumably, Paxton's spectacular elevation from a lowly surveyorship of customs to a commissionership on the American board). Needless to say, propagandist evocations of history did not center on 1760-61 to the exclusion of other suitable epochs of *Sturm und Drang.*[13] In terms of traumatic shudder 1760-61 had nothing on the years of Edward Randolph, Governor Andros, and the Dominion of New England. What does come across, though, is a sense that it had been a time perceptibly out of the ordinary.

On any reckoning it had been a time in which a great deal happened, and in a setting made for trouble. American horizons were generally bright enough, with conclusive military success against the French; but life as it was lived had more to do with economics, and on this front Massachusetts, and Boston in particular, had less to be pleased about. As a port, Boston was running a diminishing third to Philadelphia and New York. In March 1760 it had suffered a calamitous fire. But what particularly oppressed and aggrieved the Bostonians was a chronic trading disadvantage relative to neighboring Rhode Island. In Massachusetts custom officers enforced the acts of navigation and trade — notably the Staple Act, under which transatlantic imports had to be shipped from a port in Great Britain — but in

12. See pp. 172-73 above.

13. Continuity in Bostonian controversy is interestingly illustrated in the *Massachusetts Spy* and *BG* report in April 1773 (see pp. 237-38, 471 above) on a writ of assistance expedition recently conducted by a Royal Navy Party led by one Parker. Massachusetts was contrasted with "those provinces, who have not suffered such a monster of monsters to prowl about their streets for prey": a link back to the apprehensiveness about revenue search manifested in the lampoon pamphlet against the province excise bill in 1754, *The Monster of Monsters: A true and faithful NARRATIVE of a most remarkable Phaenomenon lately seen in this METROPOLIS* . . . (which in turn echoed something similar in the agitation against Walpole's excise scheme in England two decades earlier): *cf.* p. 113 above, also, Abstract-Otis's "these monsters of the law live forever", p. 347.

Rhode Island they did not. The root cause of the disparity had much to do with the enforcement sanction: seizure of the offending ship and cargo. Seizure needed to be followed by a court process of condemnation, by which the owner of the seized property was divested of his title. In a common law court condemnation of a litigated seizure depended upon the verdict of a jury, which in the New England experience could be expected to favor the smuggler. Such was the situation in Rhode Island: seizure would have been at best a waste of time (at any rate, in cases likely to be contested). In Massachusetts, on the other hand, the condemnation process had become established as proper to the vice-admiralty court, which, because it belonged to the Roman rather than to the English tradition of jurisprudence, operated without a jury and left the decision to the judge, an appointee of Westminster. Plainly identifiable with the province's adverse trading position, and for other reasons, the vice-admiralty court was a focus of erupting discontent among the Boston merchants in 1760-61. The more so because of adventitious circumstances. Merchant hostility to the vice-admiralty court was fanned and nourished by the head of the Boston custom house, Collector Benjamin Barons, who had private reasons for disliking the court. In the fall of 1760, soon after his return from England and a period of suspension from office, he took to ferreting out information about the court's condemnation jurisdiction which, circulated among the merchants, was certain to inflame their resentments still more. At the time that Barons was thus subverting the institutions of customs law enforcement his colleague at the next port up the coast made a move which, though entirely innocent and of a piece with his official responsibilities, was to help activate trouble in roughly the same area. James Cockle, newly arrived as collector of customs at Salem, sought occasion when the Superior Court visited there on circuit in October 1760 to ask for a writ of assistance. (Cockle had departed from England badly off, and no doubt part of his motivation was to seek out as many seizures as possible, thus maximizing his profits from the customs officer's statutory one-third share.) A snag awaited him, however. Since the Superior Court last issued a writ of assistance, some months previously, an article had appeared in the *London Magazine*, a periodical regularly imported from England, which indicated that the writ of assistance in England was issued only for the one sworn and specific occasion; and which accordingly implied that the writ of assistance the Superior Court of

Massachusetts had been issuing these five years past was wrong in law, because it was general and available for use at the customs officer's discretion. The recently deceased chief justice of the Superior Court, Stephen Sewall, was said to have had doubts about the Massachusetts writ, and his surviving brethren on the bench, who presumably were infected with the same uncertainty, postponed the Salem collector's application for consultation and advice back in Boston.

Meanwhile trouble was brewing in yet another quarter, involving another new arrival in the province. Among the first duties of of Governor Francis Bernard, transferred to Massachusetts from New Jersey in August 1760, was to fill the vacancy on the Superior Court resulting from the death of Chief Justice Sewall. The appointment went to Lieutenant Governor Thomas Hutchinson, much to the rage of James Otis, whose father had been an aspirant (and it was a point of special gall to the Otises that Hutchinson had allowed them to believe they had his support). Otis, hitherto a more or less apolitical barrister, felt added dissatisfaction in his own position, that of acting advocate general. This office, by which he was one of the principal men in the vice-admiralty court, made him a natural target for the disapproval of the marauding Barons. And inasmuch as it was a government job it lent a certain incongruence to his antiestablishment expostulations over the judgeship affair. What with one thing and another, probably including the active ill will of the offended Governor Bernard, it was not long before Otis quit. But any expectation of the former acting advocate general simply fading from the scene would have been a considerable error. Otis's resignation from the government side of affairs swung him straight into opposition politics. His preparatory dispositions toward a seat in the House of Representatives began in short order. By year's end he had become marshal and spokesman of the merchants' discontents against the vice-admiralty court, and — as Governor Bernard put it — "Mr Barrons faithfull Councellour." In one of the lawsuits egged on by Barons for the debilitation of the vice-admiralty court, *Erving v. Cradock,* Otis did not show up as a participant. But the staff work behind the province's action against the vice-admiralty enrichments of Charles Paxton was very much Otis's doing, as was the conduct of the proceedings.

And the last days of 1760 projected an even better opportunity for the up-and-coming lawyer-politician to shine in the eyes of an admiring electorate. The unresolved question of a writ of assistance for Collector Cockle at Salem was swept up in a larger development. The news of the death of George II meant that all writs of assistance that had been issued in his name would be dying too. Accordingly, and quite soon, the Superior Court would have to consider their problem — the problem posed by the sign in the *London Magazine* that they had been wrong to make the writ general and open-ended — by reference not to the solitary inquiry from James Cockle but to replacements for the existing writs that were about to expire. Otis was aware of the Superior Court's problem, having been consulted on it when he was still advocate general. However, what had then seemed a matter for more or less informal debate in private session was a lot larger now. In prospect was a whole batch of new writs giving customs officers the freedom of every man's landed property throughout the many years the young George III could be expected to reign. As if to show that hope need not be given up, in January 1761 one of the Boston newspapers reproduced the *London Magazine* article. At whose instance this topical item was thus made known to a wider public, is impossible to say. What can be said is that an agent of deliverance was quick to appear, in the form of James Otis presenting to the Superior Court a petition from numerous "Inhabitants" of the province to the effect that the writ of assistance be the subject of a public hearing.

"Out of this election will arise a d-d faction, which will shock this province to its foundation," John Adams heard a leading establishmentarian, Timothy Ruggles, exclaim when Boston put Otis into the House of Representatives in May 1761. Adams commented fifty-odd years later: "Ruggles' foresight reached not beyond his nose. That election has shaken two continents...."[14] Otis was washed up politically and in most other ways long before the American Revolution broke the first British empire asunder, but in the 1760s, despite all his swerving and backpedaling, he had no equal as an agitator of Boston excitements; so that, in whatever degree the discontents and tensions of that one town energized the movement of events toward American independence, Otis ranks proportionately in the accomplishment. In the same way it could be said that the events that propelled so prodigious a phenomenon into politics also partook of

14. *LWJA* X, 248.

the distinction — not only Otis's election to the Massachusetts Assembly, it must be clear, but similarly the happenings and circumstances that had a bearing on it.

In retrospect that grew more and more vivid with time, John Adams spotlighted Otis's speech in the February hearing of the writs of assistance case as the lustrous centerpiece of the events of 1760-61: every man of a crowded audience "appeared to go away, as I did, ready to take up Arms against Writs of Assistants." One would never have thought it, though, from the scant evidence of contemporary materials. In terms of what the speech set out to do, it was a failure. Otis's ingenious endeavors to fill out the *London Magazine* article with respectable legal learning, to embolden the doubters on the beach into definitive abandonment of the general writ, came to nothing. The winner at the February hearing was Chief Justice Hutchinson, who persuaded his hesitant colleagues into a deferment — a second deferment, counting the one at Salem back in October — while he contacted Agent Bollan for absolutely authentic information on the practice in England. Although, as was seen in the last chapter, the subject of general customs search did not wholly cease to interest Otis, whatever disappointment he felt at the February setback probably was soon shrugged off. It could even be that the comparative pallor of his performance at the resumed hearing in November is explicable not only by the collapse of his substantive position (Agent Bollan having, in effect, contradicted the *London Magazine* article), but also by his not trying quite so hard. There had been a sense in which Otis's failure to carry the day in February was positive and absolute defeat, no matter that the decision of the court was merely to adjourn and that the ultimate result might yet be in his favor: Chief Justice Hutchinson's success in urging the other judges against an immediate switch from the general writ of assistance to the special meant that Otis — whose potential as a political enemy must have been apparent to Hutchinson, and an additional motivation for the chief justice to thwart him — would not be able to present himself in the May election as a triumphant defender of the rights of hearth and home and the very man to speak for the people in the House of Representatives. However, none of this had mattered in the end: the Boston voters put him top of the poll anyway. Of course, ultimate victory would have been pleasant; and a triumphant and vindicatory press write-up (as projected by John Adams's

Abstract, perhaps) preferable to preparing a noisy rearguard squib for the *Boston Gazette;*[15] but Otis as arrived politician could get by without these bonuses.

Well could 1760-61 have imprinted itself on Bostonians of the period, by the sheer volume and weight of so many things happening at the same time (and the run-down a few paragraphs back did not list them all). But what with their very density, their tendency to complex interrelatedness, and the obfuscating fact that some of the most operative of them (Cockle's move for a writ of assistance, say) were not fully on public view, these crowded occurrences cannot but have been very much a confusing blur in a great many eyes and memories. Such, manifestly, was the case with John Adams. As one of the true begetters of "the child Independence" (and few did more toward the establishment of the United States than that insufficiently honored man), Adams may have undergone some sort of pentecostal experience when listening to James Otis's speech in February 1761. All the same, his understanding of the controversy was seriously imperfect. Much of what he knew and remembered of the circumstances of the writs of assistance case — the Cockle application at Salem, for example, and the doubts of Chief Justice Sewall — is valuable material; but there are patches of muddle, and important elements in the situation, notably the *London Magazine* article and the resumed court hearing in November, seem to have been totally unknown to him. Of course, Adams's tales of the writs of assistance case were told mostly when he was pretty old, and he had a polemical purpose as well (the priority of Massachusetts and James Otis in point of revolutionary chronology, over Virginia and Patrick Henry). But at no time did he check back thoroughly and see if his facts were accurate and complete. Perhaps it was that the picture lodged in his mind since early manhood so satisfied and suited him that he preferred to see no reason to disturb it. It is unfortunate, though, that too much of the picture consisted of scraps of information, hearsay, and rumor that chanced to reach the ears of a novice country lawyer of twenty-five years. Despite his friendly contacts with leaders of the Boston bar Adams was not yet close enough to the metropolitan inner circle to pick up everything that went on.

John Adams peered back through the smoke of 1760-61 and

15. *Cf.* pp. 377-78 and 417 above.

beheld the shining figure of James Otis. Other contemporaries saw Thomas Hutchinson.[16] But there is testimony still to be mentioned, from a man who had been much closer to the center of events than the young Adams, or Harbottle Dorr, or the Stamp Act rioters, or the later newspaper propagandists. To Edmund Trowbridge, formerly attorney general, latterly a Superior Court judge, and in 1779 a morose neutralist, meditation upon 1760-61 conjured forth both Otis and Hutchinson:

> What O- said, "that he would set the province in flames", has come to pass. He, poor man! suffers; and what are we coming to? I thought little of it at the time. I made every exertion in favor of Mr H, and think he was the best man to be there, if the people had been satisfied, and he had never looked beyond it. But now I think it was unhappy for us all. And I freely believe this war would have been put off many years if Governor H had not been made Chief Justice.[17]

Trowbridge discerned in the events in Boston in 1760-61 a link with the origins of "this war." To John Adams they came to be the setting for the birth of "the child Independence." A common focal reference, the revolutionary breakaway; but different perceptions. Whereas Adams concentrated his approving gaze upon James Otis and the writs of assistance case, the disconsolate Trowbridge went a little farther back, to the appointment of Thomas Hutchinson as chief justice.

Nevertheless, the Trowbridge testimony got within range of corroborating John Adams's large claim for the writs of assistance case. Because of the *London Magazine* article and the Cockle application at Salem, the writs of assistance question was in the offing when Governor Bernard made the fateful chief justice appointment. Even aside from the fact that Bernard and Cockle were old friends from past days in England, it is as near certain as can be that a Superior Court affirmation of the general writ of assistance was part of the governor's calculation. The greater the freedom for customs officers

---

16. Notable, perhaps, is a long and bitter admonition by "HYPERION" in *BG* 18 November 1771, addressed "To the Man Whom Conscience forbids to stile my Governor"; it included reference to "an indefinite number of revenue officers, invested with such powers as destroy utterly the notion of a man's house being his castle, and this too augmented by the virtue of those baleful death warrants to the constitution, called writs of assistance . . . ." The pen-name Hyperion was favored by Josiah Quincy junior, reporter of the resumed writs of assistance hearing in November 1761 (though Professor Bailyn — n. 2 above, *Ordeal of Thomas Hutchinson*, p. 199 — identifies the writer on this occasion as Dr. Thomas Young).

17. Cited from "Hutchinson" in *New England Biographical Dictionary* by J. K. Hosmer, *The Life of Thomas Hutchinson* (Cambridge, Mass., 1896), 48.

to search for seizures the more seizures they would make, and the larger the profits — including, proportionately, the gubernatorial one-third share accruing to the desperately impecunious Governor Bernard. There probably was a writ of assistance connection, too, in Attorney General Trowbridge's sponsorship of Hutchinson for the chief justiceship. Trowbridge had been the draftsman, if not the originator, of the general writ of assistance that the *London Magazine* was now casting a shadow over. Might not Trowbridge's "every exertion in favor of Mr H" have been the more strenuous from hope that an appreciative chief justice would vindicate the doubted instrument, and hence the professional reputation of the law officer who had inspired it?

Satisfactory resolution of the writs of assistance question was not the only consideration that accounted for Thomas Hutchinson's appointment as chief justice. It may not have been even the dominant one. Yet there does remain a possibility that, but for this awkward bit of business, difficult legally and sensitive politically, the senior puisne judge of the Superior Court, the unmettlesome Benjamin Lynde, would have bidden for promotion. Or that Governor Bernard would have been more strongly inclined toward a conciliatory judgeship for the dispirited Pownallite faction: William Brattle, as it might have been (who finally teamed up with James Otis in political opposition); or, as Bernard afterward mused, Benjamin Prat.[18]   In short, the imminence of the writs of assistance question might have been what tilted an otherwise open choice in the direction of the dependable Hutchinson. So that, were it not for the writ of assistance application pending in the Superior Court in the fall of 1760, on the testimony of one knowledgeable contemporary the Revolutionary War would have been slower in coming; and, on John Adams's reading of events, "the child Independence" would have had to be born some other time.

18. See pp. 221-222 above

21

~~~~~~~
~~~~~~~

Tailpiece

~~~~~~~
~~~~~~~

T HE ORIGIN of the writs of assistance case is traceable to an anonymous article in the *London Magazine* for March 1760, which had said that

> a writ of assistance from the exchequer . . . never was granted without an information upon oath, that the person applying for it has reason to suspect that prohibited or uncustomed goods are concealed in the house or place which he desires to search . . . .

And the central question in the case was whether the judges of the Superior Court of Massachusetts should not accept the *London Magazine* statement as true law, tailoring down their own writ of assistance, hitherto general and open-ended, to be good for the one sworn occasion only.

Nothing came of this in the end. The London agent for Massachusetts, William Bollan, having been commissioned by the chief justice to make inquiries, reported that the English writ of assistance was general and that it could be had from an official of the Court of Exchequer for the bare asking. Thus reassured, the Superior Court of Massachusetts decided that the general writ of assistance was in order and carried on more or less as before.

But there is something that jerks back attention to these beginnings from elsewhere and a later time. In an exchange of letters between Governor William Pitkin of Connecticut and William Samuel Johnson, agent of that colony in England, the subject was the writ of assistance being wished upon America under the Townshend legislation of 1767. On 11 March 1768 Pitkin had asked Johnson to "Transmit an Account Relative to Writs of Assistants issued under the Seal of his Majesty's Court of Exchequer: in what Manner application is made in order to obtain them, and whether general Warrants are issued &c &c." Johnson replied on 23 July:

> I have made all the enquiry I could . . . concerning Writs of Assistance to Custom House Officers, but cannot yet perfectly satisfie myself with respect to them. It is surprising how little Attention Gentlemen here pay, & how slender Intelligence they can give out, relative to things not Immediately within their own departments. It seem'd to be clearly the Opinion of several Lawyers, that I spoke with upon the subject, that they were not issued but in particular Cases, and upon Information on Oath, not in general Terms, nor to be made use of as general Warrants, at the Discretion of the Officer, which appeared to me to be the only legal and reasonable Method. But upon application to the Clerks of the Excheqr. for Copies of the usual Writs Issued here in Cases of this Nature, they have furnish'd us with the enclosed, which you will see are very general, and not grounded upon any particular Fact, or Information, & they add, that all the additional Instruction, beside what the Writs express & direct, is that the King's Officer, take unto him a Peace Officer . . . .[1]

These perplexities expressed by Agent Johnson of Connecticut in 1768 exhibit the very same contrariety of factual statement as had manifested itself in Massachusetts in 1760-61. Particularly noticeable is how closely "the Opinion of several Lawyers" corresponded to what the *London Magazine* had said about writs of assistance being granted only on sworn and specific information.

That the error in the *London Magazine* was still being fallen into years later shows that it was not just one man's personal nonsense, and encourages exploration of where the error lay.

From time to time it naturally became necessary for the corpus of customs enforcement law in Great Britain to undergo legislative overhaul and toning up. The year 1719 produced a miscellaneous package of adjustments and innovations, none of them specially eye-catching, in an *Act for preventing Frauds and Abuses in the publick Revenues.*[2] One of the items in the jumble, spreading through sections 39 to 43, had as its object the destruction of a racket whereby owners of imported merchandise promoted false rumors of it having been smuggled, with a view to mulcting customs officers in damages for unjustifiably seizing it. The act erected a series of procedural hoops through which a claimant against a seizure must jump, and gave the seizing customs officer appropriate protec-

---

1. This Pitkin-Johnson exchange is as cited in *Quincy's Reports,* 502, from the Trumbull Papers in MHS. See also *MHSC* fifth series, vol. 9 (1885), 292-93.

2. 6 Geo. 1, c. 21.

tion from successful suit. However, these protective measures were not blanket in scope or free from limiting conditions. Where they applied was governed by circumstances of the seizure. The seized goods had to be waterborne, or in process of removal from waterside without a customs officer in attendance. A third alternative related to "prohibited or customable Goods" that might

> upon the Information of one or more credible Person or Persons, be found in any House, Shop, Cellar, Ware-house, Room, or other Place, on a Search there made in such Manner as in and by an Act made in the fourteenth Year of the Reign of the late King CHARLES the Second, intituled, *An Act for preventing Frauds, and regulating Abuses in his Majesty's Customs,* is mentioned and directed . . . .

The 1719 act thus extended its protection to seizures resulting from a writ of assistance search under the Act of Frauds of 1662; subject to the condition, however, that the search had been made on credible information. Here, all but buried in low-key legislative verbiage, is an important clue to what the *London Magazine* said about writs of assistance in March 1760.

A clue only, of course. The 1719 enactment was far short of the *London Magazine* notion that the writ of assistance was issued on sworn specific information in the Court of Exchequer. It cut nothing away from the generality of the power of search given by the act of 1662, and it made no difference to the issuance or the scope of the writ of assistance that the 1662 act bespoke. On the contrary, the 1719 act went on to be more or less explicit that the customs officer had the option of rooting around with his writ of assistance as freely as before (and at that time there still was no reported judicial decision to warn him against searches that proved unproductive of a valid seizure). If he wanted the protection of the act his search must be backed by credible information; but it was up to him. The 1719 act impinged not on the power of writ of assistance search itself but on the use made of it.

And the relevance of the 1719 act to the *London Magazine* piece is as much practice as law. In reality, the customs officer's legal freedom to search without a 1719-style information was an empty figment. Illustration of this is in an authoritative manual of English customs procedures, Henry Crouch's *Complete Guide to the Officers of His Majesty's Customs in the Outports,* published in 1732:

> An Officer of the Customs may not enter or go into an House, Shop, Cellar, Warehouse, Room or other Place, to search for *prohibited* or *uncustomed Goods,* without a particular Information from one or more

credible Persons, in writing if possible, giving an Account of the Species or Package of the Goods, when and where run, or where concealed;
and then only in the Day-time, and not without a Writ of Assistants,
and a Constable, Headborough, or other publick Peace-Officer next
inhabiting . . . .[3]

Crouch made footnote reference to the acts of 1662 and 1719, but
the stipulations about the form and particularities of the customs
officer's information were not to be found in any statutory text. In
fact, they were not law at all. It is important to remember that the
customs officer was not a wholly independent agent. He was down
the line in an organization presided over by a board of customs
commissioners, and he had to do as the commissioners told him.
Whatever power he might possess in strict law, how he used it was
subject to directive from his departmental superiors. The words set
forth in Crouch's *Guide* signified an administrative instruction by the
customs commissioners tantamount to a ban on their subordinate
officers opting out of the protection of the 1719 act. Moreover, as if
to make doubly sure of compliance with the act, the commissioners
interposed rules of their own. The customs officer contemplating a
search was not left to decide for himself that his information was
good enough for the purposes of the act. He had to get it particularized, and "in writing if possible." In London (Crouch's book had to
do with the outports) the commissioners were more exacting still. A
minute dating from 1733 ordained that

Officers are not to enter Houses or peruse [*sic*] Informations unless
procured from Persons of repute & on Oath if it can be had; & then not
without Leave of the Board, taking with them a Writ of Assistance, &
Peace Officers . . . .[4]

Light dawns on the *London Magazine* article. The writer of the
article evidently had heard something about writ of assistance search

3. (London), p. 280. Writ of assistance search, as set forth by Crouch, was available for
goods either by being prohibited or by being uncustomed; his justification presumably was
the "prohibited or customable Goods" formula used in the 1719 act (see p. 513 above),
which at last expanded the constrictive "prohibited and uncustomed" of 1662 (a likely
contributor to the still more unsatisfactory 1696 legislative text for customs search in
America: pp. 46-50, 108-111 above) into something better in keeping with practicalities.
    As is indicated in note 2 to Appendix C, the 1719 sleight-of-hand got by without
arousing embarrassing attention. Insiders did not overlook it, however: chapter 18, n. 20.
    4. Customs 29/1: "Seizures" entry, 2 November 1749. (The Customs 29 series are in the
London custom house archives, not in the Public Record Office itself.)

being preceded by an information on oath. But, not realizing the true provenenace of this information — the act of 1719 and the customs department's internal procedures pertaining to it — he veered off into error. A part-legislative and part-administrative regime that had the effect of subjecting the use of the writ of assistance to sworn specificity he mistakenly represented as the Court of Exchequer's process for issuing the writ. (The lawyers whom William Samuel Johnson consulted in 1768 seem to have been muddled in much the same way; their practice clearly had not brought them into close touch with customs enforcement matters.)

Agent William Bollan's report to the chief justice of Massachusetts in 1761 was faulty in a related sense. His statement that in England writs of assistance were general and "upon any application of the commiss'rs of the customs to the proper officer of the court of exchequer . . . made out of course by him, without any affidavit or order of the court"[5] was true as far as it went. But it fell well short of correcting the imperfect picture of writ of assistance practice in England formed by Boston readers of the *London Magazine*. In fact, by omitting to signal anything of the 1719 enactment and its administrative accretions it put the picture out of focus in a different way. What the *London Magazine* made too much of Bollan was too silent about.

It looks as if Bollan's inquiries centered upon the office of the king's remembrancer, the agency of the Court of Exchequer where writs of assistance were issued into the hands of the customs authorities. One is reminded of the Connecticut inquiries of a similar sort some years later, and Agent Johnson's comment on "how little Attention Gentlemen here pay, & how slender Intelligence they can give out, relative to things not Immediately within their own departments." Perhaps, though, it was not to be expected that clerks working for the king's remembrancer should have familiarized themselves with the regulatory procedures, mostly internal to the customs organization, that governed how the writs of assistance they issued were afterward used. If Agent Bollan was aiming at comprehensive accuracy for his report to Chief Justice Hutchinson he would have done well to turn up Crouch's *Guide,* which indicated clearly that

5. See p. 392 above.

writ of assistance search in England had more to it than appeared at first sight. And, of course, he would have done still better to take discreet soundings in the quarter that could have told him everything, the London custom house.[6]

Their diligent labors on the writs of assistance case notwithstanding, no sign exists of the Bostonians having lighted upon the truth about the English practice for themselves. And it is impossible to conjecture that they did so. Even if some sharp eye spotted the 1719 enactment in the statute book (and, characteristically of legislative utterances on writ of assistance search,[7] wordy and opaque draftsmanship shielded it from instant recognition in a quick riffle), what signified still more, the regulatory superstructure erected on it by the customs commissioners, was all but unknowable in Boston. Something of it was on view in Crouch's *Guide,* but that work, specifically related to custom house business in England, is unlikely to have been a ready-to-hand source of reference in the colonies. And that really telling clue to how the *London Magazine* had gone wrong, the commissioners' 1733 directive that information supporting writ of assistance search should be "on Oath if it can be had," its application limited to the port of London, most probably had no printed circulation at all.[8]

What would have happened if an accurate and complete account of writ of assistance search in England had somehow been vouchsafed to the merchants, lawyers, and judges of Massachusetts Bay in 1760-61 is beyond speculation. One might-have-been is worth an airing, however.

The customs commissioners' administrative inhibitions upon writ of assistance search in England were not wholly explained by a concern to secure the protection of the 1719 act. Also reflected was an independent and long-standing anxiety lest footloose violation of residential and other property, which public and legal opinion had

6. If only in a nominal and absentee way, Agent Bollan himself had been a member of the customs commissioners' staff, as collector at Salem, Mass. Another irony is that the controversy Bollan was now helping sort out began as it did because Bollan's successor as collector, appointed in the belief that Bollan had died (p. 138 above), had promptly sought a writ of assistance. To which the further twist was added, that while Collector James Cockle at length got the writ he wanted, Bollan, whose services in that regard had been of decisive importance, was ousted from the agency job too (p. 436 above).

7. 11 and 12 Gul. 3, c. 10 (1700) is an example.

8. Talk in the Malcom episode of sworn information (p. 447 above) perhaps shows that word of the London practice had reached Boston by then.

never taken kindly to, cause departmental embarrassment. Years before the 1719 act the commissioners were warning their officers against searching houses "without first acquainting the board; and having their Leave to do so" (another instruction intended for London only, one surmises, given the unpracticality of headquarters clearance for searches at distant outports).[9] In 1714 the commissioners partly foreshadowed the 1719 act, with an order that certain searches for prohibited East India textiles should be on "Information in Writing signed by some Gentlemen of the Trade."[10] In 1728 officers engaged on such work were "cautioned to do their Duty with Civility."[11] At length, in the early nineteenth century, the commissioners went so far as to restrict the use of writs of assistance to cases where the officer had sworn to the quality and trustworthiness of his information before a magistrate.[12]

Geography dictated that in America the workaday mechanics of customs enforcement were controlled less by detailed directive from the commissioners than by the proconsular surveyors general. Yet one cannot help wondering whether, if the commissioners had had it put to them that promiscuous customs search could be as provocative of trouble in America as they plainly recognized it to be in England, they might not have intervened. It was immaterial that the 1719 legislation did not apply in America: witness the administrative curbs imposed long before it was enacted. There was no reason in principle, and not much in common sense, why the commissioners' quiet-life policy on writ of assistance search should not have held good on both sides of the Atlantic. However general the power of search of a customs officer in America might seem in point of law, and regardless of the generality of any concomitant writ of assistance issued to him there, the commissioners might have directed their American officers to limit the actual use of the search power — or of the writ of assistance (it came to the same thing, of course) — to suitably authenticated occasions.

9. Customs 29/1: entry *sub. cap.* "Informations and Informers," 9 June 1710.
10. *Ibid.*, 10 July 1714.
11. *Ibid.*, "Land Carriage Officers," 28 November 1728.
12. Cf. *Quincy's Reports*, 535, where Horace Gray cites a minute by the commissioners in 1817 to the effect that officers in charge of custom houses were not to allow the use of a writ of assistance to a subordinate unless he had sworn before a magistrate as to the specificity and dependability of his information. This minute, which in fact referred to the act of 1719, made general a practice which had begun as for London only, in a minute dated 4 April 1815 (for which see "Customs Regulations Minutes 1719-1826" in the Customs and Excise departmental library, King's Beam House, London).

In 1761, attitudes and atmosphere were not yet soured by the matters that five years later led the customs commissioners to bestir themselves on writ of assistance search in America.[13] If the commissioners had been consulted by Agent Bollan, deviling on the writs of assistance case for the pertinacious chief justice of Massachusetts, might they not have scented big trouble in that notoriously tetchy province? Taking sufficient alarm, perhaps, to blow the whistle on a bothersome item of Boston courtroom contentiousness they would rather had not begun?

A parting glance at the words of John Adams by which the writs of assistance case is most often remembered:

> Then and there was the first scene of the first Act of Opposition to the arbitrary Claims of Great Britain. Then and there the child Independence was born . . . .

Inspired imagery, and for all the world as though legal theater had already caught the national fancy. Top marks to Adams as publicist for Massachusetts and James Otis, respectively seedbed and begetter of Revolution. Not to Adams the historian, however. Charismatic verbalizing has a way of letting factual accuracy slip, and so it did here. Those "arbitrary Claims of Great Britain" were imaginary.

It had not been some new-fangled imposition from across the sea that evoked the oratory Adams was commemorating. The general writ of assistance assailed by Otis in February 1761 had taken its rise several years previously, right there in Massachusetts. The customs surveyor who back in 1755 applied for it, the attorney general who drafted it (probably having thought of it in the first place), and the judges who granted it were to a man New Englanders born and bred.

If London had engineered this, the draftsmanship of the Massachusetts writ certainly would not have been so poorly off for source material that it had to parrot a wholly inapt and legally dubious precedent from a superannuated law manual. Something of the same

---

13. See p. 450 above, for the commissioners recommending "the interposition of Parliament" for customs officers in America to be given "the proper power" of search there. Their tone did not convey overmuch eagerness or thrust even then. It could be that the attorney general's advice (p. 442) that the existing legislation did not bite forced them on to a subject they would have preferred, given their traditional caution toward it, to keep under wraps. On the other hand, America would soon become someone else's worry. (The customs commissioners did not formally suggest a separate board for America until 30 April 1767 — T1/459 — but an idea of that magnitude probably would have been around, if not half-decided upon, long enough for them to anticipate it in the fall of 1766.)

goes for the travails of 1761: a colonial customs establishment briefed to execute a positive policy forged and directed by the British government would have known enough about modern English writ of assistance practice not to be fazed or wrongfooted by part-truth in the *London Magazine.*

Actually, there is no sign of British influence in any of these events. Nor was it remotely likely. Writ of assistance search had been a worrisome subject for the customs commissioners practically time out of mind; and even allowing for three thousand miles of comfortable distance, they had no ground for supposing that what in England was moderated by wary procedural regard for the sensitivities of private property could operate in America like a battering ram. Indeed, to judge by their attitudes at home, had it reached the commissioners how in Massachusetts writ of assistance search was being left to unregulated enterprise in the low-to-middling ranks they would have ordered a tightening up. A more realistic probability, of course, is that they gave customs search in America scarcely a thought until it thrust itself on them for treatment in the Townshend legislation of 1767.

The writs of assistance case in 1761 signified not too much British assertiveness in America but, if anything, too little. The initiatives that had brought forth the Massachusetts writ and the exertion now sustaining it were not contrivances of London; they came from within the province itself. It was those local zealotries in the crown service, not "arbitrary Claims of Great Britain," that supplied the setting for the nativity tableau immortalized by John Adams. In that light, they were something the first British empire would have been better without.

A

Case for the Opinion
of Attorney General De Grey, 1768

.... WHETHER the Superior Courts of Justice in the British Colonies or Plantations in America, ought not upon Application to Issue Writs of Assistants in the same manner as is Practised in the Court of Exchequer in England, and what Steps should be taken by Government in Order to Enforce the Issuing of these Writs, for the Protection of the Officers of the Customs Abroad.

There can be no Doubt, but that the Superior Courts of Justice in America are bound by the 7. G. 3. to issue such Writs of Assistance, as the Court of Exchequer in England issues in similar Cases, to the Officers of the Customs.

As this Process was probably new to many of the Judges there, & They seem to have had no opportunity of Informing Themselves about it, it is Perhaps in some Measure excuseable that They wished to have Time to consider of it & to enquire into the practise of the Court of Exchequer & of other Colonies; & I think it can only be because the Subject was entirely misunderstood & the Practise in England unknown, that the Chief Justice of Pensilvania, Who is generally well spoken of, cou'd Imagine, that "He was not warranted by Law" to issue a Writ commanded by the Legislature; wch. Writ was founded upon the Common Law, enforced by Acts of Parliament & in dayley use in England, & wch. from the General Import of the 7. W. 3. ought to have been set on Foot from that Time in America; & wch. Statute the Late Act only meant to explain. & it appears accordingly, that in Boston, where a very able Judge presides & some Experience had been had upon the Subject, no difficulty was made in granting it.

I think therefore it is adviseable that the Form of the Writ issued by the Court of Exchequer in England shd. be sent over to the several Colonies in America, together with the Manner of applying for it & of granting it. By wch. They will see, that the Power of the Custom House Officer is given by Act of Parliament, & not by This Writ, wch. does nothing more than facilitate the Execution of the Power by making the disobedience of the Writ a Contempt of the Court; The Writ only requiring all Subjects to permit the Exercise of it & to aid it. The Writ is a Notification of the Character of the Bearer to the Constable & others to Whom He applies & a Security to the Subject agst. others Who might pretend to such authority. Nobody has it but a Custom-House officer armed with such a Writ.

The Writ is not granted upon a Previous Information, nor to any Particular Person, nor on a special occasion. The Inconvenience of That was experienced upon the Act of 12. C. 2. C. 19, & the Present Method of Proceeding adopted in Lieu of what That Statute had prescribed.

Wm. de Grey

Aug. 20. 1768

(From T1/465)

B

*Case for the Opinion
of Attorney General Thurlow, 1771*

. . . . What Measures are proper to be taken to oblige such of the Supreme Courts of Justice in America as have refused so to do, to grant Writs of Assistants according to the Directions of the . . . Act of the 7th. Geo. 3rd. and agreeable to the Opinion of the late Attorney General, And also whether it may be proper to take any and what Measures to oblige the supreme Court of Justice in Virginia to grant the Writ agreeable to the form used in the Court of Exchequer in England, in lieu of that which they have proposed to grant?

I know of no direct, and effectual means, in the ordinary course of Law, to compel the Judges of the chief courts in the Colonies to award the writ of assistance, according to the exigence of the acts of 7 & 8 W.3 and 7 G.3., For, this, in the form of their constitution, They are not Sovereign Courts, yet, as they are not within the body of the realm, no mandamus will lie to controul them. It has been usual for the Privy Council to issue orders of this sort; but it is not obvious, how that jurisdiction is founded; or what consequence would follow upon disobedience to such orders. Upon a case of obstinate and contumacious refusal to execute an English act of Parliament, I apprehend the Judges might be impeached. But this is a measure of punishment, not of controul.

The Supream Court of Virginia seems to have proceeded upon a meer mistake of the Law. They have issued an illegal warrant, founded on an expired Law, the 12 C. 2 c. 19; at the same time refusing to issue a lawful one, on 13th C.2 c.11; not observing, as it should seem, that the first act has a different object, and proceeds by different means. These were found useless, and inconvenient; and, to remedy the mischief, the second act was made, on which the present writ of assistance in England is founded. This head of authority has been in constant use above a century; has often been recognised, and confirmed by judicial decisions: And it seems strange indeed, that any Judge in the Colonies should think the Laws of the Mother Country too harsh for the temper of American Liberty. I am therefore inclined to suppose that they proceed upon a meer mistake of the Law.

E. Thurlow

31 Aug. 1771

(From T1/501)

C

Writ of assistance (English)
of George III, 1761[1]

George the Third by the Grace of God of Great Britain France & Ireland King Defender of the Faith and so forth To all & every the Officers and Ministers who now are or hereafter shall have any Office Power or Authority from or under the Jurisdiction of the Lord High Admiral of our Admiralty of England To all & every our Vice Admirals Justices of the Peace Mayors Sheriffs Constables Bailiffs Headboroughs And all other Our Officers Ministers & Subjects within every City Borough Town and County of England the Dominion of Wales & Town of Berwick upon Tweed And to every of you *Greeting Know Ye That Whereas We* by our Letters patent under our Great Seal of Great Britain bearing date the Eighteenth Day of August in the Sixth Year of our Reign *Have* Constituted Appointed & Assigned our Trusty and Well beloved Saml. Mead, Edwd. Hooper, Henry Pelham, Jno. Frederick, Henry Bankes Esqrs., Sir Wm. Musgrave Baront., Joseph Pennington, Corbyn Morris & Jas. Jeffreys Esqrs. Commissrs. for Managing & causing to be collected & Levied our Customs Subsidies & other Duties in the sd. Ltrs Patent mentd. during our Pleasure And by our Commissn. afsd. *We* have Given & Granted to our sd. Commissrs. or any four or more of them full power & Authority to Manage or Cause to be Levied & Collected all & every the Customs Subsidies Duties of Tonnage & Poundage and all other Sums Growing & Becoming due & payable to us for or by Reason of any Goods Wares or Merchandizes Imported or brot. into England the Dominion of Wales & Town of Berwick upon Tweed or Exported out of England the Dominion of Wales or Town of Berwick upon Tweed by way of Merchandize according to the Tenor & Effect of a certain Act or Reputed Act of Parliament made at Westminster the Twentyfifth Day of April in the Twelfth Year of the Reign of the late King Charles the Second Ratified & Confirmed in & by anor. Act of Parliamt. made at Westmr. the Eighth Day of May in the Thirteenth Year of the Reign of the sd. late King Charles the Second[2] & according to the sevl. partlar. Rates & Values of the sd. Goods Wares merchandizes mentd. & Engrossed in a certain Book of Rates and certain Rules Orders Directions & Allowances to the sd. Book of Rates annexed And in & by the sd. Acts or one of them Enacted Approved Ratified and Confirmed and according to the Tenor & Effect of anor. Act of Parliament made in the first Year of the late King James the Second Intitd. an Act for the Settling the Revenue on his Maty. for his Life wch. was settled on his late Maty. for his Life *And Also* full power and Authority to Manage & Cause to be Levied & Collected all & every the Customs Rates Subsidies Duties Paymts. & Sums of Money Arising & Growing due & Payable to us according to the Tenor & Effect of sevl. Acts of Parliamt. in the sd. Letters Patent mentd. As also full Pow'r & Authority to Manage & Cause to be Collected & Levied all other the Customs Rates Duties & Paymts. wch are or shall be in any wise due or payable to us for or upon the Importation or Exportation of the same Goods Wares or Merchandizes into or out of England the Dominion of Wales or Town of Berwick upon Tweed *And Further* by our sd. Letters Patent We have Given & Granted to our sd. Comissrs. or any four or more of them during our Pleasure afsd. full Pow'r & Authority to Cause to be put into Execution all & every the Clauses in the same or in any other Act or Acts of Parliamt. contained touching or Concerning the Collecting Levying Receiving or Securing of the Dutys therein mentd. or any of them or any part or parts thereof And to do all othr. Mrs. or Things wtsoever or wch by any the Commissrs. for the time being Intrusted wth. the Rect. & Management of our Customs can or may be Lawfully done *And Further* by our Commissn. afsd. We have given full pow'r & Authority to our sd. Commissrs. or any four or more of them from time to time to Constitute & Appoint by any Writing undr. the Hands & Seals of them or any four or more of them such Inferiour Officers in all & every the Ports of England the Dominion of Wales or Town of Berwick upon Tweed as by Nomination Warrt. & Direccon from the Commissrs. of the Treasy then or for the time being or from the Lord Trear. for the time being as our said Commissrs. shall Direct And them from time to time to Suspend Remove & displace as to our said Commissrs. or any four or more of them shall seem necessary or Expedient for our Service in the

Premises *And Further* That all & every the Customs & Subsidies of
Tonnage & Poundage & all & Singular the Sums of Money & other
the Premises may be duly paid to us And we may be truly &
faithfully Answered the Same We have given & Granted to our sd.
Commissrs. or any four or more of them And to all & every the
Collectors Dpty Collectors Ministers Servts. or other Officers serving
& Attending in all & every the Ports of England the Dominion of
Wales or Town of Berwick upon Tweed full pow'r & Authority from
time to time at their & every of their Wills & Pleasure as well by
Night as by Day to Enter & go on Board any Ship Boat or other
Vessl. Ryding Lying or Being within & Coming to any Port Creek or
Haven of England the Dominion of Wales or Town of Berwick upon
Tweed And Such Ship Boat & Vessl. then & there found to Search &
Look into And the Psons therein being strictly to Examine touching
or concerng. the Premes. afsd. As also in the day Time to Enter into
the Vaults Cellars Warehouses Shops & other places where any Goods
Wares or Merchandizes Lye Concealed or are Suspected to be Con-
cealed for wch the Customs & Subsidies & other the Duties & Sums
of Money afsd. are not or shall not be duly & truly Answd. Satsfied
& Paid to the Collectors Dpty Collectors Ministers Servts. & other
Officers afsd. respively or otherwise agreed for according to the true
Intent of the Law And the same Vaults Cellars Warehouses Shops &
other Places afsd. to Search & Look into And all & every the Trunks
Chests Boxes & Packs then & there found to break open And to do
all other Mrs. wch shall be found necessary for our Services in such
Cases agreable to the Laws & Statutes of England as in the sd.
Commissn. among othr. Things is more fully Contained *Therefore We
strictly Injoin and Command* You and every one of You That all
Excuses apart You & every one of You permit the sd. Saml. Mead,
Edwd. Hooper, Henry Pelham, Jno. Frederick, Henry Bankes Esqrs,
Sir Wm. Musgrave Baront., Josph. Pennington, Corbyn Morris & Jas.
Jeffreys Esqrs. and the Deptys Ministers Servts. & other Officers of
the sd. Commissrs. & every one of them from time to time as they
think proper as well by Night as by Day to Enter & go on Board any
Ship Boat or Vessl. Ryding Lying or being within & coming to any
Port Creek or Haven of England the Dominion of Wales & Town of
Berwick upon Tweed & such Ship Boat & Vessl. then & there found
to Search &   ³ and the Psons. therein being strictly to Examine
touching & concerning the Premes. afsd. according to the Tenor &
Effect & true Intent of our Commissn. & the Laws & Statutes of

England in that Behalf made & provided And in the day time to Enter & Go into the Vaults Cellars Warehouses Shops & other Places where any Goods Wares or Merchandizes lye Concealed, or are Suspected to be Concealed for which the Customs & Subsidies of Tonnage & Poundage & other the Sums of Money are not or shall not be duly & truly Answd. Satisfied & paid to our Collectors Dpty Collectors Ministrs. Servts. & other Officrs. respively. or otherwise Agreed for accordg. to the true Intent of the Law to Inspect & Oversee & Search for the sd. Goods Wares or Merchandizes *And further* to do & Execute all Things wch of Right accordg. to the Laws & Statutes of England in this Behalf shall be to be done accordg. to the Effect & true meaning of our Commissn. afsd. & the Laws & Statutes of England *And We further strictly Injoyn and Command* You and every one of You That to the sd. Saml. Mead, Edwd. Hooper, Henry Pelham, Jno. Frederick Henry Bankes Esqrs. Sir Wm. Musgrave Baront. Josph. Pennington Corbyn Morris & Jas. Jeffreys Esqrs. Our Commissrs. & their Dptys Ministers Servts. and other Officers & every one of them You & every one of You from Time to Time be Aiding Assisting & Helping in the Execution of the Premes. as is Meet And this You or any of You in no wise Omit at Your perils. *Witness* Sir Thos. Parker Knt. at Westmr. the Fourteenth Day of April in the First Year of Our Reign by the Remembrance Rolls & so forth And by the Barons. —

Masham

(From T1/465)

Notes

1. Although the form of this writ of assistance was authorized in 1761 it continued to serve, with no amendments of substance, for later issuances in George III's reign.

2. In a letter not otherwise related to writs of assistance William Bollan wrote Charles Townshend, 2 February 1767: "The writ of assistance which issues out of the court of exchequer appears to be wholly confined to uncustomed goods, and gives no authority to the persons authorised by it to search for and seize prohibited goods; and so does not conform to the act of the 14th of Charles the 2d cap. 11. which, in my humble opinion, is a matter worthy

of special consideration": SRO GD224/297/4. Bollan was unaware, apparently, of the influence of 6 Geo. 1 c. 21, discussed in
chapter 21.

3. The blank is for a word (seemingly single, and possibly abbreviated) the present writer has been unable to decipher.

D

Customs search warrant from
Conductor Generalis

Warrant to search for goods
(for which Customs ought to be paid) which are
privately conveyed away and concealed.
To the Constables of the Parish of Stepney, in the County of Middlesex

Midd. ss. WHEREAS *Andrew Bull,* of *Woodbridge,* in the said County, Gent. hath this Day made Oath before me, that on *Monday* last past, about the Hour of Ten at night, *John Badblood* of *Stepney* aforesaid, landed at the *New Dock,* from the Ship *Union,* lately arrived from *Coracoa,* two Casks of Liquor, about the Size of Quarter-Barrels, and conveyed them to his House situate in *Stepney* aforesaid; and the said *Andrew Bull,* having searched the Custom-House Books, and finding no Entry made of the said Barrels of Liquor, or any agreement made with the Collectors for the Customs thereof; and the said *John Badblood* being no way concerned by Profession, or otherwise, in foreign Liquors, and the said *Andrew Bull,* having produced a Witness to prove that he drank Brandy and Red Wine, on *Wednesday* last, at the House of the said *John Badblood,* who hath proved the same accordingly; all which being considered, there is good Reason to suspect that the said *John Badblood* hath concealed Liquors, for which Duties are payable to the Crown, with intent to defraud his Majesty, and contrary to the Statutes in that Case made: These are therefore in his Majesty's Name, to require and authorize you to assist the said *Andrew Bull* in the entering of the said House, and to enter with him into the House of the said *John Badblood,* and search for the said Barrels of Liquor, or any other foreign Liquors, for which Customs ought to be paid, which may be concealed there; and in Case you meet with any Resistance, that you do enter the said House by Force; and if you

find any such Liquors, that you do seize the same as forfeited, &c.
Given under my hand and Seal, *etc*

(Reproduced in *Conductor Generalis: or the Office, Duty and Authority of Justices of the Peace, etc.*: New York, 1749)

Note

This warrant also appeared in a 1750 (Philadelphia) edition of *Conductor Generalis.*

An extensively revised edition by James Parker in 1764 (Woodbridge, N.J.) left it out. Included however (pages 384-87) was a section arguing the unlawfulness of general search warrants. This pitted Hawkins, and, more particularly, Hale, against the general warrant for stolen goods in Dalton's *Countrey Justice* (somewhat as James Otis had done in the writs of assistance case: see chapter 16). Parker's inspiration presumably was the current furor in England over general warrants and John Wilkes.

It may have been another sign of the times that whereas earlier editions of *Conductor Generalis* had sections on customs law enforcement (unlawfully resisting customs officers, for example), Parker's had virtually nothing.

Draft, by Attorney General Edmund Trowbridge, of the Massachusetts writ of assistance, ordered by the Superior Court in August term 1755

Province of the Massachusetts Bay } George the Second by the Grace of God of Great Britain, France and Ireland King Defender of the Faith &c.

To all and Singular Justices[1] of the Peace Sheriffs and Constables and to all other Our Officers and Subjects within said Province & to Each of You Greeting

Whereas the Commissioners of Our Customs have by their Deputation dated the 8th. day of January 1752 Assignd Charles Paxton Esqr: Surveyor of all Rates duties and Impositions arising and Growing due within the Port of Boston in said Province as by said Deputation at large Appears We therefore Command You and each of You that You[2] permit the said *CP* and his Deputy's and Servants from time to time at his or their will as well in the day as in the night to Enter & Go on board any ship Boat or other Vessell riding lying or being within or coming to the said port or any places or Creeks appertaining to[3] said Port, Such Ship Boat or Vessell then and there found to View & Search and strictly to examine in the Same touching the Customs and Subsidies to Us due, And Also in the day time together with a Constable[4] or other publick Officer inhabiting near unto the place to Enter & Go into any Vaults Cellars Warehouses Shops or other places to Search & See whether any Goods

Wares[5] or Merchandizes in the same Ships Boats or Vessells Vaults Cellars warehouses Shops or other places are or shall be there hid or concealed having been imported, Ship't or laden in order to be exported from or out of the said Port or any creeks or places appertaining to the same Port, And to open any Trunks Chests Boxes fardells or Packs (made up or in Bulk) whatever in which any Goods Wares[6] or Merchandizes are Suspected to be pack't or concealed And further to do all things which of Right & according to Law & the Statutes in such Cases provided[7] is in this part to be done: And we strictly Command You and every of You that you from time to time be Aiding and assisting to the sd: *CP* his Deputys & Servants and every of them in the Execution of the prem^{n}es in all things as becometh: Fail not at your Peril. Witness Stephen Sewall Esqr. Etc

(SF 171001)

Notes

This is the draft in its final form, of course; except that the numbers have been added. They denote points in the manuscript — other than mere slips — where Trowbridge altered what he had first written, and correspond to the notes below.

1. Originally included was "Officers of Vice-Admiralty within said Province" (underlined). That Paxton — the man the writ ordered to be assisted — was himself the only executive officer (marshal) of vice-admiralty may have been a reason for the deletion of this. But the shortened formula became standard, apparently: *cf.* Appendix L.

2. The words "that You" are an insertion, which itself was amended from "that without any excuse You."

3. This is an amendment from "thereto" ("said Port" running on after the deletion: an immediate second thought, obviously).

4. Trowbridge started to continue, "Headboro," but struck it out. *Cf.* Appendix O, note.

5. "Wares" substitutes for "things" in the original.

6. Ditto.

7. Here "of England" was struck out from the original, and "in such Cases provided" inserted.

Cf., generally, pp. 107-8.

E(ii)

Model for the 1755 Massachusetts writ:
"Breve Assisten' pro Officiar' Custum' "

REX, &c. Omnibus & singulis Officiar' & Ministr' qui nunc habent aut imposterum sunthabitur' aliquod Officium potestatem vel aucto- ritatem ab vel super Jurisdiction' Dom̄ Magni Admiralli seu Admiral- itat' regni nostri Angliae Omnibus & singulis Vice-admirallis Justiciar' nostris as pacem Major' Vic' Constabular' Ballivis les Headboroughs ac omnibus aliis Officiar' Ministris & Subdit' nostris de & infra quemlibet Civitatem Burgum Villam & locum hujus regni Angliae dominii Walliae & vill' Berwici super Twed' & vestrum cuilibet salutem   Cum nos per literas Paten' sub magno sigillo nostro Angliae geren' dat' tertio die Decembris anno regni nostri vicesimo septimo Assignaverimus dilectos nobis T.V. & R.B. Ar' Collector' Custum̄ nr̄ar̄ infra Port' Dover & in omnibus locis & crecis eidem Portui &c. (*take the granting word in the Patent*) prout per easdem literas Paten' inter alia plenius liquet & apparet Vobis igitur & cuilibet vestrum praecipimus & firmiter iujungengo mandamus quod omni excusatione cessante permittatis & quilibet vestrum permittat praefat' T.V. & R.B. & eorum alterum deputat' & servien' eorum & eorum quemlibet de tempore in tempus ad eorum & cujuslibet eorū volunt' & placitum tam nocti quam die intrare & ire Anglice *to goe on board* aliquam navem cimbam vel aliud vas fluctuan' Anglice *riding* jacen' vel existen' infra vel venien' ad Portum praed' aut in aliquas Portus loca seu crecas eidem Portui adjacen' talem navem cimbam vel vas tunc & ibidem invent' videre scrutare & supervidere ac person' in eisdem stricte examinare tangen' vel concernen' Custum̄ & Subsid' nobis debit' Ac etiam in tempore diurno unacum Con- stabular' Praeposito Anglice *Headborough* aut alio publico officiaro prope inhabitan' intrare & ire in aliquas Cellas Anglice *Vaults* Cellur' Repositor' Anglice *Warehouses* Shopas vel alia loca scrutare & videre utrum aliqua bon' res vel merchandizas in eisdem navibus cimbis vel vasis cellis cellur' repositor' shopis vel aliis locis sint vel erint ibi abscondit' vel concelat' existen' fact' vel induct' vel eskippat' vel onerat' ad transportand' ab vel extra Port' D. p̃d aut aliquos Portus vel crecas eidem Portui adjacen' Ac aperire aliquos riscos Anglice *Trunks* cistas pixid' fardell' Packs fatt' vel de le Bulke quecunque in quibus aliqua bona res vel merchandiz' erint suspect' fore paccat' vel concelat' Ac ulterius ad faciend' et exequend' omnia ea que de jure & secundum legem & statut' hujus regni Angliæ in hac parte fuerit faciend' Ac vobis & cuilibet vestrum præcipimus & firmiter injungend' mandamus quod eisdem T. V. & R. B. deputat' & fervien' eorum & eorum cuilibet in executione præmissorum de tempore in tempus auxiliantes assisten' & adjuvan' sitis & quilibet vestrum auxilians assistens & adjuvans sit prout decet Et hoc nullattenus omittatis & quilibet vestrum omittat periculo incumbente Teste, &c.

(From *The Practice of his Majesties Court of Exchequer at Westminster*, published in 1699 as the second edition of William Brown, *Compendium of the Several Branches of Practice in the Court of Exchequer at Westminster* (London, 1688): cf. *Quincy's Reports*, 398; also *LPJA* II, 124 n. 57, 127 n. 6.)

F

*Text of section 6
of the Act of Frauds, 1696*

And for the more effectual preventing of Frauds, and regulating Abuses in the Plantation Trade in *America*, be it further enacted by the Authority aforesaid, That all Ships coming into, or going out of, any of the said Plantations, and lading or unlading any Goods or Commodities, whether the same be His Majesty's Ships of War, or Merchants Ships, and the Masters and Commanders thereof, and their Ladings, shall be subject and liable to the same Rules, Visitations, Searches, Penalties and Forfeitures, as to the entring, lading or discharging their respective Ships and Ladings, as Ships and their Ladings, and the Commanders and Masters of Ships, are subject and liable unto in this Kingdom, by virtue of an Act of Parliament made in the fourteenth Year of the Reign of King CHARLES the Second, intituled, *An Act for preventing Frauds, and regulating Abuses in His Majesty's Customs*: And that the Officers for collecting and managing His Majesty's Revenue, and inspecting the Plantation Trade, in any of the said Plantations, shall have the same Powers and Authorities, for visiting and searching of Ships, and taking their Entries, and for seizing and securing or bringing on Shore any of the Goods prohibited to be imported or exported into or out of any of the said Plantations, or for which any Duties are payable, or ought to have been paid, by any of the before mentioned Acts, as are provided for the Officers of the Customs in *England* by the said last mentioned Act made in the fourteenth Year of the Reign of King CHARLES the Second, and also to enter Houses or Warehouses, to search for and seize any such Goods; and that all the Wharfingers, and Owners of Keys and Wharfs, or any Lightermen, Bargemen, Watermen, Porters, or other Persons assisting in the Conveyance, Concealment or Rescue of any of the said Goods, or in the hindring or Resistance of any of the said Officers in the Performance of their Duty, and the Boats, Barges, Lighters or other Vessels employed in the Conveyance of such Goods, shall be subject to the like Pains and Penalties as are provided by the same Act made in the fourteenth Year of the Reign of King CHARLES the Second, in relation to prohibited or uncustomed Goods in this Kingdom; and that the like Assistance shall be given to the said Officers in the Execution of their Office as by the said last mentioned Act is provided for the Officers in *England*; and also that the said Officers shall be subject to the same Penalties and Forfeitures, for any Corruptions, Frauds, Connivances, or Concealments, in Violation of any the before mentioned Laws, as any Officers of the Customs in *England* are liable to, by virtue of the said last mentioned Act; and also that in case any Officer or Officers in the Plantations shall be sued or molested for any thing done in the Execution of their Office, the said Officer shall and may plead the General Issue, and shall give this or other Customs Acts in Evidence, and the Judge to allow thereof, have and enjoy the like Privileges and Advantages, as are allowed by Law to the Officers of His Majesty's Customs in *England*.

Extract from the

London Magazine, *March 1760*

April 26th, It was ordered that leave should be given to bring in a Bill for the more effectual preventing the fraudulent importation of Cambricks and French Lawns; and that Mr. Chancellor of the Exchequer, Mr. Nugent, Mr. West, Mr. Samuel Martin, and Mr. Charlton should prepare and bring in the same. May 3d, the Bill was presented to the House by Mr. Charlton, read a first time, ordered to be read a second time; which it was May 10th, and committed to a committee of the whole House; but before the House resolved itself into the same, that is to say, on the 21st there was presented to the House and read, a petition of the several merchants, wholesale drapers, and traders in linens, of the city of London, whose names were thereunto subscribed, on behalf of themselves, and several thousands of other wholesale drapers and traders in linen throughout Great Britain; alledging, that by the Bill then depending, all persons who should have any cambricks or French lawns in their possession after the time to be therein limited, were subjected to several penalties and forfeitures, all warehouses and dwelling-houses were made liable to search, and the persons accused, directed to be held to special bail without any previous accusation upon oath, and in case of any doubt with respect to the species or quality of the goods, or where the same were manufactured the proof was to lie upon the owner, and not upon the prosecutor; and that the petitioners conceived, several of the provisons in the said bill, if the same should be passed into a law, would be greatly detrimental to the petitioners and other traders in linens; and therefore praying, that they might have leave to be heard by their counsel, against such parts of the said bill as would materially affect them.

The prayer of this petition being granted, the petitioners were

next day heard by their counsel before the committee of the whole
house upon this bill, and whether they met with any redress will best
appear from the abstract of that act; for on that day the committee
went through the bill, after which it passed in common course, and
received the royal assent on June 2d.

As the power of searching and seizing is by this act expressed in
very general terms, it is not easy to determine whether the petitioners were right in saying that their warehouses and dwelling
houses might be searched, without any previous accusation upon
oath. It is very true, that by our laws of customs and excise, there are
many houses and places in this kingdom which may be entered and
searched by an officer whenever he pleases, and without any accusation upon oath, or so much as a suspicion upon oath; but then those
houses or places are such as in obedience to some act of parliament,
have been entered by the possessor, as a house or place where he
made or kept such goods as were by that act subjected to a duty; for
as to any other house or place he might be possessed of, no officer
can enter or search it, without a writ of assistance from the exchequer, or a warrant from the commissioners, or from a justice or
justices of the peace. As to a writ of assistance from the exchequer,
in pursuance of the act of the 13th and 14th of Charles II. cap. 11. I
believe it never was granted without an information upon oath, that
the person applying for it has reason to suspect that prohibited or
uncustomed goods are concealed in the house or place which he
desires a power to search; and as to a search warrant from the
commissioners, or a justice or justices of the peace, we must, from
the act of the 10th of his late Majesty, cap. 10, and the act of the
11th of the same reign, cap. 30, conclude that they ought, before
granting such a warrant, to have such an information: nay, that
information ought to set forth the informer's grounds of suspicion;
and if those grounds appear to be groundless, no such warrant ought
be granted; for if such a warrant should be granted without any
reasonable or solid ground of suspicion, and no such goods should
upon search be found, I am apt to *suspect*, that an action would lie
against the *grantors*, and that the plaintiff, in that action would
recover damages & costs.

Now as dealers in linen are not by this, or any other act, obliged to
enter their shops, warehouses, or other places where their linens are
kept, or exposed to sale, I am inclined to think, that no officer can,
by this act, enter and search either their shops or warehouses even in

the day time, without such an information and search warrant as I have mentioned; and I am the more inclined to be of this opinion, because, if it had been otherwise, I am persuaded our parliament would have given them relief, with respect to this part of their petition; for it would be a terrible hardship upon all dealers in linen, if officers had a .power to enter and rummage their shops and warehouses, in the day time, as often as they pleased.

(As in the *Boston Evening-Post*, 19 January 1761)

Note

The acts of 1723 and 1724 that are prayed in aid related to inland or excise duties and included provision for the commissioners of those duties, and justices of the peace, to issue specific search warrants for fraudulent concealments of the particular products — coffee, tea, etc. — the duties bore upon.

In fact, of course, these provisions had nothing to do with writ of assistance search under the customs act of 1662, which was different both in terms of fiscal regime and — *cf.* chapter 3 — juridically.

H

~~~~~~

Memorandum by William Bollan
"relating to the proceedings at Boston
with respect to illicit Trade, ec."
1761 − 62

~~~~~~

Memorandum

1761

In the beginning of this year several seizures having
been made at Boston by Mr Paxton an officer of the
customs, warm contests arose respecting the propriety of his proceedings, with those of the court of
admiralty, and a great number of merchants, encouraged by the collector, thereupon applied to the general assembly, who, after some proceedings, in effect
order'd that a suit should be commenced against
Mr Paxton by the treas^r of the province, to recover
the monies paid by him to the informers of offences
against the melasses act, which the court of admiralty
had allowed to be taken out of the kings part, which,
after being subject to the payment of charges is
granted to the province

About this time application was made to the superior court of Judicature held at Boston for a writ of
assistance to be issued in support of the officers of
the customs: divers had been granted, but their legality was now question'd, & the court doubting suspended their determination til next term

March 5th

The chief justice by letter acquainted Mr Bollan
with this proceeding, and the reason of their doubts,

& desired to know whether such writs of assistance were issue [*sic*] from the exchequer, except upon special information, & confined either to particular houses or to particular goods of which information is made.

June 13th

Mr Bollan sent him a copy of the writ of assistance, taken out of the court of exchequer, which writ is directed to the officers of the admiralty, justices of peace, mayors, sheriffs, constables, & all other his Majestys officers, ministers, & subjects in England, requiring them to permit the comissrs. of the customs, & their officers by night or day to enter on board any vessel to search &c & in the daytime to enter the vaults, cellars, warehouses, shops, & other places where any goods &c lye conceal'd, or are suspected to lye conceal'd, for which the customs are not paid, to inspect & search for the said goods &c and to do all things which according to the laws in that behalf shou'd be done, and comanding them to be aiding & assisting to the said comissrs. & their officers in the execution of the premises. On the copy sent this endorsement was made, NB. These writs upon any application of the commissrs. of the customs to the proper officer of the court of exchequer are made out of course by him, without any affidavit, or order of the court.

This copy being afterwards received by the chief justice, & produced in court, the similar writ of assistance moved for was by the court order'd to be issued.

1762
Febry.

On a trial at the superior court the action brought in behalf of the province against Mr Paxton was determined against the province. After issuing the writ of assistance, & this determination, the house of representves. not only reduced the allowance to the superior court in general, but refused to make any allowance to Mr Hutchinson as chief justice; and

March 6th

The genl. assembly presented to the governour a bill, which had passed both houses, restraining the superior court from issuing writs of assistance, except upon special information to a custom house officer, oath being first made, the informer mentioned, & the person supposed to own the goods, & the place where they were suspected to be concealed.

(SRO GD224/297/2)

Note

This memorandum, which is among the Townshend papers in the Scottish Record Office, is in the handwriting of Bollan's amanuensis. It is endorsed "Memorandum relating to the proceedings at Boston with respect to illicit Trade, &c.", but bears no signature or date. Nor is it explicitly addressed to Charles Townshend, though it clearly was intended for him (probably in 1766 or 1767).

~~~~~~

John Adams's contemporaneous notes of the writs of assistance hearing in February 1761 *

~~~~~~

Gridley. — The Constables distraining for Rates. more inconsistent with Eng. Rts. & liberties than Writts of assistance. And Necessity, authorizes both.

Thacher. I have searched, in all the ancient Repertories, of Precedents, in Fitzherberts Natura Brevium, and in the Register (Q. wt the Reg. is) and have found no such Writt of assistance as this Petition prays. — I have found two Writts of ass. in the Reg. but they are very difft, from the Writt prayd for. —

In a Book, intituled the Modern Practice of the Court of Exchequer there is indeed one such Writt, and but one.

By the Act of Palt. any other private Person, may as well as a Custom House Officer, take an officer, a Sheriff, or Constable, &c and go into any Shop, Store &c & seize: any Person authorized by such a Writt, under the Seal of the Court of Exchequer, may, not Custom House Officers only. — Strange. — Only a temporary thing.

The most material Question is, whether the Practice of the Exchequer, will warrant this Court in granting the same.

The Act impowers all the officers of the Revenue to enter and seise in the Plantations, as well as in England. 7. & 8 Wm.3, C.22, §6, gives the same as 13. & 14. of C. gives in England. The Ground of Mr Gridleys argt. is this, that this Court has the Power of the Court of Exchequer. — But This Court has renounced the Chancery Jurisdiction, wh the Exchequer has in Cases where either Party, is the Kings Debtor. — Q. into tht Case.

---

*Attempts have been made to reproduce Adams's crossings-out etc., as in *Quincy's Reports*, 469-77.

In Eng. all Informations of uncusted or prohibited Importations, are in the Exchequer. — So tht the Custom House officers are the officers of tht Court. — under the Eye, and Direction of the Barons.

The Writ of Assistance is not returnable. — If such seisure were brot before your Honours, youd often find a wanton Exercise of their Power.

At home, the officers, seise at their Peril, even with Probable Cause. —

Otis. This Writ is against the fundamental Principles of Law. — The Priviledge of House. A Man, who is quiet, is as secure in his House, as a Prince in his Castle — notwithstanding all his Debts, & civil processes of any Kind. — But

For flagrant Crimes, and in Cases of great public Necessity, the Priviledge may be [encroached?] on. — For Felonies an officer may break, upon Proscess, and oath. — i.e. by a Special Warrant to search such an House, susp sworn to be suspected, and good Grounds of suspicion appearing.

Make oath corm. Ld. Treaer., or Exchequer, in Engd. or a Magistrate here, and get a Special Warrant, for the public good, to infringe the Priviledge of House.

Genl. Warrant to search for Felonies, Hawk. Pleas Crown. — every petty officer from the highest to the lowest, and if some of 'em are com, others uncom̄ others are uncomm̄. Gouvt Justices used to issue such perpetual Edicts. (Q. with wt particular Reference?)

But one Precedent, and tht in the Reign of C. 2 when Star Chamber Powers, and all Powers but lawful & useful Powers were pushed to Extremity. —

The authority of this Modern Practice of the Court of Exchequer. — it has an Imprimatur. — But wt may not have? — It may be owing to some ignorant Clerk of the Exchequer.

But all Precedents and this am'g the Rest are under the Control of the Principles of Law. Ld. Talbot. better to observe the known Principles of Law thn any one Precedent, tho in the House of Lords. —

As to Acts of Parliament. an Act against the Constitution is void: an Act against natural Equity is void: and if an Act of Parliament should be made, in the very Words of this Petition, it would be void. The Executive Courts must pass such Acts into disuse — 8. Rep. 118. from Viner. — Reason of the Com̄ Law to control an Act of Parliament. — Iron Manufacture. noble Lord's Proposal, tht we should send our Horses to Eng. to be shod. —

If an officer will justify under a Writ he must return it. 12th. Mod. 396. — perpetual Writ.

Stat. C.2. We have all as good Rt to inform as Custom House officers — & every Man may have a general, irreturnable ~~Writ~~ Commission to break Houses. —

By 12. of C. on oath before Ld Treasurer, Barons of Exchequer, or Chief Magistrate to break with an officer. — 14th. C. to issue a Warrant requiring sheriffs &c to assist the officers to search for Goods not entrd, or prohibitd; 7 & 8th. W. & M. gives Officers in Plantations same Powers with officers in England. —

Continuance of Writts and Proscesses, proves no more nor so much as I grant a special Writ of ass. on special oath, for specl Purpose. —

Pew indorsd Warrant to Ware. — Justice Walley searc'd House. Law Prov. Bill in Chancery. — this Court confined their Chancery Power to Revenue &c.

Gridley. By the 7. & 8 of Wm. C.22. §6th. — This authority, of breaking and entering Ships, Warehouses, Cellars &c given to the Custom House officers in England by the Statutes of the 12th. and 14th of Charl. 2d, is extended to the Custom House officers in the Plantations: — and by the Statute of the 6th of Anne, ~~this~~ Writts of assistance are continued, in Company with all other legal Proscesses for 6 months after the Demise of the Crown. — Now what this Writ of assistance is, we can know only by Books of Precedents. — And we have produced, in a Book intituld the modern Practice of the Court of Exchequer, a form of such a Writ of assistance to the officers of the Customs. The Book has the Imprimatur of Wright C.J. of the K.'s B. wh is as great a sanction as any Books of Precedents ever have. altho Books of Reports are usually approved by all the Judges — and I take Brown the author of this Book to have been a very good Collector of Precedents. — I have two Volumes of Precedents of his Collection, wh I look upon as good as any, except Coke & Rastal.

And the Power given in this Writ is no greater Infringement of our Liberty than the Method of collecting Taxes in this Province. —

Every Body knows that the Subject has the Priviledge of House only against his fellow Subjects, not vs the K. either in matters of Crime or fine.

Extracts from the Acts of Parliament *

14. Car. 2nd. "And it shall be lawful to and for any Person or Persons authorized by *Writ of assistants, under the seal of his Majesties Court of Exchequer,* to take a Constable, Headborough, or other public officers inhabiting near unto the Place, and in the day time to enter and go into any House, shop, Cellar, Warehouse or Room or other Place, and in Case of Resistance to break Open Doors, Chests, Trunks and other Package, there to seize and from thence to bring any Kind of Goods, or Merchandize what soever prohibited and uncustomed and to put and secure the same in his Majesties store House, in the Port to the Place where such seizure shall be made."

7. & 8th. Willm. 3rd. "And that the officers for collecting and managing his Majesties Revenue and inspecting the Plantation Trade shall have the same Powers and authorities &c. as are provided for the officers of his Majesties Customs in England by the said last mentioned Act made in the 14th. Year of the Reign of K. Char. 2d. and also to enter Houses or Warehouses to search for and seize any such Goods. And that the like assistance shall be given to the said officers in the Execution of their office, as by the last mentioned Act is provided, for the officers in England."

Prov. Law. Page 114. Be it enacted &c. that there shall be a Superiour Court of Judicature, Court of Assize and General Goal &c. over this whole Province &c. who shall have Cognizance of all Pleas Real, Personal or mixt, as well all Pleas of the Crown &c. and generally of all other matters as fully and amply to all Intents and Purposes whatsoever as the Courts of Kings Bench, Common Pleas, and *Exchequer* within his Majesties Kingdom of England, have or ought to have.

Petition. To the honorable &c.

Humbly shews,

That he is lawfully authorized to execute the office of surveyor of all Rates, Duties, and Impositions, arising and growing due to his Majesty, at Boston in this Province and cannot fully exercise said office in such manner as his majesties service and the Laws in such Cases require Unless your Honours, who are vested with the Power of a Court of Exchequer for this Province will please to grant him a Writt of assistants, he therefore prays he and his Deputties may be aided in

---

*These extracts have not tampered with Adams's omissions and inaccuracies.

the Excution of said office within his District by a Writ of assistants under the seal of this superior Court in legal Form and according to Usage in his Majestys Court of Exchequer and in Great Britain.

C.P.

George the second by the Grace of
Province of the   God of Great Britain France and Ireland
Massachusetts Bay   King, Defender of the Faith & c.

To all and singular Justices of the Peace, sheriffs and Constables, and to all other our officers and subjects within said Province and to each of you
Greeting
Whereas the Commissioners of our Customs have by their Deputation dated the 8th. day of Jany. 1752 assigned Charles Paxton Esqr. surveyor of all Rates, Duties, and Impositions arising and growing due within the Port of Boston in said Province as by said Deputation at large appears, We therefore command you and each of you that you permit the said C.P. and his Deputies and servants from Time to time at his or their Will as well in the day as in the Night to enter and go on board any ship, Boat or Vessell riding lying or being within or coming to the said Port or any Places or Creeks appertaining to said Port, such ship, Boat or Vessell then and there found to View and search and strait to examine in the same, touching the Customs and subsidies to us due, and also in the day Time together with a Constable or other public officer inhabiting near unto the Place to enter and go into any Vaults, Cellars, Warehouses, shops or other Places to search and see, whether any Goods, Wares or Merchandizes, in the same ships, Boats or Vessells, Vaults, Cellars, Warehouses, shops or other Places are or shall be there hid or concealed, having been imported, ship't or laden in order to be exported from or out of the said Port or any Creeks or Places appertaining to the same Port; and to open any Trunks, Chests, Boxes, fardells or Packs made up or in Bulk, whatever in which any Goods, Wares, or Merchandizes are suspected to be packed or concealed and further to do all Things which of Right and according to Law and the statutes in such Cases provided, is in this Part to be done: and We strictly command you and every of you that you, from Time to Time be aiding and assisting to the said C.P. his Deputties and servants and every of them in the Execution of the Premisses in all Things as becometh: Fail not at your Peril: Witness Stephen Sewall Esqr. &c.

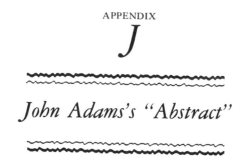

John Adams's "Abstract"

(The third speech reproduced below — that of James Otis —
is from the *Massachusetts Spy* for 29 April 1773;
the remainder of the text is from
"Israel Keith's Pleadings, Arguments, &c." as extracted
by Horace Gray on pages 479-82 of *Quincy's Reports*.)

Boston Superior Court February 1761

On the second Tuesday of the Court's sitting, appointed by the
rule of the Court for argument of special matters, came on the
dispute on the petition of Mr. Cockle & others on the one side, and
the Inhabitants of Boston on the other, concerning Writs of Assistance. Mr. *Gridley* appeared for the former, Mr. *Otis* for the latter.
Mr. *Thacher* was joined with them at the desire of the Court.

Mr. *Gridley.* I appear on the behalf of Mr. Cockle & others, who
pray 'that as they cannot fully exercise their Offices in such a
manner as his Majesty's Service and their Laws in such cases require,
unless your Honors who are vested with the power of a Court of
Exchequer for this Province will please to grant them Writs of
Assistance. They therefore pray that they & their Deputies may be
aided in the Execution of their Offices by Writs of Assistance under
the Seal of this Court and in legal form, & according to the Usage of
his Majesty's Court of Exchequer in Great Britain.'

May it please your Honors, it is certain it has been the practice of
the Court of Exchequer in England, and of this Court in this
Province, to grant Writs of Assistance to Custom House Officers.
Such Writs are mentioned in several Acts of Parliament, in several
Books of Reports; & in a Book called the Modern Practice of the

Court of Exchequer, We have a Precedent, a form of a Writ, called a Writ of Assistance for Custom house Officers, of which the following a few years past to Mr Paxton under the Seal of this Court, & tested by the late Chief Justice Sewall is a literal Translation. [Gray says that the text of the writ was given at this point, but omits it and refers to a reproduction of it elsewhere; in the present book it is set forth in appendices E and I.]

The first Question therefore for your Honors to determine is, whether this practice of the Court of Exchequer in England (which is certain, has taken place heretofore, how long or short a time so-ever it continued) is legal or illegal. And the second is, whether the practice of the Exchequer (admitting it to be legal) can warrant this Court in the same practice.

In answer to the first, I cannot indeed find the Original of this Writ of Assistance. It may be of very antient, to which I am inclined, or it may be of modern date. This however is certain, that the Stat. of the 14th. Char. 2nd. has established this Writ almost in the words of the Writ itself. 'And it shall be lawful to & for any person or persons *authorised by Writ of Assistance under the seal of his Majesty's Court of Exchequer* to take a Constable, Headborough, or other public Officer, inhabiting near unto the place, & in the day time to enter & go into any house, Shop, Cellar, Warehouse, room. or any other place, and in case of Resistance, to break open doors, Chests, Trunks & other Package, & there to seize any kind of Goods or Merchandize whatever prohibited, and to put the same into his Majesty's Warehouse in the Port where Seisure is made.'

By this act & that of 12 Char. 2nd. all the powers in the Writ of Assistance mentioned are given, & it is expressly said, the persons shall be authorised by Writs of Assistance under the seal of the Exchequer. Now the Books in which we should expect to find these Writs, & all that relates to them are Books of Precedents, & Reports in the Exchequer, which are extremely scarce in this Country; we have one, & but one that treats of Exchequer matters, and that is called the 'Modern practice of the Court of Exchequer,' & in this Book we find one Writ of Assistance, translated above. Books of Reports have commonly the Sanction of all the Judges, but books of Precedents never have more than that of the Chief Justice. Now this Book has the Imprimatur of Wright, who was Chief Justice of the King's Bench, and it was wrote by Brown, whom I esteem the best Collector of Precedents; I have Two Volumes of them by him, which

I esteem the best except Rastall & Coke. But we have a further proof
of the legality of these Writs, & of the settled practice at home of
allowing them; because by the Stat. 6th Anne which continues all
Processes & Writs after the Demise of the Crown, *Writs of Assistance
are continued among the Rest.*

It being clear therefore that the Court of Exchequer at home has a
power by Law of granting these Writs, I think there can be but little
doubt, whether this Court as a Court of Exchequer for this Province
has this power. By the Statute of the 7th. & 8th. W. 3d., it is enacted
'that all the Officers for collecting and managing his Majesty's Revenue, and inspecting the Plantation Trade in any of the said Plantations, shall have the same powers &c. as are provided for the Officers
of the Revenue in England; also to enter Houses, or Warehouses, to
search for and seize any such Goods, & that the *like Assistance* shall
be given to the said Officers as is the Custom in England.'

Now what is the Assistance which the Officers of the Revenue are
to have here, which is like that they have in England? Writs of
Assistance under the Seal of his Majesty's Court of Exchequer at
home will not run here. They must therefore be under the Seal of
this Court. For by the law of this Province 2 W. 3d. Ch.3 'there shall
be a Superior Court &c. over the whole Province &c. who shall have
cognizance of all pleas &c. & generally of all other matters, as fully &
[amply] to all intents & purposes as the Courts of King's Bench,
Common Pleas & *Exchequer* within his Majesty's Kingdom of England have or ought to have.'

It is true the common privileges of Englishmen are taken away in
this Case, but even their privileges are not so in cases of Crime and
fine. 'Tis the necessity of the Case and the benefit of the Revenue
that justifies this Writ. Is not the Revenue the sole support of Fleets
& Armies abroad, & Ministers at home? without which the Nation
could neither be preserved from the Invasions of her foes, nor the
Tumults of her own Subjects. Is not this I say infinitely more
important, than the imprisonment of Thieves, or even Murderers? yet
in these Cases 'tis agreed Houses may be broke open.

In fine the power now under consideration is the same with that
given by the Law of this Province to Treasurers towards Collectors, &
to them towards the subject. A Collector may when he pleases
distrain my goods & Chattels, and in want of them arrest my person,
and throw me instantly into Goal. What! shall my property be
wrested from me! — shall my Liberty be destroyed by a Collector,

for a debt, unadjudged, without the common Indulgence and Lenity of the Law? So it is established, and the necessity of having public taxed effectually and speedily collected is of infinitely greater moment to the whole, than the Liberty of any Individual.

Thacher. In obedience to the Order of this Court I have searched with a good deal of attention all the antient Reports of Precedents, Fitz. N. Brev. & the Register, but have not found any such Writ as this Petition prays. In the latter indeed I have found Two Writs which bear the Title of Brev. Assistenice, but these are only to give possession of Houses &c. in cases of Injunctions & Sequestration in Chancery. By the Act of Parliament any private Person as well as Custom House Officer may take a Sheriff or Constable & go into any Shop &c. & seize &c. (here Mr. Thacher quoted an Authority from Strange which intended to shew that Writs of Assistance were only temporary things.)

The most material question is whether the practice of the Exchequer is good ground for this Court. But this Court has upon a solemn Argument, which lasted a whole day, renounc'd the Chance of [Chancery] * Jurisdiction which the Exchequer has in Cases where either party is the King's Debtor.

In England all Informations of uncustomed or prohibited Goods are in the Exchequer, so that the Custom House Officers are the Officers of that Court under the Eye & Direction of the Barons & so accountable for any wanton exercise of power.

The Writ now prayed for is not returnable. If the Seizures were so, before your Honors, and this Court should enquire into them you'd often find a wanton exercise of power. At home they seize at their peril, even with probable Cause.

Otis.

May it please your honours, I was desired by one of the court to look into the books, and consider the question now before the court, concerning Writs of Assistance. I have accordingly considered it, and now appear not only in obedience to your order, but also in behalf of the inhabitants of this town, who have presented another petition, and out of regard to the liberties of the subject. And I take this opportunity to declare, that whether under a fee or not, (for in such

---

*This bracketed insertion appears to be by Horace Gray (*Quincy's Reports,* 482). *Cf.* also *LPJA II,* 139, n. 121.

a cause as this I despise a fee) I will to my dying day oppose, with all the powers and faculties God has given me, all such instruments of slavery on the one hand, and villainy on the other, as this writ of assistance is. It appears to me (may it please your honours) the worst instrument of arbitrary power, the most destructive of English liberty, and the fundamental principles of the constitution, that ever was found in an English law-book. I must therefore beg your honours patience and attention to the whole range of an argument, that may perhaps appear uncommon in many things, as well as points of learning, that are more remote and unusual, that the whole tendency of my design may the more easily be perceived, the conclusions better descend [discerned?], and the force of them better felt.

I shall not think much of my pains in this cause as I engaged in it from principle. I was sollicited to engage on the other side. I was sollicited to argue this cause as Advocate-General, and because I would not, I have been charged with a desertion of my office; to this charge I can give a very sufficient answer, I renounced that office, and I argue this cause from the same principle; and I argue it with the greater pleasure as it is in favour of British liberty, at a time, when we hear the greatest monarch upon earth declaring from his throne, that he glories in the name of Briton, and that the privileges of his people are dearer to him than the most valuable prerogatives of his crown. And as it is in opposition to a kind of power, the exercise of which in former periods of English history, cost one King of England his head and another his throne. I have taken more pains in this cause, than I ever will take again: Although my engaging in this and another popular cause has raised much resentment; but I think I can sincerely declare, that I cheerfully submit myself to every odious name for conscience sake; and from my soul I despise all those whose guilt, malice or folly has made my foes. Let the consequences be what they will, I am determined to proceed. The only principles of public conduct that are worthy a gentleman, or a man are, to sacrifice estate, ease, health and applause, and even life itself to the sacred calls of his country. These manly sentiments in private life make the good citizen, in public life, the patriot and the hero.— I do not say, when brought to the test, I shall be invincible; I pray GOD I may never be brought to the melancholy trial; but if ever I should, it would be then known, how far I can reduce to practice principles I know founded in truth. — In the mean time I will proceed to the subject of the writ. In the first, may it please your Honours, I will admit, that writs of one kind, may be legal, that is, *special writs, directed to special officers,* and to search *certain houses,* &c. *especially set forth in the writ,* may be granted by the Court of Exchequer at home, *upon oath made before* the Lord Treasurer by the person, who asks, *that he suspects such goods to be concealed in* THOSE VERY PLACES HE DESIRES TO SEARCH. The Act of 14th Car.II. which Mr. Gridley mentions proves this. And in this light the writ appears like a warrant from a justice of peace to search for stolen goods. Your Honours will find in the old book, concerning the office of a justice of peace, precedents of general warrants to search suspected houses. But in more modern books you will find only special warrants to search such and such houses specially named, in which the complainant has before sworn he suspects his goods are concealed; and you will find it adjudged *that special warrants only are legal.* In the same manner I rely on it, that the writ prayed for in this petition being general is illegal. It is a power that places the liberty of every man in the hands of every petty officer. I say I admit that *special* writs of assistance to search *special* houses, may be granted to certain persons on oath; but I deny that the writ now prayed for can be granted, for I beg leave to make some observations on the writ itself before I proceed to other Acts of Parliament.

In the first place the writ is UNIVERSAL, being directed "to all and singular justices, sheriffs, constables and all other officers and subjects &c." so that in short it is directed to every subject in the king's dominions; every one with this writ may be a tyrant: If this commission is legal, a tyrant may, in a legal manner also, controul, imprison or murder any one within the realm.

In the next place, IT IS PERPETUAL; there's no return, a man is accountable to no person for his doings, every man may reign secure in his petty tyranny, and spread terror and desolation around him, until the trump of the arch-angel shall excite different emotions in his soul.

In the third place, a person with this writ, IN THE DAY TIME may enter all houses, shops, &c. AT WILL, and command all to assist.

Fourthly, by this not only deputies, &c. but even THEIR MENIAL SERVANTS ARE ALLOWED TO LORD IT OVER US — What is this but to have the curse of Canaan with a witness on us, to be the servant of servants, the most despicable of GOD's creation. — Now one of the most essential branches of English liberty, is the freedom of one's house. A man's house is his castle; and while he is quiet, he is as well guarded as a prince in his castle. — This writ, if it should be declared legal, would totally annihilate this privilege. Custom-house officers may enter our houses when they please — we are commanded to permit their entry — their menial servants may enter — may break locks, bars and every thing in their way — and whether they break through malice or revenge, no man, no court can inquire — bare suspicion without oath is sufficient. This wanton exercise of this power is no chimerical suggestion of a heated Brain. — I will mention some facts. Mr. Pew had one of these writs, and when Mr. Ware succeeded him, he endorsed this writ over to Mr. Ware, so that THESE WRITS ARE NEGOTIABLE from one officer to another, and so your Honours have no opportunity of judging the persons to whom this vast power is delegated. Another instance is this. — Mr. Justice Wally had called this same Mr. Ware before him by a constable, to answer for a breach of the Sabbath-day acts, or that of profane swearing. As soon as he had done, Mr. Ware asked him if he had done, he replied, yes. Well then, says he, I will shew you a little of my power — I command you to permit me to search your house for unaccustomed goods; and went on to search his house from the garret to the cellar, and then served the constable in the same manner. But to shew another absurdity in this writ, if it should be established, I insist upon it EVERY PERSON by 14th of Car. II. HAS THIS POWER as well as Custom-house officers; the words are, "it shall be lawful for any person or persons authorized, &c." What a scene does this open! Every man prompted by revenge, ill humour or wantonness to inspect the inside of his neighbour's house, may get a writ of assistance; others will ask it from self defence; one arbitrary exertion will provoke another, until society will be involved in tumult and in blood. — Again these writs ARE NOT RETURNED. Writs in their nature are temporary things; when the purposes for which they are issued are answered, they exist no more; but these monsters in the law live forever, no one can be called to account. Thus reason and the constitution are both against this writ. Let us see what authority there is for it. No more than one instance can be found of it in all our law books, and that was in the zenith of arbitrary power, viz. In the reign of Car. II. when star-chamber powers were pushed to extremity by some ignorant clerk of the Exchequer. — But had this writ been in any book whatever it would have been illegal. ALL PRECE-

DENTS ARE UNDER THE CONTROUL OF THE PRINCIPLES OF
THE LAW. Lord Talbot says, it is better to observe these than
any precedents though in the House of Lords, the last resort of the
subject. — No Acts of Parliament can establish such a writ: Though it
should be made in the very words of the petition it would be void,
"AN ACT AGAINST THE CONSTITUTION IS VOID." Vid. Viner.
But these prove no more than what I before observed, that *special*
writs may be granted *on oath* and *probable suspicion.* The Act of
7th, and 8th of William III. that the officers of the plantations shall
have the same powers, &c. is confined to this sense, that an officer
should show probable grounds, should take his oath on it, should do
this before a magistrate, and that such magistrate, if he thinks proper
should issue a *special warrant* to a constable to search the places.
That of 6th of Anne can prove no more.

K

Report of the resumed writs of assistance hearing, 18 November 1761, by Josiah Quincy junior

CHARLES PAXTON , Esq., applied to the Superiour Court for the Writ of Assistants, as by Act of Parliament to be granted to him.

Upon this, the Court desired the Opinion of the Bar, whether they had a Right and ought to grant it.

Mr. Otis & Mr. Thacher spoke against.

Messrs. Gridley & Auchmuty for granting it.

Mr. Thacher first read the Acts of 14 Car. 2, ch.22, and 7 & 8 of Wm. & Mary, upon which the Request for this Writ is founded.

Though this Act of Parliament has existed 60 Years, yet it was never applied for, nor ever granted, till 1756; which is a great Argument against granting it; not that an Act of Parliament can be antiquated, but Non-user is a great Presumption that the Law will not bear it; this is the Reasoning of Littleton and Coke. Knight Service, p. 80, Sect. 108. Moreover, when an Act of Parliament is not express, but even doubtfull, and then has been neglected and not executed, in such a Case the Presumption is more violent.

Ch. Justice. The Custom House Officers have frequently applied to the Governour for this Writ, and have had it granted them by him, and therefore, though he had no Power to grant it, yet that removes the Argument of Non-user.

Mr Thacher. If this Court have a Right to grant this Writ, it must be either *ex debita Justitia* or discretionary. If *ex debita Justitia*, it cannot in any Case be refused; which from the Act itself and its Consequences, he argued, could not be intended. It can't be discretionary; for it can't be in the Power of any Judge at discretion to determine that I shall have my House broken open or not. As says Just. Holt, "There can be no discretionary Power whether a Man shall be hanged or no".

He moved futher that such a Writ is granted and must issue from the Exchequer Court, and no other can grant it; 4 Inst. 103; and that no other Officers but such as constitute that Court can grant it. 2 Inst. 551. That this Court is not such a one, vid. Prov. Law. This Court has in the most solemn Manner disclaimed the Authority of the Exchequer; this they did in the Case of McNeal of Ireland & McNeal of Boston. This they cannot do in Part; if the Province Law gives them any, it gives them all the Power of the Exchequer Court; nor can they chuse and refuse to act at Pleasure. But supposing this Court has the Power of the Exchequer, yet there are many Circumstances which render that Court in this Case an improper Precedent; for there the Officers are sworn in that Court, and are accountable to it, are obliged there to pass their Accounts weekly; which is not the Case here. In that Court, there Cases are tried, and there finally; which is another Diversity. Besides, the Officers of the Customs are their Officers, and under their Check, and that so much, that for Misbehaviour they may punish with corporal Punishment. 3 & 4 [sic] Car. 2 §8. 7 & 8 W. & M. does not give the Authority.

(Mr. Otis was of the same Side, but I was absent, while he was speaking, most of the and so have but few Notes.)

Mr. Otis 12 Car. 2, 19. 13 & 14 Car. 2, p. 56. Let a Warrant come from whence it will improperly, it is to be refused, and the higher the Power granting it, the more dangerous. The Exchequer itself was thought a Hardship in the first Constitution. Vid. Rapin, Vol. 1st, p. 178, 386, 403, 404. Vol. 2, p. 285, 375.

It is worthy Consideration whether this Writ was constitutional even in England; and I think it plainly appears it was not; much less here, since it was not there invented till after our Constitution and Settlement. Such a Writ is generally illegal. Hawkins, B. 2, ch. 1, Of Crim. Jur. Viner, Tit. Commission, A. 1 Inst. 464. 29 M.

Mr. Auchmuty. Bacon. 4 Inst. 100. From the Words of the Law, this Court may have the Power of the Exchequer. Now the Exchequer always had that Power; the Court cannot regard Consequences, but must follow Law. As for the Argument of Non-user, that ends whenever the Law is once executed; and this Law has been executed in this Country, and this Writ granted, not only by the Governor, but also from this Court in Ch. Justice Sewall's Time.

Mr Gridley. This is properly a Writ of Assistants, not Assistance; not to give the Officers a greater Power, but as a Check upon them. For by this they cannot enter into any House, without the Presence of the Sheriff or civil Officer, who will always be supposed to have an Eye over and be a Check upon them. Quoting History is not speaking like a Lawyer. If it is Law in England, it is Law here; it is extended to this Country by Act of Parliament. 7 & 8 Wm. & M. ch. 18. By Act of Parliament they are entitled to like Assistants; now how can they have like Assistants, if the court cannot grant them it; and how can the Court grant them like Assistance, if they cannot grant this Writ. Pity it would be, they should have like Right, and not like Remedy; the Law abhors Right without Remedy. But the General Court has given this Court Authority to grant it, and so has every other Plantation Court given their Superiour Court.

The Justices were unanimously of Opinion that the Writ might be granted, and some Time after, out of Term, it was granted.

(*Quincy's Reports*, 51-57; editorial notes omitted)

L

Specimen of 1762
Massachusetts writ of assistance

Province of the ⎫ George the Third, by the Grace of God, of
Massachusetts Bay ⎬ Great Britain, France and Ireland King De-
⎭ fender of the Faith &ca.

To all and singular our Justices of the Peace,
Sheriffs, Constables, and to all other our Officers and Subjects within our said Province,
and to each of You, Greeting.

Know ye that whereas in and by an Act of Parliament made in the
fourteenth year of the Reign of the late King Charles the second, the
Officers of our Customs and their Deputies are authorized and
impowered to go and enter aboard any Ship or Vessell outwards or
inward bound for the purposes in the said Act mentioned, and it is in
and by the said Act further enacted and declared that it shall be
lawfull to or for any person or persons authorized by Writ of
Assistants under the seal of our Court of Exchequer to take a
Constable, Headborough or other publick Officer inhabiting near
unto the place and in the daytime to enter and go into any House,
Shop, Cellar, Warehouse, or Room or other place and in case of
resistance to break open doors, chests, trunks, and other package
there to seize and from thence to bring any kind of goods or
merchandize whatsoever prohibited and uncustomed and to put and
secure the same in our Storehouse in the port next to the place
where such seizure shall be made.

And whereas in and by an Act of Parliament made in the seventh
and eighth year of the reign of the late King William the third, there
is granted to the Officers for collecting and managing our revenue &
inspecting the Plantation trade in any of our Plantations the same
powers and authorities for visiting and searching of Ships, and also to

enter houses or warehouses to search for and seize any prohibited or uncustomed goods, as are provided for the Officers of our Customs in England, by the said last mentioned Act made in the fourteenth year of the reign of King Charles the second, and the like assistance is required to be given to the said Officers in the execution of their Office as by the said last mentioned Act is provided for the Officers in England. And whereas in and by an Act of our said Province of Massachusetts bay made in the eleventh year of the reign of the late King William the third, it is enacted and declared that our Superior Court of Judicature Court of Assize and General Goal Delivery for our said Province shall have cognizance of all matters and things within our said Province as fully and amply to all intents and purposes as our Courts of Kings Bench, Common Pleas, and Exchequer within our Kingdom of England have or ought to have.

And whereas John Temple Esq; Surveyor General of our Customs for the Northern District of America, by his Commission or Deputation under his hand & Seal, dated at Boston the fourth day of January, in the second year of our reign, hath Deputed and Impowered Nathanial Hatch Esq; to be Comptroller of all the rates and duties arising and growing due to us at Boston in our Province aforesaid, and in and by said Commission or deputation has given him power to enter into any Ship, Bottom, Boat or other Vessell and also into any Shop, House, Warehouse, Hostery, or other place whatsoever to make diligent search into any trunk chest pack case truss or any other parcel or package whatsoever for any Goods wares or Merchandize prohibited to be imported or exported or whereof the Customs or other Duties have not been duly paid and the same to seize to our use in all things proceeding as the Law directs.

Therefore we strictly Injoin and Command you and everyone of you that, all excuses apart, you and every one of you permit the said Nathl Hatch according to the true intent and form of the said Commission or Deputation and the Laws and statutes in that behalf made and provided as well by night as by day from time to time to enter and go on board any Ship Boat or other Vessell riding lying or being within or coming to the said port of Boston or any places or Creeks thereunto appertaining, such Ship, Boat, or Vessell then and there found to search and oversee and the persons therein being strictly to examine touching the premisses aforesaid, and also in the day time to enter and go into the Vaults, cellers, Warehouses, Shops and other places, where any prohibited goods wares or merchandizes or any goods wares or Merchandizes for which the customs or other duties shall not have been duly and truly Satisfied and paid, lye concealed, or are suspected to be concealed, according to the true intent of the Law to inspect and oversee and search for the said Goods wares and Merchandize, and further to do and execute all things which of right and according to the Laws and statutes in this behalf shall be to be done. And we further strictly Injoin and Command you and every one of you that to the said Nathaniel Hatch Esq; you and every one of you from time to time be aiding, assisting, and helping in the Execution of the premisses as is meet. And this you or any of you in no wise omit at your perils. Witness, Thomas Hutchinson Esq; at Boston the third day of June, in the second year of our Reign, Anno Domini 1762. By Order of Court.

Sam Winthrop Cler

(SF 100515)

M

Article, probably by James Otis, in the
Boston Gazette for 4 January 1762

SINCE the advancement of so great a lawyer as the Hon. Mr. H-TCH-NS-N to the *first J—st—s* seat, it would be deem'd the highest impertinence for any one to express the least surprize, that the Superior Court of this province, should after *solemn hearing,* adjudge themselves authoriz'd to grant *such* a writ, as the WRIT OF ASSISTANCE; or even to doubt, whether *by law,* they have power so to do: I hope however, I may say without offence, especially as I am inform'd that this writ is not yet given out, that I heartily wish it never may —

It seems necessary to preface all our objections against such a power being given to the custom-house officers, with a formal declaration against an *illicit* trade; for to bear any *spirited* testimony against their abuse of power, and especially to offer such abuse as the strongest reason why they ought not to be trusted with more, has been represented by these very persons and THEIR PATRONS, as if we had *combin'd* to break thro' all the *just* restraints of the laws of trade, and to force a free port. — I do therefore *from principle* declare against an illicit trade; I would have it *totally* suppress'd, with this proviso only, that it may have the same fate in the other governments; otherwise all the world will judge it unequitable: it is because *we only* are severely dealt with, that we complain of unreasonable treatment; and the writ of assistance, being a further degree of severity will give us still further reason to complain —

But it is not trade only that will be affected by this new severity: every householder in this province, will necessarily become *less secure* than he was before this writ had any existence among us; for by it, *a custom house officer* or ANY OTHER PERSON *has a power given him, with the assistance of a peace officer,* to ENTER FORCE-ABLY *into a* DWELLING HOUSE, *and rifle every part of it where he shall* PLEASE *to suspect uncustomed goods are lodgd!* — Will any man put so great a value on his freehold, after such a power commences as he did before? — every man in this province, will be liable to be insulted, by a *petty officer,* and threatened to have his house *ransack'd,* unless he will comply with his unreasonable and *impudent* demands: Will any one then under *such* circumstance, ever again boast of *british* honor or *british* privilege? — I expect that some *little leering* tool of power will tell us, that the publick is now amus'd with *mere chimeras* of an overheated brain; but I desire that men of understanding, and morals, would only recollect an instance of this sort; when a late comptroller of this port, by virtue of his *writ of assistance,* FORCEABLY enter'd into and rummag'd the house of a *magistrate* of this town; and what render'd the insolence intollerable, was, that he did not pretend a suspicion of contraband goods as a reason for his conduct, but it was only because the honest magistrate had a day before taken the liberty to execute a good and wholesome law of this province against the comptroller. —

IT is granted that upon *some occasions,* even a *brittish* freeholder's house may be forceably opened; but as this violence is upon a presumption of his having forfeited his security, it ought never to be done, and it never is done, but in cases of the most urgent necessity and importance; and this necessity and importance always is, and always ought to be determin'd by *adequate* and *proper* judges: Shall so tender a point as this is, be left to the discretion of ANY person, to whomsoever this writ may be given! shall the *jealousies* and mere *imaginations* of a custom house officer, as *imperious* perhaps as injudicious, be accounted a sufficient reason for his breaking into a freeman's house! what if it shall appear, after he has put a family which has a right to the King's peace, to the utmost confusion and terror; what, if it should appear, that there was no just grounds of suspicion; what reparation will he make? is it enough to say, that damages may be recover'd against him in the law? I hope indeed this will always be the case; — but are we *perpetually* to be expos'd to outrages of this kind, & to be told for our *only* consolation, that we must be *perpetually* seeking to the courts of law for redress? Is not this vexation *itself* to a man of a well disposed mind? and besides, may we not be insolently treated by our *petty tyrants* in *some* ways, for which the law prescribes no redress? and if this should be the case, what man will hereafter think his rights and privileges worth contending for, or even worth *enjoying.*

THE people of this province formerly upon a *particular occasion* asserted the rights of *englishmen*; and they did it with a *sober, manly* spirit: they were *then* in an insulting manner asked 'whether english rights were to follow them to the ends of the earth' — we are *now* told, that the rights we contend for 'do not belong to the English' — these writs, it is said, 'are frequently issued from the exchequer at home, and executed, and the people do not complain of it — and why should we desire more freedom than they have in the mother country' — such is the *palliating* language of the great *patrons* of this writ — and who claims more liberty than belongs to us as *British* subjects? we desire no securities but such as are deriv'd to us from the *british* constitution, which is our glory — no laws but what are agreeable to the *true spirit* of the *british* laws, to which we always have, and I hope always shall yield a chearful obedience — these rights and securities, we have with other *british* subjects gloriously defended against *foreign* invasions, and I hope in God we shall always have spirit enough to defend them against all *other* invasions. — Is there then any *express* act of parliament authorizing the exchequer to issue such writs? for if there is not *plain law* for such a power, the practice of one court *against law,* or which is the same thing, *without law,* can never be deem'd a *good* precedent for another, allowing there is no reason *to doubt,* the one is *legally* vested with all the power and jurisdiction of the other: but if ALL this be matter of *uncertainty,* ought it not then forever to be determin'd in favor of common right and liberty? and would not every wise man so determine it?

BUT admitting *there is such* a practice at home, and that it is not disputed, even at this time, when there is so warm a sense of liberty there; it may nevertheless be an Infringement upon the constitution: and let it be observ'd, there may be at some times a necessity of conceeding to measures there, which *bear hard* upon liberty; which measures ought not to be drawn into precedent here, because there is not, nor can be such necessity for them here; and to take such measures, without any necessity at all, would be as violent an infraction on our liberties, as if there was no pretence at all to law or precedent. It is idle then, to tell us we ought to be content under the same restrictions which they are under at home, even to the *weakning of our best securities,* when it is tolerated then only *thro' necessity,* and there is no necessity for it here. — In *England* something may be said for granting these writs, tho' I am far from saying that anything can justify it. In *England* the revenue and the support of government, in some measure, depend upon the customs; but is this the case here? are any remittances made from the officers here? has the king's revenue, or the revenue of the province ever received the addition of a farthing, from all the collections, and all the seizures that have been made and forfeited, excepting what has been remitted by the late worthy collector *Mr. B-r-ns?* — I assert nothing: but if no benefit accrues to the publick, either here or at home, from all the monies that are receiv'd *for the use of the publick,* Is not this PECULATION? and what reason can there be, that a *free people* should be expos'd to all the insult and abuse, to the risque and even the *fatal consequences,* which may arise from the *execution* of a writ of assistance, ONLY TO PUT FORTUNES INTO PRIVATE POCKETS.

I desire it may be further consider'd, that the custom house officers at home, are under certain *checks* and *restrictions,* which they cannot be under here; and therefore the writ of assistance ought to be look'd upon as a *different thing* there, from what it is here. In *England* the exchequer has the power of controuling them in *every respect;* and even of *inflicting corporal punishment upon them for mal-conduct,* of which there have been instances; they are the proper officers of that court, and are accountable to it as often as it shall call them to account, and they do in fact account to it for money receiv'd, and for their BEHAVIOR, once every week — so that the people there have a short and easy method of redress, in case of injury receiv'd from them: but is it so here? Do the officers of the customs here account with the Superior Court, or lodge monies received into the hands of that court; or are they as officers under any sort of check from it? — Will they *concede* to such powers in the Superior Court? or does this court, notwithstanding *these* are powers *belonging* to the exchequer — notwithstanding it is *said to be vested with* ALL THE POWERS *belonging to the exchequer* — and, further, notwithstanding this *very writ of assistance* is to be granted AS a power belonging to the exchequer, will the Superior Court itself, assume the power of calling these officers to account, and punish them for misbehavior? It would be a small consolation, if we could have one instance: Have we not seen already, ONE of those officers, and he an *inferior* one too, REFUSING to account to *any power* in the province, for monies receiv'd by him *by virtue of his office,* belonging to the province, and which we are assured by the JOINT DECLARATION of the three branches of the legislature is UN-JUSTLY as well as *illegally* detain'd by him? Does not every one then see that a writ of assistance in the hands of a custom house officer here, is in reallity a *greater* power & more to be dreaded, than it is in England? *greater* because UNCONTROUL'D — and can a community be safe with an uncontroul'd power lodg'd in the hands of *such* officers, some of whom have given abundant proofs of the danger there is in trusting them with ANY?

N

Massachusetts writs of assistance bill, 1762

Anno Regni Regis Georgii Tertii Secundo

An Act for the better enabling the Officers of his Majesty's Customs to carry the Acts of Trade into Execution.

Whereas it is the Desire of this Court, that the Officers of his Majesty's Customs in this Province may be assisted in the due Execution of their Office, for the securing his Majesty's Dues, and for the preventing of Fraud.

Be it enacted by the Governor, Council and House of Representatives That upon Application of any of the Officers of his Majesty's Customs in this Province impowred by Commission to seise upon Oath made to the Superiour Court of Judicature, Court of Assize and General Goal Delivery, or to the Court of General Sessions of the Peace, or to either of the Justices of said Courts, or to any one of his Majesty's Justices of the Peace of the County, that he has had Information of the Breach of any of the Acts of Trade; and that he verily believes or knows such Information to be true; it shall be lawful in every such Case for such Court or Justice, to whom Application may be made as aforesaid upon reducing such Oath to Writing, with the Name of the Person informed against, and not otherwise, to issue ^Aa Writ or Warrant of Assistance, which Writ or Warrant of Assistance shall be in the Form following, and in no other, Vizt.

ss.

To the Sheriff and Coroner of the County of   and to their respective Deputies; and to the respective Constables of the Town of   in said County, Greeting.

Whereas A. B.   of his Majesty's Customs, hath this Day made Complaint on Oath, That (setting forth the Complaint and Oath with the name of the Person complained of) You and every of You in his Majesty's Name, upon Sight Hereof are strictly Commanded to be aiding and assisting to the said A. B. in the due Execution of his Office relating to the Information aforesaid. Hereof fail Not at your Peril, and make Return of this Warrant and of your Doings thereon unto myself in seven Days from the Date hereof. Dated at B. the Day of   In the   Year of his Majesty's Reign: Anno Domini

And be it further enacted, That it shall be lawful for any Person or Persons authorized by Writ or Warrant of Assistance in manner and Form as aforesaid, and not otherwise, in the Daytime to enter and go into any House, Shop, Cellar, Warehouse, or other Place; and in Case of Resistance, to break open Doors, Chests, Trunks and other Packages, them to seize and from thence to bring any Kind of Goods or Merchandize whatsoever prohibited and unaccustomed there found and them secure. And all his Majesty's good Subjects are required to be aiding and assisting in the due Execution of said Writ or Warrant of Assistance, and all such shall hereby be defended and saved harmless.

In Council Feby. 20. 1762. Read a first time
Read a second time and passed to be engrossed
Sent down for concurrence
A Oliver Secy

In the House of Repves Feby 22 1762

> Read a first time
> 25th a second time
> March 5 1762 Read a third time and concurd
> with the Amendmt at A.

Sent up for concurrence

James Otis Speaker
In Council March 5. 1762. Read and Concurred
A Oliver Secy

Note

What appears to be the original document is in Massachusetts Archives 66, at folios 191-93. A photostat in the possession of the present writer shows "A" as marked, but no amendment there. Horace Gray, however, was able to supply "Informing and the place" (*Quincy's Reports,* 495).

~~~~~~

Post-Townshend writ of assistance drafted and printed for American board of customs commissioners 1768–69

~~~~~~

Province of }

GEORGE *the Third, by the Grace of* GOD *of* Great-Britain, France *and* Ireland, KING, *Defender of the Faith, and so forth.*

To all and every the Officers and Ministers who now have or hereafter shall have any Office, Power or Authority, from or under the Jurisdiction of the Lord High Admiral of our Admiralty of England, *to all and every our Vice Admirals, Justices of the Peace, Sheriffs, Mayors, Constables, Bailiffs, Head Boroughs, and all other our Officers, Ministers and Subjects, within every City, Town and County within our said Province.*

KNOW YE, That whereas We by Our Letters Patent under Our Great Seal of *Great-Britain,* bearing Date the eighth Day of *September,* in the Seventh Year of Our Reign, have constituted appointed and assigned Our trusty and well beloved *Henry Hulton, John Temple, William Burch, Charles Paxton,* and *John Robinson,* Esquires, Commissioners for managing and causing to be collected and levied Our Customs and other Duties in Our said Letters Patent mentioned, during Our Pleasure, and by Our Commission aforesaid, We have given and granted to Our said Commissioners, or any three or more of them, full Power and Authority to manage and cause to be levied and collected, all and every the Customs and other Duties, and all other Sums growing and renewing, due and payable to Us, for and by Reason of any Goods, Wares or Merchandizes, imported or brought into any of Our Colonies, Plantations and Provinces, lying and being on the Continent of *America*, . . . [this recital from the board's commission of appointment continues at exhaustive but purposeless length] . . . Therefore, We strictly injoin and command you, and every one of you, that (all Excuses apart) you and every one of you, permit the said *Henry Hulton, John Temple, William Burch, Charles Paxton,* and *John Robinson,* Esquires, and the Deputies, Ministers, Servants and other Officers of the said Commissioners and every one of them, from Time to Time as well by Night as by Day, to enter and go on board any Ship, Boat, or Vessel, riding, lying or being within, and coming to, any Port, Creek or Haven, within our said Province, and such Ship, Boat and Vessel then and there found, to search and oversee, and the Persons therein being strictly to examine touching and concerning the Premises aforesaid, according to the Tenor, Effect, and true Intent of our Commission, and the Laws and Statutes of *England*, in that Case made and provided; and, in the Day Time, to enter and go into the Vaults, Cellars, Warehouses, Shops and other Places, where any Goods, Wares or Merchandizes lye concealed or are suspected to be concealed for which the Customs and other the Sums of Money are not or shall not be duly and truly answered, satisfied and paid to our Collector, Deputy Collectors, Ministers, Servants, and other Officers respectively, or otherwise agreed for, according to the true Intent of the Law, to inspect and oversee and search for the said Goods, Wares or Merchandizes; and further to do and execute all Things which of right and according to the Laws and Statutes of *England* in this behalf shall be done according to the Effect and true Meaning of our Commission aforesaid, and the Laws and Statutes of *England*. And We further strictly injoyn and command you and every one of you, That to the said *Henry Hulton, John Temple, William Burch, Charles Paxton,* and *John Robinson,* Esquires Our Commissioners, and to their Deputies, Ministers, Servants and other Officers, and every one of them, you, and every one of you, from Time to Time be aiding and assisting and helping in the execution of the Premises as is meet, and this you, or any of you, in no wise omit at your Perils.

Witness   *Esq; at*
    the   *Day of*   *in the*
    Year of Our Reign.

(SF 89801)

Note

The Massachusetts Archives, vol. 44 (and see *Quincy's Reports,* 455), have a letter from the American customs commissioners to Chief Justice Hutchinson, 20 December 1768, asking whether "a form of a Writ of Assistants" they enclosed were "such as you would choose to issue to our several Officers within the Province of Massachusetts Bay." Hutchinson replied (*ibid.*) affirmatively, though indicating a preference that mayors and headboroughs be omitted from the addressees of the writ because those functionaries did not exist in Massachusetts (a preference reflected in his own text of the 1761-62 writ: see Appendix L and *cf.* p. 107 and Appendix E(i), n. 4). It seems likely that the above text was much as the commissioners' solicitor, David Lisle, first drafted it, and that the consultation of Hutchinson made little practical difference.

Hutchinson added that he would like to speak with the other judges before actually issuing writs in the new style, and: "I imagine no inconvenience can arise by deferring the matter . . . your Officers being already furnished with Writs as agreeable to the form proposed as the Circumstances of the Colonies before your Board was constituted would admit . . . ."

Index

Table of Cases

Table of Statutes

Design:	Wolfgang Lederer
Composition:	Trend Western Technical Corp.
Lithography:	Publishers Press
Binder:	Mountain States Bindery
Text:	IBM Composer Journal Roman
Display:	Linocomp Garamond
Paper:	Natural book, basis 50